Ancient Macedonia

"This authoritative, well-written narrative history of ancient Macedonia, from its early days to absorption by Rome, is sorely needed and will become a staple of university courses to do with ancient Greece and Macedonia. The numerous illustrations help to bring the text alive, and a stand-alone chapter on the Macedonian military helps to show how and why the army was the most feared and successful before that of Rome."

Professor Ian Worthington, University of Missouri, USA

The first English-language monograph on ancient Macedonia in almost thirty years, Carol J. King's book provides a detailed narrative account of the rise and fall of Macedonian power in the Balkan Peninsula and the Aegean region during the 500-year period of the Macedonian monarchy from the seventh to the second century BCE. King draws largely on ancient literary sources for her account, citing both contemporary and later classical authors. Material evidence from the fields of archaeology, epigraphy, and numismatics is also explored.

Ancient Macedonia balances historical evidence with interpretations—those of the author as well as other historians—and encourages the reader to engage closely with the source material and the historical questions that material often raises. This volume will be of great interest to both under- and post-graduate students, and those looking to understand the fundamentals of the period.

Carol J. King is Associate Professor of Classics at Grenfell Campus, Memorial University of Newfoundland, Canada. King is an alumna of the American School of Classical Studies at Athens, Greece (Regular Member 2001–2002, Senior Associate Member 2013–2014), and earned her PhD in classics from Brown University, Providence, RI in 2004. She has taught classics and ancient-history courses at several universities in the US and Canada. Her primary research focuses on the historiography of Alexander the Great and the literary evidence for ancient Macedonia more broadly. In addition to political and military history, she has also published on divination practices in ancient Macedonia.

Ancient Macedonia

Carol J. King

LONDON AND NEW YORK

First published 2018
by Routledge
2 Park Square, Milton Park, Abingdon, Oxon OX14 4RN

and by Routledge
711 Third Avenue, New York, NY 10017

Routledge is an imprint of the Taylor & Francis Group, an informa business

© 2018 Carol J. King

The right of Carol J. King to be identified as author of this work has been asserted by her in accordance with sections 77 and 78 of the Copyright, Designs and Patents Act 1988.

All rights reserved. No part of this book may be reprinted or reproduced or utilised in any form or by any electronic, mechanical, or other means, now known or hereafter invented, including photocopying and recording, or in any information storage or retrieval system, without permission in writing from the publishers.

Trademark notice: Product or corporate names may be trademarks or registered trademarks, and are used only for identification and explanation without intent to infringe.

British Library Cataloguing-in-Publication Data
A catalogue record for this book is available from the British Library

Library of Congress Cataloging-in-Publication Data
Names: King, Carol J.
Title: Ancient Macedonia/Carol J. King.
Description: New York, NY: Routledge, 2017. | Includes
bibliographical references and index.
Identifiers: LCCN 2017001654 | ISBN 9780415827270 (hardback: alk. paper) | ISBN 9780415827287 (pbk.: alk. paper) | ISBN 9781315177410 (ebook)
Subjects: LCSH: Macedonia–History–To 168 B.C. | Macedonia–Civilization.
Classification: LCC DF261.M2 K56 2017 | DDC 938/.1–dc23 LC record available at https://lccn.loc.gov/2017001654

ISBN: 978-0-415-82727-0 (hbk)
ISBN: 978-0-415-82728-7 (pbk)
ISBN: 978-1-315-17741-0 (ebk)

Typeset in Bembo
by Sunrise Setting Ltd, Brixham, UK

 Printed in the United Kingdom
by Henry Ling Limited

**In remembrance of my parents
Don and Deanie King**
Καιρὸν γνῶθι

Contents

List of figures viii
Preface x
Acknowledgements xii
List of abbreviations xiv
Chronology of the Macedonian monarchic period xvi
Maps xix

1 Early Macedonia 1

2 Macedonia and the Argead monarchy in the fifth century 24

3 Macedonian succession and survival, 399–360 49

4 Philip II, 360–336: consolidation and expansion 70

5 Macedonian military 107

6 Alexander III and Macedonia, 356–334 131

7 Alexander and the Macedonians beyond Macedonia, 334–323 151

8 Antipater and the early wars of the Successors, 334–319 178

9 Between dynasties, 319–279: wars of the Successors 205

10 The Antigonids, the Greek Leagues, and Rome, 278–167 235

Bibliography 269
Index 292

Figures

1.1	Balkan Peninsula, satellite image, August 25, 2011	2
1.2	Marble lion, Aiani, early fifth century BCE	6
1.3	Strymon bridge, conserved wooden piles of the substructure	10
1.4	Western Pieria, Haliacmon River, view southeast from Eordaea	18
2.1	Silver *tetradrachm* (4 drachm) of Alexander I	32
2.2	Silver *tetrobol* (4 obol) of Perdiccas II	32
2.3	Silver *didrachm* (2 drachm) of Archelaus	32
2.4	Gold necklace with knot of Heracles, Amphipolis, end of fourth century BCE	33
2.5	Ionic capital of a half-column from the palace at Pella	42
3.1	Grave *stele*, copy (original in Musée du Louvre, Paris), Aiani, early fourth century BCE	53
3.2	Elimeia, Haliacmon River, view north towards Mt Bermion	59
3.3	Amphipolis, Strymon River, view north towards Mt Orbelos	63
4.1	Philippi, Via Egnatia	76
4.2	Ivory head of bearded man, miniature from Tomb II, thought to be a portrait of Philip II, Vergina (Aegae), fourth century BCE	81
4.3	Marble statuette of a horseman, Pella	87
4.4	Marble head of Aristotle, Roman copy of a Greek original, c. 320 BCE	91
4.5	Theatre at Aegae	97
5.1	Modern *Sarissa* monument, Thessaloniki waterfront	111
5.2	Kinch Tomb, drawing of a wall painting, Lefkadia, 310–290 BCE	117
5.3	Alexander Sarcophagus, Sidon, end of fourth century BCE	118
5.4	Boeotian bronze helmet, found in the Tigris River, Iraq, late fourth century BCE	119
5.5	Gold oak-leaf wreath (one of many found in Macedonian tombs), Amphipolis, end of fourth century BCE	123
6.1	Nymphaion, Mieza, stone benches of Aristotle's School	133
6.2	Marble head of Alexander, Pella/Yannitsa, late fourth century BCE	136

6.3	Marble head of Alexander with lion pelt of Heracles, Kerameikos, c. 300 BCE	145
7.1	Dion shield and cuirass monument, façade of a Hellenistic building	152
7.2	Ionic tomb of Amyntas (son of Hermagias), ancient Telmessus, Lycia, bearing resemblance to Macedonian tombs of similar date, fourth century BCE	154
7.3	Alexander mosaic, House of the Faun, Pompeii, first century BCE	155
7.4	Alexandria's east harbour, view east towards the Ptolemaic palace quarter	157
7.5	Tigris River, near Alexander's ford, Cizre, Turkey	159
7.6	Marble votive relief to the heroized Hephaestion, Pella, late fourth century BCE	171
8.1	House of Dionysus, mosaic floor of an antechamber, Pella, last quarter of fourth century BCE	191
8.2	Lion Hunt mosaic, floor of an *andron* (banquet room), House of Dionysus, Pella	192
9.1	Bust of a Kore or Goddess, Amphipolis, Hellenistic cemetery	210
9.2	Façade of Tomb II, Vergina (Aegae)	215
9.3	Lion of Amphipolis, late fourth century BCE	215
9.4	Romaios Tomb, Vergina (Aegae), 310–290 BCE	216
9.5	Pindus Mountains, Epirus, region of Tymphaea	222
10.1	Panel from the Villa Boscoreale fresco, first century BCE	238
10.2	Acrocorinth, gateway to the Peloponnese, one of the three Macedonian 'fetters' of Greece	240
10.3	Orchomenos, Arcadia	245
10.4	Inscription of a treaty between Philip V and the citizens of Lysimacheia, 202–197 BCE	252
10.5	Top of an inscribed *stele*, recording a treaty between Perseus and the Boeotians, 172 BCE	257
10.6	Phakos, once an island in Lake Loudias by Pella, stronghold of the royal treasury	260

Preface

This aim of this book is to offer a narrative account of the rise and fall of Macedonian power in the Balkan Peninsula and Aegean region during the 500-year period of the Macedonian monarchy, from the seventh century BCE, when the Argead dynasty begins to emerge, to the dissolution of the Antigonid dynasty by the Romans in 167 BCE. The narrative is meant to be both informative and explorative, and hopefully not too overburdened with the many Gordian knots of historiography. It is hoped the book will be accessible to undergraduates and non-specialist readers, while at the same time of value as a resource for graduate students, scholars, and serious history enthusiasts.

The narrative is based primarily on the ancient literary evidence for Macedonia. No Macedonian narrative accounts have survived, so the perspective is mainly that of contemporary and later classical authors who mention almost exclusively the actions of the kings. Most valuable of these authors are the Greek historians Herodotus, Thucydides, Xenophon, and Polybius; the Athenian orators Demosthenes and Aeschines; the Sicilian Diodorus; the Roman historian Livy; the Greek biographer Plutarch; and the 'Alexander historians', five authors—Arrian, Curtius and Justin, along with Diodorus and Plutarch—whose narrative histories give abundant evidence for Alexander (III) the Great and some for his Successors. Many others, such as Polyaenus and Pausanias, also provide valuable information. I have made use as well of material evidence from archaeology, epigraphy, and numismatics, and I refer the reader, where appropriate, to the works of those who are more expert than I am in these areas. A good place to begin, for archaeology, though now somewhat dated, and though some of his conclusions are vigorously contested, is Manolis Andronikos' *Vergina. The Royal Tombs and the Ancient City* (1984). His discovery of two unplundered tombs in 1977–1980 was arguably 'the' key stimulus to the opening up of ancient Macedonian studies, and his descriptions of the artifacts and art are positively delightful.

A vast scholarship has been and continues to be generated by the investigation of the history of ancient Macedonia. It has been nearly thirty years, however, since a monograph narrative history of ancient Macedonia was published in English. Nicholas Hammond's *The Macedonian State. The Origins, Institutions and History* (1989) is a synthesis of his monumental three-volume *A History of*

Macedonia (1972–1988; Vol. II co-authored with G. T. Griffith, Vol. III with F. W. Walbank; see the abbreviations). Malcolm Errington's *A History of Macedonia* (1990; a translated and revised version of his 1986 *Geschichte Makedoniens*) covers the monarchic period. Also influential have been Eugene Borza's *In The Shadow of Olympus. The Emergence of Macedon* (1992), covering only to 338 BCE, and, less accessible, Miltiades Hatzopoulos' two-volume epigraphic study *Macedonian Institutions under the Kings* (1996). Many other edited volumes, collections of articles and papers by multiple scholars, as well as biographies of various Macedonian figures and studies of narrower periods of history, have greatly contributed to our understanding of ancient Macedonia. Constraints of space have compelled me to limit the bibliography mainly to scholarship of the past forty years (in English), and at that it is hardly exhaustive, since that would constitute a volume in itself. For spelling, I have Latinized familiar names (e.g. Olympus), while trying to keep Greek 'k' and 'os' for topography and less familiar names (e.g. Phakos).

The evidence for the history of Macedonia is full of historical questions, gaps, and notorious cruxes that one cannot hope to resolve definitively. Thus I vigorously encourage readers of this book to read also the major works of the leading historians in the field of study as well as the ancient sources. Ideally, a student of history would like to have definitive facts. The best that historians can offer, however, often comes down to a convincing argument based on all available evidence. I have necessarily formulated my own views on contentious questions. Some of these views I express outright, though I have tried to keep my own judgments to a minimum, so as to allow the reader to weigh the evidence. It is hoped that this book will be useful in the classroom and beyond as a tool for developing skills in critical thinking while also making accessible the fascinating history of the ancient Macedonians.

Carol J. King, November 2016

Acknowledgements

This book was conceived at the invitation of Routledge. The opportunity to write the history of ancient Macedonia has given form to a long personal journey, originally a search for Alexander, that has lured me far afield to many diverse places and people and experiences. I have had the good fortune to trek the highlands and lowlands, the passes and gorges, and to visit sites and museums of Macedonia in the company of people who have indulged and informed my passion for all things Macedonian. I owe acknowledgment and gratitude first of all to my parents who made possible my first visit to southern Greece in 1977—eight months before Andronikos' sensational discovery of the first of the unplundered Macedonian tombs at Vergina—and later, in 1983 and 1986, again made it possible and accompanied me on my earliest trips to Pella, Amphipolis, Philippi, and Aegae/Vergina. The tombs were not yet re-enshrined in their museum tumulus, and the recently restored silver vessels, gold *larnakes*, crowns, and even the contentious 'bones of Philip' were on display in the Thessaloniki Museum. Thus the passion was ignited.

    I later had the great privilege to study closely many of the archaeological sites under the expert tutelage of (past) Mellon Professors of the American School of Classical Studies at Athens, Merle Langdon and Margie Miles, first in the company of my fellow Regular Members of the ASCSA in 2001–2002 (I still picture them seated like sons of the great Macedonian nobles on the ancient stone benches at Mieza!) and then with knowledgable fellow alumni on the Macedonia and Thrace trip in 2011, re-examining much of Lower and Eastern Macedonia from Dion to Amphipolis. As a participant in the Institute for Balkan Studies (IMXA) International Summer School in 2013, under the leadership of program director Professor Konstantinos Dimadis, I was privileged to survey those sites again and to traverse the cantons of Upper Macedonia: Eordaea, Elimeia, Orestis, and Lyncus. In winter 2014, nearly thirty years after crossing the Pindus mountains together, my friend Jane Counter chauffeured and explored with me up one side and down the other of the Haliacmon (and prompted my first feast on Macedonian wild boar). At Pella, Professor Ioannis Akamatis graciously arranged access to the extended excavations, and Lefteris Eletheriadis (site worker) kindly transported us through a swampy farmer's field to the Phakos mound, once the island stronghold of the Argead and Antigonid royal treasury. Jane indulgently chauffeured again and trekked the sites with me on our 'Macedonians in the Peloponnese' tour in spring 2015.

Memorial University has generously funded research trips and granted a sabbatical in 2013–2014 that allowed me an extended stay in Greece with time and resources to begin writing this book. Thanks to Wendy Stephenson for furnishing me with a lovely flat in a quiet Attic deme. Dr James Wright, director of the ASCSA, kindly granted my appointment as Senior Associate Member, and I am indebted to the ASCSA staff, especially in the Blegen Library, and to Margie Miles (again) and Nick Blackwell for allowing me to tag along on winter day trips to see Macedonian fortifications around Athens and Attica, to other Associate and Regular Members and Friends of the School for great discussions, especially Jake Morton who enthusiastically shared his insights into topography, Olga Palagia (University of Athens), who shared her vast knowledge of Macedonian art, and Chloe Balla (University of Crete) for introductions to scholars. This book could not have been completed without the staff in the Ferriss Hodgett Library at Grenfell Campus (Memorial), especially Crystal Rose, who helped me access online resources and digitize images. My gratitude to Erika Stonehouse, who has expertly redrawn the Kinch tomb painting, and to Gabe Moss (Ancient World Mapping Center) for creating the maps. And to Edward Anson (University of Arkansas, Little Rock) I am greatly indebted for agreeing to read an earlier draft of the manuscript. His many valuable suggestions have helped me improve the text, notes, and bibliography. Any failings are purely my own, despite his careful read and advice.

Abbreviations

Ancient authors and works

Ael.	Aelian, *On the Nature of Animals* (*NA*); *Various Histories* (*VH*)
Aeschin.	Aeschines, *Against Timarchus* (1); *On The Embassy* (2); *Against Ctesiphon* (3)
App.	Appian, *Illyrian Wars* (*Ill.*), *Macedonian Wars* (*Mac.*), *Syrian Wars* (*Syr.*)
Arr.	Arrian, *Anabasis of Alexander* (*Anab.*); *Indica* (*Ind.*); *Events After Alexander* aka *Successors* (*Succ.*)
Arist.	Aristotle, *Economics* ([*Oec.*]); *Politics* (*Pol.*)
Ath.	Athenaeus, *The Learned Banqueters*
Curt.	Q. Curtius Rufus, *Histories of Alexander the Great*
Dem.	Demosthenes, *Orations*
Diod.	Diodorus Siculus, *Library of History*
Diog. Laert.	Diogenes Laertius, Lives of Eminent Philosophers
Front.	Frontinus, *Stratagems*
Hdt.	Herodotus, *Histories*
Heid. Epit.	*Heidelberg Epitome*
Isoc.	Isocrates, *Panegyricus* (4); *To Philip* (5); *To Antipater* (L 4)
Just.	Justin, *Epitome of the* Philippic History *of Pompeius Trogus*
Liv.	Livy, *From the Founding of the City*
Marm. Par.	*Marmor Parium*
Nep.	Cornelius Nepos, *Eumenes* (*Eum.*); *Phocion* (*Phoc.*)
Paus.	Pausanias, *Description of Greece*
Philoch.	Philochorus, *Atthis*
Plin.	Pliny, *Natural History* (*HN*)
Plut.	Plutarch, *Aemilius Paullus* (*Aem.*); *Alexander* (*Alex.*); *Aratus* (*Arat.*); *Demetrius* (*Demetr.*); *Demosthenes* (*Dem.*); *Eumenes* (*Eum.*); *Titus Flamininus* (*Flam.*); *Pelopidas* (*Pel.*); *Phocion* (*Phoc.*); *Pyrrhus* (*Pyrrh.*); *Moralia* (*Mor.*); *De fortuna Alexandri* (*De Alex. fort.*)
Polyaen.	Polyaenus, *Stratagems*
Polyb.	Polybius, *Histories*

Steph. Byz.	Stephanus Byzantius, *Ethnica*
Str.	Strabo, *Geography*
Theophr.	Theophrastus, *On the Origin of Plants* (*Caus. pl.*); *On the History of Plants* (*Hist. pl.*); *Characters* (*Char.*)
Theopomp.	Theopompus, *Hellenica*, *Philippica*
Thuc.	Thucydides, *History of the Peloponnesian War*
Trogus	Pompeius Trogus, *Prologues* (*Prol.*)
Xen.	Xenophon, *Hellenica* (*Hell.*)

Modern authors and works

Archaia Makedonia	*Archaia Makedonia/Ancient Macedonia*, I–VII, Papers Read at International Symposia Held in Thessaloniki (1968–2002, published 1970–2007). Thessaloniki, Greece: Institute for Balkan Studies.
Austin	Austin, M. M. 2006. *The Hellenistic World from Alexander to the Roman Conquest*. Second Edition. Cambridge: Cambridge University Press.
BNJ	Worthington, I. ed. *Brill's New Jacoby*.
Burstein	Burstein, S. 1985. ed. and trans. *The Hellenistic Age from the Battle of Ipsos to the Death of Kleopatra VII: Translated Documents of Greece and Rome 3*. Cambridge: Cambridge University Press.
CAH[2]	*Cambridge Ancient History*. Second Edition.
FGrH	Jacoby, F. 1926–1958 *Fragments of the Greek Historians* [*Die Fragmente der griechischen Historiker*]. Berlin: Weidmann; Leiden, Netherlands: Brill (reprinted 1954–1969).
HM I	Hammond, N. G. L. 1972. *A History of Macedonia. Vol. I.* Oxford: Clarendon Press.
HM II	Hammond, N. G. L. and G. T. Griffith. 1979. *A History of Macedonia. Vol. II*. Oxford: Clarendon Press.
HM III	Hammond, N. G. L. and F. W. Walbank. 1988. *A History of Macedonia. Vol. III*. Oxford: Clarendon Press.
Harding	Harding, P. 1985. ed. and trans. *From the End of the Peloponnesian War to the Battle of Ipsus: Translated Documents of Greece and Rome 2* Cambridge: Cambridge University Press.
IG	*Inscriptiones Graecae*. 1877–. Berlin: de Gruyter.
RO *GHI*	Rhodes, P. J. and R. Osborne. 2003. eds. *Greek Historical Inscriptions, 404–323 BC*. Oxford: Oxford University Press.
SEG	*Supplementum Epigraphicum Graecum*.
Syll.[3]	Dittenberger, W. 1915–1924. ed. [*SIG*] *Sylloge Inscriptionum Graecarum*. 4 vols. Leipzig: Hirzel.
Tod *GHI*	Tod, M. N. 1946–1948. *Greek Historical Inscriptions*. 2 vols. Oxford: Clarendon Press.

Chronology of the Macedonian monarchic period

(*in relation to Greece and Persia*)

c. 700–c. 498   Early Argead dynasty in Pieria to death of Amyntas I
            (all dates BCE)
Perdiccas I, Argaeus, Philip I, Aeropus I, Alcetas, Amyntas I (Herodotus' king list)

Greek Archaic period c. 800–499, Ionian Revolt (*alternatively −479, end of Persian invasion)

Persian Achaemenid rule est. 550 by Cyrus the Great; reign of Darius I: 522–486
c. 513–510   Megabazus' expedition in north Aegean; Persian embassy to Amyntas I

c. 498–c. 310   Argead expansion, Alexander I to Alexander IV, end of Argead dynasty
c. 498–c. 454   Reign of Alexander I: expansion east, acquisition of mineral and timber resources
480–479   Alexander I an ally of Xerxes; Macedonia independent after Xerxes' defeat
c. 454–c. 413   Reign of Perdiccas II: shifting alliances with Athens, Sparta, Odrysian Thrace
c. 413–399   Reign of Archelaus: strengthening of defense, capital moved from Aegae to Pella
399–393   Succession struggles: Orestes, Aeropus II, Amyntas II, Pausanias
393–369   Reign of Amyntas III: plagued by Illyrian threat, brief rule of Argaeus II
369–360   Succession of Amyntas' 'sons': Alexander II, Ptolemy of Aloros, Perdiccas III
360–336   Reign of Philip II: consolidation of Upper and Lower Macedonia, military reforms, expansion into Thrace, Thessaly, and Illyria, hegemony over Greek states
338   Philip II and Alexander defeat Athenian/Theban alliance in battle at Chaeronea
336–323   Reign and campaigns of Alexander III: Macedonian conquest of Persian Empire
333, 331   Alexander III defeats Darius III in battle at Issus and Gaugamela

| 334–319 | Regency of Antipater based at Pella; early Wars of Successors from 323 |
| 323–c. 310 | Reigns of nominal kings Philip III Arrhidaeus (to 317) and Alexander IV |

Greek Classical period 499/479*–323, death of Alexander III at Babylon
499–479	Persian Wars: victories at Marathon 490, Salamis 480, Plataea and Mycale 479
431–404	Peloponnesian War: Athens and allies vs. Sparta and allies
404–371	Spartan Supremacy in Greek peninsula and north Aegean
371–362	Theban Hegemony

Persian Achaemenid rule 486–330, Xerxes I to Darius III, end of Achaemenid dynasty
492	Mardonius' first expedition in north Aegean, aborted at Athos, Macedonia
480–479	Invasion of Xerxes, victory at Thermopylae
386	King's Peace (Peace of Antalcidas) imposed by Artaxerxes II on Greek states
336–330	Reign of Darius III

c. 310–277 **Between dynasties: Antipatrids and Successors**
316–297	Rule of Cassander (son of Antipater) in Macedonia, as 'king'? from c. 304
306–304	Other Successors take title 'king': Antigonus Monophthalmus (One-Eyed) in Asia Minor, Ptolemy Soter in Egypt, Lysimachus in Thrace, Seleucus Nicator in Persia
301	Successor kings battle at Ipsus, death of Antigonus
297–294	Unstable rule of Cassander's sons Philip IV, Antipater I, Alexander V
294–288	Demetrius I Poliorcetes (son of Antigonus) takes throne from Antipatrids
288–285	Pyrrhus (of Epirus) and Lysimachus drive out Demetrius, partition Macedonia
285–281	Lysimachus drives Pyrrhus out of western Macedonia, annexes it to Thrace
281	Seleucus defeats Lysimachus in battle at Corupedion
281–279	Ptolemy Ceraunus (son of Ptolemy) kills Seleucus, claims Macedonian throne
279	Gauls kill Ptolemy Ceraunus; brief rules of Meleager, Antipater II Etesias
279–277	Interregnum under military commander Sosthenes

277–167 **Antigonid dynasty to Roman conquest and dissolution of monarchy**
| 277–239 | Reign of Antigonus II Gonatas (son of Demetrius I), with brief interruption |

xviii   *Chronology of the Macedonian monarchic period*

274–272	Pyrrhus' second rule; Antigonus holds 'fetters' Demetrias, Chalcis, and Corinth
239–229	Reign of Demetrius II (son of Antigonus II): losses to Aetolian-Achaean alliance
229–221	Antigonus III Doson rules on behalf of Demetrius' under-age son Philip
221–179	Reign of Philip V; First and Second Macedonian Wars with Rome
197	Roman consul Flamininus defeats Philip V at Cynoscephalae
179–168	Reign of Perseus; third Macedonian War with Rome
168	Roman consul Aemilius Paullus defeats Perseus at Pydna
167	Roman Senate dissolves the Macedonian monarchy
[150–148	Andriscus or 'false Philip' VI briefly revives the monarchy]

Greek Hellenistic period 323–30, Roman capture of Alexandria after battle of Actium

322–229	Athens under Macedonian dominance, garrison at port of Piraeus
312/304–63	Seleucid dynasty in Persia and Syria, to Roman conquest
304–30	Ptolemaic dynasty in Egypt, to death of Cleopatra VII
290–189	Aetolian League dominant in Central Greece
282–133	Attalid dynasty in Pergamon, to death of Attalus III
280–146	Achaean League federal Greek alliance in Peloponnese
229–228	First Illyrian War marks first Roman intervention in Greek states

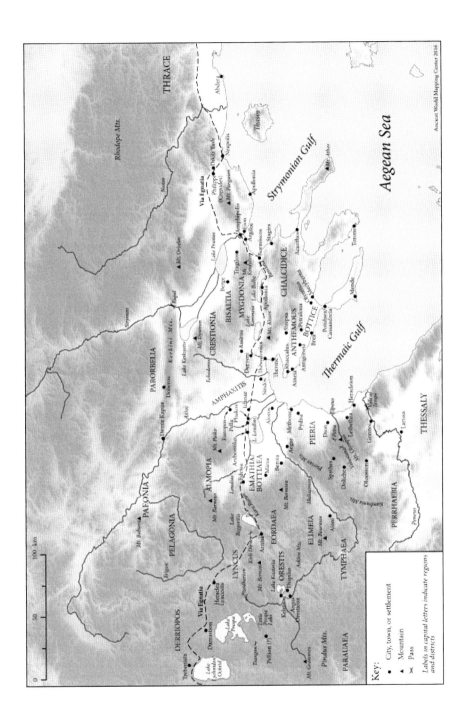

Map 1.1 Macedonia

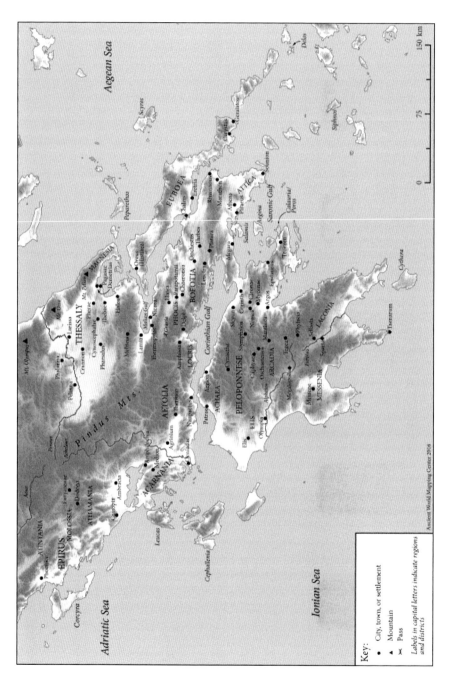

Map 1.2 Southern Balkan Peninsula

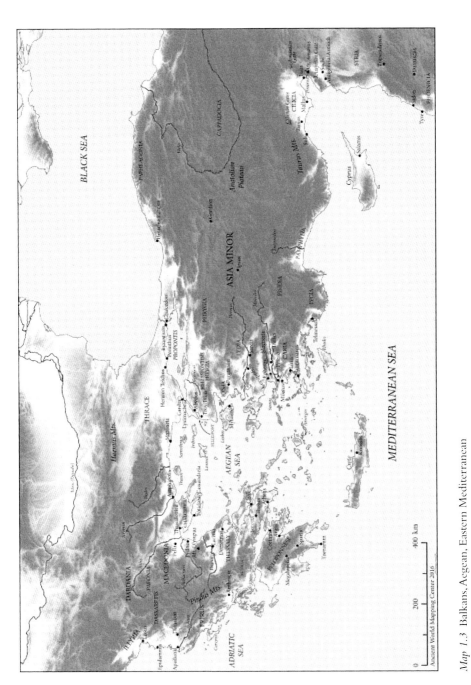

Map 1.3 Balkans, Aegean, Eastern Mediterranean

1 Early Macedonia

In a single decade late in the fourth century BCE Alexander III ("the Great") with his conquests in the east expanded Macedonian-controlled territory from the Hellespont to the Hyphasis, or, in modern terms, from the Dardanelles to the borders of India, thus ushering in an entire new age, the Hellenistic age, and immortalizing himself as one of the most famous figures of all antiquity. Before Alexander his father, Philip II, was described in his own times as the greatest man Europe had yet produced.[1] Philip, it was thought, had brought a backwater Macedonia out of the shadows and into the political limelight at a time when the great Greek city-states—Sparta, Athens, and Thebes—after centuries of incessant power struggles and battles with each other were experiencing exhaustion and decline as military and political powers. Philip was "greatest" because he compelled the bellicose Greek states to unite under his hegemony and harnessed their potential with his own might to challenge the greatest power of the day, the Persian Empire, though its conquest was left to Alexander. But Philip II is not the beginning, nor is Alexander III the end, of Macedonian history. It is an unfortunate mischance that apart from a few inscriptions no Macedonian accounts survive of the 500-year history of the monarchy, and thus a narrative history must be reconstructed mostly from the perspective of classical Greek authors who viewed the Macedonians as being of only peripheral interest, at least prior to Philip. Yet the Macedonians already had a long and complex political and cultural history in their relationships, not only with their southern Greek neighbours—it would not be far off the mark to say that the Athenians owed their fifth-century empire to Macedonian timber—but also with neighbouring peoples to the west, north, and east of their location in the Balkans.

Macedonia sits at a geographical crossroads, where the greater Balkan mass intersects with the Greek peninsula (Figure 1.1). The region serves as both the bridge between continental Europe and the southern Balkan Mediterranean zone and also the land link between the Adriatic, Aegean, and Black Seas. Since the earliest human migrations, major travel and trade routes have taken their course through a varied landscape of high mountain passes, corridors, river valleys, and coastal plains. The region's richness in natural resources attracted settlers, bringing influences from as far afield as the Near East, the Russian

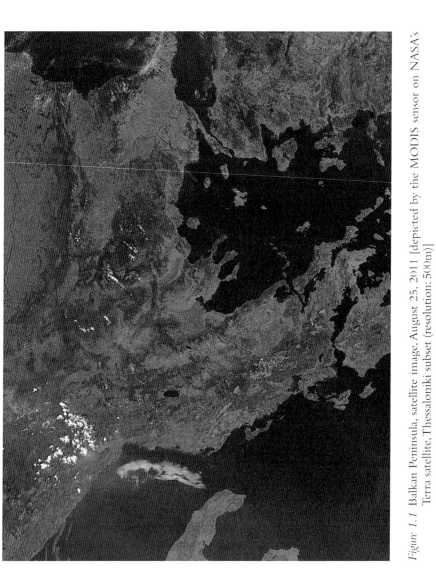

Figure 1.1 Balkan Peninsula, satellite image, August 25, 2011 [depicted by the MODIS sensor on NASA's Terra satellite, Thessaloniki subset (resolution: 500m)]

Source: NASA satellite image repository (selected and interpreted by GFMC: http://www.fire.uni-freiburg.de/GFMC new/2011/08/26/20110826_gr1.htm).

Steppes, central Europe, and Crete, and also attracted outside powers looking to control resources and trade. Much of the history of ancient Macedonia revolves around the struggle to control its strategic, physical, and economic advantages.

The archaeological record shows the broad geographical area of the Balkan bridge to have been inhabited from Paleolithic times. The earliest traces of humans in the southern Balkans were discovered in the Petralona cave of Chalcidice and date back nearly half a million years,[2] while sites dating to the Neolithic period have been uncovered across the region, including Dispilio in the western highlands, Nea Nikomedia on the western edge of the central plain, and Dikili Tash in the eastern plain. Later in the archaeological record, near the close of the sixth century BCE, evidence from the gold-rich burials at Sindos on the Thermaic Gulf, Aiani on the middle Haliacmon River, and Trebenista beside Lake Ochrid suggests considerable continuity of culture throughout the wider region, despite there being multiple tribes that controlled various parts of the whole.

Within that greater bridge region, in historical times Macedonia served as a buffer zone between the Greek city-states and neighbouring 'barbarians': that is, all non-Greek speakers, who to Greek ears uttered unintelligible 'bar bar'. Such a view begins to emerge from the Homeric *Catalogue of Ships*, a geographical list of contingents in the expedition to Troy. The list of Greek ship crews terminates in Thessaly, just southwest of Mount Olympus, while Homer places the westernmost Trojan allies along the Axios River. Thus the region between Mount Olympus and the Axios, which defines 'Macedonia' in the late Archaic period, appears a 'no man's land' in Homeric geography. According to early Greek authors, such as Homer and Herodotus, it was during the Bronze Age that the people known to history as Macedonians migrated to the Pindus Mountains, where the name "Macedones" identified them as "people of the highlands."[3] In the Iron Age (Archaic period) some of these Macedones migrated east to the slopes of the Pierian range and Mount Olympus and to the coastal plain beyond. The territory over which these Macedones took control from then on bore the name "Macedonia."

The land

The northernmost contingent fighting on the side of the Greeks at Troy came from Oloosson (Elassona) in Thessaly, north of the Peneus River. The river's narrow outlet through the Vale of Tempe allowed access between the Thessalian plain and the coast of the north Aegean, while the river itself, along with the mountains flanking the northern edge of the plain, formed a natural frontier. The most formidable natural barrier is the height of Mount Olympus, rising on the north side of Tempe and touching with its foothills the Thermaic Gulf of the Aegean. At 2,917 m (9,570 ft) it is the highest point in the Greek peninsula, a fitting home for the Homeric gods. For the ancients, Mount Olympus defined a boundary between the Greek states and Macedonia.[4]

Northwest of Olympus, peak after peak rises, undulating up into the central Balkans. Here the mountains are generally higher and more impenetrable than elsewhere in the Greek peninsula; the forests are denser and more varied. From the north face of Olympus a series of mountains rings a large plain, the central part of which looks southeast across the Thermaic Gulf to the three-pronged Chalcidice peninsula. The smaller, lower part of the plain is nearly enclosed by Mount Olympus and the abutting Pierian range. Both plains were suitable for grazing and farming, with access to the sea. East of the central plain rolling hills rise to a series of mountain ridges running northwest to southeast. These mineral-rich ridges drop on their east faces into the valley of one of Macedonian's great rivers, the Strymon (Struma). East of the Strymon another imposing mountain range running nearly parallel to the shoreline forms a natural frontier between the Thracian coast of the north Aegean and the central Balkans. All this expansive territory was at one time part of geographical Macedonia, which ancient historians (and modern) have divided into three distinct regions: Upper (Western) Macedonia, Lower (Central) Macedonia, and the Thraceward region (Eastern Macedonia).

Upper Macedonia

Upper Macedonia is the mountainous region north of Thessaly. It lies west of the mountains bordering the central plain (Olympus, Pierian, Bermion), east of the ridge of the Pindus range, mainly south of the Erigon (Crna) River, and comprises the watershed of the Haliacmon.[5] Early names for the upper and middle Haliacmon regions, "Maceta" and "Macednia," both mean "highland."[6] In the Classical period, by referring to *anō*, or "upper," Macedonia, the historians Herodotus and Thucydides distinguish the high mountains, valleys, and lakes that are "up" away from the coast, from the low-lying plains "down" by the coast in *katō*, or "lower," Macedonia.[7]

The territory between the upper Pindus range and the mountains bordering the central plain is divided by another parallel chain of mountains, on either side of which a wide corridor, the Haliacmon to the west and the Bitola–Kozani to the east, runs from the Kambunia Mountains, north of Thessaly, up into the central Balkans,[8] both major thoroughfares in antiquity. In the upper Haliacmon Corridor on the shores of Lake Kastoria are the remains of the Late Neolithic settlement Dispilio (5600–4000 BCE) (all dates are BCE, unless otherwise noted). Excavations since 1992 (CE) have uncovered traces of wooden stilts that supported houses at the lake's marshy edges, traces of a flat-bottomed dugout boat, and other evidence indicative of a rather sophisticated society that combined fishing, hunting, cultivation, and stock-raising. Such finds, though dating several thousand years before the earliest historical Macedones, challenge the perception of Upper Macedonia as an uncivilized wilderness.[9] The major site from Archaic and Classical times, Argos Oresticon, is also near the lake, a short distance southwest of Dispilio.

The most defining geographical feature of the landscape is the Haliacmon River itself. Rising on both the east facing slopes of the Pindus range and the western slopes of Mount Bernon (Vitsi), the upper course carves its way southeast through the Haliacmon Corridor, then rounds the southern extent of Mount Bourinos, along the north flank of the Kambunia range. In its middle course it flows northeast to cut a deep gorge between the Pierian range and Mount Bermion, thence making its way into the central plain to reach the Thermaic Gulf.[10]

The Lake Kastoria area, south of the Pisodherion Pass (over Bernon) and the Haliacmon Corridor, forms the canton of Orestis. This is one of several districts of Upper Macedonia that were inhabited by tribal peoples, each tribe giving its own name to (or receiving it from) the territory it controlled. Over the centuries, the Orestae sometimes fell under the rule of the Epirotes to the southwest, though for most of the Classical period Orestis was either independent or under the control of the ruling house of Lower Macedonia,[11] the Argeadae; and many of the legends surrounding the Argead monarchy link its origins to this district. It marks the western frontier of Upper Macedonia, and the Illyrians beyond its border were a persistent threat to the stability of the kingdom.

Over the mountains northeast of Lake Kastoria, beyond the Pisodherion Pass, is the district of Lyncus, or Lyncestis. This district comprises an upland valley about 650 m (2133 ft) above sea level, which is part of the Bitola–Kozani Corridor. Prior to the foundation of Heraclea Lyncestis in the mid fourth century, there were perhaps no towns of any size. We hear only of "villages," which is the typical settlement pattern of tribal peoples.[12] About 450 a royal dynasty claiming descent from aristocratic Bacchiad exiles from Corinth, who came to the region via Corcyra (a Corinthian colony) and Illyria, established itself and ruled over Lyncestian Macedones.[13] Under King Arrhabaeus, son of Bomerus, Lyncus was the strongest tribal state in Upper Macedonia in the second half of the fifth century. The major east–west route as well as one of the north–south routes passed through the heart of Lyncus, making it of great strategic importance.

A low spur of Bernon cuts northeast across the Bitola–Kozani Corridor, separating Lyncus from the district of Eordaea to the south, which is accessible by the Kirli Dirven Pass. Eordaea comprises the southern valley between Bourinos and Bermion, including Lake Begorritis and several smaller lakes.[14] An aggressive takeover probably in the sixth century that expelled the Eordaeans from Eordaea was the earliest conquest of the Argeadae in Upper Macedonia.[15]

South of Eordaea and Orestis in the region of the middle Haliacmon is the district of Elimeia, or Elimiotis. Elimeia lies on both sides of the river, here running roughly west to east, and on the southern side several passes from Elimeia lead south into Thessaly and west into Epirus. So this district also sat astride well used communication and trade routes. The Elimiotes, like the Orestae, are sometimes associated with Epirus, but in the Classical period they are identified as Macedonian.[16] The capital Aiani has been excavated in recent years, and discoveries have confirmed a major urban settlement occupied continuously from the Neolithic period to the first century, with impressive public

6 *Early Macedonia*

Figure 1.2 Marble lion, Aiani, early fifth century BCE
Source: author, 2014.

architecture, multi-storeyed private dwellings with staircases and drainage conduits, and monumental tombs dating to the Archaic and Classical periods.

Archaeologists have concluded that long before consolidation of Upper and Lower Macedonia in the mid fourth century Aiani experienced a high standard of living and culture, sharing many characteristics with the Greek world.[17] Among the small finds are local wares, as well as Mycenaean, Corinthian, and Attic pottery, sculpted marble lions (Figure 1.2), and gold sheets with the eight- or sixteen-point sun or star, which has come to symbolize ancient Macedonia. By the last quarter of the fifth century Elimeia was perhaps a subject ally of the king of Lower Macedonia, and the two royal houses had become intertwined by marriage. Nevertheless, it retained its own strong ruling dynasty and continued to exercise some independence until the mid fourth century.[18]

The districts Orestis, Lyncus, Eordaea, and Elimeia formed the heartland of Upper Macedonia in the Archaic and early Classical periods. On the periphery of this territory other districts were also absorbed by the expansion of the Argeadae Macedonians, and by the late Classical period these also came to be regarded as part of Upper Macedonia. To the northwest of Lyncus in the region of the Prespa Lakes is Derriopos, and to the northeast is Pelagonia, extending north of the Erigon River to Mount Babuna.[19] South of Orestis in the Pindus foothills is Tymphaea, a district of Epirus up until its incorporation into greater Macedonia.[20] Farther south and east is Perrhaebia, geographically contiguous with and originally subject to Thessaly; but perhaps already by the close of the fifth century it had been ceded to the Argead king.[21]

Lower Macedonia

To the north and east of Mount Olympus two coastal plains, Pieria and Emathia, the latter extending as far as the Axios River, comprise Lower Macedonia. According to Thucydides (writing in the last quarter of the fifth century), Pieria was the first Macedonian conquest in the coastal region, and Bottiaea, another name for Emathia, the second.[22] From antiquity until modern times, one of the main routes from central Macedonia to points west and north, as well as into southern Greece (a branch leading through the Volustana Pass into Thessaly was the main route between Macedonia and the south), followed the Haliacmon up the gorge between the Pierian Mountains and Mount Bermion. Archaeological evidence indicates the strategic importance and continual use of this route from the Middle Neolithic through the post-Byzantine period,[23] and it is in all likelihood the route the Macedonians followed east.[24] Another narrow coastal route passed through the southern Pierian plain east of Olympus and through the Vale of Tempe. Just south of the Haliacmon's exit from the western mountains is situated the most important political centre of early Macedonia, Aegae. It was probably near here that the Haliacmon was bridged in antiquity. By choosing this site as their base, the Macedonian kings would have been able to control the east–west route through the gorge and the north–south route that crossed the bridge.

North across the Haliacmon on the lower slopes of Bermion and looking east across the plain is Beroia, one of the most important towns during the Hellenistic and Roman periods. Some 12 km northwest is Mieza, identified as the site of the Nymphaion, where the philosopher Aristotle once instructed the young Alexander the Great. Farther north at the eastern edge of the Kara Burun Pass between Bermion and Barnous (Voras) is Edessa, which lay astride the great east–west thoroughfare, the Via Egnatia in Roman times, stretching from the Adriatic to the Black Seas (Figure 4.1, page 76). With key settlements at Aegae, Beroia, and Edessa, the early Macedonian kings controlled two of three major routes through the central plain and were well positioned to control the entire plain. The third route follows the valley of the Axios River up into the central Balkans, this being the main route for trade and communication between central Europe and the eastern Mediterranean.

From the eastern extent of the Barnous range the headland of Mount Paiko juts southward out into the central plain and drops along its east flank down into the valley of the Axios. Its west flank partly encloses a valley sheltered in the southern reaches of Barnous. This upper valley was the region called Almopia, and the Macedonians drove the Almopes out of here perhaps in the latter half of the sixth century.[25] It is excellent grazing land for goats and sheep and is protected on three sides by steep mountains. Barnous and Paiko give rise to the Loudias River, which flows south from Almopia through the Emathian plain between the Haliacmon and Axios. The Loudias today is not a significant river, except that its heavy deposits of silt continue to push the coastline farther and farther into the Thermaic Gulf. In antiquity it facilitated the transport of timber from the forested mountains to the coast for export, and from the later Classical through to the Roman period it was an important link between the port at Pella and the sea.

Pella was the greatest of the Macedonian cities at the height of Macedonian power in the fourth century. It is located east of the Loudias River on a low rise in the central part of the plain, south of Paiko. In the mid fifth century it lay in the region of Bottiaea and replaced an earlier settlement called Bounomos ("grazed by cattle"), which may have been located on the island of Phakos, in Pella's harbour.[26] Phakos is no longer an island, and Pella no longer has a harbour; in fact today Pella lies about 28 km (17 miles) inland. However, core samples taken in the central Macedonian plain have revealed that around 6200 BCE either the open gulf or a large lake extended as far west as the Early Neolithic site at Nea Nikomedeia, 11 km (6.8 miles) northeast of Beroia.[27] Herodotus and Thucydides both describe Pella as being situated on a narrow strip of coast, which must have been the inner curve of the Thermaic Gulf, around the third quarter of the fifth century.[28] Then, rapidly, within about 100 years, silting at the mouths of the Haliacmon, Loudias, and Axios rivers enclosed an inner bay of the gulf and all but cut it off from the sea.[29] The inland bay became a lake fed by the upper Loudias and the Axios, with the lower Loudias allowing access to the sea. Perhaps Macedonian engineering manipulated the riverbeds to facilitate bringing timber down to port.[30] At any rate, the distinctive situation provided for Pella a protective harbour for merchant ships and naval dockyards, with the island (later a promontory) of Phakos serving as a fortress.

Another important city was Dion, situated at the northeastern foot of Olympus in Pieria, on the coastal route to Tempe. Dion was a sanctuary, similar to Olympia in the Peloponnese, where religious festivals were held in conjunction with athletic competitions. Here the *Olympia* festival in honour of Zeus Olympios and the Pierian Muses was held from at least the late fifth century, and the *Hetairideia* in honour of Zeus Hetaireios ("of the Companions") was celebrated jointly with the nearby Magnetes of Thessaly.[31] The sacred city also housed major sanctuaries of the goddess Demeter (and later Isis) and Dionysus, and archaeological evidence indicates that other deities were also worshipped there, among these the goddesses Aphrodite and Athena.[32] Dion, Pella, and Aegae were all strategically located on or near the main routes, and control of these centres facilitated the expansionist policy of the Macedonian kings. By the mid fifth century expansion was well advanced east across the Axios.

The Thraceward region (Eastern Macedonia)

In the course of Macedonian expansion a third Thraceward region opened up. "Thraceward" is the term of contemporary Greek sources for lands east of the Axios that were inhabited by or had once belonged to Thracian tribes. The region over which the Macedonians first assumed control lay between the Axios and Strymon rivers. East of the Axios a short distance is the fourth river of the central plain, the "gold bearing" Echedoros. The land along the west bank of the

Axios and eastward between the Axios and Echedoros was known by the second century as Amphaxitis.[33] Through Amphaxitis ran the major communication and trade route between the north Aegean and the European interior. Before Macedonian expansion the Paeonians held it, but the Macedonians are said to have destroyed the Paeonian capital at Amydon on the Axios (westernmost of Troy's allies in the Trojan War) when they expanded into Amphaxitis.[34]

Beyond the Echedoros River a low mountain range running northwest to southeast separates the Axios valley from the valley of the Strymon, and towards the south the lakes Koroneia and Bolbe partially segregate the Chalcidice peninsula, though this region also is referred to as Thraceward. In the northwestern reaches lay the district Crestonia, where the Echedoros River rises; in the central region on the highest ridges and eastern slopes facing the Strymon basin lay Bisaltia; and south near the lakes lay Mygdonia, stretching east to the Strymonian Gulf and west to the Thermaic Gulf. Evidence suggests that the Macedonians first took control of Mygdonia by driving out the Edones, a Thracian tribe, and then, turning north, entered Crestonia and Bisaltia, aggressively taking control of the region's ore deposits and timber but evidently not displacing the inhabitants.[35] A pass near the northernmost peak, Mount Dysoron, was said to be the "straightest inland route" into Macedonia.[36]

South of Mygdonia in Chalcidice facing west towards the Thermaic Gulf is Anthemous, a fertile valley lying in the curve of Mount Kissos. It almost certainly was in Macedonian hands near the close of the sixth century,[37] while other districts of Chalcidice—Crousis, and Bottice—came under Macedonian control in the mid fourth century.

East of Mygdonia and Bisaltia is the rich and strategic Strymon basin,[38] the most hotly contested region in all of the north Aegean in the late Archaic and Classical periods. It is accessible through the Kumli Valley north of Dysoron and through the Rendina Pass, a narrow passage between Mount Kerdylion at the southeastern end of the Dysoron range and the easternmost heights of Chalcidice. Through Rendina the Via Egnatia took its course after passing south of lakes Koroneia and Bolbe. Here in the Strymon valley at a settlement whose name, Ennea Hodoi ("nine ways"), is indicative of the region's strategic location the Athenians established the long-fought-over colony Amphipolis ("two-way city"). Along with the Athenians, the Thracians, Spartans, and Macedonians all fiercely contested control of Amphipolis, coveting its location guarding the crossing of the Strymon as well as its proximity to sources of timber for shipbuilding and to the gold and silver mines of nearby Mount Pangaion. Remnants are still visible today of an ancient bridge that once spanned the Strymon (Figure 1.3), where the Via Egnatia intersected with another major route heading up the Strymon valley (through the Rupel Gorge) and linking the north Aegean with the central Balkans. Radiocarbon dating estimates that the wooden bridge was first constructed in the Archaic period and, with periodic maintenance and repairs, continued in use for 2,500 years up until the Ottoman period.[39]

Beyond the Strymon and the plain of Crenides, through the western reaches of the Rhodope Mountains, the Nestos River cuts its way to enter the Aegean

10 Early Macedonia

Figure 1.3 Strymon bridge, conserved wooden piles of the substructure
Source: author, 2011.

Sea opposite the mineral-rich island of Thasos. The geographer Strabo (first century) regarded the Nestos as the eastern boundary of Macedonia in the middle of the fourth century, and around that time the plain surrounding Crenides was drained and a major settlement planted. However, given the heavy Thracian presence, it is questionable whether Macedonia proper ever did extend as far as the Nestos River.[40]

The territory occupied and directly controlled by the Macedonians was not, of course, a fixed entity.[41] What began as a small region in the western mountains gradually expanded through conquest, annexation, and alliance until, at the height of its power in the second half of the fourth century, it stretched from Lake Lychnidos in the west to the plain of Crenides in the east, from Olympus to the Babuna range in the north, while the political sphere of Macedonia's monarchs often outstripped the kingdom's geographical boundaries.

The people

Who were the ancient Macedonians? Even before the subdivision of the Ottoman Macedonia region in 1913 of the modern era scholars were questioning, on grounds of linguistics, whether the Macedonians were Greeks, akin to Greeks, or other than Greeks.[42] New evidence does periodically come to light, as it did in 1986, when a lead curse tablet dating from the first half of the fourth century was discovered in a grave at Pella.[43] While the text is the most significant so far uncovered (it is the earliest and longest) and is written in a previously unknown northwest Doric Greek dialect, to call this one text conclusive evidence for the language of all Macedonians, if by "Macedonians" one means people living in Macedonia, seems untenable.[44] Allowing that there were living in ancient Macedonia throughout the Archaic, Classical, and Hellenistic periods people who were Greek, people who were akin to Greeks, and people who were not Greek, if one seeks historical truth about an ancient people who have left no definitive record, one may have to let go of the hope for a definitive answer. The ancient Greeks themselves differentiated between "Greeks" and "Macedonians," and if the difference was not one of written language, then it ought to be constructive to consider what factors *did* differentiate the Macedonians—in the opinion of ancient Greeks.[45]

Macedonians

The Macedonians are never mentioned in Homeric epic, which is generally dated to the mid eighth century (though poems and poet are impossible to date, and parts such as the *Catalogue of Ships* are considerably older), but Homer does describe Hera's descent from Olympus to Troy by way of Pieria and Emathia, which is an earlier name for the central Macedonian plain.[46] Then, in the Hesiodic *Catalogue of Women*, which may date to the end of the eighth century, Macedonia's eponymous founder Macedon, the first "Macedonian" (son of Zeus' daughter Thyia), and his brother Magnes, first of the Magnetes, are described as "dwellers in mansions around Pieria and Olympus."[47] Herodotus, in speaking about early peoples and migrations, says the Hellenes (Hellen in Hesiodic myth is uncle to Macedon and Magnes) were driven west from Olympus and Ossa to the Pindus Mountains, where they took the name Makednoi, and some of these later migrated to the Peloponnese.[48] This early mythology reflects to some degree a period of instability throughout the eastern Mediterranean in the Late Bronze Age that saw the collapse of the Mycenaean palace system in the Greek peninsula and of the Hittite Empire in Anatolia. This triggered movements of people, though it is not possible to confirm whether these movements brought the Macedones into the region of the Pindus Mountains or Pieria and Olympus. A Late Bronze Age cemetery at Spathes on the west-facing slope of Olympus has yielded grave goods similar to Mycenaean finds in Thessaly, but no associated settlements have yet been uncovered, and the affiliation of the dead remains unknown.[49] Around the same time as the traditional date of the Trojan War (1180) a migration from central Europe into the southern Balkans via the Axios Gorge and Pelagonia brought a people called Bryges into the central and western Macedonian regions. The Macedonians in the fifth century claimed the Bryges were their neighbours up until they migrated east to Anatolia and took the name Phryges/Phrygians.[50] Most of the Bryges were gone, evidently, when the early Macedonians began their expansion into the central plain, since the local peoples whom they encountered and drove out were Pieres (a Thracian tribe), Bottiaeans (who were said to be settlers from Crete, including descendants of Athenian slaves), and Almopes (a Paeonian tribe).[51]

The British historian of ancient Macedonia Nicholas Hammond has vigorously argued that the Macedonians were transhumant pastoralists and sought to gain pasturelands by their advance into the plain.[52] The goat appears on early coinage (Figure 2.1, page 32) and in the name of their early capital Aegae ("place of goats"), though expansion into the plain probably resulted in the development of farming. The early Macedonians were great hunters of wild game, especially lion and boar, as is evident from firmly embedded traditions of later times and hunting scenes in Macedonian art (Figure 8.2, page 192). The last king of the fourth century, Cassander, embarrassingly at age thirty-five still could not recline at banquet since he had not yet speared a wild boar without the aid of a hunting net.[53] Banquets (*symposia*) were a vital part of Macedonian society, with heavy drinking and prostitutes, both female and male.[54] This did not distinguish them from Greeks, except that the drinking was probably heavier, as the wine was usually "unmixed" (undiluted). But unlike many of the southern Greeks they were not seafarers, though they did turn to the sea by necessity, both for economic purposes and for war; even then, it was mostly other seafaring peoples, such as the Phoenicians and Cretans, who manned the ships. One of the most differentiating characteristics of the Macedonians was their kingship, which stood in contrast to the city-state system of the south, with its aristocratic, oligarchic, and democratic forms of government.[55]

The tribe of Macedones or ruling family which took over the central plain was known, according to later sources, as Argeadae. The Argeadae were thought to have originated in Orestis, and despite the later power struggles between the ruling monarchy of Lower Macedonia and the tribes of Upper Macedonia, each with their own ruling families, they were considered "kin" due to their common origin in the western mountains and their common language, common haircut, short cloak, and other customs,[56] which would have included religious cults, stock-herding and -breeding, hunting, and horsemanship. All written records so far uncovered are in forms of Greek, and by the mid fourth century it appears the Argead royal court preferred spoken Greek as its official language, though there are also references to a "Macedonian" (*makedonisti*) language or dialect, which predominated within the army and was unintelligible to Greek speakers from the southern part of the peninsula.[57] Since the Macedonians had regular contact with neighbouring peoples—Illyrians, Paeonians, and Thracians in addition to Greeks—certainly some Macedonians could communicate in these languages. Many, evidently, were bilingual, speaking both the language of the Macedonians and that of the Illyrians.[58] In Lower Macedonia, since the Argeadae imposed their rule over peoples not fully displaced, the population very likely was one of mixed languages, religions, and traditions. Proximity to the sea in Lower Macedonia also exposed the Argeadae to a broader range of cultural influences than their mountain kin.

Neighbours

Most ancient Greek authors relegated Macedonia to the fringes of the Greek world.[59] However, over the heights of Kambunia and Olympus from earliest times several routes facilitated trade and travel between Macedonia and Thessaly. The plain of Thessaly, the largest in all of Greece, stretches east from the Pindus mountain range (which forms a natural spine down the middle of the peninsula) almost to the Aegean, where it is enclosed by the peaks of Ossa and Pelion. The Thessalians, great herders of cattle and horses, lived in independent city-states divided into four administrative districts, or tetrarchies. Although aristocratic rule had superseded kingship in Thessaly before the Classical period, occasionally a powerful aristocrat was elected as *tagos*, whose chief role was overall military leader. Rival Thessalian aristocratic factions often sought backing against each other at the Macedonian court, and eventually this invitation to intercede led to their subservience to Macedonian rule.[60] Moreover, it was in the interests of the Macedonian kings to protect their southern flank by nurturing strong ties with Thessaly. Between the Macedonians and Thessalians lived two other tribal groups, the Magnetes and Perrhaebi,[61] both included in Homer's *Catalogue of Ships*. To the south Thessaly is separated from central Greece by mountains that leave only a narrow pass by the sea at Thermopylae ("hot gates").

Farther west the mountainous region of Epirus between the Pindus Mountains and the Adriatic Sea, although more remote than Thessaly and lying beyond Greece proper,[62] was tied firmly to the Greek world through its oracle of Zeus at Dodona and also through the legend that Neoptolemus, son of Achilles, settled there on his return from Troy. Strabo says that of fourteen Epirote tribes the Chaeones and the Molossians were the most prominent.[63] The Epirote tribes were more akin than Thessalians to early Macedonians in that they lived in villages rather than city-states and were ruled by kings.

To the east of the Greek peninsula the three-pronged Chalcidice peninsula reaches into the north Aegean. It is contiguous with the Thraceward region east of the Axios yet is somewhat segregated by the two lakes on its north/landward side. Its good harbours, in close proximity to natural resources, as well as its location on the grain route from the Black Sea to southern Greece, attracted Greek colonists as early as the ninth century, and so from earliest historical times it was always considered part of the Greek sea faring world.[64]

Neighbours on the northwest frontier of Upper Macedonia posed the greatest threat to the stability of the Macedonian kingdom. Both Orestis and Lyncus bordered the Illyrian-controlled region of the two Prespa lakes.[65] The Illyrians, so identified by the Greeks, were a cooperating but independent group of tribes inhabiting the regions beyond the lakes as far as the Adriatic Sea in the west and the Istros (Danube) River in the north. They probably spoke a common Illyrian language (although this is not certain), and by the late fifth century they so excelled in warfare that even the Spartans preferred peaceful settlement to confrontation in battle. The Encheleae, Taulanti, and Dardani were particularly powerful tribes, who clashed early with the Macedonians. The Taulanti are said to have invaded Macedonia after the untimely death of the Macedonian king Philip I early in the sixth century, when—or because—his successor Aeropus I was still an infant. As the story goes,[66] the Macedonians were initially defeated, but after placing their infant king in his cradle at the rear of the battle-line they fought with such courage in the child's defence that they slaughtered many Illyrians and drove off the rest. Illyrian tribes habitually invaded Macedonia whenever they perceived the throne was weak, especially upon the death of a king and before his successor could become firmly established. The story reflects the great veneration of Macedonians for their kingship.

On the northern frontier of Macedonia Paeonian tribes continued to inhabit the middle Axios valley, from Demir Kapija north to Skopje, as well as the upper and middle Strymon, after they were driven out of the lower reaches of both rivers late in the sixth century, when their wealth in gold and silver mines drew the attention of the Macedonians and of the distant Persians. Periodically they threatened Macedonia's northern frontier, particularly when the throne was changing hands. Like the Illyrians, Thracians, and Macedonians, they were a tribal organization with monarchic rule,[67] but their kings eventually became subject to the Macedonian ruling dynasty. An inscription dating from the first half of the second century bearing the name of the Paeonian healing god Darron testifies to the Macedonian adoption of the Paeonian cult and worship of Darron at his own sanctuary at Pella.[68]

The eastern neighbours of the Macedonians were Thracian tribes inhabiting (generally) the north Aegean coast from the Theramic Gulf all the way to the Black Sea and the interior as far as the Danube River, although, as with Macedonia, the geographical boundaries fluctuated.[69] The tribes included the Pieres who were driven out of Pieria, the Edones and Mygdones, the Triballians, and the powerful Odrysians. The Thracians were included in Homer's list of Trojan allies and were particularly famous as warriors, their skilled horsemen eventually being incorporated into the Macedonian cavalry. Cultural influences are evident especially in the shared cults of the Thracian Rider, Bendis (goddess of the moon and hunt), and Orpheus,[70] as well as in art.

The great advantage the Macedonians had over their tribal neighbours was that they did not continue to function as independent tribes but rather began to be consolidated from an early date—much earlier than the Paeonians and Thracians, while the Illyrians never truly consolidated[71]—under the dynastic rule of one tribe, the so-called Argeadae.

The legends

Legends of a shadowy time before historical record (and verification) belong to virtually all societies. The Athenians had their Theseus, the Romans their Romulus, and it should go without saying that use of such legends, especially given their tendency to veer off into the realm of myth, for the purpose of arguing 'origin' is so fraught with difficulties that any such arguments can only be speculative. Legends do have historical implications, however, with respect to the evolution of self-perception and how a people wishes to be perceived by others.[72] We have already met Macedon, the eponymous founder of Macedonia around Olympus and Pieria.[73] Hesiod adds a defining detail, that Macedon "delighted in fighting on horseback" (*hippiocharmes* could also mean "from a horse-drawn chariot"). Many of the earliest Macedonian royal coins, *octodrachms* and *tetradrachms* of Alexander I, bear the image of a mounted armed horseman (Figure 2.1, page 32). Thus both the earliest literary reference and the earliest coinage (c. 475) identify the Macedonians as horsemen.

Before the development of narrative history there was genealogy, and for early Macedonia genealogy is almost all we have. Herodotus, who fathered history on genealogical lists, gives the lineage for Alexander I (he plays a conspicuous role in Herodotus' account of the Persian invasions), naming his six immediate ancestors in ascending order, son to father: Amyntas, Alcetas, Aeropus, Philip, Argaeus, and Perdiccas, founder of the kingship.[74] All the names recur in Macedonian royal genealogy after Herodotus' time, and the list may well be the 'official' list from the Macedonian court in the mid fifth century.[75]

Herodotus also gives what is evidently the Macedonian court's account of how Perdiccas, a descendant of Zeus and Heracles through Temenus of Argos, established the royal dynasty.[76] Three exiles from Argos in the Peloponnese went to Illyria. They were brothers, descendants of Temenus: Gauanes, Aeropus, and Perdiccas. From Illyria they crossed into "upper Macedonia" and came to the town of Lebaea.[77] There they worked for wages for the local king, one tending horses, one oxen, and the youngest, Perdiccas, the lesser stock, presumably goats and sheep. Since the ruling family was poor, just like the common people, the king's wife baked their bread, and when she saw that Perdiccas' bread always doubled in size she told this to the king. Recognizing an omen of great meaning, the king ordered the brothers out of his territory. The brothers, thinking they at least deserved their pay, demanded it, but the king simply indicated the patch of sunlight shining through the smoke-hole as their reward. His older brothers were tongue-tied, but Perdiccas said he accepted the gift, drew a line around the sunlight with his knife, gathered it three times into his garment, and left with his companions. One of the king's "attendants"—evidently a *mantis*, interpreter of omens—explained the significance of what the youngest brother had done by accepting the gift. The interpretation is left unstated, but the king was enraged and sent horsemen to kill them. The brothers escaped when they crossed a river and it rose in spate behind them so the pursuing horsemen could not follow. Herodotus says the descendants of the Temenid brothers offer sacrifice to this river as their deliverer, though he does not name the river (perhaps the Haliacmon). The brothers, Herodotus says, came to "another part of Macedonia" and lived near the Gardens of Midas beneath Mount Bermion. When they had taken possession of this land, they went out from there and began to subdue "the rest of Macedonia."

References to three parts of Macedonia—upper, another, and the rest—are vague and puzzling.[78] One interpretation would be that they reflect three phases of Macedonian expansion up to Herodotus' day: arrival in Orestis and displacement of the indigenous rulers; relocation to Mount Bermion and possibly western Pieria; and expansion into the central plain. The occupations of the three brothers, tending horses, oxen, and sheep and goats, seems to reflect a Macedonian tradition of pastoralism, while the homely nature of the kingship or ruling family (the wife making her own bread) suggests social simplicity. It is significant that, given the great importance of cavalry throughout Macedonian history, the king has horsemen ready to act at his command, and in the sun we recognize the so-called Vergina sun, symbol of Macedonian sovereignty that has parallels in both Paeonia and Thrace.[79]

In all the later genealogies or king lists,[80] Caranus appears first, three generations before Perdiccas, and he appears to be entrenched as founder of the dynasty by the early fourth century, though he is apparently unknown to Herodotus.[81] According to this legend,[82] before the first Olympiad, dated to 776, Caranus of Argos gathered a force of Argives and Peloponnesians to advance against the "territory of the Macedonians." The king of the Orestae, who was fighting against the Eordaeans, asked Caranus for an alliance and as a reward offered him half his land. Caranus obliged, ruled as king for thirty years, and was succeeded in turn by Coenus, Tirimmus, and then Perdiccas. Wishing to enlarge his kingdom, Perdiccas consulted the oracle at Delphi, who instructed him to go to Bottiaea and in the place where he saw white-horned goats to offer sacrifice to the gods and found the capital city of his kingdom, this being "goat place," or Aegae. Caranus thus replaces Perdiccas as the man from Argos who settles in Orestis (the settlement Argos Oresticon appears to reflect an Argive connection), while Perdiccas, with Delphic sanctioning, is the first king to establish rule in Lower Macedonia.[83] As with the earlier Perdiccas legend, the implication is that the Macedonians and their eventual rulers were not of the same stock, and this is clearly how Alexander I promoted himself. Herodotus at one point calls Alexander I "a Greek man, ruler of Macedonians."[84]

The consensus among modern historians is that Caranus (along with Coenus and Tirimmus) was a fabricated ancestor, a tampering with the genealogy by one of the kings, perhaps to support a tenuous claim to the throne.[85] In the closing decade of the fifth century King Archelaus invited to the Macedonian court the famous Athenian tragedian Euripides.[86] While there Euripides wrote at least four plays, including his masterful *Bacchae*, a lost *Temenus*, or *Temenidae*, and, surviving only in fragments, the *Archelaus*, honouring his patron with the invention of a mythical Archelaus, son of Temenus, as founder of the royal house.[87] The play includes elements of the Perdiccas legend—the exiled descendant of Heracles, the attempt of the local king to kill the hero, the flight to another part of Macedonia—but this is blatant flattery, not serious tampering with genealogy.

Two descriptions of early Macedonian expansion mention the "so-called Argeadae": that they established themselves as rulers over a number of (non-Macedonian) tribes in what became central and eastern Macedonia, and that they destroyed the Paeonian stronghold Amydon on the Axios.[88] Though the descriptions come from Strabo in the first century, and no author of the Classical period ever refers to the Argeadae, it is possible Strabo's source was writing in the late sixth century before the reign of Alexander I,[89] thus predating Herodotus' king list. A later Roman source says the Argeadae Macedones were "so-called" because they came from Argos in Orestis,[90] which suggests a tribe comparable to the Lyncestian Macedones of Lyncus.[91] An even later Byzantine source claims they were named after Argeas, son of Macedon.[92] Also, in an excerpt from an alleged letter of the late fourth century from the mother of Alexander III to her son, she mentions the performance of *Argadistica* and *Bacchica* sacrifices.[93] Could Argeadae possibly derive from Argaeus, second in Herodotus' royal genealogy?[94] Two pioneering details are recorded about Argaeus: first that he was instructed by his father Perdiccas to establish a place of burial for his father's bones and the bones of all the succeeding kings, thus linking him to the foundation of the royal cemetery at Aegae, and second that he was the first to build walls in Macedonia.[95] It is tempting in this light to consider Argaeus, literally "man of Argos" (Oresticon), as the eponymous founder of the Argead royal dynasty.

Most modern historians refer to the first Macedonian royal dynasty as the Argead dynasty.[96] Hammond, however, has insisted that the Argeadae were a tribe and that the royal dynasts were properly called Temenidae, or the anglicized Temenids, based on the fact that both Herodotus and Thucydides call the Macedonian kings descendants of Temenus of Argos. Temenus was a legendary hero of the Peloponnese, one of the Heraclids, the descendants of Heracles who returned to the Peloponnese after a period of exile and reclaimed the lands out of which the sons of Heracles had been driven.[97] Temenus, as ancestor of the historical Argaeus, provides the important link with Heracles, another man of Argos and one of the principal deities in the Macedonian pantheon. An inscription found in the *tholos* room of the palace at Aegae reads: ΗΡΑΚΛΗΙ ΠΑΤΡΩΙΩΙ (*to Heracles Progenitor*). However, Heracles may be a relatively late arrival to Macedonia.[98]

Early expansion

If the legends of the origin of the Macedonians and their kings reflect any sort of historical actuality, then we may well look for the earliest identifiable location of the people known to later history as the Macedonians in the region of Pindus, where Herodotus says there was a people in the Late Bronze/Early Iron Age called Makednoi. By the middle of the Archaic period, a ruling family had emerged that was strong enough to organize local tribes into some sort of confederacy for the purpose of expansion. Legend insists that the founder of the ruling family came as an exile from Argos in the Peloponnese and was a descendant of Heracles, and this genealogy was accepted in the fifth century by Herodotus and Thucydides and by officials at Olympia.[99] It was important in the ancient world for kings to trace their ancestry back to divinity, since a claim to divine descent legitimated the family's status as rulers. But they can only have held onto a position of authority through exceptional leadership. The nature of leadership in tribal societies is multifaceted: a *basileus*,[100] king or headman of a tribe, was expected to perform rituals of religious observation on behalf of his people, to hear complaints and arbitrate in matters of justice, and to lead in war. An aggressive eastward advance probably originating in Orestis (the upper Haliacmon) in the early Archaic period and resulting in the takeover of western Pieria (Figure 1.4) would have required organized, military leadership. The device of a horseman on the earliest Macedonian coins could suggest that expansion was won and maintained by a strong cavalry force. Some Macedonians were living in Pieria and around Olympus before the mid seventh century, as attested by the Archaic composition *Catalogue of Women*, whose author thought these Macedonians "delighted in fighting on horseback" and were related to the Thessalian Magnetes. The latter inhabited the district around Mount Pelion, which was famous for its mythical centaurs, while in Homeric epic the finest of the Achaean (Greek) horses, aside from the immortal horses of the Thessalian Achilles, were those of another Thessalian, Eumelus, king of Pherae.[101]

From the highlands of western Pieria the Macedonians began to make their expansionist moves.[102] The earliest king, Perdiccas I, according to fifth-century historians, established a foothold on the edge of the Emathian plain by taking over an existing settlement and using it as a seat of royal power. This settlement was renamed Aegae and has been identified with the remains of a palace complex, theatre, and necropolis of vaulted chamber tombs, along with other graves,

Figure 1.4 Western Pieria, Haliacmon River, view southeast from Eordaea
Source: author, 2014.

near the modern villages of Vergina and Palatitsa ("little palaces"). Aegae had been inhabited since the Early Bronze Age, and even in the Early Iron Age before it came into Macedonian hands it was "immensely rich and populous."[103] It sits in a highly strategic location close to major routes both east–west and north–south, is near the crossing of the Haliacmon, and has a commanding view of the plain. The Macedonians used this strong position to take control of nearly all coastal Pieria from a tribe of Thracians who inhabited the southern part of the central plain. These Thracian Pieres were driven out of their homeland and resettled near Mount Pangaion, east of the Strymon. The Macedonians thus attained their first Aegean access on the western shore of the Thermaic Gulf, where two Greek colonial ports, Methone and Pydna, were already established. At a later time the Macedonians established their own coastal or riverine settlement farther south at Dion, which became the religious capital of the kingdom. In a second move from the Pierian highlands the Macedonians crossed the Haliacmon into Eordaea, and after killing most of the inhabitants they assumed control of the district; a few Eordaean survivors settled near Physca in Mygdonia. The Macedonians continued their expansion into the central plain by taking control of Bottiaea between the Haliacmon and Axios, of Almopia to the northwest, and part of the territory controlled by the Paeonians along the lower Axios.[104] We do not know the timeframe of the conquests, but all can reasonably be assigned to the latter half of the Archaic period, from about 650 to about 510.

In the latter half of the sixth century Amyntas I held the Macedonian Argead kingship for more than forty years. From the commanding position of Aegae at the edge of the Emathian plain he and the Macedonian nobility loyal to him controlled the part of Upper Macedonia immediately to the west, both western Pieria and Eordaea west of Mount Bermion, as well as the central plain from Mount Barnous above Almopia down to the coast of the Thermaic Gulf, with the exception of the Greek coastal cities Methone and Pydna, and, by the end of his reign, to the east as far as the lower Axios. Paeonians and Thracians had long been the dominant powers in the north Aegean, but the balance of power was about to shift to the great advantage of the Macedonians.

Notes

1 Polyb. 8.9.1; Diod. 16.95.1.
2 On the Petralona skull and ongoing controversy surrounding the skull's date see Runnels 1995: 706; Harvati 2009.
3 Anson 1985b.
4 See Roisman and Worthington 2010: xvi; cp. Hatzopoulos 2011b: 53; and cf. n59. Elevations are from the *Road Editions* S.A. topographic map: Macedonia 2010.
5 For the extent of Upper Macedonia before Philip II see e.g. Hammond *HM* I 1972: 37–122; Borza 1992: 31–38; Hatzopoulos 1996: 77–104; Thomas 2010: 74–76; Xydopoulos 2012b.
6 Hammond in *HM* II 1979: 24.
7 Hdt. 7.128.1, 173.1, 4; 8.137.1; Thuc. 2.99.1.

8 Borza 1992: 33–36.
9 Archibald 2011: 85. Dispilio: Hourmouziadis 2002; Theodoulou 2011; Facorellis *et al.* 2014.
10 For settlement sites identified along, and now under, the lake-like middle Haliacmon (result of the Polyfytos Dam built in the mid 1970s), dating from the Early Neolithic period through to the Late Bronze Age, see Andreou *et al.* 1996: 565–566.
11 Str. 7.7.8; 9.5.11; Thuc. 2.99.1-3. Anson 2015b: 235 n72.
12 Thuc. 4.124.1.
13 Thuc. 4.83.1.
14 Begorritis: Liv. 42.53.5; also known as Ostrovo.
15 Thuc. 2.99.5: Temenids from Argos; Diod. 7.15.1: Caranus from Argos. See 'Legends' section below.
16 Str. 7.7.8, 9.5.11; Steph. Byz. s.v. "Elimia"; cp. Thuc. 2.99.2. Karamitrou-Mentessidi 2011: 93–96.
17 Karamitrou-Mentessidi 2011: 96–112.
18 Thuc. 2.99.2.
19 Pliny (*HN* 4.35) includes the Pelagones, Eordaeans, and Almopes among the Paeonian tribes.
20 Hammond *HM* I 1972: 118, following Str. 7.7.8. Pliny (*HN* 4.35) includes Tymphaea in his description of Macedonia, as it was in his day.
21 Thuc. 4.78.6. Hammond in *HM* II 1979: 40–41; Borza 1992: 164–5.
22 Thuc. 2.99; cf. Plin. *HN* 4.33–39.
23 Kottaridi 2002: 75; cf. n10.
24 *Contra* Borza 1992: 79.
25 Thuc. 2.99.5.
26 Steph. Byz. s.v. "Pella"; Petsas, entry in Stillwell *et al.* (1976).
27 Bintliff 1976; Fouache *et al.* 2008.
28 Hdt. 7.123.3; Thuc. 2.99.3–4.
29 Hdt. 7.127; Bintliff 1976: 254–255.
30 Greenwalt 1999: 175; cp. Borza 1987; 1995: 89.
31 Diod. 17.16.3–4; Ath. 13.572d; cp. Arr. *Anab.* 1.11.1. Bosworth 1980a: 97; Borza 1993; Christesen and Murray 2010: 430; Mari 2011: 456; cp. Hatzopoulos 1982: 38–42.
32 Pingiatoglou 2010; Pandermalis 2016.
33 Polyb. 5.97; Str. 7 fr. 11; but Thucydides (2.99.4) considers it part of the Thracian territory of Mygdonia.
34 Homer *Iliad* 2.848–9; Str. 7 fr. 11, 20. Amydon was later called Abydon, tentatively identified as Axiochorion.
35 Thuc. 2.99. Hammond *HM* I 1972: 179 (see his map 1 for ore deposits); Borza 1992: 46.
36 Hdt. 5.17.2, 7.124–126. Inland route into eastern Macedonia: Hammond *HM* I 1972: 193–194 (passing south of Mount Dysoron); Borza 1989 (passing north).
37 Chapter 2 n23, n24.
38 On the disputed nomenclature of the two lakes in the basin, Kerkinitis and Prasias, see Borza 1989; Vasilev 2015: 99–103.
39 Lazaridis 1997: 32–36; Maniatis *et al.* 2010.
40 Archibald 2010: 333, and see Hatzopoulos 1996: 184–186. Str. 7 fr. 33, 35. Draining the plain of Crenides/Philippi: Theophr. *Caus. pl.* 5.14.5–6.
41 On the difficulty of determining territorial boundaries see Hammond 1995. Hatzopoulos 2011a: 43: nearly 90 per cent of ancient Macedonia proper now lies within the borders of present-day Greece. Scupi (Skopje) was a Paeonian settlement

(Hammond *HM* I 1972: 82; *HM* III 1988: 386), and Paeonia became subject to the monarchy of lower (coastal) Macedonia about the mid fourth century.
42 For more recent discussions see: Dascalakis 1965; Kalléris 1988; Borza 1992: 90–97; Hammond 1994c; Engels 2010; Giannakis 2012; and Hatzopoulos 2013, citing pre-1913 arguments.
43 *SEG* 43.434; Voutiras 1998; Lilimbaki-Akamati and Akamatis 2012: 17.
44 E.g. Borza 1999: 42 n27.
45 Borza 1996; Hall 2001; Engels 2010; Hatzopoulos 2011b.
46 Homer *Iliad* 14.226; Str. 7 fr. 2; Just.7.1.1. Justin (7.1.3) calls the pre-Macedonian inhabitants of Emathia Pelasgians, the name applied by Homer, Herodotus, and other authors to an indigenous population of the Greek peninsula and Aegean before the arrival of Greek-speaking people.
47 Hesiod *Eoiae* 3/7; cf. Str. 7 fr. 11. The *Catalogue* is ascribed to Hesiod c. 700 (e.g. Janko 1982: 85–87), although even in antiquity the authorship was questioned, and West (1985: 130–137) dates it as late as c. 540. Janko's dating (still maintained) is here preferred.
48 Hdt.1.56, 8.43, cf. 7.20.
49 Andreou *et al.* 1996: 573–574.
50 Hdt. 7.73. Hammond *HM* I 1972: 407–414.
51 Pieres: Thuc. 2.99.3; Bottiaeans: Str. 6.3.2, 7 fr. 11; Plut. *Theseus* 16.2, *Mor.* 298f–299a; Almopes: Plin. *HN* 4.35.
52 Hammond *HM* I 1972: 15, 1989a: 1–12.
53 Ath. 1.18a. Paus. 6.5.5: lions on Mount Olympus; the lion is prevalent in Macedonian iconography. On hunting scenes see e.g. Palagia 2000; Borza and Palagia 2007, plates 4–7; Franks 2012.
54 On Macedonian *symposia* see Sawada 2010: 393–399; Pownall 2010.
55 Ferrario 2014: 286–287.
56 Str. 7.7.8.
57 For bibliography on "language" see Engels 2010: 93 n35.
58 Str. 7.7.8.
59 Weiler 1968; Mari 2011: 79–82. The perception still exists in modern times, as cited in Borza 1992: 13 n23.
60 Westlake 1935: especially 51–52 and 56–58 (Archelaus), 85–87 (Amyntas III), 129–133 (Alexander II), 166–168, and 176–216 (Philip II); Larsen 1968: 12–26. *Tagos*: see also Chapter 4 n73.
61 Hammond 1989a: 37-38.
62 Str. 7.7.1.
63 Str. 7.7.5.
64 On Greek settlement see Tiverios 2008.
65 Through larger Prespa runs the present-day border between Greece, Albania, and the Former Yugoslav Republic of Macedonia. Theodoulou 2011: 62: archaeologists working in the three countries have discovered to date just in the Prespa region alone more than seventy prehistoric villages, attesting to a dense settlement pattern in early times.
66 Just. 7.2.6–12.
67 On the Paeonians see Str. 7 fr. 4; Merker 1965; Hammond *HM* I 1972: 78–80; 1989a: 40–41.
68 Lilimbaki-Akamati and Akamatis 2003: 141.
69 On Thrace and Thracians see Balcer 1988; Archibald 2010.
70 Engels 2010: 97. On the Orphic papyrus from Derveni see Betegh 2004.
71 Following Hammond 1966: 241–242; Dell 1967: 97; *contra* Papazoglou 1965; cp. Wilkes 1992: 156–180.

72 See e.g. Asirvatham 2010: 100–104.
73 Hesiod *Eoiae* 3/7, n47. On the myth of Macedon cf. Steph. Byz. s.v. "Makedonia" (Hellanicus); Marsyas *FGrH* 135–36, F13; Ael. *NA* 10.48. Hammond 1989a: 12–15; Engels 2010: 89–97.
74 Hdt. 8.139.
75 Cf. Hdt. 5.22.
76 Hdt. 8.137–8.
77 Hammond 1989a: 3 identifies Lebaea with the village Alebea. See also Hatzopoulos 2003.
78 For discussion see Hatzopoulos 2003, citing earlier bibliography.
79 Greenwalt 1986: 121; 1994.
80 Theophilus (second century CE) citing Satyrus [*FGrH/BNJ* 631, Gambetti], Eusebius (late third/early fourth century CE) citing Diodorus (7.13–17), and Synkellos (late eighth/early ninth century CE). Diodorus' genealogy stops shy of Philip III Arrhiadaeus and Alexander IV, which suggests a date c. 325 for his source. He gave a total of 24 kings from Caranus to Alexander III, but seven are missing in Eusebius' citation, notably Perdiccas II and Amyntas III, though both are mentioned elsewhere by Diodorus. Cf. also Paus. 9.40.8; Velleius Paterculus 1.6; Hesychius s.v. "Karannos" and "Korannos."
81 Diod. 7.17; Plut. *Alex.* 2.1; cf. Paus. 9.40.8–9, Just. 7.1.7–2.1 (only one generation between Caranus and Perdiccas).
82 Diod. 7.15.1 (writing in the first century); Synkellos, Adler and Tuffin 2002: 288.
83 A scholiast on Clement of Alexandria, *Protrepticus* 11.8, citing Euphorion F35 (mid third century BCE), claims Caranus, son of Poanthes, consulted Delphi about a colony from Argos to Macedonia, and founded Aegae by renaming Edessa.
84 Hdt. 5.20.4. All translations (here slightly modified) from the Greek and Latin texts are those of the Loeb Classical Library unless otherwise noted.
85 E.g. (following Macan) Greenwalt: 1985; Vassileva 2007; Ogden 2011: 57–71.
86 *Contra* Scullion 2003.
87 For the fragments and discussion of *Archelaus* see Hyginus *Fab.* 219 and Collard *et al.* 2004: 330–362; for parallels between the Caranus/Perdiccas, Caranus/Archelaus stories see especially 335. See also Harder 1985.
88 Cf. n34.
89 Hecataeus of Miletus, so Hammond *HM* I 1972: 176.
90 App. *Syr.* 63 (Appian of Alexandria, writing in the second century CE).
91 Thuc. 4.83.1.
92 Steph. Byz. s.v. "Argeou." Cp. Plut. *Mor.* 326d–345b: Alexander (the Great) is referred to as "rich and *Argeades*."
93 Ath. 14.659.
94 Sprawski 2010: 130. For the suggestion that Perdiccas I is the invented ancestor of Perdiccas II see Ogden 2011: 65.
95 Just. 7.2; Synkellos, Adler and Tuffin 2002: 310.
96 E.g. Badian 1982b; Greenwalt 1985, 1986; Errington 1990: 2–3; Green 1991: 3–6; Borza 1992: 82–83; Bosworth 2002: 29–30; Carney 1994, 2008; Vasilev 2011.
97 Plato *Laws* 3.683d; Apollodorus 2.8; Paus. 2.18.7; Diod. 7.13 (note parallels with Ael. *NA* 10.48).
98 Greenwalt 1985: 49 n16. Andronikos 1984: 38–39 dated the palace to the end of the fourth century BCE (reign of Cassander); Kottaridi's (2011: 301–304) higher dating to the third quarter of the fourth century (reign of Philip II), is contested, though the 'old' capital presumably had a royal residence—see Saatsoglou-Paliadeli 1999: 360.

99 Hdt. 5.22; see Chapter 2.
100 Cf. e.g. Hdt. 8.137.2, 9.44.1; Thuc. 2.99.2. King 2010: 375–376.
101 Homer *Iliad* 2.763–767.
102 Theories of Macedonian expansion, based on Thuc. 2.99: e.g. Edson 1970: 20–24; Hammond *HM* I 1972: 436–439, 1989a: 8–12, 51–52; Errington 1990: 5–7; Mari 2011: 83–84; Vasilev 2011.
103 Kottaridi 2002: 76. Hammond first suggested ancient Aegae should be identified with the modern villages of Vergina and Palatitsa; *contra* Faklaris 1994.
104 Bottiaeans: Thuc. 2.99.3; Hdt. 8.127; Flensted-Jensen 1995: 106, 109–110. Almopes: Plin. *HN* 4.35. Paeonians: Plin. *HN* 4.35; Merker 1965.

2 Macedonia and the Argead monarchy in the fifth century

Macedonia was obliged, by virtue of its geographical situation, to be involved in major political and military developments in the north Aegean. The three kings whose reigns span the fifth century were not mere pawns, however, for their shrewd responses to foreign powers earned economic and political significance for the kingdom. When the Persians invaded the southern Balkans (492, 480–479) Alexander I (c. 498–454) diplomatically balanced his allegiance to Persia and friendship with Athens; then in the wake of the Persian defeat with eastward expansion he gained access to valuable sources of silver, gold, and timber. During the Peloponnesian War (431–404) Perdiccas II (c. 454–413) managed duplicitous alliances with Sparta, Athens, and the Chalcidians, at the same time defending his throne against foreign-backed pretenders and the encroachment of the Odrysian Thracians. Later in the same war Archelaus (c. 413–399) strengthened the kingdom's infrastructure with roads, fortifications, ports, and important improvements to the military.

Alexander I and the Macedonian response to Persia

Alexander I, son and successor of Amyntas I, makes a grand entrance in the pages of history. He appears in Herodotus' account of Persian advances into Europe as a bold and clever man in his dealings with both Persians and Greeks, playing the dangerous role of middleman at the crossroads between east and west. The stories Herodotus tells about Alexander's responses to the Persian encroachment quite possibly came from someone close to the king, if not the king himself, during a personal visit to the Macedonian court in the middle years of the fifth century.[1] By that time, the famous battles of Thermopylae and Plataea were long over and the Greeks of the southern city-states had capitalized on their decisive victory over the Persians with their own advances into the north Aegean. Prior to the war the Macedonian king had been subject to and allied with Persia, but after the latter's defeat he found himself in the awkward position of needing to excuse his 'medism'—that is, cooperation with the Persians/Medes. This circumstance colours what Herodotus tells us about the 'philhellene' Alexander.

The historical context of Alexander's first appearance is about 510, during the reign of Amyntas I. As the story goes,[2] seven Persian envoys arrived at the

Macedonian court to demand 'earth and water', the customary tokens of submission to Persian suzerainty.[3] They were sent by King Darius' general in Europe, Megabazus. Amyntas I, as the reigning king, cooperatively gave the tokens, or agreed to give them, and then hosted the envoys to a banquet (*symposium*), which, in true Macedonian style, was followed by plenty of after-dinner drinking. As the drinking progressed, the Persian guests, claiming it was their own custom at home to have their wives and concubines join them after dinner, requested the company of women. Amyntas explained that it was not the Macedonian custom for women to dine with men,[4] but he did agree to bring in some women. When the women arrived and were forced to sit beside the now intoxicated envoys, the Persians began to grope and kiss them, an outrage the king endured in silence (Herodotus says he was terrified of Persian power), but his young son promptly intervened with heroics. Alexander suggested first that the elderly Amyntas should quit his wine and go to bed, and then that the women should be sent to bathe before the Persians had their way with them. Using this clever ploy Alexander got the Macedonian "mothers and sisters" out of the hall. By the time the freshened-up women returned, the Persians were too thoroughly drunk to notice that the women were not women at all but rather beardless Macedonian youths dressed in women's clothes, and so they were caught completely unawares by the hidden daggers and slaughter that followed. All the Persian envoys, Herodotus says, and their entire entourage of servants were slaughtered and together with the baggage train made to disappear without a trace. As would be the logical sequel, a search party came looking for the missing envoys. Alexander exercised his cunning again by pacifying them with a large sum of money and—most ironic, given his heroic defence of the Macedonian womenfolk—with the marriage of his own sister Gygaea to the leader of the search party, Bubares, son of Megabazus.[5]

Most historians reject the historicity of this episode on grounds of improbability.[6] Alexander's heroism strongly suggests self-promotion much later during his own reign, and surely he would not have *boasted* about annihilating a Persian embassy prior to Persia's defeat at Plataea in 479. However, if we reject the embassy *and* the story of its disappearance as entirely fiction, then we may conclude that tokens of earth and water were not demanded in 510; but if we accept the episode as is, we must allow that earth and water were never delivered to the Persian king.[7] So either way, we are left to conjecture about Macedonia's relationship with Persia prior to 492.[8] Some historians, rejecting only the murder of the envoys and not the embassy itself, assume that Macedonia became a vassal state about 510, while others argue that Macedonia held semi-autonomous status until 492. According to Herodotus, it was in 492, when Darius sent another expedition under the command of Mardonius, that Macedonia formally submitted: "[the Persian] land army added the Macedonians to the slaves that they had already; for all the nations nearer to them than Macedonia had been made subject to the Persians before this."[9] Herodotus neglects to say *who* is on the Macedonian throne at the time of Mardonius' invasion, though it is assumed to be Alexander I. While the tendency has been to charge Herodotus with gullibility,[10] we cannot deny the historicity of the marriage—and this ancient diplomatic practice is one the Macedonians are especially noted for— since Herodotus makes a later reference to a son of Bubares and Gygaea, named Amyntas, being given rule of a city in Asia Minor.[11] So rather than expunge the entire episode, looking to the broader historical context we might credit Herodotus with revealing the ambivalent position of Macedonia between east and west in relation to two major shifts in power in the north Aegean, one late in the sixth century and the other near the end of the first quarter of the fifth century.[12] The first shift is a consequence of the encroachment of Persian interests and a military advance into Europe from Asia. The second shift comes about with the defeat of the Persians on Greek soil and waters some thirty years later and the subsequent rise of Athenian naval supremacy. By concerning himself with these shifts in power in his investigation of the great east–west confrontation in the so-called Persian Wars, Herodotus has demonstrated a complexity of relationships between eastern and western powers.[13]

The first shift in power was triggered when Darius I, the Great King of Persia, led an expedition across the Hellespont from Asia to Europe in about 514, with the aim of subduing the most powerful tribe in the central Balkans, the Scythians, who inhabited regions along the Istros/Danube and around the shore of the Black Sea. The expedition was a resounding failure, so in a move that would help restore losses both in military reputation and finances Darius left behind in Europe his general Megabazus with instructions to reduce the Thracians and Paeonians along the north Aegean.[14] His intention was to extend Persian power into the Balkans. The Paeonians, Macedonia's northern neighbours, had long been a powerful presence in the valley of the Axios River, and more recently they had moved into the valley of the Strymon. Between 513 and 510 Megabazus defeated and deported several Paeonian tribes along the Strymon that had been mining silver and gold at Mount Pangaion near the river's mouth. Though not all the tribes were defeated, the deportation to Asia of the leading tribes and families at this time broke Paeonian power for good. The Macedonians, if they could avoid similar subjugation, were in a position to benefit from the new political situation, though it appears they already may have taken control from the Paeonians of Pella, Ichnae, and the district of Amphaxitis, along the lower Axios, before Megabazus' campaign: Megabazus found the Paeonians along the Strymon, not on the Axios, where they had been in Homer's *Catalogue*, and it was the Macedonian ruling Argeadae who destroyed the Paeonian stronghold Amydon on the Axios.[15]

Megabazus' march back to Asia Minor with the deported Paeonians is the context for Herodotus' story of the seven envoys and the demand for earth and water. In another version of the story,[16] Macedonia was to be added to Megabazus' conquests, but there is no mention of earth and water; rather, the envoys asked Amyntas for hostages as a guarantee of future peace. In this version Bubares' mission was punitive, but the marriage to Gygaea (in a romantic twist he fell in love with the king's daughter) averted war, and Bubares "entered into a regular family relationship with Amyntas." A marriage alliance at this time between the Macedonian king's daughter and a son of the Persian king's top general would have been a token of Amyntas' cooperation with Persia,[17] and it was that tie with Persia that secured Macedonia's stability in the north Aegean for the next thirty years.[18] Amyntas also acted as Darius' *hyparchos*, possibly his provincial ruler.[19] Bubares stayed in Macedonia for some time, perhaps guarding the crossing of the lower Axios and the route into the region from the north via the middle Axios valley.[20] Amyntas is said to have died soon after Bubares' departure,[21] but it is not known when or why Bubares departed. When the Ionian Greeks revolted from Persian control in 499 there may have been a greater need for Bubares' presence in Asia Minor.[22] About 505, a few years after the democratic revolution in Athens and exile of Hippias, last of the Peisistratid tyrants, Amyntas offered Hippias for refuge the district of Anthemous east of the Axios.[23] Anthemous must have been under Macedonian control at the time,[24] and Amyntas must still have been alive and ruling. So Alexander probably came to the throne between 505 and about 498.

By 494 the Ionian Revolt had been put down and Darius was looking to Europe again, resolved both to punish the Athenians and Eretrians for sending ships and men in support of the revolt and to restore Hippias as tyrant in Athens. In 492 he sent his nephew and son-in-law Mardonius as general of an expedition to secure the land and sea route along the north Aegean coast in preparation for a march into the Greek peninsula. This brought Mardonius into eastern Macedonia, and, according to Herodotus, this is when the Macedonians became subject to Persia.[25] Mardonius' campaign had a disastrous outcome, however. His fleet was caught in a storm rounding Mount Athos, the tip of the easternmost prong of Chalcidice, 300 of his ships were destroyed, and some 20,000 men lost in the sea, while his land army encamped in Macedonian territory was attacked by Thracian Brygi.[26] Mardonius himself was wounded and after avenging himself on the Brygi he retreated to Asia. Two years later, in 490, a Persian naval force, with Hippias aboard, crossed the southern Aegean directly to Eretria in Euboea and from there to Marathon in Attica, east of Athens.[27] The astonishing Athenian victory provided the precedent for successful resistance to Persian ascendancy in the Balkans.

Apart from Mardonius' brief occupation in 492, from the departure of Bubares perhaps in 499–498 until the arrival of Xerxes in 480 there is no mention of a Persian overseer (satrap or other) in or responsible for Macedonia.[28] Whether Alexander became *hyparchos* in his father's place we do not know. Herodotus calls him *strategos* (general) and *basileus* (king) of the Macedonians.[29] Subservience of some sort to Persia is clear, but the nearest Persian garrison was possibly the one under the *hyparchos* Boges at Eion, at the mouth of the Strymon. Alexander, so long as he did not act counter to Persian interests,[30] might have had considerable freedom to exercise a foreign policy as he saw fit and to boost the Macedonian economy by trade, especially given that for much of that time Persian attention was diverted elsewhere, by revolts in Ionia and Egypt and by the death of Darius and accession of Xerxes. It was possibly for the supply of timber for building ships (maybe the very ships that defeated the Persian fleet at Salamis in September 480)[31] that Alexander was honoured at Athens as *proxenos* and *euergetes*, "friend" and "benefactor" of the city.[32] The benefaction, whatever it was, must date before late 480, when Mardonius chose him as ambassador to the Athenians by reason of his simultaneous marriage connection with Persian nobility and his high standing at Athens.[33]

Xerxes' invasion of Greece in 480 resumed his father's plans for punishment and subjugation. In preparation he sent men ahead to construct a bridge across the Strymon and establish military supply bases in Thrace and Macedonia, and in 483 Bubares returned to Macedonia as one of the overseers of a project to cut a canal across the Athos peninsula, a precaution against treacherous storms.[34] Traces of the canal are only barely visible today. When William Leake was logging his travels through northern Greece in October 1806 he described the canal as not more than 60 ft wide and silted up from the surrounding heights. He wrote that the currents and gales are so strong half the year around Mount Athos that no locals, even for a high price, would sail around the peninsula. "Xerxes, therefore, was perfectly justified in cutting this canal."[35] When Xerxes' army marched and sailed into Macedonia in the spring of 480, the presence of such a large force must have stretched Macedonia's resources to the limit, and the Persians reportedly drank the Echedoros dry.[36] Alexander was required to muster and outfit a fighting force of Macedonians to be incorporated into the Persian ranks; this was likely cavalry, though it is not stated.

In the days and months that followed Alexander appears to have played a double game. The allied Greeks had chosen the Peneus River in the Vale of Tempe—the perceived 'frontier' of the Greek world, where a narrow coastal route leads into Lower Macedonia—as their first line of defence, and Alexander sent messengers there to advise them not to try to hold their present position.[37] What Xerxes was up to was having a wide path cut across the mountains so his army could cross west of Olympus to enter Thessaly at Gonnoi, behind the Greek lines.[38] Alexander's motives, alas, are the historian's guessing game,[39] but two effective outcomes may give it away. His advice effectively served the Persians in that the Greek retreat left Thessaly undefended with little option but to medize; and it effectively served Alexander's self-interest since it got the Persian army and inevitable fighting out of his territory.[40] Herodotus expresses his opinion that fear of being outflanked was the true reason for the Greeks' withdrawal, since they discovered, independent of Alexander's messengers, that farther inland another pass led from Macedonia into Thessaly. The Greeks escaped Tempe unscathed, only to be outflanked at Thermopylae.

Playing the double game again at Plataea the following year, Alexander was commanding the Macedonian contingent in the Persian army (now under Mardonius' generalship after Xerxes retreated to Asia following the defeat of his fleet at Salamis) and was about to face the Athenians in battle.[41] After a ten-day stand-off in the plain near Plataea, with sacrificial omens advising both the Persians and the allied Greeks against offensive action, Mardonius decided despite the omens—and since Greek reinforcements kept streaming in, while he himself was low on supplies—to attack the following morning. Under cover of darkness, a lone horseman approached the Athenian camp and hailed the guards, identifying himself as Alexander the Macedonian. Alexander asked to speak to "the generals," or more specifically to Aristides, one of the ten annually elected Athenian *strategoi* (generals), whom he perhaps knew personally from a previous visit to Athens.[42] Alexander revealed Mardonius' plan for a dawn attack and stressed the secrecy of the information. He ended by expressing a wish to be remembered for his actions on behalf of the Greeks and then rode off behind enemy lines. The tip-off prompted a meeting of the Athenian generals with the Spartan Pausanias, overall commander of the allied Greeks, and a change of deployment was implemented.[43] On the following day, both sides shifted and counter-shifted their deployments, so it was the second morning before the battle finally unfolded. Mardonius was killed in his battle with the Spartans; his Greek contingents, with the exception of the Thebans, who stood and fought, retreated from engagement with the Athenians, and while they escaped, shielded from pursuit by the Boeotian and "other" cavalry (perhaps including the Macedonians), the Persian army fled to their fortified camp, where thousands were slaughtered by the victorious Greeks.[44]

Historians, not surprisingly, have expressed serious doubt about the plausibility of a secret night visit to the Athenian camp.[45] Yet Alexander did have good reason to play both sides in self-interest, and a serious objection may, and should, be made to dismissing all of Herodotus' exciting tales as so much romantic invention by recalling that history is, in fact, full of daring episodes. In 1944 the English adventurer Patrick Leigh Fermor devised a daring scheme to capture the German commander in Crete, General Kreipe. It was a reckless and, given the reprisals, costly enterprise, but he did pull it off.[46] What truly transpired between Alexander and the Athenians at Plataea we can never know.

In between Alexander's two warnings to the Greeks he acted as Xerxes' agent. Shortly after his messengers advised the Greeks at Tempe he sent Macedonian officers to cities in Boeotia to safeguard the population during Xerxes' march through central Greece in the summer of 480.[47] The presence of the Macedonian officers was the 'official' sign to the Persian army that the Boeotian cities were cooperating with the Persians and should not be treated as hostile. While his actions did help to protect the Greeks, Alexander was acting on Xerxes' instructions to arrange submission in advance. Then over the winter of 480–479 Alexander (by reason of his status at Athens as *proxenos* and *euergetes* and his connection through his sister's marriage with Persian nobility) went in person to Athens as an emissary of Mardonius to negotiate an alliance whereby the Persians sought to gain control of the Athenian fleet which had so recently defeated them at Salamis. Brought before the Athenian Assembly, Alexander recited the terms of the alliance offered by Mardonius and stressed the advantages to the Athenians in accepting it. Then he added his own reasons why the Athenians would be wise to accept. In this speech there is no hedging on the part of the Macedonian king; in fact he is eloquently persuasive.[48] The Athenians, for their part, were not won over by his speech or by Persian promises, and before another year had passed Mardonius lay dead on the battlefield at Plataea, the remnants of his defeated army were fleeing through Thrace back to Asia, and Alexander was home in Macedonia pondering how to take advantage of the newly created power vacuum in the north Aegean.

Though possibly Alexander's 'reward' for hosting Xerxes' army had been the extension of his kingdom from Mount Olympus to Mount Haemus, this may rather have resulted from Alexander's own opportunism.[49] He wasted no time in making decisive moves on the heels of the fleeing Persians. East of the Axios River, the districts of Crestonia, Bisaltia, and Mygdonia all came under Macedonian control.[50] A year or two later Alexander attacked the Persian military outpost on the Strymon and from the spoils he set up a gold statue at Delphi.[51] Its placement alongside the Greek dedication from the spoils taken at Salamis was an emphatic statement, whatever the facts, that he staked a claim in the panhellenic victory.

Many historians view Alexander's acts of philhellenism as they appear in the pages of Herodotus as self-aggrandizement.[52] He had, however, made considerable inroads with his Greek southern neighbours even before the Persian defeat and despite his kingdom's vassalage to Persia. For Alexander personally, being accepted as a Hellene was of great importance. According to Herodotus, he "proved" his Greek ancestry to the *Hellenodicae* (officials) at Olympia so that he could compete in the most prestigious of the panhellenic games.

> Now that these descendants of Perdiccas are Greeks, as they themselves say, I myself chance to know and will prove it in the later part of my history; and further, the Hellenodicae who manage the contest at Olympia determined that it is so. For when Alexander chose to contend and entered the lists for that purpose, the Greeks who were to run against him wanted to bar him from the race, saying that the contest should be for Greeks and not for foreigners; but Alexander, proving himself to be an Argive, was judged to be a Greek. So he competed in the furlong race and ran a dead heat for the first place. This, then, is approximately what happened.[53]

Alexander's proof must have involved some sort of authentication of the ancestry of Perdiccas I that connected the Macedonian king list back through three centuries and some ten generations to the legendary Heraclid Temenus of Argos. If later genealogies agreed on the descendants of Temenus—there are no fewer than three distinctly different traditions—more confidence could be placed in what Herodotus transmits, but, as it is, historians have much debated Alexander's ancestry and the historical problems associated with his participation in the games.[54] While Herodotus states that Alexander was admitted as a competitor in the games, he offers no hint as to the date of the Olympiad (guesses range from 504 to 476, with some speculation that he participated in more than one),[55] and even more problematically he says Alexander finished first in a dead heat in the sprint, while the extant Olympic victors lists do not record the Macedonian king among the victors.

Alexander's admittance into the panhellenic games at Olympia is regularly brought into discussions of the Greekness or otherwise of the Macedonians.

What Herodotus' text suggests is that the royal house of Alexander was acknowledged as Greek by an official judgment at Olympia, probably in the 490s, and that there was a perception at that time in antiquity that the Macedonians were distinct from the southern Greeks, for which reason other competitors objected to Alexander's participation and he was required to produce proof of his Greek descent.[56] The rest of the Macedonians were excluded; only the king, it seems, was permitted to compete.

The resources

After the battle of Plataea Alexander I brought great economic benefits to his kingdom through expansion eastward in the wake of the Persian retreat. His advance saw first the conquest of territory inhabited by the Thracian Edones and Bisaltae, including the capture of gold mines at the head of the Echedoros River and on the southeastern face of the Dysoron range. One silver mine alone near Dysoron reputedly generated a talent of silver per day for the Macedonian king.[57] Exploitation of the Strymon region "where are forests aplenty for ship-building, and much wood for oars, and mines of silver"[58] was also an objective of the neighbouring Thracians and Thasians as well as the Athenians. One of the earliest missions of the newly formed anti-Persian alliance, the Athenian (or Delian) League, was the Athenian general Cimon's conquest, about 476, of Eion, a port at the mouth of the Strymon formerly in Persian control.[59] Seizure of the port, which gave the Athenians an outlet for exporting the region's resources, marks the beginning of the second of two major shifts in power in the north Aegean, as the Athenians proceeded through conquest and colonization to monopolize sources of timber and precious metals in order to maintain their strong fleet. Sooner or later conflict was bound to happen, though our sources are nearly silent on Macedonian activity in the region for the next half a century.[60]

Once he had gained control of mining interests, Alexander began to mint silver coinage in his own name. At first he simply altered coins of the Bisaltae by replacing their two-letter identification with the first two letters of his own name, ΑΛ. Then he continued to mint an adaptation of their 'Ares types' depicting a warrior (or hunter) horseman either standing behind or sitting astride his horse and carrying two spears, an echo perhaps of Homer's Pelasgians or Paeonians (Figure 2.1).[61] The coins held value as bullion based on the weight of the metal in each coin. Using one measure of weight for trade with the Thracian tribes and the Persian east (*stater*) and another for trade with the Greek colonies of the north Aegean, Alexander seems to have made an innovation by minting on a double standard, and the practice is reflective of Macedonia's position at a geographical and trading crossroads.[62] A temporary loss of the silver mines in Bisaltia is suggested by the minting of only small coins (*tetrobols*) during Perdiccas II's reign (Figure 2.2).[63] Larger issues do reappear under Archelaus (Figure 2.3), although there is a devaluation of the coinage towards the end of the century, when bronze issues begin to circulate with token value rather than

Figure 2.1 Silver *tetradrachm* (4 drachm) of Alexander I. 1963.268.40
Source: courtesy of the American Numismatic Society.

Figure 2.2 Silver *tetrobol* (4 obol) of Perdiccas II. 1944.100.12144
Source: courtesy of the American Numismatic Society.

Figure 2.3 Silver *didrachm* (2 drachm) of Archelaus. 1905.57.65
Source: courtesy of the American Numismatic Society.

by weight; this also may suggest a shortage of silver.[64] The high point of Macedonian wealth in terms of mineral resources did not come until the fourth century, when Philip II gained control of the Pangaion mines and began minting gold *stater* "philippics" in imitation of Persian gold "darics." Using coin to pay mercenaries and for bribes became a common practice of Macedonian kings. In 463–462 the Athenians brought a charge against Cimon of accepting a bribe from Alexander, since Cimon had allegedly left Macedonian interests untouched when he was annexing Thasian and Thracian territory in the Strymon/Pangaion region. He was acquitted, though only barely, and Alexander fell out of grace with the Athenians.[65]

Figure 2.4 Gold necklace with knot of Heracles, Amphipolis, end of fourth century BCE
Source: author, 2013.

Alexander surely would have used his mineral resources to invest in defence, and quite possibly he had the military in mind when in the early 460s, after Argos captured Mycenae, he welcomed Mycenaean refugees fleeing to Macedonia. An influx of crown-supported settlers, especially ones trained in Greek hoplite tactics, certainly had military potential.[66] New settlers would require tools at minimum, and in the western mountains deposits of copper and iron provided raw materials for making both tools and weapons. Silver and gold were used for practical and luxury items. As evidenced in the splendid grave goods from Tombs II and III at Vergina, vessels of many kinds, mostly silver, were used for banqueting and bathing, while beaten gold was used for decoration and as a symbol of status (Figure 2.4).[67] The importance of minerals to the Macedonian economy, and especially to the power of the kings, was so vital that after the Roman conquest in 168 the Senate prohibited the mining of gold and silver.[68]

Timber was another vital resource from a very early date, and here again the Romans after their conquest of Macedonia placed a total prohibition on cutting timber for shipbuilding.[69] The western mountains in particular were covered with forests of beech and oak. The great rivers, the Haliacmon, Axios, and Strymon, as well as the lesser Loudias, were conduits for transporting the timber from the upland mountain slopes down to the coast for export. Well before Pella was developed as a major Macedonian seaport, Alexander I appropriated the Greek port of Pydna. In the early 460s he gave refuge there to the Athenian exile Themistocles, former hero and mastermind behind the panhellenic naval victory at Salamis, and secured him safe passage to Ionia. This act has suggested a close relationship between Alexander and the Athenian naval strategist that would support the view that Alexander supplied shipbuilding timber for the victorious fleet.[70] Like the Strymon region, Pydna became another bone of contention between Macedonia and Athens. Timber suitable for shipbuilding was scarce in southern Greece, especially in Attica, so demand for Macedonian timber was high and often dictated politics, much as oil does today.[71]

In the early days of the kingdom the herding of goats and sheep seems to have been prevalent, with transhumance between lowland and upland pastures being the way of life for many Macedonians.[72] In the sixth and fifth centuries it is probable that the Emathian plain was suitable as pasturage for cattle and horses, and by the mid fourth century possibly some swampy areas were being reclaimed for growing cereal crops. It was about the middle of the fourth century that the plain of Crenides/Philippi was drained for agriculture, and at the end of the fourth century grain, even if only in modest quantity, was available for export.[73] The port at Pella and the exceptionally large *agora* in the centre of the city, right on the main east–west thoroughfare, attest to vigorous trade in a variety of commodities from the end of the fifth century.

Alexander I harnessed both the natural and human resources of his kingdom, and in doing so he did much to establish Macedonia as a player in the north Aegean power game. After 463–462 (Cimon's trial), we hear nothing of his activities, however. Concurrent with his reign, Teres king of the Odrysian Thracians was establishing a powerful kingdom to the east of Macedonian territory, and his son Sparadokos appears to have eclipsed Alexander's power in the Strymon region after 465.[74] Given that the numismatic evidence suggests a decline in the coinage after about 460, it is possible that Alexander experienced a major reversal late in his reign. It has been assumed, based on the attribution to him of a forty-four-year reign, that he died in the mid 450s.[75] There is a (dubious) suggestion that he died violently,[76] though allowing an age of about twenty at the time of Megabazus' campaign, he must have been close to eighty years old by this time. All of this calls into question the stability of the Macedonian kingdom in the mid fifth century. Five sons survived Alexander, but no clear successor emerges until the 430s.

Perdiccas II on three fronts: The Greek city-states, Thrace, and the western frontier

Perdiccas II was the eighth king to hold the Macedonian throne, and his father Alexander had been the seventh. This is on the authority of their contemporaries Thucydides and Herodotus,[77] both of whom may have had personal contact with the Argead court (Thucydides owned property near Macedonia in Thrace and spent considerable time in the region). Though we should expect Perdiccas to have succeeded Alexander about 454, he does not appear on the historical scene until the mid 430s, when he is found defending his throne against his brother Philip and Philip's son Amyntas. What troubles occurred in Macedonia with the kingship in the intervening two decades is a mystery with few clues.

Sometime before 433 Perdiccas deprived Philip of control over territory (*archē*) east of the Axios in Amphaxitis. He also deprived another brother, Alcetas, of control over territory (*archē*, locale and date unknown). A fourth brother, Menelaus, is known to have been politically active, since he is listed as an oath-taker in a treaty between Perdiccas and Athens, while the fifth brother, Amyntas, was not involved in public life.[78] (It is from Amyntas' line of descent, however, that the kings of the fourth century come: Amyntas III down to the last Argead, Alexander IV.) The actions of Perdiccas indicate that a period of internal weakness occurred, but that by the mid 430s Perdiccas had sole title to the kingship.[79] Hammond claims that following the "violent" death of Alexander three of his sons, Philip, Alcetas, and Perdiccas, simultaneously succeeded, *all as kings* by election of the Assembly; but his reconstruction of this period goes well beyond the evidence.[80] Three kings of one (not large) kingdom are two too many, and the division of Macedonia into three kingdoms seems not only improbable but also disproved by Perdiccas' actions.[81] Alexander I's ultimate fate and what appears to be a twenty-year-long succession struggle involving at least three of his sons are obscured in a frustrating 'dark age' in Macedonian history. Both Herodotus and Thucydides must have known what was going on and yet are completely silent about it.

Alexander's successor undoubtedly had to deal immediately with trouble on his borders with Illyria and Thrace, as habitually arose at the accession of a new king.[82] And by the time Perdiccas emerges on the scene many of his father's gains in the east were lost. Ennea Hodoi, reportedly a gain of Alexander I, was already back in the hands of the Thracians by 465, when the Athenians attempted their first settlement there.[83] In the 450s the Athenians established a strong foothold by attaching to their League Argilos on the Bisaltic coast and Berge inland on the Strymon and by sending 1,000 settlers to Bisaltia.[84] An Athenian colony at Brea followed in the 440s, and then in 437, after several attempts, the Athenians finally established a colony at Ennea Hodoi which they renamed Amphipolis.[85] Soon after the 'founding' of Amphipolis, the Athenians began to increase the tribute paid into their League by member states in the north Aegean, particularly the Chalcidian cities of Potidaea and Torone.[86] General unrest of League members quickly led to revolt and subsequently to catastrophic war.

Perdiccas' moves to protect his own interests against Athenian encroachment in the north contributed in no small measure to the outbreak of the Peloponnesian War. This war between the two most powerful Greek city-states, Athens and Sparta, and involving most of the Aegean and southern mainland Greek states as allies of one side or the other, lasted nearly thirty years, from 431 to 404. For Macedonia, the consequences were more beneficial than detrimental, since continual naval activity meant that Macedonian ship timber and pitch were constantly in demand and thus war generated healthy revenue; and since the two Greek powers continually wore each other down, Macedonia's own relatively weak military situation was mitigated.

Some years earlier, before the war broke out, Perdiccas had been an "ally and friend" of Athens.[87] Details are unknown, but the alliance likely involved the supply of timber for Athens, presumably with economic benefit to Perdiccas. Then, about 433, for reasons unknown, Perdiccas' alliance dissolved into enmity when the Athenians formed a separate alliance with Philip and Derdas. Derdas was probably of the Elimiote royal house, perhaps king at the time, and a cousin of Perdiccas and Philip.[88] We do not know whether Philip went seeking the support of Athens or whether Athens sought out Philip with the intention of stirring internal dissention to keep Macedonia weak. As a matter of self-preservation, since the Athenians were about to send thirty ships and 1,000 heavily armed hoplites to support Philip's bid for the throne, Perdiccas sent to Sparta hoping to provoke a war with Athens in the south. He also sent to Corinth to get help in fomenting revolt in Potidaea, which was a colony of Corinth but also now a dissatisfied tribute-paying member of the Athenian League. And he sent to the Chalcidians and Bottiaeans, urging their revolt from the League.[89] The Potidaeans, Chalcidians, and Bottiaeans were all located on his borders, and by making them his allies Perdiccas hoped to strengthen his military situation against the combined forces of Philip, Derdas' Elimiotes, and the Athenians.

The Potidaeans did join the Chalcidians and Bottiaeans in revolt, and Perdiccas, to strengthen his position further, persuaded the Chalcidians to abandon their many coastal cities around the peninsulas and to settle together in one location inland at Olynthus, where they could better protect themselves and not be picked off one by one by the Athenian fleet. He won them over by the diplomatic offer of use of Macedonian lands in Mygdonia around Lake Bolbe.[90] It was a move that would come back to haunt the Macedonian kingship, but at the time it was effective in weakening the Athenian hold on the region. Despite the open revolt, the Athenians first opted to proceed with their expedition to support Philip, and sailing to the Macedonian coast they joined forces with Philip and Derdas' brothers who had already invaded Lower Macedonia from Elimeia.[91] The Corinthians had meantime sent out 2,000 hoplites to protect their colony. By the time this force arrived the Athenians had already captured Therme, on the eastern coast of the Thermaic Gulf, and were now besieging Perdiccas at Pydna. The siege dragged on, and with the Corinthians' arrival at Potidaea demanding counteraction, the Athenians had little choice but to come to terms with Perdiccas and end the siege. Now technically in alliance with both Perdiccas and Philip, they took a force of allies including 600 Macedonian cavalry from the army of Philip and Derdas' brother Pausanias and proceeded to the westernmost prong of Chalcidice.[92] The turn of events was not in Philip's favour, and he soon sought support from the Thracians.

In a matter of days Perdiccas again broke his alliance with Athens by accepting appointment as commander of the cavalry defending Potidaea. Entrusting affairs in Macedonia to Iolaus (otherwise unknown), he rode for Potidaea at the head of 200 Macedonian horsemen.[93] These were stationed along with the Chalcidians and other allies about 11 km (7 miles) from, but within sight of,

Potidaea at Olynthus, on orders to attack the Athenians in the rear as soon as the battle at Potidaea began. However, the Athenian general Callias ordered the 600 Macedonian cavalry of Philip to ride towards Olynthus to keep the cavalry there in check. When the signal came that the Athenians were victorious in that day's battle (though Potidaea did not fall to Athens until winter 430–429) both sides retreated, with neither contingent of Macedonian cavalry having engaged.[94]

The Athenians' clash with the Corinthians over Potidaea along with other aggressive actions led to the Spartan declaration of war the following winter, 432–431. In their efforts to regain control in the north the Athenians sought an alliance with Sitalces, king of the powerful Odrysian Thracians on the eastern border of Perdiccas' kingdom. Perdiccas' priorities were to protect Macedonian interests and to hold onto his throne, so he made a promise, the nature of which is unknown, to Sitalces "on condition that he [Sitalces] should reconcile him [Perdiccas] to the Athenians and should not bring back his brother Philip, who was hostile, to make him king."[95] Sitalces' brother-in-law Nymphodorus, a Greek of Abdera, negotiated the alliance between Sitalces and Athens, whereby Sitalces promised he would put an end to the Chalcidian revolt and the Athenians promised to support him by land and sea. Nymphodorus also persuaded the Athenians to give Therme back to Perdiccas and to form a new alliance with the Macedonian king.[96] Perdiccas immediately joined the Athenian general Phormio in a campaign against his recent allies, the Chalcidians. However, the following summer, unbeknownst to the Athenians, Perdiccas sent 1,000 troops to fight for Athens' enemy Sparta in Acarnania (though the Macedonians showed up too late to join the battle).[97]

By the fall of 429 Perdiccas had not yet honoured his promise to Sitalces, nor had Sitalces yet ended the Chalcidian revolt, and the Athenians were asking Sitalces to support Perdiccas' rival. So the Thracian king mustered a large army—some 150,000, about 50,000 of which were cavalry—from his own Odrysians and from subject Thracian and Paeonian tribes, and then from Doberos in Paeonia he descended down the Axios valley into Lower Macedonia against Perdiccas and the Chalcidians. Sitalces had with him Philip's son Amyntas, intending to put him on the throne. What became of Philip we do not know, but since he is never heard of again it is assumed he was dead. Also with Sitalces were some Athenian envoys who had come to him on the matter of the Macedonian throne, presumably provoked by Perdiccas' support of Sparta. Perdiccas' infantry forces were far too inadequate to risk a battle, so they retreated to what few strongholds and fortresses they had. Sitalces' army first invaded the territory that had formerly been under Philip's control, taking some towns by storm while others came over out of loyalty to Amyntas. Next Sitalces marched into the part of Macedonia immediately east of Pella (not into Bottiaea or Pieria) and then devastated the districts of Mygdonia, Crestonia, and Anthemous, at which point Perdiccas sent for additional reinforcements of cavalry from his allies in Upper Macedonia.[98] Who precisely his allies were and how many cavalrymen we are not told. Together with his own cavalry they made attacks on the Thracians as opportunity presented, and though they were excellent horsemen and well armed, they were greatly inferior in number to the Thracians and so gave up their attacks.[99] Sitalces had expected support from the Athenian fleet, which the Athenian envoys evidently had promised in return for his help in Chalcidice, but the fleet had not shown up. So sending off part of his army to lay waste Chalcidice and Bottice, Sitalces entered into negotiations with Perdiccas. It was late in the campaign season with the cold of winter coming on and he was running out of food. The ever resourceful Perdiccas, as if reaching into his father's bag of tricks, won over Sitalces' nephew and top general, Seuthes, by offering him his sister Stratonice in marriage and a large sum of money.[100] Thus Sitalces' campaign, like Bubares' nearly a century earlier, had its conclusion in a wedding. Perhaps Herodotus had this contemporary marriage alliance in mind when he was telling the story of Gygaea and the Persian envoys.[101] After a campaign of thirty days Sitalces returned to his kingdom east of the Strymon.

Five years later, Seuthes succeeded as king of the Odrysians, and with the Macedonian and Thracian kings now bound by marriage ties, for the time being Macedonia's eastern frontier was pacified. Athenian activity continued to plague Perdiccas' interests. When the Athenians issued several decrees (the so-called "Methone Decrees") intended to prevent Perdiccas interfering in the trade of the Greek port Methone (near Pydna),[102] he together with the Chalcidians induced Sparta to send an army north. A personal friend of Perdiccas, Niconidas of Larissa, was one of several Thessalians who helped escort the force of 1,700 hoplites under command of the Spartan general Brasidas through Thessalian territory to Dion in Lower Macedonia in the summer of 424. This put Brasidas somewhat in Perdiccas' debt, for it was considered a hostile act for one Greek state, without permission, to march an army through the territory of another state.[103]

As soon as the Athenians learned of Brasidas' arrival, they declared war on Perdiccas for inviting their enemy into the northern theatre. While Perdiccas had legitimate concerns about Athenian encroachment, his ulterior motive in getting Brasidas to come was to secure a strong ally for his intended campaign against Arrhabaeus, king of the Lyncestian Macedonians of Upper Macedonia.[104] The two kings were in dispute, the nature of which is unknown, but part of Perdiccas' kingdom, Eordaea, bordered that of Arrhabaeus, who at this time exercised complete independence from the ruling house of Lower Macedonia.[105] Although Perdiccas' envoys to Sparta had indicated that if Brasidas came north, Perdiccas would win over his neighbours to the Spartan alliance, Brasidas could now see Perdiccas' personal agenda. Moreover, Arrhabaeus had contacted Brasidas to say he would be willing to have the Spartan arbitrate in the dispute. So when Perdiccas and Brasidas with their combined forces arrived on the border of Lyncus Brasidas announced that before marching into battle he wished first to negotiate with Arrhabaeus and try to bring him into the Spartan alliance. Perdiccas objected—he was, after all, paying half of Brasidas' expenses—but Brasidas proceeded to negotiate with Arrhabaeus anyway, and Arrhabaeus persuaded him to abandon the campaign. Taking his 1,700 hoplites and marching back to the coast, Brasidas then entered on a campaign with the Chalcidians, who happened to be paying the other half of his expenses. Since Perdiccas was unable to take on Arrhabaeus on his own, he was forced to quit the campaign. In retaliation, he cut his funding of Brasidas from half to one third.[106]

The following winter Brasidas with his allies marched on Amphipolis, where one of two Athenian *strategoi* stationed in the Thraceward region that year was in command. A non-Athenian faction, having been won over by either Perdiccas or the Chalcidians, was willing to betray the city. Just about dawn on a stormy morning with the element of surprise in his favour Brasidas seized the bridge and overran the outer town. An urgent request for relief reached Thucydides, the other Athenian *strategos* stationed half a day's sail away at Thasos, and he set sail immediately with seven triremes in bad weather. But before he could reach Amphipolis the inner city capitulated to Brasidas' generous terms. Entering port downstream at Eion Thucydides held it against Brasidas' attacks and gave refuge there to Athenians and Amphipolitans, who were permitted to leave Amphipolis. It was for his failure to save Amphipolis that the Athenians exiled Thucydides for the next twenty years, and he turned his hand to writing the history of the war. Perdiccas arrived immediately after the fall of Amphipolis and gave his assistance to Brasidas.[107]

Perdiccas probably continued to support Brasidas' successful campaign in Thrace and Chalcidice, perhaps footing much of the bill, as city after city was detached from the Athenian League.[108] Then a truce between Sparta and Athens nearly put Brasidas out of action, so he marched a second time with Perdiccas against Arrhabaeus. With a force at least double the size of the campaign the previous year—3,000 Greek hoplites (some were Greeks living in Macedonia fighting in Perdiccas' army, some the Peloponnesians of Brasidas, the rest his allies), 1,000 combined Macedonian and Chalcidian cavalry, and a large number of native troops—Perdiccas and Brasidas marched into Lyncus against Arrhabaeus' army of cavalry and hoplites. Both armies took up position on a hill, their cavalry going into action first in the plain between then the hoplite infantry following. Suffering heavy losses, the Lyncestians were routed and retreated to higher ground. Perdiccas and Brasidas set up a trophy, but did not follow up their victory, a consequence of the lack of cooperation between the two commanders. For several days they awaited the Illyrian mercenaries who were supposed to join Perdiccas' forces, with Perdiccas wanting to move out and attack the villages of Arrhabaeus, and Brasidas being reluctant to engage without the reinforcements and anxious to get back to Chalcidice.[109] Then word came that the Illyrians had broken their deal and joined Arrhabaeus instead. When these reputedly fierce warriors arrived on the scene, yelling and using every kind of 'barbarian' intimidation tactic, the invading army lost courage and decided to retreat, though there was no agreement as to how to execute it. Darkness fell on indecision, and in the night panic seized the Macedonian and native troops and they fled en masse for home. Perdiccas took flight also, without even informing Brasidas, whose camp was staked some distance away. At daylight Brasidas awoke to find himself deserted by half the army and facing the formidable combined forces of Lyncestians and Illyrians. It was something of a reverse of the year previous, when he had left Perdiccas to his own devices. Brasidas formed his troops into a defensive square and executed a difficult retreat through the Kirli Dirven Pass into Eordaea inside Perdiccas' kingdom.[110] There his army took revenge for the desertion by killing any Macedonian cattle they came across and appropriating all the gear and kit the Macedonians had tossed aside in panic during their midnight flight. Perdiccas now had a greater enemy in Brasidas and the Peloponnesians than he ever had in the Athenians. It was time to renegotiate with Athens.[111]

A cessation of Athens' declaration of war against Perdiccas came about through negotiations with the Athenian general Nicias. The suggestion that Perdiccas actually became subject to Athens seems highly improbable, though he may have suffered substantial territorial losses, as the Athenians added to their League Bormiscos in Mygdonia, Tragilos in Bisaltia, and Heracleion in Pieria.[112] Subsequent to the new alliance, Perdiccas' friends in Thessaly created such a problem for reinforcements trying to reach Brasidas from the Peloponnese that the army did not even make the attempt to cross the border, and only a few officers got through.[113] The following year, in 422, one of the Athenian generals posted to the north, Cleon, requested that Perdiccas honour his new alliance by bringing his army to Eion, where Cleon was preparing an attack on Brasidas' position at Amphipolis. But before Perdiccas arrived the Athenians attacked, were routed, and Cleon was killed. Brasidas also was fatally wounded in the battle.[114]

The deaths of Brasidas and Cleon dampened enthusiasm for war, and in 422–421 Nicias negotiated a Peace.[115] One of the terms was that Amphipolis be given back to Athens. However, the residents refused to submit to Athenian governance and so Amphipolis did not now, or in fact ever, return to Athenian control. And the Peace was hardly a peace at all, as hostilities persisted and alliances continued to shift. Perdiccas seized the opportunity to realign himself in 417 when the Spartans were able to convince Argos to break a recent treaty with Athens and form a united (oligarchic) Peloponnesian front. Both Sparta and Argos sent envoys to Thrace and to Perdiccas to persuade the two northern kingdoms to take an oath of allegiance to their new alliance. Perdiccas agreed, as Thucydides says because Argos had broken with Athens and because Argos was the native city of his ancestors,[116] but he kept his intentions secret from Athens. When the Athenians found out they promptly blockaded Macedonian ports, complaining not only that he had sworn allegiance to Sparta and Argos but also that he had not performed his role in an Athenian expedition against the Chalcidians and Amphipolis (a futile attempt to enforce the terms of Nicias' Peace), and so because of him the whole operation had fallen apart.[117] Once again Perdiccas was declared an enemy of Athens, and hostilities continued in 416 when the Athenians sent a force made up of their own cavalry and some Macedonian exiles living in Athens to Methone for the purpose of ravaging Macedonian territory.[118] It was in the winter of 416 that the Athenians decided to send an expedition to Sicily, and it may have been the need for ship timber to refurbish and build new triremes that brought about yet another reconciliation with Perdiccas. By the summer of 414, at any rate, Perdiccas was on the

Athenian side again and making up for at least one past transgression by joining forces with the general Euetion in an attack on Amphipolis.[119] That is the last that is heard of Perdiccas. His fate, like his father's, is unknown.[120]

Archelaus and the restructuring of the Macedonian kingdom

By 413 Archelaus, son of Perdiccas, had succeeded to the throne. His accession was timely, for that summer an Athenian fleet of 120 triremes, after an ill considered two-year campaign in Sicily, was annihilated in Syracuse's harbor.[121] This meant the Athenians had to begin once again to rebuild their fleet, and being in desperate need of Macedonian timber and pitch they were all too eager to be on good terms with the new Macedonian king. It also meant that the Athenians, who from the time of Xerxes' invasion had continually competed with Macedonia for control of ports and resources in the north Aegean, for now did not constitute a serious threat to Macedonian interests (though they persisted in their efforts to regain Amphipolis). On the eastern frontier the independent Thracians were checked by the power of Seuthes, and he, king of the Odrysians, was connected by marriage to the Macedonian throne. And if the increase in silver coinage minted during Archelaus' reign is any indication, it seems that the Macedonians regained control of Bisaltia and its silver mines. In the west Archelaus evidently inherited Perdiccas' conflict with the Lyncestians. However, by marrying his eldest daughter to the king of Elimeia, he secured a firm Upper Macedonian ally for his war with Arrhabaeus and the latter's ally Sirras.[122] This marriage was arguably a major diplomatic coup, since the king of Elimeia was the son of that Derdas (if not Derdas himself) who had supported the bid of Perdiccas' brother Philip for the Macedonian throne.

Over the fourteen years of his reign Archelaus restructured the Macedonian kingdom in the areas where he would have observed first hand that it had been weakest under his father's rule. Unfortunately, few details are known. Thucydides lived through the entirety of his reign; however, his history of the Peloponnesian War breaks off in the year 411 and he makes only one reference to the king: a brief and favourable summary of his accomplishments.

> Archelaus, son of Perdiccas, when he became king, built those [fortresses] that are now in the country, and cut straight roads, and in general organized his country for war by providing cavalry, arms and other equipment beyond anything achieved by all the eight kings who preceded him.[123]

We hear elsewhere that Archelaus immediately eliminated his rivals for power, namely his uncle Alcetas (whom Perdiccas had deprived of a territory), Alcetas' son Alexander, and an underage half-brother.[124] So whereas Perdiccas had had to contend with internal rivalry in addition to the constant external threat of Athens, the removal of both complications meant Archelaus could proceed to unify what had been perhaps for half a century a fragmented kingdom.

Timber was a great source of revenue for funding infrastructure. The Athenian orator Andocides credits Archelaus for honouring an ancestral tie between Andocides' family and the Macedonian royal family by allowing Andocides, when the Athenian fleet was stationed at Samos during the oligarchic coup at Athens in 411, free access to cut Macedonian timber for oars and to export them to Samos.[125] Export of timber had always necessitated access to a good port, and for this reason Alexander I early in the fifth century had taken control of Pydna, and Perdiccas had intervened at Methone. Pydna later briefly did regain its independence and Archelaus had to retake it in 410, ironically with the help of the Athenians. He promptly moved the city 20 *stadia* (4 km or 2.5 miles) inland.[126] This move no doubt was to allow him complete control over the port facilities, and not long after, in 407–406, the Athenians honoured Archelaus for providing a dockyard for Athenian shipwrights to build triremes close to the source of timber.[127]

It is not known where Archelaus' dockyards were located—perhaps at Methone or Pydna, or perhaps at Pella,[128] since the timber trade is surely one of the reasons for the Macedonian capital being relocated from Aegae in the Pierian foothills to Pella near the coast of the Thermaic Gulf. A tantalizingly brief geographical account written in the third quarter of the fourth century describes Pella as "a city with a royal seat (*basileion*) in it, and there is a voyage upstream to it up the Loudias."[129] "Royal seat" implies that Pella became the administrative, commercial, and military capital as well as permanent royal residence (Figure 2.5), while Aegae maintained its importance as a second

Figure 2.5 Ionic capital of a half-column from the palace at Pella
Source: author, 2013.

royal residence and a centre for religious ceremonial and royal burials. Though evidence is inconclusive, it is generally accepted that it was Archelaus who effected the move near the close of the fifth century; sources claim Archelaus hired the Greek painter Zeuxis to decorate his new palace with fine paintings.[130] He may also have been concerned to prevent any possible threat from Amphaxitis, a base of power from which Philip and Amyntas had challenged Perdiccas for the throne, and generally to protect Macedonian territory east of the Axios.[131] Pella was well positioned for trade, straddling the main east–west thoroughfare running from the shore of the Adriatic to Byzantium on the Black Sea, and it was not far from a strategic crossing of the Axios, where the east–west route intersected with the major north–south thoroughfare linking the north Aegean, via the Axios valley, to the interior of the central Balkans. Within a generation of Archelaus' reign Pella was acknowledged as the greatest of the Macedonian cities on account of its size and commercial prosperity.[132]

By the close of the fifth century the Macedonian kingdom was strong both economically and militarily, and Archelaus could look to resume the expansion and conquests of his predecessors. This is what he had in mind when the opportunity presented itself to intervene in politics to the south in troubled Thessaly. It was common practice for states in the midst of civil conflict to seek outside arbitration, as, for instance, Arrhabaeus of Lyncus had invited the Spartan Brasidas to arbitrate in his dispute with Perdiccas. About 400 the powerful aristocratic Thessalian family, the Aleuadae, sought Archelaus' aid in putting down a democratic movement which had ousted them from power at Larissa. Putting his improved military resources to the test, Archelaus successfully captured Larissa and put the Aleuadae back in control.[133] His removal of ten sons of leading men as political hostages and placement of a Macedonian garrison in Larissa were enough to announce Macedonia as a rising political and military influence in Thessalian affairs. The greatest gain for Macedonia (albeit short-lived) was control over Perrhaebia, the northernmost Thessalian territory bordering on Archelaus' kingdom in western Pieria as well as on the kingdom of his ally and son-in-law in Elimeia. What might have come next for Archelaus in Thessaly is a matter of speculation, for his days were numbered.

Archelaus died on a hunting expedition in 399 at the hands of a male lover, either by accident, as once source claims, or, on the authority of Aristotle, who was reared at the Macedonian court only a generation later, by an act of vengeance.[134] Is it coincidence that one of the men Aristotle names as being involved in Archelaus' 'murder' was a man of Larissa? Archelaus evidently had designated as his successor his son Orestes, but Orestes was only about three years old when succession fell to him prematurely. The Macedonian throne was thus left vulnerable to a series of succession struggles that undid virtually all Archelaus had gained and weakened the kingdom not only internally, with Macedonian loyalties divided between competing branches of the ruling house, but also against external threat for the next forty years.

Notes

1 So e.g. Hammond 1989a: 46;Vasilev 2015: 110; but Scaife 1989: 129 n3 is cautious; Badian 1982b: 44 n6 assumes an Athenian source; Greenwalt 1994: 3 suggests contact occurred during Perdiccas' reign. Herodotus' phrase "the Macedonians say" need not imply the royal court.
2 Hdt. 5.17–22.
3 Kuhrt 1988; Rung 2015.
4 Carney 2015b.
5 Hdt. 7.22. On the identification of Megabazus, father of Bubares, see Badian 1994a: 110–111.
6 E.g. (following Macan, How and Wells) Hammond in *HM* II 1979: 99; Errington 1981: 143 (should be expunged from serious history); Badian 1982b: 34 and 1994a: 108; Scaife 1989: 132; Borza 1992: 102; Fearn 2007: 115; Sprawski 2010: 136 with n19;Vasilev 2015: 109; but Dascalakis 1965: 151–157 ("slightly exaggerated").
7 So Errington 1981: 140; Borza 1992: 102; but see Badian 1994a: 109–110.
8 See Hammond in *HM* II 1979: 58–60, 1989a: 42–43; Errington 1981; Balcer 1988: 4–6; Borza 1992: 104–105; Vasilev 2015: 228–229. Cawkwell 1978: 24, 2005: 52: two stages to Macedonian subjugation to Persia (suggesting the Gygaea story reflects multiple marriages akin to Alexander III's mass weddings at Susa in 324). Cf. n16, n17.
9 Hdt. 6.44. Synkellos, Adler and Tuffin 2002: 359: Alexander gave earth and water at the time of Xerxes' expedition in 480. On Synkellos' reference see Borza 1992: 105 and Badian 1994a: 112 with n9.
10 E.g. Hammond 1989a: 99; Borza 1992: 102. Fearn 2007 offers a perceptive consideration of Herodotus' narrative purpose.
11 Hdt. 8.136; cf. n17.
12 Fearn 2007: 103, 108: "[Alexander's] actions throughout the narrative characterize him as neither obviously Greek nor as entirely Eastern either." Scaife 1989: 130: "Herodotus was not engaged in a post-war cover-up of Alexander's past." See also Badian's assessment 1994a.
13 Fearn 2007: 98; Scaife 1989: 132–133.
14 Hdt. 5.1.1–17.1.Vasilev 2015: 86–109.
15 Hammond in *HM* II 1979: 56, 59; 1989a: 42–43. See Chapter 1 n34.
16 Just. 7.3.2–9. Balcer 1988: 5 argues that the *Yaunā takabarā* ("Ionians with a hat as a shield") mentioned in an inscription on Darius' tomb "were, indeed, the patasos-wearing Macedonians" and that they held semi-autonomous status for two decades. See Xydopoulos 2012a: 28; and cp. Vasilev 2015: 116–117.
17 Hdt. 4.143.2. The date of the marriage is much disputed. Hammond 1989a: 42: Amyntas gave Gygaea to Bubares c. 510. Badian 1994a: 112: c. 511. Borza 1992: 103 n15 favours a date during the reign of Amyntas, because a marriage c. 510 would allow the male offspring of the marriage, Amyntas, to be of age (c. 29) to receive from the Persian king rule of a city (Alabanda in Caria) by about 480, the time of Xerxes' invasion. Kertész 2005: 119 rejects a marriage c. 510. Errington 1981: 141: after 498 because Alexander must have been on the throne when he gave his sister in marriage. Sprawski 2010: 137 suggests 492 when Mardonius reached Macedonia.
18 Just. 7.4.1–2.
19 Hdt. 5.20.4. Badian 1994a: 114 defends "satrap" as the meaning *contra* Balcer 1988: 2–4, 6, 15; Xydopoulos 2012a: 27 and n52 maintains Amyntas was not a satrap. See also Briant 2002: 145; Sprawski 2010: 134–136; Olbrycht 2010: 343; Vasilev 2015: 116.
20 Hammond 1989a: 42.

21 Just. 7.4.1. Justin's praise of Amyntas I "for the excellent abilities of his son Alexander" suggests again Alexander's self-promotion.
22 Hammond in *HM* II 1979: 60; Borza 1992: 103. See Vasilev 2015: 124–127.
23 Hdt. 5.94.1. Hippias had other options and declined. For Peisistratus' earlier settlement at Rhaecalus on the eastern Thermaic Gulf (now identified as Peraea—Xydopoulos 2012a: 23 n9), and his mining interests in the lower Strymon, cf. Arist. *Athenaion Politaea* 15.2; Hdt. 1.64.1. Cole 1975.
24 Hammond *HM* I 1979: 58–59, 1989: 42–43; Zahrnt 1984: 360; Borza 1992: 87–89; Xydopoulos 2012a; Vasilev 2015: 116.
25 Hdt. 6.44.1. Balcer 1988: 6: only in 492 was Macedonia subordinated to a satrapy.
26 Hdt. 6.43.4-45.
27 Hdt. 6.94–140.
28 Cole 1978: 41–42; Balcer 1988: 6, 8; Sprawski 2010: 137–138.
29 Hdt. 9.44.1. For the *hyparchoi* in Thrace cf. Hdt. 7.106–107. Balcer 1988: 14–15.
30 Cole 1978: 42.
31 Edson 1970: 25–44.
32 Hdt. 8.136.1. Badian 1994a: 119–123 supposes these titles were separately bestowed, but see Cole 1978: 40–42. On Alexander's proxeny status at Athens see Wallace 1970 (especially 199 with n13) and Gerolymatos 1986.
33 Hdt. 8.136.1.
34 Hdt. 7.42, 25.2, 22.1.
35 Leake 1835/1967: 145.
36 Hdt. 7.127, cf. 7.119–120.
37 Hdt. 7.173.
38 Hdt. 7.131. Pritchett 1961.
39 E.g. hedging his bets: Hammond 1989a: 44–45; Borza 1992: 113; Badian 1994a: 118.
40 For discussions of Alexander's role at Tempe see Robertson 1976; Cole 1978; Scaife 1989; Vasilev 2015: 188–190.
41 Hdt. 9.31.5.
42 Hdt. 9.44–45; Plut. *Aristides* 15.
43 Hdt. 9.46; Plut. *Aristides* 16.
44 Hdt. 9.59–68; Plut. *Aristides* 18–19.
45 E.g. Borza 1982b: 9–10, 1992: 110; Scaife 1989: 131. But see Badian 1994a: 118–119; Cloché 1960: 40–49; Errington 1990: 12–13; Flower and Marincola 2002: 188–191.
46 Leigh Fermor 2014.
47 Hdt. 8.34.
48 Hdt. 8.136–144. Cp. Plut. *Aristides* 10: Aristides gives the Athenian answer "to the messengers of Mardonius" with no hint that Alexander is their spokesman or even present; Diod. 11. 28: no mention of Alexander as Mardonius' spokesman; but confirmed by Dem. 6.11. For discussion of Alexander's speech see Scaife 1989: 134–137.
49 Just. 7.4.1. On Justin's claim see Hammond 1989a: 43; Borza 1992: 115 n38; Vasilev 2015: 198. See also Heinrichs and Müller 2008: 291.
50 For Mygdonia see Hammond in *HM* II 1979: 59 and 1989a: 42–43.
51 Hdt. 8.121.2; Dem. 12.21, but cp. Hdt. 9.89.4. Saatsoglou-Paliadeli 2007: 346–349.
52 E.g. Errington 1981; Badian 1982b: 34–36; Borza 1992: 130–131; Fearn 2007 (115: professed aim of Herodotus' narrative to present Alexander as "philhellenic" is undermined by details). See also Mari 2011: 85–86; Vasilev 2015: 197–206.
53 Hdt. 5.22.
54 On the Temenid ancestry see especially the contrasting arguments of Dascalakis 1965: 110–113 and Badian 1982b: 34–37. Sceptical of the Olympia episode: Borza 1982b: 10–11; Xydopoulos 2012a: 30 n47. On the problem of date and victory:

46 *The Argead monarchy in the fifth century*

Cole 1978: 39 (in 504 or 500); Hammond in *HM* II 1979: 60, 435 (in 496 competed in pentathlon as well as sprint); Badian 1982b: 34 (in 476); Borza 1992: 111–112 ("fraught with too many difficulties to make sense of it"); Roos 1985: 165 (lost in a run-off); Scaife 1989: 133–134 (n15: no good reason to doubt his participation); Errington 1990: 9, 266 n3 (in 496); Kertész 2005: 117 (in 496). On Macedonians and sports in general see Adams 2008.
55 Just. 7.2.14. Cf. arguments in n54.
56 For differing views see Dascalakis 1965: 157–167; Badian, 1982b: 34–37; Borza 1992: 110–113; Cosmopoulos 1992: 13 (with ix–x); Hatzopoulos 2011b: 56–58.
57 Hdt. 5.17.2. Hammond in *HM* II 1979: 69–73 and 1989a: 41–45. See also Kremydi 2011: 160. Hdt. 8.116: king of the Bisaltae fled into Rhodope Mountains at time of Xerxes' invasion.
58 Hdt. 5.23.2. On resources in general see Borza 1982a.
59 Hdt. 7.107; Thuc. 1.98.1; Plut. *Cimon* 7.2–8.3.
60 On the conflict in the Strymon region see Picard 2006, Osborne 2007; cp. Roisman 2010: 146–147; Archibald 2010: 333–337.
61 'Ares types': Price 1974: 9; hunter: Hammond in *HM* II 1979: 109, 1989a: 46; Pelasgian or Mycenaean imagery: Tačeva 1992: 64–69.
62 On minting and the value of the metal coinage see Dahmen 2010 with bibliography; Kremydi 2011.
63 Raymond 1953: 134–148; Price 1974: 19; Hammond in *HM* II 1979: 119–120; Kremydi 2011: 163.
64 Price 1974: 16–17, 20.
65 Plut. *Cimon* 14.2–4. See Cole 1978: 49 n26.
66 Paus. 7.25.6. Cole 1978: 47.
67 Andronikos 1984: 146–162, 168–197, 208–217; Hatzopoulos 1994: 32–38; Gill 2008.
68 Liv. 45.29.10–11. On economy and finance see Hatzopoulos 1996: 431–435; Touratsoglou 2010.
69 Liv. 45.29.13.
70 Thuc. 1.137.1; Plut. *Them.* 25.2. Cole 1978, *contra* Meiggs 1982: 123–126.
71 Plato *Laws* 705c; Thuc. 4.108; Andocides 2.11; *IG* I² 71, 105. On the export of Macedonian timber see Meiggs 1982: 356–357; on timber and politics see Borza 1987.
72 See Chapter 1 n52.
73 Theophr. *Caus. pl.* 5.14.6; Diod. 20.96. 3.
74 Tačeva 1992: 69–74.
75 Synkellos, Adler and Tuffin 2002: 359.
76 Hammond 1989a: 71; but cp. Borza 1992: 133–134; Atkinson 1994: 244. Cf. n80.
77 Thuc. 2.100.2; Hdt. 8.139.
78 Philip: Thuc. 1.57, 2.100.3; Alcetas: Plato *Gorgias* 471b; Menelaus: *IG* I³ 89 = *SEG* X 86; Amyntas: Synkellos, Adler and Tuffin 2002: 383. Cp. Thuc. 4.128.3.
79 Hammond in *HM* II 1979: 120–123; Errington 1990: 15–20; Borza 1992: 134–135; Badian 1993: 180. Perdiccas' name appears on Macedonian coinage by 438: Raymond 1953: 142, cf. 150. Sources assigned varying lengths to his reign, ranging from twenty-three years to forty-one: Ath. 5.217e.
80 Hammond 1989a: 71, but *HM* II 1979: 115 is closer to the evidence. Errington 1990: 15 rejects Geyer's suggestion of a division of the kingdom. Cole 1974 makes a plausible case for Alexander's policy of unity gone wrong. Curt. 6.11.26 is cited as evidence for Alexander's violent death (cf. n76); however, it is not clear whether the reference is to Alexander I or II, the latter known from multiple sources to have been

assassinated (Dem. 19.194–195; Diod. 15.71.1, 16.2.4; Ath. 14.629d; Just. 7.5.4). On Perdiccas' alleged illness and the Argead guest-friendship with the Asclepiad family of Hippocrates of Cos cf. *Suda* s.v. "Hippocrates"; Rubin-Pinault 1992: 61–77; Jouanna 1999: 28–31, 42–45; Nelson 2007.
81 Though cp. the sons of Cotys in Odrysian Thrace, Chapter 4 n82.
82 E.g. Diod. 16.2–4 Philip II and 17.8.1 Alexander III.
83 Dem. 12.21; Thuc. 1.100.3. Hammond in *HM* II 1979: 102–103.
84 Plut. *Pericles* 11.5. Meiggs 1972: 538–561.
85 Cole 1974: 59–60.
86 Errington 1990: 17; see Meiggs in n84.
87 Thuc. 1.57.2–3.
88 A scholiast to Thuc. 1.57.
89 Thuc. 1.57.4–6. On Perdiccas' involvement with the Greek city-states at the outbreak and during the Peloponnesian War see Cole 1974; Hoffman 1975; Chambers 1986; Badian 1993.
90 Thuc. 1.58.1–2.
91 Thuc. 1.59.1–2; 61.4; cf. n92.
92 Thuc. 1.60.1–61.5. Schol. to Thuc. 1.61.4: uncertainty whether Pausanias is Derdas' brother or son, but cp. 59.2. On the disputed route, Beroia to Strepsa, see Hatzopoulos 1987; Badian 1993: 174–178, citing earlier scholarship.
93 Thuc. 1.62.2: Iolaus appointed *archon*, but the text is ambiguous about whether Perdiccas or Iolaus led the cavalry; see Hornblower 1997: 105. See Chapter 8 n2.
94 Thuc. 1.62.3–63.2. Fall of Potidaea: Thuc. 2.70.
95 Thuc. 2.95.
96 Thuc. 2.29.
97 Thuc. 2.80.7.
98 Thuc. 2.99–100. Cp. Diod. 12.50.3–7: Sitalces placed Amyntas on a throne, but he cannot mean Perdiccas'; possibly Amyntas was restored to Philip's *archē*. See Badian 1993: 179–181; Mitchell 2007: 64–66 (but both without reference to Diod.). Cf. Diod. 12.50.1–2 on Sitalces' power.
99 Thuc. 2.100.5.
100 Thuc. 2.101; Diod. 12.51.1–2.
101 Cole 1974: 65 also notes the parallel.
102 Tod *GHI* 61 = *IG* I^3 61 = Fornara 128. Mattingly 1961; Burstein 1999; Roisman 2011 no. 26.5.
103 Thuc. 4.78.1–79.1.
104 Thuc. 4.79.2, 82.1.
105 Cf. *IG* I^3 89, which also shows that Derdas of Elimeia and Antiochus of Orestis are allies, not subjects, of Perdiccas. Thuc. 2.80.6: Antiochus of Orestis in 429 acted independently of the Macedonian king when he sent 1,000 men to fight for Sparta.
106 Thuc. 4.82–83.
107 Thuc. 4.102.1–107.3.
108 Plato (*Rep*. 336a) includes Perdiccas, along with Periander and Xerxes, in his list of very rich and powerful men.
109 Thuc. 4.124. Perdiccas' Greek hoplites: following Hammond 1995: 126 n20.
110 Thuc. 4.125.1–128.3. Brasidas came first to Arnisa in Eordaea. Hammond *HM* I 1972: 104–106; Borza 1992: 152.
111 Thuc. 4.128.4–5.
112 Hammond in *HM* II 1979: 132–133; cp. Cole 1974: 55 n4; Borza 1992: 156.
113 Thuc. 4.132.1–2.
114 Thuc. 5.6.1–11.1.

48 *The Argead monarchy in the fifth century*

115 Thuc. 5.17.2–20.1; Plut. *Nic.* 9.2–10.1.
116 Thuc. 5.80.2.
117 Thuc. 5.83.4.
118 Thuc. 6.7.3–4. Cole 1974: 70 suggests the exiles were former supporters of Philip and Amyntas.
119 Thuc. 7.9.
120 On the date of Perdiccas' death: Diodorus (14.37.6) says his successor Archelaus died in 399 after a reign of seven years, which would date Perdiccas' death to 406, but this is contradicted at 13.49.1, since in 410 Archelaus is king. Therefore "seven" has been emended to "seventeen," which agrees with Diod. 7.15.2 as preserved in Eusebius, though 416 cannot be correct either, since Thuc. 7.9 requires a date not before 414 for Perdiccas' death. Archelaus' reign is corrected by Synkellos to fourteen, which brings the date of Perdiccas' death to 413. The only notice of Perdiccas II's death is the *Marmor Parium* [*FGrH/BNJ* 239 A61, see Sickinger 2016], which places it in 421–420, and this we know from Thucydides is incorrect.
121 Thuc. 7.59–71.
122 Arist. *Pol.* 5.1311b. If not the same Arrhabaeus then probably his successor of the same name, and Sirras was probably Arrhabaeus' Illyrian ally. Hammond in *HM* II 1979: 139; Greenwalt 1988: 36; Errington 1990: 27; Borza 1992: 164. See Chapter 3 n15.
123 Thuc. 2.100.2.
124 Plato *Gorgias* 471; see Chapter 3.
125 Andocides 2.11.
126 Diod. 13.49.1–2.
127 Tod *GHI* 91 = *IG* I^3 117 = Walbank 1978 no. 90—a fragmentary Athenian inscription, with restorations "Archelaus" and "shipwrights" universally accepted. Borza 1992: 163; Blackman 1990: 47–48.
128 Respectively Borza 1992: 163 n9; Greenwalt 1999: 175.
129 Pseudo-Skylax 66, dated to the upper 330s, translation Shipley 2011.
130 Ael. *VH* 14.17; Plin. *HN* 35.62.
131 Borza 1992: 140; see Greenwalt 1999: 159.
132 Xen. *Hell.* 5.2.
133 Thrasymachus of Calchedon *For the Larissaeans*; Ps.-Herodes *Peri Politeias*; Westlake 1935: 51–59.
134 Diod. 14.37.6; Arist. *Pol.* 5.1311a–b. Carney 1983; Greenwalt 2003.

3 Macedonian succession and survival, 399–360

The forty years following the death of Archelaus constitute a period of great instability for the Macedonian monarchy and kingdom. The rapid turnover of five kings within the first decade, three by assassination, reveals a flawed system of royal succession, and this in turn raises questions about custom and law, and about the structure of the Macedonian state. Amyntas III (393–369) seized the weakened throne by force but was vulnerable to external powers. With the Illyrians briefly depriving him of his kingdom, the neighbouring Chalcidic League forcing concessions in trade and territorial control, and the major Greek states all intervening in Macedonian affairs as they jostled for hegemony in the north, his rule was precarious at best. His sons who succeed him held promise, but Alexander II (369–368) was very soon assassinated, and Perdiccas III (365–360) was killed in battle, so the kingdom's hopes fell upon the youngest son, Philip II.

Problems of succession

Archelaus earned ample praise from Thucydides for having strengthened his kingdom's defences and military capability, and at the time of the king's untimely death Macedonia was secure and on the rise as a regional power. Half a dozen years and five kings later the Illyrians were pouring in from the northwest, the Olynthians from the southeast, and the current king was on the run. Succession had not gone smoothly, that is clear, but how succession *should* have gone, that remains unclear. About ten years after Archelaus' death, and after the succession fiasco of the nineties, Plato, in one of his Socratic dialogues, passes vilifying judgment on the king's accession. It comes in the *Gorgias*, where Socrates' interlocutor is speaking as if Archelaus is "presently" on the throne, though the dialogue was written about 390.

> Archelaus, son of Perdiccas ... had no claim to the throne which he now occupies, being the son of a woman who was a slave of Perdiccas' brother Alcetas, and in mere justice he was Alcetas' slave; and if he wished to do what is just, he would be serving Alcetas... he invited this very master and uncle of his to his court, as if he were going to restore to him the kingdom [*archē*] of which Perdiccas had deprived him; and after entertaining him

50 *Succession and survival, 399–360*

and his son Alexander—his own cousin, about the same age as himself—and making them drunk, he packed them into a carriage, drove them away by night, and murdered and made away with them both . . . a while later he refused to make himself happy by bringing up, as he was justly bound, his brother, the legitimate son of Perdiccas, a boy about seven years old who had a just title to the throne, and restoring the kingdom to him; but he cast him into a well and drowned him, and then told his mother Cleopatra that he had fallen in and lost his life while chasing a goose.[1]

Plato's portrait of Archelaus as a murderer, a liar, and a usurper is heavily doused in calumny, yet as a contemporary commentary it ought to reveal something about Macedonian succession.[2]

It is likely that Archelaus was the eldest of Perdiccas' sons, and by rule of primogeniture one would expect him to have been the rightful heir. Yet the murder of Alcetas and his son (surely not Plato's invention) can only mean that at the time of Perdiccas' death Alcetas posed a challenge to Archelaus' succession. In the fragments of an inscription recording a treaty between Perdiccas and Athens, dated (uncertainly) in the 420s, Alcetas' name appears next after Perdiccas, then Archelaus' name is third, suggesting he is the eldest son but subordinate to Alcetas, and Perdiccas' brother Menelaus appears sixth. Two names are missing between Archelaus and Menelaus, one of which could be the fourth brother, Philip, though Philip was probably already dead.[3] The order of names (Hammond deems this "clearly an order of court preference"[4]) supports Plato's criticism that Archelaus should have played second fiddle to Alcetas. Why should this have been so, when father-to-son succession had always been the tradition?

Plato's objection to Archelaus' succession has nothing to do with primogeniture. He objects that Archelaus was the son of a slave, significantly Alcetas' slave, Simache,[5] and he was therefore not "justly" entitled to the throne. If this is not pure slander, or a Greek misunderstanding of Macedonian customs,[6] then the problem for Plato is one of legitimacy. In Plato's view, Perdiccas' son by his wife Cleopatra, though only aged seven, was the legitimate heir. How many royal children were the offspring of slaves is anyone's guess, but evidently there were few slaves in Macedonia at this time and it is quite possible that the Macedonians held a very different view from our Athenian sources about slaves anyway.[7] At any rate, it is clear from the inscription that Perdiccas did not regard Archelaus as being unworthy of authority. An underage heir required, of course, someone to rule on his behalf until he came of age: a regent or guardian.[8] And this raises the question of who qualified to act in that capacity: was it the deceased king's brother, who might well be the eldest living male Argead? If so, then the role should have fallen to Alcetas, and that would explain Archelaus' prompt removal of him.

The accession of Archelaus *as Plato tells it* indicates that with Alcetas eliminated it fell rightfully to Archelaus (he "was justly bound") to act as guardian for the "legitimate" seven-year-old son of Perdiccas. Instead, Archelaus killed the boy, married the boy's mother (his own father's widow),[9] and took the throne for himself. This demonstrates the risk that any king would take if he were to designate a minor as heir over an adult, for a child heir was vulnerable and so consequently was the throne. Yet Archelaus' heir, in turn, was also a minor, his son Orestes by his father's widow Cleopatra, though, like Perdiccas, he seems to have had an older son. Since primogeniture appears to be ruled out, we must ask whether it was the king's right of choice to designate his successor.

Few men were better placed to offer perspective on Macedonian succession in the fourth century than Aristotle, Plato's student and long-time resident at the Macedonian court in Pella; his father, Nicomachus, was court physician to Amyntas III and he himself tutor to Alexander III. Contrary to the later account of Diodorus (first century BCE) purporting that Archelaus' lover "Craterus" unintentionally killed the king when they were hunting,[10] Aristotle says it was deliberate and perpetrated from personal motive, though there is a strong hint *as he tells it* of political motive as well. Aristotle mentions the assassination of Archelaus by his lover "Crataeas" in a discussion of revenge regicide.

> [F]or [Crataeas] was always resentful of the association, so that even a smaller excuse became sufficient, or perhaps it was because [Archelaus] did not give him the hand of one of his daughters after agreeing to do so, but gave the elder to the king of Elimea when hard pressed in a war against Sirras and Arrabaeus, and the younger to his son Amyntas, thinking that thus Amyntas would be least likely to quarrel with his son by Cleopatra; but at all events Crataeas's estrangement was primarily caused by resentment because of the love affair. And Hellanocrates of Larisa also joined in the attack for the same reason; for because while enjoying his favors Archelaus would not restore him to his home although he had promised to do so, he thought that the motive of the familiarity that had taken place had been insolence and not passionate desire ... Also Decamnichus took a leading part in the attack upon Archelaus, being the first to stir on the attackers; and the cause of his anger was that he had handed him over to Euripides the poet to flog, Euripides being angry because he had made a remark about his breath smelling.[11]

Aristotle's discussion seems to imply that in addition to two married daughters Archelaus at the time of his death also had at least one grown son, Amyntas, who might oppose the king's legitimate or preferred successor, Cleopatra's young son Orestes.[12] And indeed, before the decade was out, an Amyntas (two, actually) would seize the throne. But why would a child be preferred as heir over a grown son?

Cleopatra was the mother of two "legitimate" *underage* heirs. If this is not coincidence, then we might assume she had something to do with the legitimacy of the heir, though we do not know what constituted "legitimate." The name Cleopatra is common for Macedonian females in the fourth century and later, and possibly this early Cleopatra was an Argead. Macedonian kings, as we know from evidence for the fourth century, could take multiple wives, usually for political reasons, and evidently without needing to repudiate an earlier wife for a newer one. But how these royal wives were ranked is unclear, as is the ranking of royal children. Obviously, since polygamy helped to secure succession by increasing the likelihood of male offspring, a wife or wives who bore sons would almost certainly gain higher status. Two wives of Philip II bore him sons so close in age that it is uncertain which was elder. Olympias, mother of Alexander III ("the Great"), though probably Philip's fourth wife and her son probably second born, may have outranked all his other wives, if only briefly, before he took as his final bride a young Macedonian, another Cleopatra.[13] Of Philip's other six wives five were from outside Macedonia and were in principle political marriages. (Olympias was an Epirote princess and her marriage served important political ends for Philip's nominal control over Epirus.[14]) His marriage to the much younger Cleopatra was a love match, we are told, and might produce, so her uncle famously toasted at the banquet, a "legitimate" heir, this being an insinuation that Alexander (III) was *not* legitimate. We are confounded, however, in the notion that a Macedonian bride outranked a foreign wife by the case of Amyntas III, Philip's father, whose part-Illyrian, part-Lyncestian wife Eurydice took precedence with her three sons (and one daughter) over three sons of another wife whose name, Gygaea, we already have met in the Argead clan.[15] The latter case has prompted a strong argument that "legitimate" children constituted only those born *after* the father succeeded to the throne, which could explain Orestes' succession,[16] but it breaks down when we come to the insinuation against Alexander III. Philip II's two sons were both born after he took the throne,[17] though a mental deficiency left the other, Arrhidaeus, out of the running to succeed. It was rumoured that Arrhidaeus' deficiency was because of some foul play on the part of Alexander's mother rather than congenital,[18] and such a rumour suggests that jockeying for status among the royal wives and offspring was seriously competitive (see in contrast, the 'close' noble family unit in Figure 3.1).

The case for merit as a factor in succession could apply in some cases, such as that of Alexander III, while in others, such as that of Orestes, the very young age of the heirs precludes it. So no clear pattern emerges. When it fell to Aeropus (II) to act as Orestes' guardian, following the lead of Archelaus he killed his ward and took the throne for himself.[19] We do not know the father of Aeropus, but his role as guardian should indicate that he was an Argead, possibly the eldest living male and perhaps another son of Perdiccas.[20] If Aeropus *was* the son of Perdiccas, and if by custom succession should now have passed to a son of the most recent king, then any living sons of Archelaus would have challenged Aeropus' rule, and this *could* explain the mayhem that followed. The fact that there were successful usurpations of royal power by guardians of an underage heir suggests strongly that a system of succession was never prescribed by law; no law protected those children. A *traditional custom* of succession may have been as far as Macedonian law went. Evidence does not support Hammond's assertion that the Assembly made the decisions—and mistakes—regarding succession, though army assemblies are recorded as 'acclaiming' successors.[21] The predominant practice in the Macedonian royal dynasty was father-to-son succession, evidently at

Figure 3.1 Grave *stele*, copy (original in Musée du Louvre, Paris), Aiani, early fourth century BCE
Source: author, 2014.

the king's discretion and taking into account factors other than primogeniture, while acclamation was a formal acceptance of the king's choice.

When Aeropus II died of illness after a reign of six years (two or three of those years as guardian for Orestes) his intention likely was that his own son Pausanias should succeed him.[22] But in 394–393 in addition to Pausanias two kings named Amyntas also came to the throne.[23] The duplication of the name "Amyntas," one of the most common names in ancient Macedonia,[24] coupled with the short duration of all but one of these reigns in the 390s has left considerable confusion (and omissions) in the sources. The first Amyntas (II) should be the one whom Aristotle says was assassinated by Derdas: "[the attack] on Amyntas the Little by Derdas [was] because he mocked at his youth."[25] (This is part of the revenge regicide passage cited above.) Derdas might well be the Elimiote king who married Archelaus' eldest daughter, and Amyntas might be Archelaus' son, though many scholars believe he was the son of Perdiccas II's brother Menelaus.[26] A late chronographic source says this Amyntas (II) was deposed by the Macedonians,[27] but whatever his fate, and his claim to succession, his reign probably lasted only a couple of months. Then Pausanias, son of Aeropus, ascended the throne, but within the year he was assassinated by another Amyntas. The latter Amyntas (III) is identified as a grandson of Amyntas, son of Alexander I, the non-political brother of Perdiccas II, and it is clear he came to the throne by force.[28] Since neither his father (Arrhidaeus) nor grandfather (Amyntas) had ever been on the throne, his accession is possibly an anomaly within the

Argead clan. Though his reign *spanned* twenty-four years, it was not continuous.[29] He lost the throne at least once, and a period of two years' rule is attributed to Argaeus (II), whose claim to succession is also unclear, after which Amyntas recovered the throne.[30] Amyntas III died an old man in 369, one of the few kings of Macedonia known to have died of natural causes.[31] Upon his death, father-to-son succession resumed down to the end of the Argead line—or sort of. Three of Amyntas' sons, all within a decade, came to the throne after him: Alexander II, Perdiccas III, and Philip II. But the succession problems of the 390s had left the Macedonians divided in their loyalties to two or more branches of Alexander I's descendants, so the sons of Amyntas experienced serious challenges to their succession.

Alexander II was the eldest son of Amyntas III and probably the designated heir.[32] An inscription dated to 375 or 373 recording an alliance between Amyntas III and Athens names Alexander as co-oath taker with his father.[33] If he was born after his father ascended in 393, he was just coming of age at the time of the alliance and only in his early twenties at the time of his accession. Almost immediately he faced a challenge from Ptolemy of Aloros, who seems likely to be the Ptolemy named in the same inscription as one of Amyntas' three ambassadors to the Athenians; he would in that case have held one of the most prominent and trusted positions at court. Though he is called "son of Amyntas" and "brother" of Amyntas' sons Alexander and Perdiccas, he was certainly not a full brother, and "brother-in-law" (or "adopted son") is more likely;[34] most assume that he was the traitorous husband of Amyntas' daughter Eurynoe. Within two years Ptolemy had assassinated Alexander II and seized power for himself.[35] Ptolemy evidently intended to rule as king in his own right, perhaps through his connection with the Argead women, if he was not himself an Argead, but he was compelled by outside arbitration to agree to a form of guardianship for Alexander's underage brothers.[36] Although Ptolemy does appear in the king lists, his rule lasting three years until Perdiccas III came of age, no coinage from his reign has come to light.[37] Around the same time another contender, an Argead in exile in Chalcidice, challenged for the throne. It is not certain from which branch of the Argeadae this Pausanias came or why he was exiled, though we are told it was Amyntas III who had exiled him.[38] Pausanias was driven out of Macedonia, and Perdiccas III as soon as he came of age promptly took revenge for his elder brother by killing Ptolemy and claiming the Argead throne.[39] His reign appears to have been uncontested, but after five years he was killed in battle,[40] leaving behind a young son, Amyntas.

Amyntas could not have been more than eight years of age and was probably quite a bit younger, and a child-king was certainly not practical with external threats and internal weaknesses rampant.[41] The one surviving son of Amyntas III and Eurydice, Philip, was now about age twenty-three. In 360–359 both Argaeus,[42] presumably the same who had ruled during Amyntas III's exile, and Pausanias,[43] who had challenged Ptolemy of Aloros, reappeared as contenders.[44] Had either of them with foreign backing been successful in seizing the throne, the history of Macedonia surely would not have unfolded in the spectacular way in which it did in the second half of the fourth century. Philip, son of Amyntas, became king, though whether he assumed the kingship right away or after a period of guardianship lasting up to three years has been hotly debated;[45] and his ward Amyntas, surprisingly perhaps, survived to adulthood.

If it is possible to draw any conclusions about the royal succession, one must be that only an Argead could legitimately hold the Macedonian throne; that is, until the Argeadae were wiped out, and a new dynasty was established in the third century.[46] Herodotus' simplified king list and Thucydides' uncritical acceptance of it leave the early succession seemingly neat and tidy, more so than it might have been in fact. Yet one surely may conclude that father-to-son succession, however formal a custom,[47] was the traditional practice from the beginning of the dynasty, even if the son was much underage. The greatest succession problem seems to have lain with the guardianship for a minor heir. As a position of trust it was readily breached once the party who had extended that trust, the king, was dead. That this occurred several times strongly weighs against Hammond's insistence that the *choice* of succession lay with a formal Army Assembly. Also weighing against the Assembly's choice is the fact that the matter of the throne was twice in the 360s determined by external arbitration (as we will see below). For if the "people" (Macedones) had joint authority in the state with the king, as adherents to a "constitutional" theory of governance argue,[48] why did the Assembly not settle the question? Admittedly, there appears to have been, at least from the time of Philip II, and perhaps before, a formal acclamation ceremony in acceptance or acknowledgement of a new king.[49] But it seems clear that the choice already had been designated by the previous king.

That the Macedonian throne did not go up for sale to the most powerful foreign interest is to the credit of Amyntas III and his quick-witted sons. While the Athenians and Thracians backed (respectively) the challengers Argaeus and Pausanias, even greater external pressures faced the Macedonians from the Illyrians in the northwest and the Chalcidians to the immediate south and east.[50]

The Illyrian threat and the Chalcidic League in the reign of Amyntas III

Both Perdiccas II and Archelaus had been at war with Arrhabaeus of Lyncus, and it was likely for this reason, in addition to forming a marriage alliance with Elimeia (his daughter to the king),[51] that Archelaus strengthened the borders of his kingdom with fortifications and made overall improvements to the military. His innovations seem to have kept the Illyrians temporarily at bay, and he had so bolstered the confidence of the monarchy in its cavalry strength that some years later, in the summer of 394, Aeropus II, when approached by the Spartan king Agesilaus for free passage through Macedonia, at first refused to grant it, evidently believing the Spartans were so inferior in cavalry strength that they could not force the issue. But force it they did, and under treaty the Spartans did pass from Thrace to Thessaly through Macedonia unchallenged.[52] Macedonia did not have the military strength to prevent a foreign invasion.

A short while later, a few years at most—and, significantly, following the succession problems of the 'year of the three kings'—Illyrian tribes had pressed to the point that Amyntas III made a treaty with the Chalcidic League: a mutual alliance of support for fifty years in the event of foreign invasion for the purpose of war. The Chalcidic League was a federal organization of city-states in the Chalcidice peninsula that had formed after Perdiccas II convinced many of the smaller city-states there to resettle at Olynthus, and Olynthus headed the League. The treaty was signed perhaps soon after Amyntas' accession late in 393 in hopes of preventing an invasion or perhaps later as a consequence of invasion.[53] Alternatively, the treaty, which is inscribed on two sides of the stone, may be interpreted as two-part: the first part suggests that Amyntas was on equal terms with the Chalcidic League, which may best reflect the situation in 393 when he first came to the throne, while the second part suggests Amyntas was at a significant disadvantage and forced to concede on economic grounds, as he would be after an Illyrian invasion and after handing over use (and revenues) of his land bordering Chalcidice. The second part could reflect the situation in the mid 380s, by which time the Chalcidians were the dominant power in the north Aegean and were actively developing their own naval capacity.[54] That Amyntas does not have full control of the Macedonian timber trade is indicated by a clause in the second part of the inscription stating that the Chalcidians may export pitch and timber, and even the restricted fir, so long as they inform Amyntas and pay appropriate fees.

Amyntas' situation is indeed ambiguous, one of many uncertainties about the history of Macedonia in the first half of the fourth century resulting from the poor documentation of this period. Diodorus *twice* records that the Illyrians invaded Macedonia and drove Amyntas out, forcing him to relinquish his kingship, and on both occasions he says Amyntas granted to the Olynthians control over his territory where it bordered on theirs.[55] The precedent had been set by Perdiccas' grant of land around Lake Bolbe to those Chalcidians who abandoned their coastal cities to congregate at Olynthus.[56] Amyntas perhaps was hoping to prevent the revenues of the region from falling into the hands of his Illyrian enemies, who around this time were beginning to mint a new silver coinage from mines at Damastion and were perhaps trying to establish trading links with Chalcidice via Macedonia.[57] The first reference to an Illyrian invasion is placed among events of 393, the second reference in 383, and since the events are so similarly described some historians have doubted that they occurred twice. Thus it is difficult if not impossible to assign a date to the invasion and exile, or invasions and exiles, and also to determine the length of the exile(s).[58] The contemporary Athenian orator Isocrates, in a letter written either in 366 or 356, mentions one "barbarian" invasion and the loss of *all* Macedonia. But instead of exile he says Amyntas seized one of the Macedonian forts and with help from the Thessalians was able to regain the throne in a matter of three months, after which he held the throne for the rest of his life.[59] Isocrates says Amyntas was "inspired" by Dionysius, the tyrant of Syracuse, who in 396–395 with only a small force made an unexpected recovery of his power in Sicily by thwarting a Carthaginian siege; but the "inspiration" might be more rhetorical than actual. Assuming a date of 393 for a first (if not only) Illyrian invasion, Amyntas must have made a quick recovery with Thessalian aid. This certainly could have occasioned a treaty of defensive alliance with the Chalcidians and also a marriage alliance with the Illyrians and their Upper Macedonian allies the Lyncestians: Amyntas III's wife Eurydice was granddaughter of Arrhabaeus and daughter of Sirras, who was probably Arrhabaeus' Illyrian ally.[60] A date for the marriage of Amyntas and Eurydice surely cannot be later than 393–391, since the eldest son of the union by 375–373 was old enough to sign a treaty with Athens.

We are still left with the question of a two-year regnum of Argaeus before Amyntas recovered his kingship,[61] unless there was a second invasion and consequent exile (which Isocrates failed to mention). It is conceivable that the Illyrians backed Argaeus on the throne in return for his cooperation with their economic interests, especially if Amyntas was attempting to block them, but it is also conceivable that the Chalcidians backed him.[62] An Illyrian invasion about 385, however, would coincide with a known invasion of Epirus at that time. The Illyrians, in alliance with Dionysius of Syracuse, invaded Epirus with the intention of installing on the Molossian throne the exiled king Alcetas, who would facilitate Dionysius' plans to establish ports along coastal Epirus. Though in the end unsuccessful, they had left as many as 15,000 Molossians dead before being driven out again following Spartan intervention.[63] It is not known precisely when the Illyrian chief Bardylis came to power, but probably he was spearheading Illyrian aggression in the mid 380s and could well have been already active in 393.[64]

How Amyntas came into an "unexpected" position of renewed strength after recovering his "whole kingdom" we do not know, but that is the context in which we find Amyntas asking the Olynthians for his borderland back. Since they had been profiting from the region's resources they refused to cede it to him, and at this time—the context is late in 383—Amyntas turned to the Spartans for aid against Olynthus and the Chalcidic League.[65] The Chalcidic League in the mid 380s was a formidable power in the north Aegean and a cause of concern not only to the king of Macedonia but also to the leading Greek states who had interests in the north, particularly Athens, Sparta, and Thebes, and closer to home the Thessalians.[66] The threat was arguably greatest for Amyntas, however, for by 383 the Chalcidians by exercising economic and political control in Macedonian territory had taken over or ostensibly "freed" several Macedonian cities, including, remarkably, Pella.[67] And to think that this Chalcidic League, which now threatened the very existence of the Macedonian kingdom, was a Macedonian creation of sorts.[68]

Only a decade after Perdiccas II had encouraged the consolidation of a number of smaller coastal cities into a centralized position of strength at Olynthus, Olynthian control over the peninsula was perceived as such a threat to southern Greek interests in the north that both Athens and Sparta swore in the Peace of Nicias (signed in 421 as a respite in the Peloponnesian War) to make the city-states of Chalcidice independent and revert to paying the tribute to the Athenian League that had been assessed in 478 when the League was formed. The Chalcidic (or Chalcidian) League was never dissolved in practice, however, since neither Athens nor Sparta truly honoured the terms of the Peace, and by 415 cautious-minded Athenians on the eve of the Sicilian expedition considered Chalcidian power in the north a weighty concern.[69] How the rise of Chalcidian power affected Macedonia in the last quarter of the fifth century is not clear, but it did not prevent Archelaus from developing a healthy trade with Athens. In the last few years of Archelaus' reign and through the first half of the 390s Sparta's preeminence and interest in the north Aegean seem to have curbed Chalcidian power, and when the Corinthian War broke out in 395 in opposition to Spartan hegemony the Chalcidians joined the anti-Spartan alliance of Athens, Corinth, Argos, and Boeotia (Thebes).[70] Soon after this, during the Corinthian War when the southern Greek city-states were concentrating attention on the situation in the Peloponnese, Amyntas III formed his defensive alliance with the Chalcidians. It is debatable whether the Chalcidians were party or not to the Peace of Antalcidas, or so-called King's Peace, imposed by the Persian King Artaxerxes II, which brought the Corinthian War to an end in 387–386, but almost certainly Macedonia was not party to it. The diffusion of power caused by a return to autonomous status of all Greek city-states affected by the King's Peace seems to have left the Olynthians looking for gains beyond Chalcidice proper, for it is soon after the Peace that we see them treating with the "Thracians without a king" towards the Strymon region and encroaching on Macedonian territory.[71]

By the time Amyntas turned to the southern Greeks for aid late in 383 or early in 382 the Olynthians had taken control of the "greater" power of Macedonia.[72] "Greater" must mean much or all of Lower Macedonia—at the very least the part including the capital at Pella—since the Spartans warned Derdas in Elimeia that "lesser" (Upper) Macedonia may be next. If this is the occasion for the exile of Amyntas lasting two years it is hard to say who is responsible for his loss of the kingdom, since the ancient sources give tantalizingly conflicting hints and little in the way of concrete evidence. Possibly there was a second foreign invasion, or possibly the Thessalians forced him out,[73] something that could have transpired after Jason of Pherae overpowered the Argead-friendly Aleuadae in Thessaly. And perhaps the Olynthians took advantage of the situation to seize even more Macedonian territory than Amyntas had previously granted them, beginning with territory closest to Chalcidice. It should not be surprising that around this time Athens sought alliance with Olynthus, doubtless with the aim of securing a supply of Macedonian timber.[74]

In response both to Amyntas' plea for help and to an appeal from two city-states in Chalcidice (Acanthos and Apollonia) for aid against the federalist aggression of the Chalcidic League the Spartans delegated an army to proceed north.[75] Amyntas also gathered an army, probably consisting of both Macedonian cavalry and mercenaries,[76] and joined forces with the Spartans in the Olynthian War. Sparta also won the alliance of Derdas of Elimeia. Derdas was acting independently and not as a subject ally of Amyntas. (A Latin inscription surviving from the time of Trajan, early second century CE, refers to an earlier arbitration by Amyntas in a border dispute between Elimeia (Figure 3.2) and Doliche in Perrhaebia; presumably he acted as an *external* arbitrator.[77]) In the initial attack on Olynthus[78] Derdas' contingent of 400 Upper Macedonian cavalry was given a position of honour near the Spartan commander Teleutias. The contemporary historian Xenophon credited this cavalry troop with having secured the first Spartan victory as well as with foiling an Olynthian raid on Apollonia in the following campaign season.[79] Both Xenophon and Teleutias thought highly of the Upper Macedonian king and the capabilities of his cavalry, but Amyntas' war effort goes unacknowledged.

In the fall of 379 Olynthus fell to the besiegers and the Chalcidic League was dissolved. For Sparta, victory was tempered by the high cost of the campaign both in lives (including Teleutias and a Spartan king) and in reputation: that is, for aiding an absolute monarch in his conflict with autonomous Greek city-states.[80] The Athenians were not long in turning the situation to their own advantage. In 378 the Second Athenian League was formed with the aim of re-establishing the Athenians as the dominant power in the Aegean world. They were particularly eager to regain control of Amphipolis, which had been awarded to them in the Peace of Nicias but which had never in fact returned to their hands, largely because the Amphipolitans refused to submit to Athenian rule. Never ceasing in their efforts, they must now have courted Amyntas, who,

Figure 3.2 Elimeia, Haliacmon River, view north towards Mt Bermion
Source: author, 2014.

being relieved of the Olynthian threat and with his power restored, could finally hope to stabilize and strengthen his kingdom. For reasons unknown, though economic interests were probably a large factor, he shifted his alliance from Sparta to Athens.[81]

The sons of Amyntas and relations with the Greek city-states

About the time Amyntas first came to the throne in 393 the Athenian general Iphicrates was making a name for himself in the Corinthian War with his innovative light shock troops called peltasts and their successes against Spartan hoplites. Then, shortly after the King's Peace of 387–386, Iphicrates, who had recently been deployed to the north Aegean, married a daughter of the Thracian king Cotys I.[82] Iphicrates stayed in the north for the next decade, his military skills facilitating Cotys' revival of the Odrysian kingdom (Cotys came to the throne about 384 and was still in power in 360, but by then he was an enemy of Athens). When Amyntas likewise sought mercenary support to maintain his hold on the throne, he "adopted" Iphicrates as his son, and this alliance, of sorts, might have opened up Macedonian–Athenian relations, though other states also pressured him for alliances throughout the latter half of his reign—for everyone, it seems, was trying to get their hands on Macedonian timber in a scramble to build ships: the Athenians for their Second Sea League and others in opposition to the resurgence of Athenian naval supremacy.[83]

The formal alliance Amyntas made with Athens in 375 or 373 was probably a trade deal that would secure timber for the new Athenian fleet and money for Amyntas to pour into much needed military support.[84] It seems more likely that the Macedonian king was returning to the foreign policy of his predecessors in the fifth century, who all at one time or another enjoyed "the friendship of the city of Athens," rather than that Macedonia was being brought into the Athenian League.[85] And the friendship was as precarious for Amyntas as it had been for his predecessors. The Athenians were hoping to remove one obstacle to their recovery of Amphipolis, and they were able to persuade Amyntas to break with long-standing Macedonian policy regarding the Strymon region. This he did by the fall of 371 at the latest, when his representative at the so-called Spartan Congress voted in favour of the Athenian claim to Amphipolis.[86] The voting participation of a Macedonian delegate at a congress of Greek city-states was unprecedented, so far as we know, and thus stands to mark the progress of Macedonia's integration into the Hellenic world. Also by about 371 Jason of Pherae had got himself elevated to the office of *tagos* in Thessaly, a periodically elected position of overall authority and supreme command in war that allowed him, with a military strength that could potentially overrun any who might refuse, to compel neighbouring kingdoms into tribute-paying alliances.[87] Amyntas was forced into some such subject alliance and finished out his days in a compromised position, dictated by the weak military strength of his own kingdom.[88]

When both Jason and Amyntas died, in 370–369,[89] the door ever so briefly opened for Amyntas' successor Alexander II to try to pull the Macedonian kingdom out from under Thessalian domination.[90] Jason had ousted from power the long-time political allies of the Macedonian kings in Thessaly, the Aleuadae, and this old aristocratic clan now sought Alexander's aid in restoring them to power at Larissa. Moving swiftly and with an element of surprise, while the new tyrant of Pherae, also named Alexander, was preparing to invade Macedonia,[91] the Macedonian king together with the Larissaean Aleuadae marched an army into Thessaly and took control of Larissa and Crannon, supporters of the Aleuadae in both cities welcoming him as their liberator from tyranny. Alexander did not, however, hand the cities over to the Thessalians as agreed, but having taken control by siege of the acropolis in Larissa he installed a garrison, thereby asserting *his* control over the city, and returned home—a rather hasty and urgent return, since his absence had occasioned Ptolemy of Aloros' first bid for the throne. It was possibly a consequence of Alexander II's breach of trust that those Thessalians wanting to be rid of the tyranny of Alexander of Pherae sent also to Thebes to ask for aid. When the Theban Pelopidas arrived at Larissa with a Boeotian army he found Alexander II's garrison in control of the acropolis. After obtaining the surrender of the garrison he went himself straight to Macedonia, where he arranged terms with Alexander and took his youngest brother Philip as hostage, presumably as a guarantee of the king's non-interference in Thessalian affairs.[92] The two Macedonian factions agreed to Pelopidas' arbitration in their war for the throne. Contemporary sources are silent, however, on Alexander's aggression in Thessaly and his betrayal of the Aleuadae,[93] so we might question how successful he was in temporarily relieving Macedonia from Thessalian domination. It is possible that Alexander had already come to mutual agreement with the Thessalians and Pelopidas before his withdrawal,[94] and Thebes feared a powerful Thessaly more than Macedonia.

Given Alexander's trouble at home and on other fronts, he could hardly give due attention to Thessaly. The Illyrians evidently were about to invade Macedonia again at the very beginning of his reign and he bought them off with a financial settlement, agreeing to pay tribute and handing over hostages. Sources say he handed over Philip, but it seems incredible that Philip could have been sent as hostage to both Illyria and Thebes within a matter of months.[95] Philip, at any rate, was sent to Thebes before the end of 368 and spent about three years there, during which time he learned much about warfare, leadership, and diplomacy that would soon turn the Theban and in fact the entire Balkan world on end.

On the home front, when Ptolemy of Aloros seized the opportunity of Alexander's absence to challenge for the throne it must have come as a scandalous surprise. It seems that Ptolemy somehow got himself into a union with Alexander's mother Eurydice, and, according to one source, he married her.[96] Allegedly, Eurydice previously had taken as her lover the husband of her daughter Eurynoe (no source names him, but it is speculated he was Ptolemy) and together they plotted to overthrow Amyntas III, but Eurynoe exposed the plot.[97] Since there was hardly time for a marriage to have transpired between the old king's death and Alexander's campaign in Thessaly, *if* the marriage did in fact occur, possibly it was during Alexander's absence and thus Eurydice's (apparent) collusion in the attempted seizure of the throne.[98] However, the entire story of Eurydice's treason is suspect.[99] Surely Alexander would not have left the kingdom vulnerable to a known rival, so either Ptolemy had not yet shown his traitorous hand, or he and his supporters had been exiled before Alexander went to Thessaly, for Pelopidas when he settled the dispute for the throne brought back the exiles.[100] The contemporary Athenian orator Aeschines says that after the deaths of Amyntas and Alexander Eurydice was betrayed by those pretending to be friends, which could imply Ptolemy's abuse of trust. Friends of the dead king called on Pelopidas to intervene again, and in desperation Eurydice appealed to Iphicrates to defend the throne for her own two remaining sons.[101]

Perhaps it was as early as the war between Alexander and Ptolemy that the exiled Argead Pausanias began to take advantage of the kingdom's compound weaknesses to seize territory on the southeastern fringes of the realm; he took control of Anthemous, Therma, and Strepsa, all near the eastern Thermaic Gulf, and "certain other places, at a time when the Macedonians were not united, but most of them favoured Pausanias."[102] These were possibly the same places the Olynthians had taken some fifteen years earlier,[103] and possibly Pausanias had Olynthian support, since they were beginning to recover from their defeat at the hands of the Spartans. The Spartans themselves by 368 were not in a position to intervene in northern affairs, having been catastrophically defeated by Theban-led Boeotian League forces at Leuctra in 371.[104] In the situation at the time of Alexander's murder there were no fewer than three Macedonian political factions. Internal instability left Macedonia time and again prey to foreign powers.

By the early 360s the Athenians had vigorously renewed their efforts to try to recover control of Amphipolis, which efforts, as we noted, Amyntas had agreed to support, and Alexander may not have had time to alter his father's policy. The Athenians sent Iphicrates to counter the moves of Pausanias whose growing support base posed a threat not only to the Macedonian throne but also to Athenian interests in the Strymon region. So when Eurydice summoned Iphicrates to the Macedonian court and appealed to him as "adopted son" of her deceased husband and as "brother" to her two surviving sons, Perdiccas and Philip, to help secure the throne for their succession, Iphicrates responded by successfully driving Pausanias and his Greek forces out of the kingdom.[105] What his dealings might have been with Ptolemy we do not know. A break from the pro-Athenian policy of Amyntas ensued, occasioned on the one hand by Iphicrates' recall to Athens and on the other by a second intervention of Pelopidas when the friends of the murdered king objected to the rule of his assassin. When Pelopidas showed up with mercenaries Ptolemy managed to buy these off, though he offered no challenge to Pelopidas' terms of settlement and request for hostages: Ptolemy handed over his own son Philoxenus and fifty

Figure 3.3 Amphipolis, Strymon River, view north towards Mt Orbelos
Source: author, 2011.

nobles as guarantee that he would act as guardian for the two younger sons of Amyntas.[106] His alliance with Athens' enemy Thebes in and of itself equated to an anti-Athenian policy. Ptolemy also supplied timber to the Theban general Epaminondas,[107] the victor at Leuctra, who aimed to challenge Athenian naval supremacy, and he worked against Athens in the interest of Amphipolis (Figure 3.3).[108]

Relations between Macedonia and Athens followed a similar course when Perdiccas III eliminated Ptolemy and took the throne for himself. At first Perdiccas maintained the policy of his father (and presumably his older brother) by forming an alliance with Athens and agreeing to help the Athenians regain Amphipolis.[109] But later Perdiccas took the side of the Amphipolitans, installed a garrison there, and in 362 fought in battle for Amphipolis against the Athenians until the latter made a truce with him.[110] When the Athenian *strategos* who made the truce was recalled and put to death, another, Timotheus, sent out in his place, captured the important Macedonian-controlled ports Pydna and (briefly) Methone,[111] but he was unable to dislodge the Macedonian garrison at Amphipolis. As for Perdiccas, disaster struck in yet another clash with the Illyrians, in 360, when King Perdiccas may have been the aggressor, leaving him and 4,000 of his Macedonian soldiers dead on the battlefield.[112]

Diodorus claims that at Perdiccas III's death Macedonia was a virtual slave to the Illyrians,[113] and though most of that conflict has, alas, gone unrecorded the

Illyrian threat was undoubtedly Macedonia's greatest external concern during the first half of the fourth century. The time was ripe for Perdiccas' younger brother Philip to prove himself the most powerful and effective king the Macedonian kingdom had yet experienced.

Notes

1 Plato *Gorgias* 470d–471e. Alcetas' *archē* appears subordinate to the *basileia* (kingship) of Perdiccas. See Chapter 2 n78, n79.
2 On these events and the 'authenticity' of Plato's account see Hammond in *HM* II 1979: 135–136; Borza 1992: 161–162. Socrates is said to have declined an invitation from Archelaus to join the Macedonian court.
3 *IG* I³ 89 = *SEG* X 86. For suggested restorations see Mattingly 1968: 472–475 and Hammond in *HM* II 1979: 134–136. See also Meiggs 1972: 428–430. Combinations of names that could fit into the lacuna between Archelaus and Menelaus (if there were 100 letters per line) include: 'Philip son of Alexander, Amyntas son of Philip' and 'Aeropus son of Perdiccas, Alexander son of Alcetas'. For Philip's probable death see Chapter 2.
4 Hammond in *HM* II 1979: 134; and see Errington 1990: 25; Borza 1992: 161.
5 So Ael. *VH* 12.43, but see Carney 2000: 17: probably of the Macedonian elite and married to Perdiccas. Cf. also Ath. 11. 506e.
6 Hammond in *HM* II 1979: 199.
7 Hammond in *HM* II 1979: 154, 198.
8 For the distinction between 'regent' and 'guardian' see Anson 2009a, especially 280–281.
9 So Badian 1982a: 106; Carney 2000: 21; *contra* Hammond in *HM* II 1979: 169 n2.
10 Diod. 14.37.6.
11 Arist. *Pol.* 5.1311b. Cp. [Plato] *Alcibiades* 2.141d–e; [Plut.] *Amatorius* 768f; Ael. *VH* 8.9.
12 Cf. n26.
13 Plut. *Alex.* 9.7; Ath. 13.557d. See Carney 1992: 171–174; and Chapter 6.
14 See Chapter 4 n61.
15 Str. 7.7.8: Eurydice was a granddaughter of Arrhabaeus, from the ruling house of Lyncus, and a daughter of Sirras, a patronym confirmed in three inscriptions from Vergina (Andronikos 1984: 49–51; further bibliography in Mortensen 1992: 165; Carney 2000: 269 n10). At least two other sources [*Suda* s.v. "Karanos," Libanius *Vita Dem.* 9; cf. Plut. *Mor.* 14c] call Eurydice Illyrian, which ought to indicate that Eurydice's father Sirras was an Illyrian and not another Lyncestian, as some believe. This follows Carney 2000: 41, who cites the sources and earlier bibliography on the debate; add Kapetanopoulos 1994 and Worthington 2008: 178 to those favouring Sirras' Lyncestian origin, and see the summary of Greenwalt 2010: 286. Given the parallel of the Sirras–Arrhabaeus alliance against Archelaus soon after the Illyrian–Lyncestian alliance against Perdiccas II, an Illyrian origin for Sirras is here preferred. For Eurydice and Gygaea and the role of women in succession in general see Carney 2000, especially chapters 1 and 2, and on Macedonian polygamy see Greenwalt 1989. Justin (7.4.5) is the only source to mention three additional sons of Amyntas III by Gygaea: Archelaus, Arrhidaeus, and Menelaus. Whether this marriage was first or second, the sons older or younger than or even concurrent with Eurydice's, is disputed. Apart from Justin's (8.3.10–11) further claim that Philip II attacked and destroyed Olynthus in 349–348 for having harboured two of his half-brothers after he had eliminated the third (Justin's accusation of fratricide charges Philip with the murder of all three), curiously they do not turn up in the

succession struggles, and no contemporary author so much as alludes to them. On these half-brothers see Ellis 1973.
16 Hatzopoulos 1986: 283.
17 Just. 9.8.3: a suggestion that other sons of Philip died of natural causes or in war is unconfirmed.
18 Plut. *Alex.* 77.8. Carney 1992: 172–173; see Chapter 8 n73.
19 Diod. 14.37.6; Synkellos, Adler and Tuffin 2002: 383.
20 So Hammond in *HM* II 1979: 134–136, followed by Hatzopoulos 1986: 283; Errington, 1990: 28; Borza 1992: 178; Roisman 2010: 158. Carney 1980: 25 suggests he was a Lyncestian prince.
21 Hammond 1989a: 71–76; cp. Anson 2009a: 279–280, citing previous scholarship. Cf. n49.
22 So Diod. 14.84.6; but cp. Synkellos, Adler and Tuffin 2002: 379.
23 Synkellos (n22): Aeropus ["Archelaos" is a mistake] 4 years; Amyntas [II] 1 year; Pausanias 1 year (we should understand only part of a year for each); Amyntas [III] 5 years; Argaeus 2 years; Amyntas [III?] 12 years. Justin (7.4.2–8) bypasses at least five kings by skipping from Alexander I to Amyntas, father of Philip II.
24 Tataki 1998 lists twenty-nine; and see Heckel 2006a: 23–26 (eleven).
25 Arist. *Pol.* 5.1311b. Possibly the text is corrupt, and "little" applies to Derdas. Cf. Ael. *VH* 12.43. On the Elimiote dynasty see Liampi 1998.
26 So Hammond in *HM* II 1979: 168–169, 1989a: 72, based on Just. 7.4.3 and Ael. *VH* 12.43 (cf. n28), *contra* "Beloch, Geyer and others" (1979: 168 n2) arguing he was a son of Archelaus based on Arist. *Pol.* 5.1311b. The debate centres on the text of line 14 in Aristotle's passage and whether one should read "of Amyntas" or "to Amyntas." Hammond is followed by Hatzopoulos 1986: 282; Borza 1992: 178; Roisman 2010: 158. Following Beloch and Geyer are Ellis 1971: 17; Errington 1990: 28.
27 Synkellos is not entirely clear on the ascension of the Amyntases but seems less confused than Diodorus and Justin.
28 Synkellos, Adler and Tuffin 2002: 384: Amyntas, son of Arrhidaeus, son of Amyntas, son of Alexander I seized the throne, and was at one time imprisoned. Just. 7.4.3, Ael. *VH* 12.43: "Amyntas" was the son of Menelaus (perhaps conflating II and III). Tod *GHI* 111 = RO *GHI* 12: an inscription naming Amyntas, son of Arrhidaeus, as king of the Macedonians, for the date cf. n53.
29 Diod. 14.89.2: Amyntas, who assassinated Pausanias, ruled for twenty-four years; but 92.3–4: Amyntas was driven from the throne by the Illyrians, and "some say" Argaeus then ruled for two years. How Pausanias succeeded Amyntas II is nowhere mentioned in the extant sources.
30 Diod. 14.92.3–4. Borza 1992: 297.
31 Just. 7.4.8; cp. Diod. 15.60.3.
32 Diod. 16.2.4; Just. 7.4.8; cp. Aeschin. 2.26, eldest of the brothers: but were they six or three?
33 The inscription (cf. n84) is thought to record an alliance formed either during the campaign of Chabrias in 375–374 or of Timotheus in 373–372.
34 Diod. 15.71.1, 77.5. In Sherman's Loeb translation "brother" is corrected to "brother-in-law." All sources agree Alexander had only two full brothers (and three half-brothers? Just. 7.4.5, cf. n15). Two brothers of Perdiccas II, Philip and Menelaus, both had sons named Amyntas, and Ptolemy could conceivably be the son of either of these, one of whom was possibly Amyntas II. Hammond in *HM* II 1979: 182 makes Ptolemy a son of Amyntas II; Macurdy 1932: 18, 20 and Mortensen 1992: 157 suggest he is an illegitimate son of Amyntas III; Stylianou 1998: 465 insists he cannot be a son of Amyntas III. For recent discussion with bibliography see Anson 2009a: 282–283.

35 Demosthenes (19.194–195), making no mention of Ptolemy himself, names Apollophanes of Pydna as one of the men who killed Alexander. Later sources—Diod. 15.71.1, 16.2.4, Plut. *Pel.* 27, and Ath. 14.629d (citing Marsyas' *History of Macedon* [*FGrH* 135–136])—hold Ptolemy responsible for Alexander's death, while Justin (7.5.4–5) lays the blame on a plot of Eurydice.
36 Plut. *Pel.* 27.3.
37 Aeschines (2.29) says Ptolemy was made "guardian" (*epitropos*) but Diodorus (15.71.1, 77.5) says he ruled as king (*basileus*). Anson 2009a: 282 believes the lack of coinage suggests that he was never king and the demotic Aloros that he was not an Argead. Greenwalt 2017: 89 also concludes he was not king.
38 *Suda* s.v. "Karanos." Hammond in *HM* II 1979: 1975–1976 suggests both Pausanias and Argaeus were sons of Archelaus. It is just as plausible (Ellis 1976: 39; Müller 2010: 167) that Pausanias was the son of King Pausanias, who held the throne briefly in 394–393 and was supplanted by Amyntas III. If that is correct, he was a grandson of Aeropus II.
39 Aeschin. 2.28–29; Diod. 15.77.5; discussed below.
40 See below and n112.
41 Diod. 16.2.4–6.
42 Diod. 16.3.3–6; Theopomp. F29 [*FGrH/BNJ*] 115, Morison 2014]; Dem. 23.121. On the political implications of Argaeus' bid for the throne see Heskel 1996.
43 Diod. 16.2.6, 3.4; Theopomp. F29 (for Theopompus see also Shrimpton 1991).
44 Hammond's argument (n38) that they were both sons of Archelaus is not widely accepted. Borza 1992: 178–179 has three branches of the Argeadae killed off by the end of the 390s including that of Perdiccas II, with only the lines of Amyntas and Menelaus surviving.
45 See Chapter 4 n9.
46 Cf. Liv. 40.9.8–9 and Chapter 10. On the importance of personal relationships in succession see Mitchell 2007.
47 Anson 2009a: 277–278.
48 King 2010: 374–375.
49 Cf. n21. Diod. 16.3.1: granted to Philip; 16.35: denied to Argaeus (not Amyntas' choice). Just. 7.5.9–10: granted to Philip, Amyntas' son, in dire circumstances. Curt 10.6.1–4: granted to Arrhidaeus, son of Philip (preferred over Alexander III's unborn and bastard).
50 Just. 7.4.6.
51 Cf. n15 and Chapter 2 n122.
52 Polyaen. 2.1.17. Cf. Polyaen. 4.4.3; Xen. *Hell.* 4.3.3–8; *Agesilaus* 2.1–2; Plut. *Agesilaus* 16.2.
53 Tod *GHI* 111 = Harding 21 = RO *GHI* 12, date uncertain. Tod: 33 and Ellis 1969: 3 favour a date 393; Hammond in *HM* II 1979: 174 favours 391; March 1995: 280 places it between 393 and 388. Zahrnt 1971: 122–124 proposes two treaties with two dates; followed by Harding 21; and see Errington 1990: 31.
54 Xen. *Hell.* 5.2.16. But cf. RO *GHI*: 57.
55 Diod. 14.92.3–4, 15.19.2.
56 Thuc. 1.58.2.
57 Greenwalt 1988, 2010: 284.
58 For discussion see Hammond in *HM* II 1979: 172–178, arguing against a doublet; March 1995: 265–274, arguing for a doublet—he re-dates the Illyrian invasion to 388–387 (272) and believes Argaeus not Amyntas III gave the land grant to the Olynthians (274). See also Stylianou 1998: 211–213, allowing two invasions; Parker 2003: 127–132 on a "spurious doublet"; Rhodes 2010: 26, favouring the doublet, i.e. one Illyrian invasion.

59 Isoc. 6.46; cp. Ael. *VH* 4.8; Diod. 14.92.3–4.
60 Carney 2000: 41. Cf. n15.
61 Diod. 14.92.4.
62 Illyrian support of Argaeus: e.g. Hammond in *HM* II 1979: 172; Greenwalt 1988: 35–37; Errington 1990: 30. Olynthian support: Tod *GHI* II: 33; Ellis in *CAH*² VI: 748. See also Borza 1992: 296–297; March 1995. Diod. 16.2.2: a third reference to Amyntas being defeated by the Illyrians, when the king was forced to pay tribute *and* to surrender his youngest son Philip as hostage, cannot be reconciled with the earlier date, since Philip was not born until about 383; but few accept that Philip was ever an Illyrian hostage, *contra* Greenwalt 2017: 89. Cf. n95.
63 Diod. 15.13.1–3.
64 Hammond in *HM* II 1979: 172; Greenwalt 2010: 284
65 Diod. 15.19.2–3; Xen. *Hell.* 5.2.11–13.
66 Xen. *Hell.* 5.2.16.
67 Xen. *Hell.* 5.2.11–13.
68 Psoma 2011: 113–115.
69 Thuc. 6.10.
70 Diod. 14.82.3.
71 Xen. *Hell.* 5.2.16–17. *Contra* Cartledge 1987: 270: the "Chalkidian Confederacy" was not yet formed at the time of the King's Peace in 386. See Badian 1991: 44: Olynthus was not party to the Peace; but Parker 2003: 119 n21 allows the possibility. On the relationship between Olynthus and the Chalcidians see Stylianou 1998: 213–215, citing earlier bibliography.
72 Xen. *Hell.* 5.2.38.
73 Dem. 23.111, schol. Aeschin. 2.26.
74 Tod *GHI* 119 = *IG* II² 36.
75 Xen. *Hell.* 5.2.11–24; cp. Diod. 15.19.2–3; Isoc. *Paneg.* 125–126. Parker 2003: 123: the Acanthian ambassador's speech is Xenophon's and no one else's (*his* interpretation of and background for Spartan policy) but this does not mean the embassy is not historical. On the conflicting accounts of Xenophon and Diodorus of the outbreak of the Olynthian War (e.g. Xenophon says Amyntas was dispossessed of his kingdom at the outbreak, while Diodorus says he had already recovered the whole of it) see Parker 2003 *passim* and 133–135 on the evidence of Isocrates and the scholia.
76 Xen. *Hell.* 5.2.38; Diod. 15.19.3.
77 *BSA* (*Annual of the British School at Athens*) 17 1910–11: 193–204; Hammond in *HM* II 1979: 178; Errington 1990: 34.
78 Delayed until spring 381 (after the Spartans themselves violated the Peace by establishing a garrison in the Theban Cadmea on their march north). For the chronology of the Olynthian War see Stylianou 1998: 209–211.
79 Xen. *Hell.* 5.2.40–3.2.
80 Isoc. 4.126.
81 Greenwalt 1988: 39 n31: "In short, Sparta provided no market for Macedonian products in the 370s, whereas Athens did—and Amyntas needed the income." See also Hamilton 1986.
82 Sears 2013: 126–128.
83 Xen. *Hell.* 6.1.11.
84 Tod *GHI* 129 = *IG* II² 102 = Harding 43; cp. Xen. *Hell.* 6.1.11. The inscription is too fragmentary to be certain of the terms, and the date (n33) is open to debate. See e.g. Cargill 1981: 85–87, who would allow it to be as late as 370–369, though the earlier date of 375 seems more logical *if* the terms secured timber for the Athenians; Xenophon claims the Macedonians *were* supplying timber to the

Athenians in 375. Also for timber supplies to Athens (privately to Timotheus) cf. Dem. 49.26–30.
85 On this disputed point and the nature of Athenian alliances in the 370s see Cargill 1981: 85–87; see also Hammond in *HM* II 1979: 179; and on the vexed question of the Macedonian king paying tribute to Athens see especially Harding 2006: 231–232.
86 Aeschin. 2.32.
87 Xen. *Hell.* 6.1.5–12, 18–19.
88 Diod. 15.60.1–2. On Diodorus' date of 371 as preferred over Xenophon's of 375 for Jason's assumption of the office of *tagos* see Cargill 1981: 84 and Sprawski 1999: 15–23.
89 Stylianou 1998: 449–450: Jason was assassinated in August 370; Amyntas died closer to summer 369.
90 Diod. 15.60.3–6; cp. Isoc. 5.20, Arr. *Anab.* 7.9.4. Greenwalt 2017.
91 He had killed his uncle Polyphron to avenge the latter's murder of his own father Polydorus, both of whom were brothers of Jason and had succeeded him: Xen. *Hell.* 6.4.33–35.
92 Diod. 15.61.3–5, 67.4; cp. Plut. *Pel.* 26.
93 Cp. Aeschin. 2.26–30; Xen. *Hell.* 6.4.34–35. Cf. also Plut. *Pel.* 26–27.
94 Buckler 1980: 113–114 and 246 argues Alexander II made a deal with the Thebans and Thessalians *before* withdrawing his garrison from Larissa in return for Theban aid against Ptolemy of Aloros and his supporters; rejected by Stylianou 1998: 423, whose view is closer to Diodorus' account.
95 Just. 7.5.1–2. Cp. Diod. 16.2.2, contradicting his own claim elsewhere (15.67.4) and other claims (Plut. *Pel.* 26.4; Just. 7.5.2, cf. 6.9.7) that it was Alexander, not the Illyrians, who surrendered Philip to the Thebans. Borza 1992: 189 with n28: the chronology is too tight. The claim of Aeschines (2.26–29) that Philip was handed over later by Ptolemy, despite being a near contemporary reference, seems less preferable since Philip can hardly have been a safe surety for the conduct of Ptolemy, who clearly hoped to rid himself of the remaining sons of Amyntas. On the controversy over *who* handed Philip over see Stylianou 1998: 456–457, citing earlier scholarship. See also Griffith's argument for Ptolemy in *HM* II 1979: 204–205.
96 Schol. Aeschin. 2.29.
97 Just. 7.4.7. On Eurydice and her alleged plots see Badian 1982a; Borza 1992: 192–193; Mortensen 1992; Carney 2000 chapter 2. Justin is the only source to identify Eurynoe, but he does not name her husband.
98 Macurdy 1932: 21–22 suggests the marriage was forced on Eurydice, and we have a parallel in Cassander's marriage to Thessalonice some fifty years later. Mortensen 1992: 165–166 suggests the marriage occurred after Alexander was murdered and could have been Eurydice's calculated though repugnant move to protect her other two sons from murder.
99 Cf. Just 7.5.4–9.
100 Plut. *Pel.* 26.
101 Aeschin. 2.26–29.
102 Aeschin. 2.27; cf. Dem. 23.149.
103 Xen. *Hell.* 5.2.13.
104 On the Boeotian League and Leuctra see Buckler 1980: 15–69.
105 Cf. n101.
106 Plut. *Pel.* 27.2–4. Nobles are actually *hetairoi*/companions; see Chapter 5.
107 *SEG* 34 (1984) 355(1); Hammond in *HM* II 1979: 185–188; Borza 1987/1995: 110 n59.
108 Aeschin. 2.29.

109 Polyaen. 3.10.14; Dem. 2.14. Heskel 1996: 41–43.
110 Diod. 16.3.3; Aeschin. 2. 29–30. Heskel 1996: 42–43 argues against Aeschines' claim that Perdiccas was defeated.
111 Dem. 4.4; Dinarchus 1.14.
112 Diod. 16.2.2–5; cp. Just. 7.5.6–8. See Chapter 8, Antipater's *Perdiccas in Illyria*.
113 Diod. 16.1.3. Cp. Illyrian advances into Epirus: Front. 2.5.19.

4 Philip II, 360–336

Consolidation and expansion

During his twenty-four-year reign Philip II raised Macedonia to be the dominant power in the Balkans. He achieved this by mixing diplomacy with force, combining marriage, trade, and other alliances with battles, sieges, and garrisons. First as a nation builder, he revitalized the monarchy by unifying Upper and Lower Macedonia, invigorated the military with innovations, subjugated the bordering kingdoms, and enhanced economic growth. Then setting his sights on empire, he expanded into Thrace, gained political and military influence as *archon* in Thessaly, and after settling rivalries of the Greek city-states in the Third Sacred War and bringing them under a common peace, as *hegemon* over the resultant League of Corinth he organized a military offensive against Persia, though he was assassinated before he could cross to Asia.

Consolidation of Upper and Lower Macedonia

Philip was twenty-three years old and possibly in command of the Macedonian garrison at Amphipolis when he got word that his brother the king and more than 4,000 men lay dead somewhere on the western frontier.[1] We do not know what precipitated Perdiccas' battle; perhaps he reneged on paying the tribute that his predecessors had been forced to pay to keep Illyria at bay, or possibly his campaign was aggressive. He had been strong enough to eliminate his rival for the throne, to blunt Athenian ambition to recover Amphipolis by taking control of it himself, and he had increased revenues into the Macedonian coffers by doubling the harbour dues.[2] The fact that he had so many men in the field suggests he was capable of flexing significant military muscle.[3] So at Philip's ascension the Macedonian kingdom may not have been on the brink of annihilation.[4] However, the military defeat was indeed catastrophic and the surviving troops demoralized and terrified, as it was expected the formidable Illyrian king Bardylis would follow up his victory with an invasion of Lower Macedonia. All foreign powers with interests in Macedonia's resources and geographic advantages were poised to capitalize on the kingdom's vulnerability.

Philip sprang into the breach. He had learned a great deal during his three-year sojourn as hostage in Thebes, where he was housed with the skillful general Pammenes.[5] Later tradition could not resist insisting that he had lived in the house of the more famous Theban general Epaminondas and that as contemporaries they had studied Pythagorean philosophy together.[6] Philip, however, was only a lad of about twelve when Epaminondas was crushing the Spartan hoplites in the battle at Leuctra. What Philip observed and absorbed during his teen years was warfare and politics. He had rubbed elbows with the elite Theban Sacred Band and its commanders and studied observantly the oblique order of battle. In politics he had gained first-hand experience of the inner workings of a democratic Greek *polis* (city-state), so he knew both its strengths and its weaknesses. Perdiccas managed to obtain his younger brother's release, possibly when Philip turned eighteen, and very likely Philip was already putting his experience into practice in Macedonia before his brother's death.[7] Perdiccas' philosopher friend and advisor, Euphraeus of Oreus, a former student of Plato, persuaded the king to give Philip a territory to oversee with his own forces. The territory is not identified, but it would make sense if it were in the eastward reaches beyond the Axios and towards the Strymon, where Perdiccas needed to safeguard mining and timber interests.[8] Back in Pella, the son of Perdiccas, Amyntas, who at this date cannot have been more than eight years old and perhaps was considerably younger, was in line to succeed to the throne. Whether Philip in his early days acted as guardian for this nephew or whether from the start he ruled as king in his own right has long been a problem for scholars.[9] Though most historians reject a period of guardianship, it does not seem possible with the available evidence to answer that question definitively, and the answer would not alter the fact anyway that Philip immediately assumed the *duties* of the ruler of the kingdom, the most vital of which in the circumstances was to lead in war. Like both of his older brothers, he acted swiftly and decisively. As war leader, in addition to replenishing the loss of more than 4,000 men it would be imperative to rebuild troop morale. But before he could give the military his full attention and deal with the troublesome frontier he had to fend off at least two exiled Macedonian royals eager to assume the kingship in his stead.

Pausanias and Argaeus were long-time rival contenders from lateral branches of the Argead clan, and Argaeus already had briefly held the throne.[10] Perdiccas' death presented an opportunity for both, with backing from foreign powers keen to exploit the region, to try to oust the line of Amyntas III. For Philip, everything was happening at once and in every direction, and needing more forces to defend the kingdom he immediately withdrew the garrison from Amphipolis, probably in October of 360, and left the city autonomous.[11] The Athenians, hoping to regain control of Amphipolis themselves by backing a candidate who would assist or at least not oppose their efforts, swiftly dispatched a force of 3,000 hoplites to help put Argaeus on the throne.[12] Pausanias was probably based at Calindoia in Chalcidice,[13] and he had obtained the military support of a Thracian king.[14] But Philip bought off the Thracian king, and also, with a combination of bribes and promises, he persuaded the Paeonian king and his war leaders, who were beginning to raid along the northern frontier, to observe a period of peace for the time being.[15] With the north and east temporarily secured, he hurried west towards Pieria, heart of the old Argead homeland, where the Athenian forces with some Macedonian exiles had already disembarked at Methone, and Argaeus, having marched a force inland, was attempting to get himself instated as king at the old capital Aegae. Argaeus might have expected considerable support there, especially if that is where his previous period of rule had been based, and if the kingship itself was still open to question—that is, if Philip had not yet been acclaimed king but rather was acting as guardian for a minor heir.[16] But the Macedonians at Aegae rejected Argaeus' overtures. On the short retreat back to Methone, Philip surprised the party, either by the unexpectedness of his swift arrival or by ambush,[17] engaged them in battle, and defeated them. The survivors sought a truce, and on agreement the Macedonian exiles in Argaeus' service were handed over to Philip (sources do not say whether Argaeus was among them), and all non-Macedonians were allowed to depart, mainly Athenians to whom Philip made restitution for their losses.[18] Argaeus is never heard of again. Nor is Pausanias. Philip had dealt promptly and effectively with the two most serious challenges to the Macedonian throne. His success was due both to military competence and to diplomacy. He was careful to conciliate the Athenians, first by not retaining captives and second by ostensibly agreeing to recognize their claim to Amphipolis.[19] It bought him time, and now with potential rivals eliminated—it is said he also executed one of his half-brothers[20]—he put that time to profitable use by applying his Theban education to a complete overhaul of the army.

Over the winter of 360–359, while Philip's envoys were at Athens negotiating peace on terms whereby Philip would relinquish (so he said) his claim to Amphipolis "for all time,"[21] Philip himself was busy recruiting, training, and outfitting a phalanx of heavy-armed foot soldiers.[22] When news reached him perhaps in the summer that the Paeonian king Agis had died, Philip seized the moment of weakness to invade the neighbouring kingdom. His victory in battle brought about not only a reversal of the terms of the previous year with the Paeonians now promising allegiance to the Macedonians,[23] but more significantly it boosted the morale of the newly reformed Macedonian army. Within another year, in addition to the ever competent cavalry Philip had a well trained and well equipped infantry force sufficiently confident, under his command, to confront head-on that formidable enemy on the northwestern frontier. Bardylis would not be collecting tribute from Philip.

Philip steeled his army for a march into Illyrian-occupied territory in the spring or summer of 358. Bardylis, now far advanced in years, dispatched envoys to Philip in an effort to negotiate peace on terms of each keeping what they presently held. What prompted the old king to take this uncharacteristically cautious stance, and why he had not yet followed up on his victory of nearly two years previous, is unclear.[24] Philip's recent victory over the Paeonians might well have given Bardylis pause, but also Philip at some point entered into a marriage alliance by taking the Illyrian princess Audata to wife,[25] and if this occurred soon after Perdiccas' defeat in 360, a cessation of hostilities ought to have followed, since that was one purpose of inter-dynastic marriages. Audata did produce a daughter, Cynnane, but the date is unknown and nothing more is heard of the marriage. Anyway, Philip now refused to come to terms and insisted on recovering what he regarded to be rightfully Macedonian territory; Bardylis held some Macedonian towns, though sources do not name them. Battle it was, then, and a near even match, with no fewer than 10,000 infantry and 600 cavalry under Philip's command against the same number of foot and 500 horse under Bardylis.[26] The Illyrians quickly adopted a defensive square against Philip's assault, which consisted of both a frontal infantry attack and a relentless attack by his cavalry on their flank. The Illyrians finally broke and took to flight, and in the wake of the rout more than 7,000 Illyrians lay dead. Bardylis submitted to peace and the Illyrians withdrew from all occupied Macedonian territory.

Philip's victory not only avenged Perdiccas' defeat but it also overturned decades of Macedonian subjugation to Illyrian power. Guy Griffith is correct to remark that the importance of the victory would be hard to overestimate, that the impact on the north Aegean of this "landmark in Macedonian history" may be compared to the impact on southern Greece of the Theban victory over Sparta at Leuctra in 371,[27] from which Sparta never recovered. It was, in actuality, a turning of the tide, as the rise of Macedonia's power under the leadership of Philip began its unstoppable encompassing sweep over the southern Balkan peninsula. What is more, Philip's success won over the Macedonians, those dissident factions that had supported rival contenders for the throne now seeing in Philip the brightest prospects for the future of the kingdom.[28] This battle also marks a turning point in the relationship between Lower and Upper Macedonia. Only twenty years earlier the Elimiote cavalry of Derdas II had been regarded as Macedonia's finest, and Philip probably did not go into battle in western Macedonian against the Illyrians without first reaffirming the long-standing alliance of Lower Macedonia with Elimeia. His marriage about this time to Phila, Derdas II's daughter—in the words of one ancient source Philip married "according to war"[29]—likely hinged on the incorporation of Upper Macedonian cavalry into his new army, just as the marriage of Archelaus' daughter to an earlier Elimiote king (Derdas I) had secured an ally in the war against Sirras and Arrhabaeus. At the time of the battle Elimeia and Eordaea were probably the only two districts of Upper Macedonia allied with Lower Macedonia. Orestis by around 370 had joined with Epirus, while about the same time the king of Pelagonia was honoured independently as *proxenos* and *euergetes* of the Athenians.[30] In 363–362 another Pelagonian, one Menelaus (almost certainly a royal), was supplying funds to the Athenian general Timotheus against Amphipolis and Perdiccas' Macedonians.[31] The rest of Upper Macedonia evidently had been under the sway of Bardylis. As a result of his victory, Philip is said to have subjugated all territory as far as Lake Lychnidos (Ochrid),[32] northwest of the Prespa Lakes region in Derriopos. Details are lacking, and consolidation of Upper and Lower Macedonia would not have happened overnight, but soon after 358 Pelagonia and Lyncus were annexed,[33] Orestis once again became Macedonian,[34] and Tymphaea, which was previously oriented towards Epirus, was also incorporated into Philip's greater Macedonia.

Consolidation meant altered political circumstances for Upper Macedonians. While some would have accepted or even welcomed Philip as their liberator from Illyrian domination,[35] others resisted any suggestion of subordination. Philip conciliated many of the royals and nobles of the upper districts by incorporating them into his court and army as officers, generals, and Companions. The Companions were an institution of the king's honoured associates, men who ate and drank with him, advised him, and hunted and fought alongside him.[36] Others opted to flee the region, while a few preferred to conceal resentment and await opportunity. Menelaus of Pelagonia, for instance, is found a few years later as an exile holding Athenian citizenship and in 351 fighting against Philip in Thrace.[37] Philip's new general Parmenio, on the other hand, whatever his prior position,[38] adapted well to the turn of events, for he (and later his sons) held high military rank for the next twenty-eight years. Parmenio's generalship helped Philip gain and maintain the upper hand over the Illyrians nearly as far as the Adriatic Sea.[39] And with the Illyrian threat under control, through land grants, population exchanges, fortified towns, and settlements Philip brought change and stability to the western reaches of his kingdom.[40] That some resentment and regionalism lingered, however, is quite likely.[41]

Once the west and northwest were notionally secure, Philip turned his attention back to what he had been about when Perdiccas' death first opened the floodgates: Amphipolis. Philip needed funds, and, as everyone knew, there was gold in the hills just a stone's throw from Amphipolis' protective walls, in Mount Pangaion. An anti-Macedonian party inside the city, dreading the imposition of another Macedonian garrison, sent two envoys to Athens to appeal to the Athenians to come and take over the city.[42] When Philip found himself shut out of Amphipolis, bringing up his battering rams he proceeded to demonstrate the effectiveness of his innovations in siege warfare. The walls were breached, and the Macedonians entering in a tide of slaughter seized control of the city from its defenders. Those who did not resist the takeover were treated fairly, but the anti-Macedonian party was exiled.[43] In addition to local mining interests Philip assumed control of the crossing of the Strymon, and Amphipolis soon became a Macedonian *polis* in the Greek sense, albeit not independent.[44]

After Amphipolis fell it was rumoured at Athens that during the siege a 'secret' negotiation was arranged whereby Philip would help the Athenians recover the coveted city in exchange for their non-interference (or help) in his own recovery of Pydna.[45] Whether or not Philip was guilty of such duplicity, the Athenians did not in fact send aid to Amphipolis, and it became apparent almost immediately that Philip had no intention of handing Amphipolis over to anyone. As for Pydna, Philip soon took control of that port anyway without much difficulty.[46] He was little concerned that anyone would or could stop him since just at this same time the Athenians were becoming embroiled in their so-called Social War (357–355), triggered when some of their east Aegean allies revolted from the Second Athenian Sea League. In order to protect their interests in the Chersonese, the Athenians promptly signed a treaty with the three neighbouring Thracian kings whereby one party or the other would collect the taxes and revenues from the Greek cities there.[47] There is no mention of Philip in the fragment of the treaty, but, as we shall see, within a year he would be a threat to both Thracian and Athenian interests near the Hellespont. Already in 357 with Philip in possession of two key northern cities he was now affirmatively at odds with Athens. Not only had he reneged on whatever the Athenians thought his intentions were with regard to Amphipolis *and* retaken a Thermaic Gulf port, which they coveted for access to timber supplies, but Philip had also outmanoeuvred the Athenians in the competition for alliance with Olynthus and the Chalcidic League. When Athens declared war on Philip over Amphipolis[48] he countered by forming an alliance with the Olynthians and offering to take over Potidaea on their behalf—a deal certain to aggravate hostility between Athens and the Chalcidians since Potidaea was full of Athenian settlers.[49] When Potidaea fell to Philip the following summer he removed the Athenian garrison, but again diplomatically he sent the Athenian captives unharmed home to Athens. The remaining inhabitants of Potidaea he sold into slavery, earning substantial revenues in the process, and then he handed the city as well as its surrounding estates over to the Olynthians as agreed.[50] Against all of Philip's moves the Athenians, since the greatest weight of their manpower and resources in these years had to be put into the war with their revolting allies, proved ineffectual. The Chalcidians were already allied with Philip and content at present not to be his target, while both Sparta and Thebes, the other Greek powers whose interests had dominated north Aegean events in recent decades, were in decline and, like Athens, heavily committed elsewhere. All of them were becoming embroiled in the Sacred War in central Greece, a war into which the Thessalians were about to draw Philip as their ally.

Expansion into Thessaly and Thrace

By midsummer 356 Philip had begun his intervention in Crenides, the Thassian colony founded just a few years earlier east of Mount Pangaion. The evidence is not clear, but evidently the inhabitants sought Philip's aid against Thracian raids,[51] and the situation, which involved King Cetriporis being reduced to vassal status, offered Philip his first Thracian foothold. After draining the swampy plain around Crenides and settling a large number of new inhabitants in the colony Philip promptly increased production from nearby gold mines and raised their revenues to more than 1,000 talents per year.[52] Pangaion gold, now accessed from both Amphipolis and Crenides, was put to use to pay mercenaries (typically used for garrison duty) and to 'buy' political supporters in the Greek city-states. Sometime later Philip renamed Crenides Philippi after himself (Figure 4.1). It was clear from his actions that Philip was purposefully intent upon expansion into Thracian territory, and on July 26, 356, the Athenians joined a coalition of three northern kings against Macedonia: the Thracian Cetriporis and his brothers (the sons of Berisades), the Paeonian Lyppeius (or Lycceius), and the Illyrian Grabos.[53] Grabos had formed an alliance with the Olynthians the previous year, but the Olynthians had broken that deal when Philip offered them Potidaea.

Figure 4.1 Philippi, Via Egnatia
Source: author, 2011.

That same summer, just as Philip was concluding his victorious siege of Potidaea in the Chalcidian August heat, news reached him of two other victories: his general Parmenio had been victorious over the Illyrian Grabos on the western frontier, and his *keles* (single horse with rider) entry had won the crown at Olympia.[54] This may have been only the second competition of a Macedonian at Olympia since Alexander I had claimed the right to compete nearly a century and a half earlier. Archelaus reputedly won in the *tethrippon* (four-horse chariot race) in 408, and Philip now won the first of three crowns in successive Olympiads; the latter two evidently were in the *tethrippon* in 352 and the *synoris* (two-horse chariot race) in 348. Philip commemorated each victory with an issue of coins.[55] News also reached Philip at Potidaea that back in Pella his fourth wife, the Epirote princess Olympias, had given birth to a son, Alexander.

The chronology of Philip's early activities cannot be precisely reconstructed, but it is estimated that the siege of Amphipolis was undertaken about nine months after the defeat of Bardylis, in the spring of 357, and that already in the interim Philip had made his first venture into Thessaly.[56] It must have been in the winter of 358–357 that Philip met the Larissaean Philinna, for their offspring, Arrhidaeus, was of marriageable age by 337 and so surely cannot have been born much later than late 357.[57] But precisely what Philip was doing in Thessaly at this time is unknown.[58] Over that winter the tyrant Alexander of Pherae was assassinated by his wife's brothers, and one of the tyrannicides,

Tisiphonus, soon assumed the role of tyrant himself.[59] Possibly there was a brief period when the anti-Pheraeans hoped to regain control of the government with Philip's support. Philip did not, however, establish a significant foothold in Thessaly at this early date. By the fall of 357 Philip was solidifying an alliance farther west with the Molossians of Epirus by taking Olympias as a wife. Olympias' father, Neoptolemus, together with his younger brother Arybbas had held the Molossian kingship after their father, Alcetas, died.[60] By the time Olympias married Philip in 357 Neoptolemus was dead and her uncle Arybbas was sole ruler and her guardian. Arybbas' rule was not strong or popular, however, so Philip's marriage to Olympias effectively gave him control over greater Epirus.[61]

Not long after, probably in 355, once again the Aleuadae of Larissa called on their long-time friendship with the Macedonian Argeads to assist in the overthrow of the Pheraean tyranny. Turning invitation into opportunity, Philip marched an army into Thessaly and won a victory over the brothers Tisiphonus and Lycophron.[62] Once again it was only a temporary gain, and Philip still did not establish a secure foothold in Thessaly, although he certainly won popularity with the Aleuadae for the victory and perhaps at this time took his second Thessalian wife, Nicesipolis of Pherae.[63] Their daughter was Thessalonice, whose name means 'Thessalian victory'. Philip returned to Macedonia, and sometime over the next winter began his siege of Methone, the only remaining Greek city on the Thermaic Gulf. The Athenians sent aid but too little too late. By midsummer of 354 Methone had fallen to Philip, and though he lost an eye when an arrow struck him in the face, the capture of the city was a major gain, since it shut out the Athenians completely from the Thermaic and Chalcidian ports. The citizens of Methone were forced to abandon their city, the city itself was razed, and Philip distributed their property among the Macedonians.[64]

By this time in central Greece the Third Sacred War (356–346) had erupted when the Amphictyonic Council, the controlling body of the sacred sanctuary of Apollo at Delphi, decided to act against the Phocians, who had seized control of the sanctuary in order to avoid paying an exorbitant fine for cultivating sacred land.[65] The Thebans were behind the imposition of this fine as well as a fine on the Spartans for a much older grievance, and together with the Locrians they were fighting to dislodge the Phocians from their entrenched control of Delphi. The war soon embroiled many of the Greek states, since Delphi was the most important sanctuary of the Greeks collectively, and many of the central and northern states held votes in the Amphictyony. The Boeotians (or the Boeotian League, a confederacy of states in Boeotia headed by Thebes), the Locrians, and the Thessalians supported the Amphictyons, while Sparta (the Phocians waived her fine) with some of her allies in the Peloponnese and Athens (enemy of Thebes) took the side of the Phocians. Philip became involved at the invitation of the Aleuadae, after the Thessalians, already in civil strife between two rival federations, became divided in their support for the war. First, the tyrants of Pherae, at the request of the Locrians, marched a force of 6,000 Thessalians and allies into central Greece in support of the Amphictyons, but the Phocian commander Philomelus with a large army of mercenaries defeated them. This probably took place while Philip was besieging Methone. Then late in 354 the Phocians and their allies were in turn defeated by a large force of Boeotians, and rather than be captured Philomelus hurled himself from a cliff.[66] He had been the instigator, so the Thebans hoped his death meant the war was over.[67]

Turning their attention elsewhere, early in 353 the Thebans sent their general Pammenes, Philip's former host, with 5,000 soldiers to Phrygia to fight for the local satrap Artabazus in his revolt from Persian sovereignty.[68] Philip went along as far as central Thrace. There, continuing his policy of cutting off or controlling Athenian access to north Aegean ports, he captured the Greek coastal towns Maroneia and Abdera, both on the Athenian grain route and wealthy from trade with Thrace. It is during this campaign that we first hear of Philip having anything that might be called a fleet (an unknown number of "light" raiding ships), but this surely would have been requisite for his efforts to control the northern ports.[69]

When Philip returned from his campaign with Pammenes, he entered Thessaly again. By this time, summer 353,[70] Tisiphonus was out of the picture (his fate is unknown) and his brother Lycophron had won the support of the Phocians, perhaps by promising them a share in the governance of Thessaly; reciprocally, Philomelus' successor Onomarchus had bribed Lycophron to support his own control of Delphi.[71] Philip fought and defeated 7,000 Phocian allies under the command of Onomarchus' brother Phayllus and drove them out of Thessaly. Onomarchus responded by leading his full military force into Thessaly to back Lycophron, and this time Philip was defeated in battle twice, many of his Macedonian troops were killed, and the rest were on the point of deserting him. It was a shocking reversal for the hitherto successful king. Onomarchus had out-generalled him, luring the Macedonians into the recess of a mountain and firing on them from elevations all around with stone-throwers. The Macedonians took what was probably their first defeat in six years extremely hard.[72] It was arguably the lowest point of Philip's entire reign.

Back in Macedonia, the king had some work to do to rebuild his army and restore his troops' confidence in his leadership, but this he did over the course of the winter months, and in 352 he marched south once again into Thessaly against Lycophron of Pherae. Onomarchus marched again from Phocis to Lycophron's aid with 20,000 infantry and 500 cavalry. At this point in time, it appears, the other Thessalians who were supporting the Aleuadae of Larissa in the civil war agreed to make Philip supreme commander in their war against Lycophron and Onomarchus by naming him *archon* of the rival Thessalian League.[73] Philip thus had put at his disposal 20,000 infantry and 3,000 cavalry. For the Thessalians it was an all-out bid for freedom from tyranny in their civil war. For Philip there was another edge to it, as he assumed a role in the Sacred War as avenger of sacrilege committed against the god Apollo. Emboldening his troops by impressing them that they should think of themselves as fighting on behalf of the Delphic god, he commanded them to don the laurel wreaths sacred to Apollo and wear them into battle. It was the Thessalian cavalry in

Philip's army that won the day. They were superior in number but more significantly proved themselves superior in skill, and from this date for the next twenty years the Thessalian cavalry was to play a leading role in Macedonian military supremacy. The fierce battle took place at what is called the Crocus Field, located in the coastal plain about 13 km (8 miles) south of Pherae. An Athenian fleet, perhaps with the aim of supporting Onomarchus, was sailing just off shore at the time of the battle, and many of the Phocians, having shed their arms, attempted to swim out to the ships but in the attempt were slaughtered or drowned to the number of 6,000. Onomarchus was among the slain.[74] With this victory to validate his election as *archon* of Thessaly, Philip finally took control of Pherae and sent into exile both Lycophron and his brother Peitholaus.[75] He also captured the port at Pagasae, the only good harbour on the coast of Thessaly (most of which is mountainous), and soon after he assumed control of the territory of Magnesia.[76]

At last Philip had a foothold in Thessaly. With Pagasae in hand he controlled the revenues from the harbour and market, and he could curtail the meddling in Thessalian affairs of the Athenian fleet, while at the same time he had a convenient base for his own piratical raids (it was probably from Pagasae that he raided Geraistos and Marathon in about 351).[77] Magnesia was of strategic value for controlling north–south traffic, and Philip began to fortify it. Through Perrhaebia lay the two southern approaches to Macedonia, one via Gonnoi and the other through the Vale of Tempe, and this territory also came under his control. All these territories held votes in the Amphictyonic Council that were now his to manipulate.[78] While the Thessalians had thought to gain their freedom by inviting Philip to conduct their wars, the Macedonian king had his own uses for Thessalian revenues and military resources.[79] Fresh from his victories in Thessaly he marched south to Thermopylae with the intention of pressing the war against the Phocians, now under Onomarchus' successor, Phayllus, but the Athenians blocked the narrow pass into central Greece and Philip did not press the issue—for now.[80]

Instead, he turned east for another campaign in Thrace.[81] At this time Thrace was divided, which greatly facilitated Philip's eventual annexation of the whole of Thrace. Three contenders, probably all sons of Cotys I, had fought for sole control of Odrysian Thrace after Cotys' assassination in 360, but they had settled by treaty on a three-way division of the once powerful kingdom: in western Thrace Berisades was soon succeeded by his own son Cetriporis, who ruled briefly until Philip seized control in the region of Crenides/Philippi; Amadocus and then his son of the same name ruled central Thrace; and in eastern Thrace Cersobleptes ruled.[82] When Philip passed through Thrace in the spring of 353 with Pammenes Amadocus resisted the army's passage, but Cersobleptes made a deal with Philip to allow the Theban army to march through his territory unopposed.[83] Cersobleptes also had a treaty with Athens, however: the treaty Athens had formed with the three Thracian kings whereby she regained control in the Chersonese with the exclusion of independent Cardia.[84] The Athenians had not forgotten that control of this peninsula had been key to the Spartan victory in the Peloponnesian War, when Athens was starved into surrender because Sparta had cut off her grain supply from the Black Sea. By the fall of 352 alliances had shifted. The Athenian general Chares had defeated some mercenaries of Philip stationed in Thrace under the command of Adaeus (possibly the garrison at Crenides/Philippi),[85] Cersobleptes had broken with Philip and reaffirmed his alliance with Athens,[86] and Philip was now giving military support to Amadocus as well as to two Greek cities in eastern Thrace, Perinthus and Byzantium, against the aggressions of Cersobleptes. If Philip was primarily concerned with protecting his interests around Philippi and the gold and silver mines of Pangaion, he also had an eye for an opportunity for expansion. He was successful in forcing Cersobleptes to treat with him again—he took the Thracian king's son as hostage back to Macedonia—and in replacing several other Thracian rulers with his own supporters.[87] The result was effectively an annexation of most of Thrace.[88]

Following the Thracian campaign Philip quite possibly was forced into an extended convalescence at Pella, for while he was besieging Cersobleptes' fortress at Heraion Teichos he took ill and evidently very seriously ill since it was rumoured at Athens that he was dead.[89] This perhaps was when he put out tenders for a number of building projects—walls, shrines, and temples in the various territories over which he now had control—but for some reason, though contractors arrived at court to bid for the projects, no contracts were granted.[90] Urgency likely recalled him to war. Sources hint at campaigns against the Paeonians, Illyrians, and Epirotes that seem to belong to this time period, though no details are offered.[91] Uprisings could easily have been prompted by news of Philip's illness—or rumour of his death. Philip would have relied on competent generals such as Parmenio to deal with some fronts, but Epirus he must certainly have handled himself. It was about 350 that Philip took Olympias' young brother Alexander away from Epirus to Pella. There the prince was kept, a 'favourite' of Philip, until he came of age, when he could be put on the Epirote throne. King Arybbas at this time was either deposed or reduced to vassal status.[92]

By the late 350s both the Chalcidic League and Athens were seriously alarmed by Philip's increasing power all across the north Aegean. The Macedonian king controlled not only his own consolidated kingdom all the way from west of the Pindus Mountains to the Strymon River, but he also held sway beyond the Strymon nearly as far as the Chersonese. Moreover, he had so far kept all the kingdoms on his northern borders in subjugation or at bay, and to the south in Thessaly he held the highest office (*archon*) in the state. The Olynthians, not surprisingly, by 352 had infringed their treaty established with Philip in 357 by renewing 'friendship' with Athens, and the Athenians' overture for 'alliance' in addition would have been particularly attractive once Philip began aggressively campaigning in Chalcidice, which he did probably as early as 351.[93] Philip did not trust the Olynthians, nor the Olynthians Philip,[94] and there is the question of Philip's half-brothers, two of whom allegedly took refuge in Olynthus after Philip had murdered the third,[95] the implication being that the Olynthians

Figure 4.2 Ivory head of bearded man, miniature from Tomb II, Vergina (Aegae), thought to be a portrait of Philip II, fourth century BCE, 3.2 cm high. Archaeological Museum of Vergina

Source: De Agostini Picture Library; G. Dagli; courtesy of Bridgeman Images.

hoped to install one of them on the throne just as they had earlier backed Pausanias. Within Olynthus there was a pro-Philip as well as an anti-Philip faction, and when the leader of the latter party, Apollonides, favoured shifting the state's alliance from Philip to Athens, the pro-Philip faction managed to secure his exile.[96] At Oreus and Eretria in Euboea (the island lying along the flank of eastern Attica) the situation was similar: Philip's men, Greeks whom he had bribed with Pangaion gold,[97] were advocates for compliance with Philip because, they thought, that would keep peace, whereas cooperation with Athens, the cry of the 'democratic' opposition, meant war.[98] The Macedonian connection with Oreus, formerly called Histiaea, went back to the reign of Perdiccas II, when the Histiaeans had migrated to Macedonia after the Athenians confiscated much Euboean land for their cleruch settlers.[99]

In 349 Philip began a concerted campaign against the cities of Chalcidice, first besieging and razing the fortress of Zereia and then forcing some other small cities to submit.[100] His strategy was to weaken the overall power of Olynthus and the Chalcidic League by taking out their weaker supporting states. Thus, with due cause, Olynthus now formalized an alliance with Athens in a desperate plea for military support, and the Athenians sent a fleet of thirty triremes with 2,000 peltasts (light-armed skirmishers) under command of Chares.[101] But the fates of Amphipolis and Methone should have been a warning to Olynthus that reliance on Athenian aid was chancy. The first Athenian force soon proved insufficient, and a second (eighteen triremes and 4,000 peltasts) dispatched in the winter under Charidemus also proved inadequate against Philip's strategy.[102] Early in 348, by treason and without battle, Philip captured Mecyberna, the port of Olynthus, and also Torone, near the southern tip of the Sithonia peninsula, the central of the three prongs of Chalcidice. This must have shut out the Athenian fleet from harbouring anywhere along the central prong and thus rendered naval support for Olynthus entirely ineffectual. By this time Euboea also had revolted from the Athenian League (Philip's involvement is suspected), and the Athenians would have been forced to divide attention. Then taking the field with a large army Philip attacked Olynthus directly. After defeating the Olynthians in two battles he was able to confine them to the defence of their walls. The siege raged throughout the summer, and in the continuous assaults on the city's walls Philip suffered many casualties in his ranks. Finally, in the fall, "for [Philip] had learned from experience that what could not be subdued by force of arms could easily be vanquished by gold,"[103] two leading officials of Olynthus, Euthycrates and Lasthenes, commander of the cavalry, having been bribed by Philip, betrayed the city to him.[104] The Olynthian women and children were enslaved and the men and property sold to raise revenue to pay his soldiers and as a scare tactic to frighten other states from opposing him. His own soldiers who had distinguished themselves in battle he rewarded with gifts, thus sending a clear message that it was most profitable to fight on Philip's side.

To mark his victory with great fanfare, Philip celebrated the Macedonian *Olympia* festival at Dion with *symposia* (banquets) and artistic competitions and lavished many of the foreigners who attended with gifts to win their support as his *xenoi* (guests) and *philoi* (friends).[105] On this occasion it is said the famous actor Satyrus was asked by Philip why he alone did not ask for a gift from the king, and when Satyrus said it was because he thought the gift he truly wanted would be denied him Philip agreed to give him whatever he asked for. The gift Satyrus sought was the release of two girls taken captive at Olynthus, daughters of his friend Apollophanes, a man of Pydna who had been murdered when the girls were young children. Both girls now were of marriageable age and Satyrus wanted to arrange dowries and husbands for them, so that they would not become servants or slaves. Philip kept his promise and released the girls, despite the fact that their father Apollophanes had been involved in the regicide of his brother Alexander II.[106] Philip also acquired some Athenian captives at Olynthus, and these he held onto until they became a useful bargaining chip in peace negotiations with Athens.[107] The Chalcidic League is not heard of again. Philip most likely disbanded it, and some Chalcidian territory he granted to Macedonians,[108] although many Chalcidian cities did continue to exist. Olynthus was razed to the ground.[109] And, as Philip intended, this utter destruction of a once great and powerful city sent shock waves throughout the Greek and Balkan worlds.

Expansion into southern Greece and war with Athens

Philip's power now thoroughly alarmed the Athenians.[110] His interests clashed with theirs not only in the north Aegean but also in central Greece, where he had entered the Third Sacred War on the side opposing Athenian interests, and furthermore he was suspected of having supported or even instigated unrest in Euboea. The Athenians had long had interests and alliances in Euboea, and in 357 they took control of most of the island. In about 349 the ruler of Eretria, Plutarchus, called in Athenian military aid against a rival, Callias of Chalcis, who was gaining considerable influence throughout the island, and Callias in turn called on Philip for aid. Though Callias was defeated and fled to Macedonia, Plutarchus had suspiciously undermined the Athenian military operation and was exiled.[111] Philip certainly had influence in Euboea, and when some Euboean envoys went to Athens to negotiate peace Philip, at the time still besieging Olynthus, arranged through them a first overture for his own peace with Athens. Philip soon after sent a second message about his desire for peace, and when the Athenians welcomed the envoy's report a proposal was brought forward by Philocrates, whose name would be attached to the eventual peace, that Philip be permitted to send to Athens a herald and envoys to negotiate terms, and the proposal was approved.[112] However, a charge was promptly brought against Philocrates for having made an illegal proposal, and, although he was acquitted, negotiations for peace cooled for the time being.[113] Athens' ally Olynthus by this time had fallen to Philip, and late that fall or early winter Eubulus passed a decree in the Athenian Assembly whereby embassies were to be sent out to the Greek states seeking support for a common Hellenic alliance *against* Philip.[114] This countercurrent to peace at Athens was the main reason why Philip would hold tightly to his Athenian captives as the proposed peace talks stalled for another year and a half.

In the meantime Philip's attention shifted to the Third Sacred War again. In the summer of 347 in central Greece the Boeotians were suffering heavy defeats to the Phocians, and three Boeotian strongholds had been seized. In desperation the Thebans appealed to Philip to intercede. But why help the Thebans win the war, if he could bring it to a close on his own terms by appearing to be the righteous champion of Apollo? Philip sent only a small force, yet it was enough to help the Theban-led Boeotians press the Phocians into flight, killing many who took refuge in the sanctuary at Delphi.[115]

About the same time Athenian action in the Chersonese further undermined peace by prompting Philip to send his general Antipater with an army to Apros and Hieron Oros, Cersobleptes' stronghold on the Thracian coast.[116] There in the second half of 347 Antipater forced many Athenian settlers to flee the Chersonese, while Philip's raiding ships harassed other Athenian settlers at Lemnos, Imbros, and Scyros, and Philip himself seized control of some Thracian silver mines.[117] By winter Philip was again concerned about Athenian intervention in Thessaly. Halos, a town on the Gulf of Pagasae, had come into dispute with its neighbour Pharsalus in Phthiotic Achaea. Since Pharsalus was under Philip's sphere of influence, he sent Parmenio to besiege Halos, the capture of which would close yet another port to the Athenian fleet. Moreover, the siege gave Philip a justification for moving a large army into position not far from the strategic pass at Thermopylae, and whoever controlled the pass controlled the gateway between central and southern Greece and Thessaly.[118]

Earlier the same winter the Athenians approached Philip about the release of the prisoners taken at Olynthus. Philip had a reputation for being a great patron of the performing arts, so the Athenians chose as their envoy Aristodemus, an actor who was on friendly terms with the king. Though Philip told Aristodemus he wanted not only peace but also alliance, the actor did not report to the Assembly until midwinter, after Philip released without ransom a captive named Iatrocles, who brought yet another message regarding Philip's desire for peace.[119] Meantime the Athenians had passed a second decree to send out embassies to the Greek states to encourage support for war against Philip. But late in the winter, when Philocrates again came forward and proposed that an embassy of ten Athenians be sent to Macedonia to discuss peace and common interests with Philip, the Athenians voted in favour of the peace; they were unsure of gaining support against Philip and they feared Philip would bring a large army south of Thermopylae as he had attempted in 352. Also about this time the Phocians spurned their alliance with Athens.[120] This First Embassy leading to the eventual Peace of Philocrates included Philocrates himself, the orators Aeschines and Demosthenes (the "Philip-hater," as Aeschines calls him), the actor Aristodemus, and the released captive Iatrolces.[121] The Embassy passed through enemy lines at Halos under Parmenio's supervision, and at Larissa a Macedonian herald met them and escorted them to Pella.[122] The envoys had decided they should each speak in order of descending age, which meant Demosthenes, the youngest though most talented orator among them, was last to speak, and, according to Aeschines, he lost his nerve and not only bungled his speech but collapsed in a faint.[123] Demosthenes suffered from a speech impediment and therefore always spoke from a written script, though perhaps this was not possible on the occasion. But also, prior to this embassy Demosthenes had publicly delivered the first of his four *Philippic* speeches and three *Olynthiacs*, all of which vilified Philip, so he did have just cause for anxiety. Philip's reply to the Athenian envoys is unrecorded, but it left them impressed with the Macedonian king's charm, eloquence, and skills of memory.[124] As for Demosthenes, he returned to Athens extremely bitter about how the embassy had gone.

When the First Embassy left Pella to return to Athens about the beginning of spring Philip, with a promise that he would *not* take an army into the Athenian-controlled Chersonese while negotiations were still underway, left for Thrace to replace Antipater in dealing with Cersobleptes.[125] Antipater he sent to Athens along with Parmenio and probably Eurylochus, another trusted general, to act as his envoys.[126] Philip himself avoided Athens. The terms of peace were to be dictated by Philip and were not at all satisfactory to the Athenians; both sides were to retain their current possessions, which meant Athens would not get Amphipolis over which it had declared war on Philip in the first place.[127] Members of the Second Athenian League were to be included in the peace; not included were Phocis and Halos, neither ever having been a League member.[128] After a two-day debate the Athenians voted to accept the peace, and a Second Embassy (the same ten envoys) was dispatched to Pella to receive Philip's oath and the oaths of his allies and to negotiate the release of the captives.[129]

The Phocians by now had called upon their Spartan alliance for reinforcements in central Greece, so the Thebans were counting on Philip's support again as soon as he should return from Thrace. Already an embassy from Thebes had been present at Pella at the same time as the First Athenian Embassy, appealing to Philip for aid and also seeking alliance.[130] When Philip, after defeating the Thracians at Hieron Oros and subordinating Cersobleptes to vassal status,[131] returned to Pella in the late spring a crowd of embassies from the Greek states, including the Second Athenian Embassy, awaited him.[132] It was a tricky matter for Philip to negotiate alliances with both Thebes and Athens, who had been fighting on opposing sides in the Sacred War for nearly ten years.[133] Philip was anxious to play his best hand in the affairs of the greater Greek powers, all of whom were now inviting his involvement, so he delayed ratifying the peace with Athens as long as possible. At the same time, though evidently agreeing to a Theban alliance, he worked to appropriate from a weakened Thebes the honour of settling the Third Sacred War.[134] Philip set out for central Greece with a large army, ostensibly to deal with the situation of Halos. On his march south, with the Athenian Embassy in tow, at Pherae in Thessaly Philip finally gave his oath to the Peace of Philocrates.[135] His delaying tactics and reticence about his intentions with regard to Phocis and Thebes kept the Athenians guessing long enough to prevent them from committing aid to their ally Phocis before Philip could secure the pass at Thermopylae. This he had accomplished by the time the Second Embassy arrived home and gave their report to the Assembly just before mid July.[136] The Athenians now could do nothing to stop his advance;[137] moreover, they were obligated by treaty of alliance to honour a request for reinforcements—against their former ally Phocis—which Philip's envoys delivered to Athens a few days later. While the Athenians hedged on sending the reinforcements, through negotiations Philip secured the surrender of the Phocian commander Phalaecus together with his mercenaries (who were freed to retreat to the Peloponnese) and the Phocian forces. Philip thus in the tenth year ended the Third Sacred War without a battle. Diplomacy was ever as much Philip's method as open warfare.[138]

The bloodless victory on behalf of Apollo was a major coup for Philip. Later that summer he convened a special meeting of the Amphictyonic Council, to which, by right, since he was not yet a member, he left the final settlement of the war. The Phocians and their Spartan allies were deprived of their Amphictyonic membership and the Phocians were severely punished, though it did not spare Philip any criticism that his terms were not so harsh, perhaps, as those the Thebans might have offered.[139] The Athenians were not expelled; that much they had gained from their treaty with Philip, though dissatisfaction with the Peace of Philocrates was already brewing. Philip also, finally, released the captives taken at Olynthus.[140] The grateful Amphictyony awarded to Philip and his descendants—not to Macedonia—the two Phocian votes. Though notionally Thessaly and Thebes now held the major voting power in the Amphictyony, because of his unique position as *archon* Philip effectively controlled the votes of the Thessalian tribal state members (Magnesia, Perrhaebia, Dolopia).[141] With the additional favourable sentiments of other members grateful for his resolution of the war, from now on he heavily influenced council decisions.[142] One of the first decisions of the Amphictyony, as a measure of its high regard for his settlement of affairs, was to grant to Philip the presidency over the Pythian games to be held, for the first time in three cycles (twelve years), at Delphi in the fall of 346.[143] Philip presided as the most powerful individual in the Greek world. His new allies, the Athenians, did not welcome his authority or membership in the Amphictyony, and they refused to attend the games.[144]

What the Macedonians thought of their king's eminence in the broader Greek world one can only speculate, since our sources offer only an Athenocentric perspective on the king's substantial inroads into Greek politics. But with affairs of the Greek states now settled (for the time being) in Philip's favour, the king returned to Macedonia and turned his attention to further strengthening and expanding his kingdom.[145] The winter of 346–345 is as likely a time as any for the setting of the famous story of Philip's son, Alexander, now ten years old, and the taming of his warhorse Bucephalus (Figure 4.3). Horse traders from Thessaly came to Philip with a herd among which was a large black stallion with a white mark in the shape of an ox head emblazoned on his forehead. The animal was wild—too wild Philip thought to be tamable—but the boy asked to approach, and when he did the horse did not balk or shy away from him. Instead,

Figure 4.3 Marble statuette of a horseman, Pella
Source: author, 2014.

Alexander calmed the agitated animal, then mounted and rode him much to the amazement of all bystanders and to the especial delight of his father, and so Philip let him keep it.[146] The king himself can have spent very little time mentoring his son, yet, if we may judge by Alexander's practices later in Asia, the son observed his father's policies with attentiveness. Over the next few years Philip strengthened defences by means of large transfers of population and settlement of war captives into cities along his borders and frontiers.[147] Philip's intention was to break up potential internal factions by dispersing tribal groups and mixing these populations together. The heaviest concentration of settlement was likely in the Thraceward region, where Philip had recently won substantial territory. However, his preoccupation in the east left Macedonia vulnerable on its traditionally troublesome western frontier. Philip's attention was drawn again to the long-time Illyrian threat, and he was compelled to invade Illyria with a large army. In a battle against Pleuratos Philip, still leading from the front, sustained yet another severe wound, this time a broken right collarbone.[148] The Macedonians were victorious and succeeded in capturing many towns in addition to much loot.[149]

Soon after, in 344, affairs in Thessaly provoked Philip to apply a firmer hand in his role as *archon*. Some Thessalian cities had fallen again into the hands of tyrants, and Philip proceeded to expel them.[150] But when he took Pherae by siege and installed a Macedonian garrison the Thessalians became alarmed that in Philip they had summoned as much a foreign master as a champion of their own causes.[151] They objected particularly to his personal use of the revenues from port taxes. Moreover, Philip's position as *archon* gave him full use of Thessalian military power, and both the military and the revenues were now being channeled into his own wars that were not of interest to Thessaly. To tighten his control Philip reorganized the political structure, returning to the traditional division of Thessaly into four administrative districts, or tetrarchies, and putting in place governors of his choosing over each.[152] Although Thessaly now effectually lost its freedom to Philip, in return he offered the Thessalians unprecedented opportunities, not least management of the Amphictyony and profitable employment in his army.

In the latter half of the 340s Philip became increasingly involved in southern Greek affairs. In the Peloponnese a number of states long overshadowed by Sparta and seeking ways to keep her from regaining some of her former supremacy hoped to find in Philip a protector. Pro-Philip factions arose in Argos and Messene as well as in Elis and Arcadia, though it is questionable how active Philip himself was in the internal politics of these states.[153] In Euboea ongoing factional strife between oligarchs and democrats drew Philip's intervention there, as several of his political supporters, men who had been won over to his purposes by substantial financial rewards, sought his military backing to assume control in their respective cities. At Eretria Cleitarchus and his party received military support from Philip's general Hipponicus, and at Oreus Philistides and his party received support from Parmenio.[154] Perdiccas III's influential advisor Euphraeus of Oreus had recently made himself offensive at the Macedonian court and of late was the leader of the pro-Athenian faction at Oreus. He now fell into the hands of the pro-Philip party and committed suicide.[155] At Chalcis Callias, though Philip had previously supported and sheltered him and even made him a Companion, was unsuccessful in winning over either the Macedonian king or the Thebans to his personal political aims, and so he turned to the Athenians for support in establishing an anti-Philip Euboean alliance.[156] The Euboeans, having already fought to get out from under Athenian domination, now wanted their autonomy. Philip's aggressions caused them due concern, though it has been suggested that he mainly wanted a diversion for the Athenians away from his campaign in eastern Thrace.[157] As was his policy with Athens, Philip personally stayed away from Euboea, attending to affairs elsewhere.

In Epirus early in 342 Philip finally placed on the throne Olympias' brother Alexander.[158] Farther southwest in the coastal region between Epirus and Aetolia Philip reduced several independent Greek cities and left them under Alexander's control. This action brought him into war with neighbouring Ambracia, a Corinthian colony, and Corinthian complaints served to fuel a growing anti-Macedonian movement in the Peloponnese[159]—much to the delight of Demosthenes. In Athens Demosthenes' voice was proclaiming loudly against a perceived Macedonian menace. After the Second Embassy he had taken it upon himself to try to destroy the Peace of Philocrates, and he saw to it that two fellow envoys were charged with accepting Philip's bribes: Philocrates went into self-exile to avoid a death-sentence conviction, and Aeschines was acquitted, though barely.[160] Philip continued his efforts to make the Peace work. He sent Python of Byzantium to Athens to attempt to revise it, but the Athenians countered by sending to Philip Hegesippus as negotiator of their own changes.[161] Demosthenes nonetheless vigorously undermined Philip's power and succeeded in winning over Greek states to an anti-Philip alliance.[162] Even the anti-Philip factions in Argos, Messene, and Megalopolis persuaded their governments to ally with Athens, though this was not in fact a reneging of any prior agreements with Philip, since Philip too was an ally of Athens.[163] In Euboea the pro-Macedonian "tyrants" were overthrown, and the Athenians were instrumental in the establishment of a Euboean League, which did upset Philip's influence there.[164]

Despite Demosthenes' persistent cries apropos Philip's alleged aim of depriving all Greeks of their freedom, the king's greater interest had always been towards the east, first in the mineral-rich Strymon region and then farther into central and eastern Thrace. Philip's expansion into Thrace appears to have been calculated, with successive campaigns in 352, 346, and a longer campaign beginning in 342, eventually bringing the whole of the former powerful Odrysian kingdom under his control. In the second half of 342 Philip marched into Thrace at the head of a large army, this time with every intention of securing eastern Thrace all the way to the Hellespont and the Black Sea.[165] Cersobleptes, along with Teres, who had replaced Amadocus as king of central Thrace, had been attacking the coastal cities which Philip had secured on his previous campaign in 346, and Philip now proceeded to recover the cities and reduce the Thracian kings to tribute-paying status. His strategy involved pressing Cersobleptes on two fronts, and he accomplished this by obtaining a military alliance with the Getae, a Thracian tribe inhabiting the region between Cersobleptes' northern flank and the Istros (Danube) River.[166] It was a mutually beneficial alliance, for Cothelas, king of the Getae, needed Philip's aid against his northern Scythian neighbour, Atheas. The alliance was sealed by marriage, Philip now taking as his sixth wife Meda, the daughter of Cothelas. Meda was added to Philip's court at Pella, though nothing further is heard of her.[167] The campaign was long and hard, especially hard because as it continued throughout the winter months it was plagued by bad weather and illness, and Philip had to send for reinforcements from both Macedonia and Thessaly.[168] By the following summer Cersobleptes (again) and Teres were reduced to vassalage, and Philip successfully secured the region with garrisons and new settlements, notably Philippopolis on the Hebrus River, mixing transplanted Greek settlers in with local Thracians.[169] Some coastal Greek city-states, now freed from Thracian raids, joined Philip in alliance.[170] The campaign continued into the second half of 341 and through the winter, though sources are all but totally silent on Philip's whereabouts. He seems to have been campaigning on the shores of the Black Sea near the mouth of the Istros.[171] Activity in that region would have posed enough of a potential disruption to the grain trade to raise concern at Byzantium, for Byzantium benefitted greatly from its proximity to the mustering point for the great convoys before they headed out through the Propontis and Hellespont to the

Aegean. A decade earlier both Byzantium and its neighbour Perinthus had become Macedonian allies when Philip gave them military aid against Cersobleptes. However, Philip's recent gains in coastal Thrace were alarming, and the alarm was also sounded at Athens. In the fall of 341 Demosthenes paid a visit to Byzantium specifically to fan anti-Macedonian flames, and it appears that around or by this time Perinthus made a clear break with Philip.[172] But it was over another Greek *polis*, Cardia, on the Chersonese peninsula, that Philip, an ally of Cardia since before the Peace of 346, came into direct conflict with Athens.[173]

About a year earlier, when the Athenian general Diopeithes attempted to appropriate land from Cardia for the use of Athenian cleruch settlers, the Cardians resisted and complained to their ally Philip, who in turn wrote a letter of complaint to the Athenian *demos* (citizenry). Philip complained of many aggressions and effective violations of the Peace, not least the abduction from Macedonia of his herald Nicias, who was taken to Athens and imprisoned for ten months, and the capture, torture, and ransom of his envoy Amphilochus, sent to negotiate the release of prisoners taken by Diopeithes in his Thracian raids.[174] The Athenians for their part claimed Philip was the aggressor, that Cersobleptes and Teres were both allies of Athens, and that Philip had seized Halonnesus and sacked Peparethus, both islands full of Athenian cleruchies.[175] Underneath all the accusations on both sides lay the threat Philip posed to the Athenian grain route through his alliance with Cardia and encroachment into the Chersonese, and it was that threat that finally led to the Athenian declaration of war in 340.

During these years of Philip's absence from Pella the education of his son Alexander, who turned thirteen in summer 343, was entrusted to Aristotle of Stagira (in Chalcidice), an eminent philosopher of the day (though not yet of the enormous fame that posterity has granted him) (Figure 4.4). Aristotle's father Nicomachus had been court physician to Amyntas III, and Aristotle himself had grown up at the Macedonian court as a contemporary of Philip.[176] At age seventeen he had gone to Athens to study at Plato's Academy, where he stayed for twenty years until Plato's death in 347. Though other philosophers had hoped for Philip's generous patronage and the honour of teaching the likely heir to the Macedonian throne, Aristotle's already strong connection to the court made him a natural choice. A formal school was established at Mieza, a day's ride from Pella, and there for three years Aristotle taught and nurtured Alexander along with a number of similarly aged sons of Philip's Companions. By 340 Philip's campaign in Thrace had no end in sight, so Alexander, now turning sixteen, was recalled from Mieza to assume the regency at Pella under the supervision of Antipater. The lessons in political theory that Aristotle had inculcated in the young prince would now be put to practical test. His military skills would see their first trial too. In the king's absence teenage Alexander conducted a punitive military campaign against a rebellious Thracian tribe in the upper Strymon region, the Maedi, successfully putting down the revolt and establishing (like Philippopolis on the Hebrus) a military colony of mixed

Figure 4.4 Marble head of Aristotle, Roman copy of a Greek original, c. 320 BCE. Kunsthistorisches Museum, Vienna

Source: author, 2015.

population. The settlement bore his own name, Alexandropolis. Perhaps the king approved the naming, but if not, it may have prompted Philip to summon his son to join him in the Chersonese.[177]

In the summer of 340 Philip entered a new phase of the campaign, turning to the attack of the same Greek coastal cities that in the past he had defended against the raids of Cersobleptes. Material profit from looting might have been a motive, though it seems the Perinthians probably had refused to support Philip's recent subjugation of Cersobleptes, and for some reason they had broken their prior alliance with Philip and now favoured the friendship of Athens.[178] Perinthus was strategically situated on the grain route and at the crossing between Europe and Asia. It was positioned facing the Propontis on a small peninsula, which Philip now undertook to besiege by sea.[179] In the past Philip had been alarmingly successful with sieges: Amphipolis, Pydna, Methone, and Olynthus had all succumbed to his battering at their walls—or to the combination of his battering and the jingling of his coin purse. Perinthus succumbed to neither. Philip did breach the walls, but the Perinthians built counter-walls, fighting and firing back, first under their own catapult power, then with reinforcements and arms from nearby Byzantium, and finally, just as supplies were running out, the Persian king, Artaxerxes Ochus, instructed his Hellespontine satraps to spare no expense in giving aid to the Perinthians: more mercenaries, money, foodstuffs, missiles, and other supplies somehow slipped through Philip's cordon of 30,000 men and into the besieged city.[180] With Perinthus thus reinforced, despite pounding away both day and night with siege engines over 100 feet high the Macedonians were unable to force their way up the steep streets of the fiercely defended city. Leaving behind a force sufficient to continue harassment of the walls, Philip himself advanced to the attack of Byzantium.[181] The Macedonians had in their arsenal state-of-the-art siege engines, yet once again they proved unsuccessful in making a decisive breach. Philip's military reputation had already suffered a blow at Perinthus, so he had somehow to recover both from the tarnish of that failure and what was now looking like a second unprofitable siege—and he was desperately in need of supplies and money for war expenses. Also, the Athenians were dangerously close to engaging on the enemy side, so Philip decided to show them what kind of foe they faced should they not abide by the terms of the Peace.

The primary interest of Athens in the Hellespont was the security of her grain fleet. The multi-state convoys had their gathering point at Hieron on the Asiatic shore of the Bosporus about 25 km (17 miles) north of Chalcedon. Their passage through the Propontis and Hellespont that fall was to be safeguarded by an Athenian war fleet under the admiralship of Chares. About September of 340 Chares took a short leave from his fleet at Hieron to attend a meeting with Artaxerxes' satraps. Philip saw his opportune moment. His own fleet, trying but failing to capture the grain boats, proved no match for the Athenian warships. Undaunted, Philip had his admiral Demetrius disembark troops on shore, under cover of night, from where they attacked totally by surprise, seizing all the grain boats together with their goods and crews.[182] The total number of ships captured was a staggering 230, of which 180 were Athenian. Philip let the ships belonging to the Rhodians and Chians go (hoping to gain their neutrality), but others he broke up as 'spoils of war' and used the timber for construction of more siege engines. The grain and other goods were used to feed and refurbish his army, while the sale of captives raised some 700 talents for war expenses. It was a stunning comeback, to say the least, and it sent a clear message that he could, if he chose, grab the Athenians by the throat. Message received. That which is carved in stone can in fact be broken, and the Athenians now officially and emphatically declared war by throwing down the *stele* recording the Peace of Philocrates.[183] Although Chares' fleet had been sent to guard the Hellespont, prior to the seizure of the grain fleet the Athenians had not directly intervened in Philip's sieges of Perinthus or Byzantium. Now, with the direct threat to their grain supply, for which they held Chares responsible, they sent out Phocion, who had not long since successfully driven Philip's partisans out of Euboea.[184] Phocion was a competent commander and Philip's campaign suffered for it.

The Macedonian siege of Byzantium continued into winter with little profitable result until finally Philip decided it was best to cut his losses, raise both sieges, and get out of the Hellespont for now. From the Athenian perspective it was their victory, though Philip no doubt thought this was business he could finish later when the situation was more in his favour.[185] What terms Philip came to with the Byzantines or Perinthians we do not know, but certainly he did not make peace with Athens while the shattered fragments of Philocrates' *stele* were still settling in the dust. Though the island fleets of Chios, Cos, and Rhodes do not appear to have given Philip any more grief, that he did not settle with *all* the Greeks is clear from the difficult time he had extricating his own fleet, for only by stratagem could Demetrius get it free and clear of the Hellespont, and then only after he was defeated in a sea battle by the Byzantines and some of his ships were captured by Phocion.[186] The implication was not lost on Philip: his Macedonian fleet could not stand up in a naval battle of any size, so it was certainly not capable of controlling the Aegean. And if Philip was intending to cross from Europe into Asia, if that was his aim when he undertook the sieges of Perinthus and Byzantium, then he did need to control the Aegean. He needed Athenian naval power *for* rather than *against* him.

Philip's plans for Persia

Sometime towards the late 350s there came to the Macedonian court two exiles who had been responsible for a revolt against the Persian king a few years earlier: Artabazus, former satrap of Hellespontine Phrygia, and Memnon of Rhodes, Artabazus' brother-in-law.[187] They stayed at court for several years until Memnon's brother Mentor secured their pardon and they were recalled by Artaxerxes.[188] What influence these two exiles might have had on Philip's eventual plans for an invasion of Persia is a matter of speculation.[189] The idea of a Macedonian—or Hellenic—subjugation of Persia certainly did not originate with Philip. Even for Isocrates, who had been promoting the idea several decades before he advocated such action pointedly in his address *To Philip* in 346, the idea was not novel.[190] Jason of Pherae in the 370s seemed to think that Persia by reason of habitual servility would be an easy conquest, particularly if he had control of Macedonian timber supplies.[191] And the Spartan king Agesilaus is said to have been on the very brink of carrying war into the heart of Persia just as he was recalled to Sparta to assist in the Corinthian War in 394.[192] If an invasion *was* among Philip's ambitions as early as 346, he must have kept his intentions as much to himself as possible, for the earliest certain public notice that he had plans for an invasion of Persian territory is found in Demosthenes' *Fourth Philippic*, delivered in 341.[193] The implication of this speech is that by 342, together with Hermias, tyrant of Atarneus in northwest Asia Minor (Aristotle's father-in-law), Philip was plotting some action or other against the Great King. Hermias was soon arrested, taken to Susa in chains, and tortured, allegedly to obtain information about Philip's plans. Though he divulged nothing, and maybe there was nothing for him to divulge, he was nonetheless executed for treason.[194]

In light of the so-called Hermias affair the Thracian campaign undertaken by Philip in the same year does look like an attempt to establish a secure land route and supply and communication line for crossing the Hellespont. When the sieges of Perinthus and Byzantium failed Philip marched his land forces straight to upper Thrace, where his generals Antipater and Parmenio had been sent the previous fall (340),[195] and where Alexander also possibly joined his father in the field.[196] Details about the Thracian campaign have not survived. We have the names of some tribes which the king and his generals subdued—the Tetrachorites, whose city Angissus (or Agessus) Antipater captured by storm, the Danthalitae, the Melinophagi—but what instigated the conflict is obscure.[197] Perhaps trouble arose as the Thracians' fearful reaction to Philip's subjugation of the Odrysian kings Cersobleptes and Teres or to Macedonian aggression in pushing their frontier towards the boundary of the Istros/Danube River. Then, too, by seizing control of territory on the Black Sea near the mouth of the Danube and getting a stranglehold on sources of grain Philip did weaken Byzantium's position. Over the winter of 340–339 while the siege of Byzantium was still under way the Scythian king Atheas had agreed to supply Philip's army in exchange for military support against his neighbours the Histrians. The promised supplies never materialized, however, and by the time the Macedonian relief force arrived on the scene the king of the Histrians had died, war was no longer a threat, and Atheas, no longer needing Macedonian support, had dismissed the reinforcements without pay or covering expenses. The Scythians were reputedly wealthy and Philip needed supplies, more even than those he had already asked for, so he proceeded to find a roundabout way of getting another armed force into Atheas' territory. He requested permission to set up a statue of his ancestor Heracles at the mouth of the Danube, and when Atheas refused to allow Philip to come with his army to do so Philip took it as his pretext for war. The Scythians were defeated, ninety-year-old Atheas was killed in battle, and Philip gained control of the territory as well as considerable plunder: captives, horses, and cattle but no hoped-for silver and gold.[198]

The Thracian campaign of 339 had resulted in the extension of Macedonian-controlled territory all the way to the Danube River and the Black Sea. It would be difficult to maintain control of the region, however, and perhaps the greater gain was the 20,000 brood mares sent back to Macedonia for breeding. On the triumphal march back to Pella with the same number of captives in tow the Macedonians met with unexpected trouble from the Triballians, a Thracian tribe who inhabited a region between the Danube and the Haemus range. When they demanded a share of the plunder as toll for passage through their territory Philip refused, and in the ensuing confrontation the captives were stolen or abandoned, while Philip himself sustained another severe war wound when a javelin pierced his thigh, killing the horse he was riding.[199]

The king, so far as we know, had not been in residence at Pella for three full years, but again it was to be a short stay and convalescence. Soon after his return, in the fall of 339, the Amphictyons called upon Philip to lead an army in the Fourth Sacred War, this time against Amphissa.[200] Amphissa had been charged with sacrilege by the Athenians while Philip was still in Scythia.[201] Before winter set in Philip marched at the head of a Macedonian army into central Greece, causing great panic in the city-states. Philip was accustomed to campaigning in winter; the Greeks were not. The Thebans had already ejected the Macedonian garrison at Nicaea in the attempt to block Thermopylae (which Nicaea guarded), but Philip bypassed the Gates and Nicaea, skirting the western side of

Mount Callidromos, and entering the Cephisos valley he seized Elatea in Phocis on the border with Boeotia. From there he could easily reach Amphissa, but he was also in striking distance of Thebes and Athens. The Athenians sounded the alarm throughout the city and promptly sent Demosthenes off to Thebes at the head of an embassy to negotiate a last-ditch alliance against Philip. Philip also sent envoys and a skilled orator to Thebes, technically still his ally, but Demosthenes achieved the greatest oratorical accomplishment of his life by talking the Thebans, Athens' long-time bitter rivals, into an anti-Macedonian alliance.[202] The Athenians and Thebans quickly mobilized an army, sending 10,000 mercenaries to Amphissa and entrenching their own citizen armies at Parapotamii and the Gravia Pass, where they kept Philip at bay at Elatea until spring.[203] Then Philip pulled a classic ruse by having fall into the hands of the Greek generals a letter to Antipater falsely informing him that Philip was pulling out his army to deal with rebellion in Thrace. The Greeks—their schooling in Homer ought to have taught them better!—relaxed their guard, and Philip slipped back under cover of night, seized the Gravia Pass, and then went on to capture Amphissa. The Sacred War was settled in a matter of a day.[204] What Thebes and Athens feared most did not follow. Philip did not march on either city-state; he turned instead to diplomacy by opening negotiations for a peace settlement.[205] At Athens Demosthenes vigorously opposed any kind of settlement with Philip, and since Thebes opted to honour the new alliance with Athens, by midsummer negotiations finally broke down.

Battle it had to be, then, and in the event a great battle, one to turn the tide of history for the Greek city-states irrevocably. On an early August morning about dawn the two armies met on the plain at Chaeronea in Boeotia. The field of battle was somewhat confined, defined on the east by the Cephisos River and on the west by Mount Thourion, a situation the Greeks perhaps hoped would restrict Philip's use of superior cavalry. We are told he brought to Chaeronea 2,000 horse and 30,000 foot.[206] Diodorus' account is the only narrative description we have of the battle and it is a poor one.[207] Philip entrusted to eighteen-year-old Alexander, with his best generals stationed close by, command of the Macedonian left (we assume) by the river, opposite the famed infantry of the Theban Sacred Band on the Greek right. Philip commanded the Macedonian right wing (we assume) against the Athenians on the Greek left. The Macedonians were in better fighting trim, and Philip deliberately prolonged the battle with his tactics to tire the Greek hoplites;[208] these were citizens, not professional soldiers, and were accustomed to battles of short duration, the typical hoplite battle lasting hardly an hour and a half. Diodorus gives a vague description of father and son both fighting to victory on the field of battle. It is the common assumption that the decisive point came when Alexander led a cavalry charge that broke the Sacred Band, though this is not explicitly stated in the sources. Plutarch, a native of Chaeronea, claims that Alexander *broke into* the formation of the Sacred Band and that Philip after the battle acknowledged the Band's bravery against the Macedonian *sarissai*, the elongated pikes that Philip had introduced.[209] Another source claims that Philip held back his line on the right, withdrawing until he enticed the Athenians out of contact with their centre and right, then turning to charge.[210] If he *did* do this, it would have opened up a gap for Alexander to charge with the Companion Cavalry against the left flank of the Thebans. What we can say for certain is that the Macedonian phalanx proved superior to the Greek hoplites and this spelled decline for the Greek city-state, the survival of which had always been dependent upon its hoplite forces. Demosthenes' contemporary enemies accused him of indictable behaviour for a hoplite—cowardice and fleeing the battlefield—but in fact many Greek hoplites fled for their lives in the rout.[211]

A marble lion marks to this day one of two mass graves of brave men who fought and died in the battle at Chaeronea.[212] In the *polyandrion* marked by the lion are 254 skeletons buried in rows. Though the argument has been made that this is the grave of the Macedonian dead, most historians believe these are the remains of the Sacred Band of 300.[213] In addition to the dead many captives were taken, among them some 2,000 Athenians.[214] The latter were later released without ransom as a conciliatory gesture when Philip arranged terms for peace and alliance with Athens, the so-called Peace of Demades (named for the orator Demades, who was among the prisoners and helped negotiate the peace). He also sent back the ashes of the Athenian dead in the care of Antipater, Alexander, and Alcimachus.[215] Philip's 'peace and alliance' with Athens spelled the end of her hegemony over the islands, and she lost her influence in the Chersonese as well,[216] though she did not become a subject state. In contrast, Philip's treatment of Thebes was markedly harsh: the replacement of the democratic government with an oligarchy of 300 and the installation of a garrison in the Cadmea.[217] Garrisons were also soon installed at Corinth and Ambracia.[218] Philip's control of Greece was tightening, control he needed before he could proceed securely with his plans for Persia.

With the two most powerful city-states decidedly subdued, Philip marched into Spartan territory, and assuming authority over outlying regions that Sparta had previously wrested from her neighbours he handed control back to those states.[219] Individual settlements were arranged with a few states, then over the winter of 338–337 he extended invitations to all the states to send representatives to Corinth to hear his general settlement and plans for a panhellenic war against Persia. Only Sparta dared decline and sent no representative. What Philip could not do was annex the Greek states to Macedonia, nor could he impose on the Greeks monarchical rule. For his own purposes, though, for war in Asia, he needed to bind the states to each other jointly and to himself collectively, and this was the premise of the so-called League of Corinth that he established that winter, a *koine eirene* (common peace) with himself elected as *hegemon* (leader supreme). Whether his settlement also consisted of an alliance is not clear, but the Common Peace was meant to guarantee that the Greeks could not cause Macedonia or Philip trouble in his absence: autonomy with constraints.[220] The terms of the Peace have not survived, but we do have substantial fragments of the oath sworn to maintain it.[221] From this we know that the members swore loyalty to the Peace; not to attack any other member taking the oath, but to make war together against any member violating the terms of the Peace; and not to overthrow the kingdom of Philip and his descendants or the constitution of any member state as it existed at the time of the oath. Representatives from the states were to meet as a *synedrion* (council). It was at a meeting of the *synedrion* that the representatives heard Philip's proposal for a war of revenge on the Greeks' behalf: punishment for destruction of the temples (namely the temple of Athena in Athens) at the hands of the Persians under Xerxes and Mardonius in 480–479. For this war the Greeks elected the Macedonian king *strategos autokrator* (general with full powers) and Philip began to levy Greek forces.[222]

The following summer Philip conducted yet another campaign in the west against the Illyrians, a tribe under King Pleurias.[223] The revolt quite possibly took its motivation from domestic turmoil at Pella, when Philip alienated Olympias and Alexander by taking his seventh wife, a much younger Macedonian noblewoman named Cleopatra. The marriage itself and then a fight at the wedding banquet over an insult to Alexander's legitimacy caused such mayhem in Philip's domestic situation that his greatly anticipated campaign was stalled.[224] It took more than a year for Philip to reconcile with his son and heir, who fled to the Illyrians, and to pacify Epirus, whose king was brother of the jilted Olympias. Meantime, in the spring of 336, Parmenio and Attalus (Cleopatra's guardian) with an advance force of about 10,000 crossed the Hellespont and proceeded to establish a bridgehead for Philip's crossing with the larger army.[225] But the greatest man Europe had ever produced would never take up command of

Figure 4.5 Theatre at Aegae
Source: author, 2001.

98 *Philip II, 360–336*

the war against Persia. Early in the fall of 336, in full view of the throngs of Macedonians and guests who had gathered in the theatre at Aegae (Figure 4.5) for the high-profile wedding of his daughter Cleopatra to her uncle Alexander king of Epirus, Philip was assassinated by one of his bodyguards, a disgruntled former lover.[226] The veteran Macedonian army stood ready but was now in need of a new commander, and Macedonia was in need of a new king. Philip II, who by military strength and diplomacy had raised his kingdom out of subservience to its Balkan neighbours, had overturned its role as pawn in the power plays of the Greek city-states, and had elevated it to the greatest power in all of Europe, would be a hard act to follow.

Notes

1 Philip's whereabouts is not recorded; Griffith in *HM* II 1979: 208 argues, given his military skills, that he must have commanded forces in the battle (cf. Diod. 16.2.4–6), yet his first recorded action is withdrawal (of the garrison) from Amphipolis. For Philip's age (probably born 383–382) cf. Just. 9.8; Paus. 8.7.6.
2 Arist. [*Oec.*] 2.1350a 16–22; see Chapter 3 n110.
3 Ellis 1976: 47 suggests that Perdiccas' 4,000 dead "represented probably one third and possibly one half of the available manpower under arms."
4 *Contra* Hammond in *HM* II 1979: 188, 203; cf. Diod. 16.2.5.
5 Plut. *Pel.* 26.5.
6 Diod. 16.2.2–3; Just. 7.5.3; cf. Ael. *VH* 13.7.
7 *Contra* Ellis 1976: 43–44, who argues Philip was too young to learn much while in Thebes. But for Theban influence on Philip's tactics in 358 see Markle 1978: 486. See also Anson 2010b: 58.
8 Cf. Ath. 11.506e–f. Ellis 1976: 46 suggests Philip's "territory" was Elimeia, but Elimeia was almost certainly not Perdiccas' to give. Other suggestions: Worthington 2008: 19 Amphaxitis; Anson 2010b: 58–59 Mygdonia. Euphraeus' advice: Speusippus' letter *To Philip*, written by Plato's nephew and successor at the Academy c. 343–342. For the letter see Natoli 2004. See also Anson 2013: 48–49.
9 Just. 7.5.8–10 *contra* Diod. 16.2.4. E.g. Griffith in *HM* II 1979: 208–209 (followed by Borza 1992: 200–201), Worthington 2008: 20–21, and Anson 2013: 22–24 argue Philip was king from the start, while Hammond in *HM* II 1979: 651 n1 argues he was regent before becoming king. Ellis 1971: 22: "The point simply, I suggest, is that we are not *compelled* to assume the intervention of a regency after Perdikkas' death either because it is to be expected or because Justin says it was there." But, however much "we are justified in rejecting Justin" (Ellis p22), we still must account for *IG* VII 3055, an inscription from Lebadaia of uncertain date restored as "Amyntas son of Perdiccas King of the Macedonians," on which see Pafford 2011. Tronson 1984: 126 allows the possibility that the Satyrus fragment at Ath. 13.557b–e (n29) is evidence for a period of regency (guardianship). For discussion, with bibliography, see Anson 2009a.
10 On their probable identity see Chapter 3 n38.
11 Diod. 16.3.3; cf. Just. 7.6.4. Heskel 1996: 44–46 dates Philip's accession to October 360, his withdrawal from Amphipolis also to October 360, and his defeat of Argaeus (below) to November 360. On dates see also Hatzopoulos 1982.
12 Diod. 16.2.6. Griffith in *HM* II 1979: 236; Heskel 1996: 46.
13 *IG* IV² 1 94; Hammond in *HM* II 1979: 193–194.
14 Diod. 16.2.6, 3.5 (king unnamed). Ellis 1976: 45 and n5 (250) favours Cotys, but Heskel 1996: 44–46 argues this took place after King Cotys died. Cotys' death:

Arist. *Pol.* 5.1311b; Dem. 23.119; cf. Theopomp. F307 [*FGrH/BNJ* 115, Morison 2014]; Diog. Laert. 3.46. On the date see Delev 2015: 48.
15 Diod. 16.3.4.
16 Cf. n9.
17 Ambush: Just 7.6.6. See Anson 2010b: 55–57.
18 Dem. 23.121; Diod. 16.3.5–6; Libanius 15.42, 20.23.
19 Polyaen. 4.2.17.
20 Just. 8.3.10; cp. Ath. 11.506e–f. The eldest half-brother was Archelaus, Just. 7.4.5.
21 Diod. 16.4.1.
22 Diod. 16.3.1: with "suitable weapons." Cp. Polyaen. 4.2.10: Philip's soldiers were trained to carry *sarissai*. The introduction of the *sarissai*, 16 to 20-foot pikes, is not securely dated; on the debate see Anson 2010b (he favours the early date) citing earlier bibliography. See Chapter 5.
23 Diod. 16.4.2.
24 Ellis 1976: 47: curious; Griffith in *HM* II 1979: 211: enigma. [Lucian] 12.10: Bardylis was in his nineteeth year yet still fought on horseback in this battle.
25 Ellis 1976: 48 suggests the marriage was part of the terms in 360–359. See also Tronson 1984: 121; Carney 2000: 57–58.
26 Diod. 16.4.3–7; Just. 7.6.7.
27 Griffith in *HM* II 1979: 214; echoed by Anson 2010b: 54.
28 Diod. 16.8.1.
29 Satyrus at Ath. 13.557b–e [Roisman 2011 no. 38.5; Schorn 2004 F21; on the ambiguity of "Satyrus" see Gambetti 2012] gives a list of Philip's seven wives (and some offspring), all but the final wife being taken "according to war." Tronson 1984: 117–118 argues that Satyrus was a student of Aristotle and thus a near contemporary of Philip (the general view is that he was active somewhat later, in the third century), but that he was not a reliable historian and (124) that Athenaeus reworked his source rather than quoted it verbatim. Whether Satyrus' list may be regarded as chronological has been much discussed (Tronson 1984: 116 cites earlier scholarship); he puts Phila (otherwise unattested) second but very soon after Audata. For the view that Phila was Philip's first wife see Ellis 1976: 38; Griffith in *HM* II 1979: 214; Worthington 2008: 19. See also Borza 1992: 206–208; Carney 2000: 59–60.
30 Orestis: *SEG* 23.471, 13; Hammond in *HM* II 1979: 185. Pelagonia: *IG* II^2 190.
31 Tod *GHI* 143 = *IG* II^2 110 = RO *GHI* 38; cf. Tod *GHI* 148 = *SIG*^{3} 188. See Bosworth 1971a: 98; Ellis 1976: 59; Hammond in *HM* II 1979: 186.
32 Diod. 16.8.1.
33 Bosworth 1971a: 99: "the annexation by Philip is obscure and undatable."
34 Str. 9.5.11. Griffith in *HM* II 1979: 215 guesses that Orestis was Olympias' dowry in 357. See also Bosworth 1971a: 98.
35 Bosworth 1971a: 102; Ellis 1976: 59; Errington 1990: 41.
36 King 2010: 382; see Chapter 5.
37 Dem. 4.27 and n31. Bosworth 1971a: 98–99; Worthington 2008: 34.
38 Ellis 1976: 60 suggests he was the former king of the Pelagonians; not followed by Heckel 1992: 13–14, 2016: 44–45; but see Dahmen 2010: 47 n25. Cf. Plut. *Mor.* 177c.
39 Isoc. 5.21; cf. Dem. 1.13, 23.
40 Dem. 4.48; Just. 8.3.7–8, 5.7; Polyaen. 4.2.12; cf. Theopomp. F224 = Ath. 4.167a–c. Hammond 1988a.
41 Walbank 1940: 3; Bosworth 1971a: 102; Errington 1990: 43; Worthington 2008: 35.
42 Dem. 1.8.
43 Diod. 16.8.2; Tod *GHI* 150 = RO *GHI* 49.

44 On the importance of Amphipolis in the development of Macedonian cities see Errington 2007.
45 Dem. 2.6, cf. 23.116, [Dem.] 7.27. For sources and bibliography see Harding 61.
46 Dem. 1.9; Diod. 16.8.3.
47 Tod *GHI* 151 = *IG* II^2 126 = Harding 64 = RO *GHI* 47.
48 In 357–356. Isoc. 5.2–3; Aeschin. 2.21, 70, 3.54; Tod *GHI* 157 = *IG* II^2 127, l. 41 = Harding 70 = RO *GHI* 53.
49 Tod *GHI* 158 = Harding 67 = RO *GHI* 50; Dem. 23.108, 2.14, 6.20; Diod. 16.8.3–4. Griffith in *HM* II 1979: 244.
50 Diod. 16.8.4–5.
51 Steph. Byz. s.v. "Philippoi"; Just. 8.3.14–15. The foundation of Crenides by the Thassians was probably in 360, *IG* IV^2 1.9; cf. Diod. 16.3.7. See Cawkwell 1978: 43–44.
52 Theophr. *Caus. pl.* 5.14.5–6; Diod. 16.8.6–7. For the Persian practice of resettlement see Balcer 1988: 9–10, his n29.
53 Tod *GHI* 157 (date: 168) = *IG* II^2 127 = RO *GHI* 53. Cp. Diod. 16.22.3.
54 Plut. *Alex.* 3.8; Just. 12.16.6.
55 On the coinage see Dahmen 2010: 52, with further references, and plate 5 in that volume. On the Olympic victories see Romano 1990; Adams 2008: 59–61.
56 Just. 7.6.8. On chronology see Griffith in *HM* II 1979: 216; but Griffith (225–226) argues Justin is wrong that Philip took Larissa and conquered Thessaly in 358. For Philip's siege of Pharcedon (Polyaen. 4.2.18) Griffith (271) prefers 353–352; so also Ellis 1976: 86.
57 Ath. 13.557c; Plut. *Alex.* 10.1. For the tradition that Philinna was of low birth, a dancing girl and/or prostitute, and Arrhidaeus a bastard cf. Just. 9.8.2 and 13.2.11. More likely Philinna was from a noble Larissaean family; see Carney 2000: 61–62, citing bibliography; Ogden 1999: 17–27. On the question of the marital status of Philip's Thessalian "wives" see also Tronson 1984: 121–122.
58 Just. 7.6.8–9: after defeating the Illyrians, Philip took Thessaly by surprise, wanting to incorporate the Thessalian cavalry into his army. Philip may have firmed up relations with the Aleuadae (by taking a bride) but he did not 'capture' Larissa.
59 Xen. *Hell.* 6.4.35–37; Diod. 16.14.1–2. Cf. Plut. *Pel.* 35. On Diodorus' erroneous date for the assassination see McQueen 1995: 77.
60 Plut. *Pyrr.* 1.3; Just 17.3.13–14 (omitting Alcetas). Greenwalt 2008: 97 suggests Philip was betrothed to Olympias during the reign of Perdiccas III; cp. Plut. *Alex.* 2.2.
61 Just. 7.6.10–12.
62 Diod. 16.14.1–2.
63 See Tronson 1984: 116 (n57); Carney 2000: 60–61.
64 Diod. 16.31.6; 34.4–5; Just. 7.6.13–16. Cf. also Dem. 4.35, Polyaen. 4.2.15; *IG* II^2 130.
65 Third Sacred War: Diod. 16.23.1–33.4, 35.1–36.1, 37.1–40.2, 52.9–60.5; Paus. 10.2.1–3.2; Ath. 13.560b; Just. 8.1.1–2.7, 5.1–6.
66 On the date cf. n70.
67 Diod. 16.30.1–31.5; Paus. 10.2.4; Just. 8.1.12–13. Buckler 1989: 45.
68 Diod. 16.34.1–2.
69 Polyaen. 4.2.22; Dem. 4.22. See Hammond 1992: 32 and Chapter 5.
70 So Ellis 1976: 78; Cawkwell 1978: 61, 64; Griffith in *HM* II 1979: 267–268; Worthington 2008: 58; *contra* McQueen 1995: 102. On the disputed chronology see Buckler 1989: 148–158.
71 Diod. 16.35.4, 31.5, 33.3; Just. 8.1.14. Tisiphonus: Xen. *Hell.* 6.4.37.
72 Diod. 16.35.1–2; Polyaen. 2.38.2. See Worthington 2008: 61–62.

73 Buckler 1980: 116, 247–248 suggests Pelopidas introduced the office of *archon* to thwart Alexander II's position in Thessaly in 369. The office of *archon* existed at latest by 361–360: Tod *GHI* 147 = *IG* II² 116 = Harding 59 = RO *GHI* 44. For further discussion of the offices of *tagos* and *archon* see Westlake 1935: 77–83; Larsen 1968: 14–19, 24; see Chapter 3 n88.
74 Diod. 16.35.3–6; Paus. 10.2.3; Just. 8.2.1–7. On Diodorus' ambiguity regarding the number of slain, the drowned, and the captives see Griffith in *HM* II 1979: 276–277.
75 Diod. 16.37.3.
76 Dem. 1.12–13; Isoc. 5.21. The order of Philip's conquests in Thessaly as given by Demosthenes: Pherae, Pagasae, and Magnesia, all after his capture of Methone. Diodorus (16.31.6) puts the capture of Pagasae *immediately* after Methone.
77 Dem. 4.34; Just. 8.3.13.
78 Aeschin. 2.115.
79 Dem. 1.22; Polyaen. 4.2.19; Just. 8.1.3, 3.1–5.
80 Dem. 19.84; Diod. 16.38.1–2; Just. 8.2.8–12.
81 Dem. 1.13; Aeschin. 2.81; cp. Just. 8.3.6.
82 Dem. 23.8–12, 170; cf. Just. 8.3.14–15 and n14. See Archibald in *CAH*² VI: 459–471.
83 Dem. 23.183; Diod. 16.34.1–2; Polyaen. 5.16.2; Front. 2.3.3. It has been suggested that the father Amadocus resisted Philip in spring 353, but in fall 352, with the father either deceased or possibly deposed by Philip, the son allied with Philip, Theopomp. F101. See Griffith in *HM* II 1979: 282–283; *contra* Errington 1990: 50 with n15.
84 Cf. n47; Dem. 23.173.
85 Theopomp. F249.
86 Schol. Aeschin. 2.81; Diod. 16.34.4.
87 We might assume one was the younger Amadocus (n83). On the hostageship of Cersobleptes' son see Badian 1983: 62 (down-dating to 346); Hammond 1994b: 83–84.
88 Just. 8.3.6.
89 Dem. 1.13, 3.4–5. Heraion Teichos: Isaac 1986: 203.
90 Just. 8.3.7–9.
91 Dem. 1.13, 4.48; Isoc. 5.21.
92 Just. 8.6.4–8; cf. 7.6.12 and n158. The date of the war with Arybbas is unknown, but must predate early 349 when Demosthenes delivered his *First Olynthiac*, where he mentions it (1.13). Arybbas' status: Griffith in *HM* II 1979: 305–308; Hammond 1994b: 50–51 (vassal); *contra* Heskel 1988; Errington 1990: 44 (exile). This also may have been the occasion of annexation by Philip of the Epirote territories Tymphaea and Parauaea; so Ellis 1976: 91.
93 Dem. 3.7, 23.109. Demosthenes (23) *Against Aristocrates* (the Olynthians had formed a "friendship" with Athens and *promised* "alliance") was delivered in 352. Libanius *Hypothesis* to Dem. 1: Philip was "away" when the Olynthians sent ambassadors to Athens, though he had "men" in Olynthus who kept him informed. By terms of the treaty with Philip of 357 neither side could form a separate peace with Athens.
94 Dem. 4.17, cp. 23.108.
95 Just. 8.3.10.
96 Dem. 9.56, 66; cf. Dem. 4.37–38, Philip's letters to the Euboeans.
97 Diod. 16.8.7: "betrayers of their native lands."
98 Dem. 9.63–66.
99 Str. 10.1.3; Thuc. 1.114.3.

100 Diod. 16.52.9; Dem. 19.266. Diodorus' claim at 52.9 that Philip also had to expel Peitholaus from Pherae again is possibly a doublet of either 16.37.3 or 69.8; so McQueen 1995: 121, *contra* Westlake 1935: 183. "Zereia" is an emendation of a corruption in the manuscripts; an alternative emendation of "Stageira" is more doubtful given that Diodorus calls the place a fortress. See Buckler 2003: 436.
101 Philoch. F49 [*FGrH/BNJ* 328, Jones 2016].
102 Philoch. F50.
103 Diod. 16.54.4.
104 Diod. 16.53.2–3; cp. Dem. 8.40, 9.56, 19.265, 342; Philoch. F156; *Suda* s.v. "Karanos."
105 Diod. 16.55.1–2; Dem. 19.192. See Chapter 1 n31.
106 Diod. 16.55.3; Dem. 19.193–195.
107 Dem. 19.230; Aeschin. 2.15. Derdas, probably brother of Philip's wife Phila and heir to the now defunct throne of Elimeia, was also a captive at Olynthus, Ath. 10.436c = Theopomp. F143.
108 *Syll.*³ 1.332.
109 Just. 8.3.11.
110 Diod. 16.54.1.
111 Aeschin. 3.85–88; Dem. 5.5; Plut. *Phoc.* 12–13. On Philip's involvement see Ryder 1994: 235–238.
112 Aeschin. 2.12–14.
113 Aeschin. 2.109.
114 Dem. 19.304; Aeschin. 2.8, 79; Diod. 16.54.1. For activity in the Peloponnese see Dem. 19.10–11, 303–307.
115 Diod. 16.56.2–8, 58.1–6. On Philip's motives see Buckler 1989: 113.
116 Theopomp. F160; Aeschin. 2.90. Apros: Archibald 2004: 893. Hieron Oros: Isaac 1986: 211.
117 Aeschin. 2.72–73; Just. 8.3.12.
118 Dem. 19.36 (with schol.), 334. Griffith in *HM* II 1979: 291–293; Buckler 1989: 119; Worthington 2008: 88.
119 Aeschin. 2.15–17. For chronology and details of the negotiations see Ellis 1976: 100–119 (note Buckler 1989 does not follow his strict Julian chronology, and see Ellis' own caveat, 266 n70); Worthington 2008: 89–99. On the debate over Philip's intentions with regard to Thebes and Athens in 346 see Buckler 1989: 121–125. For more on chronology debates see Buckler 1996.
120 Aeschin. 2.132–135.
121 Aeschin. 2.18–21, 47; 2 *Hypothesis* to Dem. 19; Just. 8.4.1. On the nature of the evidence for the Peace of Philocrates and its biases see Ellis 1982: 43–44; Worthington 2008: 89–90.
122 Dem. 19.163.
123 Aeschin. 2.22, 34–35.
124 Aeschin. 2.38, 42, 48, 51–52.
125 Aeschin. 2.82.
126 Theopomp. F165; Dem. 19.69; 2 *Hypothesis* to Dem. 19, 5; Aeschin. 3.72, 76; Just. 8.4.2. Eurylochus: Dem. 9.58; Just. 12.6.14; (?) *Syll.*³ 242 B6.
127 Aeschin. 2.70.
128 On the dubiousness of Demosthenes' later reference to Philip's "exclusion-clause" (Dem. 19.159, 174) see Buckler 1989: 134, 137. On the terms of the Peace see [Dem.] 7.26 and Buckler 2000: 121–132. Halos was captured and destroyed in summer 346; so Dem. 19.36, 39, 334.
129 Aeschin. 2.97, 103, 108; Dem. 19.154. On the Second Embassy in general see Aeschin. 2.97–118; Dem. 18.25–32, 19.150–176.
130 Diod. 16.59.1–2; Dem. 19.139–140; Aeschin. 2.140; Just. 8.4.3–4.

131 Aeschin. 2.90; Dem. 19.156, 158.
132 Aeschin. 2.112.
133 Dem. 19.318, 321.
134 Dem. 5.20, 22; cf. Isoc. 5.53–55.
135 So Dem. 19.158; but cp. 18.32 and 2 *Hypothesis* to Dem. 19, 7: Demosthenes is not clear on whether Philip gave his own oath at Pella or Pherae.
136 Just. 8.4.12. On Philip's reticence see Cawkwell 1978: 102–104. On the third (to confirm ratification of the Peace) and fourth (to plead fair treatment for the Phocians) Athenian embassies see Ellis 1976: 118, 122; Worthington 2008: 99–104. For Athenian fear of Philip's broader intentions cf. Isoc. 5.74.
137 Dem. 18.32, 19.315–324.
138 Dem. 19.53–66; cp. Diod. 16.59.2–3. On Philip's diplomacy see Ryder 1994; Mitchell 2002: 148–166.
139 Diod. 16.59.4–60.3; Paus. 10.3.1–2, 8.2; *Hypothesis* to Dem. 5. On Philip's treatment of the Phocians see the hostile view of the sources, e.g. Dem. 6.15, 19.128; Just. 8.5.1–6.
140 [Dem.] 7.38, 19.168–170.
141 Dem. 19.50; Paus. 10.3.2. Westlake 1935: 188–190; Cawkwell 1992; Buckler and Beck 2008: 213–223; Worthington 2008: 103. Cf. Aeschin. 3.124, 128 with schol.; Dem. 5.23, 18.151 with schol.
142 The Delphic Pythia was accused of Philippizing; see Hunt 2010: 88–89.
143 Diod. 16.60.2; Just. 8.5.4–6.
144 Dem. 19.111–113, 128.
145 Dem. 19.89.
146 On the significance of the episode see Willekes 2015: 54–57.
147 Just. 8.5.7–6.2.
148 Dem. 18.67; Didymos 12.64–13.2. Ellis 1976: 136 suggests Pleuratos was king of the Ardiaei. Griffith in *HM* II 1979: 469–474; Wilkes 1992: 121–122; Harding 2006: 238–240. On Philip's wounds see Riginos 1994.
149 Diod. 16.69.7; Just. 8.6.3.
150 Diod. 16.69.8; Dem. 6.22, 18.48.
151 Dem. 8.59, 9.12, 19.260, [Dem.] 7.32.
152 On Philip's political reforms in Thessaly, the possible establishment of a decadarchy, or Board of Ten system (Dem. 6.22, 18.48, but cp. Harpocration s.v. "Tetrarchia" and "Dekadarchia" = Harding 87, cp. no. 62), and then a return to the traditional Group of Four tetrarchy division (Dem. 9.26; Theopomp. F208–209) see Westlake 1935: 191–199; Griffith in *HM* II 1979: 523–544; Sprawski 2003. References to a tyranny at Larissa under the Aleuads (Arist. *Pol.* 5.1306a; Dem. 1.22 schol. = Harding 62D; Dem. 2.14 schol.; Polyaen. 4.2.11) are undated. Demosthenes (18.48) claims Eudicus and Simus betrayed Larissa to Philip.
153 Dem. 6.15, 19–27, 19.260–261. On Demosthenes' biased representation of Philip see Ryder 2000. On Philip's "designs" see Buckler and Beck 2008: 267–269; Anson 2016.
154 Cf. especially Dem. 8.36, 9.12, 33, 57–66, 18.71, 19.87. Euboea in Philip's hands: Dem. 19.22, 220, 326.
155 Dem. 9.59–62; but cp. Ath. 11.508e.
156 Aeschin. 3.89–93; Dem. 8.18. Demosthenes (19.204, 326, 334) implies widespread Macedonian control in Euboea, but other than Eretria and Oreus we have no specific details.
157 Ellis 1976: 165–166; Worthington 2008: 125.
158 [Dem.] 7.32; Just. 8.6.7–8, and cf. n92. Diod. 16.72.1 is mistaken; Arybbas died in exile at Athens: Tod *GHI* 173 = *IG* II² 226 = RO *GHI* 70; Just. 7.6.12.

159 Theopomp. F206–207; [Dem.] 7.32, 9.34, 10.10, 18.244.
160 *Hypothesis* to Aeschin. 2.
161 [Dem.] 7.18–23, 30–32.
162 *Hypothesis* to Dem. 6; 9.72; Aeschin. 3.83 schol. and *IG* II² 225 = Harding 89. Harris 1995: 107–123.
163 Ellis 1976: 158.
164 Diod. 16.74.1; Philoch. F159, 160 = Harding 91–92.
165 Dem. 8.35: by spring 341 (when Demosthenes delivered *On the Chersonese*) Philip had been in Thrace ten months.
166 Theopomp. F216; Steph. Byz. s.v. "Getia."
167 Satyrus at Ath. 13.557d (n29). Carney 2000: 68.
168 Dem. 8.14, 35, 44; cf. Polyaen. 4.2.13 (undated).
169 Dem. 8.44, 10.15; cf. Theopomp. F110 (undated). Ellis 1976: 170–171 suggests that this was the circumstance of Philip establishing a new administrative position of 'General in Thrace', although the title is not heard of until 336–335; cf. Arr. *Anab*. 1.25.2 with Bosworth 1980a: 160. Demosthenes' (9.26) claim that Philip had destroyed thirty-two Thracian cities may refer to this campaign, though possibly he refers to the campaign in Chalcidice (i.e. the Thraceward region) between 351 and 348.
170 Diod. 16.71.1–2; Just. 9.1.1. It is unclear which cities.
171 Ellis 1976: 173–174; Worthington 2008: xvii.
172 Dem. 18.244, 302; Arr. *Anab*. 2.14.5.
173 Dem. 8.2, 58, 64, 9.16, 35, 10.60, 65, 12.11. For the clash in the Chersonese in general cf. Dem. 8, 9, 10, with 7.39–77 and 23.181–183 (= the Athenocentric view).
174 The letter is preserved as Dem. 12. Dem. 12.2–3; Philoch. F158.
175 Dem. 7.2, 8.5–9, 12.8, 18.70.
176 Diog. Laert. 5.2; *Suda* s.v. "Nikomachos."
177 Plut. *Alex*. 9.1; Just. 9.1.8; cf. Isoc. L 4. Hamilton 1969: 22–23.
178 Just. 9.1.1; Diod. 16.74.2.
179 Diod. 16.74.2–5; Philoch. F53–54.
180 Diod. 16.75.1–76.4; [Dem.] 11.5; Arr. *Anab*. 2.14.5; Paus. 1.29.10.
181 Diod. 16.76.3; Just. 9.1.2–6; Dem. 18.87, 93, [Dem.] 11.5; for Perinthus *and* Byzantium cf. Theopomp. F217; Philoch. F54; Didymos 10.34–62; for Selymbria see Ellis 1976: 178 and the 'spurious' document attached to Dem. 18.[77–78], translated in Yunis 2005: 220. The motive Justin (9.1.2) ascribes to Philip for the siege of Byzantium was to secure a base for land and naval forces; Didymos (10.40–45) says it was to deprive the Athenians of bases for a war against him and to interrupt their grain supply.
182 Dem. 18.73 (with schol.), 139; Theopomp. F292 and Philoch. F162 (= Didymos 10.34–11.5), cf. Harding 95; Front. 1.4.13; Just. 9.1.5–6. On Philip's need to reassert himself see Ellis 1976: 179; Griffith in *HM* II 1979: 570, 578; but cp. Worthington 2008: 134.
183 Philoch. F55 = Harding 95C; cf. [Dem.] 11, 12. *Contra*, Worthington 2008: 128–129 argues Philip had already declared war; more recently see 2014: 67–80 (especially 79).
184 Plut. *Phoc*. 14.
185 Cf. *Suda* s.v. "Leon." Diodorus' (16.77.2) statement that Philip now made a treaty with "the Athenians and other Greeks" is not accurate. As Diodorus himself explains (76.5–6), one of the primary sources he has been following for Philip, Ephorus of Cumae, has ended his narrative with the description of the siege of Perinthus, and from that point on Diodorus must follow another source or sources, one of whom he identifies as the Athenian historian Diyllus. One immediately

discerns a less sympathetic view of Philip. On Diodorus' sources here see Bosworth 1971a: 94–95.
186 Plut. *Phoc.* 14; Front. 1.4.13; Hesychius F7.26–28 [*BNJ* = *FGrH* F1.27–28].
187 Diod. 16.22.1, 34.1, 52.3; cf. Ath. 6.256c–e.
188 Ellis 1976: 172 supposes Artabazus was still at Pella in 341. For Artabazus as *xenos* of Philip cf. Curt. 6.5.2. Diod. 16.52.3: Artabazus had twenty-one children by the sister of Mentor and Memnon; cf. Arr. *Anab.* 2.1.3, 3.23.7, 7.4.6; Curt. 3.13.13, 6.5.4; Plut. *Alex.* 21.7–9. In his *First Philippic* delivered in 351 Demosthenes mentions a rumour that Philip had sent an embassy to the Persian king (Dem. 4.48), and Arrian (*Anab.* 2.14.2) records a letter of Darius III to Alexander III after the battle of Issus in 333 claiming that there had been an alliance (at some point) between Philip and Artaxerxes, though historians are sceptical of the authenticity of both letter and alliance.
189 Ellis 1976: 92; Olbrycht 2010: 346–347.
190 Isoc. 5. On the letters of Isocrates and Speusippus to Philip see Markle 1976 and Natoli 2004. On the idea of Panhellenism and Philip's plans see Sakellariou 1992.
191 Xen. *Hell.* 6.1.11–12; Isoc. 5.119.
192 Plut. *Agesilaus* 15.
193 Dem. 10.31–34; Diod. 16.60.5.
194 Diod. 16.52.6–8; Didymos 6. On Hermias see Green 2003, especially 41–42.
195 Theopomp. F217.
196 Just. 9.1.8 (n177). The claim is unsupported; rejected by Ellis 1976: 183, accepted by Griffith in *HM* II 1979: 583.
197 Theopomp. F217, 221, 223.
198 Just. 9.1.9–2.16; Brown 1988.
199 Just. 9.3.1–3; Didymos 13.3–7; Plut. *Mor.* 331b. Worthington 2008: 140; Gabriel 2010: 12–13.
200 Aeschin. 3.128–129; Dem. 18.151–152. Worthington 2008: 140–147.
201 Griffith in *HM* II 1979: 585–595: Philip instigated the war to target Athens, cf. Dem. 18.156–168.
202 Aeschin. 3.140–144; Dem. 18.169–173, 211–213; Philoch. F56 = Didymos 11.37–51, see Harding 96; Diod. 16.84.2–85.4; Plut. *Dem.* 18; Just. 9.3.4–8. On Demosthenes' role see Cawkwell 1978: 140–144; Worthington 2008: 142–145.
203 Dem. 18.215–216; Dinarchus 1.74.
204 Polyaen. 4.2.8, cp. 4.2.14; Aeschin. 3.146–147; cf. Diod. 18.56.5.
205 Aeschin. 3.148–151; Plut. *Phoc.* 16.1–2.
206 On numbers of troops cf. Diod. 16.85.5–6, cp. Just. 9.3.9, with McQueen 1995: 160.
207 Diod. 16.85.5–86.6; Plut. *Dem.* 19–20.3, *Alex.* 9.2–3, *Pelop.* 18.7, *Cam.* 19.5, *Mor.* 845f (Chaeronea is Plutarch's hometown); Just. 9.3.9–11; Paus. 9.40.10. For discussion see Hammond 1938; Pritchett 1958; Griffith in *HM* II 1979: 596–603; Buckler and Beck 2008: 254–258; Sears and Willekes 2016; cf. n209.
208 Polyaen. 4.2.7; Front. 2.1.9.
209 Plut. *Alex.* 9.2–3; *Pelop.* 18.7, cp. Diod. 16.86.3. Some historians have vigorously denied that horses can be made to charge head-on into serried rows of spear points and a solid mass of men; see Rahe 1981: 85; Buckler and Beck 2008: 256 (both citing earlier scholarship, though Buckler and Beck omit Rahe). *Contra*, see Willekes 2015: 52–53; Sears and Willekes 2016: 1031–1035. *Sarissai*: cf. n22.
210 Polyaen. 4.2.2; Buckler and Beck 2008: 257 question this.
211 E.g. Aeschin. 3.159; Dinarchus 1.12; Plut. *Dem.* 20.2, *Mor.* 845f.
212 Paus. 9.40.10; Str. 9.2.37.

213 Plut. *Pelop.* 15, 16, 18. Macedonians: e.g. Hammond 1938: 31–33. Sacred Band: e.g. Pritchett 1958: 310–311; Ma 2008; Sears and Willekes 2016: 1021.
214 Diod. 16.86.5–6. For Philip's post-battle behavior cf. Diod. 16.87.1–2; Theopomp. F236; *contra* Just. 9.4.1–3.
215 For Alcimachus see Tod *GHI* 180; Arr. *Anab.* 1.18.1; Harpocration s.v. "Alkimachos"; Heckel 2006a: 9–10. Release of prisoners and return of ashes: Diod. 16.87.3; Just. 9.4.4–5; Polyb. 5.10.4–5. Terms of Peace: [Demades] 9; Diod. 18.56.7; Paus. 1.25.3, 1.34.1, 7.10.5; cf. Plut. *Dem.* 21.1–3, *Phoc.* 16; Tod *GHI* 181; McQueen 1995: 165–166 with source references. Aeschin. 3.131: Philip did not invade Attica because the omens were unfavourable.
216 Griffith in *HM* II 1979: 607.
217 Diod. 16.87.3; Just. 9.4.6–10; Paus. 9.1.8, 6.5; cf. Dinarchus 1.19; Diod. 17.8.3–7; Arr. *Anab.* 1.7.1; Plut. *Alex.* 11.10; Paus. 4.27.10, 9.37.8. On Philip's settlements with the Greek states see Cawkwell 1996; cf. n220 below.
218 Plut. *Arat.* 23; Polyb. 38.3.3.
219 Polyb. 9.28.6–7, 33.8–12; Paus. 8.35.4; Liv. 38.34.3. Hamilton 1982.
220 For the League of Corinth see especially Ryder 1965: 102–106; Griffith in *HM* II 1979: 623–646; Heisserer 1980: xxiii–xxvii; Perlman 1985; Hunt 2010: 217–236. Historians debate the existence of 'alliance' in addition to peace (cf. Arr. *Anab.* 3.24.5), e.g. Griffith in *HM* II 1979: 629 concludes no alliance; Perlman 1985: 169: Common Peace with elements of hegemonic alliance; and see Heisserer 1980: 3–20.
221 Tod *GHI* 177 = Harding 99 = RO *GHI* 76; cf. [Dem.] 17.
222 Diod. 16.89.2–3; Just. 9.5.1–7; Polyb. 9.33.7; cf. Dem. 18.200–201; Aesch 3.132; *Oxyrhynchus Papyri* F5; Plut. *Mor.* 240a. Two questions arise from the inadequate sources: (1) whether Philip convened two meetings, the first to establish Common Peace and the second at which he was elected full military powers and declared war; (2) whether the *synedrion* elected Philip *strategos autokrator* (Diod. 16.89.3) or *hegemon autokrator* (Arr. *Anab.* 7.9.5) for the war with Persia; see Ellis 1976: 208; Griffith in *HM* II 1979: 629–631; McQueen 1995: 169–170.
223 Diod. 16.93.6.
224 See Chapter 6.
225 Diod. 16.91.2, 17.2.4; Just. 9.5.8–9; Polyaen. 5.44.4.
226 Diod. 16.91.4–95.1; Just. 9.6.1–7; Plut. *Alex.* 9.5–11, 10.6–8; Arist. *Pol.* 1311a–b. The bibliography on Philip's assassination is extensive; the 'classic' discussion is Badian 1963, revisited 2007. See also Bosworth 1971a: 93–97; Fears 1975; Griffith in *HM* II 1979: 676–691; Develin 1981; Ellis 1981; Hammond 1991: 399–403, 407–412; Carney 1992; Worthington 2008: 172–186, 2014: 109–115; Antela-Bernárdez 2012; Heckel, Howe and Müller 2017.

5   Macedonian military

Macedonia's *hetairoi* Companion Cavalry was already reputable by the late fifth century, but Philip II greatly improved military effectiveness by fine-tuning cavalry tactics, incorporating auxiliary contingents, and transforming the Macedonian infantry, by equipping them with the innovative *sarissa* spear, into a phalanx of *pezhetairoi* Foot Companions that would prove invincible for the next two centuries. This professional standing army under the generalship of Alexander III won all its major set battles in the east, but encounters with unfamiliar methods of warfare compelled Alexander to reorganize the cavalry *hipparchiai*, develop new techniques to confront guerrilla fighting, adopt the war elephant, and compensate for attrition with native recruits (*epigoni*) trained in Macedonian weaponry and tactics. Almost immediately upon Alexander's death, the seasoned Macedonian phalanx units were incorporated into the armies of the fledgling breakaway Hellenistic kingdoms, usually as minority but elite contingents, while the cavalry declined in importance.

Macedonian military before Philip II

Well before Philip II's reign the kings of Macedonia, always serving as military leaders, had developed a cavalry force of such strength that with it they were capable of winning and maintaining supremacy in the Pierian and Emathian plains. Probably from an early date the cavalry bore the name *hetairoi*, for those who were nobles, owned a horse, and fought battles for the king, also hunted, dined and drank with, and advised the king as his chosen companions, or *hetairoi*. The nobles—the landowners—probably provided not only own horses but also arms, consisting of helmet, greaves, spear, short sword, and the *chlamys* (military cloak), and some also wore a cuirass. While in the early days the military and social aspects of society were virtually inseparable, in later times "Companions" also referred to an institution of the court that included non-Macedonians and non-combatants. The court Companions have been compared to the Achaemenid Persian royal "friends" and to the *hetairoi* of the Sicilian tyrant Gelon, a contemporary of Alexander I.[1] As the military evolved under Philip II and Alexander III, court Companions numbered in the hundreds, though the king maintained a smaller inner circle of perhaps eighty or ninety intimate associates.[2] The Companion Cavalry remained the elite military corps of heavy-armed horsemen, mainly enlisted from the Macedonian nobility.

When Alexander I was required to contribute a contingent to the Persian forces at Plataea in 479 it was almost certainly cavalry, for he was stationed with the Thessalian and Theban (Boeotian) cavalry contingents.[3] Perdiccas II was appointed commander of the allied cavalry defending Potidaea when it revolted from the Athenian League in 432. Perdiccas contributed his own contingent of 200 cavalry, and these nearly came to blows with the 600 cavalry led by his brother Philip and the Elimiote Pausanias, who were fighting on the Athenian side.[4] When the Thracians invaded Lower Macedonia in 429 the Macedonians did not even attempt to defend themselves with an infantry force. Perdiccas sent to his Upper Macedonian allies for reinforcements of cavalry.[5] His few cavalry were such "good horsemen and protected by cuirasses" that no one could stand up to them when they hazarded raids on the Thracian ranks, but they were heavily outnumbered and gave up their attacks. A few years later, in 423, Perdiccas led all his Macedonian cavalry, which combined with Chalcidian cavalry totaled 1,000, against Arrhabaeus of Lyncus, who also had cavalry of an unspecified number. In the ensuing battle the cavalry, engaging first in the plain between two hills on which the infantry were held in reserve, functioned as the primary fighting unit on both sides.

Both Perdiccas and Arrhabaeus also had some hoplite infantry, Perdiccas' consisting of some Greeks, not many, living in (Lower) Macedonia;[6] but the bulk of their forces consisted of "barbarians," probably mainly light infantry, slingers, and skirmishers. Perdiccas undertook the campaign only after securing as allies 1,700 Peloponnesian hoplites under Brasidas. The pressing need for effective heavy infantry might well be the reason why Alexander and Perdiccas were willing to resettle Greek refugees (Mycenaeans in 468, and exiles from Histiaea about 446).[7] However, the scant evidence suggests that the Macedonians from earliest times depended on cavalry for military success, and this is what tactically distinguishes the Macedonian army from the classical hoplite armies of the Greek *poleis* (city-states). As is evident from the clash between Perdiccas and Arrhabaeus, in Macedonian warfare the cavalry was a striking force, the phalanx (heavy infantry) a holding force. But cavalry alone proved inadequate against the large infantry forces of the Thracians and Illyrians.

Archelaus did more than any of his predecessors to strengthen the Macedonian army and the kingdom's defences. He saw to the building of fortresses, such as Demir Kapija guarding access to the lower reaches of the Axios from the Central Balkans,[8] organized the construction of "straight roads," which facilitated movement of troops, and made improvements to cavalry and armament. We are not told precisely what Archelaus' reforms were, but one could speculate that improvement of "horses" refers to horse breeding, which would allow for more men to be mounted as cavalry, and improvement of "arms" to state funding of infantry arms supplied to Macedonians who could not afford them. In Thucydides' opinion Archelaus organized his kingdom for war, and one should think this included some sort of infantry that was more reliable than Perdiccas' terrified hordes of "barbarians."[9] Archelaus' efforts were, alas, undone by the succession problems that weakened the kingdom following his death, and after Aeropus was forced to back down from his initial stance of thinking he had sufficient cavalry to challenge a Spartan march through his territory[10] no Macedonian force of either cavalry or infantry seems to have been able to protect the homeland from Illyrian or any other raids for the next forty years.

When Amyntas III requested Spartan aid against Olynthian incursions into Macedonia in 383–382 he was advised by Sparta to recruit an army and to seek alliances in Upper Macedonia. The kingdom was virtually defenceless. Although we do see some depictions of Macedonian infantrymen and equipment in the archaeological record that could date from this period, the infantry Amyntas mustered was probably mostly mercenary,[11] and his own contribution of cavalry was clearly inferior in skill if not in number to the 400 Upper Macedonian cavalry of Derdas II, whose alliance he won. Derdas' cavalry were given the position of honor in battle and secured the first Spartan victory.[12] Yet not much more than a decade later, in 369, when Alexander II together with the Larissaean Aleuadae marched an army into Thessaly, he quickly took control of both Larissa and Crannon. No record survives of the composition of his forces, though it is likely he had some Macedonian cavalry, these being chiefly his Companions, and some Thessalian cavalry loyal to the Aleuadae; but what about infantry? He had little time to accomplish any major reforms during his very short reign, yet the swiftness and success of his aggression in Thessaly suggest a confidence in reliable forces.

The *pezhetairoi* are not heard of until the reign of Philip II; however, there is some reason to suggest they were already in existence before Philip came to the throne. Anaximenes, one of two historians contemporary with Philip to mention them, attributes to "Alexander" the training of the "most renowned men" as cavalry and also the division of the infantry into *lochoi* (probably companies of 100 men) and *dekades* (files of ten men) with the overall designation *pezhetairoi*, or Foot Companions.[13] On the social level, the foot, many probably coming from a rising middle class made possible by increased trade and generous land grants, would thereby become privileged along with the wealthier upper-class landowners who comprised the horse.[14] Theopompus, the other historian, describes the *pezhetairoi* as the tallest and strongest of all the Macedonians, suggesting that these were an elite royal guard of spear-bearers.[15] A small unit of the tallest and strongest *pezhetairoi*, whose original duty was to stand guard on the king, was transformed over time into the force of elite shock infantry later known as the Hypaspists.[16] By the time of Alexander III's Asian campaign the term *pezhetairoi* seems to apply to the foot in general,[17] while the Hypaspists are given separate notice as the elite infantry or king's guards. It seems indisputable that the Foot Companions were well established by 349, ten years into Philip's reign, since Demosthenes also mentions them in a speech delivered to the Athenian Assembly that year. He acknowledges that by reputation the *pezhetairoi* were "admirable soldiers" and "well grounded in the science of war," though in his derisive view they were really no better than other soldiers.[18] Scholars have long debated the identification of "Alexander": was he Alexander I or II or III, or has Anaximenes mistakenly written "Alexander" for "Philip"? Arguments have been offered for all four candidates with no certain conclusion.[19] Alexander II's reign was short, but the fact is in 358 Philip levied 10,000 foot for battle against the Illyrians, by which date he had had hardly more time than his brother to institute major reforms.[20]

We have too little information to reconstruct clearly the development of Macedonian military power before Philip or in fact even during his reign. It is a mistake, however, to assume that it all began with Philip. The cavalry was effective throughout the fifth century, and while the infantry was later in development, it appears to have been a substantial force in the time of Perdiccas III. About Perdiccas III we know very little other than that he established a garrison at Amphipolis and was killed in battle along with 4,000 of his troops. And Perdiccas seems to have granted to Philip, when he returned from his hostageship at Thebes with valuable first-hand knowledge of the tactics of two of the greatest military commanders of the era, Epaminondas and Pelopidas, the authority to put this knowledge to good use.[21]

Philip II's military reforms and innovations

Immediately upon Perdiccas' death Philip undertook the reorganization and training of the army.[22] Recruitment was the first order, to replace the recent casualties; next came outfitting, since most recruits would have been herdsmen and farmers and unlikely to be able to afford their own arms; and then Philip applied rigorous conditioning to get the soldiers in fighting trim. Marches of 300 stades (56 km, or 35 miles) carrying arms and kit—helmets, shields, greaves, and spears as well as food and utensils—were instituted to accustom the troops to the hardships of campaign. Some of these early recruits were outfitted as peltasts, a type of light-infantry style adopted from the Thracians. Peltasts were distinguished by their smaller shield (*pelte*), and because they were lighter equipped (Philip's light infantry even lacked the weight of a breastplate) they were more mobile than the heavy-armed hoplites of a traditional Greek phalanx.[23] One of Philip's objectives in consolidating Upper and Lower Macedonia was to strengthen his military capacity. Through his marriage to the Elimiote princess Phila presumably he was able to assimilate into his forces the reputable Elimiote cavalry, but consolidation also broadened his recruitment catchment for infantry.

Philip's great innovation in weaponry was the *sarissa*, a pike varying in length from 4.5 to 5.5 m (15 to 18 ft) (Figure 5.1). *Sarissai* had wooden shafts with iron tips at both ends: at the head a heavy point and at its butt end a slightly lighter point, which, in addition to the practical functions of counter weight to the heavy weapon head and spare fighting point in the case of a broken head, was planted in the ground for better stability against an enemy attack, especially against the momentum of cavalry.[24] Finds from the tombs at Vergina have suggested that some *sarissai* were constructed in two pieces, with an iron fitting to

Figure 5.1 Modern *Sarissa* monument, Thessaloniki waterfront
Source: author, 2014.

attach them midway down the shaft; this allowed them to be dismantled for easier transport during long marches and then reassembled for battle, while the fitting also helped to keep the long wooden shaft from bowing.[25] Though some shafts may have been made of ash, the harder cornel from the Macedonian forests seems to have been more commonly used.[26] At what date Philip introduced the *sarissa* to the panoply of his infantry we do not know. Despite an abundance of weapons, including spearheads, butt-pikes, arrowheads, and sling bullets found at Olynthus and dating to Philip's siege of 349–348, no *sarissa* points have been indisputably identified.[27] The earliest archaeological evidence comes from one of the mass graves at the battlefield of Chaeronea, though it was likely quite long in use by that late date.

The effect of the innovation, whenever it was introduced, was tremendous, for initially at about double the length of the hoplite spear the *sarissa*-armed Macedonian phalanx had the advantage over a regular hoplite phalanx by distancing themselves 2.5 m (8 ft) or so from the first row of spear points of the enemy line while two rows of their own points were already finding flesh.

By the end of the fourth century some *sarissai* measured as long as 6 m (20 ft),[28] but the increased length rendered the *sarissa* almost too unwieldy to be effective, and it could at times be a serious impediment. The total weight of the *sarissa*, depending on variations in length and point weights, is estimated at 5.5 to 6.5 kg (12 to 14.5 lbs), about seven times heavier than a traditional hoplite spear.[29] Two hands were required to wield these long and heavy weapons, which meant that for the *sarissa*-bearer a regular *hoplon* shield with an armband in the centre of the concave and a handgrip inside the rim was impossible to manage. So a smaller lighter shield, measuring roughly 70 cm (24 in) in diameter to the *hoplon*'s 95 cm (30 in), was used since it could be slung over the left shoulder by a strap (*telamon*).[30] While probably initially it was for economic reasons that the light infantry were not outfitted with breastplates, Philip's innovation to the pike rendered chest protection virtually unnecessary anyway.[31] While the great strength of the *sarissa*-armed phalanx was the five-deep (or six-) serried hedge of armour-piercing pike points projecting in front of the first line of infantrymen,[32] its weakness was that the formation, encumbered by the long pikes boxing each infantryman into his tight position, was extremely difficult to manoeuvre and only effective on level ground. It was disastrously vulnerable if forced away from ideal terrain and unprotected by light cavalry or other light troops (slingers or archers) on its flanks.[33]

In addition to Macedonian forces who made up the *pezhetairoi* Foot Companions and *hetairoi* Companion Cavalry Philip incorporated Greek and non-Greek allies and subject peoples, notably skirmishers from the Paeonians and Agrianians. He also hired mercenary soldiers, using these especially for garrison duty.[34] Philip's political position in Thessaly put at his disposal a large number of Thessalian forces. The numbers recorded for his victory in Thessaly over the Phocians in 352 are 20,000 infantry and 3,000 cavalry.[35] These numbers indicate that in hardly more than half a dozen years Philip more than doubled his available manpower for war. A rare glimpse into the composition of his army comes from a comment of Demosthenes made in 341 during the final Thracian campaign: "you hear of Philip marching unchecked, not because he leads a phalanx of heavy infantry, but because he is accompanied by skirmishers, cavalry, archers, mercenaries and similar troops."[36] While during his reign more and more Macedonians were actually armed and trained as heavy infantry, most of these probably were not as heavily armed as the typical hoplite, and heavy infantry was not Philip's primary fighting force. A mobile standing army was what Philip needed and developed over time as he became increasingly more involved in affairs outside Macedonia and more ambitious in his imperialistic aims.[37]

Philip's great tactical innovation was the cavalry wedge formation, an adaptation of the 'diamond' used by Jason of Pherae and of the Scythian and Thracian 'wedge'. Philip is credited with being first to use the wedge to cut through a hoplite phalanx, and it is a widely held assumption that a charge of the Companion Cavalry in wedge formation against the elite infantry of the Theban Sacred Band on the Greek allied right was the winning stroke at Chaeronea. The implication of the claim of Chaeronea native Plutarch that the Sacred

Band fell facing the Macedonian *sarissa* suggests that Philip's cavalry must have been armed with *sarissai* in that battle, too, though some historians seriously contest this.[38]

In the latter part of Philip's reign significant advances were being made in siege warfare. We have no details about the types of engine Philip used for his successful sieges of Amphipolis, Pydna, and Methone, and while excavations at Olynthus have yielded a few catapult bolt-heads bearing the unmistakable stamp ΦΙΛΙΠΠΟ (Philip's), it was treachery that achieved that city's capture. It is very likely, however, that during the siege of Olynthus Philip was experimenting with new engines.[39] In 353 he had lost not only a battle but also the confidence of his troops when they came under the heavy artillery fire (stone-throwers) of the Phocians, and it is suggested that this defeat was the prompt for Philip to hire an engineer and to invest resources in artillery design.[40] Some fifty years earlier Dionysius of Syracuse had introduced the catapult into Greek warfare,[41] but it seems most probable that it was in Macedonia that the torsion catapult was designed. This was first employed at Byzantium in 340–339, after Philip had nearly given up on his unsuccessful siege of Perinthus. For the latter we have our only detailed description of Philip's siege techniques, but most of the equipment mentioned would have been long in use: scaling ladders (*klimakes*), battering rams (*krioi*), arrow-shooting catapults (*oxybeleis*) "many and varied," missiles (*beleis*), siege engines (*mechanai poliorketikai*), and siege towers (*pyrgoi*), these at 36.5 m (120 ft) high towering over the walls of Perinthus.[42] During the siege of Byzantium Philip's chief engineer, the Thessalian Polyidus, tested a fledgling torsion catapult,[43] but Byzantium's defences and defenders withstood the assault. The fine-tuning of siege techniques was left to Alexander III and his corps of engineers.

In support of Philip's sieges of Perinthus and Byzantium a fleet of some sort, albeit ineffective against the Athenian naval presence at the Hellespont, offered protection and probably brought supplies to Philip's land forces.[44] No firm evidence puts the Macedonians at sea before Philip II, yet to assume that Philip was the first Macedonian king to develop a fleet is an argument from silence.[45] Considering that ship timber was ever abundant and shipwrights must always have been at hand, it is conceivable that the development of a naval force was part of Archelaus' plan when moving the royal seat from inland Aegae to Pella, with its access to the sea. The general weakness of Macedonia's military strength for the next forty years, however, would have crippled progress. Only six years into Philip's reign we hear of him having a fleet of "many ships," according to a Macedonian author of military stratagems, Polyaenus, who describes an episode near Neapolis, opposite Thasos, when Philip avoided a naval battle with "twenty triremes" under command of the Athenian Chares.[46] The contrast between Philip's "many" and Chares' "twenty" ships could suggest that the Macedonians had more than twenty, but given that they were no match for triremes these were very likely pentaconters and triaconters, small and fast ships such as used for piratical raids (Philip was returning from a raid at the time).[47] Philip sent his four lightest and fastest ships out to sea as a decoy, and when

Chares went in hot pursuit Philip got the rest of his fleet safely away, while Chares failed to catch the other four. Even if only to protect commercial shipping, a naval force of sorts probably already existed before Philip, but he certainly expanded Macedonia's naval capacity. In addition to acquiring dockyards at Amphipolis, Methone, and other ports Philip almost certainly also had dockyards at Pella.[48] And Demosthenes gives due warning of his ongoing shipbuilding and naval activities, marking a progression from piratical raids to the construction of triremes.[49]

Along with reforms to weapons and tactics Philip also is responsible for an important reform involving the *paides basilikoi*, or Royal Pages. This institution prepared the youths of the upper class for social integration into the ranks of the king's *hetairoi* (Companions) and in this respect it may have been an age-old custom, possibly influenced by the Achaemenid practice of having the sons of Persian nobles raised at the king's court.[50] The story of Archelaus' demise is suggestive of *paides* at court by the end of the fifth century,[51] so the institution is possibly not Philip's creation. However, its evolution may have been significantly influenced by Philip's personal experience as a hostage in Thebes during his adolescent years. These young sons of nobles were 'hostage' in the sense that their residence at court obligated the good behaviour of their fathers,[52] and this would have been critical in the process of Philip's consolidation of Upper and Lower Macedonia, when some of the Upper Macedonian elite would have been of questionable loyalty. Moreover, to meet the demands of Philip's increased military activity, the institution of the *paides* provided a training ground for young officers by preparing them to take on various roles of command within the military structure once they reached the age of service, probably at eighteen.[53] They were the king's men, his servants, and rigid military discipline and obedience to the king were strictly enforced. When one of Philip's *paides* broke rank to get a drink because he was thirsty Philip had him flogged; another he executed for disarming after he had given the youth a direct order to remain under arms.[54] Another means of securing the loyalty of the nobles while simultaneously strengthening the military infrastructure was the gift of land grants, these being given generously to men who displayed the ambition and competence to assume important commands in the army.[55]

By the time of Philip's death Macedonia boasted a professional standing army that was capable of marching wherever and whenever the king wished, summer or winter,[56] and it had already proved to be the supreme fighting force in the central and southern Balkans.

Alexander III and the Macedonian army

The units of the Macedonian army that are best known from Alexander III's reign were already in place when he came to the throne in 336: the *hetairoi* Companion Cavalry; the *pezhetairoi* Foot Companions of the phalanx; the Hypaspist infantry guards; the Thessalian Cavalry; Thracian, Paeonian, and Agrianian scouts and skirmishers; and the Cretan archers.[57] It was essentially this army of Philip that Alexander led on his Balkan campaign against the Triballians and Illyrians when they seized the opportunity of Philip's assassination to revolt.[58] That campaign postponed by about a year and a half the resumption of Philip's plan for a war against Persia, and whether Alexander made any significant changes to Philip's military organization in the interim is questionable. Once Alexander embarked on the Asian expedition, over the next eleven years he made substantial innovations to both cavalry and infantry as well as to siege warfare and the naval program. Many changes were dictated by terrain and by the methods of warfare of the peoples he encountered. Sieges and guerrilla fighting became the norm, and his army actually fought only four set battles: at the Granicus River, near the Hellespont (Dardanelles), in 334 against the satraps and generals of the Persian king Darius; at Issus, on the Syrian coast, in 333 against Darius; at Gaugamela, near ancient Nineveh (northern Iraq), in 331 against Darius again; and at the Hydaspes River, in the Indus Valley (Punjab), in 326 against Porus.

When Alexander set out for Asia in the spring of 334 he took with him 12,000 Macedonian infantry and 1,800 Macedonian cavalry, while another 12,000 infantry and 1,500 cavalry remained in Macedonia with Antipater to defend the homeland.[59] The allies (Greek city-state members of the League of Corinth) contributed another 7,000 foot, the mercenaries 5,000, and these together with the Macedonian infantry were all under the command of Parmenio, Philip's long-time tried and trusted general who had led the advance force into Asia Minor and established the bridgehead. Of the subject peoples, Odrysians, Triballians, and Illyrians numbered 7,000 combined and Agrianians 1,000, for a total infantry force of 32,000. In addition to the 1,800 Macedonian cavalry there were the same number of Thessalian cavalry, 600 allied Greek cavalry, and 900 Thracian and Paeonian *prodromoi*, or mounted scouts.[60]

At the outset of the campaign Alexander's Companion Cavalry was organized in eight squadrons or *ilai*, each *ile* led by an *ilarches*, or cavalry officer.[61] Seven of the squadrons, if figures given for earlier periods are any indication (multiples of 200), consisted of 200 horsemen each, while the eighth squadron, the *basilike ile*, or Royal Squadron, perhaps comprised the remaining 400 of the total 1,800.[62] These squadrons also often fought in sub-units, depending on terrain.[63] Though there were several other *ilai* of cavalrymen called *sarissophoroi* who carried a lighter weight *sarissa* and probably did not wear a breastplate (they were not Companions, perhaps not even Macedonian),[64] the main cavalry force likely wielded the *xyston*, a thrusting lance which would have been less cumbersome than the two-handed *sarissa*, and unlike the *sarissa* it did not have a butt end but rather a second spearhead.[65] Originally, squadrons were organized by tribe or territory. The squadrons from Bottiaea and Amphipolis led the cavalry strike in the battle with the Triballians in 335;[66] the squadron from Apollonia led the first cavalry charge at the Granicus;[67] and the squadron from Anthemous and the so-called Leugaian squadron (otherwise unknown) were instructed to cover Darius' flanking move on the right at Issus.[68]

As the Companion cavalrymen were of the land-owning class, the ilarchs would have been members of the most prestigious Macedonian families. Cleitus "the Black" was the most distinguished of the ilarchs, for he commanded the Royal Squadron. Nothing is known about his father, Dropidas, but his sister Lanice was Alexander's wet nurse,[69] so the family must have been in highest regard. Cleitus was fighting nearest the king in the first battle on Asian soil at the Granicus when two Persian nobles charged Alexander at the same time from different angles; and after one struck the king a heavy blow on the helmet, splitting it in two, Cleitus severed the arm of the other just as he was poised to strike, thus saving the king's life.[70] One of the sons of the illustrious Parmenio, Philotas, was overall commander until 330 of Alexander's Companion Cavalry.[71] Philotas fought under Alexander in the Balkan campaign in 335 as commander of cavalry from Upper Macedonia, and before that he had been high in Philip's esteem.[72] Aside from Parmenio's own role as commander of the entire left wing, command of the Companion Cavalry was the most prestigious position within the army.

After Alexander's final victory over Darius at Gaugamela in 331, when reinforcements arrived from Macedonia, the cavalry *ilai* were each divided into two *lochoi*, or companies (these had existed previously for infantry but not for horse), each under the command of a *lochagos*, or company-captain.[73] Subsequent reorganization of cavalry may have been a practical adaptation to changing battle conditions—from pitched battles to long pursuits and guerrilla fighting—or it may reflect the incorporation into the Companion Cavalry of non-Macedonians from conquered territory, necessitated by attrition.[74] By the time Alexander reached India in 327 the royal squadron numbered 300. It is sometimes referred to as the *agema* (guards), a name also used for elite infantry that continued in use under the Successors.[75] At this time we also begin to hear of cavalry *hipparchiai* (brigades or regiments).[76] At the battle at the Hydaspes in 326 five *hipparchiai* are mentioned in addition to the *agema*,[77] but it is unclear whether these six cavalry units replaced the former eight *ilai* or whether the *ilai* were somehow subsumed into the hipparchy structure. Of the eight ilarchs in command at Gaugamela only one (Demetrius) reappears as *hipparches* (brigade commander), all the others perhaps having been killed, wounded, or possibly reappointed.[78] The new hipparchs included some of Alexander's closest personal friends: Hephaestion, Craterus, Perdiccas, and Coenus.[79] Perdiccas and Coenus had already proved their worth as infantry commanders before the Asian expedition began and Craterus, if not before, then from the battle at the Granicus, while Hephaestion perhaps not until Gaugamela or later.[80] Soon after the Hydaspes battle Cleitus "the White" appears as a hipparch,[81] possibly replacing Coenus, who died around that time. When Alexander's favorite, Hephaestion, died in 324 no one was officially appointed to replace him as hipparch, and the hipparchy retained the name "Hephaestion's."[82]

A magnificent painting of a cavalryman dating from the time of Alexander's Successors, late fourth or early third century, was discovered in 1887 on the inner wall of a Macedonian tomb at Lefkadia, near ancient Mieza: the so-called Kinch Tomb, named for the Danish architect who first studied and sketched it (Figure 5.2). The painting itself faded after exposure, so it survives only in the coloured sketch which Kinch made of it at the time. The rider in flowing

Figure 5.2 Kinch Tomb, drawing of a wall painting, Lefkadia, 310–290 BCE

Source: redrawn by Erika Stonehouse, 2016.

Figure 5.3 Alexander Sarcophagus, Sidon, end of fourth century BCE. Istanbul Archaeological Museums, Turkey

Source: http://visionforanewworld.com/pictures/olympus-digital-camera-8/.

chlamys cloak wields a leveled cavalry *xyston* as the horse in full gallop charges a Persian foot soldier holding a round shield with the 'Vergina sun' embossed on its face. The cavalryman wears a helmet but no breastplate and uses only an animal skin for a saddle. Although the horseman's legs and feet were already lost when Kinch first discovered the painting, ample evidence found in other representations indicates that cavalrymen did not use stirrups.[83] Coincidentally, a group of sarcophagi was also discovered in 1887 in a necropolis at Sidon in Lebanon, among them the now famous so-called Alexander Sarcophagus (Figure 5.3). Bas-reliefs on the sarcophagus depict Alexander and other (stirrup-less) cavalrymen in both battle and hunting scenes together with the dead man whom the carvings honor. It has long been thought he is the last king of Sidon, Abdalonymus, who was installed on the throne in 332 by Hephaestion on Alexander's order, though this view has been challenged.[84] The depictions of the horsemen are more stylized than in the painting, with the *chlamys* cloak used to great artistic effect. Evidence suggests that a purple or purple-bordered *chlamys* was a mark of distinction for the Companions.[85] In the left-side view of the Macedonian horseman far right the *kopis* (curved blade) or *xiphos* (straight double blade) short sword, such as Alexander carried at Gaugamela,[86] is visible in its sheath, and he wears the Boeotian style helmet (Figure 5.4).

In deployment for Alexander's great battles the Companion Cavalry were stationed on the right wing, over which Alexander himself held command. Protecting their flank were light cavalry, the Paeonian lancers and the *prodromoi*; the latter are to be equated with the *sarissophoroi* lancers, mentioned above.[87]

Figure 5.4 Boeotian bronze helmet, found in the Tigris River, Iraq, late fourth century BCE. Ashmolean Museum, Oxford, UK

Source: https://en.wikipedia.org/wiki/Boeotian_helmet#/media/File:Boeotian_helmet.jpg.

On the left wing under Parmenio's overall command (until 330) were the Thessalian, Thracian, and Greek heavy cavalry, but at the Granicus the commanders of all three units were very likely high-status Macedonians, judging from their Macedonian patronyms.[88] The mounted Companions were the strike force, and the job was highly paid.[89] The *prodromoi* and the Paeonian lancers, probably four squadrons of the former and one of the latter, were commanded at the Granicus by a Macedonian from Lyncus, Amyntas, son of Arrhabaeus,[90] though the Paeonian squadron itself was under the command of Ariston, certainly a Paeonian and probably royal.[91] So both high-status Macedonian nobles and allied kings were incorporated into Alexander's officer corps, where he could keep his eye on them.[92] The *prodromoi* scouts are last heard of during the campaign against the Scythians in 329,[93] after which they may have been incorporated into the Companion Cavalry.

Occupying the center of the Macedonian battle-line in full deployment was the phalanx of *pezhetairoi*, and to their immediate right the Hypaspists.[94] The heavy infantry were similar to Greek hoplites, and like hoplites they sometimes fought independent of cavalry in terrain where cavalry was ineffective.[95] But, as noted above, most of them were lighter equipped, having no breastplate and a smaller shield, though archaeological evidence suggests some Macedonian foot used the *hoplon*.[96] Lighter equipment allowed them to be much more manoeuvrable than a hoplite phalanx, or at least until later in the Hellenistic period when the *sarissa* became so elongated as to be cumbersome and restrictive. Smart manoeuvring was possible because the battalions of infantry were subdivided into *lochoi* and *dekades* (Alexander later increased *dekades* from ten men to sixteen), all highly trained from the time of Philip.[97] The *pezhetairoi*, like the Companion Cavalry, were originally organized territorially in battalions, or *taxeis*, each *taxis* consisting of approximately 1,500 men. (*Taxis* is the usual term for a unit of infantry, but it can be used of any formation.) Of the six *taxeis* Alexander took east in 334 at least three were from Upper Macedonia: one from Elimeia under the command of Coenus, one from Orestis and Lyncus commanded by Perdiccas, and a Tymphaean *taxis*, which by 331 was under the command of Polyperchon.[98] Two of the remaining taxiarchs were also Upper Macedonian, Amyntas (son of Andromenes) from Tymphaea and Craterus from Orestis, but the place of origin of the troops in their *taxeis* is not known. Amyntas in 331 was commanding "foreign" foot, though 6,000 infantry reinforcements arriving at that time were distributed in *taxeis* according to region of origin.[99] By the time Alexander invaded India a seventh battalion had been added.[100] The sixth *taxiarches*, Meleager (son of Neoptolemus), was possibly from Epirus. The composition of the six (or more) *taxeis* that stayed behind with Antipater is unknown. The infantry battalions that *were* from Upper Macedonia, such as the one commanded first by Coenus and later by Peithon, were specially designated *asthetairoi*, an obscure term that has been variously explained; possibly they had special training or equipment, such as a shield with distinctive device.[101]

For both the infantry and cavalry units there was a daily rotating command, so that on different days different commanders had opportunity to demonstrate skill in leadership as well as bravery and possibly earn reward.[102] Since Craterus, Perdiccas, and Coenus, after the reforms to the cavalry, were promoted to *hipparches*, well before the battle at the Hydaspes new commanders of *pezhetairoi* appear: Attalus, Gorgias, Cleitus the White, and Alcetas (brother of Perdiccas).[103]

The remaining 3,000 of the Macedonian infantry were Hypaspists (shield-bearers). They seem to have evolved out of the king's personal guard, the original *pezhetairoi*, and being 'elite' in size and strength they were not recruited by territory. They formed a distinct corps, and like the Companion Cavalry they had a royal battalion or *agema*,[104] 1,000 strong, and two more divisions of 1,000, which perhaps were organized in sub-units of 500.[105] The Hypaspists fought on the right near the king in the set battles and as shock troops on other campaigns. Parmenio's son Nicanor commanded Alexander's Hypaspists from the Balkan campaign until his death in 330, and later at the Hydaspes they were under the command of Seleucus (later founder of the Seleucid Dynasty). At some point, perhaps during the Indian campaign, as a mark of distinction and reward for outstanding service the Hypaspist veterans were given special shields with silver ornamentation, and from this they took the title *Argyraspides*, or Silver Shields.[106]

The Hypaspists, or the *agema* of Hypaspists, are sometimes referred to as *somatophylakes*, bodyguards of the king, and probably they had responsibility for security at his quarters in camp.[107] This term also often refers to an elite group of only seven men, the most elite group of all, *the* Bodyguards, the king's closest Companions and his intimate advisors.[108] The elite Seven Bodyguards were responsible for the protection of the king both on and off the battlefield, though certainly this was not their exclusive role, and they were not *all* at his side always. When Alexander personally came under heavy fire while attacking a town in the territory of the Mallians, reputedly the most warlike of the tribes in India, only one *somatophylax*, Leonnatus, was at his side to protect him. A second Bodyguard, Aristonus, arrived on the scene after the king was wounded.[109] However, two, Ptolemy (later founder of the Ptolemaic Dynasty) and Hephaestion, were off leading forces elsewhere,[110] likewise perhaps Peithon, while Lysimachus may have still been recovering from a serious wound received in the siege of Sangala.[111] Perdiccas also was present at the town, but Alexander had split the attack forces and Perdiccas was in command of the other half. It is clear here (and during the Bactrian campaign) that the Bodyguards of Alexander in addition to protecting and advising the king also commanded independent forces and expeditions.

The Mallian episode is one of the most colourful and famous of the entire eastern campaign. Alexander, though gravely wounded, drew criticism from his Companions for deliberately putting himself, and consequently his entire army, at grave risk.[112] Frustrated with the slow action of his Macedonians towards the assault, Alexander grabbed hold of a scaling ladder and throwing it up against the town wall went up crouched under his shield. Behind him went Peucestas, a Royal Hypaspist, carrying the sacred shield, this being the one Alexander took from the temple of Athena at Troy when he crossed into Asia.[113] It was a kind of talisman, an 850-year-old relic of Alexander's ancestor Achilles, or at least it symbolized that heroic ancestry. Third up the same ladder went one of the Bodyguards, Leonnatus, and by another ladder a 'double-pay' soldier called Abreas, or in another version Limnaeus, another Royal Hypaspist.[114] Then in full sight of both his own tardy troops and the town's defiant defenders the Macedonian king stood exposed on the wall. The Hypaspists scrambled to get up on the wall to protect the king, but in their mad haste they broke the ladders, the men attempting to climb fell to the ground, and the others had no means at hand to scale the wall. As he stood there in a hail of enemy fire the thought came to Alexander (says our source) that to remain where he was would be dangerous, but if he jumped down into the town he might accomplish heroic deeds worthy of remembrance![115] And jump he did, while the Hypaspists looked on in desperation. The three men on the wall with Alexander all jumped down after him. As they all came under heavy close-range fire, Abreas/Limnaeus[116] was struck in the face by an arrow and killed, and Alexander was also struck, the arrow piercing his corselet and puncturing his lung, air and blood mixing together round the shaft with each exhale. Leonnatus and Peucestas, soon joined by Aristonus, stood covering the king,[117] who was now slumped over his shield in a faint from loss of blood, trying to protect him with their shields against hordes of townsmen who, in turn, were defending their lives, their citadel, and their women and children against these Macedonian invaders. Finally a few Hypaspists got over the wall, some using climbing pegs and others hoisting each other on their shoulders, and rushed to the rescue of the king and his heroic defenders, themselves all now suffering wounds. Others broke open the gate and went for the townspeople; men, women, and children alike paid the price for Alexander's bold leap. No mercy this day.

Rumor spread like wildfire that the king was dead, the greatest fear for the Macedonian soldiers. It was tradition for the Macedonian king to lead his army into battle, to fight usually in the van or at the very least alongside his men. One imagines that is how Perdiccas III met his end on the Illyrian frontier, and it is certainly how Philip II lost his right eye and got a game leg. This was only one of many wounds Alexander received in the course of the campaign as he took his risks along with the rest.[118] Professional medical personnel were never far from the field of battle,[119] and it was expedient that some medics also be fighting men, or that fighting men also be adept at emergency medical procedures; in fact, Alexander himself was well educated in the healing arts.[120] Perdiccas was possibly first to give Alexander medical attention,[121] then once the king was transported to his tent one of the army doctors cut the barbed arrowhead, about 5 × 7.5 cm (2 × 3 in), from the wound.[122] Sources do not agree on the doctor's name, but if Critobulus is to be preferred over Critodemus,[123] then it is possible that he was the same physician who had cut the arrow out of Philip's eye at Methone in 354.[124] Alexander, a man very hard to keep down, was laid up a mere seven days before he re-embarked on his voyage down the Indus so he could put to the lie as quickly as possible the rumors of his death.[125] This was critical in the circumstances and indicative of Alexander's generalship, for the natives would be quick to revolt if they believed him dead, while the Macedonian army, despite having many competent officers who proved to be excellent generals in their own right, feared being left leaderless deep in enemy territory. The bravery and loyalty to the king of Peucestas especially are exemplary of Macedonian military ethos, and he was subsequently crowned with a gold wreath (Figure 5.5) and made an honorary eighth Bodyguard.[126]

The siege of the nameless Mallian town was in some respects like countless other sieges the Macedonians carried out, although it was more a storming than a siege with no siege equipment at hand apart from a few ladders,[127] and it was over quickly. Well before this date one of Alexander's engineers, Diades (who along with Charias was a student of Polyidus), had invented mobile siege towers for use by Alexander's army. These could be taken apart in sections and transported for reuse.[128] They had been used for the siege of Miletus and subsequently transported to Halicarnassus, dismantled, taken to the Syrian coast for use in the seven-month-long siege of Tyre, and transported again from there to Gaza.[129] At Gaza, though, and other sandy places the Macedonian army found it more effective to use sapping operations to undermine the walls and create breaches by collapse. The defenders of Gaza thought their position impregnable, but no position could hold out against the Macedonian army at the gate.

Figure 5.5 Gold oak-leaf wreath (one of many found in Macedonian tombs), Amphipolis, end of fourth century BCE

Source: author, 2011.

Most of Alexander's Asian campaign kept him away from the sea. However, a Macedonian navy remained active in the Aegean helping to keep supply and communication lines open and transporting new recruits from various points in the Balkan peninsula across to the Asian coast. Philip's advance force had gained naval control of the Hellespont before Alexander took the main army across,[130] and it was with a Macedonian fleet of sixty warships in addition to a Greek fleet of 160 that Alexander sailed in 334.[131] The latter fleet was disbanded later in 334, but within months Alexander realized his mistake, reconstituted his Greek fleet, and then in 332, during the siege of Tyre, he acquired a large fleet when the Cypriot kings with their ships went over to his side. The capture of Tyre was achieved by a combination of siege equipment and fleet, with the ships used to platform the engines and bring them in close to the fortress walls. When his campaign took him away from the sea ships often were cut apart, transported, and reassembled. At the Indus Alexander had new ships built for the crossing; of these the triaconters were larger, having to be cut into three sections for portage to the Hydaspes, while the "shorter" boats were cut in two.[132] When Alexander began his great voyage down the Indus Nearchus (of Cretan origin) was appointed admiral of the whole fleet, Oneisicritus (a Greek islander of Aegina or Astypalaea) helmsman of Alexander's ship, and the trierarchs, or financiers of *ships* (evidently there were no triremes), were all, with the exception of the Persian Bagoas, Macedonian or Greek.[133] The ships' crews, however, were not Macedonian; rather they were Phoenicians, Cypriots, Carians, and Egyptians who had joined the expedition, as well as some Greek islanders.[134] The flotilla included eighty *triacontoroi*, an unspecified number of *hemioliai*, some 200 *aphractoi* ("open" ships), horse transports and *kerkouroi* (merchant ships), and various other transport vessels.[135] Essentially, the fleet served as a floating, mobile fortress on the long route to the sea through extremely hostile territory. We have no record of the composition of the Indian Ocean fleet, but none of those ships, so far as we know, engaged in naval combat. When Alexander returned to Babylon both the fleet of Nearchus and another fleet he had summoned from Phoenicia were already present, Nearchus' having sailed up the Euphrates and the latter having been broken up and brought overland from the Phoenician coast to Thapsacus, put back together, and sailed down to Babylon; these included two Phoenician quinqueremes, three quadriremes, twelve triremes, and about thirty *triacontoroi*. At the time of his death Alexander was in the process of building a third fleet at Babylon from Babylonian cypresses, crews for which were being brought from Phoenicia and the rest of the coast, with the ultimate goal of 1,000 ships of war using Babylon as home port.[136] Picking up from Alexander's abruptly extinguished ambitions, his Successors soon made astonishing advances in naval design, and great sea battles would be a hallmark of the Hellenistic period.[137]

By the time of Alexander's death the nature of the Macedonian army had already undergone major changes. Many Asiatics, tens of thousands, had been incorporated or absorbed into the army, many of them integrated into formerly purely Macedonian units. At Opis on the Tigris in 324 the *Epigoni*, 30,000 Persian youths trained in Macedonian warfare and outfitted in Macedonian equipment, were introduced into the phalanx.[138] And the war elephant had been adopted during the Indian campaign, so the battle-line had a different face, the elephant now for the first time becoming a 'weapon' in Macedonian and Greek warfare.[139] After Alexander's death the Macedonian army at Babylon immediately began to fragment, beginning with a violent rift between the Companion Cavalry and the increasingly unruly infantry, and soon various troop contingents were allocated to various satraps in far-flung corners of the now vast empire. In the armies of the Successors the Macedonian fighting units were soon in the minority, though like Alexander's *Epigoni* many native troops in these armies were trained in Macedonian tactics and arms.

The greatest innovations to warfare after Alexander came in naval and siege craft, which together with the composite Hellenistic armies we will encounter in later chapters.[140] Suffice it to say here that long after the wars of the Successors were over it was still customary for the Hellenistic kings to have Macedonian or Macedonian-trained units in their armies. Even as late as 202 a Macedonian phalanx fought on Hannibal's side at Zama.[141] As for the armies of the subsequent kings of Macedonia, we know little about composition and structure. The Companion Cavalry is less important, and the heavy phalanx is the principal unit. The historian Polybius draws a comparison between the Roman legion and the Macedonian phalanx when he gives, in his opinion, the reason for the defeat of Philip V's army by Flamininus in 197 at Cynoscephalae. As he concludes:

> I thought it necessary to speak on this subject at some length because many Greeks on the actual occasions when the Macedonians suffered defeat considered the event as almost incredible, and many will still continue to wonder why and how the phalanx comes to be conquered by troops armed in the Roman fashion.[142]

Perseus' defeat to Roman legions at Pydna three decades later marks the end of the long supremacy of the Macedonian phalanx. But let us now turn to Alexander III.

Notes

1 Sekunda 2010: 448. On the court aspect of the *hetairoi*, especially in the time of Alexander III, see Borza 1983/1995 and Heckel 2003a. On cavalry equipment see Karunanithy 2013: 81–99.
2 Compare the treaty between Perdiccas II and Athens, containing about eighty-five oath-takers, *IG* I³ 89. King 2010: 383–384.
3 Hdt. 9.31.5, 9.44, cf. 7.185, 196, 9.69.
4 Thuc. 1.61.4, 62.2–4, 63.2. See Chapter 2.
5 Thuc. 2.98, 100.5.
6 Thuc. 4.124.1. See Chapter 2 n109.
7 Thuc. 1.114.3; Str. 10.1.3; Paus. 7.25.6.
8 Hammond in *HM* II: 1979: 146.
9 Archelaus: Thuc. 2.100.2. Perdiccas: Thuc. 4.124.1, 125.1.

10 Polyaen. 2.1.17.
11 Xen. *Hell.* 5.2.38; Diod. 15.19.3. See Chapter 3.
12 Xen. *Hell.* 5.2.40–3.2. See Chapter 3.
13 This vexing passage survives from the lost *Philippica* of Anaximenes of Lampsakos, an orator and historian contemporary with Philip II and Alexander III: Anaximenes *FGrH/BNJ* 72 F4, cited by Harpocration and the *Suda* s.v. "pezhetairoi." See Anson 2009b; cp. Greenwalt 2017.
14 Greenwalt 2007 argues for a rising middle class and development of Macedonian hoplite infantry during the reigns of Archelaus, Amyntas III, and Alexander II.
15 Theopompus in his *Philippica* [*FGrH/BNJ* 115 F348], quoted by a scholiast to Dem. 2.17; like the fragment of Anaximenes cited by Harpocration it is taken out of context. On the hazards of lost context see Develin 1985: 496 and Erskine 1989: 391.
16 Anson 2009b: 89, 92, *contra* Erskine 1989: 393–394.
17 Arr. *Anab.* 1.28.3, 7.2.1, 7.11.3.
18 Dem. 2.17.
19 E.g. Alexander I: Brunt 1976: 151 and Sekunda 2010: 447; Alexander II: Milns 1967, Bosworth 1973: 245, 250, and Greenwalt 2017: 81–84; Alexander III: Griffith in *HM* II 1979: 406, 705–709 and Develin 1985: 496; and Philip II: Cawkwell 1978: 30–33 and Anson 1985a, 2009b. One could even argue for Archelaus. See discussion of Williams 2013 [*BNJ* s.v. Anaximenes 72 F4] summarizing the arguments [Bosworth 1973 correctly is "'Ἀσθεταίροι," and add Erskine 1989]. Anaximenes attributes both the training of cavalry and the division of infantry with overall designation *pezhetairoi* to the same 'Alexander', though perhaps all these reforms are not attributable to one individual.
20 Ellis 1976: 53. Cf. Diod. 16.4.3. Brunt 1976: 153: the reforms must predate Philip. The reference does occur in the *first* book of Anaximenes' history, where he was most likely to have given background to his history of Philip (cf. F5, F27), so Greenwalt 2017: 83. But cp. Develin 1985: 494; Anson 2008a: 17–18.
21 Ath. 11.506e–f. Worthington 2008: 26: Philip was already instituting reforms under Perdiccas.
22 Diod. 16.3.1–2; Arr. *Anab.* 7.9.2; Polyaen. 4.2.10.
23 On infantry equipment see Karunanithy 2013: 100–115.
24 Butt: Markle 1977: 323–324; Manti 1994: 77. Evidence for varying *sarissa* lengths: from 4.5 m/15 ft to 5.5 m/18 ft (Asclepiodotus *Tactica.* 5.1; Theophr. *Hist. pl.* 3.12.2); cf. also Arr. *Tactica* 12; Aelian *Tactica* 12. For detailed studies of the *sarissa* see Andronikos 1970; Markle 1977, 1978; Manti 1994; Sekunda 2001 (challenging the standard view of size and weight).
25 Andronikos 1970: 106: the suggestion is challenged but not disproved.
26 Cornel: Markle 1977: 324; see Theophr. *Hist. pl.* 3.12.2 and Arr. *Anab.* 1.15.5. Sekunda 2001: 22–25 and 2010: 450 argues that ash was used primarily. If Markle is correct that *sarissa* shafts were constructed in two sections, then Sekunda's argument that cornel did not grow tall enough to supply the necessary length loses conviction, and Sekunda himself admits that ash has a tendency to warp.
27 Markle 1978: 487; Sekunda 2001: 16. See Chapter 4 n22.
28 Polyaen. 2.29.2.
29 Markle 1977: 324–325.
30 Markle 1999: 219–220, 246–51; 1978: 492: "two-foot targets." Polyaen. 4.2.10: *peltes, sarissai.* Asclepiodotus *Tactica.* 5.1.
31 Markle 1977: 327. In the Hellenistic period the Macedonian officer panoply included a cuirass and half-cuirass, Hatzopoulos 1996 II no. 12 = Austin 90.

32 Diod. 17.84.4 (Alexander's army in 327); Polyb. 18.29–30 (Philip V's army in 197); Plut. *Aem.* 20.3–4 (Perseus' army in 168); cf. Asclepiodotus *Tactica.* 5.1.
33 Polyb. 18.32; Markle 1977: 331–333. See Chapter 10.
34 Cf. e.g. Dem. 19.81, 260; 9.17, 32; Didymus 11.46.
35 Diod. 16.35.4–5.
36 Dem. 9.49.
37 Cf. Dem. 1.4; 9.50; 18.235. On Philip's generalship see Griffith 1992.
38 The wedge: Arr. *Tactica.* 16. For text and translation see DeVoto 1993 (note Sekunda's cautionary review in *CR* (1996) 46.1: 156–157). *Sarissai* at Chaeronea: Plut. *Pel.* 18.5; Markle 1978: 488–491, 497. On the cavalry charge at Chaeronea see Sears and Willekes 2016.
39 Marsden 1977: 212–218. Cf. Dem. 9.50.
40 Marsden 1969: 58–59, 1977: 212, 215; Campbell 2011: 681.
41 Diod. 14.42.1.
42 Diod. 16.74.2–76.4. See Marsden 1969: 58–60, 1977: 216–217.
43 Athenaeus Mechanicus W 10.5–10.
44 Philoch. F53–54; cf. Front. 1.4.13. Hammond 1993b: 17–19.
45 Hauben 1975 argues Philip was first.
46 Polyaen. 4.2.22. See Chapter 4.
47 Hammond 1992: 32: "considerably more than twenty." But Ellis 1976: 175: Philip's fleet was "small and unskilled." The evidence for a fleet comes mostly from Alexander III's reign (e.g. Arr. *Anab.* 2.7.2, 2.20.2, 2.21.6).
48 Hammond 1992: 34. Cf. Thuc. 4.108.1.
49 Dem. 4.22 (351), 19.286 (343), 7.16 (342).
50 Xen. *Anab.* 1.9.2–5. Olbrycht 2010: 345–346. On terminology see Carney 2008: 145–146.
51 Hammond 1990: 263.
52 Ellis 1976: 162: "benign form of hostageship."
53 Curt. 5.1.42, 8.6.6; cf. 8.6.2–5, possibly echoing the older tradition. Arrian (*Anab.* 4.13.1) attributes the institution to Philip, while Curtius (8.8.3) implies it was an age-old custom (cp. Valerius Maximus 3.3 ext. 1). See Hammond 1990; Heckel 2003a: 205–206; Carney 2008; Sawada 2010: 403–406.
54 Ael. *VH* 14.48; cf. Front. 4.2.4.
55 *Syll.*[3] 332 (estate to Polemocrates of Elimeia, father of Coenus); Diod. 16.34.5; Theopomp. F224–225. "Gifts": Diod. 16.3.3, 53.3, 93.9. Cf. Dem. 19.145; Plut. *Alex.* 15.3; Just. 11.5.5. Anson 2008a.
56 Dem. 18.235, 8.11, 9.49–50.
57 Dem. 9.49; Ath. 10.421c. On the molding of the army see Lloyd 1996. For Alexander's army see Sekunda 2010; Heckel 2016: 260–280 (not all his conclusions are accepted).
58 E.g. Arr. *Anab.* 1.2.4–5.
59 Diod. 17.17.3–5. The figures are generally trusted, cp. Just. 11.6.2: 32,000 foot and 4,500 horse; Arr. *Anab.* 1.11.3: "not much more than" 30,000 foot and 5,000 horse; Plut. *Alex.* 15.1: acknowledges discrepancies in three contemporary sources, at low end 30,000 foot and 4,000 horse and at high end 43,000 foot and 5,500 horse. Cp. Plut. *De Alex. fort.* 327d–e: Aristobulus: 30,000 foot and 4,000 horse, Ptolemy: 30,000 foot and 5,000 horse (these are Arrian's two main sources), and Anaximenes: 43,000 foot and 5,500 horse. Anaximenes' totals may include Philip's advance force (with the allied Greek cavalry?). Sekunda 2010: 454 sees no compelling reason to assume the cavalry left behind were Macedonian, but cp. Brunt 1963: 35–36.

60 Diodorus' total for horse, 4,500, may exclude the 600 Greek cavalry, which he says were commanded by Erigyius, a Mytilenaean-born Greek, who had been granted land at Amphipolis; but see Heckel 2006a: 119. For subject and allied forces see also Diod. 16.1.5.
61 Arr. *Anab.* 1.12.7, 3.11.8.
62 Squadrons of 200: e.g. Arr. *Anab.* 1.18.1. So Hammond 1998: 405, 409. *Contra* Brunt 1963: 41; Heckel 2016: 261. Hammond 1998: 408 with n13: the *basilike ile* 300 strong in 334, the remaining 100 consisting of "close Companions"; Heckel 2016: 261 with n6: "8 × 225."
63 Arr. *Anab.* 3.18.5. Brunt 1963: 28–32; Sekunda 2010: 452–454.
64 E.g. Arr. *Anab.* 1.14.1, 4.4.6; Curt. 4.15.13. Fuller 1958: 51 suggests these were Thracians, but Hammond 1998: 411 suggests they were "Macedonians" in the geographical rather than political sense. See also Brunt 1963: 27; Heckel 2008: 25; 2016: 261–2.
65 Arr. *Anab.* 1.15.5–8, 16.1; Plut. *Alex.* 16.11. Sekunda 2001: 37–39, 2012: 8–9. *Xystophoroi* in the Hellenistic armies of Alexander's Successors: e.g. Diod. 19.82.2.
66 Arr. *Anab.* 1.2.5; cf. 3.11.8. On the location of Bottiaea, central plain or Chalcidice, and Anthemous, city or region, see Hammond 1998: 414–415, *contra* Bosworth 1980a: 58–59.
67 Arr. *Anab.* 1.12.7, 14.6.
68 Arr. *Anab.* 2.9.3.
69 Arr. *Anab.* 4.9.3; Curt. 8.1.20–21.
70 Sources are not consistent: Arr. *Anab.* 1.15.7–8; Diod. 17.20.1–7; Plut. *Alex.* 16.7–11; Curt. 8.1.20.
71 Arr. *Anab.* 1.14.1, 3.11.8; Diod. 17.17.4.
72 Arr. *Anab.* 1.5; Plut. *Alex.* 10.3.
73 Arr. *Anab.* 3.16.11.
74 Arr. *Anab.* 7.8.2. See Brunt 1963: 28–32.
75 Arr. *Anab.* 4.24.1, 6.14.4; Diod. 19.28.3, 29.5.
76 Cf. Arr. *Anab.* 6.21.3. Brunt 1963: 29: references to hipparchies prior to 328, e.g. Arr. *Anab.* 1.24.3, 3.29.7, 4.4.6–7, are anachronistic.
77 Arr. *Anab.* 5.12.2.
78 Arr. *Anab.* 5.16.3, 21.5, 6.8.2; Curt 4.5.9.
79 Arr. *Anab.* 5.11.3, 5.12.2, 5.16.3; cf. Curt. 6.8.17.
80 Diod. 17.61.3. Wrightson 2010 suggests Alexander's infantry commanders commanded on horseback from the rear.
81 Arr. *Anab.* 5.22.6, 6.6.4; cf. Ath. 12.539c.
82 Arr. *Anab.* 7.14.10.
83 See also Hatzopoulos and Loukopoulos 1992, figure 48: a Macedonian grave *stele* from Alexandria. On the painting see Miller 1993b: 109–110 and Palagia 2000: 200–201. Plin. *HN* 35.93: contemporary paintings of Apelles included one of Cleitus the Black charging into battle.
84 Heckel 2006b.
85 Diod. 17.77.5; Just. 12.3.9; cp. Curt. 6.6.7.
86 Plut. *Alex.* 32.10.
87 Cf. n64.
88 Arr. *Anab.* 1.14.3: Calas, son of Harpalus, Agathon, son of Tyrimmas, and Philip, son of Menelaus respectively.
89 Curt. 7.5.27.
90 Arr. *Anab.* 1.12.7, 14.1, 6; cf. 1.28.4, 4.4.6. Plut. *Alex.* 16.3: thirteen *ilai* in total deployed.

91 Arr. *Anab.* 2.9.2; Plut. *Alex.* 39.2; cf. Curt. 4.9.25. He is not to be confused with an *ilarches* of the same name.
92 Front. 2.11.3; Just. 11.5.3. Cf. Arr. *Anab.* 1.28.4: Sitalces commanding Thracians.
93 Arr. *Anab.* 4.4.6. Brunt 1963: 27–28. For Ariston see Hammond 1998: 411 with references.
94 Alexander's deployments in the great set battles: Granicus: Arr. *Anab.* 1.14.2–3; Issus: Arr. *Anab.* 2.8.3–4; Gaugamela: Arr. *Anab.* 3.11.9–10; Hydaspes: Arr. *Anab.* 5.11.3–12.2, 16.3, 17.3–18.1. For discussion of the battles see e.g. Fuller 1958: 147–199; Hammond 1996 (1980); Devine 1985, 1986, 1987, 1988; Heckel 2008: 47–51, 57–65, 75–80, 115–120.
95 Arr. *Anab.* 1.28.3–4.
96 Markle 1999: 242: Alexander's Hypaspists carried the *hoplon*; Anson 2010a: 81–82.
97 Anaximenes F4 (n19); Front. 4.1.6, 2.4.
98 See Arr. *Anab.* 1.14.2–3 with Diod. 17.57.2.
99 Foreign foot: Curt. 4.13.28, but see Heckel 2009: 106–108. Distribution by region: Arr. *Anab.* 3.16.11.
100 Bosworth 1973: 249 n4; Heckel 2016: 269.
101 Arr. *Anab.* 2.23.2, 6.6.1; see also 4.23.1, 5.22.6, 6.21.3. Bosworth 1973 restored the manuscript reading *asthetairoi*, which long before had been emended to *pezhetairoi*. See Heckel 2009, examining various theories proposed to explain "*ast*-"; Anson 2010a, suggesting distinctive equipment.
102 Arr. *Anab.* 1.14.6, 1.28.3, 5.13.4.
103 Arr. *Anab.* 4.16.1: Attalus and Gorgias; 4.22.7: Gorgias and Cleitus; 4.27.1, 5: Alcetas.
104 Arr. *Anab.* 3.11.9, cp. 1.8.3. Heckel 2016: 253–256.
105 Arrian (*Anab.* 3.29.7, 5.23.7; cf. 4.24.10) calls the divisions *chiliarchiai*, which indicates 1,000 men, and (4.30.5–6; cf. 1.22.7) names two *chiliarchoi* of Hypaspists in association with three *chiliarchiai*, which suggests three units including the *agema*. But Curtius (5.2.2–5) says eight chiliarchs competed in 331 to win their appointments over units of 1,000 men each, these *chiliarchiai* replacing older units of 500. The Hypaspists, however, appear to have remained at about 3,000 into the period of the Successors (Diod. 19.28.1). On the problem see Milns 1971: 189–193; Bosworth 1980a: 148–149; Sekunda 2010: 454–456; Heckel 2016: 270–272.
106 Just. 12.7.5; cf. Curt. 8.5.4, 9.3.21; Arr. *Anab.* 7.11.3. Diod. 17.57.2 and Curt. 4.13.27 are evidently anachronistic, cp. Arr. *Anab.* 3.11.9. Anson 1981; Roisman 2012a; Baynham 2013.
107 Arr. *Anab.* 3.17.2, 4.3.2, 4.30.3: the "(royal) bodyguards" are the *agema* of Hypaspists. See Heckel 1986, 2016: 251–252, 271. Hammond 1991: 399 suggests the camp guards are a separate unit.
108 See especially Arr. *Anab.* 6.28.3–4.
109 Curt. 9.5.15, 18.
110 Arr. *Anab.* 6.11.8, 13.1; Curt 9.5.21.
111 Arr. *Anab.* 5.24.
112 Arr. *Anab.* 6.9.1–13.5; Diod. 17.98.1–99.4; Curt. 9.4.26–6.1; Plut. *Alex.* 63, *Mor.* 327b, 343d–345b. See Bosworth 1988: 136–137; Worthington 2004: 162–163, 2014: 253–256; Rogers 2004: 216–220.
113 Arr. *Anab.* 1.1.7–8; Diod. 17.18.1. See Chapter 7.
114 Arr. *Anab.* 6.9.3; Plut. *Alex.* 63.5. Soldier's pay: Arr. *Anab.* 7.23.3–4.
115 Arr. *Anab.* 6.9.5; Diod. 17.99.1; cp. Plut. *Mor.* 344a–c; Curt. 9.5.1–2.
116 Cp. Curt. 9.5.16: Timaeus. But see Heckel 2006a: 128 and 152.

117 Sources agree on Peucestas, not on Leonnatus; Arrian (*Anab.* 7.5.4–5) says both were later crowned for shielding the king. Arrian (following Ptolemy) omits Aristonus, doubtless because he sided with Perdiccas, Ptolemy's enemy, in the first war of the Successors. See Heckel 2006a: 50.
118 Plut. *Mor.* 327.
119 Cf. Curt. 3.6.1.
120 Plut. *Alex.* 8.1. On medical care and medics in the army see Karunanithy 2013: 164–170.
121 Arr. *Anab.* 6.11.1.
122 The shaft was 90 cm (3 ft), cf. Plut. *Mor.* 341c; Curt. 9.5.9.
123 Respectively: Curt. 9.5.25–28; Arr. *Anab.* 6.11.1; but cf. Arr. *Ind.* 18.7.
124 Plin. *HN* 7.37. So Heckel 2006a: 100 with n264.
125 Curt. 9.6.1; Arr. *Anab.* 6.12.1–2
126 Arr. *Anab.* 6.28.4, 7.5.4.
127 Plut. *Mor.* 344a. On Alexander's sieges see Kern 1999: 201–226.
128 E.g. Arr. *Anab.* 2.26.2.
129 Diod. 17.24.1; Arr. *Anab.* 1.23.6; 2.27.3.
130 Trogus *Prol.* 9 (translated in Yardley and Develin 1994: 276–277).
131 Hammond 1992 has argued conclusively that these fleets operated separately between 334–332, and sources for Alexander suggest the Macedonian fleet was distinctive for its smaller ships; cf. Dem. 17.27; Curt. 4.4.6; Polyaen. 4.2.22. Pentecontors and triaconters: Arr. *Anab.* 2.7.2, 2.20.2, 2.21.6. Hauben 1976: 79.
132 Arr. *Anab.* 5.3.5, 8.4–5, 12.4.
133 Arr. *Anab.* 6.2.3, *Ind.* 18.3–10.
134 Arr. *Anab.* 6.1.6, *Ind.* 18.1–2.
135 Arr. *Anab.* 6.1.1, 2.4; Diod. 17.95.5. Cp. Arr. *Ind.* 19.7: the whole fleet for the Hydaspes/Indus voyage totaled 800, including ships of war, merchantmen, and horse transports.
136 Arr. *Anab.* 7.19.3–4.
137 Morrison 1995.
138 E.g. Arr. *Anab.* 7.6; Diod. 17.108.1–3; Plut. *Alex.* 71.1. Bosworth 1980b; Olbrycht 2010: 361–366.
139 Epplett 2007; Charles 2010.
140 E.g. Ptolemy against Demetrius at Gaza in 313, Diod. 19.80.4. Hammond 1990: 281–282.
141 Liv. 30.33; cp. Polyb. 15.11. Derow 2003: 58 argues for unlikelihood, though I see no reason why Livy could not be correct.
142 Polyb. 18.28–32.

6 Alexander III and Macedonia, 356–334

Alexander III with his unprecedented campaign of conquest in the east was to win much more fame than his father Philip, but before ever embarking on that campaign he had already achieved no few successes. Upon accession he faced the same challenges as other kings before him, yet he quickly assumed political and military control in the Greek peninsula, having himself affirmed as *archon* in Thessaly, overseer of the Amphictyony at Delphi, and *hegemon* of the League of Corinth. His swift and competent actions in the northeast against the Triballians, in the northwest against the Illyrians, and then in the south in reaction to the revolt of Thebes firmly established him as a worthy heir to Philip II's legacy.

It is because of Alexander's enormous 'success' in overthrowing Persian power, which had long dictated or manipulated affairs in the eastern Mediterranean, that he ranks as the most famous of the ancient Macedonians. In his own times no one would have been unaffected by his actions, and all kinds of records were generated, from daily logs to narrative histories to soldiers' memoirs to popular quasi historical novels. It is not that other Macedonian kings lacked records of their deeds and lives (Theopompus wrote about Philip II, Antipater about Perdiccas III), but Alexander inspired a greater number of accounts, and a perpetual interest in his life has resulted in the preservation of a substantial body of source material. Later generations, recognizing the profound impact that Alexander's conquests had on the subsequent course of history, continued to rehash, re-evaluate, and even to rewrite the record; that trend has not ceased.[1] It was the Romans (evidently) who gave Alexander the epithet *magnus*, Caesar who wept over his own meagre accomplishments at the age of thirty-two when compared with Alexander, who at that age had already conquered the world, and Augustus who, having vanquished the last Ptolemaic/Macedonian ruler, Cleopatra, asked the Alexandrians to show him the embalmed body of Alexander so he could crown it with a gold diadem.[2] Whether one admires or abhors him, one cannot deny the personal legacy of Alexander, his tremendous influence through the centuries on military leaders, kings, would-be autocrats, and even in present times corporate moguls. The accounts we have of his career that survive from antiquity, chiefly the five narrative histories of the so-called Alexander historians—Diodorus (Book 17), Curtius (*Histories of*

Alexander the Great), Plutarch (*Life of Alexander*), Arrian (*Anabasis of Alexander*), and Justin (*Epitome of the* Philippic History *of Pompeius Trogus* Books 11–12)—were all written in late Republican and early Roman Imperial times, some 300 to 500 years after the events they describe.[3] These, then, are 'second-hand' re-workings of now lost earlier works, which themselves were of varying quality and purpose. Alexander wanted his Asian expedition to be recorded and to be reported back to the Greek world as it was unfolding so that he could 'prove' the triumph of and maintain support for his panhellenic crusade against Persia; and one can well imagine that this was done with considerable bias and propaganda. His official chronicler was Aristotle's philosopher/historian nephew Callisthenes, though when Callisthenes fell out of favour part way through the campaign, both his chronicle and his life came to an end. Unofficially, several of Alexander's generals and staff wrote histories or memoirs of their experiences on the campaign, with their king as the central figure, though of these 'eyewitnesses' some, notably the general and Bodyguard Ptolemy, who became a king himself, did not write until late in life, when the passage of time and the failing of memory cannot have helped but cloud factual detail. There were others who mainly observed from a distance, among these the popular sensationalist Cleitarchus; they wrote what they heard or imagined and did so with considerable embellishment. Alexander was such a figure as to invite and incite embellishment, and even within his own lifetime his doings were distorted and mythologized.

Alexander, son of Philip

Alexander was born in late July 356 amidst a flush of midsummer victories for his absent father: Potidaea fell to Philip's siege, Philip's race horse entry won at Olympia, and Philip's general Parmenio defeated the Illyrian Grabos.[4] It is said that on the coincidence of the three victories with the birth of his son the diviners at the Macedonian court, chief among them Aristander of Telmessus, prophesied to Philip that the child himself was destined always to be victorious.[5] There is no reason to reject a court prophecy associated with the birth of a royal male offspring, but Alexander's later great fame certainly encouraged elaboration and fabrication of stories about his birth and childhood, and stripping away accretions and distortions has ever plagued his modern historians. It is not certain but likely that Alexander, born to Philip's fourth wife, Olympias, was the king's second son, though his half-brother Arrhidaeus can not have been elder by more than a year.[6] As an adult Arrhidaeus suffered a mental affliction, though when that affliction first became evident we do not know. Thus we cannot say whether in their childhood one prince was preferred to be Philip's successor.

Many tutors were responsible for supervising the early education of Alexander (Philip, after all, was rarely at Pella), and since Plutarch claims this was "customary" practice we may assume the same was true for Arrhidaeus and any other royal sons, including Perdiccas III's son Amyntas.[7] Chief among Alexander's tutors were Leonidas, a relative of Olympias, and Lysimachus of Acarnania. Training in horsemanship, as exemplified in the story of the taming of Alexander's warhorse Bucephalus, must have begun very early and been of highest importance for royal sons, just as it was for the sons of nobles who would one day join the ranks of the Companion Cavalry. Macedonian horsemen rode, whether hunting or fighting, with neither stirrup nor saddle, so their skill level needed to be high. By his early teens Alexander was removed from the influences of the palace at Pella (perhaps particularly because of his mother's influence) to study under Aristotle at Mieza, where a school was established for that purpose (Figure 6.1).[8] Alexander was now, it seems, being groomed for succession, but whether Arrhidaeus was also being educated we do not know. Alexander's formal Greek education was surely shared with sons of leading nobles from both Lower Macedonia and the upper cantons, youths who later campaigned with him as his Companions, military officers, and administrators. Probably among them were his dearest lifelong friend, Hephaestion, Ptolemy, and Leonnatus, all three later promoted to the elite group of Seven Bodyguards, as well as Harpalus the treasurer and Nearchus, admiral of Alexander's fleet at the Indus. They considered themselves his equals in many respects, and in that sense some of them were later deservedly his Successors. Literature was part of the Macedonian curriculum, and Alexander especially admired Homer; it was Aristotle's annotated copy that he carried with him on his Asian expedition, the so-called "casket" *Iliad* because of the elaborate chest in which he stored it.[9] In addition to ethics and politics

Figure 6.1 Nymphaion, Mieza, stone benches of Aristotle's School
Source: author, 2011.

the youths at Mieza were taught science and medicine and what Alexander later called "acroamantic" (unpublished or esoteric) philosophy.

Alexander's formal study came to an end in 340 when Philip called him away to assume the regency.[10] This ought to have dispelled any doubt that by this time, if not prior, Alexander was the designated heir. Philip was not, however, entirely entrusting the rule of Macedonia to his sixteen-year-old son; rather he entrusted Alexander to the care of Antipater, who would further the young heir's education beyond Aristotle's theoretical kingship into practical kingship. Practical kingship meant active military campaigning, experience that Alexander soon gained against the Maedi. At age eighteen under Philip's generalship Alexander led a charge, probably at the head of the Companion Cavalry, against the elite Theban Sacred Band at Chaeronea. This for Alexander was education in the school of Philip. After the battle Philip entrusted to Alexander the important role of the king's ambassador to Athens (again with Antipater) to handle the post-battle settlement and return of the Athenian dead.[11]

Alexander's sudden departure from Macedonia into self-exile a year after Chaeronea marks a drastic turn of events. Great disagreements between father and son arose, according to Plutarch, out of troubles in the women's quarters. Domestic troubles might be expected to have gone hand in hand with Philip's polygamy, but Plutarch singles out Olympias as being exceedingly jealous and surly. Strife erupted publicly when Philip took to wife a young Macedonian noblewoman, Cleopatra.[12] At the wedding banquet the bride's guardian, her uncle Attalus, a nobleman who was to be co-commander of Philip's advance force into Asia Minor,[13] called upon the Macedonians to beg of the gods that from Philip and Cleopatra there might be born a "lawful" successor to the kingdom. In Attalus' view, Alexander's eligibility as heir to the Macedonian throne was questionable, and sources say he confronted Alexander with a charge of illegitimacy.[14] Yet nothing prior to this episode suggests there was any question about Alexander's paternity or eventual succession. Though few facts can be pulled from the mythologized stories associated with his birth, for Olympias to put it about that Philip was *not* Alexander's father—while Philip was still alive and Alexander his heir apparent—was to put her son's succession most foolishly at risk. The story of Zeus-Ammon in the guise of a snake visiting her bedchamber surely post-dates this episode, at any rate.[15] If it was Alexander's half-Epirote blood that was potentially a disqualifier, that made him hardly less legitimate than Philip, whose mother was part Illyrian; and inter-state marriages resulting in mixed-blood offspring were traditional royal policy. Or did Attalus suggest that Philip's polygamy was unlawful, that Olympias was not a lawful wife? Were that the case, and surely it was not, we might wonder why Philip put all that effort into grooming a bastard. Supposing Cleopatra had produced a son (no guarantee) and if indeed the male offspring of a Macedonian bride 'lawfully' out-legitimated all other royal offspring by foreign wives or concubines, then Philip had a long time to wait for his 'lawful' successor. Too long, as past events had proved. Wild times it must have been at Macedonian *symposia*, if Plutarch has captured even the essence of it with his anecdote: Alexander threw first an insult then a cup at Attalus, while Philip drew his sword and charged after his son, but "fortunately" being too intoxicated to keep his balance he tripped and fell. Alexander hurled one last rebuke at his father: the man preparing to cross to Asia from Europe could not even manage to cross from couch to couch. Then he fled the kingdom, taking his mother with him. He left Olympias with relatives in Epirus, while he himself went to live among the Illyrians.

A breach with Alexander on the eve of the king's carefully planned invasion of Asia Minor put Philip in a bad way, particularly if Olympias in her exile was trying to stir up Epirote opposition against him.[16] Philip soon arranged for the marriage of his daughter Cleopatra, Alexander's full sister, to Olympias' brother Alexander, whom he had placed on the Epirote throne in 342.[17] It has been suggested prince Alexander was also stirring up opposition among Philip's long-time enemies the Illyrians,[18] though there is no specific evidence and we simply do not know where he was or what he was doing.[19] Some months after the wedding fracas reconciliation was brought about between Philip and Alexander by Demaratus the Corinthian, a guest-friend of the king and a man of considerable influence with Alexander.[20] Alexander accepted his father's recall very reluctantly,[21] though on what terms our sources are silent. It is hard to imagine Alexander agreed to any terms that did not include a confirmation of his status as heir apparent. There was still the issue of Olympias' displacement by the young Macedonian Cleopatra, however, and the two men remained wary of each other.[22]

A second (questionable) episode of discord between father and son is the so-called "Pixodarus affair."[23] When Philip in preparation for his invasion of Asia Minor entered into negotiations for a military alliance with the Hecatomnid dynast and satrap of Caria, Pixodarus, he made a deal for an inter-state marriage between Pixodarus' elder daughter and his own son Arrhidaeus, a deal that never came to fruition. Plutarch claims it was stories and false accusations coming to Alexander from his friends and mother (coming to him where, though: was he still in exile when Philip's negotiations first began?), namely that Philip was now intending to elevate Arrhidaeus to the succession, that stirred the son to rash action. It seems implausible that Alexander ever seriously saw a rival in the simple Arrhidaeus ("only over my dead body," one might imagine him taunting), but his mother and his friends were stirring him to or supporting him in something, though we do not know what their involvement was. What Alexander did, rashly, was usurp the king's prerogative to negotiate foreign alliances, and in secret he sent a tragic actor, Thessalus, as his emissary to Pixodarus, with a counter offer of himself as groom in place of the "bastard" and "idiot" Arrhidaeus. When Philip learned of Alexander's offer he evidently regarded it to be an act of treason. He demanded Thessalus be sent back to Macedonia in chains (the actor shows up later in Alexander's entourage in Asia), and he banished several of the prince's friends: Harpalus, Ptolemy, Nearchus, and the brothers Erigyius and Laomedon (the latter three were naturalized Macedonians from Amphipolis) all remained in exile until after Philip's death. Alexander did subsequently recall them, and all eventually were elevated to high positions.[24] As for Alexander,

Philip perhaps reprimanded him,[25] though the recent stint of several months living independently among the "barbarians" had firmly established Alexander as a man come of age and one not to be demeaned. The formal reconciliation, whenever and however it came about, held up. The last thing Philip needed was to send Alexander back into exile with his troublesome friends, and Alexander would not have wanted to throw back in Philip's face his restored status.

Within a year came the assassination of Philip, too close on the heels of these events to keep Alexander and Olympias free and clear of suspicion of complicity, though Aristotle lays the blame firmly on the assassin himself, the Bodyguard Pausanias, whose motive was a personal grudge.[26] Moreover, one of Philip's own most trusted men, Antipater, stood by Alexander in support of his succession to the throne. Antipater's son-in-law Alexander Lyncestes (possibly of the royal house of Lyncus or a collateral branch of the Argeads) also stood beside Alexander, hailing him the new king.[27] And so at age twenty Philip's son, so carefully groomed for the role, was officially acclaimed the Argead successor as Alexander III. It was far from being as simple as that sounds, however, and the question of the army's (or Assembly's) role in 'acclaiming' the new king is complex, as we see more fully in the context of Alexander's death. We know little about the present

Figure 6.2 Marble head of Alexander, Pella/Yannitsa, late fourth century BCE
Source: author, 2013.

circumstances. In assembly Alexander assured the Macedonians that only the name of the king had changed and that his own governance would not fall short of his father's. It is possible that he granted some concessions to the Macedonians in order to win their support for his rule,[28] and that he would need to do so speaks to the fact that succession was never an absolutely certain deal. Arrhidaeus was clearly not a rival. If there were any other half-brothers, though it is generally agreed there were not, a rival could have had political support from an anti-Alexander faction, such as the one Attalus represented. There is one lone reference to Caranus, a half-brother by an unidentified stepmother of Alexander; however, the silence of other sources has left most historians reluctant to accept his existence,[29] and he would almost certainly have been junior. Alexander's cousin, Amyntas, son of Perdiccas III, is a different matter; clearly he did have political backing as a legitimate Argead claimant to the throne. We know too little about him, however, to say whether he personally wanted the kingship or made a serious bid for it, or to suggest when, how, or on what official grounds Alexander eliminated him. He was put to death before Alexander left for Asia.[30] Olympias at some point was recalled from Epirus, and both mother and son settled scores. She viciously vented her excessive jealousy on the young widow Cleopatra and her infant daughter Europa by having them both killed.[31] Alexander sent one of his friends, Hecataeus, to the advance forces in Asia Minor to arrest Attalus on a charge of treason. With Parmenio's cooperation Attalus was executed without trial, and thereby Parmenio, who was Attalus' father-in-law as well as co-commander, affirmed in no uncertain terms his loyalty to the new king.[32] Rumour had it the two generals had been approached by Demosthenes about rebelling against Alexander, and Parmenio may have needed to clear his own name from suspicion.[33] Attalus could hardly expect similar grace after his previous "bastard" taunt, and given that he was quite popular with the army, a trial would have been a bad gamble for Alexander. Alexander also had two brothers of Alexander Lyncestes executed for complicity in Philip's assassination (the specifics are unknown), but Lyncestes himself was rewarded for his declaration of loyalty by being promoted to *strategos* of Thrace.[34] So much for sweeping out the courtyard.

Beyond the courtyard news of Philip's death had left Macedonia and the Greek and Balkan world in uncertain anticipation.[35] No one, surely, could fill Philip's greaves. And Philip had many pairs. First, from the Thessalians Alexander gained confirmation in his father's prior role as *archon* of the Thessalian League.[36] While the Aleuadae of Larissa, the Argeads' long-time allies, no doubt supported him, not all Thessalians did, and initially some tried to block his approach at the Vale of Tempe. He got around them by the stratagem of cutting stairs into the side of mount Ossa[37] and securing Thessaly in their rear. Next, he met with the Amphictyonic Council at Thermopylae, where it regularly convened, and, again, was voted the same privileges Philip had held.[38] At Thermopylae when he met with envoys from Ambracia in western Greece he chose to forgive rather than to challenge their recent expulsion of a Macedonian garrison,[39] but such leniency may have sent the wrong message to other Greek states bristling against objectionable garrisons. When Alexander marched on from there into central and southern Greece he did so at the head of an army with the intention of intimidating any would-be dissident states,[40] and probably he stopped at Thebes to check on the garrison that after Chaeronea Philip had installed in its citadel, the Cadmea.[41] He may have thought it also advisable to give the Athenians another look at the army that had defeated them at Chaeronea.[42] Finally, he marched to Corinth where he convened a meeting of the representatives of the member states of the League of Corinth, which Sparta again refused to join. Both Thebes and Athens must have been represented. Alexander, though already entitled to Philip's position by inheritance, nevertheless had confirmed by vote his roles as "*hegemon* of the Greeks" and "general with full powers" (*strategos autokrator*) for the war with Persia.[43] The League's purpose in declaring war on Persia was twofold: to free the Greek cities of Asia Minor from Persian rule and to avenge the wrongs done to the Greeks (Athenians above all) during the Persian invasion of 480–479.[44] For Alexander as for Philip the freedom of Greek cities and revenge for age-old wrongs to Greeks were not truly Macedonian concerns.[45] It was the Common Peace imposed by the League that guaranteed, theoretically, the protection of Macedonia and Macedonian interests in Greece (members swore an oath to a common peace whereby they could not march against Macedonia or each other) in the absence of the king and a large part of his army for an extended campaign that had at its heart Macedonian imperialistic aims. It also provided him with additional land forces and a powerful fleet so long as he needed them. But the peace was precarious. Sparta had already said "no" to Macedonian hegemony, and Athens and Thebes were both itching to find a way out from under it.[46] With affairs only seemingly settled in the south, Alexander returned to Macedonia to prepare for a spring invasion of Asia.

Alexander's Balkan campaign

Spring brought a different campaign from the one anticipated, for the transition of the throne had incited trouble along his northern borders, and once again the Persian expedition had to be put off. With Antipater left as regent at Pella,[47] and Parmenio (presumably) still in Asia Minor, the unseasoned Alexander assumed the kingly duty of army commander-in-chief.[48] The Triballians, the Thracian tribe that had ravaged Philip's retreat from the Danube in 339,[49] were said to be in revolution. Setting out from Amphipolis and crossing the Nestos River, within ten days the army had passed over the Rhodope range and was heading up the pass (probably the Shipka) to cross the Haemus Mountains when the infantry ran into trouble. Some Thracians (a different tribe) had poised themselves defensively on the higher slopes behind heavy carts, and they intended to roll these down the slopes to overrun the Macedonians and throw the ranks into confusion.[50] Alexander gave orders to those still on the level to break formation and step out of the way and to those already in the defile either to crouch or to lie down and cover themselves with their shields so that the carts could pass harmlessly over and around them.[51] Amazingly, his strategy worked and no casualties were reported (though there must have been no few bruises and possibly some broken bones). In the ensuing battle 1,500 of the Thracians were killed and the women and children all taken captive.

Crossing over the Haemus Alexander came upon the Triballians near the Lyginus River, three days' march from the Istros/Danube.[52] They had managed to double around behind him, but when he discovered their position he formed up his phalanx in deep formation and then, leading it in person and using archers and slingers to flush the Triballians out from a wooded area where they had taken cover, he ordered Philotas (son of Parmenio) to lead the Upper Macedonian cavalry in a charge against the enemy right and two of his ilarchs to lead their squadrons of cavalry against the left. Alexander again proved himself a sound strategist, with 3,000 of the enemy dead and only eleven cavalry and forty infantry of the Macedonians.[53] The survivors, among them the Triballian king Syrmus, he pursued all the way to the Danube. There a few warships joined him by way of Byzantium and the Black Sea, and with these he tried to assail those who had taken refuge on an island in the river, but the fugitives repelled every attempt at landing. The Danube was a boundary beyond which Philip had never extended his sphere of power, and it seems, by the prearrangement of ships, that Alexander had planned in advance to cross. On the farther shore were Celtic tribes, and one of these, the Getae (Dacians), appeared on the bank in force with 4,000 cavalry and 10,000 infantry to challenge any attempted crossing. It was a challenge Alexander could not resist. With the few warships at hand and local riverboats and tents stuffed with straw the Macedonians—1,500 cavalry and 4,000 infantry—made the crossing in a single night, much to the astonishment of the Getae. At daybreak the Macedonians materialized out of a grain field, the infantry with their *sarissai* held oblique and levelling the grain to make way for the cavalry. In the attack this time Alexander led the cavalry and ordered Nicanor (son of Parmenio) to lead the phalanx in "rectangular" (*en plaisio*) formation.[54] Overwhelmed by the combined assault of the Macedonian phalanx and cavalry, the Getae fled at the first charge.[55]

After these Macedonian successes Syrmus and some other tribal leaders sent envoys to Alexander's camp to offer terms. Alexander accepted and his agreements with them resulted in more troops being put at his disposal for the Asian expedition.[56] Then he headed towards the Paeonians and Agrianians,[57] his subject allies on the upper Strymon. Alexander would have wanted to confirm himself as Philip's successor to the Macedonian throne and to reaffirm the prior relationships Philip had with these tribes. Langarus, king of the Agrianians, had befriended Alexander while Philip was still alive and he had already joined Alexander's army with his hypaspists. While he was with these allies Alexander learned of the revolt of two Illyrian chieftains, Cleitus, son of Bardylis (either the same or a descendant of the Bardylis who had defeated and killed Perdiccas III), and Glaucias, king of the Taulanti.[58] He also learned that the Autariates, another Illyrian tribe, living northwest of the Paeonians, were intending to attack him on the march. Langarus offered to advance against the Autariates while Alexander went to deal with Cleitus and Glaucias, and in appreciation Alexander offered to Langarus as a bride his half-sister, Cynnane, Philip's daughter by the Illyrian Audata. Langarus kept his end of the deal, but he died of illness before the marriage could be realized.[59] The marriage offer coming at this time, in the late spring or early summer of 335, surely can only mean that Cynnane was already widowed of Amyntas, son of Perdiccas, to whom Philip had given her in marriage.[60] Alexander evidently had taken care to pre-empt a potential *coup* by eliminating a viable Argead candidate before heading out on the Balkan campaign.

Advancing southwestward by way of the Erigon River (Crna) towards Illyria, Alexander arrived at Pellion on the Eordaicus river. Neither Pellion nor the Eordaicus is positively identified, though the Pellion of Alexander's fight with the Illyrians may be the same as the Pelium mentioned in connection with the Roman campaign against Philip V in 200.[61] Philip II had extended his control into the region around the lakes Prespa and Lychnidos (Ochrid) after defeating Bardylis in 358,[62] but Cleitus, who had been a subject king of Macedonia since at least 349, when Philip suppressed an Illyrian uprising, was now acting independently and had taken control of Pellion as the most defensible place in the region. The tribe of Cleitus (and Bardylis) is nowhere named, but it is probably the Dardani,[63] meaning Pellion would have been south of their territory near the western border of Lyncus, a good vantage for raids into Upper Macedonia.

Alexander arrived at Pellion before Glaucias could join forces with Cleitus, but Cleitus' forces already held the heights around the city, from which vantage they could attack the Macedonians if the Macedonians tried to attack the city. On the second day Alexander advanced to the attack anyway. After sacrificing three boys, three girls, and three black rams, which the Macedonians discovered hours later (thus we can be quite certain we have an eyewitness account), Cleitus' forces abandoned their positions and most took refuge inside the city walls. Alexander now hoped to blockade them, but the following day Glaucias arrived with a large army, occupied the heights, and the Macedonians found themselves at a significant disadvantage in numbers, with fighting men now stationed both inside and outside the fortified city. After Glaucias' forces caught a Macedonian foraging party some distance from the main camp and Alexander had to go with Hypaspists, archers, Agrianians, and 400 cavalry to relieve them, the situation was such that the young general was confronting a battle the odds suggested he could not win, so he made the rational decision to withdraw.[64] Alexander's line of retreat was a track narrow and forested, the river on one side and mountains with cliffs on the other not leaving room for even four men abreast. In this compromising circumstance Alexander shrewdly put Philip's superbly trained phalanx through such deft manoeuvres that the enemy declined engagement. He formed his phalanx 120 deep (a Greek hoplite phalanx was typically eight or sometimes sixteen men deep, and Epaminondas' stacked phalanx that smashed the Spartans at Leuctra was fifty deep), with 200 cavalry on either wing. On Alexander's command in total silence the footmen raised their *sarissai* upright and then lowered them as if for the charge, swinging their spear points right and then left. On command again the whole phalanx advanced, wheeling right and left alternately, and after a quick drill of many difficult formations the left section of the phalanx formed into a wedge (*embolos*) and, with Alexander leading, suddenly charged. The Illyrians on the nearer hills abandoned their positions and fled to the mountains. Alexander then ordered the Macedonians to give their battle cry and clash spears on shields. At this most of the Taulanti withdrew from the terrifying noise back to the city, and with his Hypaspists and Companions Alexander drove the remaining few from the last hill overlooking his line of retreat. Then, with 2,000 Agrianians and archers and the Companions covering the retreat from the vantage of the hill he had just taken, Alexander ordered the Hypaspists to cross the river and the rest of the phalanx to follow. The Taulanti who had fled to the mountains now rushed down to harass the crossing, and Alexander with the Agrianians and archers charged them from one direction while the part of the infantry already across reformed and came charging at them back across the river. The Illyrians broke and ran, and Alexander getting across the river himself ordered artillery to be set up and fired across to prevent a further attack.[65] Not a man was lost in the retreat.

The Illyrians thought Alexander had retreated in fear, and he likely had been forced to abandon his baggage train. But Alexander could not afford to leave Illyrians hostile on his frontier, much less leave Philip's army thinking he had backed out of the fight. Three days later, when Alexander learned the Illyrians were camped with little precaution against attack, taking the Hypaspists, Agrianians, archers, and infantry of Perdiccas and Coenus, and instructing the rest of his force to follow, he launched a surprise night attack. His opponents had misjudged him. Some were caught in their beds, many killed or taken captive, and the rest took to flight. Cleitus set fire to Pellion and then fled to Glaucias' kingdom.[66] The Illyrians were subjugated once again, and when Alexander set out for Asia the following spring Illyrians were numbered among his forces.[67]

The Balkan campaign was more than a military victory for Alexander. The northern frontier was decisively secured for the present, and he had proved to Macedonia's traditionally troublesome neighbours that the new king was just as formidable an opponent as the previous king. Moreover, to the Macedonians the brash but capable son had proved himself to be a worthy successor to his illustrious father as commander-in-chief of the army. One cannot help but wonder, though, whether there was some lingering criticism of his 'Trojan horse' victory. There is a famous scene some years later between Alexander and Parmenio on the eve of the battle at Gaugamela when Parmenio goes to Alexander's tent and advises him to attack Darius' overwhelmingly superior numbers at night. Alexander's reply is that it would be dishonourable to steal the victory.[68] As for Alexander in the eyes of the Greeks, well, he was out of sight among the Thracians and Illyrians a good while, four or five months, long enough to fuel rumours in the south about his whereabouts and doings. He could be dead, for all they knew.

The revolt of Thebes

Rarely is there a breathing space in war. News reached Alexander probably when he was just beginning his march back from Illyria that Thebes was in revolt and that the Macedonian garrison was besieged in the Cadmea.[69] Some Theban exiles had slipped into the city at night and together with members of the anti-Macedonian party they had killed two unsuspecting members of the garrison, Amyntas and Timolaus. The garrison was largely made up of mercenaries, and an attempt funded by Persian gold to bribe them to surrender the Cadmea had failed. The ringleaders then appeared in the Theban Assembly insisting that Alexander had died in Illyria and stirring up the citizens to throw off the detested Macedonian yoke by besieging the Cadmea. To keep the revolt from spreading to other restless states Alexander needed to act swiftly, so marching past Eordaea and Elimeia and crossing the mountains of Tymphaea and Parauaea he was at Pelinna in Thessaly on the seventh day. Another five days' march and he was through Pylae (the Gates, Thermopylae)[70] and had arrived together with his whole army inside the Boeotian frontier at Onchestus. The next day he was before the walls of Thebes.[71] The leaders of the revolt continued to insist to the populace that Alexander the king was dead and that the Macedonian army must be Antipater's forces under command of Alexander (Lyncestes), son of Aeropus.[72]

It was September 335, just three years since the Thebans had suffered defeat at the hands of the Macedonian army at Chaeronea. But Chaeronea was nothing compared to the defeat they suffered now. It was the kind of catastrophe that in the aftermath not even those who participated could (or would) sort out the truth of the whole of it. Arrian preserves what is probably the eyewitness account of Ptolemy,[73] but the account is problematic in that Ptolemy sanitizes and heroizes Alexander's role *and* points a finger at Perdiccas, his later mortal enemy, as having initiated battle by leading the first charge without orders from Alexander.[74] Diodorus, whose sources clearly gave a Greek perspective, is also problematic;[75] he states explicitly that Perdiccas acted on Alexander's order when well into the battle he charged an abandoned postern gate and broke into the city.[76] It is likely true that, with or without an order, Perdiccas did lead a charge, followed by Amyntas, son of Andromenes, and in the event was badly wounded and had to be carried from the field. Sources agree, however, that when Alexander arrived in Boeotia he gave the Thebans time to come to terms without a battle;[77] such diplomacy was in the style of Philip. Alexander, it is said, by herald's proclamation invited any Theban defenders to return with amnesty to the Macedonian-led Greek alliance (League of Corinth), and the Thebans replied with their own proclamation that any man fighting for the Macedonians who wanted to join Thebes in freeing the Greeks and destroying the "tyrant of Greece" should come over to their side.[78] In exchange for two Theban rebels whom Alexander was demanding the Thebans demanded that the Macedonians hand over Philotas, commander of the garrison, and Antipater (perhaps a different Antipater, not the regent).[79] From the time they first besieged the garrison the Thebans would have had perhaps three weeks to prepare for Macedonian retaliation, and they had built a palisade in front of the city as well as a deep trench and heavy stockade around the Cadmea so the garrison had no hope of reinforcements or supplies getting through.[80] Thebes is famously seven-gated, and Alexander moved camp from the sanctuary of Iolaus around to the gate leading to Eleutherai and Attica;[81] here he could camp near the Cadmea, which it was his primary objective to relieve. Strategically, Alexander needed to intercept any reinforcements coming from Athens, as he would have been informed of their sympathies and that Demosthenes was running weapons.[82] Diodorus claims Alexander divided his forces in three segments, one to attack the outer palisade, another to face the Theban battle-line, and a third to be held in reserve,[83] and he numbers Alexander's forces at more than 30,000 infantry and at least 3,000 cavalry, all Philip's veterans.[84] Once the battle was in full swing, when the Macedonians began to tire Alexander ordered the reserve unit into action against the battle-weary Thebans.[85] This is when, says Diodorus, Perdiccas, on Alexander's order, charged a deserted postern gate, evidently leading the fresh reserve relay of Macedonian forces, and they now got inside the city. Arrian (Ptolemy) says the Macedonians who first broke in—that is, the infantry of Perdiccas and Amyntas with the archers—got the worst of it and retreated, and Eurybotas, commander of the Cretan archers, and seventy of his men were killed. Then Alexander—hero of the piece—brought up the phalanx and turned the battle. At this point in both accounts the Macedonian garrison bursts out.[86] Perdiccas' order from Alexander, or his intent if he acted on his own initiative, evidently was to relieve the besieged garrison. After that, it was all but over for the Thebans.

Of the Thebans more than 6,000 were dead and 30,000 taken captive, and of the Macedonians more than 500 were dead.[87] Alexander buried the latter on site. The fate of Thebes Alexander put before the Greeks, but whether this means representatives of the League of Corinth or only his Boeotian allies who participated in the battle (who, he well knew, had their own axes to grind with Thebes) is not clear.[88] Thus we have the concurrence of sources that it was the Phocians, Plataeans, and other Boeotians more than the Macedonians who slaughtered or meted out punishment in retaliation for past wrongs done them by the Thebans.[89] The official condemnation was Theban complicity with the Persians during Xerxes' invasion of 480–479, the very invasion which the League of Corinth had voted to avenge by attacking Persia under the supreme command of first Philip and now Alexander. No one would have dared bring up, I suppose, the complicity of Alexander I and the Macedonians with the Persians in that same invasion. It was a truly ironic position for the Macedonian king to be in. But we should note that the grievance was actually current, since the Thebans were (by accepting bribes) complying with Persia (Macedonia's and the League's enemy) in the present revolt. By decree the captives were sold, bringing a revenue of 440 talents in silver;[90] all Theban exiles were outlawed from Greece, and consequently Greek states were banned from taking in any fugitives; the garrison was reinstalled on the Cadmea;

and the city itself was razed with very little spared, the land redistributed to Alexander's allies, Thebes' wronged neighbours.[91] Exempted from punishment were the priests, the guest-friends of the Macedonians, the descendants of the great poet Pindar, who a century and a half earlier had written an encomium of Alexander I, and those who voted against the revolt; these were all freed,[92] and the temples and the house of Pindar were left standing on Alexander's order.[93] Exception was made also for Timocleia, sister of the Theban general Theagenes, who had led the Theban forces against Philip at Chaeronea; Alexander let her and her relatives go.[94]

The Athenians had every reason to fear Alexander's next move. He, however, was anxious to set his course for the east, and he needed the Athenian fleet, so he settled with them quickly and more leniently than the Athenians might have expected. It was no secret they were letting Theban fugitives slip over the border into Attica, and in mourning they cut off mid festival their celebration of the Eleusinian Mysteries, a most exceptional act. The only notable repercussion was Alexander's demand for some eight anti-Macedonian orators and generals to be handed over to him, Demosthenes among them.[95] When the Athenians protested Alexander relented, but at his insistence they did exile Charidemus, the mercenary commander and long-time enemy of Macedonia, who ran straight to the service of the Persian king.

Not a few Greek states deeply resented Thebes, and justly so, but the severity of punishment caused widespread empathy for her in her destruction and lasting condemnation of Alexander for an unjust act.[96] In truth, though he kept his own hands behind his back, the fate of Thebes was his to sanction or not. Yet the fact remains, while many Greek states pitied Thebes' plight, and some including Athens had rallied and been ready to assist the revolt,[97] neither Athens nor any other state actually came to Thebes' aid once the Macedonians appeared in force; the Greeks left her to her fate. The objective of the punishment was to instill fear,[98] and the Macedonian king thus gave due notice to the rest of the Greek world that he would not tolerate revolt from the Common Peace between the Greeks and the Macedonian king. The son of Philip made perfectly clear that he could wear Philip's greaves. He was twenty-one.

Alexander returned to Macedonia and spent the remainder of that fall and winter (335–334) making his final preparations for the long-anticipated Asian expedition. He would have had to assess his financial resources, adding the recent income from the sale of Theban captives to revenues from mines, timber, and harbour dues. He had already begun to mint coinage in his own name, his earliest coins depicting Heracles as ancestor of the Argeads on the obverse (cp. Figure 6.3).[99] At Dion he offered the annual traditional sacrifices to Olympian Zeus and celebrated the Macedonian *Olympia* games in honour of Zeus and the Pierian Muses, one day of celebration for each of the nine muses.[100] A lavish public festival was a good way for Alexander to win over the Macedonians to the prospect of the campaign, so he spared no expense in erecting a large tent with room for 100 dining couches and inviting Companions, officers, and envoys from the various cities to his banquets. He also held a meeting of military commanders

Figure 6.3 Marble head of Alexander with lion pelt of Heracles, Kerameikos, c. 300 BCE. National Archaeological Museum, Athens

Source: author, 2008.

and advisors regarding the Asian expedition, and one tradition holds that Antipater and Parmenio (though it is not certain the latter was in Macedonia) advised Alexander to postpone the expedition until he had produced an heir.[101] It was, of course, a corollary of eliminating rivals that, if we discount the incompetent Arrhidaeus, no eligible Argead now survived to continue the dynasty in the case of Alexander's own untimely demise. Though Philip also had eliminated most of his potential rivals, he had kept alive his nephew (and son-in-law) Amyntas. One other important matter had to be attended to before Alexander headed off to war. Philip in observation of a time-honoured tradition had sent an envoy to Delphi to consult the oracle before his anticipated Persian campaign, and legend holds that Alexander attempted to do the same, perhaps on his return from Corinth late in 336. But arriving on a day that was *apophras* (no oracles), he insisted upon an exception,[102] which he might have thought he was entitled to by virtue of his role in the Amphictyony. The priestess refused to prophesy, and when he began to drag her to the temple anyway, in frustration she uttered, "You are invincible, my son."[103] He accepted that as his prophecy.

Alexander is often criticized for abandoning his kingdom at this point. He did leave with every intention of being gone for an extended period, yet he did so only after securing his Balkan frontiers and settling affairs with the Greek states; no Greek city-state, in reality, was going to invade Macedonia with an army and seize control, though given an opening any one of the more powerful states was likely to attempt to confine Macedonia's influence to within its own borders. To guard against this he left the kingdom in the hands of a trusted and competent regent. Perhaps what no one could have foreseen in the spring of 334 was just how long and how far his campaign would actually go on; or that the Macedonian king would be absent from his kingdom for the rest of his life; or how much it would impact not just Macedonia and Macedonians, but the world, as they knew it, for centuries to come.

Notes

1 Biographies of Alexander abound. Lane Fox 1973 and Bosworth 1988 are among the most influential in the last half-century. Also influential are the papers of Badian, collected 2012.
2 *Magnus*: Plautus, *Mostellaria* 775; cp. Plut. *Pyrrh.* 19.1. Caesar: Plut, *Caesar* 11.5–6; Suetonius *Iulius* 7; Dio Cassius 37.52.2. Augustus: Suetonius *Augustus* 18; cp. Dio Cassius 51.16.5. Asirvatham 2010: 112–116.
3 On fragments and epitomes see Brunt 1980; on the so-called "vulgate" see Hammond 1983: 1–4.
4 See Chapter 4 n54.
5 Plut. *Alex.* 3.9. On prophecies at Alexander's birth see King 2013: 89–93.
6 *Contra* Greenwalt 1984: 72–73. See Chapter 3.
7 Plutarch (*Alex.* 2–8), virtually our only source for Alexander's youth, probably followed Marsyas of Pella, *Education of Alexander* [*FGrH* 135–136]. Heckel 1980c.
8 See Chapter 4.
9 Plut. *Alex.* 8.2, 26.1. On Macedonian education see Carney 2003b and Worthington 2014: 93–97.

10 See Chapter 4.
11 See Chapter 4.
12 Plut. *Alex.* 9.5–14; Just. 9.7.2–6; Ath. 557d–e. Carney 2006: 31–37, citing previous scholarship.
13 Diod. 16.91.2.
14 Athenaeus' term *gnesios* (557d) has the primary meaning "lawfully begotten." Both Athenaeus and Plutarch (9.8) in reporting the dialogue of the quarrel use the antonym *nothos*, "born out of wedlock." On Olympias' fidelity see Carney 2006: 34–35. Attalus assumed guardianship of Cleopatra after her brother Hippostratus, a close Companion of Philip, was killed in battle against the Illyrians in 344–343: Didymos 12.63–13.2 = Marsyas F17.
15 Justin's (9.5.9, 11.11.4–5; cp. 9.7.2) hint about Olympias committing adultery does not fit the context of 357, when she married Philip. On the myth see Ogden 2011: 7–28.
16 Just. 9.7.7.
17 Diod. 16.72.1.
18 Ruzicka 2010: 9 with references in n21 and n22.
19 Badian 1963: 244 n8: suggests he was a guest of Langarus, king of the Agrianians; Griffith in *HM* II 1979: 472: among the Ardiaei.
20 Plut. *Alex.* 9.12–14. On Demaratus see Heckel 2006a: 107; cp. Bosworth 1980a: 122–123 (Arr. *Anab.* 1.15.6).
21 Just. 9.7.6.
22 Cf. Arr. *Anab.* 3.6.5.
23 For the Pixodarus affair (not universally accepted as historical) see Plut. *Alex.* 10.1–5 with Ruzicka 2010 and Anson 2013: 77–78, both citing previous scholarship. Plutarch places the whole affair after the reconciliation, though the two episodes are perhaps more intertwined.
24 Arr. *Anab.* 3.6.4–7. On various aspects of the relationship between Philip and Alexander see the collection of articles in Carney and Ogden 2010.
25 Plut. *Alex.* 10.3.
26 Arist. *Pol.* 1311a–b; Just. 9.7.8; Plut. *Alex.* 10.6–7; but cp. Diod. 16.93–95. On Philip's assassination see Chapter 4 n226. See also Anson 2013: 79, arguing against Alexander's involvement.
27 Arr. *Anab.* 1.25.2; Just. 11.2.2; Curt. 7.1.6–7; Ps. Call. 1.26. On Alexander the Lyncestian see Bosworth 1971a: 96; Carney 1980; Heckel 2006a: 19; *contra* Hammond in *HM* III 1988: 3, 1980a: 457–460.
28 Diod. 17.2.1–2; Just. 11.1.8–10. On the nature of the monarchy see Carney 2000: 7–8, and on 'acclamation' see Chapter 3 n49.
29 Just. 11.2.3; cp. 12.6.14, Diod. 17.2.3; Plut. *Mor.* 178e–f. E.g. Bosworth 1988: 27 n10; Heckel 2006a: 78; Anson 2013: 127; but cp. Green 1991: 103, 112, 115, 141; and see Unz 1985.
30 Just. 11.5.1–2, 12.6.14; Curt. 6.9.17; Plut. *De Alex. fort.* 327c; Tod *GHI* 164 = RO *GHI* 75. On Amyntas' alleged challenge for the throne see Ellis 1971; Prandi 1998; and Worthington 2003.
31 Paus. 8.7.7; cp. Just. 9.7.8. On the source discrepancy about the gender of the child see Carney 2000: 77–78 with references.
32 Diod. 17.2.3–6, 5.1–2; Curt. 7.1.3, cf. 6.9.18.
33 Diod. 17.3.1–2, 5.1; Plut. *Dem.* 23.1–2.
34 Arr. *Anab.* 1.25.1–2; Just. 11.2.1–2. See Chapter 7 n115.
35 Diod. 17.2.2–3: Alexander addressed Greek embassies asking for the same loyalty they had shown Philip and set the army to exercising and training; cp. Just. 11.1.

36 Diod. 17.4.1; Just. 11.3.1–2. Westlake 1935: 217–220; Grainger 2007: 68; Heckel 2008: 28; Anson 2013: 132; *contra* Harris 1995: 176.
37 Polyaen. 4.3.23. Cp. Plut. *Alex.* 17.8: "the ladder" in Pamphylia.
38 Diod. 17.4.2; cp. 16.60.1. Poddighe 2009: 101–102; Anson 2013: 132.
39 Diod. 17.3.3, 4.3.
40 Diod. 17.4.4. Hammond in *HM III* 1988: 15.
41 Diod. 17.3.4, 4.4, 9.
42 Arr. *Anab.* 1.1.3.
43 Diod. 17.4.1–3, 9; Just. 11.2.5, 3.1–2; Arr. *Anab.* 1.1.1–2, 2.14.4. Plut. *Alex.* 14.1 places the assembly after the destruction of Thebes. On Alexander and the League of Corinth see Poddighe 2009, citing previous scholarship.
44 Freedom: Diod. 16.91.2, 17.24.1. Revenge: Arr. *Anab.* 2.14.4–5, 3.18.12; Diod. 16.89.2. Squillace 2010: 76–80.
45 Polyb. 3.6.13.
46 Diod. 17.3.1–5; Arr. *Anab.* 1.1.3.
47 Arr. *Anab.* 1.7.6; Dinarchus 1.18.
48 Arr. *Anab.* 1.1.4–6.11 is our only full narrative source for the Balkan campaign; for historical commentary see Bosworth 1980a. Cf. also Plut. *Alex.* 11.1–5; Diod. 17.8.1; Just. 11.2.4.
49 See Chapter 4.
50 Arr. *Anab.* 1.1.5–13. Perhaps the Tetrachorites, so Bosworth 1980a: 54, 55 (textual problem at Arr. *Anab.* 1.1.6); *contra* Hammond in *HM III* 1988: 34 (with n2): "the republican Thracians."
51 Cf. Polyaen. 4.3.11.
52 The Lyginus is otherwise unidentified.
53 Arr. *Anab.* 1.2.4–7; cp. Plut. *Alex.* 11.5.
54 Arr. *Tactica.* 29.7.
55 Arr. *Anab.* 1.2.3.1–4.5.
56 Arr. *Anab.* 1.4.6–7; cf. Diod. 17.3.4.
57 Arr. *Anab.* 1.5.1.
58 Bardylis was said to be ninety in 358 (Chapter 4 n24), so a son ruling in 335 is possible. Presumably it was this Cleitus' son Bardylis who was king in 295, and whose daughter, Bircenna, married Pyrrhus I of Epirus sometime after 295: Plut. *Pyrrh.* 9.2–3. On Illyrian dynasties see Hammond 1966: 243 (Cleitus is a son of Bardylis' old age, but cp. 1974: 79: a great grandson). See also Wilkes 1992: chapter 5.
59 Arr. *Anab.* 1.5.4–5.
60 Arr. *Succ.* 1.22.
61 Liv. 31.40.4. On the topographical crux: Hammond 1974: 75–76 locates Pellion at Goricë. His map from personal autopsy appears in multiple publications, e.g. 1974: 72, 1977: 505, *HM* III: 42, 1989a: 51. Bosworth 1980a: 68–70 and 1982 disputes his view and places Pellion in Eordaea or Lyncus, though not precisely (and, so far as I know, without autopsy). Albanian archaeologists have argued for the tomb site at Selcë e Poshtme; see Wilkes 1992: 123–124. Winnifrith 2002: 143–148 suggests a site closer to the Tsangon Pass at Zvezdë. For the latter reference I am indebted to Jake Morton (personal correspondence); his recent autopsy leads him to favour Winnifrith's suggestion, Zvezdë over Goricë and Selcë, which he believes is too far north.
62 Diod. 16.8.1.
63 Cf. Just. 11.1.6.
64 Arr. *Anab.* 1.5.5–12.
65 Arr. *Anab.* 1.6.1–8. Fuller 1958: 226 n1: "This is the first recorded use of catapults as field artillery."

66 Arr. *Anab.* 1.6.9–11.
67 Diod. 17.17.4.
68 Arr. *Anab.* 3.10; Plut. *Alex.* 31.10–14; Curt. 4.13.3–10.
69 Revolt and sack of Thebes: Arr. *Anab.* 1.7.1–10.6; Diod. 17.8.2–15.5; Plut. *Alex.* 11.6–13.5, *Dem.* 23; Just. 11.3.6–4.8; Aesch. 3.239–240; Dinarchus 1.18–21. For a thorough discussion see Worthington 2003, citing earlier scholarship; more recently, 2014: 131–135.
70 Cp. Plut. *Alex.* 11.6. The identification of Pylae here as Thermopylae is disputed; see Yardley and Heckel 1997: 93.
71 This is the route given at Arr. *Anab.* 1.7.5, but scholars have disputed it; see especially Hammond 1980b and Bosworth 1982. The debate hinges on where Alexander was when the news reached him (Diod. 17.8.2: still engaged in settling the Illyrian rebellion; Plut. *Dem.* 23.1–2: having wrapped up the campaign, but was he then in Dassaretis? Lyncus? Eordaea? And if the latter, which Eordaea (as there were several)? [Steph. Byz., see Bosworth 1982: 82 n16]) and whether the Thebans were in fact 'surprised' by his arrival or only by the speed of it. Hammond cannot be correct that the Macedonians sneaked up on Thebes (how could they?) but is correct that Alexander fought the Illyrians in Illyria (1980: 171 n1, citing an Athenian decree mentioned at Arr. *Anab.* 1.10.3). Both Arrian (1.7.5) and Diodorus (8.3) state that Alexander had his "whole army" with him in Boeotia, but does this mean the "whole army" from the Balkan campaign, or does it include forces that would have remained with Antipater? Justin (11.2.8–10) confuses Alexander's march on Thebes and the situation arising immediately after Philip's death, cp. Diod. 17.2.2; on Justin's confused chronology for 336–335 see Yardley and Heckel 1997: 83–85.
72 Arr. *Anab.* 1.7.2–3; Just. 11.2.8, 4.1.
73 Arr. *Anab.* 1.8.1.
74 On Ptolemy's bias see Errington 1969. Cp. Arr. *Anab.* 1 proem; and cf. 1.21.1.
75 Inconsistencies, e.g. at 17.8.1–2 Alexander is in Illyria when he gets word of the revolt, then at 9.1 Alexander appears suddenly out of Thrace. Diodorus' sensationalized narrative is probably taken directly from his source; on his sources see Hammond 1983: 12–16, 25–27, 38, 51.
76 Diod. 17.12.3.
77 Arr. *Anab.* 1.7.7; Plut. *Alex.* 11.7; Diod. 17.9.2, 4; Just. 11.6–7.
78 Diod. 17.9.5; Plut. *Alex.* 11.7–8.
79 Hamilton 1969: 30; Heckel 2006a: 35–36.
80 Arr. *Anab.* 1.8.1; cp. 1.7.9–10.
81 Arr. *Anab.* 1.7.7, 9.
82 Arr. *Anab.* 1.7.4; Plut. *Alex.* 11.6; Just. 11.2.7; Diod. 17.8.5; Plut. *Dem.* 23.2.
83 Diod. 17.11.1.
84 Diod. 17.9.3.
85 Diod. 17.12.1. Cf. Polyaen. 4.3.12, contradicted by other sources; or (n79) not the regent Antipater.
86 Arr. *Anab.* 1.8.6; Diod. 17.12.5.
87 Diod. 17.14.1; Plut. *Alex.* 1.12.
88 Diod. 17.14.1 and Arr. *Anab.* 1.9.9; cp. Just. 11.3.8. On the question of allies versus *synedrion* of the League of Corinth see Bosworth 1980a: 89–90 and Hammond in *HM* III 1988: 63–66.
89 Arr. *Anab.* 1.8.8; Diod. 17.13.5; cp. Plut. *Alex.* 11.11; Just. 11.3.8.
90 Diod. 17.14.4, from Cleitarchus [*FGrH/BNJ* 137 F1 = Ath. 4.148d–e].
91 Diod. 17.14.1–4; Arr. *Anab.* 1.9.9; cp. Just. 11.4.7–8.
92 Plut. *Alex.* 11.12. For Pindar see Hammond 1989a: 46.
93 Arr. *Anab.* 1.9.10; Plin. *HN* 7.109; Dio Chrysostomus *Orations* 2.33.

94 Polyaen. 8.40; Plut. *Alex.* 12, *Mor.* 259d–260d.
 95 Arr. *Anab.* 1.10; Plut. *Alex.* 13.1–2, *Dem.* 23, *Phoc.* 17; Diod. 17.15; Just. 11.4.9–12; cf. Curt. 3.2.10. Bosworth 1980a: 92–95.
 96 Polyb. 38.2.14.
 97 Diod. 17.8.7: Athens voted to help Thebes, and the Peloponnesians sent forces as far as the Isthmus, but both waited to see how it would go; cp. Arr. *Anab.* 1.10.1.
 98 Polyb. 38.2.13; Plut. *Alex.* 11.11.
 99 Dahmen 2010: 52.
100 Arr. *Anab.* 1.11.1, mistaken about Aegae: cp. Diod. 17.16.3–4 and see Chapter 1 n31.
101 Diod. 17.16.1–2.
102 Plut. *Mor.* 292e–f, citing Callisthenes.
103 Plut. *Alex.* 14.6–7; cf. Diod. 17.93.4. Philip: Diod. 16.91.2; Paus. 8.7.6.

7 Alexander and the Macedonians beyond Macedonia, 334–323

Alexander inherited together with Philip's veteran army an invasion of Persia already in progress. That he 'conquered' nearly the entire Persian Empire and beyond in a mere decade is due to his own generalship and craving for conquest and adventure, which fueled the Macedonian army in triumph after triumph: battles won at the Granicus, Issus, and Gaugamela, 'liberation' of the Ionian Greeks and Egypt, and confiscation of rich Persian coffers. The 'war of revenge' accomplished, Alexander continued east in pursuit of further glory, until guerrilla fighting, high attrition, trials and executions for treason, his attempt to introduce *proskynesis*, monsoons, and war elephants exhausted the will of the Macedonians, and they begged a return. Back in Babylonia 10,000 veterans were discharged, 30,000 Persian youths enrolled, and new elaborate plans were launched for Arabia and the west, all suddenly overturned by his untimely death.

From Europe to Asia: enforcing liberation

Alexander marched east from Macedonia in the early spring of 334, never to return. He left Antipater as regent with forces to protect the kingdom.[1] At the Hellespont Parmenio oversaw the crossing of the main part of the army from Sestos to Abydos while Alexander went down to the tip of the Chersonese and crossed from Elaeus to Troy. He was first to step ashore on Asian soil and cast a spear, a symbolic gesture of conquest; he also marked the crossing with religious observations: a bull to Poseidon in the strait and altars set up on both sides of the Hellespont to Zeus, Athena, and Heracles, three deities especially honoured by the Macedonian kings.[2] At the famed site of Ilion (Troy) he paid homage to the heroes of the Trojan War, honouring especially his ancestors, Greek and Trojan, Achilles and Andromache.[3] Dedicating some of his own armour in the Temple of Trojan Athena, the Macedonian king took in exchange the strongest of the arms purportedly preserved from the Trojan War: a shield which the Hypaspists always carried before him into battle.[4] While his evocation of the heroic past was personal and sincere, and in keeping with the nature of Macedonian kingship, which as a descendant of Mycenaean political and military structure retained distinct heroic elements, it was also a careful cultivation of his public image.[5]

Alexander's first major battle was awaiting him some 80 km (50 miles) to the northeast, on the banks of the Granicus River. There some regional satraps and generals of the Persian king Darius III had mustered forces to quash the invasion.[6] They might indeed have given Alexander a rough start, if the Persian war council had not rejected the recommendation of Memnon of Rhodes of a scorched earth policy. This was the same Memnon who had taken political refuge at Philip's court in the 350s, and he was now in Darius' pay as commander of some Greek mercenaries.[7] After a hard fought cavalry engagement the Macedonians came away victorious, and with plenty of food and fodder there was nothing to inhibit the army's maintenance in the region.[8] Twenty-five Companion cavalrymen were killed in the first onslaught—a mad dash into the river and up a steep muddy bank—a noble sacrifice for greater Macedonian glory. Such was the message implicit in the twenty-five bronze statues Alexander commissioned the sculptor Lysippus to create in their honour (these were to be set up at Dion) and in the remission of taxes granted the parents and children of all the fallen. The message sent to Athens attached to 300 sets of armour taken from the fallen Persians and to be dedicated to Athena on the Acropolis implicitly hailed Alexander, in fulfillment of his League of Corinth mission, as the avenger of Persian wrongs: "Alexander son of Philip and the Greeks, except the Lacedaemonians, set up these spoils from the barbarians dwelling in Asia."[9] Lysippus' bronzes are gone, but there survives at Dion a wall decorated with arms in relief from some other victory monument (Figure 7.1).

Figure 7.1 Dion shield and cuirass monument, façade of a Hellenistic building
Source: author, 2011.

News ran like wildfire ahead of the victors. The commander of the Persian garrison at Sardis, seat of the Persian satrapy of Lydia, met Alexander on the road and surrendered city, citadel, and treasury, which supplied Alexander with much needed funds. Then the Greek cities of Asia Minor came into his hands: Ephesus, Magnesia, and Tralles surrendered, Priene and Iasus were won over.[10] But Miletus and Halicarnassus resisted the Macedonian offer of 'freedom', so Alexander brought his siege engines into action against their walls.[11] There is no small irony in Alexander forcefully freeing Greek city-states from their Persian-backed oligarchies and installing democracies that would owe gratitude and loyalty to the Macedonian king.[12] It had been Philip's policy to overthrow whichever of the two parties had been anti-Macedonian and install the other, and Alexander's interference with governing systems was not out of preference for democracy. The cities were relieved of paying tribute to the Persian king, but they now would be expected to make 'contributions' to his war effort. In Ephesus, though the city surrendered, there was a great deal of civil unrest and strong anti-Macedonian sentiment, manifested in the overturned statue of Philip.[13] At Miletus the citizens had first indicated surrender, but news of the Persian fleet on its way precipitated a change of heart and they begged neutrality. When the fleet failed to relieve them, however, Alexander took that as encouragement to disband his own Greek fleet of 160 ships. It was too expensive to maintain at present, too few to challenge the Persian fleet, and so he kept only a few vessels, including twenty Athenian triremes and a few others to use for transporting his siege engines.[14] It was very nearly a costly mistake. At Halicarnassus, where Memnon had taken refuge after the Granicus battle, the outer city fell to Alexander, but at the end of the summer Memnon still held a fortified citadel, so Alexander left his general Ptolemaeus in charge of the siege, and, sending Parmenio with part of the army by way of Sardis to Phrygia, he himself proceeded to campaign in the coastal regions of Caria, Lycia, and Pamphylia.[15] Could long-standing ties with the region be reflected in the name of a local dynast, Amyntas, whose rock-cut tomb sits above Telmessus' harbour (Figure 7.2)?

From Caria Alexander sent home for the winter the newly wedded soldiers under command of Ptolemy, son of Seleucus, and the taxiarchs Coenus and Meleager. They were instructed to recruit cavalry and infantry from home. At the same time Coenus' brother Cleander was sent to the Peloponnese to gather troops from the League allies.[16] Nearchus, one of Alexander's friends whom Philip had exiled, was left as governor in Lycia and Pamphylia, though he would rejoin Alexander in Bactria some four years later.[17] The longest-lasting appointment made in the course of that winter/spring campaign was of Antigonus Monophthalmus ("One-Eyed") as satrap of Phrygia.[18] Alexander secured the subdued territories by making such appointments of prominent Macedonians and by assigning them forces (mainly mercenary) to keep their regions under control. The local peoples gave these Macedonian governors a hard time of it.[19] Antigonus, however, was exceptionally successful in his battles with the subdued population, and by the time of Alexander's death ten years later he was a firmly established power in his own right in the region of greater Phrygia.[20]

Figure 7.2 Ionic tomb of Amyntas (son of Hermagias), ancient Telmessus, Lycia, bearing resemblance to Macedonian tombs of similar date, fourth century BCE. Fethiye, Turkey

Source: author, 2013.

In the spring at Gordion Alexander was rejoined by Parmenio, the forces that had wintered in Phrygia, and by those returning from winter furlough together with the recruits from Macedonia.[21] Meantime Darius had appointed Memnon general of the war with the Macedonians and sent him money to man a fleet of 300 ships for conducting naval aggression in the Aegean. Alexander was thus compelled to demand from his Greek allies a reconstituted fleet of warships.[22] As fortune would have it, before summer's end Memnon died, but Alexander had already left Aegean matters in the hands of Antipater and his admirals[23] while he himself with the land forces set out from Gordion in May, heading across the Anatolian Plateau and passing through the Cilician Gates in the Taurus Mountains and down to the coast again. Here he fell ill for a time, but by the fall he had subdued the cities of Cilicia and acquired from them considerable funds, supplies, and horses. He was at Soli when he had news of the fall of Halicarnassus, and at Mallus paying homage to his ancestor Heracles when he learned that Darius had mobilized an enormous army and was camped only two days' march east of the Assyrian Gate, one of the passes through the Amanus Mountains giving access to the coastal plain of Phoenicia. Alexander had achieved so many successes in such a short time that Darius was reasonably alarmed and was marching in person with a large army to challenge him.[24]

All along the sea coast of Asia Minor Alexander secured the ports with the intention of crippling the Persian fleet. A land battle was what he wanted. He was aware of Darius' proximity just on the other side of the Amanus Mountains, but it is unlikely he would have wanted to give up the advantages of the narrow coastal terrain and his access to supplies in Cilicia by going to meet him.[25] As he marched down the Syrian coast towards the Assyrian Gate, he was in disbelief when his scouts reported that Darius had come out to the coast behind him through the Amanian Gate, thus cutting his supply lines. Alexander had no choice but to turn around and fight. The Persian king had erred, however, in placing his army between mountains and sea where he could not make the best use of his superior numbers.[26] As the two armies faced each other across the Pinarus River near Issus, Alexander charged with the Companion Cavalry from his right, Parmenio came under heavy attack but repelled the Persian cavalry charge on the left, and in the centre the Macedonian phalanx was having a hard go against Darius' Greek mercenary hoplites[27] until some of Alexander's cavalry on the right came to their assistance, and combined they broke the Persian line. Darius fled, Alexander chasing him until dark and coming back with only the Persian king's shield and bow and a sword wound in his thigh. It is widely accepted that the Alexander Mosaic uncovered during excavations in the House of the Faun in Pompeii and now displayed in Naples (Figure 7.3) depicts Alexander's purposeful targeting of Darius in the battle at Issus, and that it is a close copy of a famous painting executed by Philoxenus of Eretria.[28] By the time Alexander returned the soldiers had captured Darius' camp, including his tent with all its rich accouterments and servants, 3,000 talents in money, and, to top it all, the king's mother, wife, two daughters, and young son! It was Persian custom to take families on campaign,[29] something Macedonians were not accustomed to do. Most of Darius'

Figure 7.3 Alexander mosaic, House of the Faun, Pompeii, first century BCE. Museo Archeologico Nazionale di Napoli, Naples, Italy

Source: https://commons.wikimedia.org/wiki/File:Battle_of_Issus.jpg.

baggage train, including many of the wives of the Persian commanders and the greater cache of money, had been sent on to Damascus, and Alexander entrusted its seizure to Parmenio.[30] The Macedonians knew something about the value of gold and silver, and among the soldiery there would have been men with experience as miners and artisans, but the effect of Persian spoils on men accustomed to living off the land was dazzling.[31] Alexander himself, when he entered Darius' tent, purportedly said, "This, as it would seem, is to be a king."[32] Among the captives taken at Damascus was Barsine, Memnon's widow and daughter of that Artabazus who with Memnon had taken refuge at Philip's court when Alexander was hardly more than a toddler; she became Alexander's mistress.[33]

Alexander's determination to secure every potential Persian stronghold on the Mediterranean seaboard kept him from impetuous hot pursuit of Darius and explains his investment in the seven-month-long siege of the island fortress Tyre.[34] When Alexander left Tyre it was an island no longer, his mole constructed for siege towers having permanently attached it to the mainland. During the siege a large number of Phoenician and Cypriot ships and a few from Rhodes defected from the Persian fleet and were instrumental in Alexander's naval assault that finally won him the city.[35] After paying homage to Tyrian Heracles and dealing with the captives Alexander used some of his ships to transport siege towers from Tyre south to Gaza, which had decided to resist him; but after two months Gaza also fell to his siege.[36]

In November 332 Alexander arrived at the Nile. Egypt in 343 had fallen a second time under Persian suzerainty and welcomed a way to be rid of their Persian satraps and garrisons.[37] Alexander was careful to present himself as a liberator, yet the first thing he did was establish his own garrison at Pelusium, the gateway from Syria, before marching up the Nile to Heliopolis and Memphis (Cairo).[38] His motives for going to Egypt, the chronology of his itinerary during the five-month-or-so stay, and the question of whether he was instated as pharaoh have been much debated, the reason being that the sources are either contradictory or are not explicit. No source, in fact, apart from the *Alexander Romance*, a quasi-historical account of Alexander's adventures, states that Alexander was crowned pharaoh, though it has often been assumed.[39] What is certain is that in addition to touring—this was an antique land, after all—Alexander established the first and ultimately the greatest of his many 'Alexandria' city foundations at the Canobic (westernmost) mouth of the Nile and that he made a journey to the Siwah Oasis in the Libyan desert to consult the oracle of Ammon, an Egyptian deity closely identified with Zeus and with the divinity of the pharaoh. In reverence for local deities, cults, and religious rites, one of his first acts upon arriving at Memphis was to sacrifice to the Apis bull sacred to Ammon, and later he arranged for the renovation of the shrine of Ammon at Luxor.[40] What his dealings were with the priestly class we do not know, but the iconography of the shrine at Luxor shows that Alexander did win approval from the priests of Ammon to be depicted as pharaoh—as the embodiment of the *ka*, or the divine entity, that infused the pharaoh upon coronation.

This recognition, which came perhaps some years after his visit to Egypt, once he had defeated Darius decisively, transpired despite the fact that he was never present for the annual renewal of that incarnation.

Alexander's choice for his site of Alexandria was wise in the practicality of a large harbour (soon made into two) protected by an offshore limestone ridge, and, as he hoped, it quickly became a port city to rival all other ports in the eastern Mediterranean,[41] as it does to this day (Figure 7.4). From there the journey to Siwah became the stuff of legend, and the inspiration for the visit to the oracle is much debated. Perhaps it was primarily personal,[42] though whether fueled by stories Olympias told about her son's conception is questionable. In the 'official' account of Alexander's court historian Callisthenes, Alexander was inspired by his desire to emulate the heroes of old, his ancestors Perseus and Heracles.[43] Siwah was one of the most important oracle sites in the ancient Mediterranean world, along with the oracles of Zeus at Dodona and of Apollo at Delphi, so possibly Alexander was seeking divine sanction for his Persian expedition.[44] Or perhaps he thought it sound political policy to promote himself in Egypt as son of Ammon; everything about Egyptian society pointed to the pharaoh, the king, as god on earth, and it was said that the priest addressed him as *o pai dios*, "o son of god."[45] Callisthenes asserted that Alexander was alone in the temple of Ammon for the consultation, in which case the accounts we have of questions and answers are imaginative. Arrian states it frankly: Alexander got the answer he desired, so he said.[46] What is clear is that Alexander came away

Figure 7.4 Alexandria's east harbour, view east towards the Ptolemaic palace quarter
Source: author, 2008.

from Siwah with the idea that there was nothing to prevent him from promoting himself as the son of Ammon. But this more than anything else he ever did was offensive to most of the Macedonian nobles, at least to Philip's old guard, as well as to the Greeks.[47]

Once Egypt was secured with garrisons under command of trusted Companions and his own appointees were put in charge of the administration system,[48] in the spring of 331 Alexander left Memphis and returned to Tyre. He in his lifetime was never to set foot in Egypt again.

Alexander "King of Asia"

Some eighteen months after he had given up the horseback chase into the foothills around Issus Alexander resumed his pursuit of Darius. Turning his back to the Mediterranean, which he left to his admirals, and leading the Macedonian army towards the very heart of the Persian Empire, undeterred by the barriers of the great Euphrates and Tigris rivers, he advanced against the enemy. Fortune favours the brave, yet boldness falters in face of the unknown. As the terrain changed and rumours flew that the enemy outnumbered the Macedonians many times over, within the ranks fear began to verge on panic, and then on the night of September 20–21 on the banks of the Tigris (Figure 7.5) an eclipse of the moon occurred that for the troops was an omen of impending disaster.[49] Alexander's diviners and astrologers understood the cause; however, one of the diviners, Aristander of Telmessus, rather than give a scientific reason, explained for the benefit of the soldiers that the moon in eclipse presaged defeat for the Persians, and a number of historical instances were recounted to reinforce the interpretation. This is one of many occasions on which Alexander, with the aid of his diviners, encouraged his troops and built up their morale in troubling circumstances.[50] Eleven days later, on October 1, 331, on the plains of Gaugamela, "House of the Camel," some 95 km (60 miles) northwest of Arbela (Erbil in northern Iraq) the Macedonian army met in battle the forces that Darius had mustered from the far corners of his empire.[51] The battlefield this time was of Darius' choosing, as wide open as Issus had been narrow, with the ground carefully cleared for his cavalry and scythed chariots, and one source says he even provided longer pikes for some of his troops because he thought the Macedonian *sarissai* had put him at a disadvantage.[52] Alexander was forced to deploy his substantially inferior numbers (outnumbered five to one by lowest estimate of the sources)[53] in a modified square formation to try to prevent encirclement, a strategy only partially successful since, as Alexander advanced with an oblique right movement, some Persians did get round his left flank into the baggage camp, probably in the attempt to recover Darius' family. Parmenio was in command of the left and a fierce cavalry engagement took place there. Alexander on the right wing, turning suddenly sharp left, led a charge of his Companion Cavalry into the thick of the Persian elite forces in the centre around the king, and for the second time he compelled Darius into flight from the battlefield.[54]

Figure 7.5 Tigris River, near Alexander's ford, Cizre, Turkey
Source: author, 2003.

The defeated Persian king fled east to Media with a few supporters, while Alexander and the Macedonians marched on the Persian capitals and, as these surrendered one by one, took possession of their treasuries. It was tradition for the Persian king to move his court seasonally from palace to palace between five capitals: Babylon, Susa, Persepolis, Pasargadae, and Ecbatana.[55] The wealth of these cities was enormous—"beyond belief"—and the total transported to Ecbatana under the supervision of Parmenio the following spring was said to amount to 190,000 talents in gold and silver coin and bullion.[56] On top of this were all the other rich spoils: furniture, gold and silver vessels, ornaments, garments, tapestries. Alexander now could give generous bonuses to his Macedonian and allied troops; indeed, he could fund a campaign indefinitely, but importantly he could reward his commanders with indulgence in the spoils of victory. At Babylon he gave his army a month-long respite, about which time Amyntas, son of Andromenes, arrived with reinforcements from Antipater. Alexander had been brought news just before he left the coast that the Spartan king, Agis, was fomenting revolt in the Peloponnese, and evidently more news now prompted him to send 3,000 talents to his regent for the war with Sparta.[57] At Susa we are told he gifted Parmenio with the opulent house of Bagoas, the powerful royal eunuch who had elevated Darius to the throne.[58] Many of the officers, because they could now afford it and thought they had earned it, began to hold outlandishly expensive banquets and to acquire large entourages of their own slaves and hangers-on. Alexander spent much of his own time reorganizing the army and the administrative control of the conquered territory.[59]

The Macedonian king had already been laying claim to the title King of Asia in his exchanges with Darius since the battle at Issus.[60] At Susa he took a seat on the Persian throne—a symbolic gesture—but if he was proclaimed "King of Asia," no coronation ceremony is anywhere described.[61] Confronted with the question of *how* to rule over the Persian empire, the policy adopted was not to disturb too much what was already in place and, whenever he thought fit, to appoint or reappoint a local ruler who, at the same time as sharing the cultural and language identity of the subjects, would now owe his position and authority, often his very life, to Alexander's clemency.[62] As a precaution and to guarantee the continued obedience of the local ruler, Alexander left a Macedonian or Greek official and a garrison under a Macedonian commander. The system was not without considerable risks. Satibarzanes, who was made satrap of Aria after surrendering to Alexander, killed his Macedonian overseer and garrison of forty javelin men and stirred up the locals to armed revolt.[63] Many Persians, on the other hand, who after Gaugamela surrendered and joined Alexander's entourage, continued to follow Persian court protocol as if he were now their king, and that protocol was much more formal and hierarchical than traditional Macedonian court practices. This was soon to lead to the alienation of a large number of the Macedonians as well as Greek courtiers.

Alexander left Susa in the early winter, and, having sent most of his allied forces with Parmenio the long way, he took with him his Macedonian cavalry, foot, and the Agrianians and fought his way through a mountain shortcut at the Persian Gates to reach Persepolis in Persis about late January. Here at Persepolis were the palaces of Darius I and Xerxes, invaders and ravagers of Greece.[64] By the time Alexander left in the spring the palace of Xerxes was a ruin of ashes. The question that has long occupied historians is whether the burning of the palace was deliberate, premeditated policy or rash impulse under intoxication.[65] The sources diverge significantly. The historian Arrian claims it was Alexander's decision, a matter of policy and one against which Parmenio advised, to burn the palace of Xerxes in retribution for Xerxes' destructions in Greece, especially the burning of the temple of Athena in Athens.[66] According to other Alexander historians (Diodorus, Curtius, Plutarch), Alexander initially granted his soldiers permission to pillage the incredibly rich city, and later, towards the end of the four-month stay, the idea to burn the palace in retribution was not Alexander's but rather that of an Athenian courtesan in his entourage, Thais, and it came during a banquet when everyone was well into the drinking. Alexander approved and threw the first torch.[67]

Historians ancient and modern agree that the burning was an act of retribution, and some scholars have reconciled the contradictory accounts by concluding that it *was* premeditated, but that Alexander seized the opportunity of Thais' intoxicated call for vengeance to carry out the act. The difficulty with a pre-meditated 'policy' is that Alexander was wise enough to realize that by deliberately destroying Persepolis he was committing a grave offense against those Persians whose support he needed, and it went against his prior policy of conciliation towards the Persian nobility. From the surrender of Sardis Alexander had been careful to treat the Persian nobles who cooperated with him with privilege and reward; just recently Mazaeus and Abulites, the satraps who surrendered Babylon and Susa respectively, were left in their posts, while Mithrenes, who four years earlier had surrendered Sardis, was now made satrap of Armenia (though this was not as cushy as it sounds—Armenia was not yet subdued). On the other hand, the ostensible purpose of the Asian expedition was to 'liberate' the Greeks—he claimed to have done that—and to seek 'vengeance' for Xerxes' depredations in Greece. After his victory at Gaugamela Alexander wrote to the Greeks: to the cities of Ionia that he had restored to them their own laws; to the Plataeans, in honour of it being on their soil that the Persians had been defeated in 479, that he would rebuild their city which had subsequently been destroyed by neighbouring Thebes; and to the Athenians that he would send back to them some of the statues stolen by Xerxes.[68] Surely the *hegemon* of the League of Corinth had fulfilled his purpose, and come spring at Persepolis the allies and Macedonians alike were restless for the triumphant return.[69] Perhaps Alexander hoped to compensate a weary rank and file by giving them over to looting, albeit the royal quarters and treasury, being the king's particular prizes of war, were excluded.[70] As archaeological evidence indicates, the palace area had been cleaned out before the fire.[71] But was it only revenge for wrongs done to the Greeks—in one account Thais says the Greeks expected it—or did Alexander also avenge wrongs done to the Macedonians? It was Macedonians who had suffered heavy losses that winter from Ariobarzanes' defence of the Persian Gates, losses generally glossed over.[72] And *if* the "Yaunã takabarã," or "Peoples of the coast wearing shields for hats," mentioned in an inscription on the tomb of Darius I at Naqsh-e Rostam and visually depicted on four tombs there, as well as on two at Persepolis, are, as some have suggested, the *kausia*-wearing Macedonians (Figures 3.1, 10.1),[73] then we might take note of a speech attributed to Darius III at about the time he might have heard news of the fire: a morale-boosting reminder to his depleted Persian army that the Macedonians had formerly paid tribute to his ancestors.[74] Did Alexander III hope to obliterate by fire any physical record of Macedonian subservience to Persia back in the days of Alexander I? Whatever the motive or trigger, he himself regretted the conflagration as a mistake, an idea he might have preferred went down in history as Thais'.[75]

Alexander rode away from the flames of Persepolis intent upon eliminating Achaemenid rule. Pasargadae had been secured during the winter,[76] so of the Persian capitals only Ecbatana remained. That is where over the winter Darius had managed to muster a small army, but at Alexander's approach he took the treasury funds and fled.[77] Darius would not be defending his kingdom in another major battle. In acknowledgment of having fulfilled the League mandate, Alexander discharged the League troops as well as the Thessalian cavalry with very generous pay. Then, hiring back any men willing to continue the campaign,[78] after instructing Parmenio to oversee the installment of the Persepolis treasury funds at Ecbatana, Alexander led his best and fastest forces on a manhunt of gruelling marches through unforgiving terrain, covering an average of 65 km (40 miles) per day and often travelling by night.[79] After passing through the Caspian Gates Alexander met deserters who told him Darius had been arrested by his satrap of Bactria, Bessus, and a few days later Alexander came upon Darius' spear-riddled body abandoned by the roadside in a hide-covered cart. Bessus' mutiny and usurpation of the royal title—he was Darius' cousin and began calling himself by the royal name Artaxerxes—was a stroke of luck for Alexander, and quickly seizing the opportunity, by the act of throwing his own cloak over the murdered king's corpse, he metamorphosed from Darius' unrelenting foe into his lawful avenger.[80] Alexander arranged a royal burial for Darius, an act that in Macedonia was the prerogative of a 'successor': a new Macedonian king upon ascension or as a declaration of succession buried his predecessor.[81]

Darius' death was a turning point. It drew a final conclusion to the war of revenge, and the Macedonians thought the war was now over for them too. However, as Darius' avenger and successor, Alexander had yet another objective: to hunt down and supplant the pretender Bessus. It required the art of persuasion for Alexander to win over his Macedonians, both officers and troops, to continuing the campaign.[82] But what did this mean for the kingdom of Macedonia, which by this time had been without its king for more than four years, and for the Macedonian officers and troops who had not seen their homeland in all that time? As one contemporary in Athens described the campaign beyond Susa, Alexander had disappeared off the map![83] Communication lines were still fluid, though, and news had reached Alexander that Antipater had put down the Spartan uprising in the Peloponnese; Macedonia and her hegemony over the Greek states were in secure hands. As for the Macedonians on campaign, many hardships lay ahead.

Treason, trials, and law

Alexander could hardly assume the role of Darius' successor without adopting Persian trappings and protocol. To some degree his Persianization was a practical policy intended to win over the administrators and subjects of the Persian Empire to his rule. In the process, many, though not all, of his close Companions took offense; for instance, when Alexander adopted Persian court dress he also issued Persian clothing to his Companions, and most disliked it.[84] The Macedonian Pages and Bodyguards remained in attendance on the king, though he began to appoint Persians both to his personal guard, among them the brother of Darius, Oxathres, and to the guard around his quarters, access to which, in Persian fashion, became increasingly difficult for the lower ranks. That restriction of access was critical for the king's protection, but it also led to the most severe rupture in Alexander's Macedonian high command.[85]

On a day late in 330, when the army (in pursuit of Bessus) was camped at Phrada, the capital of Drangiana, a Macedonian of no significant rank approached Philotas, son of Parmenio, commander of the Companion Cavalry, outside the forecourt of Alexander's royal quarters, "for nearer access was not allowed him."[86] This man, Cebalinus, had urgent need of getting word to the king that a plot against the king's life was afoot. He had been told of the plot by his younger brother Nicomachus, whose older lover, an otherwise unknown Companion named Dimnus, had attempted to suborn him into the plot. Philotas, who by this time had drawn envy and even hatred for his arrogance and high living, did not grant the man access to Alexander, and for some reason did not report the matter, despite his having audience with the king later in the day. The same thing happened the next day. Abandoning protocol, Cebalinus next approached one of the Pages, an armourer named Metron, who took his urgent word to the king. Alarmed as much by Philotas' failure to report it (and rightly so) as by the plot itself, Alexander summoned his closest friends and advisors, excluding Philotas, and they secretly arranged for Philotas to be arrested totally unawares in the middle of the night. While small bands of armed men scurried here and there to arrest everyone named by Cebalinus' brother as being in on the plot—Philotas was *not* named as a conspirator—an armed guard of 300 men under the command of Atarrhias, leader of a battalion of the Hypaspists, went to Philotas' tent and brought him in bonds, head covered by a cloak, to Alexander. The next day Alexander summoned an assembly. Six thousand Macedonian soldiers flocked to the place of assembly along with a throng of camp followers and slaves, and after Alexander primed the crowd for condemnation of the charge—before they saw who was being accused—the cloak was lifted to reveal Philotas, the "iron man," on trial for his life for treason.[87]

Much has been speculated about the so-called "Philotas Affair," as it has intrigued modern historians as much as it did the Roman Alexander historian Curtius, who gives a lengthy detailed account of the arrest, trial, and torture of one of the highest-ranking commanders in the Macedonian army.[88] It seems clear that Philotas had voiced some strong criticisms of Alexander's style of leadership, perhaps dating back to the journey to Siwah, when Alexander began to identify himself as son of Ammon; but the only 'evidence' that could be brought against him was his failure to report to Alexander the alleged plot of Dimnus, and Dimnus could not testify since he had either stabbed himself or was fatally stabbed resisting arrest. On the one hand, the charge, arrest, prosecution, and conviction all appear to have been orchestrated by a number of Alexander's close friends, who potentially stood to gain military rank from Philotas' demise. On the other hand, there had been nothing to stop these friends from rising already. Hephaestion had been elevated to command of the "bodyguards" (perhaps the Royal Hypaspists) before Gaugamela, and Craterus was increasingly being given the weightiest military assignments and arguably was being groomed for the elderly Parmenio's position.[89] Philotas was executed in the traditional Macedonian manner, though sources do not agree whether this was by stoning or hail of javelins.[90] Command of the Companion Cavalry was now divided, Hephaestion and Cleitus the Black succeeding jointly to command.

The Macedonians were still reeling from the shock of Philotas' execution when they were struck anew by news of the even more shocking assassination of Parmenio. The subsequent literary tradition built a considerable backstory of clashes between king and top general in an attempt to justify what most view as outright murder.[91] Alexander would have calculated that the execution of Philotas demanded the elimination of the father as well, for it would have been far too risky to leave the alienated old general (he was now seventy) sitting astride his communication lines.[92] Parmenio, remember, had been left behind at Ecbatana the previous spring, guarding the treasury with a sizeable force and with instructions to take forces into Hyrcania.[93] That he never did, evidently, and we next hear of him having been appointed satrap of Media, though Alexander appointed (instead?) Oxydates to that post just after he passed the Caspian Gates in pursuit of Darius. Was Parmenio not following orders?[94] A close friend of Parmenio, Polydamus, whose brothers were held hostage for his loyalty, went with two guides on fast racing camels, making what would normally be a thirty-two-day trip in only eleven days back to Ecbatana with two letters for Parmenio, one from Alexander and one sealed with Philotas' seal. As he was reading the letter from his son, three of Parmenio's own subordinate commanders assassinated him.[95]

Philotas evidently had not been popular, and the trial, in the heat of the moment at least, had convinced many that he was guilty.[96] Parmenio's assassination was a different matter. His assassins were nearly lynched by the troops under their command and disciplinary and/or cautionary measures were taken. A group openly grieved by the loss of Parmenio and hostile towards Alexander was separated out as a precaution and put in a single corps. One tradition claims that another group of malcontents had already been identified by trickery. They were encouraged to write letters home to be sent with some messengers, the letters were opened and read, and all the men who had privately penned their criticisms of the Macedonian king were then separated into a disciplinary corps called *Ataktoi* ("the out of order ones").[97] The latter episode, if true, probably occurred in Hyrcania just after the death of Darius when Alexander made his persuasive speech that convinced the Macedonians (or did it?) to continue the campaign.[98] The following spring all the volunteer Thessalian cavalry—surely another precaution—were sent home.[99] The corps of malcontents, it is said, fought most bravely to clear their records, or, alternatively, they were sent on the most dangerous missions and dispersed in the various settlements that Alexander planted. One underlying issue in all of this is that Alexander had created a situation where 'freedom of expression' could no longer be exercised with impunity; the Macedonians had been deprived of their long-standing privilege of *isegoria*. Dissention went underground rather than away, however, and that was a battle Alexander would continue to fight.

With a scent of rebellion on the wind, Alexander brought out of imprisonment Alexander Lyncestes. It is generally assumed he was Lyncestian royalty,[100] and, though his two brothers had been executed for complicity in Philip's death, he had been first to acclaim Alexander "king" in 336. Then, early in the campaign, he had been deprived of his command of the Thessalian cavalry and arrested on a charge of treason.[101] After three or four years in confinement Lyncestes was at a loss or too surprised by the suddenness of his trial to defend himself.[102] Now he also, despite being Antipater's son-in-law, was convicted and executed for the alleged crime of receiving a letter from Darius offering him the Macedonian throne in exchange for the assassination of his king.

Many, it is said, feared for their lives, for the relatives of those convicted of treason were also at risk of execution.[103] Amyntas, son of Andromenes, and his brother Simmias, because of their close friendship with Philotas, were also summoned to trial.[104] The fact that the youngest brother, Polemon, had bolted at news of Philotas' arrest did not help their case. Amyntas was brought in bound, like Philotas, and heard the charge, which contained an incrimination of him by Alexander's mother Olympias in a letter she had written her son warning him against the brothers and complaining that Amyntas had recruited against her will some of her favourites! Asking to be released from his bonds and to be granted permission to don his Macedonian military attire, which request Alexander granted, also restoring to him his *sarissa*, Amyntas stood proud and fearless before the army and made his defence.[105] Amyntas had held important commands as early as 335, so it is possible that, like Philotas, he had been one of Philip's officers before he was Alexander's.[106] His speech, as we have it, is a rhetorical piece, yet the issue of grumblings of soldiers in their tents which it addresses is probably very real; they vacillate between wanting to follow Alexander wherever he leads and longing to return to their homeland and their families. Such are the rumblings of nearly every soldier in every tent in every land in every age. Unlike Philotas, Amyntas won the approval of the assembly, among whom would have been the Macedonian infantry who long had fought under his own command, and Alexander delivered a verdict of acquittal.[107] A short while later Amyntas was killed in action, and a fourth brother, Attalus, succeeded to his position as taxiarch.[108]

At some point during these tumultuous days Demetrius, one of the elite Seven Bodyguards, was arrested and evidently executed, and Ptolemy, son of Lagos, one of Alexander's friends whom Philip had exiled, was appointed Bodyguard in his place.[109] If Demetrius was also one of Philip's men, it is hard not to suspect Alexander of a purge of high commanders who owed rank and reputation not to himself but to Philip and who surely were opposed to Alexander's insatiable desire for conquest. Philotas' brother Nicanor, commander of the Hypaspists, had died of illness a short while before,[110] so Alexander was now rid of that powerful noble family. But the question remains whether he plotted their demise or whether he was compelled to eliminate them because they did not support him—and the strength of the kingship depended on the support of the highest nobility.

These few trials were conducted within a matter of days in 330 far beyond the Macedonian homeland, and for this reason their usefulness as evidence for a formal 'constitutional' assembly and citizen rights should be questioned. From the descriptions of Philotas' trial Nicholas Hammond identified a five-step 'constitutional' procedure in cases of treason: arrest; trial before assembly of "Macedones"; the king's prosecution and the accused's defence; verdict of the Macedones; and execution of the condemned by the Macedones.[111] These steps are again observable for a trial conducted under similar circumstances in 327, when a few of Alexander's Pages, led by one Hermolaus, who held a personal grudge, were revealed to be plotting against his life.[112] However, when we look both forward and back in time most known cases of treason do not follow the pattern. To look at just one of these, in 315 Olympias was tried *in absentia*,[113] the charge evidently being that she ordered the murder of 100 of the current ruler Cassander's supporters, and the assembly of Macedonians not having heard a defence condemned her. When Olympias demanded a retrial at which she would be present to defend herself Cassander, fearing her defence might win acquittal, exposed her to the relatives of her victims and they killed her.[114] And there were no few cases of treason that did not go to trial. Of Philip II's assassins the killer Pausanias was struck down immediately with javelins, and if the two brothers of Alexander Lyncestes (sons of Aeropus) who were executed as accomplices were given a trial, there is no record of it.[115] Again, for Alexander's cousin Amyntas (son of Perdiccas III), whom Alexander accused of plotting against him, there is no record of a trial.[116] If Philotas' trial was meant to serve for both father and son,[117] Parmenio clearly was not arrested, was not brought before the Macedonians, did not hear the king's prosecution, and was not granted the opportunity of a defence. The (alleged) treasonable offense of Attalus, uncle of Philip II's final wife, Cleopatra, in 335 was that he had received a letter from Demosthenes encouraging him to overthrow Alexander (similar to the charge against Alexander Lyncestes). Supposedly he changed his mind about plotting against the king and forwarded the letter to Alexander in token of loyalty.[118] Alexander instructed Hecataeus to bring Attalus back to Macedonia alive, if he could, or kill him. He killed him; there was no trial. In the cases of the generals Parmenio and Attalus, because of their popularity the assembled troops were likely to shout in favour of acquittal, so a trial was too big a gamble.[119] They, along with Olympias (and recall Alexander Lyncestes was tongue-tied), were all deprived of a defence. As Curtius claims, "no one can be acquitted unless he has pleaded his cause."[120]

It is clear that the king did not always grant a trial before execution, so this begs the question: was he, when he acted unilaterally, acting outside Macedonian *law*? Curtius has long been accepted as an authority on Macedonian customs, but his inconsistent use of terminology prevents us from having a clear understanding of what is "law" and what is "custom."[121] For instance, at one point he says it was a "law" (*legem Macedonum*), which Alexander rescinded, at another point a "custom" (*Macedonum more*) whereby relatives of those convicted of treason were subject to execution.[122] Philip V's purge of relatives of men he had exiled or executed appears to have nothing to do with "law" (albeit that was more than a century later).[123] Alexander's personal power is what governed his trials[124] *and* what governed execution without a trial. In the speech attributed to Hermolaus for his defence he calls the execution of Philotas "unjust"—how could it be, if Alexander were following prescribed law?—and the deaths of Parmenio and others killed at that time "even more uncustomary" or "outside the law/what is just."[125] Who was to hold the Macedonian king accountable for his actions? No one. He was the law, and he could overlook or bend custom to suit himself. A fair 'constitutional' judicial system did not exist. And we cannot be sure that the Macedonians had anything that can be rightly called a legal code.[126]

Monsoons, 'mutiny', and Macedonian limits

Alexander and the Macedonian army spent the two and a half years between the trials of Philotas and Hermolaus caught up in guerrilla fighting in Bactria and Sogdiana. Hard on the trail of Bessus through the Hindu Kush, in the spring of 329 they finally got him into their hands, his capture organized with rough justice by one of his own allies, Spitamenes.[127] Accounts of Bessus' punishment are various and gruesome; most plausibly he was handed over to Darius' brother Oxathres, who punished him Persian style, cutting off his ears and nose before execution. Spitamenes then put up fierce resistance to the Macedonian occupation, regularly attacking garrisons and foraging details that left many dead, wounded, or captured.[128] The relentless fighting combined with the drudgery of eking out subsistence wore away at morale and strength.

It was at Maracanda (Samarcand) in the fall of 328 that Cleitus the Black made his fatal drunk remarks to Alexander.[129] Cleitus was another of the high command who had probably held rank since the days of Philip, and he had stayed in Alexander's favour mainly because he had saved the king's life at the Granicus. The verbal quarrel between the two is recounted in the sources, but one cannot take the speeches at face value. Speeches that occur in the ancient historians are sometimes the wholesale composition of the historian (or his source), though often they contain words considered appropriate to have been spoken on the occasion, thus approximating what was said, and always they have the benefit of hindsight.[130] The different speeches attributed to Cleitus converge on three heated points: a rebuke of Alexander taking the lion's share when other Macedonians deserved credit; Alexander demeaning Philip's exploits in contrast to his own greater achievements; and Alexander's lack of gratitude to Cleitus for saving his life. If the words are an approximation, then Cleitus reveals a general discontent and bitter resentment over Alexander's egotism. And Alexander reveals that he was beyond tolerating freedom of expression and especially expression of the greatness of Philip, for it ended with Alexander running Cleitus through with a spear. An 'official' accusation of treason was proclaimed as justification for Alexander's slaying of his general, and Cleitus was granted proper Macedonian burial.[131] In the shake-up of the high command the taxiarchs Craterus and Coenus, close Companions of Alexander, were shuffled to the top; both possibly had been commanders since Philip's time, but they were dedicated to Alexander.

Both Craterus and Coenus proved themselves deserving of high command in their handling of Spitamenes, who continued to harass the Macedonian garrisons,[132] including the one protecting Bactra (Zariaspa), where Alexander's royal entourage and other non-combatants had been left for safety. After

Spitamenes had killed no few cavalrymen and taken some officers captive Craterus arrived on the scene, defeated him, and chased the remnants of his forces into the desert.[133] Coenus afterwards inflicted such a devastating defeat on Spitamenes that the latter's allied cavalry, the Massagetae, in order to placate the Macedonians delivered Spitamenes' head to Alexander.[134] In the effort to try to stabilize the region Alexander planted numerous cities and military outposts, depositing in them his wounded and sick, captives he had not the means to support, his malcontents, and a mix of natives. Few settlers were Macedonians, though, as most of *them* when no longer fit for service were sent home under escort.[135] Ai Khanoum in Afghanistan yields evidence of the Greek conception and design of the larger of these settlements, with theatre and gymnasium and temple complex offering familiar comforts of home in a foreign landscape.[136]

The Bactrian campaign was well into its third year when Alexander captured the stronghold known as the Rock of Sogdiana. Here, so the ancient historians say, Alexander was captivated by the daughter of the warlord who had defended the Rock, and quite surprisingly he married her.[137] Modern historians argue that Alexander contracted the marriage with Roxane solely for the pacification of a region that was costing him much time and many lives. Yet Bessus and Spitamenes were by now eliminated—he had the nose and ears of one, the head of the other—and the girl's father, Oxyartes, was his hostage. Prior to this Alexander had never troubled himself with a marriage alliance or with the important kingly duty of producing an heir to the Macedonian throne. With the option open to him of marrying one of Darius' daughters, it is curious why he chose this Sogdian girl Roxane and why now. About this same time, evidently, Barsine, daughter of Artabazus, Alexander's mistress captured more than five years earlier at Damascus, gave birth to a son named Heracles.[138] The Argead successor, as it was shaping up, would be part Asian.[139] Also around this time Alexander arranged to have 30,000 sons of nobles from throughout the Persian satrapies brought together to be trained as 'Macedonian' soldiers. Like the Macedonian Pages, they were to serve as hostages for the good behaviour of their fathers while Alexander advanced into India.[140]

Before the advance to India there was another Persian matter that Alexander attempted to address. At a *symposium* with the cooperation of some of his court flatterers he tried to introduce *proskynesis* to the Macedonians and Greeks.[141] *Proskynesis* was a fundamental element of Persian court protocol, whereby the subjects of the king, by varying degrees depending on their social status, paid homage to their ruler with prostration, a bow, and/or a kiss. Since the ever increasing numbers of Persian courtiers were, as a matter of course, prostrating, bowing, or kissing Alexander, in practical terms he was attempting to impose uniformity. Yet Alexander made the attempt fully aware that *proskynesis* set the king above *all* his subjects, which is where he now saw himself: a position in the Greek world reserved for gods and heroes.[142] Herein lay the offense, for it was in the nature of Macedonian kingship to rule by acclamation, persuasion, and consultation of the elite *hetairoi* (Companions). The Companions in turn understood that, by tradition, they were entitled to an intimate camaraderie with their king. Not surprisingly Callisthenes was not the only man at banquet that night to ridicule the staged attempt to bring *proskynesis* into protocol, but he more than any other brought great odium on his own head for having spoiled the attempt. Callisthenes made a speech, variously reported, on the nature of divinity to which Alexander aspired and which Alexander sought to have recognized with obeisance, and the speech won the crowd's objection to *proskynesis*. Shortly after this, when the plot of Hermolaus, the so-called "Conspiracy of the Pages" surfaced,[143] because of his association with the conspirators as their instructor in philosophy, Callisthenes was deemed guilty by association and arrested.[144] He was imprisoned and later died in confinement. What is telling about Hermolaus' defence speech at his trial is that he exculpates the action of the conspirators by claiming they wished to kill the king of the *Persians*, not the king of the Macedonians. In his view Alexander by requesting *proskynesis* and divine honours in the manner of Persian kingship was a deserter to the enemy. Alexander is in his debt, he says, "[f]or from me you have come to know what honourable men cannot endure."[145] Hermolaus was convicted and stoned to death, but the point was taken, for Alexander did not force *proskynesis* on the Macedonians.[146]

After crossing the Indus into the Punjab region, the five-river system of the Indus valley, and advancing towards the Hydaspes, Alexander found the Indian ruler Porus with his whole army arrayed on the far bank intending to oppose his crossing. Undeterred by the high water levels of the monsoon season, on a stormy night of torrential downpour and lightning Alexander, leaving part of the army in camp with Craterus as a decoy, took a selected force out of sight upriver and made a daring night crossing. After a preliminary skirmish at the crossing[147] Alexander marched his already battle-weary forces against Porus' main army of chariots, cavalry, infantry, and 200 war elephants.[148] The elephants wreaked havoc on the Macedonian phalanx, but Alexander ordered his cavalry and infantry to regroup and surround the elephants and shoot and jab at them, while Craterus now unopposed brought fresh forces across the river. The Indian line broke when Porus was wounded and captured. Of Alexander's army as many as 700 infantry and 280 cavalry perished.[149]

As the gear of his soldiers began to rot in the rain and the wounded to die off under conditions that inhibited their healing, relentlessly Alexander advanced to the easternmost of the five rivers, the Hyphasis (Beas), intent upon subduing all of India.[150] Here, at last, Alexander lost the battle he had been fighting with his own army since Persepolis. The Macedonians had had their fill of senseless slaughter. They were dressed in makeshift Persian and Indian garments, their tattered Macedonian clothing having been discarded. Their armour was worn out, and they were short of gear and horses. It had been raining for seventy days.[151] Rumours of what lay ahead between the Hyphasis and the outer ocean, the numbers of men and elephants of even greater size, brought their morale to its lowest.[152] Alexander caught wind of secretive meetings and tried what had never failed him in the past: a speech of persuasion, reminders of all they had achieved, all they could yet achieve together, the rich plunder yet to be seized. His speech was followed by a long silence, then his second-in-command, Coenus, spoke in reply, voicing to the king the sentiment of the rank and file: they did not refuse to follow Alexander, rather they could no longer endure the hardships and the fighting; their strength and their will were spent.[153] So Alexander, after spending three days of seclusion, Achilles-like, in his tent, announced that the sacrifices for crossing the Hyphasis were unfavourable, and because of that the army would not advance. Cheers and tears of joy greeted him.

Coenus died of illness a short while later. If he was already aware of his illness and how serious it was when he took his courageous stand on behalf of the rank and file, he knew he had little to lose himself and much potentially to gain for the Macedonians.[154] So, despite the arrival of some 12,000 (at low estimate) reinforcements, 25,000 suits of armour, and abundant medical supplies, late in 326 the long retreat began, down the Indus on a large flotilla and flanked on either bank by armed forces, fighting their way through the territories of the Oxydracae and the Mallians, where Alexander made his rash leap into some nameless town and sustained a near-fatal arrow wound in the lung.[155] When Alexander reached the Indian Ocean he sailed out from the delta, and symbolic of the terminus of his Asian expedition he sacrificed bulls to Poseidon, poured libations, and threw the gold cups into the sea, just as he had done when he crossed the Hellespont nine years earlier.[156] For the return to Persia Alexander divided his army three ways, under three commanders taking three routes. Alexander himself took a third of his divided forces through the Gedrosian (Makran) desert in the attempt perhaps to supply the fleet as it made the coastal journey under command of Nearchus. Reportedly three quarters of the army he had with him perished from heat and thirst, though how many of the men who traversed the desert were Macedonian is unknown.[157]

Back in the heart of Persia Alexander, with no intention of returning to Macedonia, began to plan explorations and campaigns into Arabia, Africa, and the western Mediterranean, and to advance his policy of political integration.[158] At Susa in a mass wedding ceremony of some eighty Macedonian officers and Companions to Persian noble women he himself took as a bride one of Darius' daughters, Stateira, and a daughter of Ochus (Artaxerxes III), Parysatis, thus tying himself by marriage to two branches of the royal Achaemenids.[159] What the Macedonians thought of the imposed marriages we do not know. The only marriage we know for certain to have lasted much beyond Alexander's death is that of Seleucus to Spitamenes' daughter Apama, and from this union descended two centuries of Hellenistic kings of Syria.

It was now the summer of 324. The *Epigoni*, the 30,000 sons of Persian nobles selected three years earlier for training in Macedonian weaponry and warfare, were brought to Alexander at Susa for incorporation into the army,[160] and after sailing from Susa to Opis on the Tigris Alexander dismissed 10,000 of his Macedonian veterans whom he regarded, because of age or infirmities, as beyond effective military service. The arrival of the *Epigoni* in conjunction with the discharge of the Macedonian veterans caused an uproar in the Macedonian ranks of the army, which with the additions of Persians and subtractions of Macedonians were to be left a minority within Alexander's military forces in Asia. Criticisms of Alexander's integration practices were shouted out in assembly, and Alexander arrested thirteen of the most vocal objectors. These men were not given a trial, and it is said they were executed not by Macedonians but drowned in the Tigris by Persians.[161] Alexander reacted to the uproar by replacing Macedonians with Persians at every level, from rank and file to commanders of battalions and the Hypaspist *agema*. After three days the Macedonians asked for pardon. The discharged veterans left for home under command of Craterus, who was at this time suffering an infirmity, with Polyperchon as his second-in-command. Craterus was to replace Antipater as regent, and Antipater was to join Alexander at Babylon with new Macedonian recruits. Craterus and the veterans had advanced only as far as Cilicia by June 323, when Alexander, having suffered agonizing grief over the death to illness of Hephaestion late in 324 (Figure 7.6), and then returning to Babylon where he proceeded to establish his administrative base, himself caught fever and died. He had designated no successor. How could he? He had eliminated any potential contenders at the beginning of his reign, had produced no legitimate offspring, and the only living male Argead was his incompetent half-brother Arrhidaeus, hardly suitable for the Macedonian kingship.

Figure 7.6 Marble votive relief to the heroized Hephaestion, Pella, late fourth century BCE. Thessaloniki Archaeological Museum

Source: author, 2011.

Notes

1. Arr. *Anab.* 1.11.3–5; Diod. 18.12.1; Curt. 4.1.39; Just. 11.7.1.
2. Arr. *Anab.* 1.11.5–7; for Macedonian deities cf. e.g. Arr. *Anab.* 1.4.5; Curt. 3.12.27; Diod. 17.17.1; Just. 11.5.10. Significance of the spear: Mehl 1980/81; Squillace 2010: 77–78; Worthington 2014: 140–142.
3. Arr. *Anab.* 1.11.5–12.1; Diod. 17.17.3; Plut. *Alex.* 15.7–9; Just.11.5.12; Str. 13.1.27.
4. Arr. *Anab.* 1.11.7–8; Diod. 17.18.1. See Chapter 5.
5. On Achilles and Mycenaean elements see Cohen 1995 and Heckel 2015. On Alexander's image see Ferrario 2014: 322–331.
6. Darius' accession (shortly before the death of Philip in 336): Diod. 17.5.3–6. For Darius' reign see Briant 2015.
7. Arr. *Anab.* 1.12.9–10; Diod. 17.18.2–3. For Memnon at Pella see Chapter 4.
8. Battle of the Granicus: Arr. *Anab.* 13.1–16.7; Diod. 17.18.4–21.6; Plut. *Alex.* 16; Just. 11.6.12–13. Fuller 1958: 147–154; Badian 1977; Hammond 1980c; Devine 1988; Heckel 2008: 47–51.
9. Arr. *Anab.* 1.16.4–7; Plut. *Alex.* 16.16–18; cf. Diod. 17.21.6.
10. Arr. *Anab.* 1.17.3–18.2; Diod. 17.21.7; Plut. *Alex.* 17.1. cf. 15.2. Tod *GHI* 184–186, 190 = Harding 105, 106, 103, 114.
11. Miletus: Arr. *Anab.* 18.3–19.11; Diod. 17.22. Halicarnassus: Arr. *Anab.* 1.20.2–23.6; Diod. 17.23.4–27.6.
12. Arr. *Anab.* 1.18.2; Diod. 17.24.1. See Nawotka 2003, citing earlier bibliography.
13. Arr. *Anab.* 1.17.9–12. Bosworth 1980a: 131–132. On the potentially dangerous renegade Amyntas, son of Antiochus (friend of Amyntas son of Perdiccas), who was at Ephesus, see Heckel 2006a: 23–24 with references.
14. Arr. *Anab.* 1.20.1; Diod. 17.22.5–23.1.
15. Arr. *Anab.* 1.23.1–6. On the tomb in Figure 7.2 see Winter 2006: 86–87.
16. Arr. *Anab.* 1.24.1–2; Curt. 3.1.1. Taxiarchs: see Chapter 5.
17. Arr. *Anab.* 1.24.3–4, 3.6.6; cf. Just. 13.4.15.
18. Arr. *Anab.* 1.29.3; Curt. 4.1.35. Billows 1990: 41–48; Anson 1988.
19. E.g. Curt. 4.5.9, 8.9–10.
20. Cf. e.g. Curt. 4.1.35.
21. Arr. *Anab.* 1.29.4; Curt. 3.1.24.
22. Arr. *Anab.* 1.20.3, 2.1.1–2; Diod. 17.29.1–30.1, 31.3; Curt. 3.1.19–20.
23. Arr. *Anab.* 2.1.3, 2.2–4; Diod. 17.29.4; Curt. 3.2.1; Plut. *Alex.* 18.5. Ruzicka 1988; Chapter 8.
24. Arr. *Anab.* 2.4.1–6.1; Plut. *Alex.* 19.
25. Alexander's strategy: Arr. *Anab.* 2.6.1–2; Curt. 3.7.8–10. Bosworth 1988: 58–60.
26. Cf. Curt. 3.8.19, 23, and Cawkwell 2005: 211. Battle of Issus: Arr. *Anab.* 2.8–11; Diod. 17.33.2–34.9; Curt. 3.9–11; with criticism of Callisthenes' account: Polyb. 12.17–22. Fuller 1958: 154–162; Devine 1985; Heckel 2008: 57–65.
27. Arr. *Anab.* 2.10.6–7; Curt. 3.11.4–6.
28. Plin. *HN* 35.110; cf. Diod. 17.34.3–4; Curt. 3.11.8–9. Stewart 1993: 130–150; Cohen 1997.
29. Diod. 17.31.2, 35.3; Curt. 3.3.22–25, 8.12, 9.6.
30. Arr. *Anab.* 2.11.9–10, 15.1; Diod. 17.32.3; Curt. 3.12.27–13.17; Plut. *Alex.* 24.1–3, 25.6–26.2.
31. Plut. *Alex.* 24.3. The richest share of plunder went to the Thessalian cavalry: Diod. 17.33.2; Plut. *Alex.* 24.2.
32. Plut. *Alex.* 20.13.
33. Barsine: Plut. *Alex.* 21.7–9, *Eum.* 1.3; Curt. 3.13.14, 6.5.1–2; Just. 11.10.2–3. Carney 2000: 101–105, 149–150, 2003: 243–245.

34 Siege of Tyre: Arr. *Anab.* 2.15.6–24.6; Diod. 17.40.2–46.5; Curt. 4.2.1–4.18; Plut. *Alex.* 24–25; Just. 11.10.10–14. Worthington 2014: 173–178.
35 Arr. *Anab.* 2.20.1–3; Curt. 4.3.11.
36 Arr. *Anab.* 2.25.4–27.7; Plut. *Alex.* 25.
37 The satrap was killed at Issus: Arr. *Anab.* 2.11.8; Diod. 17.34.5; Curt. 3.11.10.
38 Arr. *Anab.* 3.1.2–3; Diod. 17.49.1–2; Curt. 4.7.1–4.
39 For the view that he was not crowned pharaoh see Burstein 1991, citing contrary views. See also Collins 2009 and Anson 2013: 104–105. Stoneman 2008: 6–21 discusses the context for the *Romance* account, Ps.Call. 1.34. On motive see Bloedow 2004, citing earlier scholarship.
40 Arr. *Anab.* 3.1.4, 16.4, cf. 7.17.1–3. Stewart 1993: 174–178; Collins 2009: 200–203. Cp. his arrival at Babylon and order that the temple of Bel-Marduk (destroyed by Xerxes) be restored. Touring: Curt. 4.8.3.
41 Just. 11.11.13. The seminal study of Alexandria *ad Aegyptum* remains Fraser 1972. The generally accepted view is that Alexander *intended* Alexandria to be a great city; *contra* Howe 2014.
42 Anson 2013: 96–107. For a different view see Collins 2014.
43 Arr. *Anab.* 3.3.2. Heckel 2015.
44 Cf. Plut. *Cimon* 18–19, possible precedent of Cimon consulting Ammon in the context of a Persian campaign; see Flower 2000: 111–112. Cp. his visit to Delphi, Chapter 6 n103.
45 Plut. *Alex.* 27.3–5.
46 Arr. *Anab.* 3.4.5. Callisthenes: Str. 17.1.43.
47 Plut. *Alex.* 28.1; and see the personal comments of Curtius at 4.7.29–31.
48 On the administration of Egypt see Burstein 2008.
49 Arr. *Anab.* 3.7.6, 15.7; Curt. 4.10.2–8; Plut. *Alex.* 31.8; Cicero *de Divinatione* 1.121; Plin. *HN* 2.180.
50 King 2013: 107–108.
51 Distance: Arr. *Anab.* 6.11.5, accepting here the shorter distance.
52 Diod. 17.53.1.
53 For numbers see Brunt *Arrian* Loeb Vol. I App. IX.3. On the overestimation of Persian armies in Greek sources see Cawkwell 2005: 237–252, especially 246–248 for Gaugamela and Issus.
54 Battle of Gaugamela: Arr. *Anab.* 3.11.3–15.6; Diod. 17.57–61; Curt. 4.12.5–16.33; Plut. *Alex.* 32.5–33.11; Just. 11.14.1–3. For discussion of the battle and discrepancies in the sources, regarding especially Parmenio's situation on the left, his messenger to Alexander (e.g. Arr. *Anab.* 3.15.1; Diod. 17.60.7; Curt. 4.16.1; Plut. *Alex.* 33.6), see Fuller 1958: 163–180; Brunt *Arrian* Loeb Vol. I App. IX (citing earlier discussions); Hammond 1996 (1980): 138–150; Devine 1986; Heckel 2008: 75–80. See also van der Spek 2003.
55 Ath. 12.513f. Allen 2005: chapter 3 (overview of the capitals with drawings and colour images of the archaeological remains).
56 Just. 12.1.3. Cp. Str. 15.3.9: 180,000. See Brunt *Arrian* Loeb Vol. 1 Appendix X.3. Quote: Curt.5.6.8. On the captured wealth see Holt 2016, especially 68–94.
57 Reinforcements: see Chapter 8 n18. Agis' revolt and the disputed chronology: see Chapter 8 n32.
58 Plut. *Alex.* 39.10.
59 Wealth, its effects, and reorganization after Gaugamela: Arr. *Anab.* 3.16.3–11; Diod. 17.64.3–66.2, 71.1–2; Curt. 5.1.10, 17–23, 36–45, 2.1–11, 16–17, 6.9; Plut. *Alex.* 34.1, 36, 39, 40.1–3; Just. 11.14.8–9; cp. Ath. 12.514e–f; and Holt 2016 (n56). For a critical view of Alexander's relations with the Persian nobility see Brosius 2003. On the transition from Achaemenid to Macedonian rule see Briant 2002: 719–726.

174 *Alexander beyond Macedonia, 334–323*

60 Three "letters" (or exchanges with envoys) between Alexander and Darius are mentioned: first after Issus: Arr. *Anab.* 2.14; Diod. 17.39.1–3; Curt. 4.1.7–14; Just. 11.12.1–2; second at Tyre: Curt. 4.5.1–8, Just. 11.12.3–4; cp. Arr. *Anab.* 2.25.1; third before Gaugamela: Plut. *Alex.* 29.7–9; Just. 11.12.9–16; cp. Diod. 17.54.1–6; Curt. 4.11.
61 Plut. *Alex.* 34.1; cp. Arr. *Anab.* 3.25.2. Accepting the proclamation, e.g. Hamilton 1969: 90; Bosworth 1980b: 5. For a different view see Fredricksmeyer 2000 and Collins 2013. See also Nawotka 2012 with bibliography.
62 Briant 2002: 842–844, 852, 869–870, 1046–1050; Worthington 2014: 196–201.
63 Arr. *Anab.* 3.25.1–2, 5–7, 28.2–3; Diod. 17.78.2–4, 83.4–6; Curt. 6.6.13, 20–32, 7.3.2, 4.34–38.
64 Cf. Diod. 17.71.3–8.
65 For a summary of older scholarship on the question see Atkinson 1994: 121–124. Badian 1967 and Borza 1972 are seminal. See also Wheeler 1968: 11–29; Sancisi-Weerdenburg 1993; Badian 1994b/2012: 352–355; Briant 2002: 733–737, 851, 2010: 107–111; Anson 2013: 153–159.
66 Arr. *Anab.* 3.18.11–12.
67 Diod. 17.70.1, 72; Curt. 5.6.1–8, 7.2–7; cp. Plut. *Alex.* 38. Cf. Str. 15.3.6; Ath. 13.576d–e.
68 Arr. *Anab.* 3.16.7–8; Plut. *Alex.* 34.
69 Cf. Curt. 5.6.13–14; Plut. *Alex.* 38.6–7.
70 Diod. 17.70.1, 71.1; cp. Curt. 5.6.11. Morrison 2001.
71 Atkinson 1994: 121–122, citing archaeological reports.
72 Arr. *Anab.* 3.18.3, cp. Curt. 5.3.17–23. Heckel 1980a: 169.
73 Cawkwell 2005: 52; Olbrycht 2010: 343–344, citing bibliography.
74 Curt. 5.8.16.
75 Arr. *Anab.* 6.30; Curt. 5.7.11; Plut. *Alex.* 38.8. On the story, here omitted, of the mutilated Greeks encountered at Persepolis see Heckel 2008: 82–83.
76 Arr. *Anab.* 3.18.10; Curt. 5.6.10; Str. 15.3.7.
77 Arr. *Anab.* 3.19.2–5; Diod. 17.73.2; Curt. 5.8.1–2, 13.1.
78 Arr. *Anab.* 3.19.5–6: dismissal at Ecbatana. Cp. Curt. 6.2.15–17, dismissal at Hecatompylos; Diod. 17.74.3–4: *before* Hecatompylos.
79 Engels 1978: 154–156.
80 Darius' death: Arr. *Anab.* 3.21.10; Diod. 17.73.3–4; Curt. 5.13.23–25; Plut. *Alex.* 43, *De Alex. fort.* 332f; Just. 11.15. Bessus "Artaxeres": Arr. *Anab.* 3.25.3; Curt. 6.6.13.
81 Cf. Diod. 19.52.5. Darius' burial: Arr. *Anab.* 3.22.1; Plut. *Alex.* 43.7. For the Macedonian practice see Chapter 9 n46.
82 Diod. 17.74.3; Curt. 6.2.18–19, 3.1–4.1 (puts speech at Hecatompylos); Plut. *Alex.* 47.1–8; Just. 12.3.2–4; not found in Arrian.
83 Aeschin. 3.165.
84 Issue of clothing: Diod. 17.77.5; Curt. 6.6.7. Alexander's Persianizing in general: Diod. 17.77.4–78.1; Curt. 6.6.1–12; Plut. *Alex.* 45; Just. 12.3.8–12.
85 On the high command see Heckel 2016, especially 52–59 for this episode.
86 Curt. 6.7.17; cp. Plut. *Alex.* 51.2.
87 Philotas Affair: Arr. *Anab.* 3.26; Diod. 17.79.1–80.3; Curt. 6.7.1–7.2.32; Plu. *Alex.* 48–49.13, cf. *Mor.* 339e–f; Just. 12.5.1–3.
88 Curt. in n87. The seminal discussions are Badian 1960 and Heckel 1977. See more recently Reames 2008 with bibliography.
89 Diod. 17.61.3. Heckel 1977: 13, *passim* "orchestration," 2006a: 133; cp. Anson 2012: 49.
90 Curt. 6.11.38; *contra* Arr. *Anab.* 3.26.3; but cp. Curt. 7.1.9.
91 For a less sympathetic view of Parmenio see Rogers 2004: 142–149.

92 Curt. 7.2.33.
93 Arr. *Anab.* 3.19.7.
94 Arr. *Anab.* 3.20.3, 4.18.3; cp. Curt. 6.2.11: appointment of Oxydates after the death of Darius. Diod. 17.80.3: Parmenio was *archon* of Media, cp. Curt. 6.8.18. See Heckel 2006a: 192: "presumably *strategos* of Media"; and n518: Parmenio's instructions "apparently cancelled"; likewise Bosworth 1980a: 337.
95 Curt. 7.2.11–18.
96 Curt. 7.1.1.
97 Reaction to Parmenio's assassination: Diod. 17.80.4; Curt. 7.2.28–38; Just. 12.5.4–8, 13. The historicity of the *Ataktoi* is generally accepted; the appointment of a former close friend of Parmenio, Leonidas, as their commander is questioned. Carney 1996a: 27; Heckel 2006a: 147.
98 Polyaen. 4.3.19. Though some of Parmenio's grievers may have been among those identified as malcontents by the opened letters, these are separate occasions, Curt. 7.2.36–38.
99 Arr. *Anab.* 3.29.5, cp. 5.27.5; Curt. 7.5.27.
100 Carney 1980: 23 n2; Heckel 2006a: 19.
101 Arr. *Anab.* 1.25; Diod. 17.32.1–2, 80.2; Curt. 7.1.5–10, 8.8.6, 10.1.40; Just. 11.7.1–2. On the apparent contradiction in the sources on the date of the arrest see Atkinson 1980: 183–187; Bosworth 1980a: 159–164; Carney 1980.
102 Diod. 17.80.2; Curt. 7.1.5–9, naming Atarrhias, who arrested Philotas, as the one demanding the Lyncestian be brought forth, "undoubtedly by previous arrangement." Cf. Just. 11.7.2. Heckel 2006a: 60.
103 Cf. n122.
104 Arr. *Anab.* 3.27.1–3; Curt. 7.1.10–2.10. Arrian says all four sons of Andromenes were tried; but Polemon had fled, and Curtius, omitting Attalus, indicates only two (*Rex solvi utrumque iubet*, 7.1.18) stood trial, i.e. before Polemon was brought back. On this trial see Atkinson 1994: 247–257 and Baynham 1998: 180–183.
105 On Curtius' use of *armigeri*, usually translated as either Bodyguard or Hypaspist, neither of which Amyntas was, see Atkinson 1994: 252.
106 Arr. *Anab.* 1.8.2. Heckel 2006a: 63 believes the Attalus named with Leonnatus and Perdiccas as one of Philip's Hypaspists at Diod. 16.94.4 is the son of Andromenes.
107 Amyntas: Heckel 2006a: 24–25. On trial assemblies, cf. n111.
108 Arr. *Anab.* 3.27.3, 4.16.1.
109 Curt. 6.7.15, 11.35–38: Demetrius was implicated, tried, and executed with Philotas; but cp. Arr. *Anab.* 3.27.5.
110 Arr. *Anab.* 3.25.4; Curt. 6.6.18.
111 Hammond 1989a: 61. On treason trials and the judicial system see Lock 1977: 95–97; Hammond 1978; Carney 1980, 1983; Adams 1986; Hatzopoulos 1996: 271–276; O'Neil 1999a; Anson 2008b.
112 Arr. *Anab.* 4.12.7–14.3; Curt. 8.6.28–8.8.20.
113 Or 316; on chronology see Chapter 9 n42. Others: Nicanor, commander of the Macedonian garrison in Munychia, in 317: Polyaen. 4.11.2; cp. Diod. 18.75.1, Chapter 9; Philip V's officers in 218: Polyb. 5.15.7–9, 16.5–7, 27.4–8, 29.6, Chapter 10.
114 See Chapter 9 n44.
115 Diod. 16.94.4; cp. Just. 9.7.10–11; and cf. Polyaen. 4.2.3: Philip exiled "Aeropus," their father? *Contra*, e.g. Hatzopoulos 1996: 272–273. On Wilcken's attempt to squeeze evidence for Pausanias' trial out of *Oxyrhynchus Papyri* 1798 see Bosworth 1971a: 93–94: it does not hold up; Pausanias was killed outright. See also Hammond 1978.
116 Curt. 6.9.17, 10.24–25; Just. 12.6.14.
117 Cf. Diod. 17.80.1; cp. Curt. 6.11.39.

118 Diod. 17.2.3–3.2, 5.1–2; Plut. *Dem.* 23.2; Curt. 7.1.3, 8.7.5.
119 Cp. Philip V's general, Leontius, cf. n113.
120 Curt. 7.2.9.
121 Here (6.8.25) as often Curtius' term for "custom" is *mos* (cp. e.g. 3.8.22, 4.6.10, 8.6, 5.4.3, 4.12, 6.10.23, 11.10, 11.38, 7.2.1, 9.21, 8.6.28, 10.3.14) which can also mean "practice," "tradition," "habit," or "usage," but rarely means "law," for which *lex* is more common and precise.
122 *Lex*: Curt. 6.11.20, 8.8.18; *mos*: 8.6.28.
123 Polyb. 23.10.8–10; Liv. 40.3.7.
124 Scholars have made much of Curt. 6.8.25, the emendation to the text, and meaning of *potestas* and *auctoritas*. See Errington 1978: 87 n30; Atkinson 1994: 226–228; Hatzopoulos 1996: 271; O'Neil 1999a: 13; Anson 2008b: 137–138.
125 Arr. *Anab.* 4.14.2.
126 Cf. Arist. *Pol.* 1324b, though again ambiguous; and cp. Dem. 18.235. For further on the question of constitutional monarchy see King 2010: 374–375, 390–391 and Roisman 2012b with bibliography.
127 Arr. *Anab.* 3.29.6–30.3; Diod. 17.83.8; Curt. 7.5.19–26; Just. 12.5.10. For the various accounts of his punishment cf. Arr. *Anab.* 3.30.4–5, 4.7.3; Diod. 17.83.9; Curt. 7.5.40–41, 10.10; Plut. *Alex.* 43.6–7; Just. 12.5.11.
128 Garrison at Maracanda: Arr. *Anab.* 4.3.6; Curt. 7.6.24. Garrison near Zariaspa/Bactra: Arr. *Anab.* 4.16.4–5. Foraging detail: Curt. 8.1.3–5. On casualties see Bosworth 1986 and Hammond 1989c. On supply as strategy see Engels 1978: 119–122.
129 Death of Cleitus: Arr. *Anab.* 4.8; Curt. 8.1.19–2.4; Plut. *Alex.* 50–51; Just. 12.6.1–8 (this falls in the large lacuna in Diodorus). Carney 1981b; Bosworth 1996b; Tritle 2003.
130 On the nature of speeches in Arrian and Curtius see Bosworth 1988: 94–134 and Baynham 1998: 46–56. Curt. 8.1.19: Cleitus recently reassigned to post of satrap of Bactria; cp. Arr. *Anab.* 4.17.3 (presumably Arrian omitted Cleitus' appointment since it was never taken up).
131 Curt. 7.7.21–8.2.40. On Cleitus' 'treason' see Anson 2008b: 138 n29.
132 Ambush of a task force: Arr. *Anab.* 4.3.7, 5.3–6.5; Curt. 7.7.31–39, 7.9.21.
133 Arr. *Anab.* 4.16.4–17.2; Curt. 8.1.3–6.
134 Arr. *Anab.* 4.17.3–7; but cp. Curt. 8.3.1–15.
135 Cf. Arr. *Anab.* 3.29.5; Curt. 7.5.27.
136 Arr. *Anab.* 4.4.1; Diod. 17.83.2; Curt. 7.3.23. Ai Khanoum: Holt 2005: 154–164. Other major settlements: Alexandria at the Caucasus (Arr. *Anab.* 3.28.4; Diod. 17.83.1; Curt. 7.3.19–23), Alexandria Eschate (near modern Khodzhent) on the Tanais/Syr-Darya/Jaxartes (Arr. *Anab.* 4.1.3–4; Curt. 7.6.13; Just. 12.5.12). On the Bactrian campaign in general see Holt 2005 with bibliography.
137 Arr. *Anab.* 4.18.4, 19.5; Plut. *Alex.* 47.7–8; Curt. 7.11, 8.4.21–30; Str. 11.11.4; Polyaen. 4.3.29 (this falls in the lacuna in Diodorus, omitted by Justin). On the Sogdian revolt see Vacante 2012.
138 Diod. 20.20.1; cp. Just. 15.2.3.
139 Cf. Curt. 8.4.29–30, 10.3.11. On Barsine and Roxane see Carney 2003a: 242–246; for the context of Alexander's marriage to Roxane see Holt 2005: 85–104.
140 Curt. 8.5.1. Cp. *Suda* s.v. "basilikoi paides": 6,000 youths had been gathered in Egypt for similar training. On the 30,000 *Epigoni* see Bosworth 1980b: 17–18.
141 Arr. *Anab.* 4.9.9–12.5; Curt. 8.5.5–24; Plut. *Alex.* 53–54 (this falls in the lacuna in Diodorus). The accounts diverge significantly. On *proskynesis* see Matarese 2013, citing earlier scholarship; Bowden 2013 agues Alexander's 'experiment' is a later invention.

142 For various views on Philip II's elevation of the Argeads above the Macedonian nobility and possible 'divine' pretensions (statues of the Twelve Olympians and a thirteenth for himself, the Philippeion *tholos* at Olympia [heroon?]) see Carney 2007; Worthington 2008: 164–166; Schultz 2009; Palagia 2010; Müller 2010: 181–182.
143 Arr. *Anab.* 4.12.7–14.4; Curt. 8.6.1–8.23; Plut. *Alex.* 55 (lost in lacuna in Diodorus). See especially Bosworth 1995: 90–101 and Carney 1981a, 2008.
144 Arrian's (4.14.1) 'trustworthy' sources Aristobulus and Ptolemy agreed that the conspirators implicated Callisthenes; Curtius' (8.6.24) source(s) vehemently claimed he was *not* implicated.
145 Curt. 8.7.12, 15.
146 Stoning: Arr. *Anab.* 4.14.3; Plut. *Alex.* 55.7. *Proskynesis* abandoned: Arr. *Anab.* 4.12.1; Plut. *Alex.* 54.3; Just. 12.7.3.
147 Arr. *Anab.* 5.12.2–15.2; Curt. 8.13.17–14.9.
148 Battle of the Hydaspes: Arr. *Anab.* 5.15.5; Diod. 17.87.3–89.3; Curt. 8.14.10–44; Plut. *Alex.* 60; Just. 12.8.3–7. Fuller 1958: 180–199; Devine 1987; Heckel 2008: 115–120.
149 Diod. 17.89.3, but cp. Arr. *Anab.* 5.18.3. The highest casualties may have been among the subject cavalry.
150 Accepting in principle Arr. *Anab.* 4.15.6, Curt. 9.2.11, 26, Diod. 17.93.1, 94.3, see Badian 1961: 20; Holt 1982: 48; Bosworth 1988: 133; Carney 1996a: 37; Anson 2013: 172–174, 2015a. *Contra* Heckel 2003b.
151 Diod. 17.94.2; Curt. 9.3.10–11.
152 Arr. *Anab.* 5.25.1; Diod. 17.93.2; Curt. 9.2.2–4; Plut. *Alex.* 62.
153 Alexander's speech: Arr. *Anab.* 5.25.2–26.8; cp. Diod. 17.94.5; Curt. 9.2.12–34. Coenus' reply: Arr. *Anab.* 5.27.2–9; Curt. 9.3.4–15. Carney 1996a: 31–33 argues for the misapplication of the term 'mutiny' both here and at Opis. For the view that Alexander staged the 'mutiny' see Spann 1999 and Heckel 2003b; for the suggestion that it is a literary myth see Howe and Müller 2012.
154 Arr. *Anab.* 6.2.1; Curt. 9.3.20. Holt 2000.
155 See Chapter 5.
156 Arr. *Anab.* 6.19.5, cp. 1.11.6; Diod. 17.104.1; Curt. 9.9.27; Just. 12.10.4.
157 Arr. *Anab.* 6.23–26; Diod. 17.104.3–8; Curt. 9.10.11–18; Plut. *Alex.* 66.
158 The views of Tarn on the "unity of mankind" or "policy of fusion" have been influential on all subsequent scholarship; see the counter-arguments of Badian 1958 and Bosworth 1980b; see also Collins 2012.
159 Susa weddings: Arr. *Anab.* 7.4.4–8; Plut. *Alex.* 70; Just. 12.10.9–10. Carney 1996b: 578, 2003a: 246–248; Brosius 2003: 176–178.
160 Arr. *Anab.* 7.6.1–2; Diod. 17.108.1–2; Plut. *Alex.* 71.1.
161 Drowning: Curt. 10.4.2; cp. Arr. *Anab.* 7.8.3. *Epigoni* and 'mutiny' at Opis: Arr. *Anab.* 7.8–11; Diod. 17.108.3, 109.1–3; Curt 10.2.12–4.3; Plut. *Alex.* 71; Just. 12.11.5–12.10; Polyaen. 4.3.7. Carney 1996a. On Alexander's speech see Nagle 1996.

8 Antipater and the early wars of the Successors, 334–319

When Alexander headed east in 334 he entrusted to Antipater the security of the Macedonian kingdom and management of affairs with the Greek states. The initial demand to supply Alexander with reinforcements left Antipater limited resources, yet he effectively guarded the traditionally problematic borders, swiftly quashed a Spartan uprising, handled the harsh backlash from Alexander's Exiles Decree of 324, and came out the winner in the Lamian War, which Athens initiated at news of Alexander's death in 323. Despite the subsequent political shake-up, the succession turmoil, and first 'settlement' of the empire at Babylon, which left Perdiccas sole regent for the two acclaimed kings, Antipater's sway over Macedonia and the Greek states was scarcely interrupted, and after he crossed to Asia and brought about a second 'settlement' at Triparadeisos following Perdiccas' death, he returned with both kings, and at his natural death in 319 he left the kingdom secure.

The regency of Antipater

Antipater, son of Iolaus, from Palioura is one of the principal figures in Macedonian history in the later fourth century.[1] He was a trusted general of Philip II and Alexander III, likely also of Perdiccas III, and probably first saw military action during the reign of Amyntas III. Antipater's family quite possibly had long held the highest honour at the Macedonian royal court: the name of his father, which is not common, is the same as that of the man (possibly he is that man) whom Perdiccas II appointed *archon* in 432.[2] In addition to important military commands and being entrusted with overseeing affairs of the kingdom during the kings' campaign absences he was one of Philip's envoys chosen to negotiate the important Peace of Philocrates between Macedonia and Athens; he was chosen again to negotiate the settlement with Athens and return of the Athenian dead after Chaeronea; and he even presided over the Pythian games on Philip's behalf in 342.[3] He was a learned man, by account a student of Aristotle (though his being Aristotle's senior casts some doubt on this) and an author of a history, *On the Deeds of Perdiccas in Illyria*, as well as two books of *Letters*, all of which are lost.[4] Uncharacteristic for a Macedonian, he had a reputation for soberness; according to one anecdote, Philip used to cheer his men into their cups with the quip: "Let's drink, it's enough that Antipater is sober."[5] Antipater mentored Alexander as a young adult and was one of the first to take his stand beside him on the day of Philip's assassination at Aegae in 336. At that time Antipater was about sixty-two years of age.[6]

For the next year and a half Antipater was a close advisor of Alexander, recommending that the young king concern himself first and foremost with securing personal alliances with the border tribes and less so with the Greek states.[7] Even if his advice was not always taken, he was held in great regard by Alexander and was one of only two men Alexander continued to address in his letters after his defeat of Darius, when he assumed the dignity of King of Asia, with the formal salutation *chairein*, or "greetings" (the other was the great Athenian statesman Phocion).[8] An alleged remark of Alexander about Antipater, "within he is all purple,"[9] is usually construed as a bitter sneer at Antipater's regal aspirations, but it is notable that although Antipater was left to manage Macedonian affairs for well over a decade, he never did attempt to usurp the throne, not even in the turmoil after Alexander's death. In fact, relations between Alexander and Antipater held steadfast for three decades, and if near the end that relationship became strained there were many extenuating factors at play. When Alexander went east, he left Antipater in charge of both Macedonia and the Greeks (League of Corinth), with an army of 12,000 foot and 1,500 horse. Antipater's title and specific duties are not clear, unfortunately. One source calls him *strategos* (general), another *praefectus* (governor or regent), and it is not certain the Macedonians even had an official title for his position or that he had clearly defined duties.[10] Given that he acted on behalf of the absent king probably in political, economic, and religious spheres as well as military,[11] it seems not inappropriate to call him 'regent'.

Initially, and until Alexander disappeared off the map (as the campaign beyond Susa was described),[12] Antipater and Alexander were mutually supportive. Alexander sent spoils home after the Granicus,[13] and the following spring at Alexander's request Antipater sent new recruits to join him at Gordion: 3,000 Macedonian infantry, 300 Macedonian cavalry, and 200 Thessalian cavalry all under command of the taxiarchs Coenus, Meleager, and Ptolemaeus, as well as 150 Peloponnesians from Elis.[14] Alexander again sent home spoils after Issus,[15] and another dispatch from Antipater of 6,000 Macedonian foot and 500 horse, along with fifty Pages, reached Alexander near Susa late in 331.[16] About the same time Alexander sent to Antipater 3,000 talents from the post-Gaugamela spoils for the war with Sparta.[17] Alexander is frequently criticized for bleeding the resources of his homeland; however, after the surrender of Sardis he probably never drew on the kingdom for financial resources, and over the years the bulk of his reinforcements were actually mercenaries and subject allies.[18]

When it became clear by the end of the first year of the expedition that Alexander had erred in disbanding his Greek fleet Antipater received instructions from Alexander and 600 talents for expenses to gather a fleet from the allies of the League of Corinth. Antipater issued orders to Proteas, son of Andronicus (probably a nephew of Cleitus the Black, son of his sister Lanice), to assemble the fleet and to protect the islands and the mainland of Greece. By the spring of 333 that fleet was ready, and with Amphoterus given command of the larger fleet and instructions to challenge Memnon at Chios and Lesbos, as at the crossing of the Hellespont in 334, two fleets again were in operation in the Aegean.[19] Proteas, sailing from Chalcis in Euboea with fifteen ships, made a surprise dawn attack on ten Persian ships anchored off Siphnos and managed to capture eight of them, while the other two and the Persian admiral got away.[20] He is not heard of again until a year later when he arrived at Tyre with a single fifty-oared ship from Macedonia.[21] Meantime Memnon of Rhodes had died, Amphoterus and Hegelochus with 160 ships had recovered Tenedos, Chios, Lesbos, and Cos, which Memnon had detached from Alexander's alliance, and Darius had sent a fleet to the Hellespont to try to retake the coast from Amphoterus' control.[22] Over the winter of 333–332 a Macedonian fleet at the Hellespont defeated a Persian squadron and captured or sank the ships.[23]

Just before that winter 100 Persian ships sailed across the Aegean to Siphnos again, where their commanders, Autophradates and Pharnabazus, met with the Spartan king, Agis III, who came with a single trireme. Agis was seeking Persian funding and as many ships as they could spare to help him recover territory in the Peloponnese that had been lost to Philip, and he could reasonably hope to gain Persian support since his activities would constitute a second front for the Macedonians in Greece. Right at the time of this meeting, however, news reached Siphnos of Darius' defeat at Issus, and an astounded Pharnabazus, taking twelve triremes, headed back across the Aegean to try to protect Chios, which at this date was still under Persian control. Autophradates gave Agis thirty talents and ten triremes, which the Spartan king sent to Taenarum, a port on the southern coast of the Peloponnese that was fast becoming a prime mustering point for mercenaries. Agis' brother took the ten Persian triremes from there to Crete, which was also a choice destination for mercenaries and exiles, and over the course of the following year he and Agis recruited some 8,000 to 10,000 mercenaries, many of whom had fled back to Greece from Cilicia after escaping the battlefield at Issus.[24]

Revolt in the Peloponnese was already a serious threat by the spring of 331, for on his return from Egypt Alexander dispatched Amphoterus with a fleet from Tyre to bring aid to those Peloponnesian city-states that were loyal to the League agreements and an additional fleet of 100 Phoenician and Cypriot ships to support him.[25] Many Peloponnesian states, including all of Arcadia except Megalopolis, and some other Greeks had joined Agis and the Spartans, but how many were defectors from the League we do not know.[26] The Athenians did not join the revolt, and that was fortunate for the Macedonians, for it could very well have tipped the scales. Alexander had been careful with regard to Athens. At Tyre, just when he was sending Amphoterus and two fleets to the Peloponnese, he finally granted the Athenian request for the release of their captives taken at the Granicus. The despatch of so many ships doubtless was intended to thwart any potential Athenian move to aid the Spartans with their triremes; a proposal to do so had recently been defeated in the Athenian Assembly.[27] Agis had mustered 20,000 infantry and 2,000 cavalry from Sparta and her allies in addition to the 8,000 or 10,000 mercenaries, and this army came to blows first with Corrhagus, a Macedonian general already in the Peloponnese, and defeated him.[28] News of Corrhagus' defeat reached Antipater while he was with his "whole" military force in Thrace trying to put down a revolt of Alexander's *strategos* of Thrace, another Memnon. This man, using the forces Alexander had assigned to him, had stirred up the Thracians against Macedonian domination.[29] It has been suggested that Memnon was working in collusion with Agis,[30] but there is no evidence for this and it may be rather that Agis simply seized the opportunity of Antipater's preoccupation to mobilize his forces. Antipater had no choice but to come to terms with Memnon as quickly as possible and redirect his forces south.[31] It took time, however (having recently sent the reinforcements of 6,000 foot and 500 horse to Alexander), for Antipater to recruit from his allies and subjects and to hire mercenaries of sufficient number to be able to confront Agis. Finally, with a force totaling not fewer than 40,000 foot and horse combined he marched on Agis' army as it was besieging Megalopolis in Arcadia.[32] In a great battle with heavy losses on both sides Agis was mortally wounded and the Spartans fell back on Laconia,[33] conceding the victory to Antipater. Though the victory was greatly to Alexander's benefit, it is said that when he received the news he belittled it as a "battle of mice."[34]

Antipater's handling of the uprising in the Peloponnese, once he got his army together, was swift and effective, tightening the dominance of Macedonia over southern Greek affairs and dealing an all but fatal blow to Sparta's hopes of recovering hegemony.[35] He deferred the post-battle settlement to the League of Corinth, which made decisions about those Peloponnesian member states that had contravened the League by actively joining the revolt. But because Sparta was not a member, the *synedrion* (council) in turn deferred its fate to Alexander, and the Spartans were granted permission to send envoys to the king to plead terms.[36]

Antipater's activities for the next seven years are not well recorded, as sources focus their attention mainly on Alexander. On the eastern frontier Odrysian Thrace evidently revolted,[37] but it seems the Greek states gave Antipater no more trouble while Alexander was alive,[38] so the garrisons and pro-Macedonian governments, though causing much resentment, were effective. While Alexander was in India communications between regent and king were perhaps infrequent, but once the king returned to the Persian capitals Antipater will not have been long hearing of the purge of the satraps. Many of Alexander's administrators and officers anticipated that he would never return alive, and the king was now bombarded by complaints of their illegal acts, their rape of Persian noble women, and their plundering of tombs and temples. Rightly, Alexander found these abuses of power unsettling and damaging to his own authority—"their greed and lust had made the name of the Macedonians hateful to the barbarians"[39]— but he was even more disturbed by the fact that some (ostensibly for protection) had acquired mercenary forces of significant size. He immediately sent orders to all his satraps and generals in Asia to disband their mercenary armies.[40]

Most alarming of all, Alexander's friend Harpalus, one of his inner circle who had been exiled by Philip and subsequently elevated to treasurer of the royal treasury (a physical condition rendered him unsuited for military service), absconded with 5,000 talents and 6,000 mercenaries, and, crossing the Aegean with thirty ships, he sailed directly to Athens to offer his money and mercenaries in their service.[41] This flight from Babylon was Harpalus' second, for he had run off on a previous occasion to Megara, near Athens, but had been recalled and pardoned by Alexander, who in his early years had a tendency to forgive and indulge his friends.[42] Harpalus had helped transfer the treasure seized at Persepolis to Ecbatana, but then he returned as overseer of the treasury at Babylon, where, being among those thinking Alexander would never survive the east, he took up a life of dissolute luxury, lavishing enormous sums on expensive prostitutes.[43] When the Athenians threatened to hand Harpalus over to Antipater, he went with his mercenaries to Taenarum.[44] Many of the men-for-hire congregated at Taenarum and in Crete were exiles from their home states, usually for political reasons, and could not return, as were the large number who were drifting about Asia now that the satraps had been forced to disband their mercenaries.[45] It appears to have been with the intent of dispersing this large pool of military resources that could be used against him that Alexander sent Nicanor of Stagira to Greece to make an announcement at the Olympic games in the summer of 324, as well as instructions by letter to Antipater to see that the announcement was enforced.

> King Alexander to the exiles from the Greek cities. We have not been the cause of your exile, but, save for those of you who are under a curse, we shall be the cause of your return to your own native cities. We have written to Antipater about this to the end that if any cities are not willing to restore you, he may constrain them.[46]

More than 20,000 exiles had travelled to Olympia to hear the proclamation, a clear indication that Alexander had already announced his intention to issue the decree (probably at Susa before he sent Nicanor).[47] The exiles received the proclamation with enthusiasm, but the states compelled to receive them back were thrown into turmoil—properties would have to be restored, old rivalries would flare up, etc.[48] The autonomy of the Greeks, which the Common Peace purported to guarantee, was blatantly flouted, and the directive to Antipater may reveal an attempt by Alexander to reassert his authority over matters on the Greek mainland that had all but disintegrated during his long absence.[49]

Rumour of the impending announcement at Olympia during the games would have reached Athens ahead of Harpalus, who arrived sometime in July,[50] and the fact that he was a long-time close friend of Alexander, his chief treasurer, and had come with a fleet of thirty ships and 6,000 mercenaries must have made his request for asylum appear dubious. The Athenians probably feared he had come to enforce the decree.[51] After his initial rebuff and withdrawal to Taenarum on his second attempt he was admitted to Athens; he had recently been honoured with Athenian citizenship for supplying the city with grain, and now returning with only a few ships and mercenaries he sought suppliant status as a citizen's right.[52] But Harpalus, son of Machatas, probably of the royal house of Elimeia and thus a very dangerous loose cannon—a royal Macedonian renegade with ample resources up for grabs—was a wanted man. Alexander's *strategos* (or *hyparchos*) of coastal Asia Minor, Philoxenus,[53] Antipater, and Olympias (these days residing in Epirus because of her political rivalry with Antipater) all demanded the Athenians hand over Harpalus.[54] It was Demosthenes, later accused of taking some of Harpalus' money, who proposed his arrest and an embassy to Alexander regarding what to do with the renegade.[55] While Demosthenes himself was attending the Olympic games and trying to work a deal with Nicanor about the non-implementation of the decree, Harpalus slipped his guard and took sail to Crete, where he was soon killed by one of his own men.[56]

The king is dead

By the spring of 323 Alexander's veterans who had been dismissed the previous year at Opis had advanced only as far as Cilicia. Craterus was leading them, and his initial instruction from Alexander had been to replace Antipater. Though he was ill when he started out, this is surely not the reason, or not the sole reason, for the slow progress.[57] The initial instruction to Antipater had been to come to Babylon with new recruits, and he was still in Macedonia. Harpalus' flight probably had forced Alexander to send new instructions to both Craterus and Antipater to prepare for trouble brewing in Athens. A number of embassies met Alexander at Babylon in the spring, among them one from Macedonia bearing complaints about Antipater.[58] This embassy had likely come from the faction of Olympias, who for some time had been in political conflict with Antipater. Letters to Alexander from his mother complained about the regent, and letters from Antipater complained about Olympias.[59] Antipater's son Cassander, who had come to Babylon, attempted to defend the charges against his father, in the process very likely not ingratiating himself with Alexander. But Cassander's lifelong hatred of Alexander more likely stems from the day when he first saw Persians performing *proskynesis* and he committed the indiscretion of laughing out loud. Alexander grabbed hold of him and banged his head against a wall, so terrifying him that many years later the mere sight of a statue of Alexander caused Cassander to shake uncontrollably, or so it was said.[60] Another of Antipater's sons, Iolaus, was also in Babylon at this time serving as Alexander's wine-pourer. Many of the embassies that came were protesting the restoration of their exiles.[61] Some historians believe embassies also came regarding Alexander's request for divine honours, though others deny that any 'request' was ever made. Sources are not explicit about a request, but cult honours do appear in the final year of his reign. Around this much debated issue of Alexander's divinity a substantial volume of scholarship has been produced.[62] Suffice it to say, leaving aside the Greeks, the Macedonians already had been resolute in rejecting Alexander's divine aspirations, though evidently his Successors granted divinity once he was dead.[63] Antipater, it is said, was the only one of them to refrain from honouring him as a god, regarding it a sacrilege.[64]

Alexander's death on June 11, 323,[65] after a ten-day fever, occurred amidst this complexity of problems attendant upon the Exiles Decree, divine honours, and complaints against Antipater. In Macedonia, where news of the king's death must have been unbelievable at first, never was there a better opportunity for Antipater to seize the throne, and he did not. At Babylon Alexander's death was catastrophic: from three wives he had produced no heir as yet; the empire of Persia, which he had subsumed as King of Asia but had not fully conquered, had no prospective ruler; the all-conquering Macedonian army, now blended with forces drawn from throughout the corners of the former Achaemenid realm, found itself a body without a head.[66] Alexander's advisors in the final feverish days are said to have asked him for some direction on how to proceed under the circumstance of his passing. The recorded replies are that they should pay him divine honours "when they themselves were happy" and that his body should be taken to Ammon; his kingdom he bequeathed to the "best" man (or strongest)—if true, an intentional apple of discord—but taking off his signet ring he passed it to Perdiccas.[67]

Perdiccas was one of the elite Seven Bodyguards and he had assumed the office of *chiliarchos* (the king's second-in-command) perhaps after Hephaestion's death late in 324.[68] According to Curtius, he and the other Bodyguards summoned Alexander's chief Companions and officers to the royal quarters, but a throng of the rank and file followed and burst into the palace area.[69] Having displayed Alexander's symbols of royal authority—his throne, crown, robe, and arms—and taking off the ring and placing it with the rest, Perdiccas spoke to those who could hear. Appropriately, he mentioned Alexander's funeral rites, then he pressed the point that a leader for the army was imperative, whether one man or more; and then pointing out that Roxane was with child (she was in her sixth or seventh month) and that a male offspring, should such be the issue, would assume the throne when he came of age (father-to-son succession is presumed) he asked them to decide how many and whom they chose to have rule in the interim. Nearchus spoke next, reminding those assembled that "only the blood and stock of Alexander was suited to royal majesty" and that Alexander had already produced a son, Heracles by Barsine.[70] This was clearly in self-interest, since he was married to a daughter of Barsine, but Heracles was illegitimate, was not present at court (he was being reared at Pergamon),[71] and the proposal was shouted down. Ptolemy, after rejecting the notion of *any* king that was part Asian, suggested that a council of advisors, probably intending the council already in existence and that had handled matters through the king's illness, should meet as needed to make decisions by majority vote and that the generals and officers should abide by their decisions. This met with some support, though not much more than Perdiccas' proposal. Then the Bodyguard Aristonus spoke,[72] and he pointed out that Alexander already had indicated who was "best" and should rule by handing Perdiccas his ring, not in private but in front of others of his inner circle; Perdiccas was Alexander's clear choice. When those assembled acceded and called for Perdiccas to pick up the ring he hesitated and withdrew behind those who had been sitting beside him. In that pause the taxiarch Meleager spewed forth such a diatribe against Perdiccas' candidacy and ambition for the supreme rule, adding the proposal that Alexander's choice be rejected and the treasuries be pillaged, that the meeting erupted into chaos. An angry mob congealed around Meleager, and the infantry demanded their say in the selection of the new king. They proposed the only living adult male Argead (who happened to be in Babylon), Alexander's mentally deficient half-brother Arrhidaeus! "If you seek a king ... next in blood, this man is the only one."[73]

The rank and file wanted above all an Argead king, but for the first time in Macedonian history there was no *viable* bloodline candidate. These were the options, all and only, available to the Macedonians for their empty throne: a fool was as fit to be king as a fetus or a bastard. Despite another of the Seven Bodyguards, Peithon, reminding the throng that Arrhidaeus was not a viable candidate, Meleager brought the startled Arrhidaeus into the palace, Arrhidaeus put on Alexander's robe, and Meleager, donning his own cuirass, staged an 'acclamation', with the rank and file clashing spears against shields in approval (though just prior this had been a signal of rejecting Nearchus' proposal).[74] The Bodyguards, generals, and Companions, evidently after Meleager and his followers had left the meeting, on the motion of Peithon took an oath of loyalty to Roxane's child, if male, in recognition of his entitlement to the succession as the deceased king's son, nominating Perdiccas and Leonnatus, both reputedly royal (though not Argead), as guardians.[75] The demand of the rank and file against the proposals of the elite persisted, bringing the army to the brink of civil war, so the elite, faced with no other option in the circumstances, accepted Arrhidaeus as nominal king.[76] Arrhidaeus' name was changed to Philip (III).

Some historians have seen in the actions of the infantry the exercise of a constitutional right to choose a king or to participate in the process.[77] However, the Macedonian monarchy and state functioned on a loose system of persuasion and consent, petition, and willing support.[78] The strength of the state depended on the strength of the person of the king. When the monarch was weak, such as when Amyntas III was driven out and the Illyrians and Chalcidians seized his territory, then the state was weak. Thus the acclamation of Arrhidaeus was a dangerous course of action. And not one Macedonian in Europe, or anywhere outside Babylon, not even Antipater and Craterus, had one whit to say in the succession.[79]

It was too late, evidently, to avert a rift in the command of the army. Perdiccas, along with the Bodyguards and others of Alexander's inner circle of advisors, was supported by the Companion Cavalry (Macedonian nobility), and Meleager, who had been one of the eight taxiarch infantry commanders since the Granicus or longer, had the loyal backing of the rank and file. The Companion Cavalry were outnumbered and disadvantaged in the city, so they fled Babylon and set up camp outside, blockading the infantry forces inside the city and cutting off their grain supply.[80] Meleager's attempt, using the authority of Philip III Arrhidaeus as king, to have Perdiccas arrested or killed failed, and arbitrators from among the Greeks at court were chosen to negotiate reconciliation. Perdiccas feigned an acceptance of Meleager as his co- or second-in-command, and by this dissimulation he brought both Meleager and Philip Arrhidaeus under his control.[81] A traditional Macedonian purification ceremony was held to reunite the two quarreling units of the army,[82] and the infantry marched out of the city to face up against the cavalry as for a mock battle. At the far end of the plain where the army was to muster a dog was disemboweled and cut in two, and the two pieces were then cast to either side of the plain. Then the infantry and cavalry under arms took up positions facing each other between the pieces of the severed carcass. As the two units approached each other as for battle, Arrhidaeus at the head of a battalion of cavalry rode up to the infantry and demanded that the ringleaders of the riot that had caused the rift be handed over. Perdiccas then singled out thirty men from the infantry ranks,[83] those who had first rallied to Meleager, threw them to the elephants, and before the eyes of all they were trampled to death.

This was the beginning of civil confrontations that were to span four decades. More immediately, Perdiccas brought resolution, Alexander-style, to a grave crisis and for the time being secured both the Asian empire and his own leading position within it. Although he had used fear to intimidate the rowdy infantry into compromise with the noble cavalrymen, by returning to a purely Macedonian tradition—the purification ritual—he mollified some of the oriental phobia many Macedonians were expressing, and the immediate critical effect was the reconciliation of the warring factions of the army. He eliminated his rival Meleager, who had jeopardized stability. Meleager was not thrown to the elephants, but he was killed shortly afterwards. Perdiccas also showed up Arrhidaeus for what he was: a pawn in the hands of whoever might be in position to manipulate him. Arrhidaeus, or, we should say, King Philip III, did precisely what Perdiccas instructed him to do, taking no action to stop the execution of the very men who had made him king and assuming no responsibility for it. The reconciliation compelled the Macedonians to concede the absolute necessity of appointing guardians or regents for the heir(s) and to consent to the rule of those appointed.

Craterus (*in absentia*) was appointed *prostates*, or regent, for Arrhidaeus, the appointment being part of the reconciliation between cavalry and infantry before the death of Meleager, and the infantry were forced to accept the possible outcome of a second king, if Roxane produced a son, whose guardians were to be Perdiccas and Leonnatus.[84] There remained the practical matter of how to govern Alexander's vast empire, so Perdiccas, now acting with the authority Alexander seems to have imparted to him, summoned an assembly and appointed the high-ranking generals and Bodyguards to commands of the various satrapies and provinces. This first settlement, the Babylon Settlement,[85] assigned to Ptolemy command of Egypt and to Leonnatus Hellespontine Phrygia, which (conveniently) distanced him from Perdiccas and the central authority and squeezed him out of co-guardianship of the unborn king; Lysimachus was assigned Thrace, the buffer between Asia and the Macedonian homeland; and Eumenes of Cardia, the Greek secretary of Philip and Alexander, was assigned the task of subduing and then governing Cappadocia. Others were reinstated in commands they already held, including Antigonus the One-Eyed in Greater Phrygia, which he had governed since 333, though he immediately proved unwilling to recognize Perdicccas' supreme command; and Antipater was confirmed as *strategos autokrator* (general with full powers) in Europe. How different this was from his position as Alexander's regent or general in Europe is difficult to say; it certainly meant subordination to the regency which Perdiccas assumed.[86] Though Craterus, initially before the settlement, was appointed to the highest office, in the several surviving lists of the settlement itself there is only one reference to him, his co-command with Antipater in Europe.[87] At the expense of both Craterus and Antipater,[88] Perdiccas became the central figure of authority acting in Philip III's name and commanding the royal army, and when Roxane came to full term, producing the anticipated son, he assumed guardianship of Alexander IV.[89]

The Macedonian rank and file had been successful in holding onto what they regarded as their traditional monarchy. But the weakness of Alexander's Argead heirs opened up a high-stakes power game among the many capable and ambitious generals who had survived his hard campaigns: his Successors, or the Diadochi. As news of Alexander's death reverberated across the known world, revolts immediately broke out around the peripheries of both the home kingdom and the greater empire. At home, Antipater was confronted with a major uprising, the backlash of Alexander's Exiles Decree.

The Lamian War: Antipater's triumph over Athens

In June 323 Antipater was in Macedonia keeping a close watch for the king on affairs at Athens. He had not defied Alexander's summons to Babylon, but rather news of Harpalus' flight to Athens in 324 surely precipitated a revocation of the summons, as is implied by Alexander's proclamation to the exiles at Olympia: "We have written to Antipater about this to the end that if any cities are not willing to restore you, he may constrain them."[90] Antipater can hardly have carried out this directive while marching to Babylon. Alexander's trust in Antipater, moreover, seems to belie the tradition that the relationship between king and regent was deteriorating, though certainly Olympias had tried to aggravate a breach between the two. She went so far at a later date as to accuse Antipater and his sons of poisoning Alexander, though there was no evidence for her charge.[91] Since the turmoil of succession at Babylon had derailed the embassies, objection to the Exiles Decree was an issue now even more in Antipater's hands. The Decree was especially objectionable to Athens, since it would mean the loss of Samos, which some forty years prior she had confiscated for cleruchies (settlements) by exiling the inhabitants, and to Aetolia, because the Aetolians had confiscated Oeniadae and exiled the native Acarnanians, and for this Alexander had already threatened retaliation.[92] The Aetolians possibly approached Antipater for an alliance in hopes that he would not enforce the Decree in their case.[93] The Athenians entertained no such hope, despite Antipater's friendship with a few prominent Athenians, among them Demades and Aristotle, who by 323 had been living at Athens for over a decade; *his* relationship with Alexander had deteriorated, yet he remained a close friend of Antipater.[94] At news of Alexander's death the Athenians, still sitting on some of Harpalus' moneybags, immediately sent the money and arms to their general Leosthenes at Taenarum.[95]

Leosthenes was an elected Athenian *strategos* and in the winter and spring of 323 he was at Taenarum aggressively recruiting mercenaries, something that was supposed to be kept a secret from Antipater, though it cannot have been much of one by the late spring.[96] At news of Alexander's death all pretenses were cast to the wind, and at Athens, though many of the aristocracy were reluctant to go to war with Macedonia, the democrats outvoted them and called for the liberation of all Greeks from Macedonian garrisons.[97] Leosthenes won the Aetolians to alliance (they committed 7,000 soldiers) as well as tribes in central Greece including the Locrians and Phocians, while the Athenians brought in some of the more dominant states in the Peloponnese, including Argos, Sicyon, and Elis. Leosthenes soon had his Hellenic war, or what came to be known as the Lamian War.[98] His first move was to seize Thermopylae, hoping to hold off a Macedonian advance until his own allies could mobilize. The Boeotians south of Thermopylae sided with the Macedonians, so the Athenians had first to defeat the Boeotian resistance, which they did in a battle near Plataea; then they advanced to Thermopylae to join the coalition. As Leosthenes intended, the land war was confined to the north.[99]

Leosthenes now had roughly 30,000 men in the field, and Antipater was hard pressed to pull together an army that could stand up to that number, so he appealed for aid to Craterus, who was still in Cilicia with the 10,000 veterans intended for repatriation.[100] Unable to await Craterus' arrival, which in the event was a long time coming, he left Sippas (otherwise unknown) as *strategos* in Macedonia with forces enough to defend the kingdom and orders to recruit, and himself marched with an army of only 13,000 Macedonian foot and a meagre 600 horse into Thessaly, doubtless anticipating considerable reinforcements there, especially cavalry. At the same time he deployed a fleet of 110 triremes (ships Alexander had sent to Macedonia shortly before his death carrying money probably to fund recruitment and shipbuilding in anticipation of this very war). These triremes were to challenge the fleet Athens was sending as naval support for Leosthenes.[101] As hoped, the Thessalians at first backed Antipater's advance, but then under Athenian persuasion the superb Thessalian cavalry, which had played such a vital role in so many of Philip's and Alexander's victories, seeing this as their opportune moment to regain independence, went over to the Greek coalition. Now seriously outnumbered, Antipater was defeated in a battle and, unable to execute a safe retreat to Macedonia, took shelter in nearby Lamia, a well fortified town in the south of Thessaly. And there the wily old general sat, besieged, busying his men with manufacture of arms and missiles and storing in food for what was shaping up to be a long winter.[102]

Craterus had not yet made his way to Europe, so Antipater appealed for aid to Leonnatus. Leonnatus had been firmly cut out of the co-guardianship and had taken up his satrapal appointment in Hellespontine Phrygia. A return to the homeland of either Leonnatus or Craterus with seasoned veterans was potentially dangerous for Antipater, yet his own pressing needs were of greater weight, and so in a diplomatic move reminiscent of Philip he offered both veteran generals a daughter in marriage. Leonnatus found himself in a high-class dilemma, for he had been in private correspondence with Alexander's full sister Cleopatra, now widow of the Epirote king Alexander, regarding marriage, and such an alliance combined with his Lyncestian royal blood would make him a powerful royal alternative to Antipater's rule in Macedonia.[103] Eumenes, whom Leonnatus had tried to win over as an ally, distrusting the latter's ambition, declined to assist his crossing at the Hellespont and then revealed the marriage negotiations with Cleopatra, to which he was privy, to Perdiccas.[104] Perdiccas was already negotiating his own marriage alliance with a third daughter of Antipater, Nicaea.[105]

Leosthenes' coalition meanwhile exulted in having the mighty Antipater holed up in Lamia. As soon as he ran out of foodstuffs, they thought, the war would be over. Prospects being such, Leosthenes' Aetolian allies pulled up stakes and went home, while Leosthenes himself kept up a daily harassment of the walls to prevent the Macedonians from getting supplies. Then in a skirmish near the walls Leosthenes was struck by a missile and died a few days later. The Athenians and their allies stayed entrenched where they were and a new general, Antiphilus, was sent out from Athens to take command. By the early spring of 322 Leonnatus had made his way to Macedonia from Hellespontine Phrygia, and, finally, after taking time to recruit more Macedonian soldiers, with 20,000 infantry and 1,500 cavalry he marched into Thessaly to relieve Antipater. Before he reached Lamia the allied Greeks decided to stake everything on a battle to prevent his joining forces with Antipater. The two armies were fairly well matched in infantry, but the Greeks had more than double the number of horse. Of 3,500 cavalry 2,000 were elite Thessalian, and just as they had bested Antipater they proved too much for the cavalry of Leonnatus. Leonnatus himself, cut off in a swamp, received multiple wounds and had to be carried from the field—dead before they got him into camp. Antipater seized the moment of the Greek army's absence to break out of Lamia, and the day after the battle he met up with Leonnatus' defeated forces. He took these under his own command and with the two armies combined began his retreat, leading them over rough terrain so as to avoid battle and to foil any attacks from the Thessalian cavalry.[106]

While the Macedonian land forces were pinned down in Thessaly, the Macedonian fleet was winning supremacy at sea, and it is these naval victories that likely decided the war. The Athenians had voted at the beginning of the war to man forty quadriremes and 200 triremes, and Antipater had sent out 110 triremes.[107] There is scant evidence for the actions of either of these fleets. By the late spring or early summer of 322 the Macedonian admiral Cleitus the White had command of the sea with 240 ships, a number matching the Athenian fleet. It is unknown whether these included Antipater's triremes or whether there were now two Macedonian fleets in operation. Cleitus, who had been taxiarch and then hipparch during Alexander's Indian campaign, recently had been in Cilicia with Craterus and the discharged veterans, and he may have been in charge of shipbuilding there.[108] It is probable that he won the Macedonian naval victory at the Hellespont near Abydos in the spring of 322. Macedonian predominance at sea now forced the Athenians to outfit more ships for their fleet, one source says bringing their total to 170.[109] They had suffered serious losses indeed, if the number is correct, since a year earlier they voted a fleet of 240. It has been suggested, however, that the Athenians were operating with two fleets.[110] Cleitus is credited with two victories over the Athenian fleet of Euetion and is said to have put many Athenian ships out of action near the Echinades islands. It is uncertain whether the latter refers to a third battle, and since the Echinades are off the west coast of Acarnania out from Oeniadae, most historians assume, though perhaps not correctly, that Echinades is a mistake for the Lichades islands, near the Malian Gulf close to Lamia, or the town Echinus in Phthiotis.[111] It is agreed that the most important Macedonian victory (presumably Cleitus') came at Amorgos early that summer. For the Athenians it was a defeat from which they never recovered, marking the end of their long naval dominance of the Aegean.[112]

Naval success evidently made possible Craterus' arrival, finally, from Cilicia with 10,000 infantry, 6,000 of these being hardened veterans of Alexander's great battles against Darius and the Bactrian and Indian campaigns, 1,000 Persian bowmen and slingers, and 1,500 cavalry. Joining forces with Antipater at the Peneus River he deferred supreme command to his soon-to-be father-in-law. The combined Macedonian army now totaled more than 40,000 infantry, 3,000 bowmen and slingers, and 5,000 cavalry.[113] Antiphilus with only 25,000 infantry and 3,500 cavalry had waited too long to make his move, but still relying on the strength of the Thessalian horse commanded by Menon, in midsummer he challenged Antipater to battle southwest of Larissa near Crannon.[114] Menon's cavalry was indeed superior, but the seasoned Macedonian infantry phalanx got the best of the Greek hoplites and mercenaries, and with 500 of their own dead on the field the Greeks decided to sue for peace.

In post-battle negotiations Antipater refused to grant the Greek request for a mass settlement, and one by one he and Craterus besieged the cities of Thessaly, forcing them to sue for peace individually and desert the Athenian coalition. When the Athenians found themselves alone facing Antipater and the Macedonian army they too finally sued for peace. Having suffered the humiliation of a defeat and winter blockade in Lamia, Antipater gave no quarter; he demanded what Leosthenes had demanded of him: full surrender.[115] Antipater and Craterus marched into Boeotia and established camp at the Theban Cadmeia, where they received Athenian envoys, among whom were Antipater's old friend Demades and the venerable Phocion. With Antipater's army sitting on the northern frontier of Attica and Cleitus' fleet controlling the grain route through the Hellespont, Athens had no choice but to capitulate. When a force of

Macedonians entered Athens in the early fall the democracy was abolished; all citizens whose wealth amounted to less than 2,000 drachmas (the non-aristocrats who had voted for the war) were disenfranchised, some 12,000 deported and offered resettlement in Thrace, and only 9,000 of the wealthier were left in Athens to govern, according to the pre-Cleisthenic constitution of Solon.[116] To ensure that Antipater's stipulations were enforced a Macedonian garrison was installed on Munychia hill in Piraeus with Menyllus as commander, a fair-dealing Macedonian and friend of Phocion.[117] The Athenians were forced to give up Samos, and Perdiccas oversaw the return of the Samian exiles. The Athenians passed a decree, proposed by Demades, condemning Demosthenes to death. Demosthenes had been exiled earlier for accepting a bribe from Harpalus, had gone only as far as Megara, and was recalled during the Lamian War. Fleeing now to Calauria (Poros), before Antipater's henchman Archias could take him captive he took poison.[118] Antipater and Craterus returned to Macedonia to embark upon cooperative rule. To solidify their political arrangement Antipater, as promised, gave his daughter Phila to Craterus in marriage. Remains of an elaborate noble's house excavated at Pella, the so-called House of Dionysus named for one of the mosaic floors it contained, may have been theirs, and another of the mosaics in the house, the Lion Hunt mosaic, is thought to depict Craterus (right) saving Alexander from a mauling by a lion (Figures 8.1, 8.2).[119]

Figure 8.1 House of Dionysus, mosaic floor of an antechamber, Pella, last quarter of fourth century BCE. The house possibly belonged to Antipater's daughter, Phila

Source: author, 2014.

Figure 8.2 Lion Hunt mosaic, floor of an *andron* (banquet room), House of Dionysus, Pella

Source: author, 2014.

Antipater and the Successors

Not long after the conclusion of the Lamian War Antipater's daughter Nicaea, escorted by her brother Iolaus, arrived in Asia Minor as the intended bride of Perdiccas. Perdiccas, with the royal army and King Philip, had been busy gaining control of Cappadocia for Eumenes and besieging two towns in Pisidia which some while back had put to death Alexander's satrap, Balacrus, son of Nicanor.[120] It was Balacrus' widow, Phila, who married Craterus. But Perdiccas now had two-brides-in waiting! After Leonnatus was killed in battle Olympias proposed to Perdiccas that he marry Alexander's sister, and so Cleopatra also now arrived in Asia Minor.[121] At this point Perdiccas chose to continue his original course of cooperation with Antipater by marrying Nicaea. His regency would be confined to Asia, while Antipater with Craterus would manage Europe. But Perdiccas now thought that the most powerful of the satraps in Asia Minor, Antigonus (the One-Eyed), posed a challenge to his regency. In the Babylon Settlement Antigonus was reconfirmed in his satrapy of Phrygia, where he had held the appointment for more than ten years and had consolidated a considerable personal power base, but he had not responded to the royal directive to give military support to Eumenes in Cappadocia.[122] Perdiccas intended to have him removed from his command by bringing him to trial, though the specific charges are not recorded.[123]

Before Perdiccas could deal with Antigonus trouble of a surprising nature presented itself, or, we should say, *her*self. Philip II's daughter Cynnane, half-sister of Alexander III and widow of Perdiccas III's son Amyntas, at the head of an armed troop managed to force her way past Antipater's guards at the Strymon, and then getting herself and her troops across the Hellespont she arrived in Asia Minor ready to battle for what she regarded as her rightful share of the Argead succession. Her mother was the Illyrian princess Audata, and like her mother she was trained in Illyrian military tactics; she is said to have led forces into battle and killed by her own stroke an enemy Illyrian queen.[124] She was not to be outdone by Antipater's and Olympias' proposed marriage alliances with Alexander's Successors, so with an audacious scheme of one-upmanship she brought to Asia her daughter by Amyntas, Adea, who was in her mid teens, with the intention of marrying the girl to her half-uncle Arrhidaeus, King Philip III. The genius of Cynnane's proposal lay in the potential for a true Argead successor to the Macedonian throne, a grandson and great-grandson of Philip II *and* great-grandson of Perdiccas III; in other words, an Argead through and through (if not a particularly bright one). Perdiccas the regent sent his own brother Alcetas to stop her, and in the confrontation somehow Cynnane was killed.[125]

The Macedonian infantry which had so forcefully declared its unwavering loyalty to the Argead line at Babylon by acclaiming Philip II's incompetent son "king" was outraged now at the death of his daughter, and when they learned that Philip's granddaughter had been intended as bride for their king, they created such an uproar that eventually, with Perdiccas hard-pressed to pacify them, they got their way again and the marriage was realized. One would love to have been nearby (but not too nearby) when Olympias heard the news. As for Perdiccas, it was time to reconsider an Argead alliance for himself.

Amidst the commotion over Cynnane's death and the royal marriage Antigonus saw fit to extricate himself from Perdiccas' summons to trial, and together with a few close associates and his young son Demetrius he took ship and crossed the Aegean to seek protection with his old friend Antipater.[126] When Antigonus arrived in the winter of 321–320,[127] Antipater and Craterus were in Aetolia on a campaign of retaliation for Aetolian involvement in the Lamian War. The Aetolian campaign was a major operation, with the Macedonians fielding an army of 30,000 foot and 2,500 horse. The Aetolians with a force of only 10,000 had been driven into the mountains and with winter upon them were on the point of surrender when Antigonus broke the news to Antipater in exaggerated detail that Perdiccas and Alcetas had killed Cynnane, and that Perdiccas was about to jilt Antipater's daughter for Cleopatra and march triumphant with the royal army into Macedonia. Antigonus' report was greatly alarming, so Antipater and Craterus quickly settled with the Aetolians. Neither Antipater nor Craterus had had any say in the Perdiccas-engineered Babylon Settlement, so *their* plan now was for Antipater to continue in his role as *strategos* of Europe, while Craterus would assume the regency in Asia. Both would take forces and cross to Asia Minor to challenge Perdiccas. They sent to Ptolemy in Egypt asking for his support, and Antipater sealed the alliance by sending his daughter Eurydice as a bride for Ptolemy.[128]

Perdiccas now had war on two fronts (the so-called First Diadoch War), since Ptolemy had already precipitated war by hijacking the funeral cortège of Alexander—two years in preparation—as it was en route to Macedonia, and diverting it to Memphis. Thus it came about that Alexander was the only Argead king not to be buried at Aegae (later the body was entombed in Alexandria).[129] Ptolemy's hostile aggression was of greater concern to Perdiccas than the challenge from Craterus, so marching with the two kings and royal army to Egypt he sent his brother Alcetas and Neoptolemus (former commander of the Hypaspists) to assist Eumenes in preventing a crossing at the Hellespont. But neither of Perdiccas' Macedonian commanders was willing to take orders from the Greek Eumenes, so Antipater and Craterus were able to cross unchallenged, and they proceeded inland towards Cappadocia.[130] Alcetas foresaw that the Macedonian infantry under his own command would refuse to go into battle against Antipater out of shame and out of respect and affection for Craterus, and he pulled out of the campaign.[131] Neoptolemus thought the same about his own infantry and was personally ashamed to fight Antipater and Craterus, so he entertained an invitation from Antipater to switch allegiance. Eumenes received a similar invitation, but in part because of a long-standing enmity with Antipater, and in part out of loyalty to Perdiccas as regent for the two kings, he rejected the overture, and suspecting Neoptolemus' imminent defection he challenged him to battle.[132] Neoptolemus lost, and with only about 300 cavalry he rode off to join Antipater, while Eumenes rounded up the defeated Macedonian infantry.[133] Ordering them to ground arms, Eumenes forced them to take an oath of allegiance to his command.

Antipater and Craterus now divided their forces, Antipater marching to Cilicia in pursuit of Perdiccas, and Craterus assisted by Neoptolemus marching against Eumenes.[134] Eumenes concealed from both his officers and his infantry the fact that they were headed into battle against Craterus, persuading them that the enemy was (only) Neoptolemus with a force of allied cavalry.[135] Thus Eumenes' Macedonian infantry, perhaps less than a quarter of his total 20,000 foot ("men of every race") were ignorant until too late that they were facing the venerated Craterus. Craterus also had 20,000 infantry, the bulk of them Macedonian, and after promising them the enemy baggage for plunder he rode into battle in the position of honour, leading the right wing with a cavalry charge, probably in all expectation that the Macedonians in Eumenes' army would desert. But Eumenes was a clever general; knowing Craterus would be leading on the opposing right he placed the bulk of his 5,000 foreign cavalry on his own left opposite Craterus, and on his right opposite Neoptolemus he himself led an elite unit of 300 cavalry. He could not trust the Macedonians, once they knew Craterus was opposite, to stand and fight, so he was counting on his superior strength in cavalry, which was more than double. Sources say Eumenes and Neoptolemus singled each other out in the thick of it for an epic duel to the finish: charging full gallop, they knocked each other off their horses and then grappled on the ground until Eumenes got the upper hand and with a sword thrust to the neck dispatched Neoptolemus. On the far side of the battlefield (depending on the source) Craterus' horse stumbled, threw its rider to the ground, and he was trampled; or a Thracian speared him and he fell from his horse; or Paphlagonians, a contingent of Eumenes' cavalry, killed him. Eumenes' general Gorgias recognized him as he lay dying, but Craterus was already unresponsive. Eumenes came away from the battle wounded but victorious, having slain two of Alexander's great generals. And for that, in Macedonian eyes, he was more to be despised than to be respected. The Macedonian infantry of Craterus were offered terms and employment in Eumenes' army, to which he bound them by oath, but most of them slipped away in the night and rejoined Antipater.[136]

While all this was unfolding, Polyperchon, whom Antipater had left as general in Macedonia (he had come from Cilicia with Craterus and the veterans), had his hands full putting down a revolt in Thessaly stirred up by the Aetolians who had entered into a deal with Perdiccas.[137] When one of Antipater's generals, Polycles, was killed, Polyperchon led a large force into Thessaly and defeated and killed the cavalry commander Menon. Antigonus had already re-crossed to Asia Minor ahead of Antipater and Craterus, landing in Caria and setting an ambush for Eumenes, but Cleopatra, now ensconced at Sardis, did some spying and tipped off Eumenes.[138] Antipater and Craterus then assigned Antigonus the task of sailing to Cyprus against Perdiccas' ally Aristonus, the former Bodyguard.[139] Antipater finally made his way to Cilicia, but by then Perdiccas was long gone, having marched to Egypt against Ptolemy.

Ptolemy had diverted Alexander's elaborate funeral cortège, as we said, and he was no longer answering to Perdiccas as representative of the kings. He had killed Alexander's administrator Cleomenes and expanded his satrapy westward to Cyrene in Libya.[140] It is good to keep in mind that the literary tradition is hostile to Perdiccas, and we might well see him as primarily attempting to keep the empire intact to prevent breakaway kingdoms.[141] In his attempt to cross the Nile and attack Ptolemy's fortified position more than 2,000 of Perdiccas' men drowned or were eaten by crocodiles, a gruesome mishap causing him to lose support among the infantry, who did not want this war to begin with. Peithon, another former Bodyguard, and a large number of officers and cavalrymen, prominent among them Seleucus, now commander of the Companion Cavalry, backed by the hostile infantry, turned on Perdiccas and assassinated him.[142] The next day Ptolemy was welcomed in the Perdiccan camp. It might have been expected that he would assume the regency, but he deferred to Peithon and Arrhidaeus (the one who had escorted Alexander's funeral cortège). News of Eumenes' victory over Craterus did not reach Perdiccas' camp until two days after his assassination, else events might well have turned out much differently.

Alexander's body, the *soma*, was the desired prize for Ptolemy.[143] Its appropriation exemplifies Macedonian veneration of any and every relic of the deceased Argead god-king and the inherent power in the possession and use of such relics and Alexander imagery.[144] Eumenes, for instance, later made the most of such veneration as a means of winning the support of the Macedonian soldiery; he habitually produced Alexander's throne, diadem, and scepter as symbolic of the dead king's presence. Now, however, the new regents Peithon and Arrhidaeus, having convened an army assembly, declared Eumenes and fifty of his chief men, including Alcetas, outlaws under sentence of death.[145] Many of Perdiccas' close friends and even his sister, Atalante, wife of Attalus, son of Andromenes, who had recently been appointed Perdiccas' admiral, were put to death. Peithon and Arrhidaeus left the Nile and marched to Triparadeisos in upper Syria. There the young wife of Philip III, Eurydice, as Adea was renamed, with the backing of the Perdiccans Attalus and Asclepiodorus,[146] was inciting the soldiers to revolt against the new regents (*epimeletai*). Peithon and Arrhidaeus, to save their necks, resigned the regency, and an army assembly, perhaps steered by a council of officers, voted to elect Antipater sole regent.[147] A few days later Antipater arrived from Cilicia only to discover the army in an uproar and greatly hostile towards him. Adea Eurydice, still fuelling revolt, had given a public speech denouncing Antipater and stirred up the rank and file to fever pitch. They demanded from Antipater their long-overdue pay, and when he said he did not have it to give they were on the point of stoning him. He escaped only by the quick thinking of Antigonus and Seleucus, who created a diversion, and fled to his own camp. Antigonus then gave a speech in support of Antipater and this had the desired effect of putting the disturbance to rest. Antipater was confirmed as sole regent.

Due to the recent elimination of several senior commanders Antipater now had to reassign some of the satrapies; this is called the Second Settlement at Triparadeisos.[148] Peithon was sent to Media, and Arrhidaeus to Hellespontine Phrygia, still vacant since Leonnatus' death. Among the 'new' satraps Cleitus in Lydia is notable, a reward no doubt for defecting to Antipater with the Hellespont fleet. Antigenes, one of the veteran commanders of Alexander's Hypaspists (he was discharged at Opis but had rejoined the royal army and had a leading role in the assassination of Perdiccas), was given command of 3,000 "most rebellious" Macedonian infantry and the task of escorting money down from Susa.[149] Philip III was assigned four Bodyguards, one of whom was Polyperchon's son Alexander; another three presumably were assigned to Alexander IV.[150] Ptolemy was reconfirmed in his satrapy, as was Antigonus in Phrygia and Lycia. Antigonus was also assigned the war against Eumenes and Alcetas. Antipater's son Cassander was appointed *chiliarchos* of the cavalry, effectively second-in-command to Antigonus; Cassander could quietly keep an eye on the satrap's ambitions and report to his father. In fact, before Antipater returned to Macedonia Cassander advised him to take with him the two kings and the troublesome Adea Eurydice and not leave them in the guardianship of Antigonus.

At Sardis on his way home Antipater met with Cleopatra and reproached her for her cooperation with Eumenes, who was now a condemned traitor.[151] She defended herself against his criticisms and they parted on good terms. When Antipater's entourage arrived back in Macedonia, for the first time in fourteen years a Macedonian king set foot inside the kingdom.[152] What King Philip III said or did through all these events is unrecorded, but once back in the familiar homeland he may have felt less intimidated by the generals, and no doubt he had a prominent public presence, likely performing daily sacrifices as he had done with Alexander. Some fallout from the war with Perdiccas lingered. When Antipater's long-time Athenian 'friend' Demades arrived at Pella seeking the removal of the Macedonian garrison at Munychia he and his son were arrested on a charge of having negotiated with Perdiccas to invade Macedonia (a letter to Perdiccas was found in which Demades called Antipater "an old and rotten thread"); both were put to death.[153]

Antipater himself was by now, in the second half of 319, not much shy of eighty years of age and in ill health. Polyperchon was not a young man either, but he was greatly revered among the Macedonians as a seasoned veteran of Alexander's campaigns and he had handled affairs competently while Antipater was in Asia. Though Cassander had returned from Asia, it was Polyperchon whom Antipater appointed just before he expired as regent for the kings and general with full powers.[154] Cassander once again was appointed *chiliarchos*, second-in-command to Polyperchon. Antipater very likely did not foresee that, like Alexander, he was setting up his own funeral games. It has been argued that his choice of Polyperchon was a poor decision.[155] However, what Antipater had in mind in 319 was the security of the throne for Argead succession. Antipater himself had never attempted to usurp the throne, and despite his enmity with Olympias he had remained to the end a supporter of Alexander III and his policies, with the exception of deification. Cassander had been no friend of Alexander; he certainly had not campaigned with him, and Antipater might have thought it better to leave the son of Alexander under Polyperchon's care. Alexander IV was just turning four; the road to majority stretched out long ahead.

Notes

1. *Suda* s.v. "Antipatros"; Kanatsulis 1968; Adams 1984; Heckel 1992: 38–49, 2016: 33–43; Baynham 1994; Blackwell 1999: 33–79. The location of Palioura is unknown.
2. Thuc. 1.62.2, chapter 2 n93. Baynham 1994: 337–338 with n23; Tataki 1998: 330.
3. See Chapter 4 n126, n215. The Athenians honoured Antipater as *proxenos* and granted him citizenship, Harpocration s.v. "Alkimachos." Pythian games: Dem. 9.32; Libanius 23.1.66. Athens: Just. 9.4.5; Polyb. 5.10.4.
4. *Suda* s.v. "Antipatros" = FGrH/BNJ 114 T1; Walsh 2012. On Antipater's relationship with Aristotle cf. e.g. Paus. 6.4.8; Ael. *VH* 14.1; Diog. Laert. 5.11–16.
5. Ath. 10.435d.
6. Antipater's age: *Suda* s.v. "Antipatros."
7. Plut. *Alex.* 11.3.
8. Plut. *Phoc.* 17.6.
9. Plut. *Mor.* 180e; cp. Curt. 10.10.14.
10. Diod. 17.17.5: he held *hegemonia*, but 17.118.1, 18.12.1: *strategos* (cf. 17.62.5, 18.12.2, and cp. Arr. *Succ.* 1.3, FGrH 156 [for translation of select fragments (summaries) with some commentary see Harding 125; Goralski 1989; Dreyer 2007.] Curt. 4.1.39: *praefectus*. Arr. *Anab.* 1.11.3: he was entrusted with "Macedonian and Greek affairs." Cf. also Just. 11.7.1. For Antipater's authority cf. e.g. Arr. *Anab.* 2.2.4, 3.16.10; Diod. 18.8.4. On the ambiguous nature of his position see Blackwell 1999: 36 and Carney 2003b: 239, 1995: 371–372. On the term 'regent' see Anson 2009a: 280–281.
11. E.g. Theophr. *Char.* 23.4.
12. Aeschin. 3.165.
13. Plut. *Alex.* 16.19.
14. Arr. *Anab.* 1.29.4; cf. Polyb. 12.19.1–4, not specifying how many are 'Macedonian'.
15. Plut. *Alex.* 25.6–8.
16. Curt. 5.1.40–42; Diod. 17.65.1; cf. Curt. 4.6.30–31; Diod. 17.49.1.
17. Arr. *Anab.* 3.16.10. The timing of Alexander's dispatch of Menes to the coast with money is disputed: from Babylon in October or from Susa in December? This complicates the chronology of events in Greece, the Spartan uprising, the date of Antipater's defeat of Agis at Megalopolis, the date when that news reached Alexander, and how it might have affected his policy. Cf. n32.
18. Arr. *Anab.* 2.20.5, Curt. 4.3.11: 4,000 mercenaries arrive at Sidon/Tyre summer 332; Curt. 5.1.41, Diod. 17.65.1: 4,380 mercenaries and 4,100 Thracians reach Susa in 331; Curt. 7.10.11–12, cf. Arr. *Anab.* 4.7.2: 22,000 arrive in Bactria in spring 328, none identified as Macedonian; Curt. 9.3.21, Diod. 17.95.4: 12,000 reach India late in 326, same; Arr. *Anab.* 7.23.1: unspecified number arrive at Babylon in 323, some Macedonian. Arr. *Anab.* 4.18.3: Sopolis was sent to Macedonia in winter 328–327 for reinforcements, but there is no record of him returning. For discussion of Alexander's demands on the homeland and whether these were detrimental see chiefly Bosworth 1986 (yes) and Billows 1995: 183–212 (no). For numbers see also Engels 1978: 146–150 and Adams 1984: 80–81.
19. Curt. 3.1.19–21; Arr. *Anab.* 2.2.4. Hammond 1992: 37–38.
20. Arr. *Anab.* 2.2.4–5.
21. Arr. *Anab.* 2.20.2.
22. Arr. *Anab.* 3.2.3–7; Curt. 4.5.14–22.
23. Curt. 4.1.36.
24. Arr. *Anab.* 2.13.4–6, cf. 15.2; Diod. 17.48.1–2; Curt. 4.1.38–40; Dinarchus 1.34; Polyb. 18.14.6–8. On Darius' naval strategy see Ruzicka 1988.

25 Arr. *Anab.* 3.6.3; cp. Curt. 4.8.15: Amphoterus is sent to Crete. On the apparent discrepancy see Badian 1994b: 268–271. See also Bosworth 1975 and Ruzicka 1988: 148–151.
26 Aeschin. 3.165; Dinarchus 1.34; Diod. 17.62.7; Curt. 6.1.20. McQueen 1978.
27 Plut. *Mor.* 818e. Badian 1967: 182.
28 Aeschin. 3.165. The location and date of the battle, and whether Corrhagus was killed, are unknown.
29 Diod. 17.62.4–6.
30 Badian 1967: 179–184.
31 If *this* Memnon reaches Alexander in India in 326 with reinforcements from Thrace (Curt. 9.3.21), then "terms" must have included pardon and possibly reinstatement.
32 Spartan Revolt: Arr. *Anab.* 2.13.4–6, 3.6.3, 16.10; Diod. 17.48.1, 62.2–63.4; Curt. 6.1.1–21; Plut. *Agis* 3.2; Just. 12.1.4, 6–11; Paus. 1.13.4; Orosius 3.18.1–2. Badian 1967, 1994b; Bosworth 1988: 198–204; Blackwell 1999: 53–79. The date of the battle of Megalopolis has been much disputed. Curtius (6.1.21) claims it was over before Gaugamela (October 1, 331) but *if* Alexander sent money to Antipater about two months after Gaugamela, this suggests he did not yet know the revolt was over. Also, Aeschines' claim (n36) that about midsummer 330 fifty Spartan hostages were still awaiting escort to Alexander in the east suggests a later date. See Borza 1971; Lock 1972; Atkinson 1980: 482–485; Badian 1994b: 268–277.
33 Diod. 17.63.3: Agis' losses 5,300, Antipater's 3,500. Cp. Curt. 6.1.16: Agis' 5,300, Antipater's "not more than 1,000 Macedonians." Adams 1984: 83.
34 Plut. *Agesilaus* 15.4; cp. Curt. 6.1.18, 10.10.14; Diod. 16.64.1.
35 Blackwell 1999: 53.
36 Aeschin. 3.133; Diod. 17.73.5–6; Curt. 6.1.19–20; Plut. *Mor.* 235b.
37 Curt. 10.1.45 with Atkinson and Yardley 2009: 104–106.
38 Baynham 1994: 342; Blackwell 1999: 110–117.
39 Curt. 10.1.4, Yardley translation.
40 Diod. 17.106.2–3; for abuses and the purge cf. also Diod. 17.108.6; Arr. *Anab.* 7.4.1–3; Plut. *Alex.* 68; Curt. 10.1.1–9; Just 12.10.8.
41 Diod. 17.108.4–8; Curt. 10.2.1–3.
42 Arr. *Anab.* 3.6.4–7; Plut. *Alex.* 35.15, 41.8; Paus. 1.37.4. On the 'purge' and Harpalus' flight see Badian 1961; Worthington 1994b; Blackwell 1999. Alexander's former leniency: e.g. Arr. *Anab.* 7.8.3.
43 Ath. 13.586b–c, 594e–595c.
44 Plut. *Mor.* 846a–c. Chelsea Gardner, who has been excavating Taenarum/Tainaron, has suggested (personal correspondence) that, because of its difficulty of access, the location had long been a refuge for run-away helots and other asylum seekers.
45 Diod. 17.111.1.
46 Diod. 18.8.4. Exclusions: Diod. 17.109.1; Curt. 10.2.4; Just. 13.5.2.
47 Diod. 18.8.2–7. On the Exiles Decree see Dmitriev 2004 and Worthington 2015, both citing earlier scholarship. Worthington 2015: 95 summarizes views on Alexander's intent.
48 See e.g. Heisserer 1980 Chapters 7–8, especially 186–193.
49 Blackwell 1999: 158. Autonomy: [Dem.] 17.8.
50 On the chronology see Worthington 1986, and see 1992: 41–58 for a summary of events at Athens.
51 Dinarchus 2.4.
52 Tod *GHI* 196; Plut. *Dem.* 25; Ath. 13.586d. Worthington 1994b: 318–319.
53 Plut. *Alex.* 22.1; Polyaen. 6.49. On Philoxenus' "overarching authority" see Heckel 2006a: 220.

54 Hyperides 5.8; Diod. 17.108.7; Paus. 2.33.4; Plut. *Mor.* 531a, 846b. Worthington 1994b: 320; Blackwell 1999: 11–31, 136–144.
55 Worthington 1994b: 321 with sources.
56 Diod. 17.108.8, 18.19.2; Curt. 10.2.3; Arr. *Succ.* 1.16; Dinarchus 1.81–82; cp. Paus. 2.33.4.
57 Diod. 18.4.1, 12.1. Anson 2012: 50–51 citing previous views; Ashton 2015: 108–112; Heckel 2016: 142.
58 Antipater's recall: Arr. *Anab.* 7.12.4; Just. 12.12.9. Cassander: Plut. *Alex.* 74. Macedonian embassy: Diod. 17.113.2; Plut. *Alex.* 74.4–5.
59 Plut. *Alex.* 39.11, 68.4–5; Diod. 17.118.1; Just. 12.14.3. On the conflict, the authenticity of these and other "letters," and their dubious value as historical evidence see Carney 2006: 53–59.
60 Plut. *Alex.* 74. Cp. Plut. *Mor.* 180f; Diod. 17.118.2; Curt. 10.10.19.
61 Arr. *Anab.* 7.19.1–2, cp. 23.2; Diod. 17.113.1–4; Just. 12.13.1–2.
62 Badian 1981, 1996 and Cawkwell 1994 are seminal; and see the recent thorough discussion of Anson 2013: 83–120 (especially 114–120), citing the principal arguments. On the question of Philip's divinity, a possible precedent, see Fredricksmeyer 1979; Worthington 2008: 200–201, 228–233; Anson 2013: 86–92.
63 Curt. 8.5.9–16, 10.5.11.
64 *Suda* s.v. "Antipatros."
65 Depuydt 1997.
66 Curt. 10.9.1–2. Cf. Just. 13.1.7: some welcomed his death. Yardley *et al.* 2011: 53–54 assume "Macedonians" here are those in Babylon, but Justin could be referring to those in Macedonia. On the "threat of chaos" see Waterfield 2011: 10–15.
67 Curt. 10.5.4–6 (quotes); Arr. *Anab.* 7.26.3; Diod. 17.117.3–4, 18.1.4; Just. 12.15.5–13; Nep. *Eum.* 2.1. Hammond 1983: 10 rejects the ring. Yardley *et al.* 2011: 69–70 accept the ring but reject the verbal responses, arguing that Alexander had lost the power of speech. See Rathmann 2005: 18–22.
68 Plut. *Eum.* 1.2; App. *Syr.* 52, 57; but cp. Arr. *Anab.* 7.14.10; Arr. *Succ.* 1.3. On the *chiliarchy* see Collins 2001 especially 262–268: an adopted Persian office (cf. Diod. 18.48.5) and distinct from the cavalry *chiliarchoi* (cf. Plut. *Phoc.* 31.1); Meeus 2009 especially 302–310 (also 289 n9): no evidence and no need for a *Macedonian* court *chiliarchos*. Arrian indicates that Hephaestion's *chiliarchy* (to which Perdiccas and then Seleucus succeeded) was that of supreme commander of the Companion Cavalry, though the position was not what it had been when Philotas had the job, Heckel 2016: 294–297. Cp. Romm 2011: 14: no "clear second."
69 For the 'meeting': Curt. 10.6.1–7.15; Just. 13.2.4–3.1; cf. Diod. 18.2.1–2. Hammond in *HM* III 1988: 101 n1 rejects the accounts of the meeting(s) as fictitious; Bosworth 2002: 35–45 also criticizes. *Contra* Atkinson and Yardley 2009: 177; and see Anson 2014: 14–18. Arr. *Succ.* 1.2 gives a list of the most eminent of Alexander's officers in Babylon when Alexander died: Perdiccas, Leonnatus, Ptolemy, then Lysimachus, Aristonus, Peithon, Seleucus, and Eumenes, all commanders of cavalry, and Meleager, commander of infantry. For discussion see also Errington 1970; McKechnie 1999; Meeus 2008; Amitay 2010: 88–89.
70 Curt. 10.6.10–11. Nearchus is not in Arrian's (*Succ.* 1.2) list, but there is no denying his high rank and closeness to Alexander in the final year of his life.
71 Diod. 20.20.1; Just. 13.2.7.
72 This lends Curtius' account an air of authenticity, since Aristonus has been almost a silent figure in the extant histories; note his position in Arrian's list, cf. n69.
73 Curt. 10.7.2. On Arrhidaeus' mental deficiency see Greenwalt 1984 and Carney 2001.

74 For Meleager and Peithon see Heckel 2006a: 159–161, 195–196.
75 Curt. 10.7.8–9: oath to the child-king; cp. Just.13.2.14: oath of allegiance to four guardians, including Craterus and Antipater. Atkinson and Yardley 2009: 191 and Yardley *et al.* 2011: 73: Curtius is to be preferred. Cf. *Suda* s.v. "Leonnatos."
76 Arr. *Succ.* 1.1: Roxane's child was the "proper heir"; *Heid. Epit.* 1.1: Arrhidaeus would be king until Roxane's child came of age. But see Heckel 1980b and Anson 2015b: 73–74.
77 On the scholarly debate over the alleged constitution see the summary of King 2010: 374–375. In the "no" camp see e.g. Lock 1977 and Anson 1985c, 2013: 19–42. In the "yes" camp see e.g. Hammond 1980a and Hatzopoulos 1996: 125–165.
78 Anson 2013: 25–26.
79 Cp. Bosworth 2002: 32; Anson 2012: 51–52.
80 Perdiccas' supporters: Curt. 10.7.16. For the civil confrontation cf. Curt. 10.7.16–9.21; Just. 13.3.2–5.8; Diod.18.2.3–4, 4.7; Arr. *Succ.* 1.2–4. Curtius (10.10.9) says the strife lasted six days, accepted by Anson 2014: 22. Cp. Ael.VH 12.64: thirty days. See Bosworth 2002: 55 and Atkinson and Yardley 2009: 231.
81 Errington 1970: 56. Curtius (10.8.22) says Meleager was to be admitted as a third regent, similarly Just. 13.4.5; but Arr. *Succ.* 1.3 indicates he was in a subordinate position to Perdiccas.
82 Cp. Liv. 40.6.1–6.
83 Diod. 18.4.7; cp. Curt. 10.9.18: 300. See Atkinson and Yardley 2009: 216.
84 Arr. *Succ.* 1.1, 3, 8; Just. 13.4.2–5. On the *prostasia* see Anson 1992, 2009a: 280–285, 2014: 21; Meeus 2009: 292–302; and *contra* Carney 2006: 70.
85 Curt. 10.10.1–5; Diod. 18.3.1–3; Just. 13.4.9–23; Arr. *Succ.* 1.5–7; Dexippus F 8.2–7 [*FGrH/BNJ* 100; F 8 = Photius 82.64, probably also based on Arrian *Events*]; *Heid. Epit.* 1.2–3; App. *Syr.* 52–53; Orosius 3.23.6–13.
86 Cf. Diod. 18.3.1; Just. 13.5.8; Arr. *Succ.* 1.7. The sources are not clear about various "offices," their titles, and their respective powers. For bibliography on offices and settlement see Yardley *et al.* 2011: 57, and for commentary 58–119. See also Atkinson and Yardley 2009: 172–230. See again (n69) Errington 1970; McKechnie 1999; Bosworth 2002: 29–63; Rathmann 2005; Meeus 2008; Anson 2014: 18–28; all citing additional bibliography.
87 Arr. *Succ.* 1.7. Cf. n84.
88 See Errington 1970: 55, 1990: 117–118. Cf. Diod. 18.23.2; App. *Syr.* 52. Cf. *Suda* s.v. "Krateros."
89 Arr. *Succ.* 1.3; cp. Diod. 18.2.4: *epimeletes* (see Anson 1992: 40–41); Dexippus 8.4; Just. 13.4.5. Bosworth 1993; Anson 2009a.
90 Diod. 18.4.4. To check Athens Alexander was preparing a fleet of 1,000 ships: Curt. 10.2.2; Just. 13.5.7.
91 Alexander and Antipater: cf. Diod. 17.118.1, but cp. Plut. *Alex.* 39.11–13. Bosworth 1971b; Baynham 1994: 343; Carney 2006: 63–64. For Olympias' charges see Chapter 9 n33, n34.
92 Diod. 18.8.6–7; Plut. *Alex.* 49.15; Just. 13.5.1–6. Athens: Poddighe 2009: 119–120. Aetolia: n93.
93 Plut. *Alex.* 49.14–15. Badian 1961: 37; Mendels 1984: 131–133; Baynham 1994: 345–346.
94 Diog. Laert. 5.11–12. On Aristotle's relationship with Alexander see Arr. *Anab.* 7.27.1–2; Plut. *Alex.* 77.3–4; Dio Cassius 77.7; Dio Chrysostom *Orations* 64.20.
95 Diod. 18.9.1–5. For Harpalus' 'contribution' to the Lamian War see Ashton 1983.
96 Diod. 17.111.1–3; 18.9.4; Paus. 8.52.5.

97 Diod. 18.11.1–2. Rhodes, acting independently, overthrew its Macedonian garrison at this time: Diod. 18.8.1.
 98 Diod. 18.8–18; Just. 13.5.14; Arr. *Succ.* 1.9; Hyperides, *Epitaphios* 1, 10–13; Plut. *Phoc.* 23–28, *Dem.* 27–28, *Pyrrh.* 1.5; [Plut.] *X orat. Dem.* 38–48; Paus. 1.1.3, 25.3–5, 29.13; Polyaen. 4.4.2; Polyb. 9.29.2–4; Str. 9.5.10; cf. Orosius 3.23.15–16; *Marm. Par.* F B9 (see Chapter 2 n120). On the name of the war see Ashton 1984.
 99 Diod. 18.11.5.
100 Diodorus (18.12.1) suggests Antipater appealed at the outset to both Craterus and "Philotas," a mistake for Leonnatus, in which case the later appeal to Leonnatus is a second appeal, so Anson 2015b: 83. Leosthenes' forces: Just. 13.5.8. For Craterus in Cilicia cf. n57.
101 Diod. 18.10.2, 12.1–2; cp. Just. 13.5.8.
102 Hyperides, *Epitaphios* 12; Diod. 18.12.3–4; Just. 13.5.8 ("Heraclea" is a mistake).
103 Plut. *Eum.* 3.6, 9. Diod. 18.14.4, cp. 12.1; Just. 13.5.14. Anson 2015b: 82–84.
104 Plut. *Eum.* 3.10–12; Nep. *Eum.* 2.4–5. Both Antipater and Antipater's messenger to Leonnatus, Hecataeus the tyrant of Cardia, were Eumenes' enemies and he possibly feared for his life.
105 Cf. n120.
106 Diod. 18.12.4–15.7; Plut. *Eum.* 3.6, *Phoc.* 25.5; Just. 13.5.12–14; Arr. *Succ.* 1.9; Str. 9.5.19.
107 Cf. n101.
108 Cf. Just. 12.12.8. Heckel 2006a: 87; n90.
109 Diod. 18.15.8–9, cp. 18.10.2, 12.2. On the naval activity cf. also: *IG* II² 398, 493, 505; Plut. *Phoc.* 25.1–4, *Demetr.* 11.4–5, *Mor.* 338a; *Marm. Par.* 9: 323–322. See (with bibliography) Morrison 1987; Bosworth 2003; Anson 2014: 34–36.
110 E.g. Ashton 1977: 9.
111 Bosworth 2003 and Wrightson 2014 defend "Echinades" at Diod. 18.15.9, though most historians, given no other evidence for a theatre of war in the west, are reluctant to allow a battle in the Ionian Sea, e.g. Anson 2014: 44 n54.
112 Ashton 1977: 9–11 dates the battle of Amorgos to late June, i.e. before the end of the Athenian archon year 323–322. See also Hale 2009: 311–318 and Anson 2014: 34–41.
113 Diod. 18.16.4–5.
114 Plut. *Camillus* 19.6, *Dem.* 28.1. Bosworth 1993: 426: August 7; cp. 2002: 10: late July 322; Wheatley 2007: 192: August 322. Cf. Plut. *Phoc.* 26.
115 Diod. 18.17.6–18.3; Plut. *Phoc.* 26. Tritle 1988: 129–131.
116 Plut. *Dem.* 28.1, *Phoc.* 28.2; cf. *Phoc.* 26. Habicht 1997: 36–42.
117 Diod. 18.18.4–5; Plut. *Phoc.* 27–28. Baynham 2003.
118 Diod. 18.13.6; Arr. *Succ.* 1.13; Plut. *Phoc.* 26.2, 27.5, 29.1, *Dem.* 27–29; Paus. 1.8.2–3.
119 On the mosaics see Petsas 1978: 52–55 and Palagia 2000: 183–186.
120 Diod. 18.16.1–3, 22.1–8. Balacrus' death is undated: see Heckel 2006a: 69.
121 Diod. 18.23.1–3; Just. 13.6.4–7; Arr. *Succ.* 1.21. On Cleopatra's several marriage negotiations with Alexander's Successors see Carney 2000: 123–128.
122 Plut. *Eum.* 3.2. Antigonus' power: Anson 1988. Perdiccas' designs: Heckel 2016: 170–177.
123 Diod. 18.23.3–4 (note the anti-Perdiccas sentiment of Diodorus/his source); Arr. *Succ.* 1.20. Billows 1990: 58–59; Anson 2015b: 92–93.
124 Polyaen. 8.60.
125 Arr. *Succ.* 1.22–23; cf. Diod. 19.52.5. Carney 2000: 130.
126 Diod. 18.23.4.
127 The chronology of the early period of the Successors is notoriously problematic, thus for many events dates are speculative rather than firm. One tradition follows a

'high' chronology at this point, placing the Aetolian campaign in the winter of 322–321, immediately following the Macedonian settlement with Athens after the Lamian War; Diodorus (18.25) describes a winter setting for Antigonus' arrival (cp. Arr. *Succ.* 1.24) among other events of 322–321. The 'low' chronology, which has Antigonus reach Antipater and Craterus the following winter, allows time for Antipater and Craterus to return to Macedonia probably in November 322, for the war-weary Macedonians to recuperate, for Craterus to marry Antipater's daughter, for Antipater to resettle the disenfranchised Athenians and negotiate with Phocion over exemptions (Plut. *Phoc.* 28–29), and for new recruits to be trained and outfitted for a spring or fall campaign. For a good introduction to the chronology problem see Wheatley 2007. See also Boiy 2007, arguing for a low-high-low chronology, taking into account cuneiform evidence; and see Meeus 2013 for a cautionary approach to gaps in the evidence. Chronology herein is largely in agreement with Anson 2014: ix–xv.

128 Diod. 18.24.1–25.5, cf. 14.2; Arr. *Succ.* 1.24, 26; Just. 13.6.7–9; Paus. 1.6.8. Carney 2013: 19–20.
129 Diod. 18.25.6–26.1, 28.2–29.1; Arr. *Succ.* 1.25; Paus. 1.6.3, 7.1; Str. 17.1.8.
130 Diod. 18.25.6, 29.1–3; Arr. *Succ.* 1.26; Plut. *Eum.* 5.1–3; Nep. *Eum.* 3.2–3; Just. 13.6.15–16.
131 On Alcetas' motives and his Macedonian forces see Roisman 2012a: 122–123 with references in n11, n12.
132 Diod. 18.29.4–6; Plut. *Eum.* 5.4–6; Nep. *Eum.* 5.1; Just. 13.8.3–5.
133 On these forces see Billows 1995: 191; Bosworth 2002: 84; Heckel 2006a: 290 n62; Roisman 2012a: 120–121. On Eumenes sending a man who spoke their "dialect" to address them (Diod. 18.29.4; *PSI* XII 1284) see Bosworth 1978 and Anson 2015b: 229.
134 Diod. 18.29.6; Plut. *Eum.* 6.1–4.
135 Cf. Nep. *Eum.* 3.4–6.
136 Diod. 18.30–32, 53.3; Arr. *Succ.* 1.27; Plut. *Eum.* 7; Nep. *Eum.* 4; Just. 13.8.6–9. Schäfer 2002: 86–91; Anson 2014: 66–68, 2015b: 119–121.
137 Diod. 18.38.
138 Arr. *Succ.* 1.40.
139 Arr. *Succ.* 24.6 (*Vatican Palimpsest*); cf. *IG* XII 2.645. Bayliss 2006: 115–116.
140 Paus. 1.6.3. On Cleomenes' office see Burstein 2008; Anson 2014: 43 n38.
141 Rathmann 2005: 32, 65.
142 Diod. 18.26–28, 33–36; Arr. *Succ.* 1.28–30; Plut. *Eum.* 8.3; Just. 13.6.18–20, 8.1–2, 10; Paus. 1.6.3; Polyaen. 4.19; *Heid. Epit.* 1.3; *Suda* s.v. "Perdikkas." Roisman 2014.
143 Str. 17.1.8. Amitay 2010: 90–92; Romm 2011: 149–152; Ferrario 2014: 5–11; Meeus 2014: 273–278; Anson 2015b: 104–106; Worthington 2016: 129–133.
144 Cf. e.g. Diod. 18.60.3–61.3. Amitay 2010: 92–100; Waterfield 2011: 48–51; Anson 2014: 95–96.
145 Diod. 18.37.2; Arr. *Succ.* 1.30; Plut. *Eum.* 8.3; Nep. *Eum.* 5.1; Just. 13.8.10, 14.1.1; App. *Syr.* 53.
146 Asclepiodorus: see Heckel 2006a: 58 (#4).
147 Diod. 18.37, 39; Arr. *Succ.* 1.31–38; Plut. *Eum.* 8.4; Polyaen. 4.6.4.
148 Cf. n147. On the Triparadeisos Settlement see especially Errington 1970; Anson 1986; Landucci Gattinoni 2008: 174–180.
149 Arr. *Succ.* 1.35, 38; Nep. *Eum.* 5.1.
150 Arr. *Succ.* 1.38. Cf. Diod. 19.52.4; *IG* II² 561 with Burstein 1977 and Heckel 1980b.
151 Plut. *Eum.* 8.6–7; Arr. *Succ.* 1.40; Just. 14.1.7.

152 *Heid. Epit.* 2.2: both kings and Roxane crossed to Macedonia; also Adea Eurydice.
153 Diod. 18.48.3–4; Arr. *Succ.* 1.14; Plut. *Phoc.* 30.8–9, *Dem.* 31.4–6. Cassander may have had a stronger hand in this than Antipater, for Antipater was already seriously ill.
154 Diod. 18.48.4.
155 Baynham 1994: 355. On the choice see also Hammond in *HM* III 1988: 130; Errington 1990: 123; Waterfield 2011: 73.

9 Between dynasties, 319–279

Wars of the Successors

Antipater's son Cassander, in fierce rivalry with the successor to the regency, Polyperchon, precipitated another Successors' war, as factions polarized around these two men whose authority resided in two ambitious royal women: Philip II's granddaughter Adea Eurydice, ruling on behalf of her husband, Philip III (323–317), and Olympias as guardian for her grandson Alexander IV (323–c.310). The elimination of both kings as well as the two royal women left Polyperchon powerless and Cassander in firm control of Macedonia, though this also emboldened the more powerful Successors, who fought each other in continuous wars throughout this forty-year period, to adopt the title "king" in their respective regions and establish their own dynasties. Upon Cassander's death the remaining Successors attempted to annex Macedonia to their own kingdoms, but after brief reigns of Demetrius I, Pyrrhus of Epirus, Lysimachus, and Ptolemy Ceraunus Macedonia was reduced to a state of anarchy, weak and open to attack.

The throne in peril: warring regents and royal women

After Antipater's death and the appointment of Polyperchon to the regency the position of *chiliarchos*, or second-in-command, was intolerable for Cassander, and he attempted to stir a revolt against the regent within Macedonia by appealing to his own circle of nobles. He also sent envoys to Ptolemy, who had recently married his sister Eurydice, asking him to send a fleet to the Hellespont, and to other satraps and generals, and to the oligarchs and garrison commanders whom his father had installed in various cities, all in the effort to raise a coalition against Polyperchon. To distract attention from his movement he organized a large hunt with his friends. Perhaps the hunt has no other particular significance, but it is said that Cassander had not by the age of thirty-five earned the right to recline at banquet, because he had not yet killed a boar without a net.[1] What he did achieve immediately upon his father's death, and this he pulled off before the Athenians heard the news, was to send out Nicanor to replace Menyllus as garrison commander at Munychia. By cleverly securing a stronghold outside Macedonia, in the form of a garrison answerable to himself and a secure harbour for a fleet, Cassander established a position from which he could challenge for the regency—or, more ambitiously, for the throne.[2]

Cassander left Macedonia in the winter of 319–318, and crossing over to Asia Minor he petitioned Antigonus for help in wresting the regency away from Polyperchon. Antigonus agreed to assist this son of an old friend, though his motivation was self-interest. Since the time of Antipater's departure from Asia the previous year, Antigonus had taken measures to consolidate his power in Asia. He had succeeded in defeating Eumenes, who was now besieged in a fortress at Nora with a mere 600 supporters, and the Perdiccans Alcetas and Attalus, and he had assumed control of the armies of all three. Antigonus' forces now totaled 60,000 foot, 10,000 horse, and 30 elephants. News of Antipater's death encouraged him to act more openly in his own interests.[3]

In anticipation of Cassander's coalition, Polyperchon, after consulting with his commanders and the most prominent nobles, in the name of Philip III issued an edict meant to undermine support for Cassander by announcing: the 'freedom' of Greek cities from garrisons and oligarchies that had been installed by Antipater; the reinstatement of the exiles (with noted exceptions) who had been banished by Antipater after Alexander III crossed to Asia; the return of Samos to the Athenians; and the instruction to the cities to obey Polyperchon in his implementation of the edict.[4] Polyperchon feared that Antipater's supporters would favour Cassander, so to diffuse that support, and to obligate political parties to himself, he wrote to Argos and other cities ordering them to exile their pro-Antipatrid political leaders. He also wrote to Olympias asking her to return to Macedonia and to assume guardianship of Alexander IV until the child should reach the age of majority.[5] Olympias did not answer the recall right away but first wrote to Eumenes (by this time relieved from Antigonus' siege) pleading with him to remain loyal to the Argead line and to support her guardianship of the kings, and asking his advice whether he thought she should trust Polyperchon. Eumenes' advice was that she should remain in Epirus until the present war, involving himself, Polyperchon, Antigonus, and Cassander (the Second Diadoch War), was over.[6] And it seems she did remain in Epirus for another two years.[7]

Polyperchon also wrote, in the name of the kings, to Eumenes asking him to challenge Antigonus in Asia. "The kings," he said, had written already to the generals and treasurers in Cilicia, instructing them to give Eumenes 500 talents and more, if necessary, and they would write also to the commanders of the Silver Shields (Argyraspids, Alexander's veteran Hypaspists), instructing them (Antigenes and Teutamus) to cooperate with him fully. He added that he would come himself with the royal army, if need be.[8] The letters from Olympias and Polyperchon encouraged Eumenes to renege on the terms of surrender he had accepted from Antigonus and he quickly headed for Cilicia to avail himself of the royal coffers and the Silver Shields.[9] Ptolemy also headed for Cilicia with the requested fleet, but he was unable to prevent Eumenes from taking up his royal commission.[10]

At Athens, the royal decree was quickly acted upon, the Assembly voting to restore the democracy, which Antipater abolished in 322. The Macedonian garrison commander, Nicanor, Cassander's man, made no move to decamp from

Munychia in the Piraeus; instead he fortified his position and seized control of the harbour. Then receiving a letter from Olympias ordering him to reopen Munychia and the harbor to the Athenians, Nicanor pretended to agree, since he had caught wind of Polyperchon's plan to restore Olympias to Macedonia, but he stalled in carrying out the order, anxiously awaiting Cassander to show up with a fleet.[11] The Athenians appealed to Polyperchon to enforce the autonomy clause of the edict, so to put pressure on Nicanor he sent an army into Attica under command of his son Alexander. But the Piraeus had to stay in Macedonian hands, so Alexander undertook negotiations with Nicanor. The Athenians in anger accused a few of the oligarchs, men who had been on good terms with Antipater, of conspiring with the Macedonians and allowing Nicanor to escape arrest for violation of the Macedonian edict. Prominent among them was Phocion, now in his eighties. Facing a sentence of exile, Phocion and a few others fled for asylum to Alexander, and he sent them on to his father, who with the kings and the royal army was camped in Phocis.[12] But Polyperchon, in a base effort to earn Athenian support, arrested the asylum seekers and sent them back to Athens. Phocion and company had first been given an audience with King Philip III, and this farcical scene of court theatrics gives a rare glimpse into the incapacity of the Argead heir. An Athenian delegation arrived to denounce the asylum seekers, and as the two parties of Athenians hurled accusations back and forth, while Phocion turned his back to Polyperchon in disgust, King Philip sent the first speaker off to immediate execution, then burst into laughter at the bickering Athenians, and when Polyperchon raised his voice in annoyance at one of the accused the king jumped up, grabbed a spear, and would have run the old man through had Polyperchon not thrown his arms around Philip and prevented it. Back in Athens Phocion and his pro-Macedonian party were tried and condemned to death by their political opponents. A short while later Cassander with a fleet of thirty-five ships and 4,000 soldiers supplied by Antigonus sailed into the Piraeus and joined Nicanor. Cassander assumed control of the harbour, and Nicanor continued to hold the fortified Munychia.[13]

Polyperchon now marched from Phocis down into Attica with a royal army that included 20,000 Macedonian infantry and sixty-five elephants. Leaving some of his forces with Alexander near Piraeus to help check Cassander, he took the greater number into the Peloponnese to enforce his edict there. By ordering the executions of oligarchs who had supported Antipater and now favoured Cassander, and by restoring democrats to power, he won a number of city-states into alliance against Cassander. When the people of Megalopolis, who had remained loyal to Antipater during his war with the Spartan king Agis, refused to abide by Polyperchon's edict he proceeded to besiege their city, using every siege tactic he had learned in the east with Alexander and, most imposingly, his sixty-five elephants. But another veteran of the school of Alexander was in charge of defending Megalopolis, one Damis, and Damis knew the elephants' weaknesses. By night he sent men outside the city to plant spiked planks concealed just below the surface of the ground, and when Polyperchon by day brought the elephants full force up to a breach he had made in the walls the weight of the animals pressing the ground caused them to snag and impale their tender feet on the spikes, resulting in shrieks of pain and the trampling of everyone and everything around them as they writhed in agony. The assault failed miserably, the troops were demoralized, and with both Cassander and Antigonus at his back Polyperchon could not afford a protracted siege. Disengaging most of his army and leaving only a small force to maintain a blockade, the regent turned to other matters.[14]

The successful defence of Megalopolis against Polyperchon's siege did serious damage to his military reputation both in southern Greece and in Macedonia, as a direct parallel between his own failure against Damis and Antipater's success against Agis was unavoidable.[15] Turning his attention to defending the kingdom, Polyperchon sent Cleitus the White with the entire royal fleet to the Hellespont, assigning him the task of preventing Antigonus from crossing to Europe. Cleitus had fled to Macedonia from his satrapy of Lydia the previous year when Antigonus began ousting Antipater-appointed satraps and replacing them with his own friends.[16] Now Cleitus stood guard at the Hellespont, having won over the cities of the Propontis in alliance with Arrhidaeus, satrap of Hellespontine Phrygia, who was defying Antigonus' attempt to wrest his satrapy away from him. In a countermove Cassander sent Nicanor to the Hellespont with his borrowed fleet of thirty-five ships, and these reunited with Antigonus' larger fleet to a total of 130 ships, all under Nicanor's command. When the two fleets finally engaged off Byzantium Cleitus was victorious, sinking seventeen and capturing not fewer than forty ships. The celebration was short-lived, however, for Antigonus arrived with land forces, quickly marshaled Nicanor's limping fleet, and with fresh infantry put on board, in a surprise pre-dawn attack by land and sea Cleitus was caught unprepared, most of his sailors and soldiers having disembarked for the night. In the early morning light amidst alarm and confusion a naval battle of sorts was fought between the few ships Cleitus could get battle-ready and the sixty remaining vessels under Nicanor. This time Nicanor was the victor. Of Polyperchon's fleet Cleitus' ship alone escaped. Soon after Cleitus put ashore on the Thracian coast, but as he was trying to make his way to Macedonia he was captured by some of Lysimachus' troops and killed.[17]

Polyperchon was losing the war, and many of the Greek city-states opted for their chances with Cassander. Even at Athens despite the autonomy edict the vote was passed to treat with Cassander. Not that there was much of an option, given that he now had them by the gullet, controlling both the Piraeus and the grain route from the Black Sea. Athens surrendered to his blockade in the spring of 317. He allowed the Athenians to hold onto their city and Attica, and their fleet and revenues, but the garrison remained in place on Munychia and oligarchic rule was reinstated, with the pro-Macedonian Demetrius of Phaleron, chosen by Cassander, set up as *epimeletes*, a kind of governor of Athens—and a good-governing one, by most accounts.[18] Cassander, however, quickly revealed his own tyrannical side when shortly after the victorious Nicanor returned to Piraeus from the Hellespont with great pomp and ceremony he had him killed after a conviction in a closed trial.[19]

Polyperchon's whereabouts during this time, late 318 through the spring of 317, is mostly a mystery. Epigraphic evidence indicates that at some point he crossed to Asia, possibly making some joint effort with Eumenes.[20] Adea Eurydice with her husband King Philip had slipped out from under his control, and when she heard Olympias was preparing for a return to Macedonia she contacted Cassander and urgently asked him to come to her aid. It is not clear whether these two already had come to some sort of alliance, but at some point between the early winter of 319–318 and the late summer of 317 Cassander made a return to Macedonia, though the only detail we know is that he captured most of Polyperchon's elephants.[21] Adea Eurydice, though barely out of her teens, because of her marriage and the incapacity of her husband, was able to wield great power and influence, and she had somehow assumed the "management of the kingship."[22] This may have been the result of her own forcefulness or it may have come about with Cassander's backing. About early fall of 317, having seized the regency, in the name of the king, her husband, she sent an order to Polyperchon to surrender his army to Cassander, claiming that King Philip was transferring "administration of the kingdom" to Cassander's care. She also wrote to Antigonus in Asia informing him that Philip was transferring administration to Cassander.[23] Since Cassander was attending to affairs in the south, however, it was she herself who was in control in Macedonia. Well before this Macedonian royal women had held a prominent public presence in the religious sphere: Eurydice, mother of Philip II, is known for her dedications at the sanctuary of Eucleia at Aegae, and she may even have been the priestess; Olympias made dedications at Athens and Olympia; and Roxane made dedications to Athena on the Acropolis at Athens. Demeter and Kore (Figure 9.1) were especially honoured in Macedonia and are clearly tied to the Macedonian belief in an afterlife, as is evident from their presence in Macedonian tomb contexts.[24] If the Macedonians wanted the Argead monarchy to be perpetuated, then they had seriously to consider embracing what Alexander and Antipater allegedly voiced as a preposterous idea: allowing a woman to rule until such time as an Argead male came of age. There was, of course, the possibility that Adea Eurydice would conceive.

The dual monarchy had split, though when or why the two kings were separated is unknown. In the early fall of 317 Adea Eurydice and Philip III were in Macedonia, Cassander was in the Peloponnese besieging Tegea, and Olympias was in Epirus with Alexander IV and Roxane. Polyperchon had been cut out of the regency and possibly Alexander IV out of the kingship,[25] so the best move Polyperchon could make was to back the child's legitimacy as heir by installing the boy's grandmother, mother of Alexander III, as guardian. Gathering military support from Aeacides, the king of Epirus (son of Arybbas and Olympias' nephew),[26] he led a forceful return to Macedonia to reinstate Alexander IV with Olympias. Adea Eurydice, assuming the kingly duty of military commander, for which she had both the training and the nerve,[27] and for which Philip III had not the capacity,[28] marched out at the head of an army to bar their advance, and a confrontation took place on the western frontier at Euia in Dassaretis, a direct route into Upper Macedonia from Epirus. Faced with the

Figure 9.1 Bust of a Kore or Goddess, Amphipolis, Hellenistic cemetery
Source: author, 2011.

presence of the intimidating Olympias, the son and heir of the divine Alexander, and the veteran of Alexander's eastern conquests, Adea Eurydice's Macedonian troops deserted her and went over to Polyperchon without a battle. Philip Arrhidaeus was captured immediately, and Adea Eurydice, having fled with her advisor Polycles, was captured a short time later as she was trying to reach Amphipolis. Olympias marched triumphant into Macedonia, having "seized the kingdom without a fight," and both Philip Arrhidaeus and Adea Eurydice were imprisoned.[29] When word got out that Olympias was treating her prisoners "unlawfully" (she walled them up in a small chamber with one tiny opening through which they were given only the bare necessities) the Macedonians made a public outcry against her actions, so Olympias decided to kill them outright. She sent some Thracians to stab the king, and to his wife she sent a sword, a noose, and hemlock, with instructions to make a choice and end her own life. Defiant to the end, it is said that Adea Eurydice, after taking care of the preparation of her husband's body for burial, chose none of Olympias' three 'gifts', but, taking off her own sash and uttering as her final words a curse that Olympias meet with a similar fate, she hanged herself.[30] Macedonia now had one king, a child aged six years who was, by tradition of father-to-son succession, the rightful heir to Alexander's kingdom. But *Alexander's* kingdom, as Alexander himself had determined, was centred in the east, while for nearly two decades Macedonia had been almost entirely managed by Antipater and his family and supporters. Cassander thus envisioned himself as heir to the kingdom of Macedonia.

Cassander and the end of the Argead dynasty

The Macedonian army had welcomed Olympias' return as wife, mother, and grandmother of Argead kings, and she might have used that veneration for the Argead clan to strengthen her guardianship.[31] Instead, she undermined her popularity with the cruel treatment and elimination of Philip II's son and granddaughter. She further undermined her popularity when she carried out personal acts of vengeance against the family of her long-time political rival Antipater. She had Antipater's son Nicanor killed (the details are unknown and nothing else is known about him).[32] She had the tomb of the youngest son, Iolaus, destroyed and his remains strewn (the cause of his death is unrecorded), alleging that Antipater and his sons, especially Iolaus, who was Alexander III's wine-pourer in his final days, were guilty of poisoning Alexander—a charge, so far as we know, never brought to trial.[33] There is some evidence to suggest that Iolaus' involvement was celebrated at Athens within a year after Alexander's death, though on other evidence it may have been several years before the rumour of the Antipatrid poisoning plot surfaced.[34] If Olympias did not invent the rumour, then she certainly propagated it as part of her anti-Cassander propaganda. And she did not stop with killing his brothers; she went on to order the deaths of 100 of the most prominent Macedonians in Cassander's circle of friends.[35]

At news of the executions Cassander broke off his siege of Tegea and marched north. Olympias appointed as general Alexander III's former Bodyguard Aristonus, and ordering him to challenge Cassander, she fled to Pydna with a large entourage. This included some Ambracian cavalry, the soldiers assigned to the royal court, and Polyperchon's few remaining elephants. Most of the entourage were non-combatants "useless in war," among them Alexander IV, his mother Roxane, Thessalonice, daughter of Philip II by his Thessalian wife Nicesipolis, Deidameia, daughter of Aeacides (she was already betrothed to Alexander IV), and a large number of other friends and their relatives—a group most vulnerable to reprisal from Cassander.[36] Pella by this date still had access to the sea but only via the long canal-like Loudias River, whereas Pydna was a port directly on the Thermaic Gulf and the city itself well fortified. Olympias hoped—in vain—for support from the sea.

Before Olympias' forces could get into position to block the coastal route, Cassander's general Deinias managed to occupy the defiles of Lower Olympus. Cassander sent another general, Callas, to challenge Polyperchon, who was preparing to block Cassander in Perrhaebia. Callas was able to bribe many of Polyperchon's men to desert, thus leaving the old veteran with a meagre ineffectual force and enabling Cassander to march through the passes of Perrhaebia and down to Pydna, where he quickly established a blockade around the city.

Cassander sent another general, Atarrhias, to occupy the passes from Epirus, which foiled Aeacides' attempt to bring military relief to Olympias, since many of his troops were marching against their will and rebelled. When these rebels returned home they incited a general revolution, the outcome of which was a decree exiling their king and a treaty of alliance with Cassander. Cassander sent Lyciscus to Epirus as regent and general. Though many of Aeacides' supporters were killed, his two-year-old son, Pyrrhus, was secreted away to safety with the Illyrian king, Glaucias, whose wife, Beroa, was Aeacid. News of events in Epirus so disheartened those Macedonians still favouring Olympias and Alexander IV that they gave up resistance to Cassander.[37]

With Aeacides deposed and Polyperchon having proved impotent both in winning allies and in providing military support for the Argead succession, Olympias was in a bad way. Eumenes, still acting in the name of the child-king, had not been able to extricate himself from his war with Antigonus, and by this time he had been forced to retreat east from the Mediterranean coast into the heart of Persia.[38] Just how long Olympias remained under siege we do not know, though it was presumably quite long as we are told she had gone to Pydna unprepared for "a very long siege."[39] Cassander put her under siege after hearing about the deaths of his friends, which was later than the slaying of the royal couple in the fall of 317 (the reign of Philip III is given as six years and four months), though how much later is hard to say. The siege may not have begun until the spring or summer of 316, and it lasted over one winter.[40] It was, at any rate, the same winter that Eumenes and Antigonus came to their final showdown in Media, in two battles fought at Paraetacene and Gabiene. When Antigonus' cavalry captured Eumenes' baggage train the Silver Shields, bargaining to get back their wives and children, betrayed Eumenes, handed him over to Antigonus, and accepted enrollment in Antigonus' army. Eumenes was executed, and the Silver Shields fared hardly much better; one of their commanders, Antigenes, was burned alive, and the ranks, now reputedly all over sixty years of age, were dispersed and assigned to dangerous missions from which they were not expected to return.[41] Such was the fate of the best infantry the Macedonians ever were to field. Over the course of the winter those besieged with Olympias were reduced to a virtual state of cannibalism. In the spring (probably of 315)[42] Olympias arranged for some of the starving soldiers to be released so as to reduce demand on the nearly exhausted food supply, and the report these men gave about conditions inside Pydna—as Cassander intended—brought home the realization that Olympias' cause was all but lost.

Apart from the ineffectual Polyperchon, Olympias had only two men of power still loyal to her cause, the governors of Pella and Amphipolis, Monimus and Aristonus respectively. Her only hope was to get to the protection of one or the other of these men, so she attempted to escape from Pydna by ship. The ship is said to have been arranged by Polyperchon, but Cassander intercepted the go-between, seized the ship, and when Olympias discovered her escape was foiled she gave herself up after negotiating terms for her own personal safety, as if such were possible, given Cassander's hatred. When Monimus heard about her capitulation he surrendered Pella without a fight. But Aristonus held out. He had just defeated Cassander's general Crateuas in the vicinity of Amphipolis, had not yet heard news of the death of Eumenes, and still hoped for help from Polyperchon and the latter's son Alexander. Olympias, however, sent him an order not to resist, so he surrendered under Cassander's guarantee of his safety. Alas, Cassander handed Aristonus over to the relatives of Crateuas, and they killed him.[43] All that kept Olympias alive now was the thin thread of her biological tie to the Argead kings Alexander III and IV, and that thread was about to snap.

Cassander now faced a dilemma: it was too dangerous for him to leave Olympias alive and too dangerous to eliminate her. So as if to keep his own hands clean he resorted to putting her fate in the hands of a judicial assembly heavily stacked with her enemies. Olympias had no recourse. The king controlled the judicial system, and at present Cassander was *de facto* king, having assumed the regency by royal command from Philip III/Adea Eurydice. It was he who stirred up the relatives of the 100 nobles, his own friends, whose executions Olympias had ordered, to bring charges against her. And, like Parmenio, she was not present to defend herself, since there was too great a risk that the mere sight of her would win over the majority of those assembled. The Macedonians present at the trial condemned her to death. Cassander, still seeking to absolve himself, offered her an escape, a secret deal for her "safe conduct" to Athens. Knowing full well that this was a death sentence of a different sort, she demanded a retrial before *all* the Macedonians, with herself present in her own defence. Cassander simply could not risk giving Olympias a voice before the greater body of Macedonians, so he sent 200 soldiers to kill her. When these men entered the royal apartments and laid eyes on her they could not do the deed, she was so awe-inspiring. It was the vengeful relatives of her victims who finally carried out the sentence.[44]

Alexander IV and Roxane were now defenceless, but again it was too dangerous to eliminate them while popular sentiment was in the boy's favour. Cassander quietly took away all Alexander's royal prerogatives, including his pages and bodyguards, and placed mother and son under guard in the citadel at Amphipolis. He then aligned himself with the Argead house by marrying Thessalonice, also now defenceless, against her will, and proceeded to exercise two royal prerogatives. He founded two cities, one in his own name, Cassandreia, a re-founding of Potidaea and Olynthus combined, and one in the name of his wife, Thessalonica, a port on the Thermaic Gulf intended to supersede the rapidly silting port of Argead Pella.[45] At Aegae, the ancient capital and burial place of all the Argead kings (except Alexander III), he buried in state Philip III Arrhidaeus and Adea Eurydice as well as Adea's mother, Cynnane. Cynnane had been dead for more than six years and the royal couple for probably the better part of two years, so this was no perfunctory chore. Traditionally, this was the public gesture of the ascending monarch: the burial of his predecessor with ceremony. Cassander was sending the clear message of his legitimacy as the successor to power, if not to the throne.[46] At the same time (taking a lesson from Alexander) he was presenting himself as the champion and avenger of the murdered king, whose murderess had met just punishment. All the while he was distracting attention from the fact that he simultaneously held hostage the all but last remaining male Argead.

Some forty years later at Aegae a band of mercenary Gauls dug up and ransacked the royal cemetery. A few tombs somehow escaped desecration, and two of these along with a third partially destroyed tomb were uncovered some forty years ago, in 1977–1978, at Palatitsa-Vergina (ancient Aegae). The two double-chambered, barrel-vaulted, unplundered tombs, discovered by Manolis Andronikos, have yielded a wealth of remarkable and some exceptionally beautiful objects: gold *larnakes* (funerary boxes still containing bones and ashes of the deceased); gold wreaths; ceremonial armour; bronze and iron weapons; silver vessels of many kinds for daily and ceremonial use; and ivory carvings from long-disintegrated furniture (Figure 4.2, page 81). The interpretation of these discoveries has been a topic of fierce scholarly debate. The general consensus (though not unanimous) is that the tombs are royal, and that Tomb III contained the remains of Alexander IV (an adolescent male); his death is recounted below. The greatest debate has been over the identity of the two occupants, a male and female, of Tomb II (Figure 9.2)—whether these are Philip II and Cleopatra, or Philip III and Adea Eurydice. Strong arguments have been made for both royal pairs, and, despite scientific analyses of the bones, the debate continues to rage. That takes nothing away from the spectacular material evidence these tombs have given us for Argead Macedonia in the late fourth century.[47] The nearby "Romaios" Tomb, with Ionic rather than Doric half-columns, is slightly later in date and is possibly the tomb of Thessalonice (Figure 9.4).[48]

The large "Kasta" tomb excavated at Amphipolis in 2012–2014 contained the partial remains of one female, together with two younger males and an infant child, as well as some cremated remains. The sheer size and extravagance of the tomb design have led some to hope that it belongs to Olympias. However, the ancient tradition is that Cassander denied Olympias burial, and while one might expect that eventually her remains were properly interred, to think that Cassander would have tolerated such an impressive monument to her memory stretches credulity. The nearby Lion of Amphipolis (Figure 9.3), fragments of which were discovered by soldiers in 1912–1913 and subsequently reconstructed, dates to about the same time, and is thought to have honoured one of Alexander III's generals. In 1937 Charles Edson came across an inscription in the village of Makriyialos, near ancient "old" Pydna, that had once marked the grave of an Aeacid descendant of Olympias. Another partial inscription from the same village (recorded but by this date lost) referred to a tomb of Olympias. This tomb, Edson thought, had been erected at Pydna perhaps by her cousin Pyrrhus (Aeacides' infant son) when later he briefly ruled Macedonia as king, a full decade after the death of Cassander.[49]

Hope was fading for Alexander IV. Polyperchon, having been besieged in Azorius in Perrhaebia by some of Cassander's forces and unable to reach Pydna, fled to Aetolia when he heard that Olympias had been killed, taking with him

Figure 9.2 Façade of Tomb II, Vergina (Aegae)

Source: https://upload.wikimedia.org/wikipedia/commons/4/44/Facade_of_Philip_II_tomb_Vergina_Greece.jpg.

Figure 9.3 Lion of Amphipolis, late fourth century BCE, funerary monument thought to honour one of Alexander III's high-ranking officers

Source: author, 2013.

Figure 9.4 Romaios Tomb, Vergina (Aegae), 310–290 BCE
Source: author, 1986.

the troops of Aeacides that had remained loyal. His son Alexander was still in the Peloponnese with a sizeable army. Since this Alexander still posed a threat to Cassander's supremacy in Greece, Cassander now marched his army south again. In Boeotia he announced his intention to rebuild Thebes, a plan for which several Greek states, including Athens, were quick to offer support. He then advanced to the Peloponnese, where some cities he won over, or rather forced into alliance, such as Argos, but when Alexander would not face him in a pitched battle, leaving a guard of 2,000 troops at the Isthmus, Cassander returned to Macedonia.[50]

Cassander and the Successors

As the wars of the Successors raged on, the satraps of Alexander's great empire—an empire barely conquered and never in fact either controlled or consolidated—each concerned himself with protecting or advancing his own interests; and long before the fate of Alexander IV was sealed there was no one left who was willing to recognize any proclaimed central authority.[51]

> For never before that time did Macedonia, or indeed any other nation, produce so rich a crop of brilliant men, men who had been picked out with such care, first by Philip and then by Alexander, that they seemed chosen less as comrades-in-arms than as successors to the throne.[52]

Antipater's grip on the homeland had been equivalent to that of a strong monarch, and as the central authority crumbled away, the other Successors set themselves up in similar positions of strength in what were turning into independent kingdoms. Antigonus was the one who most aspired to keep the empire together, though this was not from any sense of loyalty to the half-Asian heir; if he united the empire, it would be his.

When Antigonus returned from Media after defeating Eumenes he was treated as *de facto* 'Lord of Asia' by the native Persians.[53] He had already executed Peithon after accusing him of plotting revolt,[54] and Seleucus, fearing a similar fate when Antigonus arrived in his satrapy of Babylonia and demanded an account of the revenues in such a way as to presume Seleucus' subordination, fled with about 500 cavalry to Ptolemy in Egypt. He warned Ptolemy that Antigonus was aiming to seize the whole of the empire for himself, a warning soon affirmed by Antigonus presuming the authority, as Perdiccas and Antipater had done, to redistribute the satrapies.[55]

Antigonus' presumption posed a threat to the other powerful Successors, and in the spring of 314 Ptolemy sent messengers to both Cassander in Macedonia and Lysimachus in Thrace seeking an alliance. They jointly demanded that Antigonus redistribute the satrapies so that each of them received a part of Asia in addition to the regions they individually held outside Asia as well as a share of the royal treasure captured with Eumenes. If he refused, they would jointly wage war on him. Antigonus opted for war (the Third Diadoch War), and thus he and Cassander became enemies. In order to prevent Cassander from crossing to Asia Antigonus sent a land force to guard the Hellespont, and sending his general Aristodemus to the Peloponnese, he hired mercenaries and won over Polyperchon and Alexander, who were all too willing to align themselves against Cassander. Antigonus appointed Polyperchon his general in the Peloponnese and enticed Alexander to join him in Asia.[56] Antigonus' great handicap was lack of a fleet. Ptolemy essentially controlled the eastern Mediterranean, including Tyre, and Cassander now controlled the Aegean, since Antigonus had concentrated his military power in land forces, and after the success of his ships over Cleitus at the Hellespont in 317 he had not maintained a strong fleet. So marching down to Phoenicia he proceeded to build ships. With this underway he then put on the mantle of defender of the Macedonian throne—never mind that he had been dismissed as regent for the kings in Asia by Adea Eurydice in Philip III's name, and when he fought Eumenes the latter professed to be acting on behalf of the throne by order of Olympias as guardian of Alexander IV—and with Alexander, son of Polyperchon, fresh from Europe to support his claims, he brought a range of serious charges against Cassander: the murder of Olympias and the confinement of Roxane and Alexander IV; marrying Thessalonice by force; trying to claim the Macedonian throne; resettling the Olynthians at his eponymous Cassandreia; and rebuilding Thebes. He followed up the charges by issuing a decree, the so-called Decree of Tyre, declaring Cassander an outlaw if he did not destroy his new cities, release the "king" and Roxane, and acknowledge Antigonus as regent (*epimeletes*). And in a bid to win over the Greek states he decreed that they were to be free, no longer garrisoned. He sent Alexander back to the Peloponnese with 500 talents for the war while he proceeded to besiege Tyre. It was fifteen months before Tyre fell and Ptolemy's garrison was expelled. By that time Antigonus had amassed a fleet of 240 warships.[57]

Hoping to undermine Antigonus' strategy, Ptolemy issued his own autonomy decree and sent one of his generals with fifty ships to the Peloponnese to cooperate with Cassander against Polyperchon and Alexander. Cassander in turn tried to detach these two from their alliance with Antigonus. Having no diplomatic success, he marched south, seized several fortresses in the Peloponnese, dismissing Alexander's garrisons and establishing his own, and after presiding over the Nemean games (summer 313) he returned to Macedonia. When Alexander found himself losing most of the Peloponnese to Cassander he finally agreed to desert Antigonus and accept Cassander's offer to become *his* general in the Peloponnese.[58] Alexander now came into open conflict with Antigonus' general Aristodemus (where Polyperchon stood at this point is unknown) and before long some of his own allies at Sicyon, where he had his base of operations, turned on him and he was assassinated. His wife Cratesipolis assuming his military command quickly put down the revolt in Sicyon and Corinth, and she continued to control these cities for several years.[59]

Antigonus countered in western Greece by gaining the support of the Aetolians.[60] The Aetolians' involvement in a border war with the Acarnanians north of the Peloponnese posed enough of a threat to Cassander's interests that he marched from Macedonia with a large army, persuaded the Acarnanians to relocate from their villages into a few central locations, formed an alliance with them, and left an occupation force under Lyciscus. Before leaving the region Cassander formed an alliance and established a garrison at Leucas near the entrance to the Gulf of Ambracia; then moving north through Epirus along the Adriatic coast, he took Apollonia by storm and installed a garrison; and then marching into Illyria, he defeated king Glaucias in battle and concluded a treaty prohibiting Glaucias from making war on his new allies. Glaucias still had Aeacides' son Pyrrhus in protective custody, and Cassander offered him 200 talents for the child, but Glaucias would not hand him over. Leaving another garrison at Epidamnus Cassander returned to Macedonia,[61] having fortified his southwestern flank against an attack from Antigonus' fleet and the Aetolians.

Cassander's attention now turned to Asia Minor and the war against Antigonus there. When he learned that Antigonus' general (and nephew) Ptolemaeus was besieging all the Carian cities that were allied with Ptolemy and Seleucus he sent forces to support the besieged and to distract Antigonus from crossing into Europe.[62] Fearing Cassander would win Caria, Antigonus, leaving his twenty-two-year-old son Demetrius in Syria with four veteran advisors (among them Nearchus the former admiral) to block any move by Ptolemy, and summoning his fleet to patrol the Carian coast, took an army and marched up into his old satrapy of Phrygia, where they spent the winter of 313–312. Antigonus had enough forces to send some to the Black Sea to aid a revolt in Thrace against Lysimachus—though Lysimachus suppressed the revolt and captured many of Antigonus' forces, ransoming some and enrolling others in his own army[63]—and to send fifty ships and a force of infantry to the Peloponnese to enforce the autonomy clause of his Decree of Tyre. There he was successful in winning support against Cassander, and all the Greek city-states that still had garrisons installed by Alexander, son of Polyperchon, were freed except Sicyon and Corinth, which were firmly held by Cratesipolis and Polyperchon.[64]

Cassander thus lost most of the Peloponnese to Antigonus, though for now he held onto western Greece. The Aetolians, despite Lyciscus' occupation force, had risen up and slaughtered many Acarnanians at Agrinium, so Cassander sent his younger brother Philip with an army against the Aetolians. While Philip was ravaging Aetolian territory he learned that Cassander's enemy Aeacides had returned to Epirus, was pardoned by his people, and had mustered a strong army. Fearing that army would join forces with the Aetolians, he turned and marched against Aeacides and defeated him in battle, killing a large number of Epirotes and taking many more captive, including about fifty of the faction that had been responsible for Aeacides' recall; these prisoners he sent to Cassander, whose vendetta against Olympias and her kin was not yet sated. The survivors joined up with the Aetolians, and in a second battle fought at Oeniadae Aeacides was fatally wounded (he died soon after) and the Aetolians fled to the hills.[65]

Cassander, meanwhile, having failed miserably in Caria, could not come to agreement with Antigonus over the Hellespontine region, which both men feared would fall under the other's control.[66] Hoping to distract Antigonus, Cassander turned his attention to Euboea. Macedonian influence there dated back to Philip II's day, and Cassander for some time had held Chalcis with a garrison. When he now attempted to seize nearby Oreus by sea, Antigonus sent ships to check him.[67] Then Antigonus sent Ptolemaeus with a large fleet of 150 ships, 5,000 foot, and 500 horse to 'liberate' the Greeks. Cassander promptly pulled out of Oreus and sailed to Chalcis, calling in all his forces for its defence, since Chalcis was highly strategic for anyone wanting to control central and southern Greece. When Antigonus learned of Cassander's move he quickly recalled part of his fleet and then headed with his army for the Hellespont, hoping to cross to Europe and march on Macedonia undefended. Cassander, leaving his brother Pleistarchus in charge of the garrison at Chalcis, crossed to Boeotia with all his forces, made an alliance with newly re-founded Thebes and a truce with the other Boeotians, and then leaving one of his generals to protect the alliance, he hurried back to Macedonia.[68] At the Hellespont Lysimachus persuaded the Byzantines not to cooperate with Antigonus (they claimed neutrality), and so Antigonus did not cross over and instead retreated to winter quarters.[69] Ptolemaeus forced the garrison at Chalcis into submission and left the city ungarrisoned; then on the mainland he took Oropos, making captives of Cassander's troops, freed Thebes of its garrison, and in Phocis freed other cities from Cassander's garrisons. Meantime on the west coast the Corcyreans had removed Cassander's garrisons from Apollonia and Epidamnus and had handed control of the latter over to Glaucias.[70]

Cassander by this time had lost most of his influence outside Macedonia proper. Epirus he lost when Aeacides returned from exile, and after Aeacides' death the latter's older brother Alcetas, long since banished by their father Arybbas, returned to claim the throne. Cassander regained Epirus, however, after Lyciscus, having driven Alcetas into flight from Cassopia, besieged him in Eurymenae, and then, after both sides received reinforcements, together with Deinias he defeated Alcetas and his two sons. Cassander arrived, and coming to terms of 'friendship' with Alcetas, left him on the throne, probably as a client king. Then taking part of his army west to the Adriatic coast, he undertook a siege to recover Apollonia. His force was inadequate, however, and after suffering heavy casualties and with winter coming on he returned to Macedonia late in 312. After he was gone the people of Leucas also drove out their Macedonian garrison, so while Cassander regained Epirus, he lost all three of his Adriatic garrisons.[71]

To the east, late in 312, Cassander's ally Ptolemy subjected the inexperienced Demetrius, who had been left guarding upper Syria, to a plundering raid, and then in the spring of 311 Ptolemy and Seleucus inflicted a humiliating defeat on him in battle at Gaza.[72] The victors proceeded to take control of the cities of Phoenicia, and on the wave of this success Seleucus asked Ptolemy for forces so that he could march inland and reclaim his satrapy of Babylonia.[73] Seleucus set out from Syria with only 800 foot and 200 horse, but once he reached Mesopotamia he was able to recruit some Macedonians in the region, and with the additional benefit of the local population welcoming his return he easily overcame Antigonus' officers.[74] By this time Demetrius had made something of a comeback by capturing one of Ptolemy's generals who had been sent with forces to drive him out of Syria, and when Antigonus arrived in answer to his son's call for aid Ptolemy, never one to take an unnecessary risk, retreated to the security of Egypt, though in so doing he abandoned Syria and Phoenicia to Antigonus.[75]

The Third Diadoch War essentially had come to a stalemate, with the allies unable to enforce their ultimatum. So late in 311 a treaty was concluded with Antigonus on the following terms: Cassander was to be *strategos* of Europe until Alexander IV came of age; Lysimachus was to rule in Thrace; Ptolemy was to rule Egypt and the parts of neighbouring Libya and Arabia that he had previously seized; Antigonus was to hold first place in all of Asia—in other words, all the satraps (in Asia) would be subject to him; and the Greeks were to be autonomous.[76] Seleucus appears not to have been included in the treaty (he was not part of the original coalition, except as Ptolemy's ally), but when Antigonus sent Demetrius to Babylonia to reclaim the satrapy Seleucus could not be dislodged.[77] Apart from Seleucus now holding Babylonia, this was very nearly the status quo at the beginning of the war, and it tacitly acknowledged division of the empire into four virtually independent kingdoms.

For Cassander, the treaty provided little security, since in theory he was the one, and evidently the only one, who would be forced to concede power to Roxane's son Alexander. As it now stood, every man's 'kingdom' was his own to defend, and seeking to strengthen his position, Cassander went first to help the Paeonian king, Audoleon, fend off an invasion of the Autariatae; and taking 20,000 of these Illyrians, he resettled them near Mount Orbelos, his border with Thrace.[78] At the same time he engaged in negotiations with Ptolemaeus. The two formed an alliance: Ptolemaeus defected from Antigonus (his uncle) and brought over his loyal friend Phoenix, whom he supplied with forces to guard the disputed region along the Hellespont.[79] Then a year or so after the treaty was signed, when some Macedonian nobles began to agitate for the ascension of the Argead heir—he was approaching his fourteenth birthday, which may have marked a milestone for Macedonian youths—Cassander quietly ordered the murder of Alexander and Roxane, a deed he concealed for some time.[80] When it became apparent that the Argead heir had been, in fact, eliminated a forgotten player made an unexpected move. From Pergamon in Asia Minor, where he had been living with his mother Barsine, Alexander's illegitimate son Heracles, about seventeen years old, was brought across the Aegean into Polyperchon's protection at Corinth. It is hard to believe that Heracles could have left Pergamon without Antigonus' knowledge and approval, so perhaps we should see his designs at work here.[81] Antigonus had lost control of most of the Peloponnese to Cassander with the defection of Ptolemaeus,[82] and Polyperchon now asked the Aetolians, Antigonus' allies, to help him get Heracles safely to Macedonia and installed on the throne. He had raised an army he thought large enough (20,000 foot, 1,000 horse) to challenge Cassander.[83]

Polyperchon with Heracles had made it as far as Tymphaea (Figure 9.5) on the border between Epirus and Upper Macedonia (Polyperchon was a native of Tymphaea so ought to have had support there) when Cassander met them with his Macedonian army, perhaps in the late summer or fall of 309. Polyperchon, we are told, was offered return of his confiscated land grants in Macedonia as well as 4,000 Macedonian infantry, 500 Thessalian cavalry, and generalship in the Peloponnese in exchange for the murder of Heracles; he accepted the bribe and carried out the assassination quite openly at a banquet.[84] Unless Polyperchon's complicity is merely Cassander's propaganda scheme, it is startling that after years of bitter rivalry he would come to a rapport with Cassander, and evidently not a particularly profitable one, for he appears thereafter to be out of the power game.[85]

Already the treaty between Antigonus and the allies had broken down: Ptolemy accused Antigonus of subjecting some of the Greek cities to garrisons,[86] and when he declared war Cassander and Lysimachus did the same. Cassander feared Antigonus would make another attempt to cross the Hellespont and march on Macedonia, while Lysimachus hoped to expand his 'kingdom' of Thrace into Asia Minor at Antigonus' expense. As his gateway to Asia, in 309 Lysimachus founded an eponymous city, Lysimacheia, on the Propontis in the Chersonese.[87] In 308 Ptolemy made his only serious bid for control in Greece. Crossing to the Peloponnese from Asia he took control of Sicyon and Corinth from Cratesipolis, with her cooperation.[88] When he found little welcome from the Peloponnesians for his efforts to 'liberate' them, however, he formed an

Figure 9.5 Pindus Mountains, Epirus, region of Tymphaea
Source: author, 1986.

alliance with Cassander, and leaving Cassander to garrison the cities he sailed back to Egypt. About this time Ptolemy seems to have entered into negotiations for a marriage alliance with Cleopatra, who was still living at Sardis after some thirteen years under Antigonus' close watch. When Cleopatra attempted to slip away to join Ptolemy in Egypt, she was detained by force, and shortly after Antigonus had some of her female attendants murder her. Covering up his own involvement, he gave her a splendid royal funeral, one befitting the sister and daughter of Argead kings. It was a gesture, like Cassander's, intended to mark himself as successor to her royal prestige.[89]

Unable to approach Macedonia via Thrace, in the following campaign season Antigonus sent Demetrius with strong land forces and a fleet of 250 ships to 'free' the Greeks from Macedonian/Cassandrian control.[90] Coming to Attica in the spring of 307, Demetrius quickly captured the Piraeus, and after negotiating with Cassander's governor, Demetrius of Phaleron, for release of the city the latter after a ten-year rule fled and sought refuge with Ptolemy in Egypt. The Macedonian garrison entrenched on Munychia put up fierce resistance to Demetrius' siege, but when its commander, Dionysius, was captured the garrison capitulated and the fortification was razed. The Athenians honoured both Antigonus and Demetrius as "saviours" for freeing the city from Macedonian control, which it had been under since the close of the Lamian War.[91] Macedonian control had meant, for one thing, restricted access to shipbuilding timber, and Antigonus immediately filled an Athenian request for materials, enough for 100 ships.

Over the next four years Cassander made repeated attempts to try to regain control of Athens in an ongoing war with Demetrius and Antigonus.[92] And initially events in the east worked in his favour. Late in 307 Antigonus sent instructions for his son to take the fleet as quickly as possible to Cyprus against Ptolemy's forces. At Cyprian Salamis the following spring Demetrius defeated the combined fleets of Ptolemy and his brother Menelaus and took control of all Cyprus. Upon hearing the news of the spectacular victory, Antigonus—he had already founded an eponymous Antigoneia on the Orontes—"assumed the diadem and from that time on he used the style of king; and he permitted Demetrius also to assume this same title and rank."[93]

By 305–304 Ptolemy, having fended off Antigonus' massive invasion of Egypt,[94] and having earned the epithet *Soter* ("savior") for supplying the Rhodians with grain, which enabled them to withstand a siege by Demetrius (now dubbed *Poliorketes*—"city-besieger" or "city-taker"—for his use of a nine-storey-high *helepolis*),[95] assumed the title *basileus* (king); around the same time Lysimachus and Seleucus did likewise, the latter already recognized as "king" by the native population in Persia.[96] At this point the title was all that any of them lacked of authority in their spear-held kingdoms, so it was really a notice to the Greeks as well as to each other just how things stood with respect to the fragmented empire of Alexander. The great expanse of territory conquered by Alexander and the Macedonians, so long as his Successors continued to war amongst themselves for parts of it, would never be united. As for Cassander, it is debated whether he used *basileus* in Macedonia (the kings before him had not used it of themselves, not even Alexander before he crossed to Asia).[97] However, there was no ambiguity about his assumption of the kingship, whatever he called himself, and the Rhodians, who with divine approval from Ammon at Siwah now honoured Ptolemy as a god, set up statues to King Cassander and King Lysimachus.[98]

Cassander had not made peace with Antigonus and Demetrius, and in Demetrius' absence he had put Athens under siege. Demetrius sailed to Greece once again as liberator, and with the intention, once established in southern Greece, of challenging Cassander for control of Macedonia. Landing in Euboea, he seized Chalcis then crossed to the mainland and forced Cassander to lift his siege, pursuing him and his army as far as Thermopylae (or Heraclea), where Cassander stood and fought. Cassander lost, and 6,000 of his troops defected to Demetrius.[99] Macedonian soldiers had no admiration for an unsuccessful general, but these perhaps had joined him only reluctantly at Olympias' demise, and the army probably had never 'acclaimed' Cassander king, so he did not have the kind of personal loyalty that Macedonian kings in the past had from their troops. Demetrius proceeded to free Attica and then to liberate cities in the Peloponnese from control of Cassander's generals Prepelaus and the apparently still active Polyperchon.[100] At Corinth he convened a Greek congress, with the intention (on his father's instruction) of reinstituting the long-defunct League.[101] These heavy losses in southern Greece compelled Cassander to send envoys to treat with Antigonus. But when Antigonus demanded total surrender Cassander called on Lysimachus for support, and the two of them once again allied with Ptolemy and Seleucus for a joint war against Antigonus.[102] Cassander's fear was that Antigonus would seize control of Greece *and* Macedonia, and the others feared he would seize their territories one by one until he alone controlled Alexander's vast empire. It was to be Antigonus' final showdown.

After sending part of his forces to Lysimachus for the advance into Asia Cassander marched the rest of his army into Thessaly against Demetrius.[103] Cassander challenged him with 29,000 foot and 2,000 horse, but this was only about half the strength of Demetrius' army of 56,000 foot (of which 8,000 were Macedonians) and 1,500 horse. Surely this spelled victory for Demetrius and the end of Cassander's control of Macedonia in addition to Thessaly and Greece. However, Demetrius waited to hear about events in Asia before he attacked, and he soon received his father's recall. Quickly coming to temporary terms with Cassander, he took his forces and crossed to Asia.[104] Cassander immediately re-established control in Thessaly and sent additional reinforcements under command of his brother Pleistarchus to Lysimachus at Heraclea Pontica.[105] The decisive battle was finally fought at Ipsus in Phrygia, Antigonus' home ground, in the spring of 301. The two armies were fairly evenly matched in foot and horse, but Seleucus' 400 elephants tipped the scales when he placed them between Demetrius' cavalry (after they had made a successful charge and routed the opposing line) and Antigonus' infantry, so that Demetrius was cut off from returning to his own line.[106] Seleucus surrounded the exposed phalanx and they defected, while Demetrius fled with some foot and horse. As for Antigonus, he went down in a hail of javelins. He was eighty-one years old. The victors—though notably neither Cassander nor Ptolemy had actually shown up for the battle—carved up Antigonus' kingdom.[107]

Monarchy to anarchy

With Antigonus eliminated, Cassander's hold on Macedonia seemed secure, though Demetrius with the strong Antigonid fleet remained a factor. For the present Demetrius found himself shut out of Athens and went thundering off to Thrace to raid Lysimachus' territory, leaving Pyrrhus in charge of maintaining his garrisons in the Peloponnese at Argos, Sicyon, and Corinth. Pyrrhus was that Aeacid prince, son of Aeacides, whom the Illyrian king Glaucias had refused to surrender to Cassander, and Demetrius had married his sister Deidameia, formerly betrothed to Alexander IV. After the Epirotes had assassinated Alcetas out of rage over his harshness, in 307 or 306 Glaucias had placed Pyrrhus, though only about age twelve, on the throne of Epirus. In 302 at Cassander's instigation Pyrrhus was deposed and replaced by a rival Aeacid, Neoptolemus. Pyrrhus fled to his brother-in-law Demetrius for protection, and fought for him at Ipsus.[108] Demetrius' absence was an opportunity for Cassander to attempt to regain some losses in the west, namely his garrisons along the Adriatic. In 299 he brought a large fleet against Corcyra and was on the point of capturing it when Agathocles of Syracuse, coming to the aid of the Corcyreans, set fire to the Macedonian ships.[109] Cassander lost the fight to save them, and Agathocles claimed the victory without even engaging any Macedonian forces.

Two years later, in 297, Cassander died of illness.[110] The later king lists grant him a reign of nineteen years, though he began as regent when he forced Olympias into flight, and in the treaty of 311–310 he was designated *strategos* of Europe.[111] He was, unarguably, a transitional figure in Macedonian history. He had brought great odium on himself for the elimination of the mother and son of Alexander III, yet he had made every effort to evoke the legacy of Philip II, marrying (albeit by force) a daughter of Philip and overlooking tradition to name his own firstborn son Philip—his intended heir—after the maternal rather than the paternal grandfather.[112] His period of rule seems to have been relatively peaceful and prosperous: the Illyrians (evidently) did not raid across the border, he maintained the long-standing alliance with Paeonia, and though he lost Thrace to Lysimachus, who received it as his share of Alexander's empire, he had good relations with his eastern neighbour.[113] He also seems to have maintained, for the most part, Macedonian influence in Epirus and Thessaly.[114] Yet he left behind no secure state. His succession was a catastrophe, almost the end of the kingdom of Macedonia. His eldest son succeeded as Philip IV, but Philip reigned only four months before he also died of illness. Evidently, Cassander's widow, Thessalonice, then divided the kingdom between her two remaining sons, though why she would do so or on what authority is puzzling; or, possibly, the elder, Antipater I, succeeded—and then when she appeared to favour the youngest son, Alexander, after a few years (in 294) Antipater killed her and drove his brother into exile.[115] Either she or Cassander had arranged marriages for both younger sons, so both had (in theory) strong allies, Lysimachus and Ptolemy.[116] But there were too many competent and power-hungry rivals on Macedonia's borders for the kingdom to survive this kind of dynastic feud.

Alexander V promptly sent letters to Pyrrhus, who had resumed the throne in Epirus, and to Demetrius (his uncle) begging support. Pyrrhus arrived first, and in exchange for his backing he demanded the annexation to his own kingdom of Tymphaea and Parauaea, two districts which had been part of Upper Macedonia since Philip II annexed them from Epirus half a century earlier, as well as the city Ambracia, another of Philip II's gains, and the regions Acarnania and Amphilochia on his southern border; in all of these he promptly installed garrisons.[117] When Pyrrhus then challenged Antipater I for control of the rest of Macedonia Antipater fled to his father-in-law Lysimachus in Thrace. By the time Demetrius marched north Pyrrhus, Alexander, and Lysimachus (on Antipater's behalf) had come to a settlement, and so Alexander met and entertained Demetrius near the border at Dion, then told him his support was no longer needed. It was an uneasy meeting, the young Alexander V allegedly attempting to have the seasoned Besieger assassinated, and Demetrius just as keen to do away with his host. He lured Alexander to Thessaly and at a reciprocal banquet at Larissa had his bodyguards kill him.[118]

On the following day the Macedonians who were present met in assembly at Demetrius' summons, and after hearing his persuasive speech they acclaimed him "king." Then they marched with him back to Macedonia. With few options available, the Macedonians were accepting of the new king Demetrius I, preferring his military reputation to the half-Argead blood of the one remaining son of Cassander. They despised the young Antipater for slaying the daughter of Philip II, as they had resented Cassander for his murder of Olympias and Alexander IV.[119] Moreover, Demetrius' first wife, Phila, was a daughter of the long-time regent Antipater and former wife of the popular taxiarch Craterus, so in her there was at least some continuity.

Neither Lysimachus nor Pyrrhus, though they were wary of his military strength, initially contested Demetrius' accession.[120] Demetrius himself was still preoccupied with controlling Greece, so he first looked south. In Magnesia in 293 he established his eponymous city Demetrias, a port on the Gulf of Pagasae,[121] to be a naval base for his growing fleet. Then he proceeded to subdue Boeotia. When Thebes opted to side with his enemy Sparta Demetrius besieged the city and established garrisons throughout Boeotia.[122] Hearing that Lysimachus had been captured by the Thracian Dromichaetes, and thinking to seize Lysimachus' kingdom, he made a mad dash to Thrace, but the Thracians had already released Lysimachus. In Demetrius' absence the Boeotians revolted, and by the time he returned, his capable son, Antigonus, had the situation in hand. Meantime Pyrrhus had overrun Thessaly, and now the Epirote and Macedonian kings came into bitter rivalry. Demetrius left Antigonus in charge in Boeotia and marched against Pyrrhus, but Pyrrhus fled at his approach, so Demetrius left an occupation force of 10,000 foot and 1,000 horse in Thessaly and returned to his second siege of Thebes.[123]

Demetrius formerly had been Pyrrhus' protector, but after Deidameia died in Syria in 300, and after he sent Pyrrhus to Ptolemy as hostage (while there Pyrrhus married Ptolemy's step-daughter Antigone), the relationship dissolved.[124] Then, shortly after Demetrius' second siege of Thebes ended (in 291) and he returned to Macedonia, Pyrrhus' wife, Lanassa, left him and took up with Demetrius. She was the daughter of King Agathocles of Syracuse, and her dowry was the strategic island of Corcyra. Demetrius saw fit to marry her and form an alliance with Agathocles.[125] The new alliance drew Demetrius' interest to the west, and he soon made a campaign into Aetolia. From there he crossed into Epirus to challenge Pyrrhus, but Pyrrhus had anticipated him and already fallen in with Demetrius' general Pantauchos, defeated him in battle, and took 5,000 of Demetrius' men prisoner, a great humiliation for the Macedonian king.[126] Pyrrhus inflicted further humiliation when Demetrius, having returned to Pella, fell ill and Pyrrhus seized the opportunity to retaliate for depredations in Epirus by invading and pillaging the western part of Macedonia as far as Edessa. With the help of his generals, Demetrius drove Pyrrhus out again, but the Macedonians took notice of Pyrrhus' boldness. All this while Demetrius had been recruiting a large number of forces, reportedly some 98,000 foot and 12,000 horse, and constructing an enormous fleet of 500 ships, with which he now made preparation to invade Asia and reclaim the territory that had long been under his father's control. The response was inevitable: the remaining Successors of Alexander III—Lysimachus, Seleucus, and Ptolemy—formed an alliance and drew Pyrrhus into it against Demetrius.[127]

While Demetrius was away overseeing shipbuilding for his Asian expedition, in 288 Lysimachus invaded Macedonia from Thrace, Pyrrhus from Epirus, and Ptolemy brought his fleet from Egypt to challenge for Greece.[128] Demetrius immediately went against Lysimachus, but he did not trust his Macedonian army not to defect to the famed Macedonian general, and when he heard that Pyrrhus had already taken Beroia he turned his army back towards the heart of the kingdom. He was now trapped. Demetrius' constant campaigning, it was said, was because he found his Macedonians too unruly when idle (at peace).[129] But Demetrius' kingship had been problematic from the start. He was an outsider, the first 'foreign' king of Macedonia, for he had grown up in Asia Minor, had lived the life of a despot in Athens, and had no consideration for the nature of Macedonian kingship, for the judicial responsibilities inherent in it, or the customary *un*pretentious behaviour and dress of the king. The Macedonians were offended by his style of rule: difficulty of access, neglect of embassies, notoriously on one occasion tossing a bundle of petitions into the Axios, ostentatious clothing, and extravagant entertainment. As one old woman scolded him, if he had not the time to perform the *duties* of king, he should not *be* king.[130] At some point he had lost control of Amphipolis to Lysimachus, whose bribing of the garrison commander to betray the city, a principal mint, was undoubtedly a carefully targeted blow aimed at undermining finances for Demetrius' invasion of Asia.[131] Macedonia was to be Demetrius' means to a greater conquest, but the Macedonians could sense his defeat at hand and they began to slip away to Pyrrhus. When a few got up the nerve to go to Demetrius' tent and tell him that the Macedonians would no longer fight to maintain his extravagant lifestyle Demetrius changed his ostentatious robe for regular soldier's garb and thus disguised fled to join his wife Phila at Cassandreia. The daughter of Antipater, unwilling to follow her husband of some thirty years into exile, took poison. Demetrius headed south, where his son Antigonus was holding key positions among the city-states.[132]

Pyrrhus rode into Demetrius' camp unopposed to find the Macedonian soldiers looting their king's tent. Though his was a foreign conquest, Pyrrhus' style of generalship and his treatment of the many Macedonians who had been taken captive or defected earned him respect and approval; and so without any evident hesitation the Macedonian army acclaimed the Epirote cousin of Alexander III "king."[133] Lysimachus also claimed a share in the victory and in the rule of the kingdom on the strength of his fame as a Bodyguard of Alexander III and, evidently, his noble Macedonian blood (though, by one account, his father was a naturalized Macedonian from Crannon in Thessaly).[134] So the cities and land were divided between them.[135] Lysimachus now took the precaution of killing his son-in-law Antipater,[136] possibly the last trickle of Argead blood. Neither Pyrrhus nor Lysimachus was interested in relocating his seat of power to Macedonia. Rather, each saw his share of Macedonia as an appendage to his own kingdom, and so the divided kingdom was ruled from without for the next two years. Both kings made use of their territory to recruit for their armies, and, like Demetrius, Pyrrhus found the Macedonians easier to control when on campaign.[137] So long as either king thought there was a risk that Demetrius might recover his former military might they cooperated. Seleucus might yet aid Demetrius, for he had married Demetrius' daughter Stratonice (granddaughter of Antipater through Phila) shortly after Ipsus, though subsequently he had passed her on to his son Antiochus.[138] Then, after Demetrius bungled a takeover of Seleucus' territory in Cilicia and Seleucus took him captive,[139] Lysimachus marched into Pyrrhus' half of the kingdom, captured his baggage train at Edessa, and drove him out.[140] Thus by 285 Lysimachus had become the sole monarch of the whole kingdom of Macedonia, which he then attached to his kingdom of Thrace.

Over the next few years the king was heavily involved in expansionist efforts, successfully seizing Heraclea Pontica and annexing Paeonia.[141] But internal family dissention was beginning to tear apart Lysimachus' long-laid plans for succession. His son Agathocles, the intended heir, was a popular and competent general. He defeated Demetrius in Asia Minor when the latter, after his ignominious flight from Macedonia, had tried to recover from Lysimachus some territory in Caria and Lydia that had formerly been under Antigonus' control.[142] Had Agathocles succeeded to the throne he would likely have won considerable support from the Macedonian nobility, for his mother Nicaea (married to Lysimachus after Perdiccas' death) was one of Antipater's daughters. But in 284, persuaded by the accusations of treason made by his wife Arsinoe, daughter of Ptolemy, against her stepson, Lysimachus murdered Agathocles and made a purge of his many supporters.[143] Agathocles' loyal officers now defected to Seleucus, as did his widow, Lysandra (also widow of Alexander V, a daughter of Ptolemy, half-sister to Arsinoe), who incited Seleucus to invade Lysimachus' territory. Lysimachus crossed the Hellespont to stop him, and in the late winter of 281 at Corupedion near Sardis the two old generals fought for sole control of what was left of Alexander's empire. About a year earlier Ptolemy (I) had died of natural causes and was succeeded by his son Ptolemy II Philadelphus (Arsinoe's full brother), so only these two remained of Alexander's great generals. In the battle Lysimachus was struck by a spear and killed, leaving Seleucus the last Successor standing.[144]

Seleucus crossed the Hellespont, probably for the first time since 334, intending at the age of seventy-seven to reunite Alexander's empire by claiming Thrace and Macedonia as his possessions, himself to rule the European part from Macedonia and leaving Asia to his son Antiochus. He never made it as far as Macedonia. Having survived Lysimachus by a mere seven months, he was murdered near Lysimacheia by Ptolemy Ceraunus, the very man who, along with Lysandra, had encouraged his invasion of Lysimachus' territory.[145] Ptolemy Ceraunus

(Thunderbolt) was a son of Ptolemy I and had been cut out of the succession in Egypt by his younger half-brother Ptolemy II. He had fled to Seleucus for support at the same time as his full-sister Lysandra. Their mother was Antipater's daughter Eurydice, and so he fancied himself a legitimate candidate for the Macedonian throne. When he presented himself, surrounded by a formidable bodyguard, to Seleucus' army they acclaimed him "king." Right away he made effective use of Lysimachus' fleet to fend off a challenge by Antigonus, son of Demetrius (Demetrius had since died in captivity), then he entered Macedonia and assumed control. Over the next year and a half he concerned himself with the elimination of anyone he perceived to be a threat to his sovereignty: he married Lysimachus' widow Arsinoe (his half-sister), killed her two younger sons, then sent her into exile.[146]

Macedonia had been severely weakened by the division of the kingdom and subsequent years of rule from without, and though Ptolemy Ceraunus now ruled from within, he failed to strengthen the kingdom and secure his frontiers. His 'loan' to Pyrrhus of 5,000 infantry, 4,000 cavalry, and fifty elephants for the latter's invasion of Italy left Macedonia more vulnerable than it had been in some eighty years, and for the first time since Philip II the kingdom was invaded from the north. In 279 a massive invasion of Gauls put an end to Ceraunus. Having rejected (reportedly) an offer of substantial military support from the Dardani, another from the Gauls to "buy" peace (the Gauls were migrating, in search of food and land), and the advice of his advisors, when he met them in battle with troops too few and too unorganized his wounded elephant threw him, he was captured and brutally executed. Few of his army escaped; most were taken captive or killed. Macedonia, its military reputation in tatters, was now in a state of anarchy.[147]

There is scant evidence for events of the next few years. Perpetual warfare had inured the fighting men to competent leadership, but now that the crop of brilliant Successors had expired the pool of military talent was shallow. Ptolemy Ceraunus' brother (or uncle) Meleager ruled for two months, but the Macedonians deposed him and appointed in his place a son of Cassander's brother Philip, named for his grandfather Antipater. But Antipater II Etesias lasted only forty-five days (the season of the etesian winds) until the general Sosthenes, a man of uncertain origin, had him deposed in turn as being too militarily incompetent to deal with the threat of the Gallic chieftain Brennus with his horde of 160,000 invaders. Sosthenes assumed control of the army himself, with the intent to rule as supreme general and not as the acclaimed king.[148] Another Ptolemy (possibly the eldest son of Lysimachus and Arsinoe) and an unknown Arrhidaeus or Alexander are also mentioned as contenders for supreme power.[149] Perhaps the time had come to abandon monarchy altogether. What was most critical for the leadership role was military prowess, and perhaps Sosthenes modeled his rule on the role of *tagos* in Thessaly.[150] For a short time Sosthenes kept the Gauls from looting, perhaps buying them off, but then Macedonia was overrun and pillaged. The buffer zone between the northern 'barbarian' tribes and the Greeks had collapsed, and the Gauls raided all the way to Delphi.[151] For Macedonia the future looked bleak.

Notes

1 Diod. 18.49.1–3, 54.1–2; Ath. 1.18a. Eurydice: Paus. 1.6.8. Hunting: see Landucci Gattinoni 2003: 30–43; cp. Carney 2002: 65; and see Palagia 2000: 199–200. Eurydice's marriage: Paus. 1.6.8.
2 Plut. *Phoc.* 31; Nep. *Phoc.* 2.4. Nicanor was possibly the son of Balacrus, former Bodyguard of Alexander, so Bosworth 1994: 59, *contra* Heckel 2007: 402–404; see Chapter 8 n120. On the war between Cassander and Polyperchon see Yardley *et al.* 2011: 191–193, listing sources and bibliography, and Anson 2014: 83–116.
3 Diod. 18.50.1–5, 52.7–8, 53.4, 54.3–4, cf. 40–42, 44–47; Just. 14.2.1–4; *Marm. Par.* B 12 (see Chapter 2 n120). Landucci Gattinoni 2003: 39–40.
4 Diod. 18.55–56; Plut. *Phoc.* 32.1–3. Landucci Gattinoni 2008: 229–236; Poddighe 2013; Anson 2014: 87–90.
5 Diod. 18.57.1–2 (cp. 49.4, perhaps a doublet; if not, the two letters of recall were within a few months of each other), 65.1; Just. 14.5.1. On the ambiguity see Adams 1983: 20 n10 and Carney 1994: 362–363, 2006: 69–70.
6 Diod. 18.58.2–4; Nep. *Eum.* 6.1–3.
7 Carney 1994: 364.
8 Diod. 18.57.3–58.1; Plut. *Eum.* 13.1–3. Argyraspids: see Chapter 5 n106.
9 Diod. 18.50.4, 53.4–7, 58.1–59.4, 60.2–61.3; Str. 14.5.10; cp. Plut. *Eum.* 13.4–8; Nep. *Eum.* 7; Polyaen. 4.8.2. On the divergent accounts and Eumenes' alleged altered oath see Schäfer 2002: 119–121; Dixon 2007: 164–167; Roisman 2012a: 173–174; Anson 2015b: 152–154.
10 Diod. 18.62.1–2.
11 Diod. 18.64.1–65.2; Plut. *Phoc.* 32.9–10; Nep. *Phoc.* 2.4–5.
12 Diod. 18.65.5–66.1, 68.2; Plut. *Phoc.* 32.4–8, 33.4. On Phocion see Tritle 1988.
13 Diod. 18.66.2–68.1; Plut. *Phoc.* 33–37; Nep. *Phoc.* 3–4.
14 Diod. 18.68.2–72.1 (what "matters" Diodorus does not say).
15 Cp. Paschidis 2008a: 243 n36.
16 Diod. 18.52.5–6.
17 Diod. 18.72.2–9; Polyaen. 4.6.8; *Marm. Par.* B 13.
18 Diod. 18.74; Str. 9.1.20; Paus. 1.25.6; *Marm. Par.* B 13.
19 Diod. 18.75.1; Polyaen. 4.11.2. See O'Neil 1999a: 39 with n80; Anson 2008b: 146 with n76; and Chapter 7.
20 Inscription from Nasos, Aeolis, *IG* XII (2) 645. See Paschidis 2008a, 2008b: 408–413.
21 Diod. 18.75.1; Just. 14.5.4–5. Adams 1984: 86: spring 317; Paschidis 2008a: 243, 245: late spring or summer 317.
22 Diod. 19.11.1; cf. Just. 14.5.1–5. Carney 2000: 135–136; Yardley *et al.* 2011: 193–201.
23 Just. 14.5.3. Bosworth 2002: 120–121. On the chronology see Anson 2014: 99, 117.
24 Rule of women: Plut. *Alex.* 68.5; Diod. 19.11.9. Carney 1995; O'Neil 1999b (cautiously). Dedications: *SIG* 152; Hyperides 4.19; *IG* II^2 1492 A 45–57. Andronikos 1984: 49–51; Saatsoglou-Paliadeli 1999: 354 355, 361; Kosmetatou 2004; Carney 2006: 90–91. Afterlife, Demeter and Kore: Christesen and Murray 2010: 437.
25 Carney 1994: 366–369.
26 He came to the throne when Olympias' brother Alexander was killed: Liv. 8.24.
27 Ath. 560f: Macedonian armour; Polyaen. 8.60. Carney 2004: 184–186.
28 Carney 2001: 74.
29 Diod. 19.11.2–4; Just. 14.5.9–10; Paus. 1.11.3. See Carney 2004: 186–189; Adams 1984: 86: Eurydice's army "deserted … rather than face a direct confrontation without a competent commander."
30 Diod. 19.11.5–7; Paus. 1.11.4, 25.5; Ael. *VH* 13.36.

31 On Olympias' "position" in Macedonia see Anson 2014: 38, 44; *contra* Carney 2000: 138–139.
32 Adams 1983: 23: Cassander's "regent." Cp. Sippas, *strategos* for Antipater in 323–332 (Diod. 18.12.3).
33 Diod. 19.11.8. Cf. Diod. 17.118.1–2; Arr. *Anab.* 7.27.1–2; Plut. *Alex.* 77.2–5, *Mor.* 849f; Curt. 10.10.14–19; Just. 12.14. Iolaus was rumoured to be the lover of Medius of Larissa (Arr. *Anab.* 7.27.2), at whose drinking party Alexander allegedly first took his fever.
34 Plut. *Mor.* 849f, cp. *Alex.* 77.2–3. Bosworth 1971b: 113–114; but cp. Hammond 1993a: 144–148.
35 Diod. 19.11.8; Just. 14.6.1; cf. Orosius 3.23.29–38. On factional strife see e.g. Adams 1983: 19, 22–23. On Olympias' acts see Carney 2006: 75–79.
36 Diod. 19.35; Just. 14.6.2–4.
37 Diod. 19.36; cf. Plut. *Pyrrh.* 2–3; Just. 17.3.16–20.
38 Eumenes acting in the name of the king(s): Diod. 18.73.2, 19.12.1–2, 15.3–5; *Heid. Epit.* 3.2.
39 Diod. 19.35.5. Anson 2014: 107.
40 On the dates see Anson 2014: 106–107. Also Mendels 1984: 162 dates Cassander's second return to spring/summer 316.
41 Diod. 19.37–48. Roisman 2012a: 212–236; Baynham 2013; Anson 2015b: 163–206.
42 Cf. n40. High chronology dates Olympias' surrender to spring 316, e.g. Hammond in *HM* III 1988: 142; Carney 2006: xii, 80; low chronology to spring 315, e.g. Errington 1990: 128–129; Anson 2014: ix, 116–121; cf. *Marm. Par.* B 14.
43 Diod. 19.50.1–51.1 (Aristonus had slain many of Crateuas' men but reportedly let Crateuas himself go); Just. 14.6.5; Polyaen. 4.11.3.
44 Diod. 19.51.1–5, 17.118.2; Just. 14.6.6–12; Paus. 9.7.2; Porphyry F3.3 [*FGrH/BNJ* 260, Toye 2011]. Adams 1983: 22 questions her 'right' to a defence speech; but she had no 'rights' Cassander did not grant her. Possibly the case of a female (royal) brought to trial is anomalous. Hatzopoulos 1996: 273–275; Carney 2006: 82–84.
45 Diod. 19.52.1–4, 61.2; Just. 14.6.13; Liv. 44.11.2; Str. 7 fr 21, 25; *Heid. Epit.* 2.4.
46 Diod. 19.52.5; Ath. 4.155a (= Diyllos F1, *FGrH/BNJ* 73). Alonso Troncoso 2009, especially 287–288, citing earlier scholarship; Landucci Gattinoni 2010.
47 For the excavations and finds see especially Andronikos 1984, 1987. See also Saatsoglou-Paliadeli 1999. On the debate see e.g. Philip III: Borza and Palagia 2007; Gill 2008; Romm 2011: 7; Philip II: Hatzopoulos 2008; Worthington 2008: 234–241; Lane Fox 2011b, all citing earlier arguments.
48 Kottaridi 2011: 302.
49 *SEG* 12:340, 32.644. Edson 1949; Oikonomides 1982; Carney 2006: 85–87, 104–105. Amphipolis Lion: Broneer 1941.
50 Diod. 19.52.6, 53–54.
51 Diod. 18.50.1.
52 Just. 13.1.12–13. Yardley translation.
53 Diod. 19.48.1.
54 Diod. 19.46.
55 Diod. 19.55.1–56.2. Billows 1990: 105–107.
56 Diod. 19.56.3–60; Just. 15.1.1–2; App. *Syr.* 53. On the chronology see Meeus 2012 and Anson 2014: 157–162.
57 Diod. 19.58, 61; Just. 15.1.3–4.
58 Diod. 19.62.1–64.4. Cp. Diod. 20.20.1: Polyperchon's ongoing hostile relationship with Cassander. For his apparent continued good relationship with the Aetolians and Antigonus see Mendels 1984: 165–170 and Wheatley 1998: 13–14.
59 Diod. 19.66.2–67.2. Carney 2004: 187–188; Dixon 2014: 55–57.

60 Diod. 19.66.2.
61 Diod. 19.67.3–68.1; Plut. *Pyrrh.* 3.3; Just. 15.2.1–2; Polyaen. 4.11.4. For further on this campaign see Anson 2014: 136–137. On Glaucias see Wilkes 1992: 124–125. Pyrrhus' maternal grandfather was Menon, commander of the Thessalian cavalry during the Lamian war: Plut. *Pyrrh.* 1.4.
62 Diod. 19.68.2–7. Ptolemaeus: Billows 1990: 426–430.
63 Diod. 19.69, 73. On this practice see Anson 2015b: 257–258.
64 Diod. 19.74.1–2.
65 Diod. 19.74.3–6; Paus. 1.11.3–4.
66 Diod. 19.75.6; cf. Diod. 20.19.2. Caria: cf. n62.
67 Diod. 19.75.7–8.
68 Pleistarchus: cf. Plut. *Demetr.* 31.6; Paus. 1.15.1. Eupolemus: cf. Diod. 19.68.5–7. For the strategic value of Chalcis cf. Diod. 19.78.2 and Chapter 10 n3.
69 Diod. 19.77. Billows 1990: 123 doubts that Antigonus really intended to cross the Hellespont.
70 Diod. 19.78.
71 Diod. 19.88.1–89.1.
72 Dates: cp. Anson 2014: xii, and for high chronology see e.g. Bosworth 2002: 283.
73 Diod. 19.80–86.
74 Diod. 19.90–91; App. *Syr.* 9.54.
75 Diod. 19.93.
76 Diod. 19.105.1; Harding 132 = Austin 38. Mendels 1984: 175 suggests Seleucus was included in the treaty, but see Billows 1990: 132 and Anson 2014: 148–149.
77 Diod. 19.100.3–7; Plut. *Demetr.* 7.2–4. On Seleucus see Bosworth 2002: 210–245.
78 Diod. 20.19.1; Just. 15.2.1–2.
79 Diod. 20.19.2, cf. 19.5. On Ptolemaeus' defection see Anson 2014: 151.
80 Diod. 19.105.2–4; Just. 15.2.3–5 (he seems to have confused the two sons); App. *Syr.* 54; Paus. 9.7.2; Trogus *Prol.* 15; *Marm. Par.* B 18; *Heid. Epit.* 1.6. Concealed: Wheatley 1998: 17 with n23. Fourteen: Yardley *et al.* 2011: 234.
81 See e.g. Wheatley 1998: 14–15 with n14, n20.
82 Diod. 20.19.2.
83 Diod. 20.20. See Mendels 1984: 175–179.
84 Diod. 20.28.2–4. Poison: Paus. 9.7.2; strangulation: Plut. *Mor.* 530D; at dinner: Lycophron *Alex.* 800–804. Cf. Just. 15.2.3–5; Trogus *Prol.* 15; *Marm. Par.* B 18. On the sequence of the murders and Barsine's whereabouts see Wheatley 1998: 18–19.
85 Plut. *Mor.* 530d: Cassander gave Polyperchon 100 talents.
86 Diod. 20.19.3.
87 Diod. 20.29.1.
88 Diod. 20.37.1–2; Polyaen. 8.58. She perhaps thought of it as an alliance. Carney 2000: 229 suggests one of marriage; cp. Cratesipolis' subsequent dealings with Demetrius: Plut. *Demetr.* 9.5–7. Paschidis 2008a: 246–248 argues Polyperchon died c. 308 leaving her vulnerable, but cp. Diod. 20.100.6, 103.7.
89 Diod. 20.37.3–6. Carney 2000: 127. *Heid. Epit.* 4 erroneously states the marriage took place.
90 Diod. 20.45; Plut. *Demetr.* 8–9.
91 For the obsequious honors voted to Antigonus and Demetrius cf. Diod. 20.46.1–3; Plut. *Demetr.* 10–13.
92 Habicht 1997: 74.
93 Diod. 20. 46.4–53.2; Plut. *Demetr.* 15.1–17.1, 17.6–18.4; App. *Syr.* 54; Just. 15.2.10.
94 Diod. 20.73.1–2.

95 Diod. 20.48, 91, 95; Vitruvius 10.16.3–8; Athenaeus Mechanicus 23.11; Plut. *Demetr.* 21.1–3, 40.2. Marsden 1977: 212; Kern 1999: 243–246.
96 Just. 15.2.11–13. On date and title see Yardley *et al.* 2011: 244–245 and Anson 2014: 167, both citing earlier scholarship.
97 Diod. 20.53.4; Just. 15.2.12; but cf. Plut. *Demetr.* 18.4 and cp. Nep. *Eum.* 13.3. On the debate [*Syll.*³ 332] see Errington 1974 and Yardley *et al.* 2011: 245–247 with bibliography.
98 Diod. 20.100.2.
99 Diod. 20.100.5–6, 102.1; Plut. *Demetr.* 23.1–2; *Marm. Par.* B 24.
100 Diod. 20.102.2–103. Most historians (e.g. Wheatley 1998: 21) assume Polyperchon survived until 303–301; *contra* Paschidis cf. n88.
101 Plut. *Demetr.* 25.4 (cf. Diod. 20.102.1); *IG* IV² 1.68 = Harding 138. Ferguson 1948; Billows 1990: 228–230.
102 Diod. 20.106; Just. 15.2.15–16.
103 Diod. 20.107.1; Just. 15.2.17.
104 Diod. 20.110.2–111.3; Plut. *Demetr.* 28.2.
105 Diod. 20.112.1. The entrance to the Black Sea was already under Antigonus' control, and only about a third of these made it through.
106 Plut. *Demetr.* 29. Diodorus' extant narrative becomes fragmentary at this point, cf. 21.1.2. For sources and bibliography see Yardley *et al.* 2011: 297–298.
107 Diod. 21.1.4–5; Polyb. 5.67.7–10; Just. 15.4.22–23; App. *Syr.* 55; Paus. 1.6.7.
108 Plut. *Pyrrh.* 3.3, 4.1–3, *Demetr.* 25.2; Paus. 1.11.5.
109 Diod. 21.2.
110 Plut. *Demetr.* 36.1; Just. 15.4.24; Paus. 9.7.3.
111 Diod. 19.105.1.
112 Landucci Gattinoni 2010: 114.
113 Diod. 20.106.2–3; Paus. 1.10.1.
114 Errington 1990: 133–137; Adams 2010: 214–216.
115 Diod. 21.7.1; Plut. *Demetr.* 36.1, *Pyrrh.* 6.2; Just. 16.1.1–4; Paus. 9.7.3. Philip IV: for the testimonia see Oikonomides 1989 (though his poison theory is unsubstantiated).
116 See Carney 2000: 155–165; 158: suggesting they were twins. Antipater married Eurydice, daughter of Lysimachus and Nicaea (daughter of Antipater); Alexander married Lysandra, daughter of Ptolemy I and Eurydice (daughter of Antipater), i.e. both married first cousins, and all were Antipater's grandchildren. See also Landucci Gattinoni 2009.
117 Plut. *Pyrrh.* 6.
118 Diod. 21.7.1; Plut. *Demetr.* 36; *Pyrrh.* 7.1; Just. 16.1.5–8.
119 Plut. *Demetr.* 37; Just. 16.1.10–18.
120 Just. 16.1.19; but cp. Paus. 1.10.1.
121 Str. 9.15.
122 Plut. *Demetr.* 39.1–5; Polyaen. 4.7.11.
123 Diod. 21.14.1–3; Plut. *Demetr.* 39.6–40.6; *Pyrrh.* 7.2; Polyaen. 3.7.2.
124 Plut. *Pyrrh.* 4.3–4.
125 Diod. 21.15.1; Plut. *Pyrrh.* 9.2, 10.5.
126 Plut. *Demetr.* 41.1–5, *Pyrrh.* 7.3–5; *SEG* 48.588.
127 Plut. *Demetr.* 43.1–44.2; *Pyrrh.* 10.1–4, 11.1; Just. 16.2.1–2.
128 Plut. *Demetr.* 44.3–5, *Pyrrh.* 11.1. On the chronology of Demetrius' reign see Wheatley 1997.
129 Plut. *Demetr.* 41.1.
130 Diod. 21.9; Plut. *Demetr.* 41.6–42.7; Ath. 6.261b, 12.535f–536a.

131 Polyaen. 4.12.2; Paus. 1.10.2. Events at Amphipolis and the date are sketchy. See Walbank in *HM* III 1988: 226–229; Lund 1992: 16, 100; Koukouli-Chryssanthaki 2011: 418. On Demetrius' ambition see Anson 2014: 180.
132 Plut. *Demetr.* 44.6–10, 45.1, *Pyrrh.* 11.3–6; Just. 16.2.3, 6; Paus. 1.12.3; Cicero *de Officiis* 2.7.26.
133 Plut. *Pyrrh.* 11.6.
134 Just. 15.3.1; Paus. 1.9.5; but cp. Porphyry F3.8; Synkellos, Adler and Tuffin 2002: 388. For sources and arguments see Yardley *et al.* 2011: 257.
135 Plut. *Demetr.* 44.11, *Pyrrh.* 12.1.
136 Dating in agreement with Lund 1992: 100, based on Just. 16.2.4–5. Cp. Diod. 21.7.
137 Plut. *Pyrrh.* 12.5.
138 Plut. *Demetr.* 31.5–32.3.
139 Plut. *Demetr.* 47–50.
140 Diod. 21.20 (cf. Str. 16.2.10); Plut. *Pyrrh.* 12.5–7; Just. 16.3.1–2; Paus. 1.11.6.
141 Polyaen. 4.12.3; Lund 1992: 105.
142 Plut. *Demetr.* 46.4–9, 47.2; Polyaen. 4.7.12. Cf. Paus. 1.10.2: Lysimachus against Demetrius' son Antigonus.
143 Memnon of Heraclea F1 5.6–7 [*FGrH/BNJ* 434] = Austin no. 159; Just. 17.1.4–6; Paus. 1.10.3; cf. Plut. *Demetr.* 31.5. This is Arsinoe II; Arsinoe I is Lysimachus' daughter by Nicaea. On Arsinoe II's plot and Lysimachus' "senility" see Lund 1992: 184–198; see also Carney 2013: chapters 2 and 3. On the inter-dynastic marriages of this period see Gabbert 1997: 2.
144 Memnon F1 5.7; App. *Syr.* 64; Just. 17.1.7–2.1; Paus. 1.10.4–5, cf. 1.9.6; Porphyry F3.8.
145 Memnon F1 8.2–3; App. *Syr.* 62; Nep. 21.3; Just. 17.2.4–5; Paus. 1.16.2; *BCHP* (*Babylonian Chronicles*) 9.
146 Memnon F1 8.4–7; Just. 17.2.6–15, 24.1.1–3.9.
147 Memnon F1 8.8; Diod. 22.3.1–2; Just. 24.3.10–5.11; Paus. 10.19.4–7; Porphyry F3.9.
148 Diod. 22.4; Just. 24.5.12–6.3; Synkellos, Adler and Tuffin 2002: 389; included in the king list of Eusebius/Porphyry. On acclamation at this time and the broader context see Hatzopoulos 1996: 290–293.
149 Diod. 22.4; Porphyry F3.11; cf. Just. 24.2.10–3.2. On the anarchy see Walbank in *HM* III 1988: 239–258.
150 See Chapter 4 n73.
151 Diod. 22.9; Paus. 10.19.8–12.

10 The Antigonids, the Greek Leagues, and Rome, 278–167

Antigonus II Gonatas (277–239) put an end to anarchy by defeating the Gauls and implementing a policy of consolidation. His strategic placement of garrisons re-established Macedonian hegemony in the south, and Greek resistance, first in the Chremonidaean war (c. 267–262), was unsuccessful in breaking his hold, until the revamped federal states of Aetolia and Achaea began to challenge and he lost control of Corinth. He secured the throne for a new dynasty, but his successor Demetrius II (239–229) suffered further losses. Though some recovery was made by Antigonus III Doson (229–221) with victory at Sellasia, Philip V (221–179) spent his long reign reinforcing a weakened kingdom on all fronts. But as three Macedonian wars (215–205, 200–197, 171–168) proved, Macedonia could not offer serious resistance to Roman intervention in Greece. Philip's defeat at Cynoscephalae struck a blow to Macedonian military supremacy, and Perseus' (179–168) defeat at Pydna resulted in Rome's dissolution of the monarchy.

Antigonus II Gonatas: recovery and renewal

The invasion of the Gauls in 280–279 was a turning point for Macedonia. The fame of the eastern conquests had faded, and Macedonian glory was tarnished by too many would-be kings, the ineffectual scions of the great noble families. The exception was Antigonus, son of Demetrius I Poliorcetes. When Demetrius was driven from the kingship of Macedonia and found himself in captivity to Seleucus he wrote to his son Antigonus and his generals in Greece and instructed them to hold onto his "possessions."[1] Among these were garrisons and dockyards at Corinth, Chalcis, and the recently founded Demetrias,[2] three key naval strongholds from which the Macedonians for most of the next century effectively controlled Greek affairs. As later described to the Roman Senate, in explanation of the situation in Greece in 197, during the reign of Philip V: "if the king held Demetrias in Thessaly, Chalcis in Euboea, and Corinth in Achaea, Greece could not be free."[3] Philip himself called them the "fetters of Greece," and together with the Piraeus, these ports provided haven for the large Antigonid fleet. After the assassination of Seleucus in 281 Antigonus used the fleet to attempt his first advance on Macedonia, but Ptolemy Ceraunus defeated him. Two years later Ceraunus was killed in the first invasion of the Gauls, and the monarchy devolved into chaos.[4]

When the Greek states united against the Gauls at Thermopylae the following year, Antigonus sent 500 mercenaries in support of the Greek resistance.[5] The Gauls were routed and retreated north, but a band left guarding the frontier then took to raiding in the region of Thrace. The following summer, by ruse of displaying great booty to be seized from his 'unguarded' camp, Antigonus enticed the band into an ambush near Lysimacheia and slaughtered them wholesale.[6] Antigonus had already assumed the title "king" upon his father's death, though "he was 'king' of very little,"[7] and probably it was this victory that earned him sufficient respect as a military leader to win over enough Macedonians to have them acclaim him "king" of Macedonia.[8] A dearth of evidence (source material dries to a trickle for the next half century) prevents a clear understanding of how Antigonus II Gonatas (the nickname supposedly came from his having been raised at Gonnoi in Thessaly)[9] consolidated his power. It seems he had first to oust a rival claimant, Antipater Etesias, and at one point was involved in a drawn-out war with Seleucus' successor Antiochus I,[10] who possibly also challenged for the throne. Cassandreia, Demetrius' former stronghold had fallen in 278 to the tyrant Apollodorus, and Antigonus only managed to reclaim it by siege.[11]

Recovery was slow, and Antigonus had not yet consolidated his position when Pyrrhus returned from his five-year campaign in southern Italy and Sicily, where he had earned ambiguous victories over the Romans and Carthaginians, and was now looking for ways to reward his surviving troops. In 274 Pyrrhus invaded Upper Macedonia for a plundering raid with his veterans and a band of Gauls. There was also the matter of Antigonus having denied a request from Pyrrhus to send reinforcements to Italy. Pyrrhus succeeded in capturing several towns and was joined by some 2,000 Macedonian soldiers defecting from Antigonus—evidence that the Epirote king still had support inside Macedonia. So Pyrrhus' pillaging raid quickly turned into a campaign to reclaim the throne. Antigonus marched out with his superior army to challenge him, but Pyrrhus caught Antigonus' forces by surprise just as they were entering a narrow gorge and cut down the rearguard of mercenary Gauls. In the utter confusion of the surprise attack the elephant drivers surrendered their beasts, and Antigonus' Macedonian phalanx, when they saw Pyrrhus, in person, appealing to them and calling on the officers by name, defected en masse. Antigonus fled to the coast to protect his cities there while Pyrrhus advanced into Pieria and captured Aegae. Control of the ancient sacred capital was a major coup for Pyrrhus, who now claimed the Macedonian throne for a second time. He was already popular, and his popularity might have soared had he not left his band of Gauls to garrison the city. In his absence they plundered the royal tombs, a sacrilegious act that could not help but anger and disgust the Macedonians. Yet Pyrrhus did nothing to punish the Gauls for the outrage.[12] There is a story that Lysimachus had once raided Epirus when Pyrrhus was absent, destroyed the royal tombs, and scattered the bones of the dead.[13] Perhaps Pyrrhus thought one injustice justified another. The Macedonians saw it otherwise, and it spelled the end of Pyrrhus' popularity.

Antigonus, meanwhile, after losing another battle, this time against Pyrrhus' son Ptolemy, was driven out of Macedonia altogether, and fled with only seven Companions. He still had the security of his fleet, and when Pyrrhus, at the invitation of the dispossessed Spartan royal Cleonymus, went off to attack Sparta in 272 Antigonus began to recover the Macedonian coastal cities he had lost. Pyrrhus' strategy was to get control of the Peloponnese and weaken Antigonus' support there, but at Sparta his siege was repulsed (partly thanks to a general of Antigonus who had come with mercenaries to her defence) and his son Ptolemy was killed. Antigonus himself came with an army to Argos, and Pyrrhus, with his Aeacid blood fired up, challenged Antigonus to meet him in a duel outside the walls of Argos, the winner to claim the Macedonian throne, but Antigonus cautiously declined. In street fighting shortly after Pyrrhus was struck on the neck by a roof tile thrown by an old woman, captured while still in a swoon, and decapitated.[14]

Antigonus could now turn unopposed to the work of stabilizing the state.[15] Macedonian affairs long since had been inextricably entangled in the affairs of the Greek states, and he seems first to have rallied a number of those states in the Peloponnese where he had alliances going back to his father's day. In addition to the 'fetters' garrisons were maintained in other critical locations, especially around and near the Saronic Gulf, such as at Piraeus, Sounion, Troezen, and probably Hydra. Craterus, son of the famous taxiarch Craterus, and Antigonus' half-brother (Antipater's daughter Phila was mother of both), was at one time or other in charge of one or more of these garrisons, his role being perhaps *strategos* of the Peloponnese; and Ameinias of Phocis, a former pirate captain and the one who had relieved Sparta, also served as commander.[16] The garrisons both secured the maintenance of the Antigonid fleet and kept the city-states from being logistically able to unite against Macedonia. The city-state system, largely thanks to Macedonia, had become quite impotent. Hegemony in the Greek mainland was part of Antigonus' policy to honour old Macedonian traditions associated with the Argeads. He also honoured Argead traditions along cultural lines by his continuance of intellectual court *symposia* and the cultivation of Greek poets and philosophers (Figure 10.1). He was a student of the Stoic philosopher Zeno and great friend of Persaeus of Cition, whom he later appointed as commander at Corinth and as tutor to one of his sons.[17] Like Philip II and Alexander III, it seems he spent little time in Macedonia, and as soon as his son Demetrius was old enough to assume responsibility, he left him to handle much of the governing of the kingdom.

As a challenge to Macedonian hegemony, federal states were now on the rise. In central Greece the Aetolians had been instrumental in defeating the Gauls at Thermopylae in 279, and soon after that they took over control of the Delphic Amphictyony.[18] As the Aetolian federation or League began to wield increasingly greater power, it did not at first come into conflict with Antigonid interests.[19] In the district of Achaea in the north central Peloponnese some twelve cities had long ago formed a federation to help protect themselves against the former superpowers Sparta, Corinth, and Argos, but by the beginning of the third

Figure 10.1 Panel from the Villa Boscoreale fresco, first century BCE Roman copy of a Hellenistic painting group depicting (probably) Macedonian royals of the third century BCE in a court setting with a philosopher (out of frame, left). Museo Archeologico Nazionale, Naples, Italy

Source: courtesy of Bridgeman Images.

century this federation had been dissolved. Around 280 the Achaean League was revived, this being made possible by the state of anarchy in Macedonia and the consequent weakened Macedonian influence in the Peloponnese.[20] Once it was clear that Antigonus was making a substantial recovery, the cities of the Achaean League formed an alliance with a number of other southern Greek city-states, chiefly Athens and Sparta, and with Ptolemy II in Egypt, who was vying with Antigonus for naval control in the Aegean and whose sister-wife Arsinoe II still had designs on Macedonia. In response, Antigonus marched an army into Attica; the date is not secure but perhaps in 267. Events of the ensuing Chremonidean War, which took its name from the Athenian Chremonides, who proposed the alliance, and its cause are obscure.[21] But by 262 Antigonus had the upper hand, having rendered the Egyptian fleet of Ptolemy II useless, defeated and killed the Spartan king Areus at Corinth, forced Athens to surrender under siege, and installed a Macedonian garrison on the Mouseion hill, overlooking the Pnyx, where the Athenians met for assembly.[22] About this same time Pyrrhus' son Alexander II, who had succeeded to the throne of Epirus, invaded Macedonia in Antigonus' absence. He was promptly driven out again, reputedly defeated by Antigonus' son Demetrius, though the latter at this date was only about fifteen.[23]

A period of stability ensued in the south, such that in 255 Antigonus removed his garrison from Mouseion hill, and the naval conflict with Ptolemy II in the Aegean was suspended by treaty.[24] By this time Antigonus' son Demetrius was beginning to take on administrative duties within Macedonia proper.[25] Most evidence for the system of governance of the cities and towns throughout the several regions of the kingdom comes from scattered and mostly late inscriptions. These suggest that the larger cities were self-governing in civil affairs, and that each seems to have governed its affairs in its own distinct way, with assembly, council, and officials, including *epistatai* (overseers) and *dikastai* (judges). Historians have debated whether these officials were local or royal appointments, but either way it seems assured they answered to the king.[26]

If Antigonus was lulled into a sense of security, it was soon interrupted. About 252 he faced another major upheaval in the south when his commander of the garrison at Corinth, his nephew Alexander son of Craterus, revolted.[27] The garrisons at Chalcis and Eretria joined the revolt, and Alexander set himself up as "king" in Euboea, though he seems to have kept his seat of power at Corinth. The reason(s) for the revolt is not known, and about the war that ensued we know only that with the aid of pirates Alexander attempted to seize Athens, and that he died at Corinth before or about 245, allegedly poisoned by Antigonus. Around the same time as Alexander's revolt Aratus of Sicyon seized control of his native city from the Macedonian-backed 'tyranny' and brought about its membership in the Achaean League, of which he soon was elected *strategos*.[28] Alexander, rather than fighting Aratus, also aligned himself with the League.[28] The Achaean League's purpose now became the expulsion of the Macedonians and pro-Macedonian 'tyrants' from the Peloponnese.[29] When Alexander died control of Corinth devolved upon his wife Nicaea. Desperate

Figure 10.2 Acrocorinth, gateway to the Peloponnese, one of the three Macedonian 'fetters' of Greece
Source: author, 2011.

to regain command of the garrison, Antigonus proposed a marriage alliance between Nicaea and his son Demetrius. Though she consented to the marriage, she did not relinquish control of the garrison. So during the wedding celebrations Antigonus tricked the garrison guards into opening the gate on the Acrocorinth citadel (Figure 10.2) and seized control. What became of the nuptials and Nicaea is unknown.[30]

Antigonus then dealt with Ptolemy II, who possibly was the instigator of Alexander's revolt; at any rate, Ptolemy had funded Aratus' attempts to gain control of Corinth. In a naval battle off Andros Antigonus decisively demonstrated the superiority of the Antigonid fleet over the Egyptian fleet, and Ptolemy was driven from the Aegean (at the time he was also embroiled in the Third Syrian War with the Seleucids).[31] Only a couple of years later Aratus found a way to seize Corinth himself by trickery, bribing a garrison guard to reveal a weakness in the defences, then infiltrating the city by cover of night, storming and seizing the citadel, and capturing in addition twenty-five of Antigonus' ships and 500 horses.[32] The loss of Corinth was a serious blow to Macedonian dominance in the south.[33] It meant the loss of a major port and shipyards as well as control of the gateway to the Peloponnese, and it signaled to Argos and other pro-Macedonian city-states that it might be time to reconsider the power game. A Macedonian garrison did continue to hold the Piraeus, but after bringing Corinth into the

Achaean League Aratus quickly won over Megara, Troezen, and Epidaurus, thus all but shutting Antigonus out of the Saronic Gulf. Aratus then began to undermine Macedonian control of Athens by invading Salamis and Attica and trying to bring Athens into the League, though he was unsuccessful.[34] Antigonus evidently did not try to regain Corinth, and he died a few years later in the spring of 239, after a reign of nearly forty years.[35] The elevation of his son Demetrius to a prominent military and administrative role ensured a smooth succession and the establishment of a new dynasty.[36]

Demetrius II, Antigonus III Doson, and the Greek resistance

By 239 Alexander II of Epirus also had died, and his young son Pyrrhus II succeeded, perhaps under the guardianship of Alexander's widow (and half-sister) Olympias. When the Aetolians seized the hour of transition to advance into western Acarnania, which Epirus controlled, Olympias sought aid from Demetrius II. The two ruling houses, putting aside recent enmity, formed an alliance through marriage, Demetrius taking Alexander II's daughter Phthia to wife.[37] This compelled the Aetolians to ally themselves with Aratus and the Achaean League.[38] Much of Demetrius' ten-year reign was spent in the struggle to maintain Macedonian influence against this powerful Aetolian–Achaean alliance.[39] In the so-called Demetrian War Demetrius induced the Boeotians to abandon their alliance with the Aetolians,[40] and about 235 he advanced into southern Greece, hoping to hold onto Megalopolis, Argos, and a few smaller Peloponnesian cities that were still governed by pro-Macedonian factions. Argos three times fended off the attacks of Aratus,[41] and though Macedonia still had a garrison in the Piraeus, Aratus also persisted in efforts to seize Athens, forcing Demetrius to come to the city's defence.[42] But when the ruler of Megalopolis, Lydiades, decided to abandon his allegiance to Demetrius and bring his city over to the Achaean League Macedonian influence suffered a reversal. Lydiades was promptly elected *strategos* of the Achaean League,[43] and for the next few years he held the office of *strategos* in alternating years with Aratus. When Aratus was again *strategos* Demetrius' general Bithys defeated him in battle at Phylacia in Arcadia.[44] Then Demetrius' attention was drawn away by the sudden turn of events in Epirus.

In Epirus the royal line was imploding. Pyrrhus II was dead, his younger brother Ptolemy assumed the throne briefly, then he died while on campaign against Ambracia. Their mother, Olympias, died soon after, so of the royal line only two daughters of Pyrrhus remained,[45] and one of these, Deidameia, when she tried to assume control of the state was mobbed and murdered. Thus by revolution the long-reigning Aeacid monarchy was overthrown and in its place a republican government established.[46] This created something of a power vacuum that threatened to leave the western frontier of Macedonia unstable. The Aetolians promptly advanced against western Acarnania, intending to seize it from Epirote control, and the Acarnanians appealed to Demetrius for aid.

Demetrius was already committed to supplying Bithys with a large force in the Peloponnese to fight the Achaean League and was evidently occupied elsewhere (at some point he invaded and ravaged the territory of Aetolia, causing the inhabitants of Pleuron to relocate their city),[47] so he approached Agron, king of the Ardiaean Illyrians, for help and paid him to relieve the Acarnanian city Medion from an Aetolian siege. In the fall of 231 Agron with a fleet of 100 small raiding ships (*lembi*) manned by 5,000 Illyrian pirates defeated the Aetolian army at Medion and sailed away with the booty.[48] Agron died of illness soon after, and his wife Teuta assumed power. For the next three years Illyrian pirates raided up and down the Adriatic coast, including the western Peloponnese, and captured a number of positions from Epirote and Macedonian hands. In 229 in a naval battle off Paxos Teuta's Illyrians defeated the feeble Aetolian and Achaean fleet, the result being the capitulation of the Corcyraeans to an Illyrian siege, the installation of an Illyrian garrison under command of Demetrius of Pharos, and a notice to the Romans that Adriatic shipping was prey to Illyrian piracy.[49] The Romans thus had their attention first draw to the east.

Amidst the general upheaval in the northwest another tribe of Illyrians, the Dardani, under the leadership of Longarus, took advantage of Demetrius' preoccupation to invade Macedonia. Demetrius was defeated in battle and died either during the campaign or soon after, leaving behind as successor his son Philip, about nine years old.[50] Demetrius had fathered Philip about 238, a year or so after he married Phthia, and one would expect that she was the mother; however, sources that name Philip's mother call her Chryseis, who is said to have been a captive of Demetrius.[51] It is possible that Demetrius, whose first wife Stratonice, sister of Antiochus II, did not appreciate her husband's polygamy and returned home when he married Phthia, was married to both Phthia and Chryseis in 238 (if these are not two names for the same woman). The alienation of Stratonice had dire consequences, it seems, for it antagonized the Seleucid dynasty of Syria.[52] At the point of succession the kingdom was in a state of turmoil, and fearing anarchy (again) the leading Macedonians called upon Demetrius' cousin Antigonus Doson, son of Antigonus Gonatas' half-brother Demetrius (the Fair), to assume guardianship of the heir, and he married the child's mother on the condition that he would not raise any sons by her of his own.[53]

The death of Demetrius II occasioned a shift in the balance of power in the Peloponnese, when the Macedonian-backed rulers realigned themselves with the Achaean League. Demetrius had been buying their loyalty, and when that incentive was removed, and Aratus offered them other rewards—Aristomachus of Argos was soon elected *strategos* of the Achaean League—they saw no advantage in maintaining a pro-Macedonian stance.[54] It was thus at a serious disadvantage that Antigonus Doson began his period of rule. He first had to drive the Illyrians out of Macedonia and secure the northern frontier. During the Dardanian war the Aetolians had overrun Thessaly, so he next proceeded to drive them out again, and then he carried his campaign into Phocis and Doris.[55] While Antigonus was still occupied with securing the kingdom's frontiers, in 229 the

Macedonian garrison commander in the Piraeus, Diogenes, accepted the handsome price of 150 talents to surrender the garrisons in Piraeus, Munychia, Salamis, and Sounion.[56] Athens thus at long last gained her freedom, but Aratus did not win the hoped-for Achaean League membership of Athens; the Athenians assumed a position of neutrality.

Having lost both the Peloponnese and Attica, Antigonus hoped to hold Boeotia, but he was forced to cede control there as well, though he did hold onto his garrison at Chalcis in Euboea.[57] In the west three years of Illyrian pirates raiding along the eastern Adriatic had drawn the attention of Rome, and a Roman army invaded Illyria by land and sea. In this First Illyrian War (229–228) the Romans freed Corcyra, Pharos, Apollonia, and Epidamnus from Agron's widow Teuta, as well as the island Issa; and when they marched inland they brought the Illyrian tribe Atintani into alliance with Rome.[58] The Romans did not leave an occupation force, and there is no evidence of contact between Rome and the Macedonian king at this time and no reason why there might have been.[59] Macedonian influence had so drastically waned under Demetrius II that the Illyrian coast was not a Macedonian concern, though Demetrius' hiring of Agron had set in motion a chain a events that would soon bring Rome into conflict with Macedonian and Greek powers. Antigonus was successfully occupied in pushing the Aetolians back and forcing their League to come to terms, and perhaps as recognition of his success in securing the northern and southern borders of the kingdom the Macedonian army acclaimed him "king." Antigonus III Doson took up the kingship *in addition* to guardianship, rather than in place of it, for having adopted the heir Philip, and having demonstrated to the leading nobles his good leadership, Philip's succession was (theoretically) secure.[60]

While Antigonus III turned his attention and a revitalized fleet eastward in 227 to campaign in Caria,[61] the Achaean League was deeply embroiled in a war with the Spartan king, Cleomenes III, who was spearheading a resurgence of Spartan power in the Peloponnese.[62] The Cleomenic War had deep roots in social reform at Sparta, but the trigger for trouble with the Achaean League was Cleomenes' seizure of three member city-states of the Aetolian League, Tegea, Mantinea, and Orchomenos, to which the Aetolians did not object since they wanted to see Spartan power supersede Achaean. The Aetolian League had broken with the Achaeans after the end of the Demetrian war and reverted to their former hostile position, which they shared with the Macedonian king. Cleomenes also fortified the Athenaion near Megalopolis, the latter being a member of the Achaean League.[63] So the Megalopolitans, with Aratus' urging and doubtless uneasy that Macedonia would ally with the Aetolians and Cleomenes to crush Achaean power, brought before the League the proposal to appeal to the Macedonian monarchy for alliance. The proposal passed, and Antigonus agreed by formal letter to offer his assistance. But his price evidently was too high; or Aratus had thought twice about becoming indebted to the Macedonian king.[64] At any rate, Macedonian assistance was not called in at this time. Over the course of the next year the Achaeans began to suffer heavy losses, including the death of the alternating *strategos* Lydiades, and were becoming desperate, so Aratus sent his own son to renegotiate with Antigonus. But again Aratus balked at the price for aid, which now, if not earlier, was set at the handing over of the garrison at Corinth. When Cleomenes proceeded to win over many Achaean League states, among them Epidaurus, Troezen, and Argos, the Corinthians drove Aratus out and turned their city over to Cleomenes. An Achaean garrison still held the Acrocorinth, but Aratus finally thought fit to hand it over to Antigonus in exchange for military support.[65]

In the spring of 224 an army of 20,000 Macedonian veteran infantry and 1,400 cavalry under Antigonus' command marched to the Isthmus. Cleomenes was entrenched for resistance, but the proximity of the Macedonians encouraged a faction in Argos to bring about a revolt. Cleomenes tried but failed to retake Argos, and so he retreated to Sparta, leaving Antigonus free, finally, to retake possession of Corinth and the shipyards, which had been out of Macedonian control for nearly twenty years.[66] Antigonus promptly advanced to Argos and from there proceeded to capture some Spartan forts in Arcadia. At Aegion he attended the congress of the Achaean League, and out of that meeting came a new Hellenic League, or Symmachy: a league of all Greek allies committed to the war against Cleomenes. It was something of a revival of the short-lived Hellenic League of Demetrius I, and also of the League of Corinth of Philip II and Alexander III, though it was comprised not of individual city-states but rather of constituted leagues. The alliance included, in addition to the Achaeans, the Epirotes, Phocians, Boeotians, Acarnanians, Thessalians (though they were under Macedonian control), and also the Macedonian *koinon*. The Macedonian citizen population was recognized as a "commons," but the *koinon* did not act outside the authority of the king.[67] The Macedonian king was appointed *hegemon* of the League for carrying on the war.[68]

After wintering at Corinth and Sicyon, in the spring of 223 Antigonus marched to Tegea, captured the city by siege, and went on to capture Orchomenos (Figure 10.3), Mantinea, and some other Arcadian towns,[69] while Cleomenes after two attempts took Megalopolis, though only after filling out his ranks with freed helots. Of the helots Cleomenes had trained 2,000 in Macedonian weaponry to counter one of the units in Antigonus' army called *leucaspides* (white shields).[70] In something of a stalemate Antigonus spent the winter of 223–222 at Argos, having sent all his Macedonian troops home for the winter and keeping only his mercenaries.[71] In the spring, before the Macedonian and Achaean forces returned to service, Cleomenes began making trouble around Argos. But over that winter Ptolemy III had withdrawn his financial support for Cleomenes, and when the Spartan king could not provoke Antigonus into open battle he retreated to Laconia before his own troops could find out the financial situation.[72] In the early summer, after some of his 20,000 Macedonian infantry had returned, Antigonus went in pursuit. His army now totaled 27,600 foot and 1,200 horse (with a few hundred Cretan archers), of which 10,000 Macedonian infantry comprised his heavy phalanx, 3,000 were Macedonian peltasts, and 300 Macedonian cavalry.[73] The remainder included Agrianians, Gauls, Illyrians, and other mercenaries, as well as

Figure 10.3 Orchomenos, Arcadia. A Macedonian garrison held this strategic position in the late 220s

Source: author, 2015.

Greek allies from the Achaean League, Boeotia, Epirus, Acarnania, and 1,000 Megalopolitans trained in Macedonian weapons.[74] Cleomenes came as far as Sellasia to block Antigonus' advance with an army of only 20,000, consisting of Spartans, *perioecoi* (non-enfranchised Laconians), allies, and mercenaries. Cleomenes had the advantageous position on well fortified high ground, but the bold actions of a young Megalopolitan, Philopoemen, turned the tide of battle against the Spartans. Then Antigonus ordered his Macedonian foot into their unique double- phalanx formation, and Cleomenes' army was routed and defeated. Cleomenes fled to Alexandria, while Antigonus III Doson marched into Sparta and, overthrowing the recent reforms, re-established the old constitution.[75] For the first time in its long history Sparta suffered a foreign occupation. Macedonian influence was resurgent in the Peloponnese; the Greek resistance had been broken.

Only a few days after the battle Antigonus received word that the Illyrians had overrun the northern border of his kingdom. Stopping briefly at Tegea and Argos, where he received honours at the Nemean games, he made a rapid return to Macedonia. He defeated the Illyrians in a major battle, but in overexerting himself it is said he ruptured his lung and died of hemorrhage. There was no question about who was to succeed: his adopted son Philip, son of Demetrius II, who was only seventeen.[76]

Philip V: the Macedonian wars and the advance of Rome

Philip V began his long reign of forty-two years in a position of strength, though he was very young. He had been left in the care of advisors and officers whom Antigonus III had carefully chosen for the security of succession and the smooth running of the state (or so he thought). Among these were Apelles, one of the *epitropoi*, guardians of the underage heir;[77] Leontius, commander of the peltasts; Megaleas, the secretary; Taurion, general of the Peloponnese; and Alexander, commander of the Bodyguard.[78] Philip inherited Antigonus Doson's influence in the Peloponnese as well as the Macedonian garrisons at Corinth and (recently) Orchomenos, which controlled a main route into Arcadia from the northeast.[79] However, Philip came to the throne at a time when a powerful newcomer to political and military affairs in the Greek states and Hellenized east was just emerging on the western horizon. Apart from their periodic establishment of garrisons along the Adriatic coast, the Macedonian kings had never looked seriously towards the west. But it was no longer possible not to look west. The Romans had already crossed the Adriatic in 229 to deal with the raids of the Ardiaei that were threatening their shipping lanes. Again, in 219 the Second Illyrian War brought the Romans across the Adriatic, when Demetrius of Pharos violated the treaty that concluded the earlier Illyrian War by pillaging Illyrian cities that were allied with Rome and, in company with the Illyrian commander Scerdilaidas, sailing south of the treaty-stipulated boundary of Lissus with ninety Illyrian ships and raiding the coast. He was defeated by a Roman army under the consul L. Aemilius Paullus at Dimalion (inland from Apollonia), escaped, and fled to Philip.[80] Demetrius expected Macedonian support in return for the military service he had rendered Antigonus Doson. Also in 219 the Carthaginian general Hannibal Barca began the siege of Saguntum in Spain that provoked the Roman Senate into a declaration of war with Carthage, the Second Punic War (218–201), and the following year Hannibal invaded Italy from the north after crossing the Alps with his Carthaginian army, elephants and all.[81]

The period of Rome's rise as a world power and advance into the eastern Mediterranean is well documented by two major literary sources: the contemporary Greek historian Polybius, a native of Megalopolis, who in 170–169 served as *hipparchos* of the Achaean League (his father had been *strategos*) and in 167 was taken to Rome as a political hostage; and the Roman historian Livy, writing in the late Republican/early Augustan period and relying heavily upon Polybius' earlier work.[82] Polybius' history begins, as he explains, at the point when the Greeks were on the eve of the Social War and the Romans of the Hannibalic (Punic) War—an epochal time in Hellenistic history when three young kings, all within a few years, succeeded to the thrones of the three major Successor kingdoms. In addition to Philip V, in Egypt Ptolemy IV Philopator succeeded his father Ptolemy III Euergetes (grandson of the Successor Ptolemy I), and in Syria Antiochus III succeeded his brother Seleucus III (sons of Seleucus II Callinicus, great-grandson of the Successor Seleucus I).[83] All three young kings were faced with challenges such as habitually plague the transition of a throne. For Philip the initial challenge was the alliance of the Aetolian League with Cleomenes' successor at Sparta, Lycurgus, and their bid for power in the Peloponnese.

At the end of the Cleomenic War Antigonus Doson had established a general peace in southern Greece. But the Aetolians, deriding the youth of Philip V, were taking aggressive action in the Peloponnese as well as in Epirus and Acarnania. They greatly provoked both the Achaeans and Taurion, the Macedonian *strategos*, when, marching straight through Achaean territory, they invaded Messenia. The Aetolians defeated some Achaean League forces in a battle at Caphyae in Arcadia, and so the Achaeans called on their allies of the newly reconstituted Hellenic League and the Macedonian king for aid.[84] Though Taurion did give some support to the Achaeans, Philip was reluctant to end the general peace with Aetolia.[85] When the Aetolians continued to harass Achaean territory and destroyed the northern town of Cynaetha Philip, all too eager to get started on an illustrious career, then marched south with an army and called the Hellenic allies to a congress at Corinth. He presided over it himself, with his advisors at his elbow, and war was declared on the Aetolians, the so-called Social War (or War of Allies, 220–217).[86] Philip also met with Spartan envoys at Tegea, but despite their pledges to maintain peace, he did not succeed in preventing a Spartan alliance with the Aetolians.[87]

Philip spent the winter of 220–219 back in Macedonia making preparations for war and attending to his borders, since his absence had encouraged the Dardani to attempt raids across the northern frontier. This led to an alliance with Scerdilaidas, a younger brother of Agron and long-time commander of Illyrian forces, who was ambitious of carving out a large Illyrian kingdom for himself. He had gone unrewarded for his recent support of the Aetolians at Cynaetha, so he now accepted an annual payment of twenty talents from Philip to attack the Aetolians by sea.[88] In the spring the Aetolian–Spartan alliance launched a three-pronged attack against the Achaea League.[89] The Achaeans counted on Philip to come as planned, but it was approaching summer when Philip finally set out from Macedonia with an army of 10,000 heavy infantry, 5,000 peltasts, and 800 cavalry, all Macedonians, making his way through Thessaly to Epirus, where he was joined by the Epirote army, and thence to Ambracia, which was the prime objective of the Epirotes.[90] This was a costly enterprise, for the Aetolians promptly marched into Lower Macedonia, destroyed the crops in Pieria, and thoroughly sacked sacred Dion; the walls, houses, and gymnasium were demolished, the colonnade of the sanctuary burned, sacred monuments destroyed, and the royal statues thrown down.[91] When Philip heard the news he continued with his siege of Ambracia, captured it after forty days, and, handing it over to the Epirotes, invaded Aetolia, attacking towns and laying waste the countryside. He had captured Oeniadae and already put time into building a wall around the dockyards there when a dispatch reached him that the Dardani were preparing to invade Macedonia again. Abandoning his mission of crossing to the Peloponnese to help the Achaeans, he hurried back to Pella. The Dardani called off their invasion, so Philip sent his forces home to bring in the harvest and went to Larissa for the rest of the summer.[92]

That Dion could be sacked in the king's absence and that Philip had always to rush back to Macedonia at news of a Dardanian threat indicates that the bulk of military resources were being used in foreign theatres of war, while the kingdom was left insufficiently guarded. At the onset of winter 219–218 Philip re-mustered a smaller force of 3,000 *chalcaspides* (bronze shields), 2,000 peltasts, 300 Cretans, and 400 cavalry,[93] and, making a quick march to the Peloponnese via Euboea, he had defeated a small force of Eleans near Stymphalos before most of the Peloponnesians even knew of his arrival.[94] By midwinter many towns in the Aetolian alliance had either succumbed to siege or surrendered to Philip's authority.[95] He had not yet turned twenty, yet he was getting the upper hand in the Peloponnese and winning popularity. His advisors, Apelles and Leontius, aimed to re-establish Macedonian hegemony at the cost of Achaean power, naturally, and so Aratus, defensively, became uncooperative in supplying the Macedonian army with corn and pay.[96] Aratus managed a private meeting with Philip without his advisors, and Philip agreed to give Aratus political backing within the Achaean League, while the League in return gave Philip a handsome salary for his military support.[97] Philip continued the campaign with a naval attack on Cephallenia (after training his phalanx to row!), and then sailing to the Gulf of Ambracia and marching inland he thoroughly sacked Thermon in Aetolia in retaliation for the Aetolian sack of Dion.[98]

The successful cooperation of Philip with Aratus aggravated Philip's circle of advisors. After a confrontation between Aratus and Megaleas Philip arrested the latter and put him on trial. Megaleas was convicted and fined, but Leontius gave surety and Megaleas was let go.[99] Later in the summer, after a mutinous uprising of the peltasts and *agema* (royal battalion), evidently on the grounds that they were not receiving their due—Philip had sold all the booty from the recent Laconia campaign at Tegea on his return—and after they attempted "to plunder the tents of the king's most prominent friends, and even to pull down the doors and break through the roof of the royal apartments," Philip sent the peltasts away to serve under Taurion, and once Leontius, their commander, was isolated, Philip had him executed without trial.[100] Megaleas fled, and when Philip's bodyguard Alexander came to arrest him he committed suicide. Apelles meantime had taken up residence at Chalcis and was continuing to exercise administrative powers in dealing with officials from both Thessaly and Macedonia. But Philip now ventured to assume full royal authority for himself, and when Apelles returned to Corinth Philip arrested him on suspicion of treason. With no prospect of a fair trial, Apelles also committed suicide.[101] Arbitrators from Rhodes and Chios had already approached Philip and the Aetolians about ending the war, but Philip stalled, sending his Macedonians home for the winter and going himself to Demetrias, where the last of the 'conspirators', one Ptolemaeus, was tried before "the Macedonians" and executed.[102] Aratus' influence over Philip, which is far more likely to be the cause of the demise of these advisors than that they were conspiring against their king, is indicative of the manipulability that plagued Philip to his end.

While the Aetolians and Achaeans dragged the Social War on into 217,[103] Philip turned his attention to the incessant raids of the Dardani, and by taking control of Bylazora in Paeonia at the pass into Macedonia from Dardania he secured his northern frontier. Then mustering forces from Upper Macedonia, Bottia (Emathia), and Amphaxitis, with the whole force he marched to southern Thessaly, where he achieved the important goal of securing Thessaly, Magnesia, and Demetrias from Aetolian plundering.[104] Philip promptly set sail for Corinth and thence to Nemea to attend the games in July. It was there that he received a dispatch from Macedonia informing him that Hannibal had defeated the Romans in a great battle (Lake Trasimene, June 217). Envisioning himself a great conqueror, Philip was incited to wrap up the Social War as soon as possible, so he could get on with his Illyrian campaign and after that cross to Italy. His ambition was fed by Demetrius of Pharos, who was now a wanted man at Rome; a Roman embassy to Philip demanding the surrender of Demetrius was the Macedonian king's first contact with Rome.[105] Peace was signed at Naupactus between Philip on behalf of the Hellenic League, including Achaea, and the Aetolians and their allies, each side keeping what they had.[106]

Philip returned to Macedonia to find that his erstwhile ally Scerdilaidas had made significant inroads in the northwestern regions, especially in Pelagonia and Dassaretis. So he spent the rest of the season recovering his losses until time came to disband his army for the winter. Over the winter he ordered 100 ships to be built in preparation for an invasion of Illyrian territory from the Adriatic, though, as it turned out, the campaign was a fiasco, aborted when Philip heard that a fleet of Roman quinquiremes was on its way to Apollonia in support of Scerdilaidas. This was about the time the Romans suffered their defeat to Hannibal at Cannae (August 216). The Roman fleet turned out to be a mere ten ships, but Philip had already retreated to Cephallenia before he found that out, so the whole affair was embarrassing and damaging to his reputation.[107]

As the business of conquest was going well for the invaders of Italy (three major Carthaginian victories), the following year, 215, Philip made an alliance with Hannibal. The treaty, the text of which Polybius has preserved, indicates that Philip expected to keep Rome from gaining control of Illyria—that a peace agreement concluded upon the Carthaginian victory in the war should stipulate that: "the Romans shall no longer be masters of Corcyra, Apollonia, Epidamnus, Pharos, Dimale [Dimalion], Parthini, or Atintania; and that they shall return to Demetrius of Pharos all his friends who are in the dominions of Rome."[108] The Romans, discovering the treaty when they captured Philip's envoys, were legitimately concerned that Philip was indeed preparing to invade Italy, and in 214 when they learned that Philip had brought his fleet up to the Illyrian coast and was preparing to besiege Apollonia, which had been under Roman protection since the First Illyrian War, they sent M. Valerius Laevinus across the Adriatic with a fleet to stop him. A Roman detachment infiltrated Philip's poorly guarded camp by night, and the king fled to his ships on the Aous River, but when he found Laevinus' fleet guarding the river's mouth he burned his ships and with his despoiled army headed overland for Macedonia.[109] Once again Philip's ignominious retreat damaged his military reputation.

The ultimate goal of Philip, to achieve fame and glory akin to the illustrious Philip II and Alexander III, whom he *claimed* were his ancestors, though he was descended from Antipater and Antigonus I,[110] was eluding him as he suffered repeated humiliating defeats. That same year Demetrius of Pharos was killed while trying to capture Messene on Philip's behalf,[111] and Aratus, who had distanced himself from Philip (Philip was having an affair with his daughter-in-law and later married her), died in 213, allegedly by poison on Philip's orders, though the charge is doubtful.[112] Philip campaigned in Illyria again, invading overland from Macedonia, since he had lost his fleet, and when he captured coastal Lissus north of Apollonia he drew more fire from Rome.[113] The Roman Senate, deciding it was better to make war against Philip on his side of the Adriatic, sent Laevinus to Aetolia to negotiate an alliance against Philip.

The Aetolians needed little encouragement to break their peace with Macedonia, and by 211 the Aetolian League had formed an anti-Macedonian alliance with Rome and Attalus I of Pergamon, a lesser Successor kingdom in northwestern Asia Minor.[114] Laevinus returned to Rome confident that there was no need to commit a legion to Greece.[115] Philip at the time was busy rehabilitating his military reputation. With a raid on Apollonia, where he had been defeated in 214, then a raid into Pelagonia and seizure of the Dardanian city Sintia, followed by a successful campaign against the Maedi in Thrace,[116] he turned his war game around. All these raids were made to intimidate the tribes bordering on the Macedonian kingdom so that Philip could turn his attention to his war with the Aetolian League. While Philip was occupied in the north, the Aetolians renewed their old alliance with Sparta.[117] Despite this, when Philip did turn his attention south again he quickly got the upper hand in the war.[118] After presiding over the Nemean games of 209 he met with the Achaean League at Aegion and rejected proposals for peace with the Aetolians.[119] Then after a raid into Elis[120] word reached him that the Dardani were causing trouble on the frontier, so he made a hasty march back to Demetrias. By the time he arrived the Dardani had already invaded Orestis, emboldened by the false report that Philip was dead—he had broken a horn off his helmet in an earlier battle, and an Aetolian soldier had found it and carried it to Scerdilaidas, who recognized it as Philip's.[121] Philip again dealt with the Dardanian threat, while embassies flooded his court, from Achaea, Boeotia, Euboea, Acarnania, and Epirus, begging for his aid and protection against the incursions of Rome and her allies, the Aetolians and Attalus I.[122]

Attalus I in company with a Roman fleet under command of P. Sulpicius Galba had seized Oreus in Euboea, a task made easy when Philip's commander betrayed the city. The 'fetter' Chalcis was the next target, but the Macedonian garrison there remained loyal, and Philip, marching out to its defence, surprised Attalus' troops in Locris and drove them into flight. The Roman fleet gave up on Chalcis and returned to Aegina (which the Romans had captured in 210), and Attalus beat a hasty retreat to Asia Minor.[123] Though by this time arbitrators had approached Philip about a peace, his recent victories inclined him not to settle.[124] By 206, after Philip had sacked the sanctuary at Thermon a second time, the Aetolians, when Roman support appeared to have failed them, were compelled to conclude peace with Philip.[125] The Romans took issue with the peace and provoked a new confrontation with Philip along the Illyrian coast, but both sides refrained from open battle.[126] The First Macedonian War with Rome, which had lasted ten years (215–205), was concluded the following year when Philip was invited to peace talks at Phoenice in Epirus. The Peace of Phoenice in 205, which included the allies on both sides, granted to the Romans a number of small Illyrian towns on the Adriatic and to Philip Atintania in Epirus.[127] Philip had wanted to gain territory, and he had expected help from the Carthaginians, but that help never came. By this time Hannibal's brother Hasdrubal had been defeated at the Metaurus River, and Hannibal himself was hemmed in at Bruttium in southern Italy.[128] Rome had wanted to keep Philip from crossing to Italy and supporting Hannibal, and in that they were entirely successful.[129] Rome now concentrated on driving Hannibal out of Italy altogether, while Philip gave up on the west and looked east.

Before his peace with the Aetolians Philip had begun construction of 100 warships at Cassandreia.[130] These were near ready when a situation arose that prompted Antiochus III, ruler of the Seleucid Empire, to approach Philip about an alliance. Ptolemy IV died in 204, leaving his six-year-old son as successor; and when the native Egyptian population seized the occasion to revolt a weak Ptolemaic kingdom appeared ripe for the picking.[131] Antiochus invaded Ptolemaic territory in Koile Syria in 202,[132] the same year P. Cornelius Scipio defeated Hannibal at Zama near Carthage, precipitating the end of the Second Punic War.[133] Philip followed up with raids in the Aegean and Asia Minor, concluding treaties with Chalcedon and Lysimacheia (Figure 10.4),[134] and this aggressive policy put him afoul of Rhodes and Athens.[135] These two states along with Attalus I of Pergamon and Ptolemaic Alexandria now sent envoys to Rome to ask for intervention in the Aegean.[136] Rome sent warnings to both Philip and Antiochus not to encroach on Ptolemaic territory, but Philip, when the envoy reached him while he was besieging Abydos, rebuffed Rome's ultimatum and thus was ignited the Second Macedonian War (200–197).[137]

This time the Romans took the war to Philip's territory. The 'fetter' Chalcis was their first target; they attacked and sacked it, though they did not have the manpower to occupy it, while Philip ravaged Attica in retaliation.[138] Many times Philip had answered the call of the Achaeans, but they and the Aetolians, his allies by treaty, now remained neutral. The Macedonian-led Hellenic League was all but defunct.[139] The following year, 199, a Roman army marched inland from Apollonia through Illyria, where the general Galba had gained as allies Scerdilaidas' son Pleuratus and Bato, son of Longarus, king of the Dardani. Amynander, king of the Epirote Athamanes, also offered his support to the Romans.[140] In Dassaretis, where the Romans made camp, several skirmishes took place (Philip had a cavalry force of 2,000, with 20,000 foot, against Galba's estimated 25,000), but the Macedonians were shaken by their encounter with

Figure 10.4 Inscription of a treaty between Philip V and the citizens of Lysimacheia, 202–197 BCE. Dion

Source: author, 2013.

unfamiliar tactics and weapons, and when Philip's horse was wounded and threw him and he narrowly escaped with his life they retreated. Galba invaded and ran roughshod over Eordaea, Elimeia, and Orestis; then after attacking Keletron in Orestis and Pelion in Dassaretis the Romans marched back to Apollonia.[141] This was much to Philip's relief, since the Dardani had invaded Pelagonia, from which Philip had withdrawn his frontier guard for reinforcements, including his adolescent son Perseus,[142] and the Aetolians, perceiving the presence of a Roman army in western Macedonia to be a sign of Philip's waning power, in company with the Athamanes were raiding Thessaly. Philip was forced to divide his forces to deal with these simultaneously, and in both actions he was successful in driving out the enemy.[143]

Galba's replacement was utterly ineffectual over the winter,[144] so Philip, after reviving his waning popularity at home by imprisoning his admiral Heracleides of Tarentum, whose reprehensible actions had caused great resentment of Philip,[145] in the spring marched to Epirus and established a fortified position on the Aous River. The new Roman consul T. Quinctius Flamininus met with Philip at the

Aous in the summer of 198,[146] first for peace talks arranged by the Epirotes; then when Philip rejected in anger Rome's conditions for peace—relinquishing Thessaly being at top of the list—Flamininus, using a local guide, got part of his force into a commanding position behind Philip's fortified camp and, attacking from front and rear, drove the Macedonians into flight.[147] When news of the Roman victory reached the Aetolians and the Athamanes they wasted no time moving in on Philip's territory in Thessaly, and Flamininus soon followed. At Atrax north of the Peneus River the Macedonian garrison, with reinforcements sent from Philip, who entrenched himself in the Vale of Tempe, gave the Romans a taste of the famous Macedonian phalanx, with its impenetrable hedge of *sarissai*, and Flamininus was forced to retreat and seek winter quarters.[148]

A second round of peace talks was held near Nicaea in the late fall, and following that Philip sent envoys to Rome over the winter of 198–197.[149] Philip, once the "darling of the whole of Greece," now was dangerously low on allies.[150] At the time of the ultimatum before the war the Romans had demanded that Philip stop making war on Greek states. Now they demanded that the Greeks be granted their freedom and that Philip withdraw his garrisons, especially from the 'fetters' Chalcis, Corinth, and Demetrias. When Philip's envoys were specifically asked about the latter they were tongue-tied; the king was prepared to concede his conquests in Illyria, Thrace, and Asia Minor but not the possessions he had inherited in the south. By that winter Titus Flamininus' brother Lucius, in command of the Roman fleet, had seized Eretria, another of the Macedonian garrisoned cities in Euboea. Titus himself had relieved Elataea in Phocis of its garrison, taking control of most of Phocis and Locris, and had won over the Achaean League with the exclusion of Argos. The Achaeans together with Attalus and Lucius, who had already captured the Corinthian port at Cenchreae, attempted but failed to dislodge the Macedonian garrison at Acrocorinth. So Philip still held Corinth as well as Dymae, Megalopolis, and Argos. Boeotia also that winter went over to the Roman side, and Acarnania capitulated to Rome the following spring, meaning Philip was physically shut out of central and southern Greece. And since he could not protect Argos, he gave it away to Nabis, who had seized control of Sparta in 207.[151] What T. Flamininus wanted was to finish the war by spear and sword, and when he found out that his consular command was prorogued he sabotaged the peace talks.

In June 197 at Cynoscephalae in Thessaly T. Flamininus with 18,000 Roman infantry and 2,500 cavalry supplemented by 8,000 Greek allies (most of which were sent by the Aetolian League) defeated Philip's army of 23,500 infantry and 2,000 cavalry.[152] It was a battle that Philip need not have lost, but a number of factors played against him. Morale was low because of the defeat at the Aous. Many of the recent recruits to his phalanx of 16,000 either were very young, and consequently undertrained and inexperienced, or were veterans past customary age of service.[153] And both terrain and weather were unfavourable. Flamininus, having marched north from Elataea via Phthiotic Thebes, and Philip, having marched south from Dion via Larissa, had arrived in the vicinity of Pherae, where intervening hills kept the two armies out of sight of one another. A long ridge lay between them as both armies made their way towards the grain fields near Scotussa. Then a dense fog descended, so thick the standards were obscured, and when a Roman scouting party surmounted the intervening ridge (the "dog-heads") and suddenly stumbled upon a Macedonian covering troop a skirmish developed. Both commanders sent reinforcements, and from the skirmish, as the fog lifted, a full-scale battle developed in haphazard fashion, for Philip ordered his army to climb the hill and descend on the enemy. The phalanx on Philip's right wing, which he led in person up the hill, charging downhill pushed the Roman forces back, but a Roman tribune saw opportunity in the vacated high ground, and taking twenty maniples he went around behind the phalanx, which being encumbered with the long *sarissai* was unable to manoeuvre, and from the higher ground to the rear the Roman maniples began to cut the Macedonian phalanx to pieces. When Philip saw his left, which because of the terrain had not been able to form up properly, fall apart in the face of Flamininus' elephant corps he abandoned the field and fled for Tempe with whatever forces he could round up, sending an officer to Larissa to burn his documents. He left behind 8,000 Macedonian dead, and another 5,000 were taken prisoner.[154]

Polybius attributed the Macedonian defeat to a fatal flaw of the phalanx, namely that it could operate only on flat ground with no obstacles and then only as a single massed unit.[155] Philip, then, had committed the tactical error of attempting to deploy in unsuitable terrain. The grave consequence was the demise of Macedonia's long-held military supremacy. Rome had revolutionized warfare, and the Macedonians had not kept apace.

The Roman settlement was generous in that Philip kept his throne and no Roman troops remained in Macedonia.[156] However, territory was lost, including long-held Thessaly, and his power was now confined to the kingdom of Macedonia. He was required to give up his fleet—all but five warships and his uselessly oversized royal flagship—surrender hostages and prisoners, and pay a war indemnity. His son Demetrius was among the hostages sent to Rome. The upper district Orestis, which after being invaded had sided with the Romans during the war, was granted autonomy,[157] and the kingdom, reduced nearly to its pre-Philip II boundaries, mainly the central plain and Thraceward to the Strymon, was now little more than a buffer zone between the 'barbarian' tribes of the north and the Greek states.[158] The Aetolians, claiming an instrumental role in the victory at Cynoscephalae, hoped to assume hegemony in the Greek mainland in the wake of the Macedonia defeat, but Roman garrisons now occupied Chalcis, Corinth, and Demetrias.[159] The following year at the Isthmian games near Corinth Flamininus announced the "freedom" of the Greeks, though Roman garrisons continued to hold Chalcis and Demetrias.[160]

Perseus, Rome, and the end of the monarchy

Philip's second war with the Romans had left his northern frontier vulnerable to yet another invasion of the Dardani.[161] Recruitment for a frontier campaign distracted from the recent defeat, and his success in driving out the invaders was a first step towards reviving Macedonian pride. Philip now chose a path of diplomacy, and after 196 he helped Rome defeat Antiochus III of Syria.[162]

Antiochus was Philip's former ally, but notably he had not come to the Macedonian king's aid, and in the aftermath of the battle at Cynoscephalae he ominously marched towards the Hellespont. The Senate sent him a warning similar to that given to Philip at Abydos in 200. Antiochus found such presumption ludicrous, but for the next few years he refrained from antagonizing Rome.[163] The Romans for their part were facing tremendous criticism for their handling of the Greek 'liberation'. The Aetolians were angry that they had not been duly rewarded for their role in defeating Philip—that the Greeks had merely traded Macedonian masters for Roman ones. Many Greeks complained about the Roman settlement with Nabis, 'tyrant' of Sparta, and general hatred was incited in Boeotia when Flamininus turned a blind eye to the murder of the Boeotarch (general) Brachylles, a long-time friend and agent of the Macedonian monarchy.[164] Hoping to gain Greek favour, the Romans held a second congress at Corinth in 194, and they withdrew all occupying forces, including the 'fetters'.[165] When it was rumoured that the Senate intended to restore Demetrias to Philip, the Aetolians seized Demetrias by trickery, assassinated Nabis at Sparta, and tried but failed to seize Chalcis.[166] At the invitation of the Aetolians Antiochus III crossed the Aegean to Demetrias in the fall of 192 as the new 'liberator' of the Greeks. Antiochus succeeded in taking control of Chalcis as well as some cities in Thessaly and much of Acarnania. But the following spring at Thermopylae he was defeated by the Roman coalition and retreated to Asia.[167]

Philip cooperated with the Romans in exchange for the release of his son Demetrius.[168] Philip and the Roman general Baebius had taken more than a dozen towns in Thessaly, as well as Athamania, and in the wake of Antiochus' defeat Philip made more gains both in central Greece and in Thrace, all of which Rome permitted. From Thrace Philip brought settlers to be incorporated into the military, and he reopened gold mines in Pangaion, in the Strymon region.[169] He also provided protective escort and supplies for the Roman advance through Thrace against Antiochus in 190. The Roman campaign culminated the following winter in the defeat of Antiochus "the Great" at Magnesia on the Maeander River in Lydia, when Antiochus' Macedonian-trained phalanx was bested by the Roman legions.[170] The balance of power in the eastern Mediterranean for more than a century had been fairly evenly weighted among the three great Hellenistic kingdoms. Antiochus had aimed to tip the scales and had been successful in destroying Ptolemaic naval power in the Aegean. But in the end the boundaries of his own Seleucid Empire in Asia Minor were pushed back beyond the Taurus Mountains and Halys River.[171] The Peace of Apamea between Antiochus III and Rome, concluded in 188, established Rome as the undisputed dominant power in the Mediterranean.[172]

Philip had never considered his defeat at Cynoscephalae to mark the end of Macedonian power, and he now availed himself of every opportunity to re-establish

Macedonian influence in neighbouring states.[173] When the Romans went home, as was their practice (up to now) after victories, he proceeded to extend his boundaries south and east, and soon Attalus' successor at Pergamon, Eumenes, was at Rome complaining about his aggression in Thrace, and the Athamanes, Perrhaebians, and Thessalians about his seizure of, or refusal to free, their towns and territory.[174] When the command came from Rome for Philip to remove his garrisons from Thessaly, Philip's defence was that he had not acted without Roman consent. When the same command came regarding Thrace, Philip (allegedly) arranged the slaughter of all the pro-Roman and pro-Eumenes inhabitants in Maroneia.[175] Afterwards he sent his son Demetrius to Rome again, this time to defend his actions. Demetrius returned to Macedonia with the message from the Senate that Rome accepted Philip's defence *and* that he owed his reprieve to his son.[176] In Polybius' view this was the beginning of war and also the beginning of the end for Demetrius, since both his father and his elder brother Perseus resented and suspected his favour at Rome, though his good standing there was the reason Philip had sent him.[177] Philip paid little heed to Roman diktats,[178] and as he began to relocate populations within his kingdom and import Thracian settlers with a view to better defence his actions alienated the uprooted Macedonian populace as well as some of the leading nobles, who preferred peace under Roman jurisdiction to another war. Demetrius perhaps became the standard-bearer for the aggrieved, though whether he 'plotted' with the Romans to secure succession or whether he fell victim to his brother's jealousy remains a question. Early in 180 Philip had Demetrius murdered on suspicion of treason.[179] Though Livy records an earlier "hearing" of the king between his sons in their rivalry, there was no trial. Less than two years later, in the summer of 179, Philip died at Amphipolis after a short illness.[180]

Perseus' accession cannot have been smooth. The recent elimination of Demetrius must have left many Macedonian nobles disaffected and relations with Rome strained. Moreover, Philip's killing of a number of his close advisors and his later ordering of the arrests of their relatives had created an atmosphere of fear. At home Perseus likely had to make a purge of potential rivals (Antigonus, a nephew of Antigonus Doson and loyal advisor of Philip, was executed),[181] but lest the Macedonians think they had entered into a reign of terror he issued a general amnesty for past offenses against the king: he recalled exiles and restored their property, cancelled debts owed to the crown, and released prisoners held on crown offenses. Rome's prompt affirmative to his request for renewal of his father's treaty constituted foreign endorsement of his kingship.[182] Approval of the Macedonians for their new king was boosted by his immediate display of military prowess with a victory over the Thracian king Abrupolis, who seized the moment of Philip's death—the end of a forty-two-year reign—to invade the Pangaion mining region.[183] Military success was absolutely critical for a Macedonian king's standing with the nobles, who from earliest times had either backed their monarch when he kept the 'barbarians' at bay or undermined his authority with factional strife when he showed signs of weakness.

Figure 10.5 Top of an inscribed *stele*, recording a treaty between Perseus and the Boeotians, 172 BCE. Dion

Source: author, 2013.

Early in his reign Perseus formed two royal marriage alliances, himself marrying Laodice, daughter of Seleucus IV (successor of Antiochus III), and his sister marrying Prusias II of Bithynia.[184] These dynastic alliances caused alarm for Eumenes at Pergamon; Bithynia on his northern border had long been hostile, and the Seleucids were bound to try to win back their losses in Asia Minor. It was at Eumenes' expense and Rome's that Perseus began to revive Macedonian's reputation and standing with the Greeks by forming new alliances with the Thessalians, Boeotians (Figure 10.5), Aetolians, and the Rhodians, with their strong fleet.[185] After subduing the Dolopians (they brutally murdered his governor) Perseus marched with his armed force to Delphi; perhaps a bit of bravado, but he did hold two votes in the Amphictyonic Council.[186] A resurgent Macedonia was not what the Greeks wanted, however, if it cost them their autonomy. The Achaeans, by slim majority, refused to ally with him, and the Athenians maintained a ban (effective probably since 200–199) on Macedonians entering Attica.[187]

Rome's policy all along had been *not* to keep a military presence in the Aegean Greek world, but at the same time the Senate was not willing to accept Macedonia as an equal power in the east.[188] By 172, while many Greeks favoured Perseus over Rome, others were looking to Eumenes as the only power in the east that might check Macedonia. Eumenes travelled to Rome and presented to the Senate a slate of complaints against Perseus, and Rome listened. While there were "a good many senators who regarded [Eumenes'] speech as a piece of self-interested and tendentious hyperbole," Rome prepared to declare war on Perseus, the Third Macedonian War (171–168).[189]

Perseus, it is true, had built up a strong military force and was well supplied with weapons and a large store of grain, and one of the charges against him was that he was preparing to make war on Rome.[190] However, the Dardani were a perennial threat, and Philip at the time of his death had been planning a joint campaign with the Bastarnae against Dardania.[191] When the Romans sent envoys and an armed force across the Adriatic in the fall of 172 Perseus sent them a letter asking for explanation of the military presence, and when the Romans proceeded to detach Greek states from their alliances with Perseus the king sent a second message requesting diplomatic talks.[192] Q. Marcius Philippus, son of an old friend of Philip V, met with Perseus at the Peneus River. Perseus obtained from him a truce allowing time to send envoys to Rome; he also used the time to try to secure allies.[193] The Macedonian envoys were given a hearing, but when the Senate did not accept Perseus' defense they were kicked out of Italy. Rome's intentions were clear: a force had already been sent to Thessaly to garrison Larissa. When Perseus' envoys returned he held a council at the royal palace at Pella. Opinions were divided whether in the interest of peace he should resist or knuckle under to whatever Rome demanded. Perseus' decision was war.[194]

For the next three years the consular armies sent out from Rome accomplished little against Perseus' forces, though they did infiltrate territory traditionally under Macedonian control. At the outset Perseus had 39,000 infantry of which perhaps 20,000 were Macedonian phalanx, 5,000 Macedonian special light troops (including the *agema*), and of 4,000 cavalry 3,000 were Macedonian. The remaining infantry were a mix of Paeonians, Agrianians, Thracians and Odrysians, Gauls, and Cretans; only 1,000 were from the Greek states.[195] In the fall of 171 Perseus marched his army via Eordaea and Elimeia into Perrhaebia and entrenched his forces near the entrance to the Vale of Tempe, where he could defend one of the main routes into Lower Macedonia.[196] Roman forces mustering with allies (Eumenes prominent among them) to the west at Larissa were near equal in numbers. Hoping to win the advantage with superior cavalry, Perseus advanced on the Roman position and provoked a battle near a hill called Callicinus. He routed the Roman cavalry forces, but when the consul Licinius held back his heavy infantry Perseus withdrew.[197] Again he sued for peace, but he would not meet the Roman demand for unconditional surrender. After another indecisive battle near the Roman camp at Phalanna (north of Larissa) both armies withdrew to winter quarters.[198]

Perseus was active on several fronts the following year, with successes in Dardania, Thessaly, and Epirus, a naval victory at Euboea, a land victory over the consul Mancinus when he attempted to invade Elimeia from Thessaly, and a winter campaign into Aetolia.[199] But he could not keep the Romans at bay. In 169 Marcius Philippus as consul brought 5,000 reinforcements to Thessaly for a major offensive against Macedonia. Perseus sent 10,000 light troops to guard the Volustana Pass and 12,000 Macedonians (mostly his phalanx, nearly useless in mountainous terrain) to guard the route up to the Petra Pass. So Marcius, Hannibal-style, brought his forces and elephants on a trackless course over Olympus down to the coast between Heracleion and Leibethra.[200] Perseus, it is said, was taking a bath at Dion, where he was headquartered, when a bodyguard rushed in and announced that the enemy was nearly on his doorstep. Recalling both guard units from the mountain passes, he ordered everyone in Dion and the area around the southern end of the Pierian plain to relocate to Pydna, removing all the gold statues before abandoning the sacred city. Polybius the historian was with the Roman army as an envoy for the Achaean League, but all that survives of his eyewitness account is the comment that he shared in the danger of the invasion. Marcius advanced to Dion and beyond, but, fearing Perseus would cut off his supply lines, he quickly retreated to Phila, at the mouth of Tempe. When Perseus returned to Dion, now with his full army, Marcius captured Heracleion, and as winter came on the two armies sat entrenched, neither side initiating battle.[201]

In the spring of 168 Marcius' consular replacement, L. Aemilius Paullus (son of the consul of the same name who defeated Demetrius of Pharos in Illyria), arrived in Thessaly with experienced officers and enough fresh troops to bring two legions up to strength. In desperation Perseus sought alliances, but reinforcements of Bastarnae, a tribe of Celts, went home because he refused to pay their high price; and though he bought an alliance with Gentius, king of the Illyrian Ardiaei, which ought to have secured his western frontier, when the Romans on the Illyrian front pressed Gentius hard he surrendered.[202] A few traditional allies stood by Perseus: the Odrysian king Cotys IV continued to contribute cavalry even in the final engagement, and the Molossians of Epirus, the tribe of Olympias, mother of Alexander III, defected from their Roman alliance to side with Perseus.[203]

By the time Aemilius Paullus brought his forces forward to the Elpeus River Perseus had sent forces back to guard the Petra Pass, others to guard his docks at Thessalonica and the coast against the Roman fleet, and had fortified the riverbank on his side. It was a position Aemilius Paullus could not force, so by night he sent a detachment up and over Olympus; they surprised Perseus' guard at dawn, and came down, as before, near Dion, behind the Macedonian lines. Perseus withdrew to Pydna, and that is where on June 22, the day after a lunar eclipse, the fate of Macedonia was decided in battle.[204] A skirmish broke out between the outposts, and though it was late in the day, Perseus deployed his phalanx. Aemilius Paullus knew what he was up against, though this was the first time he had seen it. Later back at Rome he said "he had never seen anything more terrible and dreadful than a Macedonian phalanx, and this although he had witnessed and directed as many battles as any man."[205] The phalanx impaled or put to flight the first Italian troops to engage, then Aemilius Paullus commanded the legions to advance in small cohorts so as to infiltrate and break apart the immobile massed phalanx, while on his right he deployed his elephants and allied foot. The beasts, despite Perseus' special

Figure 10.6 Phakos, once an island in Lake Loudias by Pella, stronghold of the royal treasury
Source: author, 2014.

anti-elephant unit, began to break up the phalanx, as men dropped their weapons and ran. Perseus withdrew with the cavalry, leaving his infantry to the slaughter.

While some 20,000 were slain on the battlefield and another 11,000 taken prisoner, Perseus fled to Pella. When he met no support from the nobles and advisors he set out at night for Amphipolis. But again the people did not rally behind the king, so with 2,000 talents cash and a small entourage that included his wife and sons he crossed to the sacred isle of Samothrace,[206] where nearly 200 years earlier a young Philip II had fallen in love with an Epirote princess. Aemilius Paullus in pursuit approached Pella. After centuries of heavy silting the swamps around the lake were impenetrable, though the Loudias was still navigable between the lake and the ever receding coast. The site, to his mind, "had not been chosen to be the capital without good reason." The royal treasury had long been impregnably safeguarded on Phakos (Figure 10.6), an island in the lake that was separated from the city walls by part of the river but connected by an easily guarded bridge. It had already been emptied of all but 300 talents.[207] Pella and most of the cities surrendered immediately, the rest within a few days, on condition that the citizens would not be harmed, and few were given over to the Roman army for looting; instead, on the return to Italy the army was granted seventy towns to loot in Epirus in retaliation for the Molossian defection.[208] The royal palaces, however, were stripped of their enormous riches: silver and gold, statues, paintings, and textiles—Aemilius Paullus' spoils for the treasury at Rome.[209] Perseus surrendered at Samothrace, was taken to Rome with his sons, and paraded along with the treasures in the consul's triumph.[210]

Macedonia had always been and still was a valuable buffer state between northern 'barbarian' tribes and the southern Greek states. But leaving in place an ambitious king with Macedonia's vast resources at his disposal was a gamble Rome would not take again. The Macedonian monarchy was dissolved. The people were granted their freedom to govern themselves, though with severe restrictions. The kingdom was governed as four separate independent regions, or *merides*, which were pre-existing, each with its own capital, assembly, and elected officials, all now subject to laws imposed by Rome. The westernmost *meris* comprised "upper" Macedonia, including Elimeia, Eordaea, Lyncus, Pelagonia, Tymphaea, and Atintania around Lake Lychnidos, with the capital in Pelagonia; Orestis remained independent. The old "lower" Macedonia between the Peneus and the Axios and including Paeonia west of the Axios comprised another *meris*, with Pella as the capital. The region between the Axios and the Strymon, including Paeonia east of the Axios and Chalcidice but excluding Bisaltia, had Thessalonica as the capital. The easternmost *meris* stretched from the Strymon to the Nestos, including Bisaltia and some territory beyond the Nestos, and had Amphipolis as the capital. Excepting Lower Macedonia, which did not border on 'barbarian' tribes, the regions were permitted to garrison their frontiers, but they were not permitted to engage in inter-regional commerce or to intermarry, and the people were required to pay tribute to Rome at half the amount previously paid to the Macedonian king. Mining of silver and gold was banned, as was the cutting of timber for shipbuilding, though copper and iron mining was permitted. All of the chief royal advisors and nobles, generals, admirals, and garrison commanders, together with their sons over fifteen years of age, were deported to Italy.[211]

Some twenty years later one Andriscus, claiming to be the son of Perseus, declared himself king of the Macedonians. Perseus had died in prison a few years after the settlement and so had his son Philip, while his other son, Alexander, survived to become an artisan and magisterial secretary at Rome.[212] So who this Andriscus, or 'false Philip', was is unknown. He succeeded in seizing control of Macedonia and overran parts of Thrace and Thessaly. Then in 148 the consul Q. Caecilius Metellus defeated him in battle—the second Battle of Pydna in the so-called Fourth Macedonian War—and in 146 Macedonia became a Roman province.[213] This large province initially included the neighbouring regions of Epirus and Thessaly, as well as parts of Illyria, Paeonia, and Thrace. Macedonia prospered long under Roman rule, while the former political and military supremacy of the monarchy, especially the Argead kings Philip II and Alexander III, continued to impact the Mediterranean world and beyond for centuries to come.

Notes

1 Plut. *Demetr.* 51.
2 Gabbert 1997: 19, 25. Cf. Plut. *Pyrrh.* 12.5.
3 Liv. 32.37.2–4; cf. Polyb. 18.11; Plut. *Arat.* 16.2–6; Paus. 7.7.6.
4 Memnon F1 8.8 [*FGrH/BNJ* 434]; Just. 24.1, 25.2.2. See Chapter 9.
5 Paus. 10.20.5.

6 Just. 25.1.1–2.7; Diog. Laert. 2.141–142.
7 Gabbert 1997: 20.
8 Memnon F1 8.8; Paus. 1.16.2: Polyaen. 4.6.17.
9 Eusebius *Chronicle*. I, Schoene, Petermann (eds., Berlin: Weidmann, 1866–1875): 237.
10 Memnon F1 10.1; Just. 25.1.1.
11 Diod. 22.5.1–2; Polyaen. 6.7.1–2, 4.6.18; Trogus *Prol.* 25; Porphyry F3.12.
12 Diod. 22.11–12; Plut. *Pyrrh.* 26.2–7; Paus. 1.13.1–3; Polyaen. 6.6.1; Just. 25.3.5–7.
13 Paus. 1.9.7–8.
14 Plut. *Pyrrh.* 26.8–34.6; Paus. 1.13.7–8; Polyaen. 8.68.1; Just. 25.3.8–4.1, 4.6–5.2. Pyrrhus' sons: Plut. *Pyrrh.* 9; Just. 18.1.3.
15 Just. 26.1–3.
16 Craterus: Front. 3.6.7; Plut. *Mor.* 253a, 486a. Ameinias: Plut. *Pyrrh.* 29.6; cf. Polyaen. 4.6.18. Gabbert 1997: 33–44; Dixon 2014: 83–86.
17 Plut. *Mor.* 183d; Diog. Laert. 7.1.6–9, 36. Carney 2003b: 55–56. On the Boscoreale fresco (Figure 10.1) see Miller 1993a; Billows 1995: 45–55; Palagia 2014.
18 Paus. 10.22.2–13, 23.12–13; Just. 24.1.1–6. On the Aetolian federation see Grainger 1999 and Scholten 2000.
19 The League appears to have remained neutral in the Chremonidean War and at other times supported Antigonus, e.g. Polyb. 2.43.9–10, 9.34.6, 38.9.
20 Polyb. 2.38–43, especially 2.41.1–2; Str. 8.7.1; Paus. 7.7.1–2. Larsen 1968: 215–240.
21 *IG* II² 687 = Austin 61; Paus. 1.1.1, 30.4, 3.6.4–6; Just. 26.2.1–8; Trogus *Prol.* 26. Gabbert 1997: 45–53; Habicht 1997: 142–149.
22 Fleet: cf. Paus. 1.7.3; references to Antigonus' victory over the Ptolemaic fleet at Cos are not securely dated: Plut. *Mor.* 545b; Ath. 5.209e; Diog. Laert. 4.39 (see Gabbert 1997: 48–50, 52–53: no naval battle in this war; battle at Cos later). Areus: Plut. *Agis* 3.7; cf. Diod. 20.29.1. Athens: Polyaen. 4.6.20; Front. 3.4.2. Mouseion: Apollodorus F44 [*FGrH* 244]. On Antigonus' control of Athens after the war see Habicht 2003 and Tracey 2003.
23 Just. 26.2.9–3.1; cf. Ael. *NA* 10.34. Alexander's accession: Plut. *Pyrrh.* 9.1; Just 18.1.3.
24 *IG* XI 2 116; Paus. 3.6.6; Tracey 2003: 58–59.
25 *Syll.*³ 459, dated 248–247.
26 Cf. Polyb. 4.76.2, 5.26.5, 22.5.12, 23.10.8. Hammond 1999; *contra* Hatzopoulos 1996: 371–393.
27 *IG* II² 774; *IG* XII 9 212; Plut. *Arat.* 17.2; Trogus *Prol.* 26; *Suda* s.v. "Euphorion." Gabbert 1997: 54–58; Dixon 2014: 91–97, and on the Antigonid garrison and shipyards at Corinth in general 81–101. We do not know when Craterus died (but after 270) or whether Alexander succeeded him immediately or later.
28 *Syll.*³ 454; Polyb. 2.43.2–3, 10.22.3; Cicero *de Officiis* 2.81–82; Str. 8.6.25; Plut. *Arat.* 6–9, 16.1, 18.2; Paus. 2.8.3.
29 Polyb. 2.43.8.
30 Plut. *Arat.* 17.2–6, 18.2; Polyaen. 4.6.1; cf. Liv. 35.26.5. Carney 2000: 188–189.
31 Trogus *Prol.* 27. Plut. *Pel.* 2.4. Reger 1994: 33–35; cf. 46 n56: the date; 48: Macedonian hegemony in the Aegean.
32 Polyb. 2.43.4, 4.8.4 (cf. 50.8–9, 52.4: an underhanded trick); Str. 8.7.3; Plut. *Arat.* 16.2, 18.2–24.4; Paus. 2.8.4–5, 7.8.3; Polyaen. 6.5.1; Ath. 4.162d.
33 Walbank in *HM* III 1988: 309–310; Dixon 2014: 153; cp. Errington 1990: 172–173.
34 Plut. *Arat.* 33.2–6.
35 Polyb. 2.43.9–10, 9.34.6; Plut. *Arat.* 34.1; [Lucian] 11; Porphyry F3.12. Date of death: Wheatley 1997: 23–24.

36 Adams 2010: 222: shared kingship "probable, but not certain"; Errington 1977, 1990: 173 with n42 argues against shared kingship.
37 The dating is disputed: if Olympias proposed the marriage, presumably her husband was dead, i.e. after 243, *IG* XII 4 1. A date c. 239 is generally accepted, though fierce arguments have been made for c. 246. Errington 1990: 174 with n44; Ogden 1999: 178–183; Gabelko and Kuzmin 2008; Lane Fox 2011c: 518.
38 Polyb. 2.44.1, 46.1; Plut. *Arat*. 33.1.
39 *Syll*.³ 485.B. Walbank in *HM* III 1988: 317–336; Dixon 2014: 153–154.
40 Polyb. 20.5.3
41 Plut. *Arat*. 27.1–28.4, 29.1–6. Factions: cf. Polyb. 2.44.3–6, 9.29.5–6.
42 Plut. *Arat*. 34.1–4.
43 Plut. *Arat*. 30.1–8, *Cleomenes*. 6.7, *Mor*. 552a.
44 Plut. *Arat*. 34.2–3.
45 It is not clear whether these were daughters of Pyrrhus I or II, but Pyrrhus II is described as too young at the time of his death to have had a daughter old enough to assume power. Walbank in *HM* III 1988: 332–333.
46 Ath. 13.589f–590a; Just. 28.3.1–8; Polyaen. 8.52; Paus. 4.35.3, 5.
47 Str. 10.2.4. This campaign possibly occasioned the nickname Aetolicus, though whether the name was flattering or derogatory is unknown.
48 Polyb. 2.2.2–4.5. For the date see Walbank in *HM* III 1988: 333, and 335 for the suggestion that Demetrius was dealing with a Dardanian invasion.
49 Polyb. 2.4.6–5.1, 9.7–10.8; cf. Ael. *VH* 2.41.
50 Polyb. 2.44.2; Liv. 31.28.1–2; Trogus *Prol*. 28, Just. 28.3.9. On the Dardani (Dardanians) see Wilkes 1992: 144–146.
51 Euseb. *Chron*. I, Schoene 237–238; Synkellos, Adler and Tuffin 2002: 409 (possibly following Eusebius). See e.g. Carney 2000: 189–193, citing earlier bibliography. For the continuing uncertainty: Phthia: e.g. Adams 2010: 223. Chryseis: Lane Fox 2011b: 518. Philip's age: Polyb. 4.5.3.
52 Just. 28.1.1–4. Carney 2000: 184–187.
53 Plut. *Aem*. 8.2–3; Diod. 25.18; Paus. 7.7.4; Just. 28.3.10; Euseb. *Chron*. I, Schoene 238–239. On the nickname Doson see Green 1990: 254–255.
54 Polyb. 2.44.3–6; Plut. *Arat*. 35.1–5, 60.4; Paus. 2.8.6. Le Bohec 1993: 97–111.
55 SEG 38.1476 93–99; Paus. 6.16.2; Front. 2.6.5; Just. 28.3.14. Walbank 1989; Le Bohec 1993: 154–162.
56 *Syll*.³ 475.2–6, 497.13; Plut. *Arat*. 34.5–6; Paus. 2.8.6. Habicht 1997: 173–178 (and Rhamnous).
57 Cf. Polyb. 20.5.4–11.
58 Polyb. 2.2.1, 11.1–12, 44.2; App. *Ill*. 2.7. Hammond 1989b; Wilkes 1992: 158–161; Derow 2003: 51–54.
59 Dell 1967.
60 Plut. *Aem*. 8.3; Just. 28.3.11–16; Euseb. *Chron*. I, Schoene 237. Le Bohec 1993: 113–143.
61 Polyb. 20.5.11; Trogus *Prol*. 28. Walbank in *HM* III 1988: 343–345; Le Bohec 1993: 327–361.
62 Polyb. 2.45.2–47.2.
63 Polyb. 2.46.2, 6.
64 Polyb. 2.47.3–51.2; Plut. *Arat*. 38.11–12.
65 Polyb. 2.51.4–7, 52.1–4; Plut. *Arat*. 39.4–40.7, *Cleomenes*. 17.5–18.1, 19.1–9; Paus. 2.9.2.
66 Polyb. 2.52.5–9, 53, 59.1–60.3, cf. 4.6.5, 54.1; Plut. *Arat*. 41.7, 43.1–44.1, 6, 42.1–3, 45.1, *Cleom*. 20.1–4. The date: Dixon 2014: 151, 161.

264 *The Antigonids, the Greek Leagues, and Rome*

67 Cf. *IG* XI 4 1097, 1102 = *Syll.³* 575. Walbank in *CAH²* VII.1: 226.
68 Polyb. 2.54.2–5, 4.9.3–4, 15.1–2. Walbank in *HM* III 1988: 351–353 and Hammond 1989b: 484; Dixon 2014: 170–171. Errington 1990: 182 with n17 argues for a later date of 223–222. On federal *koina* see McInerney 2013.
69 Polyb. 2.54.6–13, 56.6–7, 57, 58.12–15; Plut. *Arat.* 45.1, 6–9, *Cleom.* 23.1. For a convenient list of Peloponnesian towns and walking distances see Shipley 2008: 59.
70 Polyb. 2.55.2–7, 5.93.2, 9.18.1–4; Plut. *Cleom.* 23.1–25.1, *Philopaemen* 5.1–5; Paus. 4.29.7–8. Sekunda 2012: 36–37.
71 Polyb. 2.54.13–55.1; Plut. *Cleom.* 25.2–3.
72 Polyb. 2.63.1–5, 64.1–7; Plut. *Cleom.* 25.4–26.6, 27.4, 32.4.
73 Polyb. 2.65; Plut. *Cleom.* 27.11. Probably 400 Cretan archers: at Polyb. 65.5 the total is 28,000 foot, but individual contingents add up to 27,600, and in the deployment at 66.6 Cretans (usually archers) are mentioned.
74 Cf. Polyb. 4.69.5.
75 Polyb. 2.66.1–70.1, 5.9.8–10, 36.1–5, cf. 9.31.3–4, 20.5.12–13; Liv. 34.28.1, 40.54.4; Plut. *Arat.* 46.1, *Cleom.* 28.1–30.1, 32.1, *Philopaemen* 6; Paus. 2.9.2–3, 3.10.7, 4.29.9, 8.49.5–6; Just. 28.4.1–15.
76 Polyb. 2.70; Plut. *Cleom.* 27.5–10, 30.1–4; Just. 28.4.16–29.1.2. On Antigonus Doson's reign cf. Liv. 32.21.25, 40.54.4–5.
77 Cp. Diod. 14.37.6, 16.38.6; Arr. *Anab.* 1.11.3. Anson 2009a: 280–282.
78 Polyb. 4.87.6–8; Liv. 40.56.4; Plut. *Arat.* 46.2–3; cp. Just. 29.1.8, 10.
79 Polyb. 4.6.5–6. Shipley 2008: 62.
80 Polyb. 3.16, 18–19, 4.16.6–7; App. *Ill.* 2.8. Wilkes 1992: 162–164.
81 Polyb. 3.6.1–2, 8.8–11, 17.9–10, 33.1–4, 54.1–56.1; Liv. 21.7.1–15.3.
82 Eckstein 2010: 225–227. For Polybius' treatment of Macedonia see Walbank 1970 and Eckstein 1995: 1–26. On Rome and Macedonia see Gruen 1984 (vol. II) chapters 11–12.
83 Polyb. 2.37, 2.71, 3.1, 39.8.5–8.
84 Polyb. 4.5.1–6.4, 6.7–7.11, 9.1–15.4; Plut. *Arat.* 47.
85 Polyb. 4.16.1–3, 19.1, 7–9, 30.6–7.
86 Polyb. 4.22.1–3, 25.1–26.8; Plut. *Arat.* 47.6.
87 Polyb. 4.22.4, 23.4–24.9, 34.1–35.5.
88 Polyb. 4.27.9–10, 29.1–7; Just. 29.1.10–11.
89 Polyb. 4.36, 57.2–60.3.
90 Polyb. 4.37.7, 57.1, 61. On their Cretan allies see Polyb. 4.55.1–6; Plut. *Arat.* 48.5.
91 Polyb. 4.62, 5.9.2, 5–6, 11.2, 8. Grainger 1999: 14.
92 Polyb. 4.63.1–66.7.
93 Polyb. 4.67.6. *Chalcaspides*: cf. Liv. 44.41.2; Plut. *Aem.* 18.5–8. Sekunda 2012: 35–36.
94 Polyb. 4.67.6–69.9.
95 Polyb. 4.70–75, 77.5–80.
96 Polyb. 4.83–87. Polybius' account, probably from Aratus, is strongly biased.
97 Polyb. 5.1.6–12; Plut. *Arat.* 48.1–3.
98 Polyb. 5.2.1–9.6.6.
99 Polyb. 5.2.7–10, 4.10–13, 14.11–16.10; Plut. *Arat.* 48.6.
100 Polyb. 5.17.8–25.7 (quote: 25.3). See Chapter 7.
101 Polyb. 5.26–27, 28.4–9; Plut. *Arat.* 48.7.
102 Polyb. 5.28.1–3, 29.1–6.
103 Polyb. 5.30.1–7, 91–96.
104 Polyb. 5.97–100; Liv. 28.7.12; Diod. 26.9.1.
105 Liv. 22.33.3. Derow 2003: 54. Eckstein 2010: 227–228 also argues against significant Roman intervention before the end of the Social War.

106 Polyb. 5.100.9–105.10, cf. 3.2.3; Just. 29.2–3.
107 Polyb. 5.108–110; Liv. 31.28.
108 Polyb. 7.9.1–17; cp. Liv. 23.33.1–34.9. App. *Mac.* 1; Just. 29.4.2–3. On Appian's claim that Philip attacked Corcyra see Walbank 1940: 299.
109 Liv. 24.40.1–17, 31.7.4; Plut. *Arat.* 51.1–2; Just. 29.4.4.
110 On Antigonid emulation of the Argeads see Walbank 1993.
111 Polyb. 3.19.11; cp. Paus. 4.29.1–5. For Philip's own attempts, both before and after, cf. Polyb. 5.7.10–14; Plut. *Arat.* 49–50; Polyb. 8.8.1–5, 12.1. On Philip and Messenia, and the uncertain chronology, see Walbank 1940: 72–74, 77–79.
112 Polyb. 8.12.2–8; Liv. 32.21.23–24; Plut. *Arat.* 52.1–54.4; Paus. 2.9.4, cf. 7.7.5, 8.50.4.
113 Polyb. 8.13.1–14.11.
114 Polyb. 11.5.1–5, 21.20.3 (Attalus), 22.8.10; Liv. 26.24.1–25.1, 37.53.7–8; Trogus *Prol.* 29; Just. 29.4.5, 7. Austin no. 77. Eckstein 2002: 271–272; Derow 2003: 55–56.
115 Liv. 26.28.1–2.
116 Liv. 26.25.2–8; cp. Just. 29.4.6; *Lindian Chronicle* F42 [*FGrH/BNJ* 532 = Burstein 46].
117 Polyb. 9.30.1–39.7; cf. Liv. 34.32.1–3.
118 Polyb. 9.41.1–42.4.
119 Polyb. 10.25.1–26.10; Liv. 27.29.9–31.8; App. *Mac.* 3.
120 Liv. 27.31.9–32.9.
121 Liv. 27.32.9–33.5; Just 29.4.6–10.
122 Polyb. 10.41.1–42.8; Liv. 28.5.1–17; Diod. 28.2.
123 Liv. 28.5.18–7.13. Aegina: Polyb. 9.42.5–8, 22.8.9.
124 Liv. 28.7.14–8.8; cp. Polyb. 11.4.1–6.10.
125 Polyb. 11.7.2–3; 18.38.8; Liv. 29.12.1–2, 31.1.9, 29.4, 16, 31.19, 33.13.11; 36.31.11; App. *Mac.* 3. On the peace of 206 see Eckstein 2002.
126 Liv. 29.12.3–7.
127 Polyb. 18.1.14; Liv. 29.12.8–15; App. *Mac.* 3; Just. 29.4.11; Trogus *Prol.* 29. Eckstein 2002: 293–294; Derow 2003: 57–58.
128 Liv. 27.45–49, 51.12–13; App. *Hannibalic Wars* 52.
129 Liv. 31.7.4–5.
130 Liv. 28.8.14.
131 Polyb. 3.2.8, 15.20.1–8; Liv. 31.14.5; App. *Mac.* 2; Just. 30.2.6–8. On the debate about the 'pact' and its authenticity see Eckstein 2005, 2008: 129–180.
132 The Fifth Syrian War, 202–195. *Koile*, or "Hollow," Syria is variously defined in the sources—generally, the Phoenician coast and valley between Lebanon and anti-Lebanon Mountains.
133 Liv. 30.26.3, 33.5, 31.1.9; see Chapter 5 n141.
134 Polyb. 15.21–23, 16.1–10, 18. 2.1–4, 54.8–10. *SEG* 38.603 (Figure 10.4).
135 Polyb. 13.4.1–2, 5.1; Liv. 31.1.10; Diod. 28.1; Polyaen. 5.17.2.
136 Polyb. 16.24.3, cf. 25–26; Liv. 31.2.1–2, 3.1–6, 5.1–6.1, 9.1–4. Derow 2003: 59–60; Eckstein 2008: 230–270.
137 Polyb. 16.30–34; Liv. 31.16–18; Diod. 28.6. For the ancient view that the 'first' and 'second' Macedonian wars, so-called by modern historians, were one continuous war see Derow 2003: 58–59. See also Walbank 1940: 138–185; Hamilton 1993; Warrior 1996 (an analysis of Livy 31, summarizing earlier scholarship); Eckstein 2008: 273–305.
138 Liv. 31.7.13, 22.4–23.12, 24, 26.5–13, 30; Diod. 28.7. On Philip's depredations in Attica during the Second Macedonia War see Habicht 1997: 194–204.
139 Polyb. 16.38.1; Liv. 31.25, 32.
140 Liv. 31.14.1–2, 27–28.

266   *The Antigonids, the Greek Leagues, and Rome*

141 Polyb. 18.23.3; Liv. 31.33.1–40.6, 32.21.19, 33.8.4; cf. Diod. 28.8. Pelion: Chapter 6 n61.
142 Liv. 31.28.5, 33.1.
143 Liv. 31.40.7–43.4, cf. 32.4.
144 Liv. 32.3.1–7, 5.9–13.
145 Liv. 32.5.1–8; Diod. 28.2, 9; cf. Polyb. 13.4, 18.7.6; Plut. *Arat.* 54.6.
146 Liv. 32.6.1–8, 9.6–11; Plut. *Flam.* 2–3. Paus. 7.7.8–9 is confused about date and name.
147 Liv. 32.10.1–12.10; Diod. 28.11; Plut. *Flam.* 4.1–5.1.
148 Liv. 32.13.1–15.9, 17.4–18.3; Plut. *Flam.* 5.2–5.
149 Polyb. 18.1–12; Liv. 32.32–37; Plut. *Flam.* 5.6, 7.1–2; App. *Mac.* 8.
150 Polyb. 7.11.8. Cf. Liv. 31.44.2–9: at Athens, *damnatio memoriae*. Bayliss 2006: 110.
151 Liv. 32.16, 19–25, 38–40, 33.1–2, 16–17; App. *Mac.* 7; Plut. *Flam.* 6; Paus. 7.8.1–2, 10.34.3–4.
152 Polyb. 18.20–26; Liv. 33.6.7–10.5; Plut. *Flam.* 8.1–4; Just. 30.4.5–15. For the numbers cf. Liv. 33.3.8–10, 4.4–5; Plut. *Flam.* 7.2. On topography see Hammond 1988b; reinvestigated by Jake Morton, unpublished paper (2014) "Of Bikes and Battles: Relocating Cynoscephalae."
153 Liv. 33.4.1–3, 3.1–4.
154 Polyb. 18.27, 33; Liv. 33.10.6–11.1.
155 Polyb. 18.28–32; Plut. *Flam.* 8.4.
156 Polyb. 18.36–39, 44; Liv. 33.13, 30; App. *Mac.* 9.2–3; Plut. *Flam.* 9.4–5, *Arat.* 54.5; Dio Cassius 18.60; Just. 30.4.16–17. Gruen 1973: 124 n1: "dubious accretions" in the later sources (Livy, Justin).
157 Polyb. 18.47.6–7; Liv. 33.34.5–6, 39.23.6, 28.2.
158 Polyb. 18.37.8–9; Liv. 33.12.9–11; App. *Mac.* 9.2.
159 Polyb. 18.34.1, 45; Liv. 33.11.4–10; Plut. *Flam.* 10.1–2; App. *Mac.* 9.1. Defeat of Philip's commander at Corinth: Liv. 33.14–15; cf. Liv. 32.40.5–6.
160 Polyb. 18.46; Liv. 33.32–33, 34.23.8–10; Plut. *Flam.* 10.3–11.1; App. *Mac.* 9.4.
161 Liv. 33.19.1–5.
162 App. *Mac.* 9.5. Gruen 1973 argues against a formal "alliance" suggested by Polyb. 18.48.3–4; *contra* Hammond in *HM* III 1988: 447. Eckstein 2008: 308–341.
163 Polyb. 18.47.1–5, 49.2–52.5; Liv. 34.57–59. Derow 2003: 61–62.
164 Polyb. 18.43; Liv. 33.28–29, 34.48–50, 35.47.3, 36.6.1; Diod. 28.13; cf. Polyb. 20.5.
165 Liv. 34.49.4–6, 50.7.
166 Liv. 35.31, 34–39.
167 Liv. 35.32–33, 43–51, 36.8–12, 15–19; Plut. *Cato Minor* 13.1–14.2; App. *Syr.* 16–20; Just. 31.6.5–6; cf. Polyb. 21.31.7. Walbank 1940: 195–201.
168 Liv. 35.31.5, 36.35.13; Diod. 28.15.1; cf. Polyb. 21.3.1–2; Liv. 36.35.12–14; Plut. *Flam.* 14; App. *Mac.* 9.5, *Syr.* 20.
169 Liv. 36.13–14, 39.23.7–24.4; Diod. 29.3.1; App. *Syr.* 17, 21.
170 Liv. 37.7.8–16 (cf. 39.28.8–9), 38–44; App. *Mac.* 9.5, *Syr.* 23, 30–37; Just. 31.8.5–7; cp. Liv. 38.40.7–8.
171 Plut. *Aem.* 7.2.
172 Rome left most of the spoils to her allies: Polyb. 21.24.7–8, 41.6–43.3; Liv. 38.38–39; App. *Syr.* 38–39; Just. 31.8.9.
173 Liv. 39.24.1; cf. Polyb. 22.14.7–8, 18.1–11.
174 Polyb. 22.6; Liv. 39.24.5–13. Philip's continued aggressions: Polyb. 23.8.1–7, 10.1–17; Liv. 39.53.12–15, 40.3.3–4.15. Subsequent complaints: Polyb. 23.9.1–7; Liv. 40.2.6–3.7.
175 Polyb. 22.11.1–4, 13.1–14.6; Liv. 39.24.5–29.3, 34.1–35.2; Diod. 29.16; Paus. 7.8.6.

176 Polyb. 22.14.9–12, 23.1.1–3.9, 7.1–7; cf. 23.8; Liv. 39.35.3–4, 46.6–48.5, 53.1–11; App. *Mac.* 9.6; Just. 32.2.3–7.
177 Liv. 20.3–22.15; Just. 32.2.8–10.
178 Gruen 1974: 231. But cf. 237: by 182 "discord [between Philip and Rome] had subsided."
179 Liv. 40.2–16, 23.1–24.8, 41.23.10–11; Plut. *Arat.* 54.6–7; Paus. 2.9.5; Just. 32.3.1–3. Gruen 1974; Dell 1983. Gruen 1974: 239: domestic strife and foreign relations are separate matters.
180 Liv. 40.56.8–9, 42.11.4; Diod. 29.25; Plut. *Aem.* 8.9–12; Just. 32.3.4–5.
181 Liv. 40.54.1–57.1, 58.8.
182 Polyb. 25.3.1–8; Liv. 40.58.8, 41.24.6, 42.25.4, 10, 45.9.3; Diod. 29.30.
183 Polyb. 22.18.2–3; Liv. 42.13.5, 40.5, 41.11–12; Diod. 29.33; App. *Mac.* 11.2, 6; Paus. 7.10.6.
184 Polyb. 25.4.8–10; Liv. 42.12.3–4; App. *Mithridatic Wars* 2, *Mac.* 11.2; *IG* XI[4] 1074 = *Syll.*[3] 639. Antiochus III was killed in a plundering expedition: Diod. 28.3, 29.15; Just. 32.2.1–2. Perseus possibly already had taken a royal bride from the northern Bastarnae tribe: Liv. 40.5.10. Meloni 1953: 38–40.
185 Polyb. 27.5, 9.1, 10.1, 4; Liv. 42.12, 13.9, 42.4, cf. 30.1–7; Diod. 29.33; Plut. *Aem.* 7.4. For Perseus' treaty with the Boeotians, and the resolution of the textual crux at Liv. 42.12.6, where "Dion" can now be securely restored, see Briscoe 2012: 191–192 and Iatrou 2016: 93.
186 Liv. 41.22.4–6, 23.13–16, 42.42.1–3; *SIG*[3] 636. These were *not* 'recovered' votes: Habicht 1987: 60–61; Hatzopoulos 1996: 223 with n8; *contra* Pugliese 2014: 148–151 (citing some earlier scholarship).
187 Liv. 41.22.7–24.20, 42.5.1–6, 6.1–2; cf. 31.44.
188 Liv. 42.39.7.
189 Liv. 41.22.4–5, 42.6.3–4, 11–14, 18, 30.8–11, 36; Diod. 29.34; App. *Mac.* 11; *Syll.*[3] 643 = Austin 93. Eumenes: Green 1990: 428; Waterfield 2014: 173–175. Quote: Gruen 1984: 410. When Eumenes on his return was seriously injured at Delphi he accused Perseus of an assassination plot, Polyb. 22.18.5; Liv. 42.15–16; App. *Mac.* 11.4.
190 Cf. Liv. 42.12.8–10, 52.3.
191 Liv. 40.57.2–58.7. Wilkes 1992: 151–153.
192 Liv. 42.37–38.
193 Liv. 42.39–43.3, 46.
194 Liv. 42.47.10, 48.1–4, 50–51.1–2. On "Citium" at Liv. 51.1–2 see Hatzopoulos 1996: 114 n5. On Perseus' pre-war relations with the Senate see Adams 1982; Gruen 1984: 408–419; Hammond in *HM* III 1988: 497–504.
195 Liv. 42.51.3–11. On the units and numbers, and textual problems in Livy, see Hammond in *HM* III 1988: 515 with n1; Briscoe 2012: 331–335. On the war see Hammond in *HM* III 1988: 505–557; Waterfield 2014: 181–193; Derow 2015: 58–77.
196 Liv. 42.53.5–54.11; cf. Polyb. 27.8.15.
197 Liv. 42.55–59; Plut. *Aem.* 9.2. On "Callicinus" see Briscoe 2012: 357–358.
198 Polyb. 27.8; Liv. 42.62, 65–67; App. *Mac.* 12.
199 Polyb. 29.19.7; Liv. 43.11.9, 21.1–23.1, 44.2.6; Plut. *Aem.* 9.3–5; Zonaras 9.22.6–8. The campaign in Illyria and Perseus' efforts to win the alliance of Gentius: Polyb. 28.8; Liv. 43.9.4–10.8, 18–20; Plut. *Aem.* 9.6, with Dell 1977. On the lacuna at Liv. 43.3 see Briscoe 2012: 397–398. Attempts at peace: Liv. 44.14.5–15.8; cf. 45.44.
200 Polyb. 28.13.1–3; Liv. 44.1–5.
201 Polyb. 28.10–11, 12.4–6, 13.1–2; Liv. 44.6.4–9, 8.1–9.11.

268 *The Antigonids, the Greek Leagues, and Rome*

202 Liv. 44.23, 26–27, 30.1–32.5, cf. 43.18.3–4, 45.43; Diod. 31.14; Plut. *Aem.* 9.6, 12.1–13.3.
203 Liv. 42.29.11–12, 51.10, 43.18.1–3, 44.42.2, cf. 45.42.6–11; cf. 45.34.1–9.
204 Polyb. 29.16; Liv. 44.32.5–11, 35.8–37.9, cf. 45.41.4; Plut. *Aem.* 15–17.
205 Polyb. 29.17; Plut. *Aem.* 19.2.
206 Liv. 44.40–45; Plut. *Aem.* 18–21, 23.
207 Liv. 44.46.4–9, quote 46.4.
208 Polyb. 30.15; Liv. 44.45.2–8, 46.1–3, 45.34.1–9, 41.6, cf. 35.5–9; Plut. *Aem.* 29.
209 Liv. 45.33.6–7, 35.3, 37.10. Plut. *Aem.* 28.10–11, 30.1–3.
210 Polyb. 18.35.4–5; Liv. 45.4.1–9.3, 28.9–11, 39.1, 4–7, 40, 42; Diod. 31.8.9–12, 11.1–2; Plut. *Aem.* 26–27, 32–34.
211 Liv. 45.18, 29, 30.3–8, 32; Diod. 31.8.1–9; Plut. *Aem.* 28.6; Just. 33.2.7. Gruen 1982. On the *merides* see Hatzopoulos 1996: 231–260.
212 Perseus and his sons: Polyb. 36.10.3; Diod. 31.9; Plut. *Aem.* 37; cp. Porphyry F3.18.
213 Polyb. 36.10, 17.13–15; Diod. 31.40, 32.15; Zonaras 9.28; Velleius Paterculus 1.11. Helliesen 1986; Ogden 1999: 189–192; Matyszak 2009: 157–174; Vanderspoel 2015.

Bibliography

Adams, W. L. 1982. "Perseus and the Third Macedonian War." In Adams and Borza, *Heritage* 1982: 237–256.
———. 1983. "The Dynamics of Internal Macedonian Politics in the Time of Cassander." *Archaia Makedonia* III: 17–30.
———. 1984. "Antipater and Cassander: Generalships on Restricted Resources in the 4th Century." *AncW* 10: 79–88.
———. 1986. "Macedonian Kingship and the Right of Petition." *Archaia Makedonia* IV: 43–52.
———. 2008. "Sport and Ethnicity in Ancient Macedonia." In Howe and Reames, *Legacies* 2008: 57–78.
———. 2010. "Alexander's Successors to 221 BC." In Roisman and Worthington, *Ancient Macedonia* 2010: 208–224.
Adams, W. L. and Borza, E. N., eds. 1982. *Philip II, Alexander the Great, and the Macedonian Heritage*. Washington, DC: University Press of America.
Adler, W. and Tuffin, P. 2002. *The Chronography of George Synkellos: A Byzantine Chronicle of Universal History from the Creation*. Oxford: Oxford University Press.
Allen, L. 2005. *The Persian Empire*. Chicago, IL and London: University of Chicago Press.
Alonso Troncoso, V. 2009. "Some Remarks on the Funerals of the Kings: From Philip II to the Diadochi." In Wheatley and Hannah, *Antipodes* 2009: 276–298.
Alonso Troncoso, V. and Anson, E. M., eds. 2013. *After Alexander. The Time of the Diadochi (323–281 BC)*. Oxford and Oakville: Oxbow Books.
Amitay, O. 2010. *From Alexander to Jesus*. Berkeley and Los Angeles: University of California Press.
Andreou, S., Fotiades, M. and Kotsakis, K. 1996. "Review of Aegean Prehistory V: The Neolithic and Bronze Age of Northern Greece." *AJA* 100.3: 537–597.
Andronikos, M. 1970. "Sarissa." *Bulletin de correspondence hellénique* 94: 91–107.
———. 1984. *Vergina. The Royal Tombs and the Ancient City*. Athens: Ekdotike Athenon S. A.
———. 1987. "Some Reflections on The Macedonian Tombs." *ABSA* 82: 1–16.
Anson, E. M. 1981. "Alexander's Hypaspists and the Argyraspids." *Historia* 30.1: 117–120.
———. 1985a. "The Hypaspists: Macedonia's Professional Citizen-Soldiers." *Historia* 34.2: 246–248.
———. 1985b. "The Meaning of the Term Macedones." *AncW* 10: 67–68.
———. 1985c. "Macedonia's Alleged Constitutionalism." *CJ* 80.4: 303–316.
———. 1986. "Diodorus and the Date of Triparadeisus." *AJPh* 107: 208–217.
———. 1988. "Antigonus, the Satrap of Phrygia." *Historia* 37: 471–477.

———. 1992. "Craterus and the *Prostasia*." *CPh* 87.1: 38–43.

———. 2008a. "Philip II and the Transformation of Macedonia: A Reappraisal." In Howe and Reames, *Legacies* 2008: 17–30.

———. 2008b. "Macedonian Judicial Assemblies." *CPh* 103: 135–149.

———. 2009a. "Philip II, Amyntas Perdicca, and Macedonian Royal Succession." *Historia* 58.3: 276–286.

———. 2009b. "Philip II and the Creation of the Macedonian *PEZHETAIROI*." In Wheatley and Hannah, *Antipodes* 2009: 88–98.

———. 2010a. "The Asthetairoi: Macedonia's Hoplites." In Carney and Ogden, *Father and Son* 2010: 81–90.

———. 2010b. "The Introduction of the SARISA in Macedonian Warfare." *Ancient Society* 40: 51–68.

———. 2012. "The Macedonian Patriot: the Diadoch Craterus." *AHB* 26: 49–58.

———. 2013. *Alexander the Great. Themes and Issues*. London and New York: Bloomsbury.

———. 2014. *Alexander's Heirs. The Age of the Successors*. Malden, MA; Oxford; Chichester: Wiley Blackwell.

———. 2015a. "Alexander at the Beas." In Wheatley and Baynham, *East and West* 2015: 65–74.

———. 2015b. *Eumenes of Cardia. A Greek Among Macedonians*. Second Edition. Leiden and Boston: Brill.

———. 2016. "Philip's Ambitions." In D. Powers, J. Hawke and J. Langford, eds., *Hetairideia. Studies in Honour of W. Lindsay Adams on the Occasion of his Retirement*, 19–29. Chicago: Ares Publishers.

Antela-Bernárdez, B. 2012. "Philip and Pausanias: A Deadly Love in Macedonian Politics." *CQ* 62.2: 859–861.

Archibald, Z. 2004. "Inland Thrace." In M. H. Hansen and T. H. Nielsen, eds., *An Inventory of Archaic and Classical Poleis*, 885–899. Oxford and New York: Oxford University Press.

———. 2010. "Macedonia and Thrace." In Roisman and Worthington, *Ancient Macedonia* 2010: 326–341.

———. 2011. "Macedonia and Thrace (Prehistoric to Roman)." *Archaeological Reports* 57: 85–99.

Ashton, N. G. 1977. "The Naumachia near Amorgos in 322 B.C." *ABSA* 72: 1–11.

———. 1983. "The Lamian War – A False Start?" *Antichthon* 17: 47–63.

———. 1984. "The Lamian War – *stat magni nominis umbra*." *JHS* 104: 152–157.

———. 2015. "Craterus Revisited." In Wheatley and Baynham, *East and West* 2015: 107–116.

Asirvatham, S. R. 2010. "Perspectives on the Macedonians from Greece, Rome, and Beyond." In Roisman and Worthington, *Ancient Macedonia* 2010: 99–124.

Atkinson, J. E. 1980. *A Commentary on Q. Curtius Rufus' Historiae Alexandri Magni: Books 3 and 4*. Amsterdam: J. C. Gieben.

———. 1994. *A Commentary on Q. Curtius Rufus' Historiae Alexandri Magni: Books 5 to 7.2*. Amsterdam: Adolf M. Hakkert.

Atkinson, J. E. and Yardley, J. 2009. *Curtius Rufus. Histories of Alexander the Great, Book 10*. Oxford: Oxford University Press.

Badian, E. 1958. "Alexander the Great and the Unity of Mankind." *Historia* 7: 287–306. Reprinted in *Collected Papers* 2012: 1–19.

———. 1960. "The Death of Parmenio." *TAPA* 91: 324–338. Reprinted in *Collected Papers* 2012: 36–47.

———. 1961. "Harpalus." *JHS* 81: 16–43. Reprinted in *Collected Papers* 2012: 58–95.
———. 1963. "The Death of Philip II." *Phoenix* 17: 244–250. Reprinted in *Collected Papers* 2012: 106–112.
———. 1967. "Agis III." *Hermes* 95: 170–192. Reprinted in *Collected Papers* 2012: 153–173.
———. 1977. "The Battle of the Granicus." *Archaia Makedonia* II: 271–293. Reprinted in *Collected Papers* 2012: 224–243.
———. 1981. "The Deification of Alexander the Great." In Dell, *Studies* 1981: 27–71. Reprinted in *Collected Papers* 2012: 244–281.
———. 1982a. "Eurydice." In Adams and Borza, *Heritage* 1982: 99–110.
———. 1982b. "Greeks and Macedonians." In Barr-Sharrar and Borza, *Macedonia and Greece* 1982: 33–51.
———. 1983. "Philip II and Thrace." *Pulpudeva* 4: 51–71.
———. 1991. "The King's Peace." In M. A. Flower and M. Toher, eds., *Georgica: Greek Studies in Honour of George Cawkwell*, 25–48. London: University of London.
———. 1993. "Thucydides and the *Archē* of Philip." In E. Badian, ed., *From Plataea to Potidaea: Studies in the History and Historiography of the Pentacontaetia*, 171–185. Baltimore, MD: Johns Hopkins University Press.
———. 1994a. "Herodotus on Alexander I of Macedon: A Study in Some Subtle Silences." In S. Hornblower, ed., *Greek Historiography*, 107–130. Oxford: Oxford University Press.
———. 1994b. "Agis III: Revisions and Reflection." In Worthington, *Ventures* 1994: 258–292. Reprinted in *Collected Papers* 2012: 338–364.
———. 1996. "Alexander the Great between Two Thrones and Heaven." In A. M. Small, ed., *Subject and Ruler: The Cult of the Ruling Power in Classical Antiquity*, 11–26. Ann Arbor, MI: University of Michigan Press. Reprinted in *Collected Papers* 2012: 365–385.
———. 2007. "Once More the Death of Philip." *Archaia Makedonia* VII: 389–406. Reprinted in *Collected Papers* 2012: 496–511.
———. 2012. *Collected Papers on Alexander the Great*. London and New York: Routledge.
Balcer, J. M. 1988. "Persian Occupied Thrace." *Historia* 33: 1–21.
Barr-Sharrar, B. and Borza, E., eds. 1982. *Macedonia and Greece in Late Classical and Early Hellenistic Times*. Studies in the History of Art, Vol. 10. Washington, DC.
Bayliss, A. J. 2006. "Antigonus the One-Eyed's Return to Asia in 322: A new consideration for a rasura in *IG* II² 682." *ZPE* 155: 108–126.
Baynham, E. 1994. "Antipater: Manager of Kings." In Worthington, *Ventures* 1994: 331–356.
———. 1998. *Alexander the Great. The Unique History of Quintus Curtius*. Ann Arbor, MI: University of Michigan Press.
———. 2003. "Antipater and Athens." In Palagia and Tracey, *Macedonians in Athens* 2003: 23–29.
———. 2013. "Alexander's Argyraspids: Tough Old Fighters or Antigonid Myth?" In Alonso Troncoso and Anson, *After Alexander* 2013: 110–120.
Betegh, G. 2004. *The Derveni Papyrus: Cosmology, Theology and Interpretation*. Cambridge: Cambridge University Press.
Billows, R. A. 1990. *Antigonos the One-Eyed and the Creation of the Hellenistic State*. Berkeley and Los Angeles: University of California Press.
———. 1995. *Kings and Colonists: Aspects of Macedonian Imperialism*. Leiden, New York, Köln: Brill.
Bintliff, J. 1976. "The Plain of Western Macedonia and the Neolithic Site of Nea Nikomedeia." *Proceedings of the Prehistoric Society* 42: 241–262.

Blackman, D. 1990. "Triremes and Shipsheds." In H. E. Tzalas, ed., *Tropis II: 2ⁿᵈ International Symposium on Ship Construction in Antiquity*, 35–52. Delphi: Helladic Institute for the Preservation of Nautical Tradition.

Blackwell, C. 1999. *In The Absence of Alexander. Harpalus and the Failure of Macedonian Authority*. New York: Peter Lang.

Bloedow, E. 2004. "Egypt in Alexander's Scheme of Things." *Quaderni Urbinati di Cultura Classica* 77.2: 75–99.

Boiy, T. 2007. *Between High and Low. A Chronology of the Early Hellenistic Period*. Frankfurt am Main: Verlag Antike.

Borza, E. N. 1971. "The End of Agis' Revolt." *CPh* 66: 230–235. Reprinted in *Makedonika* 1995: 201–210.

——. 1972. "Fire from Heaven: Alexander at Persepolis." *CPh* 67: 233–245. Reprinted in *Makedonika* 1995: 217–238.

——. 1982a. "The Natural Resources of Early Macedonia." In Adams and Borza, *Heritage* 1982: 1–20. Reprinted in *Makedonika* 1995: 37–55.

——. 1982b. "Athenians, Macedonians, and the Origins of the Macedonian Royal House." *Hesperia Supplement* 19: 7–13. Reprinted in *Makedonika* 1995: 113–123.

——. 1983. "The Symposium at Alexander's Court." *Archaia Makedonia* III: 44–55. Reprinted in *Makedonika* 1995: 159–171.

——. 1987. "Timber and Politics in the Ancient World: Macedon and the Greeks." *Proceedings of the American Philosophical Society* 131: 32–52. Reprinted in *Makedonika* 1995: 85–112.

——. 1989. "Some Toponym Problems in Eastern Macedonia." *AHB* 3: 60–69.

——. 1992. *In the Shadow of Olympus. The Emergence of Macedon*. Princeton, NJ: Princeton University Press. (updated paperback edition of 1990 hb)

——. 1993. "The Philhellenism of Archelaus." *Archaia Makedonia* V: 237–244.

——. 1995. *Makedonika. Essays by Eugene N. Borza*. C. G. Thomas, ed. Claremont, CA: Regina Books.

——. 1996. "Greeks and Macedonians in the Age of Alexander: the Source Traditions." In Wallace and Harris, *Transitions* 1996: 122–139.

——. 1999. *Before Alexander: Constructing Early Macedonia*. Publications of the Association of Ancient Historians 6. Claremont, CA: Regina Books.

Borza, E. N. and Palagia, O. 2007. "The Chronology of the Macedonian Royal Tombs at Vergina." *Jahrbuch des Deutschen Archäologischen Instituts* 122: 81–125.

Bosworth, A. B. 1971a. "Philip II and Upper Macedonia." *CQ* 21.1: 93–105.

——. 1971b. "The Death of Alexander the Great: Rumour and Propaganda." *CQ* 21.1: 112–136.

——. 1973. "ΑΣΘΕΤΑΙΡΟΙ." *CQ* 23.2: 245–253.

——. 1975. "The Mission of Amphoterus and the Outbreak of Agis' Revolt." *Phoenix* 39: 27–43.

——. 1978: "Eumenes, Neoptolemus, and *PSI* XII 1284." *GRBS* 19.3: 227–237.

——. 1980a. *A Historical Commentary on Arrian's History of Alexander*. Vol. 1. Oxford: Oxford University Press.

——. 1980b. "Alexander and the Iranians." *JHS* 100: 1–21.

——. 1982. "The Location of Alexander's Campaign against the Illyrians in 335 B.C." In Barr-Sharrar and Borza, *Macedonia and Greece* 1982: 74–84.

——. 1986. "Alexander the Great and the Decline of Macedon." *JHS* 106: 1–12.

——. 1988. *Conquest and Empire. The Reign of Alexander the Great*. Cambridge: Cambridge University Press.

———. 1992. "Philip III Arrhidaeus and the Chronology of the Successors." *Chiron* 22: 56–81.
———. 1993. "Perdiccas and the Kings." *CQ* 43.2: 420–427.
———. 1994. "A New Macedonian Prince." *CQ* 44.1: 57–65.
———. 1995. *A Historical Commentary on Arrian's History of Alexander*. Vol. 2. Oxford: Oxford University Press.
———. 1996b. "The Tumult and Shouting: Two Interpretations of the Cleitus Episode." *AHB* 10: 19–30.
———. 2002. *The Legacy of Alexander. Politics, Warfare, and Propaganda under the Successors*. Oxford: Oxford University Press.
———. 2003. "Why did Athens lose the Lamian War?" In Palagia and Tracey, *Macedonians in Athens* 2003: 14–22.
Bosworth, A. B. and Baynham, E., eds. 2000. *Alexander the Great in Fact and Fiction*. Oxford: Oxford University Press.
Bowden, H. 2013. "On Kissing and Making Up: Court Protocol and Historiography in Alexander the Great's 'Experiment with *Proskynesis*'." *Bulletin of the Institute of Classical Studies* 56.2: 55–77.
Briant, P. 2002. *From Cyrus to Alexander. A History of the Persian Empire*. Winona Lake, IN: Eisenbrauns.
———. 2015. *Darius in the Shadow of Alexander*. Cambridge, MA and London: Harvard University Press.
Briscoe, J. 2012. *A Commentary on Livy. Books 41–45*. Oxford: Oxford University Press.
Broneer, O. 1941. *The Lion Monument at Amphipolis*. American School of Classical Studies at Athens. Cambridge, MA: Harvard University Press.
Brosius, M. 2003. "Alexander and the Persians." In Roisman, *Alexander* 2003: 169–193.
Brown, T. S. 1988. "Herodotus and Justin 9.2." *AHB* 2: 1–3.
Brunt, P. A. 1963. "Alexander's Macedonian Cavalry." *JHS* 83: 27–46.
———. 1976. "Anaximenes and King Alexander I of Macedon." *JHS* 96: 151–153.
———. 1980. "On Historical Fragments and Epitomes." *CQ* 30: 477–494.
Buckler, J. 1980. *The Theban Hegemony 371–362 BC*. Cambridge, MA and London: Harvard University Press.
———. 1989. *Philip II and The Sacred War*. Leiden, Netherlands; New York; Copenhagen; Köln: Brill.
———. 1996. "The Actions of Philip II in 347 and 346 B.C.: A Reply to N. G. L. Hammond." *CQ* 46.2: 380–386.
———. 2000. "Demosthenes and Aeschines." In Worthington, *Demosthenes* 2000: 114–158.
———. 2003. *Aegean Greece in the Fourth Century BC*. Leiden, Netherlands and Boston: Brill.
Buckler, J. and Beck, H. 2008. *Central Greece and the Politics of Power in the Fourth Century BC*. Cambridge: Cambridge University Press.
Burstein, S. 1977. "I.G. II² 561 and the Court of Alexander IV." *ZPE* 24: 223–225.
———. 1991. "Pharaoh Alexander: A Scholarly Myth." *Ancient Society* 22: 139–145.
———. 1999. "I.G. I.³ 61 and the Black Sea Grain Trade." In R. Mellor and L. Tritle, eds., *Text and Tradition: Studies in Greek History and Historiography in Honor of Mortimer Chambers*, 93–104. Claremont, CA: Regina Press.
———. 2008. "Alexander's Organization of Egypt: A Note on the Career of Cleomenes of Naucratis." In Howe and Reames, *Legacies* 2008: 183–194.
Campbell, D. 2011. "Ancient Catapults: Some Hypotheses Reexamined." *Hesperia* 80.4: 677–700.

Cargill, J. 1981. *The Second Athenian League.* Berkeley, CA: University of California Press.
Carney, E. 1980. "Alexander the Lyncestian: The Disloyal Opposition." *GRBS* 21: 23–33. Reprinted in *King and Court* 2015: 127–137.
——. 1981a. "The Conspiracy of Hermolaus." *CJ* 76: 223–231.
——. 1981b. "The Death of Clitus." *GRBS* 22: 149–160. Reprinted in *King and Court* 2015: 141–151.
——. 1983. "Regicide in Macedonia." *Parola del Passato* 211: 260–272. Reprinted in *King and Court* 2015: 155–164.
——. 1992. "The Politics of Polygamy: Olympias, Alexander and the Murder of Philip." *Historia* 41: 169–189. Reprinted in *King and Court* 2015: 167–188.
——. 1994. "Olympias, Adea Eurydice, and the end of the Argead dynasty." In Worthington, *Ventures* 1994: 357–380.
——. 1995. "Women and Basileia: Legitimacy and Female Political Action in Macedonia." *CJ* 90.4: 367–391. Reprinted in *King and Court* 2015: 1–24.
——. 1996a. "Macedonians and Mutiny: Discipline and Indiscipline in the Army of Philip and Alexander." *CPh* 91.1: 19–44. Reprinted in *King and Court* 2015: 27–56.
——. 1996b. "Alexander and Persian Women." *AJPh* 117.4: 563–583.
——. 2000. *Women and Monarchy in Macedonia.* Norman, OK: University of Oklahoma Press.
——. 2001. "The Trouble with Philip Arrhidaeus." *AHB* 15.1–2: 63–89.
——. 2002. "Hunting and the Macedonian Elite: Sharing the Rivalry of the Chase (Arrian 4.13.1)." In D. Ogden, ed., *The Hellenistic World: New Perspectives,* 59–80. London: Classical Press of Wales and Duckworth. Reprinted in *King and Court* 2015: 265–279.
——. 2003a. "Women in Alexander's Court." In Roisman, *Alexander* 2003: 227–252.
——. 2003b. "Elite Education and High Culture in Macedonia." In Heckel and Tritle, *Crossroads* 2003: 47–63. Reprinted in *King and Court* 2015: 191–204.
——. 2004. "Women and Military Leadership in Macedonia." *AncW* 35: 184–195.
——. 2006. *Olympias. Mother of Alexander the Great.* New York and London: Routledge.
——. 2007. "The Philippeum, Women, and the Formulation of Dynastic Image." In Heckel, Tritle and Wheatley, *Formulation* 2007: 27–60. Reprinted in *King and Court* 2015: 61–88.
——. 2008. "The Role of the *Basilikoi Paides* at the Argead Court." In Howe and Reames, *Legacies* 2008: 145–164. Reprinted in *King and Court* 2015: 207–221.
——. 2013. *Arsinoë of Egypt and Macedon: A Royal Life.* Oxford and New York: Oxford University Press.
——. 2015a. *King and Court in Ancient Macedonia. Rivalry, Treason and Conspiracy.* Swansea, Wales: The Classical Press of Wales.
——. 2015b. "Women and Symposia in Macedonia." In Howe, Garvin and Wrightson, *Greece, Macedon and Persia* 2015: 33–40.
——. 2015c. "Dynastic Loyalty and Dynastic Collapse in Macedonia." In Wheatley and Baynham, *East and West* 2015: 147–162.
Carney, E. and Ogden, D., eds. 2010. *Philip II and Alexander the Great. Father and Son, Lives and Afterlives.* Oxford: Oxford University Press.
Cartledge, P. 1987. *Agesilaos and the Crisis of Sparta.* London and Baltimore: The Johns Hopkins University Press.
Cawkwell, G. L. 1978. *Philip of Macedon.* London: Faber and Faber.
——. 1992. "Philip and the Amphictyonic League." In Hatzopoulos and Loukopoulos, *Philip* 1992: 78–89.

———. 1994. "The Deification of Alexander the Great: A Note." In Worthington, *Ventures* 1994: 293–306.

———. 1996. "The End of Greek Liberty." In Wallace and Harris, *Transitions* 1996: 98–121.

———. 2005. *The Greek Wars. The Failure of Persia*. Oxford: Oxford University Press.

Chambers, J.T. 1986. "Perdiccas, Thucydides and the Greek City-States." *Archaia Makedonia* IV: 139–145.

Charles, M. B. 2010. "Elephants, Alexander, and the Indian Campaign." *Mouseion* 10.3: 327–353.

Christesen, P. and Murray, S. C. 2010. "Macedonian Religion." In Roisman and Worthington, *Ancient Macedonia* 2010: 428–445.

Cloché, P. 1960. *Histoire de la Macédoine jusqu'à l'avènement d'Alexandre le Grande*. Paris: Payot.

Cohen, A. 1995. "Alexander and Achilles—Macedonians and Mycenaeans." In J. B. Carter and S. P. Morris, eds, *The Ages of Homer: A Tribute to Emily Townsend Vermeule*, 483–505. Austin, TX: University of Texas Press.

———. 1997. *The Alexander Mosaic: Stories of Victory and Defeat*. Cambridge: Cambridge University Press.

Cole, J. W. 1974. "Perdiccas and Athens." *Phoenix* 28.1: 55–72.

———. 1975. "Peisistratus on the Strymon." *Greece & Rome* 22.1: 42–44.

———. 1978. "Alexander Philhellene and Themistocles." *L'Antiquité Classique* 47: 37–49.

Collard, C., Cropp, M. J. and Gibert, J. 2004. *Euripides: Selected Fragmentary Plays*, Vol. II (*Philoctetes, Alexandros, Palamedes, Sisyphus, Andromeda, Oedipus, Hypsipyle, Antiope, Archelaus*). Oxford: Aris and Phillips.

Collins, A. 2001. "The Office of Chiliarch under Alexander and the Successors." *Phoenix* 55.3–4: 259–283.

———. 2009. "The Divinity of Alexander in Egypt: A Reassessment." In Wheatley and Hannah, *Antipodes* 2009: 179–205.

———. 2012. "The Royal Costume and Insignia of Alexander the Great." *AJPh* 133.3: 371–402.

———. 2013. "Alexander the Great and the Kingship of Babylon." *AHB* 27.3–4: 130–148.

———. 2014. "Alexander's Visit to Siwah: A New Analysis." *Phoenix* 68.1–2: 62–77.

Cosmopoulos, M. B. 1992. *Macedonia. An Introduction to its Political History*. Winnipeg: Manitoba Studies in Classical Civilization.

Dahmen, K. 2010. "The Numismatic Evidence." In Roisman and Worthington, *Ancient Macedonia* 2010: 41–62.

Dascalakis, A. 1965. *The Hellenism of the Ancient Macedonians*. Thessaloniki, Greece: Institute for Balkan Studies.

Delev, P. 2015. "Thrace from the Assassination of Kotys I to Koroupedion." In J. Valeva, E. Nankov, and D. Graninger, eds., *A Companion to Ancient Thrace*, 48–58. Malden, MA; Oxford; Chichester: Wiley-Blackwell.

Dell, H. J. 1967. "Antigonus III and Rome." *CPh* 62.2: 94–103.

———. 1977. "Macedon and Rome: The Illyrian Question in the Early Second Century B.C." *Archaia Makedonia* II: 305–315.

———, ed. 1981. *Ancient Macedonian Studies in Honor of Charles F. Edson*. Thessaloniki, Greece: Institute for Balkan Studies.

———. 1983. "The Quarrel between Demetrius and Perseus: A Note on Macedonian National Policy." *Archaia Makedonia* III: 67–76.

Depuydt, L. 1997. "The Time of the Death of Alexander the Great: 11 June 323 B.C. (–322), ca. 4:00–5:00 PM." *Die Welt des Orients* 28: 117–135.

Derow, P. 2003. "The Arrival of Rome: from the Illyrian Wars to the Fall of Macedon." In A. Erskine, ed., *A Companion to the Hellenistic World*, 51–70. Oxford: Blackwell Publishing. Reprinted in *Rome, Polybius, and the East* 2015: 21–45.

———. 2015. "Rome, the Fall of Macedon and the Sack of Corinth." In P. Derow, *Rome, Polybius, and the East*. Edited by A. Erskine and J. Crawley Quinn, 47–82. Oxford: Oxford University Press. Reprinted from *CAH*^{2} VIII: *Rome and the Mediterranean to 133 BC*, 290–323.

Develin, R. 1981. "The Murder of Philip II." *Antichthon* 15: 86–99.

———. 1985. "Anaximenes ("F Gr Hist" 72) F 4." *Historia* 34.4: 493–496.

Devine, A. M. 1985. "Grand Tactics at the Battle of Issus." *AncW* 12: 39–59.

———. 1986. "The Battle of Gaugamela: A Tactical and Source-Critical Study." *AncW* 13: 87–115.

———. 1987. "The Battle of Hydaspes: A Tactical and Source-Critical Study." *AncW* 16: 91–113.

———. 1988. "A Pawn-Sacrifice at the Battle of the Granicus: The Origins of a Favorite Stratagem of Alexander the Great." *AncW* 18: 3–20.

DeVoto, J. G., ed., trans. 1993. *Flavius Arrianus ΤΕΧΝΗ ΤΑΚΤΙΚΑ (Tactical Handbook) and ἜΚΤΑΞΙΣ ΚΑΤΑ ἈΛΑΝΩΝ (The Expedition Against the Alans)*. Chicago: Ares Publishers, Inc.

Dixon, M. D. 2007. "Corinth, Greek Freedom, and the Diadochi, 323–301 BC." In Heckel, Tritle and Wheatley, *Formulation* 2007: 151–178.

———. 2014. *Late Classical and Early Hellenistic Corinth: 338–196 B.C.* London and New York: Routledge.

Dmitriev, S. 2004. "Alexander's Exiles Decree." *Klio* 86: 348–381.

Dreyer, B. 2007. "The Arrian Parchment in Gothenburg: New Digital Processing Methods and Initial Results." In Heckel, Tritle and Wheatley, *Formulation* 2007: 245–263.

Eckstein, A. M. 1995. *Moral Vision in The Histories of Polybius*. Berkeley; Los Angeles; London: University of California Press.

———. 2002. "Greek Mediation in the First Macedonian War." *Historia* 51.3: 268–297.

———. 2005. "The Pact between the Kings, Polybius 15.20.6, and Polybius' View of the Outbreak of the Second Macedonian War." *CPh* 100.3: 228–242.

———. 2008. *Rome Enters the Greek East. From Anarchy to Hierarchy in the Hellenistic Mediterranean, 230–170 BC*. Malden, MA; Oxford; Victoria, Australia: Blackwell Publishing.

———. 2010. "Macedonia and Rome, 221–146 BC." In Roisman and Worthington, *Ancient Macedonia* 2010: 225–250.

Edson, C. F. 1949. "The Tomb of Olympias." *Hesperia* 18: 84–95.

———. 1970. "Early Macedonia." *Archaia Makedonia* I: 17–44.

Ellis, J. R. 1969. "Amyntas III, Illyria and Olynthos, 393/2–380/79." *Makedonika* 9: 1–8.

———. 1971. "Amyntas Perdikka, Philip II and Alexander the Great." *JHS* 91: 15–24.

———. 1973. "The Step-Brothers of Philip II." *Historia* 22.2: 350–354.

———. 1976. *Philip II and Macedonian Imperialism*. London: Thames and Hudson.

———. 1981. "The Assassination of Philip II." In Dell, *Studies* 1981: 99–137.

———. 1982. "Philip and the Peace of Philokrates." In Adams and Borza, *Heritage* 1982: 43–59.

Engels, D. W. 1978. *Alexander the Great and the Logistics of the Macedonian Army*. Berkeley and Los Angeles: University of California Press.

Engels, J. 2010. "Macedonians and Greeks." In Roisman and Worthington, *Ancient Macedonia* 2010: 81–98.

Epplett, C. 2007. "War Elephants in the Hellenistic World." In Heckel, Tritle and Wheatley, *Formulation* 2007: 209–232.

Errington, R. M. 1969. "Bias in Ptolemy's History of Alexander." *CQ* 19.2: 233–242.

———. 1970. "From Babylon to Triparadeisos, 323–320 BC." *JHS* 90: 49–77.

———. 1974. "Macedonian 'Royal Style' and Its Historical Significance." *JHS* 94: 20–37.

———. 1977. "An Inscription from Beroea and the Alleged Co-Rule of Demetirus II." *Archaia Makedonia* II: 115–122.

———. 1978. "The Nature of the Macedonian State under the Monarchy." *Chiron* 8: 77–133.

———. 1981. "Alexander the Philhellene and Persia." In Dell, *Studies* 1981: 139–143.

———. 1990. *A History of Macedonia*. Berkeley and Los Angeles: University of California Press.

———. 2007. "The Importance of the Capture of Amphipolis." *Archaia Makedonia* VII: 275–282.

Erskine, A. 1989. "The 'πεζέταιροι' of Philip II and Alexander III." *Historia* 38.4: 385–394.

———. 2002. "Life after Death: Alexandria and the Body of Alexander." *Greece & Rome* 49: 163–179.

Facorellis, Y., Sofronidou, M. and Hourmouziadis, G. 2014. "Radiocarbon Dating of the Neolithic Lakeside Settlement of Dispilio, Kastoria, Northern Greece." *Radiocarbon* 56.2: 511–528.

Faklaris, P. 1994. "Aegae: Determining the Site of the First Capital of the Macedonians." *AJA* 98.4: 609–616.

Fearn, D. W. 2007. "Herodotus 5.17–22. Narrating Ambiguity: Murder and Macedonian Allegiance." In E. Irwin and E. Greenwood, eds., *Reading Herodotus: A Study of the Logoi of Book 5 of Herodotus' Histories*, 98–127. Cambridge: Cambridge University Press.

Fears, J. R. 1975. "Pausanias, the assassin of Philip." *Athenaeum* 53: 111–135.

Ferguson, W. S. 1948. "Demetrius Poliorcetes and the Hellenic League." *Hesperia* 17: 112–136.

Ferrario, S. B. 2014. *Historical Agency and the 'Great Man' in Classical Greece*. Cambridge: Cambridge University Press.

Flensted-Jensen, Pernille. 1995. "The Bottiaians and their Poleis." In M. H. Hansen and K. Raaflaub, eds., *Studies in the Ancient Greek Polis*, 103–132. Stuttgart: Historia Einzelschriften.

Flower, M. 2000. "Alexander the Great and Panhellenism." In Bosworth and Baynham, *Fact and Fiction* 2000: 96–135.

Flower, M. and Marincola, J. 2002. *Herodotus: Histories Book IX. Cambridge Greek and Latin Classics*. Cambridge: Cambridge University Press.

Fouache, E., Ghilardi, M., Vouvalidis, K., Syrides, G., Kunesch, S., Styllas, M. and Stiros, S. 2008. "Contribution on the Holocene Reconstruction of Thessaloniki Coastal Plain, Greece." *Journal of Coastal Research* 24(5): 1161–1173, 1217–1218.

Franks, H. M. 2012. *Hunters, Heroes, Kings: The Frieze of Tomb II at Vergina*. Princeton, NJ: Princeton University Press.

Fraser, P. M. 1972. *Ptolemaic Alexandria*. 3 Vols. Oxford: Oxford University Press.

Fredricksmeyer, E. A. 1979. "Divine Honors for Philip II." *TAPA* 109: 39–41.

———. 2000. "Alexander the Great and the Kingdom of Asia." In Bosworth and Baynham, *Fact and Fiction* 2000: 136–166.

Fuller, J. F. C. 1958. *The Generalship of Alexander the Great*. London: Eyre & Spottiswoode.

Gabbert, J. 1997. *Antigonus II Gonatas. A Political Biography*. London and New York: Routledge.

Gabelko, O. L. and Kuzmin, Y. N. 2008. "Matrimonial Policy of Demetrios II of Macedonia: New Solutions of Old Problems." *Вестник древней истории / Vestnik drevnej istorii / Bulletin of Ancient History* 1: 141–164.

Gabriel, R. A. 2010. *Philip II of Macedonia: Greater than Alexander*. Washington, DC: Potomac Books.

Gambetti, S. 2012. "Satyros of Alexandria (631)." In *Brill's New Jacoby*, Editor in Chief: Ian Worthington. http://referenceworks.brillonline.com/entries/brill-s-new-jacoby/satyros-of-alexandria-631-a631.

Gerolymatos, A. 1986. "The proxenia of Alexander I of Makedonia." *LCM* 11.5: 75–76.

Giannakis, G., ed. 2012. *Ancient Macedonia. Language, History, Culture*. Thessaloniki, Greece: Centre for the Greek Language.

Gill, D. W. J. 2008. "Inscribed Silver Plate from Tomb II at Vergina: Chronological Implications." *Hesperia* 77: 335–358.

Goralski, W. J. 1989. "Arrian's *Events After Alexander*." *AncW* 19: 81–108.

Grainger, J. D. 1999. *The League of the Aetolians*. Leiden, Netherlands: Brill.

———. 2007. *Alexander the Great Failure. The Collapse of the Macedonian Empire*. London and New York: Hambledon Continuum.

Green, P. 1990. *Alexander to Actium. The Historical Evolution of the Hellenistic Age*. Berkeley and Los Angeles: University of California Press.

———. 1991. *Alexander of Macedon, 356–323 B.C*. Berkeley; Los Angeles; Oxford: University of California Press.

———. 2003. "Politics, Philosophy and Propaganda. Hermias of Atarneus and His Friendship with Aristotle." In Heckel and Tritle, *Crossroads* 2003: 29–46.

Greenwalt, W. S. 1984. "The Search for Arrhidaeus." *AncW* 10: 69–77.

———. 1985. "The Introduction of Caranus into the Argead King List." *GRBS* 26: 43–49.

———. 1986. "Herodotus and the Foundation of Argead Macedonia." *AncW* 13: 117–122.

———. 1988. "Amyntas III and the Political Stability of Argead Macedonia." *AncW* 18: 35–44.

———. 1989. "Polygamy and Succession in Argead Macedonia." *Arethusa* 22.1: 19–45.

———. 1994. "A Solar Dionysus and Argead Legitimacy." *AncW* 25.1: 3–8.

———. 1999. "Why Pella?" *Historia* 48.2: 158–183.

———. 2003. "Archelaus the Philhellene." *AncW* 34:131–153.

———. 2007. "The Development of a Middle Class in Macedonia." *Archaia Makedonia* VII: 87–96.

———. 2008. "Philip and Olympias on Samothrace: A Clue to Macedonian Politics during the 360s." In Howe and Reames, *Legacies* 2008: 79–106.

———. 2010. "Macedonia, Illyria and Epirus." In Roisman and Worthington, *Ancient Macedonia* 2010: 279–305.

———. 2017. "Alexander II of Macedon." In Howe, Müller and Stoneman, *War and Empire* 2017: 80–91.

Griffith, G. T. 1992. "Philip as General and the Macedonian Army." In Hatzopoulos and Loukopoulos, *Philip* 1992: 58–77.

Gruen, E. 1973. "The Supposed Alliance between Rome and Philip V of Macedon." *CSCA* 6: 123–136.

———. 1974. "The Last Years of Philip V." *GRBS* 15.2: 221–246.

——. 1982. "Macedonia and the Settlement of 167 BC." In Adams and Borza, *Heritage* 1982: 257–267.

——. 1984. *The Hellenistic World and the Coming of Rome*. Vol. 2. Berkeley and Los Angeles: University of California Press.

Habicht, C. 1987. "The Role of Athens in the Reorganization of the Delphic Amphictyony after 189 B.C." *Hesperia* 56: 59–71.

——. 1997. *Athens from Alexander to Antony*. Cambridge, MA and London: Harvard University Press.

——. 2003. "Athens after the Chremonidean War: some second thoughts." In Palagia and Tracey, *Macedonians in Athens* 2003: 52–55.

Hale, J. R. 2009. *Lords of the Sea: The Epic Story of the Athenian Navy and the Birth of Democracy*. New York: Viking.

Hall, J. M. 2001. "Contested Ethnicities: Perceptions of Macedonia within Evolving Definitions of Greek Identity." In I. Malkin, ed., *Ancient Perceptions of Greek Ethnicity*, 159–186. Cambridge: Cambridge University Press.

Hamilton, C. D. 1982. "Philip II and Archidamus." In Adams and Borza, *Heritage* 1982: 61–83. Washington, DC: University Press of America.

——. 1986. "Amyntas III and Agesilaus: Macedon and Sparta in the Fourth Century." *Archaia Makedonia* IV: 239–245.

——. 1993. "The Origins of the Second Macedonian War." *Archaia Makedonia* V: 559–567.

Hamilton, J. R. 1969. *Plutarch Alexander: A Commentary*. Oxford: Clarendon Press.

Hammond, N. G. L. 1938. "The Two Battles of Chaeronea (338 B.C. and 86 B.C.)." *Klio* 31: 186–218.

——. 1966. "The Kingdoms in Illyria circa 400–167 B.C." *ABSA* 61: 239–253.

——. 1974. "Alexander's Campaign in Illyria." *JHS* 94: 66–87. Reprinted in *Collected Studies III* 1994: 1–25.

——. 1977. "The Campaign of Alexander Against Cleitus and Glaucias." *Archaia Makedonia* II: 503–509.

——. 1978. "Philip's Tomb in Historical Context." *GRBS* 18: 343–349.

——. 1980a. "Some Passages in Arrian Concerning Alexander." *CQ* 30.2: 455–476. Reprinted in *Collected Studies III* 1994: 65–92.

——. 1980b. "The March of Alexander the Great on Thebes in 335 B.C." In *Megas Alexandros*, 171–181. Thessaloniki. Reprinted in *Collected Studies III* 1994: 45–57.

——. 1980c. "The Battle of the Granicus River." *JHS* 100: 73–88. Reprinted in *Collected Studies III* 1994: 93–108.

——. 1983. *Three Historians of Alexander the Great*. Cambridge: Cambridge University Press.

——. 1988a. "The King and the Land in the Macedonian Kingdom." *CQ* 38.2: 382–391. Reprinted in *Collected Studies III* 1994: 211–220.

——. 1988b. "The Campaign and Battle of Cynoscephalae in 197 BC." *JHS* 108: 60–82. Reprinted in *Collected Studies III* 1994: 351–375.

——. 1989a. *The Macedonian State. The Origins, Institutions and History*. Oxford: Oxford University Press.

——. 1989b. "The Illyrian Atintani, the Epirotic Atintanes and the Roman Protectorate." *JRS* 79: 11–25. Reprinted in *Collected Studies III* 1994: 245–259.

——. 1989c. "Casualties and Reinforcements of Citizen Soldiers in Greece and Macedonia." *JHS* 109: 56–68.

——. 1990. "Royal Pages, Personal Pages, and Boys Trained in the Macedonian Manner during the Period of the Temenid Monarchy." *Historia* 39.3: 261–290.

———. 1991. "The Various Guards of Philip II and Alexander III." *Historia* 40.4: 396–418.
———. 1992. "The Macedonian Navies of Philip and Alexander until 330 B.C." *Antichthon* 26: 30–41.
———. 1993a. *Sources for Alexander the Great.* Cambridge: Cambridge University Press.
———. 1993b. "Philip's 'Letter' to Athens in 340 B.C." *Antichthon* 27: 13–20.
———. 1994a. *Collected Studies III. Alexander and His Successors in Macedonia.* Amsterdam: Hakkert.
———. 1994b. *Philip of Macedon.* Baltimore: Johns Hopkins University Press.
———. 1994c. "Literary Evidence for Macedonian Speech." *Historia* 43.2: 131–142.
———. 1995. "Connotations of 'Macedonia' and 'Macedones' Until 323 B. C." *CQ* 45.1: 120–128.
———. 1996. *Alexander the Great. King, Commander and Statesman.* Third Edition. London: Bristol Classical Press, reprint of Noyes 1980.
———. 1998. "Cavalry Recruited in Macedonian down to 322 B.C." *Historia* 47.4: 404–425.
———. 1999. "The Roles of the Epistates in Macedonian Contexts." *ABSA* 94: 369–375.
Harder, A. 1985. *Euripides' Kresphontes and Archelaos. Introduction, Text and Commentary.* Leiden, Netherlands: Brill.
Harding, P. 2006. *Didymos: On Demosthenes.* Oxford: Oxford University Press.
Harris, E. M. 1995. *Aeschines and Athenian Politics.* New York and Oxford: Oxford University Press.
Harvati, K. 2009. "Petralona: Link between Africa and Europe?" *Hesperia* 43: 31–47.
Hatzopoulos, M. B. 1982. "The Oleveni Inscription and the Dates of Philip II's Reign." In Adams and Borza, *Heritage* 1982: 21–42.
———. 1986. "Succession and Regency in Classical Macedonia." *Archaia Makedonia* IV: 279–292.
———. 1987. "Strepsa: A Reconsideration or New Evidence of the Road System of Lower Macedonia." In M. B. Hatzopoulos and L. D. Loukopoulos, *Two Studies in Ancient Topography*, 19–53. (Meletemata 3) Athens: de Boccard.
———, ed. 1994. *Macedonia from Philip II to the Roman Conquest.* Princeton, NJ: Princeton University Press.
———. 1996. *Macedonian Institutions under the Kings. I–II.* (Meletemata 22) Athens: de Boccard.
———. 2003. "Herodotus (8.137–8), the Manumissions from Leukopetra, and the Topography of the Middle Haliakmon Valley." In P. Derow and R. Parker, eds., *Herodotus and His World*, 203–218. Oxford: Oxford University Press.
———. 2008. "The Burial of the Dead (at Vergina) or the Unrelenting Controversy on the Identity of the Occupants of Tomb II." *Tekmeria* 9: 91–118.
———. 2011a. "Macedonia and Macedonians." In Lane Fox, *Ancient Macedon* 2011: 43–49.
———. 2011b. "Macedonians and Other Greeks." In Lane Fox, *Ancient Macedon* 2011: 51–78.
———. 2013. "The Speech of the Ancient Macedonians in the Light of Recent Epigraphic Discoveries." *Монументум Gregorianum. Сб. научных статей памяти академика Г.М. Бонгард-Левина / А.И. Иванчик (ред.).* М., 204–221.
Hatzopoulos, M. B. and Loukopoulos, L., eds. 1992. *Philip of Macedon.* Athens: Ekdotike Athenon S. A., reprint of 1981 London: Heinemann.
Hauben, H. 1975. "Philipe II, fondateur de la marine macédonienne." *Ancient Society* 6: 51–57.
———. 1976. "The expansion of Macedonian sea-power under Alexander the Great." *Ancient Society* 7: 79–105.

Hauben, H. and Meeus, A., eds. 2014. *The Age of the Successors and the Creation of the Hellenistic Kingdoms (323–276 B.C.)*. Leuven, Belgium: Peeters.
Heckel, W. 1977. "The Conspiracy against Philotas." *Phoenix* 31: 9–21.
——. 1980a. "Alexander at the Persian Gates." *Athenaeum* 58: 168–174.
——. 1980b. "*IG* II² 561 and the Status of Alexander IV." *ZPE* 40: 249–250.
——. 1980c. "Marsyas of Pella, Historian of Macedon." *Hermes* 108.3: 444–462.
——. 1986. ""Somatophylakia": A Macedonian "Cursus Honorum"." *Phoenix* 40.3: 279–294.
——. 1992. *The Marshals of Alexander's Empire*. London: Routledge.
——. 2003a. "King and 'Companions': Observations on the Nature of Power in the Reign of Alexander." In Roisman, *Alexander* 2003: 197–225.
——. 2003b. "Alexander the Great and the 'Limits of the Civilized World'." In Heckel and Tritle, *Crossroads* 2003: 147–174.
——. 2006a. *Who's Who in the Age of Alexander the Great*. Malden, MA; Oxford; Victoria, Australia: Blackwell Publishing.
——. 2006b. "Mazaeus, Callisthenes and the Alexander Sarcophagus." *Historia* 55.4: 385–396.
——. 2007. "Nicanor son of Balacrus." *GRBS* 47: 401–412.
——. 2008. *The Conquests of Alexander the Great*. Cambridge: Cambridge University Press.
——. 2009. "The *Asthetairoi*: A Closer Look." In Wheatley and Hannah, *Antipodes* 2009: 99–117.
——. 2015. "Alexander, Achilles, and Heracles: Between Myth and History." In Wheatley and Baynham, *East and West* 2015: 21–33.
——. 2016. *Alexander's Marshals. A Study of the Makedonian Aristocracy and the Politics of Military Leadership. Second Edition*. London and New York: Routledge.
Heckel, W., Howe, T. and Müller, S. 2017. "'The giver of the bride, the bridegroom, and the bride'. A study of the murder of Philip II and its aftermath." In Howe, Müller and Stoneman, *War and Empire* 2017: 92–124.
Heckel, W. and Tritle, L., eds. 2003. *Crossroads of History. The Age of Alexander*. Claremont, CA: Regina Books.
Heckel, W. and Tritle, L., eds. 2009. *Alexander the Great: A New History*. Malden, MA; Oxford; Chichester: Wiley-Blackwell.
Heckel, W., Tritle, L. and Wheatley, P., eds. 2007. *Alexander's Empire: Formulation to Decay*. Claremont, CA: Regina Books.
Heinrichs, J. and Müller, S. 2008. "Ein persisches Statussymbol auf Münzen Alexanders I. von Makedonien." *ZPE* 2008: 283–309.
Heisserer, A. J. 1980. *Alexander the Great and the Greeks. The Epigraphic Evidence*. Norman, OK: University of Oklahoma Press.
Helliesen, J. 1986. "Andriscus and the Revolt of the Macedonians, 149–148 B.C." *Archaia Makedonia* IV: 307–314.
Heskel, J. 1988. "The Political Background of the Arybbas Decree." *GRBS* 29.2: 185–196.
——. 1996. "Philip II and Argaios." In Wallace and Harris, *Transitions* 1996: 37–56.
Hoffman, R. J. 1975. "Perdikkas and the Outbreak of the Peloponnesian War." *GRBS* 16: 359–377.
Holt, F. L. 1982. "The Hyphasis Mutiny: A Source Study." *AncW* 5: 33–59.
——. 2000. "The Death of Coenus: Another Study in Method." *AHB* 14.1–2: 49–55.

———. 2005. *Into the Land of Bones. Alexander the Great in Afghanistan*. Berkeley, CA; Los Angeles; Oxford: University of California Press.

———. 2016. *The Treasures of Alexander the Great*. Oxford and New York: Oxford University Press.

Hornblower, S. 1997. *A Commentary on Thucydides*. Volume I: Books I–III. Oxford: Clarendon Press.

Hourmouziadis, G., ed. 2002. *Dispilio. 7500 Years After*. Thessaloniki, Greece: University Studio Press.

Howe, T. 2014. "Founding Alexandria: Alexander the Great and the Politics of Memory." In P. Bosman, ed., *Alexander in Africa*, 72–91. *Acta Classica Supplementum V*. Praetoria: Classical Association of South Africa.

Howe, T., Garvin, E. E. and Wrightson, G., eds. 2015. *Greece, Macedon and Persia. Studies in Social, Political and Military History in Honour of Waldemar Heckel*. Oxford and Philadelphia: Oxbow Books.

Howe, T. and Müller, S. 2012. "Mission Accomplished: Alexander at the Hyphasis." *AHB* 26: 21–38.

Howe, T., Müller, S. and R. Stoneman, eds. 2017. *Ancient Historiography on War and Empire*. Oxford: Oxbow Books.

Howe, T. and Reames, J., eds. 2008. *Macedonian Legacies. Studies in Ancient Macedonian History and Culture in Honor of Eugene N. Borza*. Claremont, CA: Regina Books.

Hunt, P. 2010. *War, Peace, and Alliance in Demosthenes' Athens*. Cambridge: Cambridge University Press.

Iatrou, M. 2016. "The Sanctuary of Zeus Olympios." In D. Pandermalis, ed., *Gods and Mortals at Olympus. Ancient Dion, City of Zeus*, 90–93. Athens and New York: Onassis Foundation (USA).

Isaac, B. H. 1986. *The Greek Settlements in Thrace Until the Macedonian Conquest*. Leiden, Netherlands: Brill.

Janko, R. 1982. *Homer, Hesiod and the Hymns*. Cambridge: Cambridge University Press.

Jones, N. F. 2016. "Philochoros of Athens (328)." In *Brill's New Jacoby*, Editor in Chief: Ian Worthington. http://referenceworks.brillonline.com/entries/brill-s-new-jacoby/philochoros-of-athens-328-a328.

Jouanna, J. 1999. *Hippocrates*. Baltimore, MD and London: The Johns Hopkins University Press.

Kalléris, J. N. 1988. *Les anciens Macédoniens. Etude linguistique et historique*, 2 vols. Athens: L'Institut Français d'Athènes.

Kanatsulis, D. 1968. "Antipatros als Feldherr und Staatsmann nach den Tode Alexanders des Grossen." *Makedonika* 8: 121–184.

Kapetanopoulos, E. 1994. "Sirras." *AncW* 25.1: 9–14.

Karamitrou-Mentessidi, G. 2011. "Aiani – Historical and Geographic Context." In Lane Fox, *Ancient Macedon* 2011: 93–112.

Karunanithy, D. 2013. *The Macedonian War Machine. Neglected Aspects of the Armies of Philip, Alexander and the Successors 359–281 BC*. Barnsley, South Yorkshire: Pen & Sword.

Kern, P. B. 1999. *Ancient Siege Warfare*. Bloomington and Indianapolis: Indiana University Press.

Kertész, I. 2005. "When did Alexander I visit Olympia?" *Nikephoros* 18: 115–126.

King, C. J. 2010. "Macedonian Kingship and Other Political Institutions." In Roisman and Worthington, *Ancient Macedonia* 2010: 373–391.

———. 2013. "Plutarch, Alexander, and Dream Divination." *ICS* 38: 81–111.
Kosmetatou, E. 2004. "Rhoxane's Dedications to Athena Polias." *ZPE* 146: 75–80.
Kottaridi, A. 2002. "Discovering Aigai, the Old Macedonian Capital." In M. Stamatopoulou and M. Yeroulanou, eds., *Excavating Classical Culture*, 75–81. Oxford: British Archaeological Reports.
———. 2011. "The Palace of Aegae." In Lane Fox, *Ancient Macedon* 2011: 297–333.
Koukouli-Chryssanthaki, Ch. 2011. "Amphipolis." In Lane Fox, *Ancient Macedon* 2011: 409–452.
Kremydi, S. 2011. "Coinage and Finance." In Lane Fox, *Ancient Macedon* 2011: 159–178.
Kuhrt, A. 1988. "Earth and Water." *Achaemenid History* 3: 87–99.
Landucci Gattinoni, F. 2003. *L'arte de potere. Vita e opere di Cassandro di Macedonia*. Stuttgart: Franz Steiner Verlag.
———. 2008. *Diodoro Siculo: Biblioteca storica: libro XVIII: commento storico. Storia. Ricerche*. Milano: Vita e Pensiero.
———. 2009. "Cassander's Wife and Heirs." In Wheatley and Hannah, *Antipodes* 2009: 261–275.
———. 2010. "Cassander and the Legacy of Philip II and Alexander III in Diodorus' Library." In Carney and Ogden, *Father and Son* 2010: 113–121.
Lane Fox, R. 1973. *Alexander the Great*. London: Allen Lane.
———, ed. 2011a. *Brill's Companion to Ancient Macedon*. Leiden, Netherlands and Boston: Brill.
———. 2011b. "Dating the Royal Tombs at Vergina." In Lane Fox, *Ancient Macedon* 2011: 1–34.
———. 2011c. "'Glorious Servitude...': The Reigns of Antigonus Gonatas and Demetrius II." In Lane Fox, *Ancient Macedon* 2011: 495–519.
Larsen, J. A. O. 1968. *Greek Federal States*. Oxford: Clarendon Press.
Lazaridis, D. 1997. *Amphipolis*. Second Edition. Athens: Hellenic Ministry of Culture.
Le Bohec, S. 1993. *Antigone Dôsôn, roi de Macédoine*. Nancy, France: Presses Universitaires de Nancy.
Leake, W. M. 1967. *Travels in Northern Greece*. Vol III. Adolf M. Hakkert, reprint of London 1835.
Leigh Fermor, P. 2014. *Abducting a General. The Kreipe Operation and SOE in Crete*. London: John Murray.
Liampi, K. 1998. "The Coinage of King Derdas and the History of the Elimiote Dynasty." In A. Burnett, U. Wartenberg and R. Witschonke, eds., *Coins of Macedonia and Rome: Essays in Honour of Charles Hersh*, 5–11. London: Spink and Son Ltd.
Lilimbaki-Akamati, M. and Akamatis, I. 2003. *Pella and Its Environs*. Thessaloniki, Greece: Athanasios A. Altintzi.
———. 2012. "Pella from the Bronze Age to the Hellenistic Age." In M. Tiverios, P. Nigdelis and P. Adam-Veleni, eds., *Threpteria. Studies on Ancient Macedonia*, 9–25. Thessaloniki, Greece: AUTH Press.
Lloyd, A. B. 1996. "Philip II and Alexander the Great: The Moulding of Macedon's Army." In A. B. Lloyd, ed., *Battle in Antiquity*, 169–198. London: Duckworth, The Classical Press of Wales.
Lock, R. 1972. "The Date of Agis' War in Greece." *Antichthon* 6: 10–27.
———. 1977. "The Macedonian Army Assembly in the Time of Alexander the Great." *CPh* 72: 91–107.
Lund, H. S. 1992. *Lysimachus: a Study in Early Hellenistic Kingship*. London: Routledge.
Ma, J. 2008. "Chaironeia 338: Topographies of Commemoration." *JHS* 128: 72–91.

McInerney, J. 2013. "*Polis* and *koinon*: Federal Government in Greece." In H. Beck, ed., *A Companion to Ancient Greek Government*, 466–479. Chichester: Wiley-Blackwell.

McKechnie, P. 1999. "Manipulation of Themes in Quintus Curtius Rufus Book 10." *Historia* 48: 44–60.

McQueen, E. I. 1978. "Some Notes on the Anti-Macedonian Movement in the Peloponnese in 331 BC." *Historia* 27: 40–64.

———. 1995. *Diodorus Siculus: The Reign of Philip II. The Greek and Macedonian narrative from Book XVI*. London: Bristol Classical Press.

Macurdy, G. 1932. *Hellenistic Queens*. Baltimore, MD: The Johns Hopkins Press.

Maniatis, Y., Malamidou, D., Koukouli-Chryssanthaki, H. and Facorellis, Y. 2010. "Radiocarbon Dating of the Amphipolis Bridge in Northern Greece, Maintained and Functioned for 2500 Years." *Radiocarbon* 52.1: 41–63.

Manti, P. A. 1994. "The Macedonian Sarissa, Again." *AncW* 25.1: 77–91.

March, D. 1995. "The Kings of Makedon: 399–369 B.C." *Historia* 44.3: 257–282.

Mari, M. 2011. "Archaic and Early Classical Macedonia." In Lane Fox, *Ancient Macedon* 2011: 79–92.

Markle, M. M. 1976. "Support of Athenian Intellectuals for Philip. A Study of Isocrates' *Philippus* and Speusippus' *Letter to Philip*." *JHS* 96: 80–99.

———. 1977. "The Macedonian Sarissa, Spear, and Related Armor." *AJA* 81: 323–339.

———. 1978. "Use of the Sarissa by Philip and Alexander of Macedon." *AJA* 82: 483–497.

———. 1999. "A Shield Monument from Veria and the Chronology of Macedonian Shield Types." *Hesperia* 68.2: 219–254.

Marsden, E. W. 1969. *Greek and Roman Artillery*. Oxford: Clarendon Press.

———. 1977. "Macedonian Military Machinery and its Designers under Philip and Alexander." *Archaia Makedonia* II: 211–223.

Matarese, C. 2013. "Proskynesis and the Gesture of the Kiss at Alexander's Court: The Creation of a new Élite." *Palamedes* 8: 75–85.

Mattingly, H. B. 1961. "The Methone Decrees." *CQ* 11.2: 154–165.

———. 1968. "Athenian Finance in the Peloponnesian War." *Bulletin de correspondence hellénique* 92: 450–485.

Matyszak, P. 2009. *Roman Conquests: Macedonia and Greece*. South Yorkshire: Pen & Sword.

Meeus, A. 2008. "The Power Struggle of the Diadochoi in Babylon, 323 BC." *Ancient Society* 38: 39–82.

———. 2009. "Some Institutional Problems concerning the Succession to Alexander the Great: "Prostasia" and Chiliarchy." *Historia* 58.3: 287–310.

———. 2012. "Diodorus and the Chronology of the Third Diadoch War." *Phoenix* 66: 74–96.

———. 2013. "What We Do Not Know about the Age of the Diadochi: The Methodological Consequences of the Gaps in the Evidence." In Alonso Troncoso and Anson, *After Alexander* 2013: 84–98.

———. 2014. "The Territorial Ambitions of Ptolemy I." In Hauben and Meeus, *Age of the Successors* 2014: 263–306.

Mehl, A. 1980/81. "ΔΟΡΙΚΤΗΤΟΣ ΧΩΡΑ." *Ancient Society* 10/11: 173–212.

Meiggs, R. 1972. *The Athenian Empire*. Oxford: Oxford University Press.

———. 1982. *Trees and Timber in the Ancient Mediterranean World*. Oxford: Oxford University Press.

Meloni, P. 1953. *Perseo e la Fine della Monarchia Macedona*. Rome: L'Erma di Bretschneider.

Mendels, D. 1984. "Aetolia 331–301: Frustration, Political Power, and Survival." *Historia* 33.2: 129–180.

Merker, I. L. 1965. "The Ancient Kingdom of Paeonia." *Balkan Studies* 6: 35–54.
Miller, S. 1993a. "Boscoreale and Macedonian Shields." *Archaia Makedonia* V: 965–974.
———. 1993b. *The Tomb of Lyson and Kallikles: A Painted Macedonian Tomb*. Mainz am Rhein: Philipp von Zabern.
Milns, R. D. 1967. "Philip II and the Hypaspists." *Historia* 16.4: 509–512.
———. 1971. "The Hypaspists of Alexander III: Some Problems." *Historia* 20.2/3: 186–195.
Mitchell, L. 2002. *Greeks Bearing Gifts. The Public Use of Private Relationships in the Greek World, 425–323*. Cambridge: Cambridge University Press. (paperback edition of 1997 hb)
———. 2007. "Born to Rule? Succession in the Argead Royal House." In Heckel, Tritle and Wheatley, *Formulation* 2007: 61–74.
Morison, W. S. 2014. "Theopompos of Chios (115)." In *Brill's New Jacoby*, Editor in Chief: Ian Worthington. http://referenceworks.brillonline.com/entries/brill-s-new-jacoby/theopompos-of-chios-115-a115.
Morrison, G. 2001. "Alexander, Combat Psychology, and Persepolis." *Antichthon* 35: 30–44.
Morrison, J. S. 1987 "Athenian Sea-Power in 323/2 BC: Dream and Reality." *JHS* 107: 88–97.
———. 1995. "Hellenistic Oared Warships, 399–31 BC." In R. Gardiner and J Morrison, eds., *Age of the Galley: Mediterranean Oared Vessels since pre-Classical Times*, 66–77. London: Conway Maritime Press.
Mortensen, K. 1992. "Eurydice: Demonic or Devoted Mother?" *AHB* 6.4: 156–171.
Müller, S. 2010. "Philip II." In Roisman and Worthington, *Ancient Macedonia* 2010: 166–185.
Nagle, D. B. 1996. "The Cultural Context of Alexander's Speech at Opis." *TAPA* 126: 151–172.
Natoli, A. F. 2004. *The Letter of Speusippus to Philip II*. Stuttgart: Franz Steiner.
Nawotka, K. 2003. "Freedom of the Greek Cities in Asia Minor in the Age of Alexander the Great." *Klio* 85.1: 15–41.
———. 2012. "Persia, Alexander the Great and the Kingdom of Asia." *Klio* 94.2: 348–356.
Nelson, E. D. 2007. "Hippocrates, Heraclids, and the 'Kings of the Heracleidai': Adaptations of Asclepiad History by the Author of the 'Presbeutikos'." *Phoenix* 61.3–4: 234–246.
Ogden, D. 1999. *Polygamy, Prostitutes and Death*. London: Duckworth, The Classical Press of Wales.
———. 2011. *Alexander the Great. Myth, Genesis and Sexuality*. Exeter: University of Exeter Press.
Oikonomides, A. N. 1982. "The Epigram on the Tomb of Olympias at Pydna." *AncW* 5: 9–16.
———. 1989. "Philip IV of Macedonia: A King for Four Months (296 B.C.)." *AncW* 19: 109–112.
Olbrycht, M. J. 2010. "Macedonia and Persia." In Roisman and Worthington, *Ancient Macedonia* 2010: 342–369.
O'Neil, J. L. 1999a. "Political Trials under Alexander the Great and his Successors." *Antichthon* 33: 28–47.
———. 1999b. "Olympias: The Macedonians will never let themselves be ruled by a woman." *Prudentia* 31.1: 1–14.
Osborne, R. 2007. "The Paeonians (5.11–16)." In E. Irwin and E. Greenwood, eds., *Reading Herodotus: A Study of the Logoi of Book 5 of Herodotus' Histories*, 88–97. Cambridge: Cambridge University Press.

Pafford, I. 2011. "Amyntas son of Perdikkas, King of the Macedonians, at the Sanctuary of Trophonius, Lebadeia." *AncW* 42.2: 211–222.

Palagia, O. 2000. "Hephaestion's Pyre and the Royal Hunt of Alexander." In Bosworth and Baynham, *Fact and Fiction* 2000: 167–206.

———. 2010. "Philip's Eurydice in the Philippeum at Olympia." In Carney and Ogden, *Father and Son* 2010: 33–41.

———. 2014. "The Frescoes from the Villa of P. Fannius Synistor in Boscoreale as Reflections of Macedonian Funerary Paintings of the Early Hellenistic Period." In Hauben and Meeus, *Age of the Successors* 2014: 207–231.

Palagia, O. and Tracey, S., eds. 2003 *The Macedonians in Athens 322–229 B.C.* Oxford: Oxbow Books.

Pandermalis, D., ed. 2016. *Gods and Mortals at Olympus. Ancient Dion, City of Zeus.* Athens and New York: Onassis Foundation (USA).

Papazoglou, F. 1965. "Les origines et la destinée de l'État illyrien: Illyrii proprie dicti." *Historia* 14: 143–179.

Parker, V. 2003. "Sparta, Amyntas, and the Olynthians in 383 B.C." *Rheinisches Museum für Philologie* 146: 113–137.

Paschidis, P. 2008a. "Missing Years in the Biography of Polyperchon (318/7 and 308 BC onwards)." *Tekmeria* 9: 233–250.

———. 2008b. *Between City and King.* (Meletemata 59) Athens: de Boccard.

Perlman, S. 1985. "Greek Diplomatic Tradition and the Corinthian League of Philip of Macedon." *Historia* 34.2: 153–174.

Petsas, Ph. 1978. *Pella.* Thessaloniki, Greece: Institute for Balkan Studies reprint of 1960.

Picard, O. 2006. "Mines, monnaies et imperialism: Conflits autour de Pangee (478–413 av. J.-C.)." In A. M. Guimier-Sorbets, M. B. Hatzopoulos and Y. Morizot, eds., *Rois, cités, nécropoles. Institutions, rites et monuments en Macédoine*, 269–283. (Meletemata 45) Athens: de Boccard.

Pingiatoglou, S. 2010. "Cults of Female Deities at Dion." *Kernos* 23: 179–192.

Poddighe, E. 2009. "Alexander and the Greeks: The Corinthian League." In Heckel and Tritle, *Alexander A New History* 2009: 99–120.

———. 2013. "Propaganda Strategies and Political Documents: Philip III's *Diagramma* and the Greeks in 319 BC." In Alonso Troncoso and Anson, *After Alexander* 2013: 225–240.

Pownall, F. 2010. "The Symposia of Philip II and Alexander III of Macedon: The View From Greece." In Carney Ogden, *Father and Son* 2010: 55–65.

Prandi, L. 1998. "A Few Remarks on the Amyntas "Conspiracy"." In W. Will, ed., *Alexander der Grosse: Eine Welteroberung und ihr Hintergrund*, 91–101. Bonn: R. Habelt.

Price, M. J. 1974. *Coins of the Macedonians.* London: Trustees of the British Museum.

Pritchett, W. K. 1958. "Observations on Chaeronea." *AJA* 62: 307–311.

———. 1961. "Xerxes' Route over Mount Olympos." *AJA* 65.4: 369–375.

Psoma, S. 2011. "The Kingdom of Macedonia and the Chalcidic League." In Lane Fox, *Ancient Macedon* 2011: 113–135.

Pugliese, A. 2014. "The Literary Tradition on King Perseus and the End of the Macedonian Kingdom: Between History and Propaganda." *AncW* 45.2: 146–173.

Rahe, P. 1981. "The Annihilation of the Sacred Band at Chaeronea." *AJA* 85.1: 84–87.

Rathmann, M. 2005. *Perdikkas zwischen 323 und 320: Nachlassverwalter des Alexanderreiches oder Autokrat?* Vienna: Der Österreichen Akademie der Wissenchaften.

Raymond, D. 1953. *Macedonian Regal Coinage to 413 B.C.* New York: The American Numismatic Society.

Reames, J. 2008. "Crisis and Opportunity: The Philotas Affair Again." In Howe and Reames, *Legacies*, 2008: 165–181.

Reger, G. 1994. "The Political History of the Kyklades 260–200 B.C." *Historia* 43.1: 32–69.

Rhodes, P. J. 2010. "Literary and Epigraphic Evidence to the Roman Conquest." In Roisman and Worthington, *Ancient Macedonia* 2010: 23–40.

Riginos, A. 1994. "The Wounding of Philip II of Macedon: Fact and Fabrication." *JHS* 114: 103–119.

Robertson, N. 1976. "The Thessalian Expedition of 480 B.C." *JHS* 96: 100–120.

Rogers, G. M. 2004. *Alexander. The Ambiguity of Greatness*. New York: Random House.

Roisman, J., ed. 2003. *Brill's Companion to Alexander the Great*. Leiden, Netherlands and Boston: Brill.

——. 2010. "Classical Macedonia to Perdiccas III." In Roisman and Worthington, *Ancient Macedonia* 2010: 145–165.

——. 2011. *Ancient Greece from Homer to Alexander: The Evidence*. Translations by J. C. Yardley. Oxford: Wiley-Blackwell.

——. 2012a. *Alexander's Veterans and the Early Wars of the Successors*. Fordyce W. Mitchell Lecture Series. Austin, TX: University of Texas Press.

——. 2012b. "Royal Power, Law and Justice in Ancient Macedonia." *AHB* 26: 131–148.

——. 2014. "Perdikkas' Invasion of Egypt." In Hauben and Meeus, *Age of the Successors* 2014: 455–474.

Roisman, J. and Worthington, I., eds. 2010. *A Companion to Ancient Macedonia*. Oxford: Wiley-Blackwell.

Romano, D. G. 1990. "Philip of Macedon, Alexander the Great, and the Ancient Olympic Games." In E. C. Danien, ed., *The World of Philip and Alexander. A Symposium on Greek Life and Times*, 61–79. Philadelphia: University of Pennsylvania Museum.

Romm, J. 2011. *Ghost on the Throne. The Death of Alexander the Great and the War for Crown and Empire*. New York: Alfred A. Knopf.

Roos, P. 1985. "Alexander I in Olympia." *Eranos* 83: 162–168.

Rubin-Pinault, J. 1992. *Hippocratic Lives and Legends*. Leiden, Netherlands; New York; Köln: E. J. Brill.

Rung, E. 2015. "The Language of the Achaemenid Imperial Diplomacy towards the Greeks: The Meaning of Earth and Water." *Klio* 97.2: 503–515.

Runnels, C. 1995. "Review of Aegean Prehistory IV: The Stone Age of Greece from the Palaeolithic to the Advent of the Neolithic." *AJA* 99.4: 699–728.

Ruzicka, S. 1988. "War in the Aegean, 333–331 B.C.: A Reconsideration." *Phoenix* 42: 131–151.

——. 2010. "The 'Pixodarus Affair' Reconsidered Again." In Carney and Ogden, *Father and Son* 2010: 3–11.

Ryder, T. T. B. 1965. *Koine Eirene*. London: Oxford University Press.

——. 1994. "The Diplomatic Skills of Philip II." In Worthington, *Ventures* 1994: 228–257.

——. 2000. "Demosthenes and Philip II." In Worthington, *Demosthenes* 2000: 45–89.

Saatsoglou-Paliadeli, Ch. 1999. "In the Shadow of History: The Emergence of Archaeology." *ABSA* 94: 353–367.

——. 2007. "Arts and Politics in the Macedonian Court before Alexander." *Archaia Makedonia* VII: 345–355.

Sakellariou, M. B. 1992. "Panhellenism: From Concept to Policy." In Hatzopoulos and Loukopoulos, *Philip* 1992: 128–145.

Sancisi-Weerdenburg, H. 1993. "Alexander and Persepolis." In J. Carlsen, B. Due, O. S. Due and B. Poulsen, eds., *Alexander the Great: Reality and Myth*, 177–188. Roma: L'Erma di Bretschneider.
Sawada, N. 2010. "Social Customs and Institutions." In Roisman and Worthington, *Ancient Macedonia* 2010: 392–408.
Scaife, R. 1989. "Alexander I in the *Histories* of Herodotus." *Hermes* 117.2: 129–137.
Schäfer, C. 2002. *Eumenes von Kardia und der Kampf um die Macht im Alexanderreich*. Frankfurt am Main: Marthe Clauss.
Scholten, J. B. 2000. *The Politics of Plunder: The Aetolians and their Koinon in the Early Hellenistic Era, 279–219 B.C.* Berkeley, CA; Los Angeles; London: University of California Press.
Schorn, S. 2004. *Satyros aus Kallatis. Sammlung der Fragmente mit Kommentar*. Basel: Schwabe.
Schultz, P. 2009. "Divine Images and Royal Ideology in the Philippeion at Olympia." In J. Jensen, G. Hinge, P. Schultz and B. Wickkiser, eds., *Aspects of Ancient Greek Cult: Ritual, Context, Iconography*, 125–193. Aarhus Studies in Mediterranean Antiquity 8. Aarhus: Aarhus University Press.
Scullion, S. 2003. "Euripides and Macedon, or the silence of the *Frogs*." *CQ* 53: 389–400.
Sears, M. A. 2013. *Athens, Thrace, and the Shaping of Athenian Leadership*. Cambridge: Cambridge University Press.
Sears, M. A. and Willekes, C. 2016. "Alexander's Cavalry Charge at Chaeronea, 338 BCE." *The Journal of Military History* 80: 1017–1035.
Sekunda, N. V. 2001. "The Sarissa." *Acta Universitatis Lodziensis, Folia Archaeologica* 23: 13–41.
———. 2010. "The Macedonian Army." In Roisman and Worthington, *Ancient Macedonia* 2010: 446–471.
———. 2012. *Macedonian Armies after Alexander 323–168 BC*. Oxford and New York: Osprey Publishing.
Shipley, G. 2008. "Approaching the Macedonian Peloponnese." In C. Grandjean, ed., *Le Péloponnèse d'Épaminondas à Hadrien*, 53–68. Paris: Ausonius/De Boccard.
———. 2011. *Pseudo-Skylax's Periplous: The Circumnavigation of the Inhabited World. Text, Translation and Commentary*. Exeter: Bristol Phoenix Press.
Shrimpton, G. S. 1991. *Theopompus the Historian*. Montreal: McGill-Queens University Press.
Sickinger, J. P. 2016. "Marmor Parium (239)." In *Brill's New Jacoby*, Editor in Chief: Ian Worthington. http://referenceworks.brillonline.com/entries/brill-s-new-jacoby/marmor-parium-239-a239.
Spann, P. 1999. "Alexander at the Beas: Fox in a Lion's Skin." In F. B. Titchener and R. F. Moorton, eds., *The Eye Expanded: Life and the Arts in Greco-Roman Antiquity*, 62–74. Berkeley, CA; Los Angeles; London: University of California Press.
Sprawski, S. 1999. *Jason of Pherae: A Study on History of Thessaly in Years 431–370 BC*. Krakow: Jagiellonian University Press.
———. 2003. "Philip II and the Freedom of the Thessalians." *Electrum* 9: 55–66.
———. 2010. "The Early Temenid Kings to Alexander I." In Roisman and Worthington, *Ancient Macedonia* 2010: 127–144.
Squillace, G. 2010. "Consensus Strategies under Philip and Alexander. The Revenge Theme." In Carney and Ogden, *Father and Son* 2010: 69–80.
Stewart, A. 1993. *Faces of Power. Alexander's Image and Hellenistic Politics*. Berkeley; Los Angeles; Oxford: University of California Press.

Stillwell, R., MacDonald, W. L. and McAlister, M. H. 1976. *The Princeton Encyclopedia of Classical Sites.* Princeton, NJ: Princeton University Press.

Stoneman, R. 2008. *Alexander the Great. A Life in Legend.* New Haven, CT and London: Yale University Press.

Stylianou, P. J. 1998. *A Historical Commentary on Diodorus Siculus Book 15.* Oxford: Clarendon Press.

Tačeva, M. 1992. "On the Problems of the Coinages of Alexander I, Sparadokos and the So-Called Thracian-Macedonian Tribes." *Historia* 41.1: 58–74.

Tataki, A. B. 1998. *Macedonians Abroad. A Contribution to the Prosopography of Ancient Macedonia.* (Meletemata 26) Athens: de Boccard.

Theodoulou, T. 2011. "Evolving Relationships Between People and Water: archaeological evidence." In T. Papayannis and D. Pritchard, eds., *Culture and Wetlands in the Mediterranean: an Evolving Story*, 62–69. Athens: Mediterranean Institute for Nature and Anthropos (Med-INA).

Thomas, C. G. 2010. "The Physical Kingdom." In Roisman and Worthington, *Ancient Macedonia* 2010: 65–80.

Tiverios, M. 2008. "Greek Colonisation of the Northern Aegean." In G. R. Tsetskhladze, ed., *Greek Colonisation. An Account of Greek Colonies and Other Settlements Overseas*, Vol. 2 [Mnemosyne Suppl. 193], 1–154. Leiden, Netherlands and Boston: Brill.

Touratsoglou, Y. P. 2010. *A Contribution to the Economic History of the kingdom of Macedonia (6th–3rd century BC.).* Athens: Society for the Study of Numismatics and Economic History.

Toye, D. L. 2011. "Porphyry (260)." In *Brill's New Jacoby*, Editor in Chief: Ian Worthington. http://referenceworks.brillonline.com/entries/brill-s-new-jacoby/porphyry-260-a260.

Tracey, S. 2003. "Antigonus Gonatas, King of Athens." In Palagia and Tracey, *Macedonians in Athens* 2003: 56–60.

Tritle, L. A. 1988. *Phocion the Good.* London; New York; Sydney: Croom Helm.

———. 2003. "Alexander and the Killing of Cleitus the Black." In Heckel and Tritle, *Crossroads* 2003: 127–146.

Tronson, A. 1984. "Satyrus the Peripatetic and the Marriages of Philip II." *JHS* 104: 116–126.

Unz, R. K. 1985. "Alexander's Brothers?" *JHS* 105: 171–174.

Vacante, S. 2012. "Alexander the Great and the "Defeat" of the Sogdianian Revolt." *AHB* 26: 87–130.

van der Spek, R. J. 2003. "Darius III, Alexander the Great, and Babylonian Scholarship." *Achaemenid History* 13: 289–346.

Vanderspoel, J. 2015. "Rome's Apparent Disinterest in Macedonia." In Howe, Garvin and Wrightson, *Greece, Macedon and Persia* 2015: 198–206.

Vasilev, M. I. 2011. "Thucydides II.99 and the Early Expansion of the Argeadae." *Eirene* 47.1–2: 93–105.

———. 2015. *The Policy of Darius and Xerxes towards Thrace and Macedonia.* Leiden, Netherlands and Boston: Brill.

Vassileva, M. 2007. "King Midas and the Early History of Macedonia." *Archaia Makedonia* VII: 773–779.

Voutiras, E. 1998. *Dionysophontos Gamoi: Marital Life and Magic in Fourth Century Pella.* Amsterdam: J. C. Gieben.

Walbank, F. W. 1940. *Philip V of Macedon.* Cambridge: Cambridge University Press.

———. 1970. "Polybius and Macedonia." *Archaia Makedonia* I: 291–307. Reprinted in *Essays and Reflections* 2002: 91–106.

———. 1989. "Antigonus Doson's Attack on Cytinium (REG 101 (1988), 12–53)." *ZPE* 76: 184–192.

———. 1993. "Η ΤΩΝ ΟΛΩΝ ΕΛΠΙΣ and the Antigonids." *Archaia Makedonia* V: 1721–1730. Reprinted in *Essays and Reflections* 2002: 127–136.

———, ed. 2002. *Polybius, Rome, and the Hellenistic World: Essays and Reflections*. Cambridge: Cambridge University Press.

Walbank, M. B. 1978. *Athenian Proxenies of the 5th Century BC*. Toronto: Stevens.

Wallace, M. B. 1970. "Early Greek "Proxenoi"." *Phoenix* 24.3: 189–208.

Wallace, R. W. and Harris, E. M., eds. 1996. *Transitions to Empire: Essays in Greco-Roman History, 360–146 B.C., in honor of E. Badian*. Norman, OK and London: University of Oklahoma Press.

Walsh, J. 2012. "Antipater and Early Hellenistic Literature." *AHB* 26: 149–162.

Warrior, V. M. 1996. *The Initiation of the Second Macedonian War*. Wiesbaden, Germany: Franz Steiner Verlag Stuttgart.

Waterfield, R. 2011. *Dividing the Spoils. The War for Alexander the Great's Empire*. Oxford and New York: Oxford University Press.

———. 2014. *Taken at the Flood. The Roman Conquest of Greece*. Oxford and New York: Oxford University Press.

Weiler, I. 1968. "Greek and Non-Greek World in the Archaic Period." *GRBS* 9.1: 21–29.

West, M. L. 1985. *The Hesiodic Catalogue of Women*. Oxford: Oxford University Press.

Westlake, H. D. 1935. *Thessaly in the Fourth Century B.C.* London: Methuen & Co.

Wheatley, P. 1997. "The Lifespan of Demetrius Poliorcetes." *Historia* 46.1: 19–27.

———. 1998. "The Date of Polyperchon's Invasion of Macedonia and Murder of Heracles." *Antichthon* 32: 12–23.

———. 2007. "An Introduction to the Chronological Problems in Early Diadoch Sources and Scholarship." In Heckel, Tritle and Wheatley, *Formulation* 2007: 179–192.

Wheatley, P. and Hannah, R., eds. 2009. *Alexander and His Successors. Essays from the Antipodes*. Claremont, CA: Regina Books.

Wheatley, P. and Baynham, E., eds. 2015. *East and West in the World Empire of Alexander. Essays in Honour of Brian Bosworth*. Oxford: Oxford University Press.

Wheeler, M. 1968. *Flames over Persepolis*. London: Weidenfeld and Nicolson.

Wilkes, J. 1992. *The Illyrians*. Oxford: Blackwell.

Willekes, C. 2015. "Equine Aspects of Alexander the Great's Macedonian Cavalry." In Howe, Garvin and Wrightson, *Greece, Macedon and Persia* 2015: 47–58.

Winnifrith, T. J. 2002. *Badlands – Borderlands. A History of Northern Epirus / Southern Albania*. London: Duckworth.

Winter, F. E. 2006. *Studies in Hellenistic Architecture*. Toronto; Buffalo, NY; London: University of Toronto Press.

Worthington, I., 1986. "The Chronology of the Harpalus Affair." *Symbolae Osloenses* 61: 63–76.

———. 1992. *A Historical Commentary on Dinarchus: Rhetoric and Conspiracy in Later Fourth-Century Athens*. Ann Arbor, MI: University of Michigan Press.

———, ed. 1994a. *Ventures into Greek History*. Oxford: Clarendon Press.

———. 1994b. "The Harpalus Affair and the Greek Response to the Macedonian Hegemony." In Worthington, *Ventures* 1994: 307–330. Oxford: Clarendon Press.

———, ed. 2000. *Demosthenes: Statesman and Orator*. London: Routledge.

———. 2003. "Alexander's Destruction of Thebes." In Heckel and Tritle, *Crossroads* 2003: 65–86.

——. 2004. *Alexander the Great*. London: Pearson Longman.

——. 2008. *Philip II of Macedonia*. New Haven, CT: Yale University Press.

——. 2014. *By the Spear: Philip II, Alexander the Great, and the Rise and Fall of the Macedonian Empire*. Oxford and New York: Oxford University Press.

——. 2015. "From East to West. Alexander and the Exiles Decree." In Wheatley and Baynham, *East and West* 2015: 93–106.

——. 2016. *Ptolemy I: King and Pharaoh of Egypt*. London and New York: Oxford University Press.

Wrightson, G. 2010. "The Nature of Command in the Macedonian Sarissa Phalanx." *AHB* 24: 71–92.

——. 2014. "The Naval Battles of 322 B.C.E." In Hauben and Meeus, *Age of the Successors* 2014: 517–535.

Xydopoulos, I. K. 2012a. "Anthemus and Hippias: The Policy of Amyntas I." *ICS* 37: 21–37.

——. 2012b. "Upper Macedonia." In M. Tiverios, P. Nigdelis and P. Adam-Veleni, eds. *Threpteria. Studies on Ancient Macedonia*, 520–539. Thessaloniki, Greece: AUTH Press.

Yardley, J. C. and Develin, R. 1994. *Justin Epitome of the Philippic History of Pompeius Trogus*. Atlanta, GA: American Philological Association and Scholars Press.

Yardley, J. C. and Heckel, W. 1997. *Justin Epitome of the Philippic History of Pompeius Trogus Vol. I Books 11–12: Alexander the Great*. Oxford and New York: Oxford University Press.

Yardley, J. C., Heckel, W. and Wheatley, P. 2011. *Justin Epitome of the Philippic History of Pompeius Trogus Vol. II Books 13–15: The Successors to Alexander the Great*. Oxford and New York: Oxford University Press.

——. 2012b. "Upper Macedonia." In M. Tiverios, P. Nigdelis and P. Adam-Veleni, eds., *Threpteria. Studies on Ancient Macedonia*, 520–539. Thessaloniki, Greece: AUTH Press.

Yunis, H., trans. 2005. *Demosthenes, Speeches 18 and 19*. Austin, TX: University of Texas Press.

Zahrnt, M. 1971. *Olynth und die Chalkidier. Untersuchungen zur Staatenbildung auf der Chalkidischen Halbinsel im 5. und 4. Jahrhundert v. Chr*. Munich: Verlag.

——. 1984. "Die Entwicklung des makedonishen Reiches bis zu den Perserkriegen." *Chiron* 14: 325–368.

Index

Figures appear in italics.

Abdalonymus, King of Sidon 119
Abrupolis, Thracian King 256
Achaean League 239, 241, 242, 243–44, 245, 246–48, 250, 253, 259
Acrocorinth 240, *240*, 244, 253
Adea Eurydice (wife of Philip III) 193, 196, 197, 205, 209–10, 213–14, 217
Aeacides, Epirote King 209, 212, 219, 220
Aegae (Vergina) 7, 8, 12; and Argaeus (II) 72; assassination of Philip II at 179; early occupation of 18–19; and legends of ancient Macedonia 16; palace/royal residence at 17, 43, 113; portrait of Philip II at 81; 'Romaios' Tomb 214, 216; royal cemetery/tombs at 17, 43, 194, 213–14, 215, 216, 236; sanctuary of Eucleia at 209; status/importance of 42–43, 113; theatre at 97, 98; Tomb II at 214, 215
Aeropus I, Macedonian King 14, 15
Aeropus II, Macedonian King 52–53, 55, 109
Aeschines (Athenian orator) 62, 84–85, 88–89
Aetolia/Aetolians 187–89, 194, 195, 237, 241–43; and Perseus 257, 258; and Philip V 247, 248–49, 250, 251–255; and wars of successors 214–15, 218–19, 221, 226
Aetolian League 237, 243, 247, 250, 253
Agathocles, King of Syracuse 225, 226
Agathocles (son of Lysimachus) 228
agema (royal battalion/guards): of cavalry 116, 120; of infantry 120, 171, 248, 258
Agesilaus, Spartan King 55, 93

Agis III, Spartan King 159, 180–81, 207, 208
Agron, Illyrian King 242, 243
Ai Khanoum 168
Aiani 3, 5–6, 53
Alcetas, Epirote King (brother of Aeacides) 220, 224
Alcetas (brother of Perdiccas the regent) 121, 193–94, 196, 197, 206
Alcetas (grandfather of Olympias) 57, 77
Alcetas (son of Alexander I) 35, 41, 49–50
Alcetas, Macedonian King 15
Aleuadae (Thessalian clan) 43, 58, 61, 77–78, 109, 137
Alexander (bodyguard of Philip V) 246, 248
Alexander (son of Alcetas, son of Alexander I) 41, 50
Alexander (son of Craterus) 239–40
Alexander (son of Perseus) 261
Alexander (son of Polyperchon) 197, 207, 213, 216, 217–19
Alexander I, Epirote King 80, 88, 98, 135, 189
Alexander I, Macedonian King: and Athens 28, 29–30, 32; and Battle of Plataea 28–30, 31, 108; and coinage 15, 31; death of 34, 35; descendants of 54; legend of 15, 16, 144; and Olympic games 30–31, 76; and Persian Empire 24–30, 143, 161; and resources 31–34, 42; self-promotion of 25, 30; and settlers 108
Alexander II, Epirote King 239, 241
Alexander II, Macedonian King 54, 61–62, 83, 109–10

Index   293

Alexander III ('the Great'), Macedonian King: and Achilles 121, 151, 170; and Alexandria 156–7, 194; and Aristotle 7, 51, 90, 133–34, 188; ascension to the throne 131, 136–37; Asian expedition 115–24, 132, 133, 144, 146, 151–70; and Athens 138, 144, 182–83; Balkan campaign 115, 116, 120, 138–41, 190; and Battle of Chaeronea 95–96, 134; and Battle of Gaugamela 115, 116, 119, 141, 151, 158–59, 160, 161, 163; and Battle of the Granicus 115, 116, 120, 151, 152–53, 167, 179, 180; and Battle of Hydaspes 115, 116, 121, 169; and Battle of Issus 115, 151, 154–56, 158, 160, 179, 180; birth of 76, 132; coinage 144; death and burial of 124–25, 171, 179, 184, 188, 194, 196, 211; divinity of 183–84, 197; education of 51, 90, 132–34; and Egypt 156–158; Exiles Decree 178, 184, 187; expansion of Macedonian-controlled territory 1, 131; fame and legacy of 131–32; fleet of 124, 153, 154, 179–80; generalship of 122; and the Greeks 137–138, 143–144, 153, 161; and Heracles 144, *145*, 151, 154, 156, 157; House of the Faun mosaic 155, *155*; and Hypaspists 109, 114, 120, 121–22, 139, 140–41, 151, 163, 165, 171, 197; and Illyrians 115, 139–41; Indian campaign 116, 120–21, 124–25, 168–70, 181, 190; as 'King of Asia' 158–62, 179, 184; legitimacy and succession of 52, 97, 134, 136–37; marble heads of 136, 145; and Mallians 121–22, 170; military forces and innovations 107, 109, 113, 114–25, 151; military skills of 90–91, 140–41; and Olympias 17, 133, 135, 136, 165, 183; and oracle at Delphi 146; and Persian Empire 1, 115–18, 124–25, 131, 138, 152–56, 158–62, 167–9, 170–71, 180–81; 'Persianization' of 162; as 'pharaoh' of Egypt 156–57; and 'Philotas Affair' 162–63; plots and rebellions against 163, 164–66, 169–70; and proskynesis 151, 168–69, 183; relations with Antipater 134, 136, 146, 179, 182–84, 187–88; relations with Parmenio 137, 141, 146, 156, 159, 164; relations with Philip II 93–94, 97, 134–36; and Siwah 156–58, 163; and Sparta 138, 159, 162, 180–81; tames Bucephalus 86–87, 133; and Thebes 131, 138, 142–44; and Thessaly 137; and Thrace/Thracians 138–39, 141; and Triballians 115, 131, 138–39

Alexander IV, Macedonian King 35, 187, 197, 206, 209, 211, 212, 213–14, 216–17, 220–21, 224, 225, 226

Alexander V, Macedonian King 225–26, 228

Alexander Lyncestes 136, 137, 142, 164–65, 166

Alexander of Pherae 61, 76

Alexander historians *see* Historians of Alexander

Alexander mosaic *see* House of the Faun

Alexander Romance (Pseudo-Callisthenes) 156

Alexander Sarcophagus 119, *118*

Alexandria (at the Nile) 131, 156–57, *157*, 194, 245, 251

Alexandropolis 91

Almopia 7, 19

Ameinias of Phocis (Macedonian garrison commander) 237

Ammon 134, 156–58, 163, 184, 223

Amorgos 190

Amphaxitis 9, 26, 35, 43, 249

Amphictyonic Council 77–78, 79, 86, 88, 94, 131, 137, 146, 237, 257

Amphipolis 9, *63*, 35, 115, 135, 138, 212, 213, 227, 256, 260, 261; Athenian claims to 35, 40, 59, 60, 62–63, 71, 72, 73, 74, 75, 85; gold necklace *33*; gold oak-leaf wreath *123*; goddess figurine *210*; 'Kasta' tomb at 214; Lion of Amphipolis 214, *215*; and Peloponnesian War 39, 40, 41; and Perdiccas II 35; and Perdiccas III 73, 110; and Philip II 70, 71, 72, 74, 75, 76, 82, 85, 91, 113, 114

Amphissa 94–95

Amphoterus (Macedonian admiral) 180

Amydon 9, 16, 26

Amynander, Athamanian King 251

Amyntas (son of Alexander I) 35, 37, 43, 53

Amyntas (son of Andromenes) 120, 142, 143, 159, 165

294 Index

Amyntas (son of Gygaea and Bubares) 26
Amyntas (son of Hermagias) 153, *154*
Amyntas (IV) (son of Perdiccas III) 54, 55, 71, 132, 137, 140, 146, 166, 193
Amyntas (son of Philip, son of Alexander I) 35, 37, 43
Amyntas I, Macedonian King 15, 19, 24–25, 26–27
Amyntas II, Macedonian King 51, 53
Amyntas III, Macedonian King 35, 51, 52, 55, 71, 90, 178; and Chalcidic League 56–59; death of 54, 61, 62; and Illyrians 56–57, 185; military forces 109; relations with Athens 59–60, 62; and succession struggles 53–54
Anabasis of Alexander 132; *see* Arrian
Anaximenes of Lampsakos 109–110
Andocides (Athenian orator) 42
Andriscus ('false' Philip VI) 261
Andronikos, Manolis (Greek arcaheologist) 214
Angissus 94
Anthemous 9, 27, 37, 62, 115
Antigenes (Macedonian general) 197, 206, 212
Antigoneia (on the Orontes) 223
Antigonus (the One-Eyed) (Macedonian Successor) 153, 187, 228; as King Antigonus I 223–224, 250; and wars of successors 193, 194, 195, 196–97, 206, 207–8, 209, 212, 217–18, 219, 220–23
Antigonus II Gonatas, Macedonian King 226, 227, 229, 235–37, 239–41
Antigonus III Doson, Macedonian King 242–45, 246, 247
Antiochus I, Seleucid King 228, 236
Antiochus III, Seleucid King 246, 251, 255
Antipater (Macedonian general and regent): and Agis' revolt 181, 207–8; under Alexander III 115, 120, 136, 138, 151, 154, 159, 162, 171, 178–79, 182–84, 209, 211; as author 131, 178; daughters of 189, 191, 193, 194, 226, 227, 228, 229, 237; and Lamian War 187–91; under Philip II 84, 85, 90, 93–94, 95, 96, 134, 142, 178–79; and successors 185, 187, 193–97, 205, 206, 217
Antipater I, Macedonian King 225, 226, 228

Antipater II Etesias, Macedonian King 229, 236
Antiphilus (Athenian general) 189, 190
Apama (wife of Seleucus I) 170
Apelles (advisor to Philip V) 246, 248
Apollophanes (Macedonian regicide) 83
Aratus of Sicyon 239, 240–41, 242–44, 248, 250
Archelaus 16; *see* Euripides
Archelaus, Macedonian King: and coinage 31, 41; death of 43, 49, 51, 114; military forces 73, 108–9; and Euripides 16; and Olympic games 76; and Plato 49–50; relations with Athens 42, 58; restructuring of Macedonian kingdom 41–43, 49, 55, 108, 113; and succession struggles 49–51, 52, 53, 109
Archias (agent of Antipater) 191
arche (control over territory) 35, 41, 49–50
archon: in Macedonia 178; in Thessaly 70, 78, 79, 80, 86, 87–88, 137
Areus, Spartan King 239
Argadistica rites 17
Argaeus I, Macedonian King 15, 17
Argaeus II, Macedonian King 54, 55, 57, 71–72
Argeadae (Macedonian ruling clan) 5, 6, 12, 14, 16–17, 26, 54–55
Argos 15, 16–17, 33, 40, 58, 88–89, 188, 206, 216, 224, 237, 240, 241, 244–45, 253
Argos Oresticon 4, 16–17
Argyraspides see Silver Shields
Aristander of Telmessus 132, 158
Aristides (Athenian general) 29
Aristodemus (actor) 84
Aristodemus (Macedonian general) 217, 218
Aristonus (Bodyguard of Alexander III) 121–22, 184, 195, 211, 212–13
Aristotle 7, 43, 51, 53, 90, *91*, 133–34, 136, 178, 188
army assemblies 35, 52, 55, 136–37, 163–66, 171, 184–85, 186–87, 196–97, 226
Arrhabaeus, Lyncestian King 5, 51, 57, 73, 108; and war with Perdiccas II 38–39, 41, 43, 55
Arrhidaeus *see* Philip III
Arrian (Alexander historian) 132, 142, 143, 157, 160

Arsinoe (wife of Lysimachus) 228, 229
Artabazus (Persian satrap) 78, 93, 156, 168
Artaxerxes II, Persian King 58
Artaxerxes III Ochus, Persian King 91, 92, 93, 170
Arybbas, Epirote King 77, 80, 220
Atarrhias (Macedonian general) 163, 212
Atheas, Scythian King 89, 94
Athena 8, 97, 121, 151, 152, 160, 209
Athenian League 31, 35, 36, 39, 40, 58, 108; Second Athenian League 59, 60, 74, 82, 85
Athenian (Attic) orators 42, 56, 62, 84–85, 95, 96, 144
Athens: and Achaean League 239, 243; and Alexander I 28, 29–30, 32, 33–34; and Alexander II 57; and Alexander III 134, 138, 143, 144, 152, 161, 180, 182–83; and Amphipolis 9, 59, 60, 62–63, 70, 71, 72, 74, 75, 85; and Amyntas III 54, 59–60, 63; and Antigonus II 239, 241; and Antipater 178, 183; and Archelaus 41, 42, 58; and Battle of Chaeronea 95–96; and Cassander 205, 206–7, 208, 216, 222–223; and Demetrius I 222–24, 227; and Demetrius II 241; and Lamian War 187–91; and Peloponnesian War 35–36, 37, 38–41, 58, 79–80; and Perdiccas II 35, 37, 38, 40–41, 50; and Perdiccas III 63, 73; and Persian wars 1, 27, 28–30; and Philip II 72, 74–75, 77–78, 79–80, 82, 83–86, 88–90, 91–92, 93, 95–96, 113; and Philip V 251; and Perseus 257; and Social War 74–75; and wars of successors 205–6, 208; *see also* Athenian League
athletic games 8; *see also* Olympia
Attalus (guardian of Cleopatra, wife of Philip II) 97, 134–35, 137, 166
Attalus (son of Andromenes) 120, 165, 196, 206
Attalus I, King of Pergamon 250, 251, 253, 256
Attica 27, 34, 143, 144, 190, 207, 208, 222, 223, 239, 241, 243, 251, 257
Audata (Illyrian wife of Philip II) 72–73, 140, 193
Audoleon, Paeonian King 221

Autophradates (Persian general) 180
Axios River 3, 7–9, 11, 13, 14, 16, 19, 26–27, 30, 33, 35, 37, 43, 71, 108, 227, 261

Babylon 124, 125, 151, 159, 161, 171, 178, 182, 183, 184, 186, 187, 193
Babylonia 217, 220
Bacchae 16; *see* Euripides
Bacchica rites 17
Bactra 167–68
Bactria 121, 153, 162, 167–68, 190
Baebius (Roman general) 255
Bagoas (Persian) 124
Balacrus (satrap of Alexander III) 193
banquets (*symposia*) 12, 25, 33, 52, 82–83, 97, 134–35, 144, 159, 160, 168–69, *192*, 205, 221, 226, 237
'barbarians' 3, 39, 56, 108–9, 136, 152, 181, 229, 254, 256, 261
Bardylis, Illyrian King 57, 70, 72–73, 76, 139–40
Barsine (mistress of Alexander III) 156, 168, 184, 221
basileion (royal seat) 42
basileus (king) 18, 27, 223
Bato, Dardanian King 251
Berisades, Thracian King 75, 79
Beroa (wife of Glaucias) 212
Beroia 7–8, 227
Bendis 14
Bessus (Persian satrap) 162, 167, 168
Bisaltia 9, 30, 31, 35, 40, 41, 261
Bithys (Macedonian general) 241, 242
Boeotia/Boeotians: and Alexander II 61; and Alexander III 142–44; and Antigonus III 243, 244, 245; bronze helmet *119*, 119; and Cassander 216, 219; and Corinthian War 58; and Demetrius I 226; and Demetrius II 241; and Lamian War 188, 190; and Perseus 257; and Persian wars 29, 108; and Philip II 77–78, 84, 95; and Philip V 250, 253, 255
Boeotian League 62, 77
Boges (Persian *hyparchos*) 27
Bottice 9, 38
Bottiaea 7, 8, 12, 16, 19, 37, 115
Bottiaeans (displaced inhabitants of Bottiaea) 36
Brasidas (Spartan general) 38–40, 43, 108

Brennus (Gallic chieftain) 229
bronze helmet (Boeotian) 119, *119*
bronze statues (Dion) 152; *see* Lysippus
Bryges (Phryges/Phrygians) (early inhabitants of Macedonia) 11
burials 3, 96, 143, 167, 210, 222; at Aegae 17, 42–43, 213–14; of Alexander III 194, 195–96; of Olympias 214; of Darius III 162; *see also* tombs
Brygi (Thracian tribe) 27
Bubares (son of Megabazus) 25, 26–27, 28, 38
Bucephalus (Alexander III's warhorse) 86–87, 133
Byzantium 43, 80, 89–90, 93–94, 139, 208; and Philip's siege 91–93, 113

Cadmea (Theban citadel) 96, 138, 142–44
Calindoia 71
Callas (Macedonian general) 211
Callias of Chalcis 83, 88
Callias (Athenian general) 37
Callisthenes (Alexander historian, Aristotle's nephew) 132, 157, 169
Caranus (mythical Macedonian King) 16
Caranus (alleged half-brother of Alexander III) 137
Cardia 79, 90
Caria 135, 153, 195, 218, 219, 228, 243
Carthage/Carthaginians 57, 236, 246, 249, 251
Cassander (son of Antipater): and Alexander III 183, 197; and Athens 205, 206–7, 208, 216, 222; as *chiliarchos* 197, 205; as king 213, 223; death of 225; and end of Argead dynasty 211–16, 221; and Epirus 212, 218, 219, 220, 221, 224; garrisons of 205, 206–7, 208, 218, 219, 220, 222, 224–25; and hunting 12, 205; and Olympias 166, 209, 211–13, 214, 217, 219, 226; and wars of successors 197, 205–9, 216–26; wife and heirs of 225–26
Cassandreia 213, 217, 227, 236, 251
Catalogue of Ships 3, 11, 13, 26; *see* Homer
Catalogue of Women 11, 18; *see* Hesiod
cavalry wedge formation 112–13
Cebalinus ('Philotas Affair') 162–63
Cephallenia 248, 249
Cersobleptes, Thracian King 79–80, 84, 85, 89–90, 91, 94

Cetriporis, Thracian King 75, 79
Chaeronea, Battle of 95–6, 111, 112–13, 134, 138, 142, 144, 178
Chalcedon 92, 251
Chalcidic League 56, 57–59, 75, 80, 82, 83
Chalcidice 3, 4, 9, 13, 27, 36–37, 38–39, 54, 56, 58–59, 80, 82, 261
Chalcis 88, 180, 219, 223, 235, 239, 243, 248, 250, 251, 253, 254, 255
Chares (Athenian general) 80, 82, 92, 113–14
Charidemus (Athenian general) 82, 144
Chersonese 74, 79, 80, 84, 85, 90, 91, 96, 151
chlamys (military cloak) 107, 116–18, *117*
Chremonidean War 239
Chryseis (wife of Demetrius II) 242
Cilicia 154–55, 171, 180, 183, 188, 190, 195, 196, 206, 228
Cimon (Athenian general) 31, 32, 34
Cleander (brother of Coenus) 153
Cleitus (son of Bardylis) 139–40, 141
Cleitus 'the Black' (ilarch) 115–16, 163, 167
Cleitus 'the White' (hipparch, admiral) 116, 121, 189–90, 196–97, 208, 217
Cleomenes III, Spartan King 243–45, 247
Cleomenes of Naucratis 195
Cleon (Athenian general) 40
Cleonymus (Spartan) 237
Cleopatra (sister of Alexander III) 98, 135, 189, 193, 194, 195, 197, 222
Cleopatra (wife of Perdiccas II and Archelaus) 50, 51
Cleopatra (wife of Philip II) 52, 97, 134–35, 137, 166, 214
Cleopatra VII (Ptolemaic dynasty) 131
Coenus (mythical Macedonian King) 16
Coenus (taxiarch, hipparch) 116, 120, 141, 153, 167–68, 170, 179
coinage 12, 15, 18, 31–32, *32*, 34, 41, 54, 56, 76, 144
Common Peace 96–7, 138, 144, 182
Companion Cavalry (*hetairoi*) 96, 107–8, 109, 112, 114, 115–16, 119, 125, 133, 134, 141, 152, 155, 158, 162, 163, 185, 196
Companions (court *hetairoi*) 74, 88, 90, 107–8, 114, 121, 144, 158, 162, 163, 167, 168–69, 170, 184, 185, 237

Companions, Foot (*pezhetairoi*) 72, 109, 112, 114, 119–20
Corinth 5, 6, 36–37, 88, 96, 138, 146, 218, 219, 221, 223–24, 235, 237, 239–41, 244, 246, 247, 248, 249, 253, 254, 255
Corinthian War 58, 60, 93
Corrhagus (Macedonian general) 181
Cothelas, Getic/Thracian King 89
Cotys I, Odrysian/Thracian King 60, 79
Cotys IV, Odrysian/Thracian King 259
Crataeas (Macedonian regicide) 51
Craterus (son of taxiarch Craterus) 237
Craterus (taxiarch, Successor) 116, 120, 163, 167–68, 169, 171, 183, 185, 186–87, 188–89, 190–91, 192, 193–95, 196, 226
Cratesipolis (wife of Alexander, son of Polyperchon) 218, 219, 221
Crateuas (Macedonian general) 213
Crenides (Philippi) 9–10, 34, 75, 76, 79, 80
Critobulus/Critodemus 122
Crocus Field, Battle of 79
Crousis 9
Curtius (Alexander historian) 131–32, 160, 163, 166, 184
Cynnane (daughter of Philip II) 72, 140, 193–94, 213
Cynoscephalae, Battle of 125, 235, 253–54, 255

Damastion 56
Damis 207–8
Danube (Istros) River 13, 14, 26, 89, 94, 138–39
Dardani 13–14, 140, 229, 242, 247–48, 249, 250, 251–52, 254, 258
Darius I, Persian King 25–28, 160, 161
Darius III, Persian King 157, 159, 160, 161, 165, 179, 180, 190; and Battle of Gaugamela 115, 116, 141, 158–59; and Battle of the Granicus 115, 152; and Battle of Issus 115, 154–56, *155*, 158, 160, 180; daughters of 155, 168, 170; death of 162, 164
Darron (Paeonian god) 14
Dassaretis 209, 249, 251–52
Decree of Tyre *see* decrees
decrees: of Alexander III (Exiles Decree) 182–83, 184, 187–88; of Antigonus I (Decree of Tyre) 217, 219; Athenian 83, 84, 191; Methone Decrees 38; Molossian 212; of Polyperchon 206; of Ptolemy I 218
Deidameia (wife of Demetrius I) 211, 224, 226
Deinias (Macedonian general) 211, 220
Delphi: Amphictyony 77, 86, 237, 257; Gallic invasion 229; oracle 16, 131, 146, 157; statue of Alexander I 30; Third Sacred War 77–79, 84
Demades (Athenian orator) 96, 188, 190, 191, 197
Demetrian War 241, 243
Demetrias 226, 235, 248–49, 250, 253, 254, 255
Demetrius (Macedonian admiral) 92, 93
Demetrius (Bodyguard of Alexander III) 165
Demetrius (hipparch) 116
Demetrius (son of Philip V) 254, 255, 256
Demetrius I, Macedonian King 194, 218, 220, 222–24, 225–28, 229, 235, 236, 244
Demetrius II, Macedonian King 237, 239, 240, 241–42, 243
Demetrius the Fair 242
Demetrius of Phaleron 208, 222
Demetrius of Pharos 242, 246, 249, 250, 259
Demosthenes (Athenian orator) 84–85, 89, 90, 95, 96, 109, 112, 114, 137, 143, 144, 166, 183, 191; *Philippics* 85, 93, 112; *Olynthiacs* 85, 109; and the Peace of Philocrates 84–85, 88
Derdas I, Elimiote King 36, 41, 53, 73
Derdas II, Elimiote King 58–59, 73, 109
Diades (engineer) 123
Diadochi (Successors) 187; and *passim* 178–229
didrachm 32
dikastai (judges) 239
Dikili Tash 3
Dimnus ('Philotas Affair') 163
Diodorus (historian, Alexander historian) 51, 56, 63, 95, 131, 142–43, 160
Diogenes (Macedonian garrison commander) 243
Dion 8, 19, 38, 225, 253, 259; Aetolian sack of 247, 248; and *Olympia* festival 8, 82–83, 144; shield monument 152, *152*
Dionysius of Syracuse 56, 57, 113

Dionysius (Macedonian garrison commander) 222
Diopeithes (Athenian general) 90
Dispilio 3, 4
dockyards *see* ships/shipbuilding
drinking/drunkenness 12, 25, 49–50, 134–35, 160, 167, 178–79

early Macedonian expansion 8, 11–12, 16, 17–19
Ecbatana 159, 161, 164, 182
Echedoros River 8–9, 28, 31
Echinades 190
economic advantages of Macedonian region 1, 3, 9, 31, 32, 33, 36, 57, 75, 80, 261
Edessa 7, 226, 228
Edson, Charles (American scholar) 214
Egypt 27, 124, 180, 186, 194, 217, 220, 222–23, 227, 229; Alexander III in 156–58; Perdiccas' invasion of 195–96; Ptolemy I as king/Pharaoh of 223; and the Ptolemaic fleet 227, 239, 240; and Ptolemaic succession 229, 246, 251
Eion 27, 31, 39, 40
Elimeia (Elimiotis) 5–6, 36, 41, 43, 55, 58–59, *59*, 73, 120, 142, 183, 252, 258, 261
Emathia, Emathian plain 7, 11, 18, 19, 34, 107, 249; *see* Bottiaea (aka Bottia)
Ennea Hodoi (later Amphipolis) 9, 35
Eordaea 5, 6, 16, *18*, 19, 38, 40, 73, 142, 252, 258, 261
Epaminondas 63, 71, 110, 140
Ephesus 153
epigoni (native recruits) 107, 124–25, 170–71
Epirus 5, 6, 13, 57, 73, 120, 241–42, 245, 247, 258, 260, 261; and Cassander 212, 218, 219, 220, 221, 224, 225; end of monarchy 241; Molossian tribe of 57, 77, 259; and Olympias 77, 135, 137, 183, 206, 209, 212; and Philip II 52, 77, 80, 88, 97–98, 225; and Philip V 247, 250, 251, 252–53; and Pyrrhus I 224, 225, 226, 227, 236, 239
epistatai (overseers) 239
Eretria (in Euboea) 27, 82, 83, 88, 239, 253
Erigyius (Macedonian general) 135
Euboea 27; Alexander son of Craterus as king of 239; and Philip II vs.

Athenians 82, 83, 88, 89, 92; and wars of successors 180, 219, 223; and Antigonids 235, 243, 248, 250, 253, 258
Eubulus (Athenian statesman) 83–84
euergetes 28, 29, 73
Euetion (Athenian general, Peloponnesian War) 41
Euetion (Athenian general, Lamian War) 190
Eumenes of Cardia (general, Successor) 186–87, 189, 193, 194–95, 196, 197, 206, 209, 217; death of 212–13, 217
Eumenes II, King of Pergamon 256–58
Euphraeus of Oreus 71, 88
Euripides 16, 51
Europa (infant daughter of Philip II) 137
Eurybotas (commander of Cretan archers) 143
Eurydice (wife of Amyntas III) 52, 54, 57, 61–62, 209
Eurydice (daughter of Antipater) 194, 205, 229
Eurynoe (daughter of Amyntas III) 54, 61–62
exiles: mercenary and political 180, 182, 183, 187, 191, 206; to Macedonia 5, 15, 93, 108; from Macedonia 40, 56, 62, 72, 256; Theban 142–143
Exiles Decree *see* decrees

Fermor, Patrick Leigh 29
'fetters' of Greece 235, 237, *240*, 250, 251, 253, 255
First Diadoch War 194
First Illyrian War 243, 246, 249
First Macedonian War 251
Flamininus, Lucius (brother of T. Quinctius) 253
Flamininus, T. Quinctius (Roman consul) 125, 252–54, 255
Fourth Macedonian War 261
Fourth Philippic 93
Fourth Sacred War 94–5

Gabiene, Battle of 212
Galba, P. Sulpicius (Roman proconsul) 250, 251–52
Gaugamela, Battle of 115, 116, 119, 141, 158–59, 160, 161, 163, 179

Gauls 214, 236, 237, 244, 258; invasions of 229, 235–36, 237
Gelon of Syracuse 107
Gentius, Illyrian King 259
geography of Macedonian region 1–3, *2*; Lower Macedonia 7–8; strategic and economic advantages 1, 3, 31, 261; Thraceward region 8–10; Upper Macedonia 4–6
Getae 89, 139
Glaucias, Illyrian King 139–141, 212, 218, 219, 224
goats 7, 12, 15, 16, *32*, 34
gold mines *see* mines/mining
gold necklace (Amphipolis) *33*
gold oak-leaf wreath (Amphipolis) *123*
gold statue of Alexander I (Delphi) 30
Gonnoi 28, 79, 236
Gordion 154, 179
Gorgias (taxiarch) 120, 195
Gorgias 49–50; *see* Plato
Grabos, Illyrian King 75–76, 132
Granicus, Battle of the 115, 116, 120, 152–53, 167, 179, 180, 185
Griffith, Guy (British scholar) 73
guerrilla fighting 107, 115, 116, 167
Gygaea (daughter of Amyntas I) 25, 26–27, 38
Gygaea (wife of Amyntas III) 52

Haliacmon River 3, 4–5, 7–8, 15, *18*, 18–19, 33, *59*
Halicarnassus 122, 153, 154
Halos 84, 85
Hammond, Nicholas (British scholar) 12, 17, 35, 50, 52, 55, 165
Hannibal 125, 246, 249, 251, 259
Harpalus (treasurer of Alexander III) 133, 135, 182–3, 187–88, 191
Hasdrubal (brother of Hannibal) 251
Hecataeus (agent of Alexander III) 137, 166
Hegelochus (Macedonian admiral) 180
Hegesippus (Athenian negotiator) 89
Hellenic League 244, 247, 249, 251
Hellespont 1, 26, 190, 255; and Alexander III 115, 124, 151, 170, 180; and Cassander 219; and Philip II 75, 89–90, 91–93, 97, 113; and wars of successors 189, 193, 194, 196–97, 205, 208, 217, 219, 221, 228
Hellespontine Phrygia 186, 189, 196, 208

Hephaestion (Bodyguard of Alexander III) 116, 118, 121, 133, 163, 171, *171*, 184
Heracleides (admiral of Philip V) 252
Heracles (god) as ancestor of Macedonian line 15, 16, 17, *33*, 94, 154; and Alexander III 144, *145*, 151, 154, 156–7
Heracles (son of Alexander III) 168, 184, 221
Hermolaus (Royal Page of Alexander III) 166, 167, 169
Herodotus 3, 4, 8, 11, 15–16, 17, 24–31, 34–35, 38, 55
Hesiod 11, 15
Hetairideia festival 8
hetairoi see Companion Cavalry
Hieron Oros 84, 85
hipparches, hipparch (brigade commanders) 116, 120, 190
hipparchiai, hipparchy (cavalry divisions) 107, 116
hipparchos (commander of Achaean League) 246
Hippias (Athenian tyrant) 27
Hipponicus (Macedonian general) 88
Historians of Alexander the Great 131–32, 142–143, 160, 163
Homer 3, 11, 13, 14, 18, 26, 31, 95, 133
hoplon (shield) 112, 119
hoplites 33, 36, 38, 39, 60, 71, 108, 110, 111–12, 119, 140; vs. Macedonian phalanx 95–96, 155, 190
horsemanship 12, 14, 15, 16, 18, 31, *32*, 37–38, 86–87, *87*, 107–8, 115–19, *117*, *118*, 133, 195; *see also* Companion Cavalry
House of Dionysus (Pella) 191, *191*, *192*
House of the Faun mosaic (Pompeii) 155, *155*
hunting 4, 12, 14, 31, 43, 51, 74, 107, 118, 133, 166, 191, *192*, 205
hyparchos (Persian governor) 27
Hydaspes, Battle of 115, 116, 121, 169
Hypaspists: Agrianian 139; of Alexander III 109, 114, 120–23, 140–41, 151, 163, 165, 171, 194, 197, 206

ilarches, ilarch (cavalry officers) 115–16, 139
ile/ilai (cavalry division) 115–16
Iliad 133; *see* Homer

Illyria/Illyrians 5, 12, 15, 261; and Alexander II 61; and Alexander III 115, 135, 139–41, 142; and Amyntas III 49, 52, 55, 56–57, 185; and Antigonus III 242–43, 244, 245; and Archelaus 41, 55; and Cassander 218, 221, 225; and Cynnane 193; and Demetrius II 242; and Parmenio 75–76, 132; and Peloponnesian War 39; and Perdiccas II 35, 39, 108; and Perdiccas III 63, 70, 73, 122, 178; and Philip II 70, 72–73, 74, 80, 87, 97, 110, 134, 140; and Philip V 247, 249, 250, 251, 253; and Pyrrhus I 212, 218, 224; and Roman Empire 242, 243, 246, 251, 259; threat to Macedonia 5, 13–14, 63–64, 74, 87, 109, 248, 250, 258; *see also* First Illyrian War, Second Illyrian War

India 1, 116, 121–22, 124–25, 168–70, 181, 190

Iolaus (*archon* of Perdiccas II) 36, 178

Iolaus (son of Antipater) 183, 193, 211

Iphicrates (Athenian general) 60, 62

Ipsus, Battle of 224, 228

isegoria 164

Isocrates (Athenian orator) 56, 57, 93

Issus, Battle of 115, 154–56, *155*, 158, 160, 179, 180

Istros (Danube) River 13, 14, 26, 89, 94, 138–39

Jason of Pherae 58, 60–61, 93, 112

Justin (Alexander historian) 132

Kambunia Mountains 4, 5, 13

'Kasta' tomb 214

Kinch Tomb painting (Lefkadia) 116–18, *117*

King's Peace (Peace of Antalcidas) 58, 60

kingship 12, 14, 15, 16, 18, 19, 134, 151, 165, 168–69, 227

koine eirene see Common Peace

kopis (curved blade sword) 118

Kore 209, *210*

Laevinus, M. Valerius (Roman general) 249–50

Lake Kastoria 4, 5

Lamian War 187–91, 194; Antipater's settlement of 190–191; death of Leonnatus 189; death of Leosthenes 189; naval activity 188, 189–90; recruitment of mercenaries for 188

Lanassa (wife of Pyrrhus I and Demetrius I) 226

Langarus, King of Agrianians 139–40

language of ancient Macedonians 11, 12

Lanice (nurse of Alexander III) 116, 179

Laodice (wife of Perseus) 257

Laomedon (brother of Erigyius) 135

Larissa 38, 43, 61, 76–77, 78, 84, 109, 137, 190, 226, 247, 253–54, 258

League of Corinth 70, 96–97, 115, 131, 138, 142–43, 152, 161, 179, 180, 181, 244

Leake, William (British topographer) 28

Lefkadia 116–18, *117*

legends of ancient Macedonians 14–17

Leonidas (tutor of Alexander III) 133

Leonnatus (Bodyguard, Successor) 121, 133, 185, 186, 189, 193, 196

Leontius (advisor, general of Philip V) 246, 248

Leosthenes (Athenian general) 188, 189, 190

Leuctra, Battle of 62, 63, 71, 73, 140

Licinius (Roman consul) 258

Life of Alexander 132; *see* Plutarch

lions 12, *32* (Fig. 2.2), *145*, 191; marble 6, 6, 96

Lion Hunt mosaic (Pella) 191, *192*

Lion of Amphipolis 214, *215*

Lissus 246, 250

Livy 246, 256

Loudias River 7–8, 33, 42, 211, 260

Loudias, Lake *260*

Lower Macedonia 4, 5, 6, 7–8, 12, 16, 28, 36, 37, 38, 58, 108, 133, 247, 258, 261; consolidation with Upper Macedonia 70–5, 110, 114

Luxor 156

Lyciscus (Macedonian general) 212, 218, 219, 220

Lycophron (tyrant of Pherae) 77, 78–79

Lycurgus, Spartan King 247

Lydiades (*strategos* of Achaean League) 241, 243

Lyncus (Lyncestis) 5, 6, 13, 17, 38–39, 43, 55, 73, 108, 120, 136, 140, 261

Lysandra (daughter of Ptolemy I) 228

Lysimacheia 221, 228, 236, 251, *252*

Lysimachus (tutor of Alexander III) 133
Lysimachus (Bodyguard, Successor, King) 121, 186, 208, 217, 218–20, 221; as King of Thrace 223–29, 236; as King of Macedonia 227–228
Lysippus (sculptor) 152

Macedon (mythical eponymous ancestor) 11, 15
Macedonian military: *passim*, see especially 107–125
Magnesia (by Thessaly) 79, 86, 226, 249
Magnesia (in Asia Minor) 153, 255
Makednoi 11, 17
Mallians 121–22, 170
Mardonius (Persian general) 25, 27, 28–30, 97
Meda (Getic/Thracian wife of Philip II) 89
Media 159, 164, 196, 212, 217
medicine/medical and healing 14, 51, 90, 122, 134, 169, 170
Medion 242
Megabazus (Persian general) 25, 26, 34
Megaleas (secretary of Philip V) 246, 248
Megalopolis 89, 180, 181, 207–8, 241, 243, 244, 246, 253
Meleager (taxiarch) 120, 153, 179, 185–86
Meleager (brother of Ptolemy Ceraunus, Macedonian King) 229
Memnon (Alexander's III's *strategos* of Thrace) 181
Memnon of Rhodes 93, 152–54, 156, 180
Menelaus (brother of Ptolemy I) 223
Menelaus (son of Alexander I) 35, 50, 53
Menelaus of Pelagonia 73, 74
Mentor (brother of Memnon of Rhodes) 93
Metellus, Q. Caecilius (Roman consul) 261
Methone 19, 38, 40, 42, 63, 72, 77–78, 82, 91, 113, 114, 122
Metron (Royal Page of Alexander III) 163
Mieza 7, 90, 116, 133–34, *133*
Miletus 122, 153
mines, mining, minerals 4, 9, 10, 14, 26, 31–32, 33, 41, 56, 71, 74, 75, 80, 84, 89, 144, 156, 255, 256, 261
Monimus (governor of Pella) 212–13
mosaics 155, *155*, 191, *191*, *192*
Mount Athos 27, 28
Mount Bermion 4, 5, 7, 15, 16, 19, *59*

Mount Dysoron 9, 31
Mount Haemus 30, 94, 138, 139
Mount Olympus 3–4, 7, 8, 10, 11, 13, 15, 18, 28, 30, 211, 259
Mount Orbelos *63*, 221
Mount Pangaion 9, 19, 26, 32, 74, 75, 80, 255
Mycenae/Mycenaean 6, 11, 33, 108, 151
Mygdonia 9, 19, 30, 36, 37, 40

Nea Nikomedeia 3, 8
Neapolis 113–14
Nearchus (Macedonian admiral) 124, 133, 135, 153, 170, 184, 185, 218
Neoptolemus (Hypaspist commander) 194, 195
Neoptolemus (son of Achilles) 13
Neoptolemus, Epirote King 77
Neoptolemus II, Epirote King 224
Nestos River 9–10, 138, 261
Nicaea (daughter of Antipater) 189, 193, 228
Nicaea (wife of Alexander, son of Craterus) 239–40
Nicaea (near Thermopylae) 94, 253
Nicanor (Macedonian garrison commander) 206–7, 208
Nicanor (son of Antipater) 205, 211
Nicanor (son of Parmenio) 121, 139, 165
Nicanor of Stagira 182, 183
Nicesipolis of Pherae (wife of Philip II) 77, 211
Nicias (Athenian general) 40, 57–58
Nicomachus (brother of Cebalinus) 163
Nicomachus (physician of Amyntas III) 51, 90
Niconidas of Larissa 38
Nymphaion 7, 133; *see* Mieza
Nymphodorus (agent of Sitalces) 37

Oloosson (Elassona) 3
Olympia festival 8, 82–83, 144
Olympia/Olympiads/Olympic games 8, 16, 17, 30–31, 76, 132, 182, 187, 209
Olympias (mother of Alexander III) 97, 157, 165, 182, 193–94, 217, 259; and Adea Eurydice 209–10; and Antipater 183, 187, 197; and Cassander 211–213, 214, 219, 225; death of 213, 214, 217, 223, 226; and education of Alexander III 132–33; legitimacy and succession of

sons 52, 134–35, 136; marries Phillip II 76–77; murder of Cleopatra and Europa 137; trial and death of 166; and wars of successors 205, 206–7, 209–11
Olympias (widow of Alexander II of Epirus) 241
Olynthus 36, 37, 62, 213; and the Chalcidic League 56, 57–60, 75; and Philip II 75, 80, 82–84, 86, 91, 111, 113
On the Deeds of Perdiccas in Illyria 178; *see* Antipater
Onomarchus (Phocian general) 78–79
Orchomenos (in Arcadia) 243, 244, *245*, 246
Orestes, Macedonian child-King 43, 51, 52–53
Orestis 5, 6, 12, 13, 16–17, 18, 73, 120, 250, 252, 254, 261
Oreus 82, 88, 219, 250
Oxathres (brother of Darius) 162, 167
Oxyartes (father of Roxane) 168
Oxydates (satrap of Media) 164

Paeonia/Paeonians 9, 12, 75, 249, 261; and Alexander III 139–40; influence on Macedonia 14, 16, 31; and Macedonian military 112, 114–15, 119, 258; Persian invasion 26–27; and Philip II 71–72, 80; subjugated by Macedonia 16, 19, 26, 72; threat to Macedonia 14, 37, 71; and wars of successors 221, 225, 228
Pagasae 79
paides basilikoi (Royal Pages) 114, 166; *see* Royal Pages
paintings 43, 116–18, *117*, 155, *238*, 260; *see also* Villa Boscoreale fresco
Pammenes (Theban general) 70, 78, 79
Paraetacene, Battle of 212
Parauaea 142, 225
Parmenio (Macedonian general): under Alexander III 115, 116, 119, 137, 138, 141, 146, 151, 153–56, 158–60, 161; death of 163–64, 166, 213; under Philip II 74, 76, 80, 84, 85, 88, 93, 97, 115, 132
Parysatis (daughter of Artaxerxes III) 170
Paullus, L. Aemilius (Roman consul) 246
Paullus, L. Aemilius (son of Paullus, consul) 259–60
Pausanias (bodyguard of Philip II) 136, 166

Pausanias (brother of Derdas) 36, 108
Pausanias, Macedonian King 53
Pausanias, Spartan King 29
Pausanias (usurper) 54, 55, 62, 71, 72, 82
Peace of Antalcidas *see* King's Peace
Peace of Apamea 255
Peace of Demades 96
Peace of Naupactus 249, 250, 251
Peace of Nicias 40, 57–58, 59
Peace of Philocrates 83, 86, 88–89, 90, 92–93, 178
Peace of Phoenice 251
Peitholaus (brother of Lycophron) 79
Peithon (Bodyguard of Alexander III) 121, 185, 196, 217
Pella 8, 11, 14, 26, 33, 34, 57, 58, 76; and Alexander III 90, 133; and Antipater 138, 197; and Philip II 80, 84–85, 94, 114, 132; royal seat/court 42–43, *42*, 51, 71, 89, 97, 113, 133, 226, 247, 258, *260*; and wars of successors 211, 212–13; House of Dionysus 191; status/importance of 42, 43, 113, 260, 261
Pelion/Pelium 140, 252
Pellion 140, 141
Pelopidas (Theban general) 61, 62, 110
Peloponnesian War 35–43, 57, 79–80
pelte (shield) 110
peltasts 60, 82, 110, 244, 246, 247, 248
Peneus River 3, 28, 190, 253, 258, 261
people of ancient Macedonia 10–14
Perdiccas (Bodyguard, hipparch and regent) 116, 120, 121, 122, 141, 142, 143, 184–87, 189, 191, 193–96, 197, 217, 228
Perdiccas I, Macedonian King 15, 16, 17, 18, 30
Perdiccas II, Macedonian King: and Athens 35–36, 37, 38, 40–41, 50; and Chalcidic League 56, 57; and coinage 31; military forces 108–9, 178; and Peloponnesian War 35–41; and settlers 82, 108; and succession struggles 34–35, 41, 43, 49–50, 51, 52, 53; and war with Arrhabaeus of Lyncus 38–40, 41, 43, 55, 108
Perdiccas III, Macedonian King 54, 62, 63, 70–71, 72, 73, 74, 110, 122, 131, 139, 178
Perinthus 80, 90, 91–94, 113

Persaeus of Cition 237
Persepolis 159, 160–61, 169, 182
Perseus, Macedonian King 125, 252, 256–60, 261
Persian Empire: and Alexander I 15, 24–30, 31, 107–8, 143; and Alexander III 1, 115–18, 124–25, 131, 138, 152–56, 158–62, 167–9, 170–71, 180–81; and Greek states 25–26, 27–30, 31, 58, 93, 97, 138, 142, 143, 144, 180–81; and Paeonians 14, 26; and Philip II 1, 32, 91, 93, 97–98, 114, 115
Petralona cave (Chalcidice) 3
Peucestas (hypaspist, Bodyguard) 122
pezhetairoi see Companions, Foot
Phakos 8, 260, *260*
phalanx (Macedonian) 72, 96, 108, 110–12, 114, 120, 125, 139, 140–41, 143, 169, 224, 236, 248; vs. Greek hoplites 95–96, 155, 190, 244–45; vs. Roman legions 253–54, 255, 258, 259–60
Pharnabazus (Persian general) 180
Pharsalus 84
Phayllus (brother of Onomarchus) 78
Pherae 18, 58, 60–61, 76–79, 85, 87, 93, 112, 253–54
Phila (Elimiote wife of Philip II) 73, 110
Phila (daughter of Antipater) 191, 193, 226, 227, 228, 237
Philip (son of Alexander I) 35–37, 41, 43, 50
Philip I, Macedonian King 14, 15
Philip II, Macedonian King: and Amphictyonic Council 77–78, 79, 86, 88, 94; and Amphipolis 74, 75, 76, 85; ascension to the throne 70, 71; and Athens 72, 74–75, 79–80, 82, 83–86, 88–90, 91–92, 95; and Battle of Chaeronea 95–96, 112–13; and Boeotians 77–78, 84, 95; and Chalcidice 82–83; challenge of Argaeus and Pausanias 71–72; and coinage 32; and Common Peace 96–97; consolidation of Upper and Lower Macedonia 70–75, 110, 114; death of 98, 136, 137, 166, 179; and Demosthenes 84–85, 88–89, 93, 95; expansion into southern Greece 83–93; fleet of 78, 92, 93, 113–14; and Fourth Sacred War 94–95; and Illyrians 72–73, 74, 87, 97, 110, 140; legitimacy

and succession of sons 52, 97, 134; loses eye 77, 122; marriage to Olympias 76–77; military forces 107–8, 109–10; military reforms and innovations 72, 110–14; and Olympiads 76; and Olynthians 80, 82–84, 86, 111, 113; and Paeonians 71–72, 80; and Perinthus 80, 90, 91–94, 113; and Persian Empire 1, 91, 93, 97–98, 115; and Phocians 77–79, 84, 85–86, 92–93, 95, 112; portrait of *81*; and Potidaea 75–76, 132; relations with Alexander III 134–36; and succession struggles 54–55; and Thebes 61, 70–71, 85, 94–95, 96, 112–13, 114; and Thessaly 76–80, 84, 86, 87–88, 112; and Third Sacred War 77, 78–79, 83, 84, 85–86; and Thrace 71, 75, 78, 79–80, 85, 87, 89–90, 93–94, 112
Philip III (Arrhidaeus) Macedonian King 52, 76, 132, 133, 135, 137, 146, 171, 185–86, 187, 193, 196, 197; and wars of successors 205, 206, 207, 209–10, 212, 213, 217
Philip IV, Macedonian King 225
Philip V, Macedonian King: and Aetolians 247, 248–49, 250, 251, 254, 255; and Antiochus III 251, 255; ascension to the throne 245, 246; and Battle of Cynoscephalae 125, 235, 253–54, 255; and Dardani 247–48, 249, 250, 251–52, 254, 258; death of 256; fleet of 251; as heir to the throne 242, 243; and Illyrians 247, 249, 250, 251; purges of 166; and Roman Empire 140, 246, 249–56; and Social War 247–49; and Sparta 247; and Thessaly 252–53, 254, 255, 256; and Thrace 255–56
Philippi (Crenides) 34, 75, 76, 79, 80
Philippopolis 89, 90
Philippus, Q. Marcius (Roman consul) 258–59
Philocrates (Athenian statesman) 83, 84, 88
Philomelus (Phocian general) 77–78
Philotas (son of Parmenio) 116, 139; and 'Philotas Affair' 162–67
Philoxenus of Eretria (painter) 155
Philoxenus (Alexander III's *strategos* of Asia Minor) 183
Phocion (Athenian general) 92–93, 179, 190–91, 207

Phocis/Phocians 77–9, 84, 85–86, 95, 112, 113, 143, 188, 207, 219, 242, 244, 253
Phormio (Athenian general) 37
Phrygia 78, 153–54, 186–87, 193, 197, 218, 224
Phthia (wife of Demetrius II) 241, 242
Pieria 7, 8, 11, 14, 15, 16, 18–19, *18*, 37, 40, 42, 43, 71–72, 107, 236, 247, 259
Pierian Mountains 3, 4, 5, 7, 19, 42
Pierian Muses 8, 144
Pindar 144
Pindus Mountains 3, 4–5, 6, 11, 13, 17, 80, *222*
Pixodarus (Carian dynast) 135
Plataea, Battle of 24, 25, 28–30, 31, 108
Plato 49–51, 71, 90
Pleistarchus (brother of Cassander) 224
Pleuratos, Illyrian King 87
Pleuratus (son of Scerdilaidas) 251
Pleurias, Illyrian King 97
Plutarch (Alexander historian) 95, 112–13, 132, 134–5, 160
Plutarchus (tyrant of Eretria) 83
Polemon (brother of Amyntas, son of Andromenes) 165
Polyaenus (Macedonian author) 113
Polybius 125, 246, 249, 254, 256
Polyperchon (taxiarch, regent, Successor) 120, 171, 195; as regent 197, 205–8; and Cassander 205–10, 211–13, 214, 217–18, 219; and murder of Heracles 221, 223
Porus, Indian King 115, 169
Potidaea 35–37, 75–76, 108, 132, 213
Prepelaus (Macedonian general) 223
prodromoi (Paeonian mounted scouts) 115, 120
proskynesis 168–69, 183
prostitutes/concubines/courtesans 12, 25, 134, 160, 182
Proteas (Macedonian admiral) 179–80
proxenos 28, 29, 73
Prusias II, Bithynian King 257
Ptolemaeus (nephew of Antigonus I, admiral) 218, 219, 221
Ptolemaeus (Alexander III's *strategos* of Caria) 153, 179
Ptolemy I (son of Lagos, Bodyguard, Successor, King) and Alexander III 121, 133, 135, 165, 184; Alexander historian 132, 142, 143; as satrap of Egypt 186, 194, 195–96, 197, 205, 206, 217–18, 220, 221–22, 222–23; as King/Pharaoh of Egypt 223–24, 225, 226–27, 228
Ptolemy II, King/Pharaoh of Egypt 228, 229, 237, 239, 240
Ptolemy III, King/Pharaoh of Egypt 244, 246
Ptolemy IV, King/Pharaoh of Egypt 246, 251
Ptolemy Ceraunus, Macedonian King 228–9, 235–36
Ptolemy of Aloros 54, 61–63
Ptolemy of Epirus (son of Pyrrhus I) 237
Ptolemy of Epirus (son of Pyrrhus II) 241
purification ritual 186
Pydna 19, 33–34, 36, 42, 63; and Philip II 74, 83, 91, 113; and Olympias 211–12, 214; Battle of (Perseus) 125, 259–60; Second Battle of (Andriscus) 261
Pyrrhus I, Epirote King 212, 214, 218, 224, 225, 226–27, 229; as King of Macedonia 227–228, 236–37
Pyrrhus II, Epirote King 241
Python of Byzantium 89

religion: deities 3, 8, 14, 16, 78, 134, 210, *210*; divine sanction 16, 146, 156–57, 223; diviners 132, 158; divinity of kings 17, 156, 168–69, 183–84, 196, 223; sacrifices 15, 16, 17, 144, 156, 170, 197; sanctuaries at Dion 8; sanctuary at Pella 14; Thracian influence 14
'Romaios' Tomb 214, *216*
Roman Empire 7, 33, 132; and Perseus 125, 257–61; and Philip V 125, 140, 235, 236, 242, 243, 246, 249–56; Via Egnatia 7; *see also* First Illyrian War, Second Illyrian War, First Macedonian War, Second Macedonian War, Third Macedonian War, Second Punic War
Roxane 168, 184, 185, 186, 187, 209, 211; confinement and death of 213, 217, 220–21, 211, 213, 217, 220, 221
Royal Pages 114, 162–63, 166, 168, 169, 179, 213

Salamis (Attica) 27–28, 29, 30, 34, 241, 243
Salamis (Cyprus) 223
Samos 42, 187, 191, 206

Samothrace 260
Sardis 153, 161, 179, 195, 197, 222, 228
sarissa (pike) 95, 110–13, *111*, 115, 120, 139, 140–41, 158, 165, 253, 254
Satibarzanes (Alexander III's satrap of Aria) 160
Satyrus (actor) 83
Scerdilaidas (Illyrian general) 246, 247, 249, 250
Scipio, P. Cornelius (Roman consul) 251
Scythia/Scythians 26, 89, 94, 112, 120
Second Athenian League *see* Athenian League
Second Diadoch War 206
Second Illyrian War 246
Second Macedonian War 251, 254
Second Punic War 246, 251
Second Settlement at Triparadeisos 196–97
Seleucus I: (Bodyguard, Successor, King) 121, 170; and wars of the successors 196, 217, 218, 220; as King 223, 224, 227, 228–29, 235, 236
Seleucus III, Seleucid King 246
Seleucus IV, Seleucid King 257
Seuthes, Odrysian/Thracian King 38, 41
Seven Bodyguards 121, 122, 132, 133, 165, 184–85, 186, 195, 196, 211, 227
shield and cuirass monument (Dion) *152*
ships 12, 78, 84, 92–93, 113–14, 124 (*aphractoi, hemioliai; kerkouroi, triacontoroi*), 139, 153, 154, 156, 180, 182–83, 207, 208, 225; 242 (*lembi*), 254; dockyards 8, 42, 114, 235, 240, 244, 247; and shipbuilding 9, 27–28, 31, 33, 34, 35, 40, 60, 113, 114, 188, 190, 217–18, 222–23, 226–27, 249, 251, 261; triremes 39, 40, 41, 42, 82, 113–14, 124, 153, 180, 188, 189–90; *see also* Catalogue of Ships
Sicily 40, 41, 56–57, 236
Sidon 119
siege warfare 74, 91–92, 113, 115, 123, 124, 125, 153, 156, 207–8, 223
Silver Shields 121, 206, 212
Simache (mother of Archelaus) 50
Simmias (brother of Amyntas, son of Andromenes) 165
Sindos 3
Siphnos 180
Sirras 41, 51, 57, 73

Sitalces, Odrysian/Thracian King 37–38
Siwah 156–58, 163, 223
Social War (Athenian) 74–75
Social War (Peloponnesian) 246, 247–49
Socrates 49
somatophylakes (bodyguards) 120–21, 162, 163, 197, 213, 226, 229, 246, 248, 259; *see also* Seven Bodyguards
Sosthenes (Macedonian general, ruler) 229
Sparta/Spartans 1, 9, 13, 55, 59–60, 75, 88, 226, 237; and Achaean League 237, 239, 243–45; and Alexander III 138, 159, 162, 179, 180–81; and Antigonus II 237, 239; and Antigonus III 243–45; and Battle of Leuctra 62, 63, 71, 73, 140; and Chalcidic League 57–59, 109; and Common Peace 96–97; and Corinthian War 60, 93; and Peloponnesian War 35, 36, 37, 38, 39, 40, 43, 79–80; and Persian wars 29, 93; and Philip V 247, 250, 253, 255; and Third Sacred War 77, 85, 86
Spartan Congress 60
Spitamenes (Bactrian/Sogdian commander) 167–68
Stateira (daughter of Darius III) 170
statues *87*, *94*, *260*; of Alexander III 183; bronze equestrian by Lysippus 152; of Cassander and Lysimachus; at Dion 247, 259; gold of Alexander I; of lion 6, *215*; of Philip II 153; stolen by Xerxes 161
stelae: grave *stele 53*; *stele* of Peace of Philoctetes 92–93; treaty of Perseus *257*
Strabo 10, 13, 17
strategic advantages of Macedonian region 1, 3, 261
Stratonice (sister of Perdiccas II) 38
Stratonice (daughter of Demetrius I) 228
Stratonice (wife of Demetrius II) 242
Strymon River 4, 8–10, *10*, 14, 19, 26, 27, 28, 30, 31, 33, 34, 35, 38, *63*, 71, 74, 80, 139, 193, 254, 255, 261
Susa 93, 159–60, 161, 170, 179, 182, 197
symposia see banquets
Syrmus, Triballian King 139

306 Index

Taenarum 180, 182–83, 188
Taulanti 13–14, 139, 141
Taurion (general of Philip V) 246, 247, 248
Tegea 209, 211, 243, 244–45, 247, 248
Teleutias (Spartan general) 59
Telmessus 153, *154*
Tempe, Vale of 3, 7, 8, 28, 29, 79, 137, 253, 254, 258, 259
Temenus of Argos 15, 16, 17, 30
Temenidae 17
Teres, Odrysian/Thracian King 34, 89, 90, 94
Tetrachorites 94
tetradrachm 15, *32*
tetrobol 31, *32*
Teuta (wife of Agron) 242, 243
Thais (Athenian courtesan) 160–61
Theagenes (Theban general) 144
Theban Sacred Band 71, 95–96, 112–13, 134
Thebes 1, 57, 58, 61, 63, 75; and Alexander III 131, 134, 138, 142–44, 161; and Boeotian League 62, 77; and Cassander 216, 217, 219; and Demetrius I 226; and Macedonian military 108, 110; and Philip II 61, 70–71, 84, 85–86, 94–96, 112–13, 114
Themistocles (Athenian general) 33–34
Theopompus (historian) 109
Thermaic Gulf 3–4, 5, 7–8, 9, 19, 36, 42, 62, 75, 77, 211, 213
Thermopylae 13; Battle of 24, 28; and Philip II 79, 84, 86, 94, 137; and Alexander III 142; and Lamian War 188; and Cassander 223; and Gauls 236, 237; and Antiochus III 255
Thessalonica 213, 259, 261
Thessalonice (daughter of Philip II) 77, 211, 213, 214, 217, 225
Thessalus (actor) 135
Thessaly/Thessalians: and Alexander II 61–62; and Alexander III 137; and Amyntas III 60–61; and Cassander 224, 225; cavalry 78–79, 109, 114, 115, 161, 164, 179, 188, 189, 190, 221; and Demetrius I 226; and geography of Macedonian region 3, 4, 6–7; and Lamian War 188, 189, 190; and Peloponnesian War 40, 43; and Philip II 76–80, 84, 86, 87–88, 112; and

Philip V 252–53, 254, 255, 256; subservience to Macedonian rule 13
Third Diadoch War 217, 220
Third Macedonian War 258
Third Sacred War 77, 83, 84, 85–86
Thrace/Thracians 4, 8–10, 14, 19; and Alexander I 31–32, 34; and Alexander III 138–39, 141; and Antigonus II 236; and Antipater 181, 191; and Cassander 220–22, 225; and Demetrius I 224, 226; and Lysimachus 186, 217, 218–19, 220, 221, 225, 227–28; and Peloponnesian War 37–38, 40; and Perdiccas II 35, 36–37; and Philip II 71, 74–75, 78, 79–80, 85, 87, 89–90, 93–94, 112; and Philip V 250, 253, 255–56; and wars of successors 208, 210, 222, 228
Thraceward region (Eastern Macedonia) 4, 8–10, 13, 39, 87, 254
Thucydides: as Athenian general 39; as historian 4, 7, 8, 17, 34, 40, 41, 49, 55, 108
Tigris River *119*, 124, 158, *159*, 170–71
timber trade 1, 7–8, 9, 24, 27–28, 31, 33–34, 35, 36, 41, 42, 56, 58, 60, 63, 144, 222–23
Timocleia (sister of Theagenes) 144
Timotheus (Athenian general) 63, 73
Tisiphonus (brother of Lycophron) 77, 78
To Philip 93; *see* Isocrates
Tomb II (Aegae) 33, *81*, 110–11, 214, *215*
tombs (and grave goods) 6, 10–11, 18–19, 116–18, *117*, *118*, *123*, 153, *154*, 161, 181, 209, *210*, 211, 214, *215*, *216*, 236
traditional custom of succession 52–53, 55
Trebenista 3
trials, treason 162–167, 169, 193–94, 208, 213, 248
Triballians 14, 94, 115, 131, 138–39
Trojan War 9, 11, 14, 151
Troy 3, 11, 13, 121, 151
Tymphaea 6, 73, 120, 142, 221, *222*, 225
Tyre 122, 124, 156, 158, 180, 217–18, 219

Upper Macedonia 4–6, 12, 13, 70–75

Vergina *see* Aegae
Via Egnatia 7, 9, 76
Villa Boscoreale fresco *238*

war elephants 125, 169, 186, 206, 207–8, 209, 211, 224, 229, 246, 259–60

Xenophon 59
Xerxes I, Persian King 27–30, 41, 97, 143, 160–61
xiphos (straight double blade sword) 118

Zama, Battle of 125
Zeno 237
Zeus 8, 11, 13, 15, 134, 144, 151, 156, 157
Zeuxis (painter) 43